ASHER'S BIBLE OF

# Executive Résumés

*and How to Write Them*

# ASHER'S BIBLE OF
# Executive Résumés
## and How to Write Them

## DONALD ASHER

TEN SPEED PRESS
Berkeley, California

1○
Ten Speed Press
P.O. Box 7123
Berkeley, California 94707

Distributed in Australia by E. J. Dwyer Pty. Ltd., in Canada by Publishers Group West, in New Zealand by Tandem Press, in South Africa by Real Books, in Singapore and Malaysia by Berkeley Books, and in the United Kingdom and Europe by Airlift Books.

Cover design by Cale Burr
Interior design by Jeff Brandenburg, ImageComp

Library of Congress Cataloging-in-Publication Data on file with the publisher

First printing, 1996
Printed in Canada

1 2 3 4 5 6 7 8 9 10 — 00 99 98 97 96

To my father, the first president of a corporation I ever met.

To my mother, who taught me how to read, the greatest gift one person could ever give another.

Some of the material in this book originally appeared in other forms in the *Wall Street Journal*'s *National Business Employment Weekly* and *Managing Your Career* magazines; these sections are adapted by permission of Dow Jones & Co., Inc. Some of this material appeared previously in *The Overnight Résumé, The Overnight Job Change Strategy, The Overnight Job Change Letter,* or *The Foolproof Job-Search Workbook.* These sections are used here with the permission of Ten Speed Press.

# Table of Contents

# Introduction

## A Message from the Author

The only difference between people who make $80,000 a year and people who make over $200,000 is in how they manage their careers. The skills required to do even moderately well in most $80,000-a-year jobs are identical to the skills that it takes to succeed in a position *significantly* further up the ladder. If you have a healthy combination of financial, interpersonal, and organizational skills, and a strong drive to succeed, you might very well be able to double your income—and double your satisfaction—in the next few years just by changing your approach to your career. In this day and age, when fear and loathing dominate most news about careers, jobs, and the labor marketplace, I continue to work with people who are busy hurdling others to find career success and happiness. I've identified several factors that these careerists exhibit.

**They are constantly looking for a new assignment.** If they don't get a promotion every eighteen months, or sooner, they make looking for that new opportunity *their top priority.* They have a career of projects, not jobs in the traditional sense. This outlook places careerists at a distinct advantage as companies themselves come to view jobs in the same way. The covenant between employers and employees has fundamentally changed, and it seems to have changed forever. Employers now view you as a temporary solution to a rapidly evolving problem. Security is a thing of the past. Years ago, the safest places in the world to work were the military, the federal government, and IBM. Think about it. (Read William Bridges's *JobShift* and Jeremy Rifkin's *The End of Work* for more on this.)

Yet in the last downturn, during layoffs by a major old-line computer manufacturer, a surprising 40 percent of the exiting executives received job offers with a little surprise bonus attached: an increase in pay. Statistically this is a very important finding: Even in an industry shedding managers from coast to coast, 40 percent of those leaving were able to improve their immediate future by changing jobs. That's two out of five. Are you above average? Look one manager to your left and to your right. If you're just a little better than those two people, you're competitive in the job marketplace. Somewhere, you're in demand—even in a tough economy.

(U.S. Department of Labor research covering the same downturn also found that 35 percent of layoff victims found a new job at equal or better pay; during the following economic expansion, some studies showed *nine out of ten displaced managers landed a job at equal or better pay.*)

Now, don't read this and give notice tomorrow. I said fast-track careerists consistently seek new opportunity. I didn't say they quit first or even that they necessarily switch companies. I've worked with one client for over ten years. She's had a meteoric rise with the same employer, but she's ready to move at any time and constantly tests the water with other employers, saying, "It gives me more confidence in dealing with my own employer to know I can walk. It's allowed me to take risks others might not have been willing to take. For me, those risks have paid off."

Changing companies takes more energy than getting promotions. These people squeeze every promotion out of an employer before they move on.

**They maintain a large network of friends and contacts.** Every career book on the market cites the need for this, and this time the cliche is 100 percent true. The point I want to make is that the fast-track careerists I've worked with *maintain* a large network. They keep their networks going *all the time,* not just when they need them. They trade stories and information and favors and courtesies with people in other departments, branches, divisions, and companies. They know people up and down the organizational chart, from the biggest bigwigs to the secretaries and supervisors. They generate exposure for themselves in industry organizations and in contacts with vendors, customers, and media, and they leverage that exposure by making business friends wherever they go. Personally, I do not care for the many mercenary presentations on networking I've read since the eighties, when the very word became an office nuisance. Networking does not mean exploiting those people with the power to further your ends. Networking, to the fast-track careerist, means maintaining a large number of business friends, in town and out of town, in your organization and in other organizations.

Maintaining these contacts inside your own organization is critical for finding a new assignment. Some employees mistakenly believe that promotions are in some way earned, or that managers are rewarded with advancement for service provided in the prior assignment. Bad thinking. Companies give people promotions because they need work done, and they search for those who can do that work. Two things are involved here: capacity and timing. Most people understand capacity: You need to be known as someone who can do the work. With the help of your business friends, you can make sure you are considered. Savvy careerists understand the more subtle factor of timing: You need to be available at the time the new project is to start. With a strong internal network, they know about the company's upcoming needs. The best careerists manage their existing assignments to make them available at the right time. It's the executive version of ready, willing, and able.

This kind of connectedness can save you from many career emergencies. My brother worked for Hewlett-Packard for seventeen years, joining the company right out of graduate school. As a family man, he was attracted to the company's promise not to lay off employees. That was a long time ago. More recently they walked into his department and said something like this: "Management has decided that your operation is redundant to another on the other coast. We are sorry to say that the other team got the nod, and yours will be eliminated entirely as soon as your materials and reports can be transferred to the other group. You each have six weeks to find another position within H-P, or we will no longer be able to employ you." My brother had friends everywhere. He got on the phone and found another position easily. Some of the engineers working for him, highly talented but insular, did not fare so well. Later, when he left the company, he again used his connections, this time outside Hewlett-Packard. His contacts were people he valued before he needed them, not because he needed them.

There's another benefit from maintaining business contacts on an ongoing basis: It makes you smarter and more effective at your job. When you *maintain* a network, you are like a spider on a web, sitting at nerve central soaking up the vibrations of business information. You literally borrow other people's knowledge and intelligence to spot trends, anticipate trouble, learn about emerging technologies, and scope out competitors. Also, you can skip over organizational channels to solve problems yourself. Call that woman you know in shipping and find out why your customer hasn't received the product. Call the CFO and find out if that project you're interested in is really going to get funding. Networks are invaluable for getting things done.

**They promote themselves and their team.** They are public. They know that doing a good job is not enough. The career track is littered with talented people who do a good job but will never advance because nobody who matters knows about this performance. If you are more talented than your own boss, you are particularly at risk. You need to get over her head, or you're on the most dangerous career path of all: the seniority system. Who wants to wait for someone to die to get a promotion?

Savvy careerists use memos and presentations to send information up the organizational chart. They trumpet their accomplishments and distance themselves from failure. The memo is the most powerful tool in business, when used with care, and the most dangerous when used carelessly. Savvy careerists use the memo and e-mail to jump organizational levels by judicious use of co-authoring and "cc:" notations. They involve a lot of people in all their communications, so when they need to jump the chart with important information no one finds it unusual. The presentation has the advantage of allowing them to "show face" to senior officers, who may want to involve them in future projects. At the pinnacle of this phenomenon, top officers use the media to promote themselves to shareholders and do battle with internal adversaries. A risky game, yes, but these people don't get there by being afraid to play.

This is not to say that you will advance rapidly if you are more interested in appearing effective than being effective. It's just that being effective—if nobody knows about it—gets you nowhere. The ability to name and claim your accomplishments is critical to job-seeking success, inside or outside the organization.

By the way, if you are interested in continuous advancement, be sure to both develop and promote your subordinates. Not only does this demonstrate a highly valued skill, it answers the question of how to achieve transition. The last thing you want to be is irreplaceable.

**They go where the action is.** Top careerists seem to have a sixth sense for the direction of the company or the marketplace. Contrary to popular mythology, this isn't some business gift that some managers have and others lack. This sense is the direct result of their connection to real-time business information sources, that is, real people doing the actual work related to their concerns. Classroom and home study cannot replace this information channel. No matter how much you read and think, books and magazines just won't feed a level of prescience that could be construed as a sixth sense. By the time the media report a trend, it's ancient news on the street. The steady flow of information from the people in their network, combined with careerists' ability to reinvent themselves fast enough to take advantage of the information, are the keys to their success.

And reinvent themselves they do. They avoid the very natural tendency to cling to old success. No matter how many accolades are heaped upon them for selling little black boxes, if they see that the future is in tying the boxes together, next week they are in the tying game. If the company is going to hell in a hurry, they become experts in downsizing or bankruptcy. If a competitor gains some structural advantage, they know how and when to cross the street. By anticipating a company's needs and repositioning themselves to serve those needs, they become business heroes.

Careerists do make mistakes, but they don't repeat their mistakes. If they find themselves in a backwater assignment, in charge of a mature product or technology, or involved in some failing endeavor, they abandon ship. What point is there in going down with the deck furniture? Next you drown. The proverbial person who stays to turn out the light may get a little bonus and a letter of appreciation from somebody who still has a job, but then he's unemployed and without career momentum. Loyalty is certainly a trait of fast-track careerists, but blind loyalty is not.

**They learn, and they learn fast.** This is an increasingly critical factor for career success. In my profession as a career specialist, I have seen waves of managers become obsolete because they refused to learn fast enough to keep up with changes in the workplace. Right now, America is running on a three-year technology curve. At least theoretically, every computer, software application, or communication device you use today will be obsolete three years from now. What are you going to do about it?

The fast-track careerists learn *on their own* and *in advance of others*. They don't wait for training; they learn first and train others. A good initial business, technical, or liberal arts education is a definite booster for any career, but the ability to learn constantly is actually much more important than any knowledge you may have picked up with a sheepskin or two. Remember, Bill Gates's job didn't exist until he dropped out of college and invented it.

Careerists embrace new technology, but I don't mean to imply that this learning is primarily technological. Revolutions in sales concepts and gender relations in recent years, to name but two nontechnical areas, have left many otherwise talented managers behind.

**They are straight shooters.** Surprised? Perhaps you were thinking these highly successful people were a tad Machiavellian? Not at all. They just see clearly where the organization's interests and their own long-term interests diverge. With a few notable exceptions, my most successful clients have all been very conscientious. They understand the value of a good business contact and are loathe to endanger one. They understand that the more successful they are, the smaller the pool they swim in. Cheaters and betrayers win battles, but not wars. Stephen R. Covey explained the business value of honest and fair dealings in *The 7 Habits of Highly Effective People,* one of the most successful career books of all times.

Executive-level job candidates get pretty thoroughly investigated these days. A few quirks and liabilities are fine, but a history of manipulation or disloyalty will earn you a pass for sure. A successful careerist benefits her employer tremendously, is appreciated for it at the time, and is fondly remembered after she leaves.

Aren't you like these people? Don't you share these traits? If you bought this book, you are at a crossroads. Are you unemployed, with a whole world of career options before you? If currently employed, should you leave, or seek an internal promotion or transfer? Should you accept that buyout or stay and risk being burned out or thrown out? Do you want to retire? Is that headhunter calling you about a real position or just jerking your chain? Can you make a living as a consultant? These are the kinds of questions you may be facing.

My message to you is, whatever the reason you picked up this book, go forward. Go for the promotion, go for advancement, go for the challenging assignment. I didn't say quit your job; I just said see a future where you do even better. I have witnessed so many careerists blossom after standing where you are standing now. Commit yourself to gaining mastery over this new job market, where change is the constant and you are your own master.

## What's in This Book and How to Use It

The career bookshelf in any bookstore or library has dozens of résumé guides, but none to date have addressed the executive résumé in a sophisticated and comprehensive manner. The documents used by executives to look for assignments are different from those used by middle managers, technicians, and college graduates. This book explicates those differences, teaches you how to write a résumé in an appropriate executive style (there are several styles), and provides hundreds of examples. You could write an unlimited number of versions of your own executive résumé by modifying the samples alone.

These samples come from three main sources: my own practice (approximately 70 percent; written by me, Tia Woodward, John Heed, David Glober, Kathleen Docherty, Kathy Priola, and Marsha Keeffer), headhunters (approximately 20 percent), and human resources professionals (approximately 10 percent). Two were given to me by the career center director at a top business school, and two were given to me by friends who own their own résumé-writing companies.

As a career coach and a professional résumé writer, I personally have written over 10,000 executive résumés, and others on my staff have written almost as many. I am not an outplacement executive, a headhunter, or a refugee from a corporate human resources department. I am a hired gun, working directly with candidates on a one-on-one basis.[1] I coach executives just like you on résumé preparation, job-search techniques, tough interview questions, and every nuance of a potential career move. I am in the trenches of executive job change, year in and year out, as an advocate for the individual candidate. Every theory or opinion in this book has been tested, retested, and verified in practice. We know these techniques work because we see them in action; our clients routinely win job offers at thousand-to-one odds.

In this book I have tried to provide a resource that captures this experience in an accessible and useful way. But to be triply sure I was giving you the best advice possible, I didn't rely on just my own expertise. I visited the offices of several friends of mine, headhunters and human resources officers of major corporations,

---

[1] Although my expertise comes from working with candidates, I also design and deliver job-search lectures and workshops for corporations in transition and for some of the best business schools in the nation. If you are interested in having me speak or consult with your organization, call my office at (415) 543-7130.

to view their résumé collections and discuss their impressions of the current state of the art of executive résumé writing. They told me that the overwhelming majority of résumés are exceptionally bad. The documents they received were poorly organized, difficult to skim, difficult to categorize, and loaded with obvious, vague, or extraneous information. Then they showed me their examples. They were right.

According to my own analysis, the main **problems** with these résumés are the following:

**The executive refused to take a stand on his particular expertise.** Either you are a management consultant or you are a chief financial officer. Although in real life you can be both things simultaneously, on paper you ought not. Résumé after résumé made overly broad claims of talent, leaving the reader with no clear indication of either the candidate's past or desired future. The problem is that the résumé reader is almost never looking for a management consultant or a chief financial officer, if you understand my point. They want one or the other. Decide what you're selling in advance. If you want to package yourself differently for different readers, that's great, but in each case, present yourself with focus.

**The executive wrote too much but said too little.** A good résumé is fact based, and business facts are based in numbers. When a recruiter looks at a résumé and doesn't see any numbers, she doesn't know how to evaluate the candidate. If a résumé lacks exactitude, it lacks verifiability and feels "slippery" to the reader. Imprecision and elusiveness are not exactly the executive traits with which you want to be associated.

**The executive continued to hang on to advice she got when she was fresh out of college.** As mentioned before, résumés at the executive level are different from entry-level and junior executive résumés. They are longer, less flashy, more conversational. These differences are covered in greater detail in the following chapter. The most common errors of this type were executives slavishly following the "one-page rule" decades after it no longer applied to them or presenting their material in a functional format (with skills and experience listed separately from jobs), a sure-fire way to get the recruiter to dissect your background with a microscope, looking for the problem you're trying to hide.

Mixed in with all these atrocious examples, my friends and contacts produced their small collection of all-time **favorite** résumés, those documents which they thought exemplified good presentations for executive candidates. These résumés likewise had some common characteristics:

**The executive implied or stated what she wanted to do next—or what she was best at—on the very top of the first page.** The reader could tell what the entire résumé was about by reading the first few lines. Key information was either evident or easy to ascertain: industry, function, level of position the candidate was qualified for. Interestingly enough there were many different literary devices used to achieve this effect.

**These résumés were easy to skim.** By their layout and design the reader was quickly and easily able to check the candidate's last position, whether the candidate was still employed, and educational credentials (the three things that are generally checked first by executive recruiters).

**They were well written, each paragraph making a distinct point or set of points.** The author anticipated the points that would be of interest to the targeted reader and dwelt on them, while the obvious or tangential was glossed over quickly.

**They were results oriented;** that is, they listed solid, quantifiable results attributable to the candidate. You could see what the candidate had done in the past and easily infer what she might do in the future.

I collected several of these examples and included them in the book, and had my contacts review the samples from my own practice. This book contains hundreds of executive résumés that are concise, precise, and represent strong candidates. These presentations worked for the candidates, helping them get positions, investors, new business opportunities, and civic or philanthropic appointments. And they have passed the muster of my informal review board of executive recruiters and human resources officers.

The book includes an overview of executive résumés (chapter 1) and a training session on how to write them (chapter 2), complete with tips for most problems you will encounter (too old, too long with one company, recent demotion, long period of unemployment, consulting, and similar disadvantages). The subsequent chapters focus on styles ranging from general management résumés to presentations for specific professions, such as curricula vitae for medical doctors, with a few notes on each style followed by examples. Chapter 13 gives a short presentation on cover letters (for more, see my *The Overnight Job Change Letter*, which is full of executive-level examples). Chapter 14 covers salary histories and reference sheets, often overlooked documents that can clinch a job offer and be worth thousands of dollars to you in the salary negotiation stage. The bibliography lists career books that I think are particularly pertinent to the executive job-seeker, and the index lets you find the examples you need quickly and easily.

**Be sure to read chapters 1 and 2 before
you attempt to write anything.**

I believe this is the largest collection of executive résumés ever published for the public. However, you must observe this disclaimer: In collecting these documents, I became privy to an incredibly large volume of personal information on candidates and confidential business information which rightfully belongs on résumés, but ought not be published. At my discretion, and sometimes at the discretion of my editors, I have changed certain signifying information to protect the privacy of candidates and companies. Unfortunately, this has also changed the flavor of some of the résumés. When a reader reads an executive résumé, he gets a lot of information from the name of the company alone. It means a very different thing to be a corporate VP at IBM than at Netscape, to live in New York than in Des Moines, to be a pioneer with a new technology than to become involved with that technology after it has been accepted worldwide. Also, you should know that these résumés were collected over a ten-year period. Suffice it to say that in many cases candidate names, dates, company names, product names, cities, and financial and statistical data have been changed. However, absolutely nothing presented is faked or inflated. These are the real accomplishments of real executives at real companies. I would have vastly preferred to run all these examples without changing so much as a comma, but that was not practicable. The very nature of my clientele makes them uncomfortable with publicity. My entire practice is entirely confidential, and so it should be. To confuse the matter further, some candidates gave permission to use their résumés verbatim and insisted that their actual names be used. In short: No person mentioned in this book should be presumed to be any particular individual, and any such assumption would be unwarranted. Company, product, and service names mentioned in this book may or may not represent the actual company, product, or service named. Likewise, any statistic or numerical reference to the companies, products, or services mentioned in this book is used only to illustrate the art of résumé writing and should not be considered to be based in fact. The candidates and their résumés are diverse, representing the highly successful and the plodding, careerists seemingly born into a career path and those individuals who happened onto a calling late in life, people dealing with a demotion and people who seemingly have never suffered a mishap in life. You will notice a wide range of educational attainment, from an engineer with no degree to managers with stacks of diplomas, many of them quite unrelated to business. Although some of the details have been disguised, these are very real people, and these are your peers, colleagues, and competitors.

## Terms Defined

Of course the most important word for me to define in a book on executive résumés is "executive." You might think this would be easy, but it is not. I know from experience that "executive" means something very different in Siloam Springs, Arkansas, where I have a vacation home, than it does in San Francisco, where I have my office. In the simplest terms, when I use the word "executive" in this book I am referring to an officer of the company, vice presidential level and up. In a small company, an executive may be someone who earns $45,000 per year and supervises three people. In an entrepreneurial setting, executive may mean someone who earns nothing and supervises no one. In a very large company it may mean someone with a compensation package worth several million dollars a year and responsibility for tens of thousands of employees. In this text, "executive" can be understood to mean someone with strategic authority, either over a department, product line, division, company or a group of companies, and generally it will mean someone who earns nearly six figures or well above that. Titles these people will hold include:

| | |
|---|---|
| Chief Administrative Officer (CAO) | Manager |
| Chief Financial Officer (CFO) | Managing Director |
| Chief Information Officer (CIO) | Owner |
| Chief Operating Officer (COO) | Partner |
| Chief Scientist | President |
| Consultant | Principal |
| Controller | Senior Vice President (SVP) |
| Director | Treasurer |
| Executive Director | Vice Chairman |
| Executive Vice President (EVP) | Vice President (VP) |
| General Manager (GM) | |

Or they may have a professional title, such as attorney, medical doctor, or certified public accountant. Of course, as one of my clients said to me, "I don't care what they call me as long as I get a piece of the action." It doesn't matter what you are called either. If you recognize yourself in the examples in this book, then you are an executive and this guide is for you.

The other terms used in this book are standard business buzzwords—such as line and staff management, benchmarking, outsourcing, and so on—and industry standard abbreviations such as P&L, ROI, TQM, and the constantly evolving alphabet soup of computer technology. These terms are not defined.

# Chapter 1

# What's Different about
# Executive Résumés

## Old Advice

You can probably still remember that university career officer ranting about the laws of résumé writing: "Keep it to one page! Use short phrases! Start each sentence with an action verb! Start each line with a bullet!" You probably even followed her advice, got a good job, and thought she was right about that résumé stuff.

Well, she was. When you were about twenty-two years old and fresh out of college.

Executive résumés are longer, less flashy, and more conversational in tone than lower-level résumés. When a company is faced with paying you $100,000 or $250,000 or over a million dollars per year for your services, they'll invest more time in reading your résumé.

## Longer

Most strikingly, executive résumés are longer, running three pages or more as a matter of routine. Traditionally, college graduates *should* stick to one page, but those with five to ten years of experience can have either one or two pages; those with over ten years of experience usually have two pages, and executives usually have two to five pages. Nothing harms an executive more than to try to explicate a complex background on one page.

As was so convincingly pointed out by John Lucht in his book, *The Rites of Passage,* when an executive shortens her résumé, the first things that go are the accomplishments. Think about it: You list the company, your title, maybe the dates, maybe a brief depiction of your employer, a short description of the job; *then* you list accomplishments. When you start cutting copy to shorten the length, the accomplishments are thrown out first, then the short description of the job, then any information about the company you worked for, in reverse order. In other words, the part of the résumé that actually sells you is the first part thrown away. Cutting your résumé's length by one-third may cut its impact by way more than half. Call your marketing department, and they will gladly tell you what they know to be true: Long copy sells.

Of course you should be brief and to the point, but not *too* brief. Your résumé should be as short as you can make it without cutting muscle with the fat. For most executives, that's two pages minimum, typically three or four pages, and sometimes even much more. With addenda on special projects, community service, speaking engagements, publications, and so on, an executive presentation can be rather long, certainly much, much longer than for a twenty-two-year-old college student.

(Two styles of executive presentation are still quite short: vitae and narrative profiles. They are discussed later in this chapter and in chapters 3 and 4.)

## Less Flashy

A management-level résumé is first and foremost a business document. It should reflect the position and decorum of the candidate. In general, you will see fewer little pointing hands on an executive presentation; bright colors are way too far out, and weird sizes and shapes are generally considered just that: weird.

There is an inverse relationship between résumé fanciness and income: the more bells, whistles, graphics, and colors on a résumé, the closer the candidate is to the bottom of the food chain. Recent college grads may need to scream and shout, but do you really want a senior financial officer whose taste in paper colors runs to hot pink?

A good background speaks for itself. Executive placements are not made by accident. In a sense, you have to trust the process. If you have a well-written presentation that conveys your good points, anything else counts against you.

By the way, those fold-out brochures that some of the résumé companies foist upon hapless middle managers are not nearly as popular with employers as they are with candidates. Headhunters and hiring managers can smell an oversold candidate at forty paces, and those brochures are a dead giveaway.

(At the end of the next chapter is detailed instruction on résumé graphics, including papers, fonts, and colors. See p. 29 ff.)

## More Conversational Tone

- Use short phrases!
- Start each sentence with an action verb!
- Start each line with a bullet!

How much of that can you read before your mind goes numb? Executive résumés spend a great deal more space on why and how a certain decision was made or accomplishment attained than junior-executive or middle-management résumés. "Reduced manufacturing cost 17%!" might be enough information to decide on the promise of a production engineer, but if you're looking for a plant manager, you'd want to know a little more, wouldn't you?

Context is important in evaluating executive backgrounds. What were the options? What were the impediments? Who was involved? What business conditions were in play? In executive résumés you will frequently find paragraphs that sound almost like conversations, paragraphs that *tell business stories*. Here is an example:

The hotel chain had had a cost-cutting program in effect for three years, and had achieved an 11% reduction in costs through the usual means—reduction in overtime, overhaul of vendor relationships, and similar—when I ran a study on the relationship between customer satisfaction and gross and net income. We discovered that every percentage point we could increase customer satisfaction was worth $22 million net income to the chain. Using this. . . .

Now *that's* interesting. That beats bullets and exclamation points all the way to the bank. Savvy résumé readers demand hard data—11%, $22 million—but at the executive level they also want context. You can use a whole paragraph to make a point, rather than just a short declarative sentence. Of course, you can't explain every damn thing you've ever done. You will see in many of the examples selected for this book a mix of styles: some bullets, some stories.

Also notice that admonitions never to use first-person pronouns don't apply to executive résumés. An occasional "I," "we," "my," or "our" can be very effective, as in the example above.

## More Differences

Briefly, here are some more differences between executive presentations and others:

You can criticize a former employer, if you do it gently. The party line for entry- to middle-level résumés is that you should never, ever, criticize a former employer. However, at the executive level you have to show leadership; one evidence of leadership is independent judgment. If your employer tried to sell ice in Alaska in January or poison a small town in Iowa, it's OK to *gently* mention that you didn't think it was a great strategic decision.

You can tell the reader why you are leaving a company, sometimes. Again, lower-level résumés should forgo any comment on this topic, but executives can some-times benefit from an early disclosure. If there is a good rationale for a short tenure or an apparent demotion, it can be better to let the prospective employer know the reason up front. You will see some examples of this technique in the résumés in later chapters (see pp. 36 and 67).

You may need to give a quick description of the company you worked for. Middle managers work in *departments,* executives work in *companies.* For this reason, on executive résumés, it is more common to give a one-sentence bio of the company before going into any description of your experience there.

You can be older, but not much older (more on this in the next chapter). Com-panies don't buy experience anymore, even for the executive suite. They buy skills, skills, and nothing but skills.

You can include personal data, but I don't recommend it. Height, weight, pic-tures, race, health, and your social security number are stylistically verboten, but executive presentations do still sometimes include hobbies/sports, age or date of birth, and marital status. These data are more common on the East Coast than on the West Coast, but are not and cannot be required anywhere in the United States or Canada. I recommend that you do not include any such information, because it can only be used against you. This is explained further in the next chapter, along with the information that goes in presentations used internationally.

## Five Main Styles

There are four styles of executive résumé presentation: **chronological**, **functional**, **vita**, **narrative profile**. The fifth style, **curriculum vitae**, is for medical personnel, scientists, and some technical specialists. Let's consider them in order.

## Chronological Is the Most Popular, with Good Reason

The overwhelming favorite of candidates and employers alike is the chronological résumé, a classic style providing a wealth of information in a format that is both easy to skim *and* digest.

The chronological résumé lists the candidate's jobs in reverse chronological order, with the accomplishments and activities of each job clearly identified with a particular company, title, and tenure. That is the defining nature of the chronological style: Each experience or accomplishment claimed is tied to a specific company and period in time, and the reader has some confidence that there is someone at that company who could verify each and every claim.

In current practice, executive-level chronological résumés frequently begin with a brief **profile** summarizing an executive's talents or a brief series of accomplishments, or **highlights**, illustrating past triumphs. Using either or both of these stylistic techniques, the most pertinent information can be presented in the first few lines of the résumé. The modern chronological résumé has the benefits of providing the most important information right up top, with room further down for extensive and detailed career data; it comes with a high "verifiability" factor, giving the reader confidence in the document and, when properly designed, it is easy to skim quickly. On p. 7 is an example of a modern, profile-headed, chronological résumé. Most of the examples in this book are chronological résumés, as these are the best presentations for qualified executives to use when applying for career-related opportunities, whether as a future employee, consultant, venture partner, or equity participant. Chronological résumés are also a frequent part of business plans and proposals (cf. the narrative profile style).

## Functional Is Most Closely Scrutinized, if at All

The functional-style résumé presents experience and/or skills claims from *all* jobs under topical headings, such as "finance," "marketing," or "management," and usually includes a separate section where the jobs are simply listed (company and title) in reverse chronological order, dates optional. The problem with this style is that it is hard to tie a specific accomplishment claim to a specific job, and proper context is obscured.

This style is a favorite with candidates who have something to hide, and for that reason it is far more popular with candidates than with employers. For example, in a functional résumé it may say under the management topic, "Headed up a crew of 14," and in the job chronology section, "XYZ Futurecorp, Vice President, Marketing." In the reader's mind, there the candidate is, working hard to lead this marketing department of fourteen, in a company large enough to have at least one marketing department of fourteen. When it comes time to interview this candidate, however, the truth comes out: XYZ Futurecorp was a start-up fantasy; the candidate was the principal and only worker; the candidate has, in fact, not worked in over a year; and the "crew of 14" refers to a one-summer stint as foreman over a warehouse crew twenty-eight years ago!

As a hiring manager, you don't have to be led down this time-wasting path very often before you are suspicious of every functional résumé. Some hiring managers will not consider candidates presenting functional formats. In the next chapter, we will explore ways to solve special problems—a dismissal, a demotion, a need to shift industries late in life—without resorting to the functional style. Although it is of great benefit to job-hoppers, ex-convicts, parents returning to the workforce after a long hiatus for childrearing, in my personal opinion the functional résumé is not an executive presentation.

(Besides, with some rare exceptions, at the executive level a candidate cannot misrepresent his way into an appointment. Instead of using a tricky résumé to get an interview, a candidate with a difficult background ought to use effective job-search techniques to get interviews. See my *Foolproof Job-Search Workbook* or *The Overnight Job Change Strategy* for how to get to the job openings before they are announced.)

The second example is a functional résumé, and since I know this candidate personally, I'll just tell you up front that he has nothing to hide. He used the functional style years ago, found success with it, and insists on continuing to present his background this way. This is one of the few functional résumés in this book (p. 9 ff.). The others are mostly engineers, pp. 333–340, who can sometimes use the style to present their projects effectively. Another example is on p. 70. Most candidates should avoid it.

## The Vita Is Brief When Brief Is Best

The English word vita is misappropriated from the Latin term *curriculum vitae,* which means the racecourse of life. Vita means, translated, "a life." Curriculum vitae, or CV, was the most common name for a job résumé prior to World War II. In modern usage, curricula vitae are résumés for doctors, scientists, and academicians (see the last style, below).

The vita style of executive presentation is very brief, more like a fact sheet than a persuasive marketing piece. It is usually one page long, listing key points only. It is used when you are so famous that you don't need to explain yourself and simply want to provide a business contact with some background; you are applying for a bank loan or financing you are 100 percent sure you will get, and they have requested a résumé as a mere formality; or you want to give someone a teaser, a sort of "calling-card" résumé, and you intend to give them more information later.

Vitas are handy to give when first meeting people, but you will want to be careful not to use a vita when you should have used a more elucidating version.

## Narrative Profile, Primarily for Marketing

The narrative profile is a third-person promotional piece, a common feature of business proposals and marketing materials. It can be written about either an individual or a company. When the subject is an individual, the profile can focus on the career or be fully biographical in scope. Some high-end headhunters write narrative profiles for all candidates they advance to an employer for consideration. When written about a company as a whole, the narrative profile is sometimes referred to as a company résumé or a corporate résumé. Public relations firms routinely prepare these as part of their services, and some résumé companies, including my own, write them.

The style is difficult to write well, and sometimes comes off as treacly praise. The goal is to present the facts with enough story to be interesting, but not so much story that the facts disappear. Due to the narrative format, it is easy to obscure any unpleasant details. The narrative profile is not a common style to use in a job-search situation, however.

## Curriculum Vitae, for Doctors, Scientists, Academicians

The curriculum vitae style, or CV style, is for clinical care providers (medical doctors, nurses, physician assistants, medical technologists, and similar professionals), scientists, and academicians. It is closely related to the vita style; jobs are listed (company, title, date), but job descriptions are truncated or omitted. It is helpful to realize that CVs are credentials-based, not performance-based. CVs usually have full listings for publications, appointments, research projects, and so on, even if that pushes the length up to a dozen pages or even more. CVs are quite understated. Accomplishments, braggadocio, and the tone of self-confidence that pervades business résumés is properly absent.

In practice, however, CVs run the entire stylistic gamut from bare-bones vitas to fully explicated chronological résumés. Medical administrators are a good example, often using documents called CVs but stylistically indistinguishable from regular chronological business résumés. The best way to tell what style is best for you is to look at the sample following, the examples in chapter 7, and the one on p. 128.

■

Following you will find one example of each of the five main résumé styles used today by top executives and professionals.

# ROBERT G. FLEMING

25 Ivory Terrace
San Francisco, California 94133

Corporate office: (415) 555-2771
Home office: (415) 555-4788
Secure e-mail: r.fleming@pur.1cwb.com

---

## PROFILE

### Purchasing / Procurement

Planned and purchased in excess of $100,000,000 per annum for banking and financial services companies, with executive authority over entire procurement process. Experience with domestic and international subsidiary corporations, branch and satellite business structures, acquisition and divestiture activities, and joint-venture/business partner endeavors.

Expertise in overseeing procurement of capital equipment, paper and printed goods, real estate, legal/advertising/consulting and other services, intellectual properties, and technology, including analysis/negotiation of sophisticated and creative lease/buy/vendor finance options.

Liaison to information services; executive committee for technology evolution planning. Recent success in overseeing development and emplacement of single-entry integrated paperless forms systems (profiled in "Only Planning Beats Paper," *Corporate Computing*, 11/17/96).

Additional expertise in inventory and automatic ordering systems.

## HISTORY

### THE COMMERCIAL WORLD BANK

**Vice President, Head of Purchasing,** 1993-present. Direct the bank's program for centralized purchase of expendable and capital goods supplied to all units corporatewide (U.S./Asia/Europe/Latin America); provide oversight and policy development to worldwide decentralized procurement practices. Annual procurement budget in excess of $100,000,000.

Forecast, strategize, and manage all procurement activity. In charge of HQ staff of 22 and decentralized staff of 103 in ordering, contract administration, accounts payable, customer support resources, forms management, IS, and corporate communications functions.

Responsible for tracking millions of pieces of inventory and thousands of open vendor contracts; chair of some two dozen task forces and planning committees; member, executive committee, long-range planning committee, president's budget advisory group, technology evolution planning committee.

Maintain officer-level relations with all major suppliers. Personally negotiate most major purchase and service agreements. Set procurement policy worldwide.

*Accomplishments:*
- Designed cost savings/cost avoidance program saving a documented $4,600,000 in first year alone, as verified by internal management audit. Earned president's commendation and performance bonus.
- Published *CWB Purchasing Policy Manual*, simplifying and standardizing procedures bankwide, to provide guidance to line managers in charge of local purchasing. Results: adherence to principle over precedence; 16% average drop in local purchasing expenses; identification of 6 cases of vendor fraud and 2 cases of employee collusion.

- Brought single-entry integrated paperless forms systems online, eliminating estimated $14,000,000 in paper/printing/handling costs and $5,500,000 in costs associated with delays/introduced errors.
- Negotiated 17 major agreements last year alone, 12 of which were with offshore suppliers. Designed system to track local contracts for possible implementation bankwide.
- Designed minority purchasing program to identify qualified minority suppliers; exceeded 15% minority contracting goal at wholly competitive rates/specifications.
- Reduced staff by 15% with concurrent *increase* in service provision.

**Assistant Vice President, Head of Forms Management**, 1989-1992. Managed and controlled over 7000 standardized commercial banking forms, as well as a portion of the bank's worldwide expendable supplies, equipment, and furniture.

*Accomplishments:*
- Implemented major reorganization and expansion of purview of bank's forms management program, spearheading a change in focus from a "printing and forms distribution" to a "technology and information integration" role.
- Formed alliance with chief information officer to serve as project leader, single-entry integrated paperless forms systems development task force. Also gained appointment as standing member, technology evolution planning committee.
- Managed a total staff of 60 engaged in software specification, forms analysis, forms design, customer programs, and reprographic services.

**Senior Purchasing Officer**, 1984-1989. Supervised buying staff in procurement of forms, supplies, mechanical equipment, vault security systems, furniture, and specialized printing.

**Forms Control Officer**, 1982-1984. Controlled the corporate process of creation, revision, and obsoletion of over 5000 forms and forms-related supply items.

**Pro-Forma Officer**, 1981. Coordinated production of bank's pro-forma manual instructing employees on how to locate and complete appropriate forms for financial and internal operations.

**Operations Officer**, Glenwood Springs Branch, 1979-1980. Supervised staff in general banking operations, with responsibility for knowing, interpreting and applying bank policies and procedures.

**Assistant Operations Officer**, Beverly Hills Branch, 1978-1979.

**Management Trainee**, Los Angeles, 1977-1978.

## EDUCATION
### STANFORD UNIVERSITY
**Bachelor of Arts, Social Sciences**

## SPECIAL SKILLS
Paperless process design, minority contracting, team building, workflow reengineering, security technology, security printing, worldwide supplier sourcing and evaluating.

# Perry Purcell

65 Fa Po Street, Flat 6-A
Village Gardens
Yau Yat Chuen
Kowloon
Hong Kong
555-1434

---

**SKILLS &
ACCOMPLISHMENTS**

Twenty-three years of increasing responsibilities in the manufacturing systems industry. Successful sales, marketing, general management and international management background. Executive leadership and organizational skills.

### General Management

As **General Manager**, Pacific Rim, responsible for unit P&L performance. Restructured unprofitable business, and achieved 20% average annual net profit.

Experienced in key business functions, including personnel, communications, business practices, strategic planning, organization, quality management, and community relations.

**Master of Business Administration** degree, with emphasis in corporate finance and business modeling. Harvard University's **Executive Development Programs**, three topics.

### Sales & Marketing Management

Fifteen years of successful direct sales and marketing of turnkey process automation hardware, software, and services in the United States, Canada, and Pacific Rim. As **Business Manager**, Northwest, responsible for marketing for 13 states, including Alaska, Hawaii.

As **Regional Manager** and senior sales operations executive based out of San Francisco, led sales and technical support team of 900 people, achieved annual revenue plan of $350 million, and managed annual expense plan of approximately $40 million.

As **Director of Marketing** based out of Los Angeles, responsible for market analysis and segmentation, marketing strategies, channel management and development, product marketing, and marketing plan management.

### International Management

As **Chief Representative** and senior operational executive resident in Beijing and Hong Kong, developed and implemented business strategies for the pan-China environment (PRC, Taiwan, HK), tailored for the unique opportunities and challenges of an emerging region.

As **Pacific Rim Strategist**, achieved operational objectives, hiring and training a local workforce, and implementing business processes suitable for a startup business unit. Experienced in establishing new businesses, both wholly-owned subsidiaries and representative offices. Responsible for company-to-government relations, U.S. export regulation compliance, and liaison with U.S. embassy.

Language skills: fluent **English** (native tongue) and **German**, conversational in **Mandarin**, basic **Japanese**. Bachelor of arts degree in German; Berlitz graduate in Mandarin.

### Organization & Leadership

Proven ability to organize and motivate employees, and recruit, retain, and develop sales, technical and management personnel. Hands-on management style, with emphasis on leadership by example and accessibility. Executive verbal and written communication skills.

### Technical Systems

Broad experience in automated and computer-controlled manufacturing and process control systems. Liaison to system development engineers. Technical author / technical trainer.

Extensive experience with IBM- and SUN-architecture control systems (mainframe-to-workstation) and Honeywell sensing technologies, as well as many other OEM providers of CPUs and sensing / control devices.

Knowledgeable on applications in most industry segments, heavy industrial to incubator-level projects.

Prior advancement based on combination of technical, sales, and management skills.

**EXPERIENCE CHRONOLOGY**

**Process Control Systems, Inc.** (22 years)
    **General Manager, Pacific Rim**, Hong Kong
    **General Manager / Chief Representative, Pacific Rim**, Beijing
    **Business Manager, Northwest**, San Francisco and Seattle
    **Regional Manager, Northwest**, San Francisco
    **Director of Marketing**, Los Angeles
    **Assistant to Group Executive of Marketing**, New York
    **Branch Manager**, Portland
    **Marketing Representative** and **Marketing Manager**, Los Angeles
    **Engineering Assistant**, Los Angeles

**Starburst Computer Corporation** (2 years)

Computer operator, programmer, and technical author for startup manufacturing control and computer timesharing company.

**EDUCATION**

**Master of Business Administration**
    University of California at Los Angeles

**Executive Development Programs** (three topics)
    Harvard University

**Bachelor of Arts, German Language & Literature**
    Amherst College

**PERSONAL**

Available for assignment worldwide. Interests include international relations, trade patterns, foreign language. Charter member, Commerce Club. Associate, Asia Business League.

# C. PARKER CLEMMONS
*Curriculum Vitae*

22 Mill Plain Road
Danbury, Connecticut 06811 U.S.A.

Office / voicemail: (203) 555-4776
Home office / message: (203) 555-8441

---

**EDUCATION**

HARVARD BUSINESS SCHOOL, Cambridge, Massachusetts
**M.B.A.,** Finance & International Business

DARTMOUTH COLLEGE, Hanover, New Hampshire
**B.A.,** International Relations

**EXPERIENCE**

WILSON & WOODWARD, INC., New York, New York
**Chairman & CEO**, 1990-Present
**President & CEO**, 1984-1990
**Vice President & Regional Manager**, 1978-1984

*also*

INTERNATION COMMUNICATION USA, LTD.,
New York, New York
**Vice President & Chief Financial Officer**

REED SECURITIES, New York, New York
**Managing Officer, Montrose Securities** (investment banking)
**President, Bragdon & Company** (consulting division)
**Treasurer & CFO, Principal** (NASD filing)

GRAHAM LOVING & COMPANY, New York, New York
**Fund Manager**

WHITE WELD & COMPANY, New York, New York
**Investment Banking Associate**

DOUGLAS AIRCRAFT, Santa Monica, California
Corporate Planning, Space and Defense Technology Division

U.S. DEPARTMENT OF COMMERCE, Washington, D.C.
International Investment Office

**CREDENTIALS &
AFFILIATIONS**

NABE (National Assoc. of Business Economists),
**President**, Northeastern Chapter

AICPA (Uniform Examination for Certified Public Accountants)

ACG (Association for Corporate Growth)

IMC (Institute of Management Consultants),
**Certified IMC Management Consultant**

AAA (American Arbitration Association), **Certified Panelist**

**PUBLICATIONS**

"The Collapse of Consulting," *Wall Street Journal*, October 27, 1996

"Treasury Function as a Profit Center," *Chief Executive*, Spring 1993

"South Africa: Unexplored Territory!" *Chief Executive*, Spring 1992

**REFERENCES**

References and additional information provided on request.

# Robertson & Associates
### ATTORNEYS-AT-LAW

3801 Melrose Avenue, Suite 1500
Los Angeles, California 90029
(213) 555-4964 or (213) 555-1713

---

## Nathaniel A. Robertson

### BIOGRAPHY

Mr. Robertson is currently the principal of Robertson & Associates, a law firm specializing in quality legal research and representation concerning matters of banking, securities, commercial credit and tax law, general business and contract litigation, professional liability, personal injury, product liability, appellate services, and such related services as negotiations, advocacy memoranda, and representation to tax, government, or regulatory authorities.

In addition to heading his law practice, Mr. Robertson serves as a private consultant to banks and fiduciary entities. He provides advisory services, structuring, and oversight for a wide range of transactions and agreements, for both corporations and financial institutions. This includes projects for such institutions as the European Industrial Development Bank and more routine assistance to such entities as the Arbuckle Consulting Group, the renowned Southern California venture capital firm.

Prior to starting his firm, Mr. Robertson was Founder and Executive Director of the Western Legal Research Institute at Stanford for seven years. WLRI is a legal "think tank" and support firm providing quality research, writing, and analysis to private practitioners, corporate counsel, and attorneys in government. Mr. Robertson built a team of dynamic young attorneys around this new concept, and this "law firm's law firm" gained quick recognition as both innovative and highly resourceful. WLRI has continued to grow, and has been touted as the model of a new breed of legal services firm.

WLRI provides litigation, research, and analysis in the areas of administrative law, automobile injury, banking, civil procedure, civil rights, commercial law and bankruptcy, constitutional law, contracts, corporate law and antitrust, criminal law and procedure, eminent domain, energy, environmental law, family law, labor law, pension benefits, copyright and trademark, personal injury, product liability, real property, securities, torts, trusts, wills and estates, and workers' compensation.

Mr. Robertson's earlier career spans assignments as research attorney for the California Supreme Court and research clerk/fellow/extern for Public Advocates, Inc., Honorable Justice Frank M. Newman, Pacific Gas and Electric Corporation, National Aeronautics and Space Administration, Legal Aid Society of Alameda County, and the U.S. House of Representatives Subcommittee on Equal Rights.

Nathaniel A. Robertson is a graduate of Stanford University and the University of California at Berkeley (Boalt Hall) School of Law. He is a member of the ABA, the NBA, and CBA, and is licensed to practice before all California State Courts, Federal District Court, and the U.S. Court of Appeals. Mr. Robertson is well known in legal and business circles in both Northern and Southern California. He has been described by at least one media source as a "major force in West Coast litigation."

**Joshua D. F. Gordon, M.D.**                                    **Curriculum Vitae**

820 Mill View Lane                                                          Telephone:
Los Altos Hills, California 94022                                    (415) 555-0132

---

## SPECIALTY

**Anesthesiology**

## CREDENTIALS

Board Certified, American Board of Anesthesiology          1996
Basic Life Support Instructor                                             1990
Advanced Cardiac Life Support                                         1990

Diplomate, National Board of Medical Examiners            1987
Federal Licensure Examination                                         1986

Medical License, State of California                                  1985
Medical License, State of Ohio                                         1984

## EXPERIENCE

**Staff Anesthesiologist**
Santa Clara Valley Medical Center, San Jose, California     1991-Present
Pacific Presbyterian Medical Center, San Francisco, California     1991-Present
Sonoma Valley Hospital, Sonoma, California                   1990
Seton Medical Center, Daly City, California                    1990

## TRAINING

**Research Fellowship** (blood bank and liver transplant anesthesia)     1990
University of California, San Francisco

**Residency** (anesthesiology)                                        1987-1990
University of California, San Francisco

**Internship** (internal medicine)                                   1986-1987
University of California, San Francisco

## EDUCATION

**M.D.**, College of Medicine                                           1986
University of Cincinnati, Cincinnati, Ohio

**A.B.**, Biochemical Sciences                                          1982
Princeton University, Princeton, New Jersey
   Thesis: *Studies on a Deletion Mutant from a Recombinant Bacteriophage Library*

Three Advanced Levels (physics, chemistry, biology)     1978
Twelve Ordinary Levels                                                   1976
Harrow School, Harrow-on-the-Hill, England

**RESEARCH**

**ARTICLES:**

"The Pharmacokinetics of Vecuronium During Liver Transplantation in Humans." J.D.F. Gordon, M.D.; J.E. Caldwell, F.F.A.R.C.S.; M.C. Prager, M.D.; M.L. Sharma, Ph.D.; L.D. Gruenke, Ph.D.; R.D. Miller, M.D. *Anesth Analg* 1995; 70: S432 (abstract, presented at the IARS 64th Congress, Honolulu, Hawaii, March 13, 1995).

"Vecuronium Plasma Concentrations During Orthotopic Liver Transplantation in Humans." J.D.F. Gordon, M.D.; J.E. Caldwell, M.B.Ch.B.; M.C. Prager, M.D.; M.L. Sharma, Ph.D.; L.D. Gruenke, Ph.D.; D.M. Fisher, M.D.; N. Ascher, M.D., Ph.D.; R.D. Miller, M.D. (submitted).

"The Effect of Aprotinin on Intracranial Pressure and Cerebral Edema in Rabbits with Galactosamine-Induced Acute Liver Failure." J.D.F. Gordon, M.D.; M.C. Prager, M.D.; S.F. Ciricillo, M.D.; M. Grady, B.A. (submitted).

"A Comparison of HTLV-1 Seropositivity in Orthotopic Liver Transplant Recipients Before and After Routine HTLV-1 Screening." J.D.F. Gordon, M.D.; E. Donegan, M.D. (in preparation).

**ADDITIONAL**

"Fibrinolysis During Liver Transplantation," in association with Dr. Marie Prager, Department of Anesthesia, Dr. Marc Schuman and Dr. Larry Corash, Department of Hematology, UCSF, 1992.

"Analysis of Lymphocyte Subset Variations Associated with Liver Transplantation," in association with Dr. Elizabeth Donegan, Director of Blood Bank, UCSF, 1991.

**AFFILIATIONS**

| | |
|---|---|
| American Society of Anesthesiologists | 1988-Current |
| International Anesthesia Research Society | 1988-Current |
| California Society of Anesthesiologists | 1988-Current |
| Northern California Anesthesia Society | 1988-Current |

**COMMUNITY SERVICE**

| | |
|---|---|
| Volunteer, Animal-Assisted Therapy Program, San Francisco SPCA | 1989-Current |
| Instructor, Basic Life Support, American Red Cross, Southwest Ohio Chapter | 1985-1986 |

**PERSONAL INTERESTS**

Interested in therapeutic aspects of animal-human relationships, especially as related to illness recovery and geriatrics. Hobbies include Weimaraner dogs and violin. Certified Grade VIII (Final) "with distinction" in violin, Board of Royal College of Music, London.

# How to Write, Edit, Enhance, Focus, and Improve an Executive Résumé

Most people who sit down to write a résumé think first about themselves: What have I done? How has my career progressed? What are my main accomplishments? Those are important considerations, but I would suggest that the first person you should think about when you sit down to write your résumé is your intended reader.

Every employer has a sentence stenciled on the inside of her eyelids: What can this candidate do for me? Every time she blinks her eyes, she sees this sentence. It is a question you had better answer. There are many choices to be made in preparing your résumé, and your guide to making those choices is always the same: What effect will this have on my intended reader?

You did not get where you are in business today without being able to anticipate how others will react to something you've said, done, or written. You must anticipate your reader's response and use it to decide among your myriad options for what information to include and how to present it.

Obviously, you will need a different résumé for every different reader. Think of your résumé as a living document. Tweak it each time you use it, and let it evolve over time and for different purposes.

In this chapter we will discuss how to write a focused résumé, in a classical business style: a profile over a reverse chronological work history. As preparation, see appendix A: personal and work history forms.

## The Heading

List your name the way you would for any important business document: Clarence Martin Darrow. If everybody in the world knows you as "Jay," list it this way: Clarence Martin "Jay" Darrow, *except* in the Northeast (New York-Boston), where nicknames are normally withheld until an introduction or a face-to-face meeting. If your gender cannot be discerned by your name, it is OK to put a Mr. or Ms. *after* your name, but smaller and in parentheses: Mica Dale Darrow (Ms.). I do not recommend withholding your gender, for two reasons: no one will be comfortable calling or writing you without knowing your gender, and you probably don't really want to work for a company where your gender will be a stumbling block. Don't put a Mr. or Ms. in front of your name, as you will seem arrogant. Don't use the title Mrs. in a business setting.

List your street address, not a post office box. If you use a post office or obvious mail drop box you will seem unstable; you do not want anyone to wonder if you live in your car. List a local address if you can come up with one at all, for example, use a mail-drop service, a summer home address, or a close relative's address. Many people list multiple addresses. Some advisors recommend that you not show an apartment or suite number, as it may indicate that you do not own your home. As a lifelong urban person, I don't agree. "Apt. 7" may cost three million dollars. Besides, with the increasing mobility of the executive class, being tied to an estate can be a liability. Don't worry too much about your address, anyway, as the only things you'll get by mail are polite brush-off letters.

List as many phone numbers as are necessary to allow someone to reach you easily. People who are interested in you will call, not write. Your largest worry is: Should I list my work number? This is not a small matter. I recently had a client who was fired for *receiving* a headhunter's call. I recommend that you do list your work number, unless the risk just makes you too uncomfortable. Placement, even executive placement, is largely a matter of timing. Minutes count. If you make someone wait twenty-four hours to get a call back, they will spend that twenty-four hours looking for someone else.

List an office phone, home office phone, home phone, car phone, fax, and beeper—the more the better. If you have teenagers at home, sit them down and tell them their entire college career depends on their ability to answer the phone and take a polite and accurate message. Better yet, list a home office telephone that only you can access. If you are looking for work nationwide, consider getting a toll-free 800 number. If you list foreign phone numbers, list all country codes exactly as one would dial it *from the country you are sending it to.*

If you have a secure e-mail address or a private home page, be sure to list it. You will achieve instant identification as someone who is technologically with it, and you will allow your contacts to use what many of them consider their communication medium of choice. If you have e-mail at work, you face the same security and confidentiality conundrum as with a work phone, except worse. E-mail is written, always recorded somewhere, and liable to be resurrected to be used against you. The best solution, of course, is to get your own provider and address.

After you complete your heading, draw a thick line across your résumé from border to border. This will guide the reader's eye, and keep him from getting bogged down reading your address. Your reader will begin reading your résumé below the bar, in your profile area, where it counts. Do not skip the bar. It matters.

Here are three samples:

## KHALID N. KHORGIAN

| *U.S.A. / permanent address:* | *U.K. address:* | *Swiss family address:* |
|---|---|---|
| 800 Pacific Heights Avenue | "The Cedar" | "Chalet Lisabeth" |
| Penthouse | 16 Copse Hill | Champ de Moulin |
| Laguna Beach, California 92651 | London SW20 ONL | 1296 Charmey |
| U.S.A. | England, U.K. | Switzerland |
| (714) 555-1381 | 44.81.568.6385 or 44.81.568.5816 | 41.29.75820 |

The reader's eye is drawn here; résumé starts here...

---

Kenomweh Miwatu (Ms.)
51089 Rolling Hills Drive
Dallas, Texas 75230
(214) 555-8078

The reader's eye is drawn here; résumé starts here...

---

RICHARD PANINI

Headquarters office/voice mail: (916) 555-5125
San Francisco office/voice mail: (415) 555-0239
Mobile: (916) 555-1896

265 Nevada Avenue
South Lake Tahoe, California 96150

Fax: (916) 555-6109
Residence/message/emergency:
(916) 555-2448
r.panini@aol.com

The reader's eye is drawn here; résumé starts here...

# The Profile

The purpose of the profile section is to inform a reader *in the fewest words possible* who you are and why he might be interested in you. The profile hooks the reader into the rest of the résumé. The profile also tells the reader what to look for in the résumé: It sets up expectations, puts a spin on the rest of the document, and provides focus. In advertising terms, the profile is the sizzle, and the experience section is the steak. It is an unbeatable approach, providing sizzle and steak in the same package.

Here are its main advantages:

- Your résumé can be sorted by an idiot, and that is always a good thing.

- Your résumé can be routed to the right decision maker without even being read.

- Whenever it is read, it will be read, right from the first line, with sincere interest.

Typical headings for this section are: PROFILE, STRENGTHS, EXPERTISE, PROFESSION, HIGHLIGHTS, SKILLS, QUALIFICATIONS.

A profile section should be as short as you can make it and should focus on hard skills, not vague, general claims of management talent. "Native fluency in German" is a specific, *verifiable,* skills claim. "Strong written and oral communication skills" will make your reader vomit. "Took three start-ups through IPO" is a specific, *verifiable,* experience claim. "Strong knowledge of finance" is not.

(By the way, an "objective" is totally passé. No reader cares about *your* objective.)

Profile sections consist of skills claims, experience claims, or a combination of both. The best way to write one is to read several first. Here are some examples, giving some idea of the variety of approaches:

---

**EXPERTISE**

> *Finance*
> Construction emphasis
> Transportation specialty

---

**PROFILE**

> P&L responsibility for companies and divisions with up to $100 million in gross revenues: financial management and capitalization during critical growth phases, bridging R&D to full commercialization, building staff and designing operational systems to control growth. *Took three start-ups through IPO.*
>
> Extensive M&A and joint venture experience, including international trade and venture agreements, licensing, technology transfer (Japan, Russia, Europe, former East Bloc).
>
> Proven catalyst, creating new business opportunities.

PROFILE General Management — Operations, Sales, Marketing

Effective combination of analytical and leadership skills, with expertise in the following operational areas:

- **Production / Inventory Management**
- **Transportation / Distribution / Logistics**
- **Import / Export**
- **Management of Broker - Dealer Organizations**

Background of accomplishment as the manager in charge under the company's executive operating officer. Available for travel and/or relocation as needed for continued career advancement. Member, American Production and Inventory Control Society.

---

## PROFESSION

*Technical Marketing Consultant*

Highlights:

- Recruited to be regional manager of start-up OEM sales group for Paradyne Corp. Created sales organization that took sales from zero to $50,000,000, establishing exclusive relationships with Burroughs, DEC, Wang, and other major OEMs.

- As regional manager for the Atlantic Seaboard, took sales from $500,000 to $7,000,000 for Universal Data Systems, a Motorola subsidiary.

- As district manager for New York City, increased district sales from $200,000 to $5,000,000 for Codex Corp., a Motorola subsidiary.

- Co-founder and director of marketing for a biotech start-up; directed feasibility studies, collaborated with R&D, engineered highly profitable sell-out to V.C. group.

- Gave seminars and symposia on nuclear and infrared devices to Ph.D.-level audiences throughout the United States and internationally on behalf of Beckman Instruments, Inc.

- Lab chief, Hanford Atomic Works, Richland, Washington, while in U.S. Army.

---

SKILLS **Administrative Management / Project Management / Construction Management Budgeting & Financial Management / Foreign Government Relations Global Purchasing & Procurement / Contract Administration**

Fluent in **English, Spanish, Hebrew**. Basic **French**.

---

A résumé is no place for false modesty. Use the profile to let the reader know what you can do for her and her company. Put the information in order of greatest interest to that reader, and you'll have a fine profile. Your profile is your first impression, and you will frequently win or lose in the first ten lines of your résumé.

As an illustration of how you can use profiles to create focus, these two profiles are for the same candidate:

**STRENGTHS**

*Total Quality Management*

Extensive internal consulting background, including designing and establishing total quality programs and applying total quality concepts to a complex organization with multiple locations and billions of dollars in equipment maintenance/readiness/distribution, logistics, human resources, and training and development aspects. Expertise in statistical analysis, continuous process improvement, statistical process control, logistics, and related information systems. Computer skills: programming, modification of off-the-shelf applications, all major spreadsheet, database, and document management functions. Multilingual.

*Training & Development*

Extensive background as teacher, lecturer, and "Evangelist" for TQM, leadership, and other areas. Can design and deliver program modules as needed. Additional HR knowledge in EEOC, diversity training, sexual harassment training, EAP, counseling, and records administration.

---

**PROFILE**

**Training & Development Specialist**

*Strengths:*

**Cultural Diversity • Sexual Harassment • Multi-Ethnic Workplace • EEO Executive Development • Management Development • Leadership • Supervisory Skills • Total Quality Management • Standard Operating Procedures**

Expertise in training and corporate education, needs assessment, design/implementation/evaluation of training programs, train-the-trainer, collateral materials design, documentation, public speaking.

**Human Resources Generalist**

Experience in most aspects of human resources administration, including employee relations, internal investigations, performance audit, EAP, career counseling, placement, etc.

---

The profile section is now standard on job-seeking résumés at the management level; however, you don't have to have one. The profile creates a level of focus that you sometimes will not want. I recommend you keep some résumés without profiles in your briefcase in case you run into an opportunity that's not straight up your career path. Also, they are rare in some industries, for example, investment banking and law.

## The Experience Section

**List jobs in order of interest to the targeted employer.** For most careerists with a logical career path, the experience section lists jobs in reverse chronological order. However, if another chronology will sell you better, you can and should reorder jobs in order of interest to the targeted employer.

Use a HIGHLIGHTS section to put important jobs on top, or split your work history into separate topics, such as MARKETING ASSIGNMENTS and ADDITIONAL EXPERIENCE, or DIRECTLY RELATED EXPERIENCE and ADDITIONAL EXPERIENCE, or ENGINEERING ASSIGNMENTS and TEACHING. Using this technique, you can achieve almost every goal of a functional résumé without falling into the pit with a gaggle of unscrupulous prevaricators.

For each job, list data in this order: company, title, dates of tenure, scope of job, accomplishments. Let us consider each in turn.

**Company.** Use the name of the company with the greatest clout. If you work for an unknown acquisition, subsidiary, spin-off, or other foster child of a larger, better-known family, consider these options:

---

**Tabletop Rockets**
(a wholly owned subsidiary of **Rockwell International**)

**Motorola Corp.** (via the following two subsidiaries)
   **Universal Data Systems**
   **Codex Corporation**

**Bank of America - Payroll Services Division**
(formerly Payroll Systems, Inc.)

---

If you worked on contract or as a consultant, consider this structure:

**Lucent Technologies, Inc.** (Technical Contract Services, Inc.)

Do not list an employer in a way that will intentionally mislead a reader. Remember, backgrounds of executive candidates are thoroughly investigated and verified prior to placement. Even an accidental misrepresentation will eliminate you from further consideration.

**Title.** Your title is usually pretty straightforward, but you can put a comment in parentheses if needed to explain your position:

**Consultant (Interim CFO)**

**Vice President (Plant Manager)**

**Group Staff Support (Project Assistant to the SVP of Human Resources)**

Do *not* change your title outright. It is extremely easy for a potential employer to verify your title.

You can stack titles with the same company, if you want to combine your description as well. This can be a good way to deal with a confusing collection of titles.

| ARROW ELECTRONICS, INC., HQ: Austin, Texas | 1990-Present |
|---|---|
| **Director of Marketing, Corporate** | 1993-Present |
| **Director of Sales, Voice/Data Sales Group** | 1995-Present |
| **Sales Manager Representative, Genie Group** | 1991-Present |
| **General Sales Director, Corporate** | 1992-1993 |
| **General Manager, Sales & Distribution, Headquarters Branch** | 1990-1992 |

*(Scope and accomplishments begin here. To see the rest of this résumé, see p. 208.)*

Or, you can stack companies, if you held essentially the same title (and especially if this was some time ago):

**COLDWELL BANKER RESIDENTIAL and
CARSON & McCULLOU REALTORS, INC.
Real Estate Broker**, 1980-1986

**Dates.** Dates should be listed year to year, without months. Listing months is for college students. List dates somewhere toward the right margin. Showing dates down the left column is old fashioned and dangerous, as dates can only count against you, not for you. Use résumé design to keep your reader focused on your skills and accomplishments, not the number of minutes you've held a particular job.

As a general rule, do not list dates older than fifteen to twenty-five years ago on a job-seeking résumé. If you want to list older jobs, go ahead, *just don't list the dates.* Examples of this technique are on the résumés beginning on pp. 37, 55, 288, 300, 343, and dozens of others throughout the book. (More on dates in the special problems section.) Do not change your dates. It is extremely easy for a potential employer to verify your dates of employment.

**Scope.** Scope is the size and nature of the job, and sometimes, the size and nature of the company, too. Scope consists of your purview of authority: whether you are a line or a staff officer, the dollar value of your sales and/or budgets, the number and titles of your staff, the titles of those you report to (directly and indirectly), your department/division/group within the larger organization, your mission, technology, and product/service. You want to establish this in the shortest possible way. Provide exact figures, obscuring only the most proprietary details:

"Directed training organization supporting the largest family restaurant chain in the United States, 400 locations, annual sales of over $1 billion, 25,000 employees, departmental staff of 50, training budget of $7,000,000 per annum."

Think of scope as static information, and accomplishments as dynamic information. Although scope can be boring to read about, it is absolutely vital to interpreting your accomplishments. It is a good idea to consider all the branches of general management responsibility, whether you decide to comment on them or not:

| | |
|---|---|
| financial | distribution |
| staffing / human resources | technology |
| production | R&D |
| marketing | strategic planning |

In practice most candidates include too much scope and not enough accomplishments, filling paragraphs with obvious minutiae that could be omitted. Remember, you're writing for an insider, someone smart, someone who knows the business.

**Accomplishments.** Accomplishments are the heart and soul of a good management résumé. You might hire a clerk because of his skills, but you hire an executive because of her accomplishments. Executives must be proven, they must have *done something* to be of interest to an employer. Creativity here is the difference between a phone call from an interested employer party and another polite rejection letter for the recycling bin.

Here are the main goals of business:

| | |
|---|---|
| more revenues | lower cost |
| faster delivery | new or better product |

Be careful listing awards. Top executives give awards, they don't receive them.

Here are a few writing tips:

1. **Don't be afraid to be a little conversational in tone**, telling business stories to your reader:

   Selected by the Chairman of the Board of Waterman Industries to turn around negative trends at National Lock, a recently acquired subsidiary. National Lock was a $17 million company with 85 employees. The company had an excellent reputation for quality, but had failed to adjust to the exit of the founder and changing market conditions.

2. **Search for the superlative: only, first, best, most, highest, least, greatest, strongest.** Even the most mundane accomplishments sound much better when described with a superlative.

   (Warning: Don't take credit for being the youngest man or first woman, African American, or person of Lithuanian descent to x, y, or z. Employers just don't care. They want to know if you can do the job, and pointing out that you've already risen well beyond others with your background is frankly alarming.)

3. **Use appropriate jargon.** Would you take a diving lesson from someone who insisted on saying "self-contained underwater breathing apparatus" in every sentence? Likewise with human resources information systems, Occupational Safety and Health Administration, Securities and Exchange Commission, return on investment, profit and loss, total quality management, radio detecting and ranging, and so on. Just say HRIS, OSHA, SEC, ROI, P&L, TQM, and radar. People don't even know what the acronyms stand for anymore. If you want to start a fight, lean out your door and ask in a loud voice, "Does IS mean information services, or information sciences?" For years now I've been trying to get an answer to this question: Does SKU stand for store keeping unit, as some reference materials say, or stock keeping unit, as say others? Better to just play it safe, and use IS and SKU and you won't be misunderstood. If you are worried about your reader, define the jargon once and then use it for the rest of the presentation: National Aeronautics and Space Administration (NASA).

4. **Present the material in order of interest to your intended reader.** If you spend 80% of your time managing ongoing operations and 10% seeking M&A, and you are applying for a job with a venture capital or management consulting firm, you had better tell all about the M&A activity before you get on to "oh, yeah, and I also ran the company." The *order* that you present the information in has almost as much impact as the information itself. Remember that.

5. **Start many** (but certainly not all) **sentences with action verbs.** Here are a few of my favorites:

| | |
|---|---|
| act as liaison | motivate |
| administer | negotiate |
| advise | orchestrate |
| analyze | organize |
| compile | originate |
| conduct | oversee |
| consolidate | plan |
| contribute | prepare |
| coordinate | produce |
| create | promote |
| design | provide |
| develop | reconcile |
| devise | reorganize |
| direct | resolve |
| ensure | restrict |
| evaluate | revise |
| execute | schedule |
| facilitate | select |
| generate | start |
| guide | streamline |
| implement | supervise |
| increase | teach |
| initiate | test |
| install | train |
| manage | troubleshoot |
| maximize | utilize |

Here are two examples of job listings. Look for the company, title, dates, scope, and accomplishments:

---

SPINDLE U.S.A. CORPORATION                                 US HQ: Cincinnati, OH
(a wholly owned subsidiary of Spindle, Switzerland)
HEALTH SYSTEMS DIVISION

**Vice President & General Manager**                                 1993-1994
P&L Phoenix/Salt Lake City, 1994
P&L California Central Valley, 1993-1994

Provided regional P&L management (distribution, sales, merchandising, operations, logistics), total staffs up to 200, two distribution centers in each assignment, and revenue responsibility close to $1 billion.

*Contributions:*

Personally oversaw relationships with all levels of management of drug companies, regional chain accounts, retail and hospitals.

Strategized major restructuring projects, achieving cost savings *and* concurrent sales increases of approximately 10%.

Reengineered sales and distribution functions. Focused on quality improvement, enhanced process control, and implementation of cross-functional teams. Ensured training and development of employees.

---

THE COMMERCIAL WORLD BANK

**Vice President, Head of Purchasing**, 1993-Present

Direct the bank's program for centralized purchase of expendable and capital goods supplied to all units corporatewide (United States/Asia/Europe/Latin America); provide oversight and policy development to worldwide decentralized procurement practices. Annual procurement budget in excess of $100,000,000.

Forecast, strategize, and manage all procurement activity. In charge of HQ staff of 22 and decentralized staff of 103 in ordering, contract administration, accounts payable, customer support resources, forms management, IS, and corporate communications functions.

Responsible for tracking millions of pieces of inventory and thousands of open vendor contracts; chair of some two dozen task forces and planning committees; member, executive committee, long-range planning committee, president's budget advisory group, technology evolution planning committee.

Maintain officer-level relations with all major suppliers. Personally negotiate most major purchase and service agreements. Set procurement policy worldwide.

*Accomplishments:*

- Designed cost savings/cost avoidance program saving a documented $4,600,000 in first year alone, as verified by internal management audit. Earned president's commendation and performance bonus.

- Published *CWB Purchasing Policy Manual*, simplifying and standardizing procedures bankwide, to provide guidance to line managers in charge of local purchasing. Results: adherence to principle over precedence; 16% average drop in local purchasing expenses; identification of 6 cases of vendor fraud and 2 cases of employee collusion.

- Brought single-entry integrated paperless forms systems online, eliminating estimated $14,000,000 in paper/printing/handling costs and $5,500,000 in costs associated with delays/introduced errors.

- Negotiated 17 major agreements last year alone, 12 of which were with offshore suppliers. Designed system to track local contracts for possible implementation bankwide.

- Designed minority purchasing program to identify qualified minority suppliers; exceeded 15% minority contracting goal at wholly competitive rates/specifications.

- Reduced staff by 15% with concurrent *increase* in service provision.

---

After detailing fifteen to twenty years of work history, you can truncate your presentation. Use a synopsis statement, or just list companies and titles (no dates). Here are two examples:

PRIOR:

Smith, Johnson & Hills, Inc., HQ: Buffalo
**General Sales Manager**
**Branch Sales Manager** (two branches)
**Sales Manager**
**Associate**

---

SYNOPSIS: Additional experience in accounting and finance, including design of all financial systems for start-up that went to $3.5 million in sales, and service as an auditor, tax consultant, and manager for a Big 6 accounting firm.

Knowing when to cut off your résumé is difficult. Not only will the case of every candidate be different, but for any given candidate every application might be different. A consultant, a jobseeker, and the new member of a philanthropic board will all have different concerns about how many dates to reveal, even if they are the same person. In general, do not give people information in preliminary contacts that will reveal your age, if it puts you at a disadvantage compared with younger, equally accomplished candidates. You can always provide more information later, but you cannot retract information already let out.

## A Warning About Consulting Engagements

If you do list a period of self-employed consulting, you must report *specific* engagements, that is, a specific client, a specific project, a specific outcome. Otherwise, employers will assume you couldn't get even a single contract, or even worse, you made the whole thing up to disguise a period of inactivity and despondency. Here's the right way to do it:

**Paul K. Pizarny dba Marketing Design Group**, 1995 – Present
Philadelphia, Pennsylvania

*Marketing Consultant*

Initiated, structured, and conducted marketing consulting projects, including all phases of business analysis, market analysis, media planning, staff training, and organizational development in support of marketing efforts. Designed marketing campaigns for two existing companies; designed entire marketing function (staff, policies, operations) for two start-up companies. Examples:

- NEW FACES, EDUCATION DIVISION — Providing organizational consulting and marketing plans for a cosmetic surgery spin-off company. Working directly with the founder of the company to develop realistic marketing budgets and plans for various business launch scenarios. Ongoing.

- EASTERN COLLEGES OF APPLIED TECHNOLOGY — Revamped marketing and advertising functions for this educational nonprofit with 15 campuses. Restructured $3 million annual ad/marketing budget. Solicited, reviewed and selected an advertising agency. Consolidated and standardized marketing, advertising, and media planning for all campuses. Achieved 41% increase in fall class with no increase in ad/marketing budget. 1995.

- CHARLOTTESVILLE STAR RESTAURANTS, INC. — Planned and conducted comprehensive review of marketing plans for five restaurants in suburban Washington, D.C./Virginia area. Wrote the company's first formal media plan. Achieved 13% increase in business with minimal increase in marketing budget. Also consulted on some operational areas to improve company image. 1995-1996.

- PAPYRUS, INC. — Retained to establish structure and internal marketing function for newly formed franchise/real estate department for an aggressive new retail chain. Provided competitive analysis, consulted on site selection, collaborated on business plan development and strategic plan for franchisee development. 1995.

If you want to get started, or just want to use your leisure time productively, volunteer your consulting expertise with educational, religious, or other nonprofit organizations. Then you'll have some projects to report on your résumé.

## Education

As a general rule, if you went to a name brand school, have a recent degree, have worked less than ten years, or are in medicine or academe, education goes before the experience section on your résumé. Otherwise, in general business applications the education section comes after experience. Here is a straightforward listing:

**EDUCATION**

THE WHARTON SCHOOL, UNIVERSITY OF PENNSYLVANIA
**M.B.A., Finance**

AMHERST COLLEGE
**B.A., Mathematics**

If you are listing recent education, you may try to milk a little extra mileage out of it by listing classes or research, as in this example:

**EDUCATION**

Golden Gate University, San Francisco, California
**M.B.A., Human Resource Management,** May 1996

Coursework / Areas of Special Interest:
- Management Theory
- HR Information Systems
- Employment Law
- Benefits Analysis
- Compensation Theory & Practice
- Issues in Outplacement & Downsizing
- Topics in HR Management
- Training Science
- EAP
- Labor Negotiations

University of Tampa, Tampa, Florida
**B.A., History,** 1978

If your major is totally unrelated to your current career, you can list the degree and omit the major. Always list the undergraduate degree, even if you have a stack of graduate degrees. You don't want to be associated with the type of graduate programs that admit students who have not completed their undergraduate programs.

If you did not complete a program, do not say "M.B.A. program, 1991-1992," which is an outright admission of failure to complete the degree requirements; instead, say something like this: "Graduate Studies in Finance and Business Modeling, 1991–1992." If you do not have a degree, use the "studies in" technique, or simply list the area of concentration, as in this example:

UNIVERSITY OF SOUTH FLORIDA
**Psychology**

For more on how to sell education, see my *From College to Career.* For most executives, however, education should be listed last and should not be emphasized. Listing your squash trophies could be evidence of arrested development. Was it really the crowning moment of your life when you won some sporting game twenty years ago?

## Publications, Affiliations, Patents, Computer Skills, References, Etc.

The bottom of your résumé is an excellent place to put miscellaneous details, such as publications, patents, foreign languages not likely to be used on the job, computer skills if not already mentioned, and so on. Keep your computer skills vague, as they evolve so quickly and it is secretarial to list each software package; try a line like this: "Experience with spreadsheet, database, and word processing packages." Remember that your reader is probably skimming by this point, so if information is pertinent to a particular reader, it should be moved to the profile or further up in the presentation. Saying "references on request" is not necessary and is now considered old-fashioned. Unless requested, withhold your references from initial contacts. References can be incorporated, as in the presentation on p. 468, or written up on a page of their own, as in the examples in chapter 14.

## Regional Differences

With executive mobility at an all-time high, regional differences in résumé styles are disappearing. A plant manager in Indiana may be from Louisiana, and the president of a company in Oregon may be from New Jersey. Nevertheless, some stylistic differences remain. Private high schools are frequently listed on finance résumés in the Northeast corridor, New York to Boston, for roughly the first ten years of employment after college. This is a practice not copied in the rest of the country. East Coast résumés tend to be strictly business. In the Midwest, the South, and on the West Coast, presentations reveal a little more personality. Résumés in general are flashier on the West Coast, and a *little* less flashy in the Midwest and on the East Coast, but not much less. In California you are safe in making strong, self-congratulatory remarks; in Boston/New York/New Jersey, a slightly understated tone is better. These are subtle differences, however, and a good résumé is a good résumé from sea to shining sea.

Whatever tone you adopt, be sure to communicate your accomplishments. Several years ago I worked with the president of a company who had made the jump from chief of sales to chief operating officer, and at the same time moved from New York to Los Angeles. He had a straightforward operations-based résumé describing the company and the product. It was boring, but utilitarian. By reading it, you could see him in the president's office, poring over reports trying to shave a point or two off of some already minuscule cost.

I knew there had to be more to the story. "What happened to gross sales while you've been president?" I asked him.

"They've more than doubled," he said.

"You achieved a 100% increase in sales," I asked him, incredulous, "and you don't think that needs to be in your résumé?"

"Well, I didn't want them to think I was bragging," he said.

"Brag," I said. "This is the time to brag. You're in L.A. now, and if you don't brag they'll think you have nothing to brag about. By the way, what happened to margins?"

"They doubled, too."

He was so eager not to seem like a salesman that he forgot to sell himself at all.

## Papers, Colors, Textures, Fonts, Envelopes

A study of executive recruiters revealed that paper color by itself was not a selection factor, but that paper weight was very important. As long as you choose a nice pearl gray, white, or light tan, you're safe on paper color. Avoid ivory, a color that was way too popular in the 80s, and avoid any of the parchment or marbled colorings, as these styles were favored for decades by a national résumé-writing organization with a less-than-stellar reputation. Do not select a dark shade, as you can expect companies to want to scan, copy, and fax your résumé. I prefer a lightly textured paper over a smooth finish, but that is a personal prejudice. Much has been made of cotton content, and once upon a time cotton was the chief indicator of high quality, but papermaking technology has taken a leap, and cotton content is no longer an indicator of anything but high cost. Paper weight, however, matters. A heavy weight paper connotes a heavyweight candidate, a manager of substance and reliability. Pick the heaviest paper you can that is not card stock, 24 lb. minimum up to perhaps 80 lb. maximum. You can print your résumés and cover letters on standard 8½ x 11-inch paper, or on Monarch-sized stationery, 7¼ x 10½ inches (but only if you have a full complement of matching envelopes).

Executives should choose a conservative, easy-to-read, serif font, size ten to twelve. Serif means the letters have tiny horizontal lines that serve as tops and bases of the vertical lines, like the letters in this sentence. Some version of Times Roman is standard on almost all word processing systems, and a good default choice for an executive presentation. Scanners and OCR software have become so sophisticated that it is no longer necessary to avoid bold and italic type in a résumé that will be scanned, although underlining can still be a problem. Do not write or design your résumé just to be scanned. Relying on scanners and databases is a notoriously poor way to look for work, especially at the executive level. Write and design your presentation to impress a human, and plan on following up with a phone call. (I don't know how many databases you've called lately, but I haven't had a good conversation with one yet.)

**Do not ever fold up an executive résumé.** It will never lie flat again, and laser printing flakes off at the folds. Instead, send out your résumés in 9 x 12-inch envelopes, either standard manila or white, or made to match your paper.

Should you ever use company stationery? Not if you're applying for a job. Use your official stationery for company business or a philanthropic endeavor, never for private business. Resist the temptation to use the office postage meter, even out of convenience. It's tacky at best and literally a petty theft; some recruiters view it as a lapse of judgment.

## Special Problems

### Too old

Do not put *any* dates on a résumé that will allow the reader to calculate your age. List jobs back ten to twenty years, then just omit dates or use the summary or prior techniques listed above. Drop ancient jobs entirely; they probably do nothing to sell you today anyway. It is perfectly acceptable to list a date with your latest educational endeavor and omit dates from older education listings. Keep the focus on your skills and accomplishments and off your age. Use hard-driving language and dynamic descriptions of your accomplishments to convey vitality. Although its not my favorite technique, you can also list activities such as mountain biking, tennis, and marathon running. When you go to the interview, dress in fashion, walk briskly, speak with enthusiasm, and consider touching up that gray.

The days of total disclosure *in advance* are over. Don't allow anyone to screen you out on age.

By the way, coming into a company as a consultant or a temporary executive is an excellent technique for older workers. Once they see how valuable you are, they'll forget all about your age.

### Overqualified

Overqualified is a code word usually meaning "too old" or "too expensive." When it means "too old," use the techniques above. When it means "too expensive," remind the employer that you've made some good investments and no longer need the kind of income you've made in the past.

When you are actually overqualified, you need to tone down your résumé. Change or omit numbers that are out of line with the targeted company. For example, if you were going from a larger company to an entrepreneurial start-up, you might describe your most recent employer not as "a $90 million company" but as "a multimillion-dollar company." Change "managed departmental staff of 120" to "managed staff." Then change experience descriptions from the strategic to the tactical level. Instead of talking about policy and company direction, talk about mundane tasks within your department. Change "designed the succession-planning process for the entire company," a policy-level description, to "wrote job descriptions for executive staff and conducted salary surveys," equally true but less threatening to the chief HR manager at a smaller concern.

Some experimentation and practice will provide you with range of presentations and the ability to present yourself as appropriately qualified for each position you seek.

## No education

See the education section, above, for techniques to deal with education. If you actually have no post-high school classroom experience whatsoever, not one single seminar or vendor-training session, omit any reference to education and make sure your résumé is at least two pages long.

By the way, never let lack of education keep you from applying for advancement. Either crack the hidden job market using books like *The Overnight Job Change Strategy* to apply for positions before they're announced, or apply anyway to all those jobs advertised as "advanced degree preferred" or "college degree absolutely required." I've placed more nondegreed executives in positions advertised like that than I can count.

Never, never, never succumb to the urge to lie about an educational program. It takes less than sixty seconds to call the registrar and verify your claim.

## Too many jobs (job-hopper)

Do not assume that you will be considered a job-hopper if you have had more than a few jobs in the last ten years. These days, mobility is seen as less of a liability than is longevity in one assignment.

Nevertheless, if you list all dates on your résumé as year-to-year, as you should, then you can omit jobs that are as long as two years without showing a gap in your résumé. Experiment with this. Do not worry if your résumé shows you leaving one job in 1991 and beginning another in 1992. See gaps, below.

Remember, a résumé is a marketing presentation. Every word must be true, but you don't have to list a single item that would count against you.

## Short tenure

Short tenure used to be a real red flag to recruiters, but it is less so now. Companies' plans change so fast, who could blame an employee for getting caught up in those changes? In general, if you can omit a short tenure it is best to do so. If you cannot, try to define it as a change in the company's plans or market, or describe what you were able to finish while you were there. Here are a couple of examples:

"This division was bought out by Microsoft six months after I was brought on board; after assisting with the integration I opted to accept a severance offer."

---

The strategic plan is now in its second year and has achieved its goal of reversing negative business trends at the bank. Available for a new challenge.

If the short tenure is due to a bad fit, and you cannot avoid listing the position, gently insinuate that the other side is at fault:

Recruited to open a chain of galleries in luxury hotels worldwide for an investment group with no prior art background. Opened in Paris, Milan, San Francisco, and Monaco with sales in excess of plan, then experienced aesthetic differences with the board and turned the project over to others.

Sometimes you can convert short tenures into interim executive or consulting engagements by negotiating a change in your status *before you leave,* but this can be risky if a prospective employer later decides you lied to them about the nature or status of the experience.

### Demotion

A demotion used to be a sign of a real loser, someone who couldn't handle a higher level of responsibility, someone not valued by the company. Now, *the exact opposite is true*. If a company doesn't value you, they just fire you. Today, a demotion means that the company thought so highly of you that they retained you when they reorganized or eliminated your position. Use language like this:

"One of the only managers retained by the acquiring company's organization. Reassigned to . . ."

---

Identified as a high potential manager and temporarily assigned to a headquarters staff position, one of the only regional directors so retained.

An excellent example of how to deal with a demotion begins on p. 155.

By the way, lateral transfers are so common now that they don't even require comment. Flatter organizational charts make them inevitable.

### Prolonged unemployment, employment gaps, and reentry issues

If you have not worked in over a year, go out and get some consulting assignments. Read the sections on consulting in John Lucht's *Rites of Passage*, or design a marketing plan for your new consulting enterprise using any of Dan Kennedy's or Jay Levinson's excellent marketing books (see the bibliography). Then you will have worked in over a year.

For truly severe cases, I recommend taking every single date off your résumé. Every human resources and recruiting professional I know swears this won't work, and every time I've done it for a client it has worked unbelievably well. Why? It removes the whole issue from the initial consideration of your candidacy. The reader knows there's probably something goofy about the work history, but she doesn't know what it is. If she likes the rest of the story, she'll call you up and ask you about the dates. Then you're talking to her; you've gotten past the first hurdle.

If there is a gap between your current job and your prior work history, list all dates for the prior history, and where dates go for your current job, just write "current."

For older gaps, just don't comment on them. If you list your dates year-to-year they may disappear anyway. 1991–1992 can mean two days or two years. Let it.

### Too long with one employer

Once upon a time, staying with the same employer demonstrated loyalty and reliability. Now, other employers fear you may be brain-dead or locked into a provincial point of view if you've not changed employers in the last ten years. To combat these stereotypes, show every title change, reassignment, relocation, or reorganization of your work duties *as if it were a separate job*. Tie your dates to your work changes, and don't report assignments that started over ten to twenty years ago.

If you switched divisions or moved from one plant to another, feature the plant name or division name, and downplay or even omit the corporate name:

**Chief Engineer,** Rocky Flats Manufacturing Facility, 1992–1994

Also, show leadership roles in industry consortia, trade groups, associations, lobbying groups, or other organizations, anything to show you interact with others outside your company. Take on a moonlighting consulting gig or write an article for an industry trade journal addressing an issue broader than your own company. If nothing else, note customer visits and vendor relationships.

Your goal is to show dynamic career growth and recent contributions, even though you've been with one employer for some length of time.

### Scandalous past or confidential present

If your employer defrauded investors of $700 million, killed off several particularly cuddly species, or made a name for itself promoting illegal prostitution, you may wish to distance yourself from the company. You can do this several ways. Most obviously, "Nasty Brothers' Lewd and Lascivious Theatres, Inc.," is perhaps better rendered "NBLL Theatres, Inc." or "NBLLT, Inc." You can also use a generic description of a company, in place of its name: "A $13 Million Diversified Entertainment Group."

Also, if your division or department was not involved in the scandal, sometimes the smartest thing to do is just point that out: "The Taiwanese branch of Bartell International was and is the most profitable in company, in contrast to the bankruptcies in Singapore and Hong Kong." One CEO I worked with wanted to let prospective employers know that he had nothing to do with the recent disgraceful performance of his company, run into the ground in just 18 months; we wrote: "After 23 years of consistent profitability, the transfer was completed in June 1995. Subsequently, owners installed entirely new management team, and the company's progress since that time has been guided by them."

### Transition into new industry or function

Transitional résumés are some of the most difficult to strategize and write. Nevertheless, here is a process that leads to success: Analyze the job you are seeking, that is, make a list of the functions you would perform on the job, and then prioritize them in order of greatest importance *in that job*. Then, break down your own recent jobs into discrete tasks and functions, identifying similarities. When you describe your current job on your transitional résumé, describe the tasks in the order of importance *in the targeted job*. This sounds simple, but it works. It's a formula for writing transitional résumés, and with it, you can create vastly different presentations, all based on the background you currently have and all true. **The order of the information completely changes its impact.**

If you are not careful, however, this process can lead to thoroughly misleading presentations, line by line literally true, but in aggregate inexcusably misleading. Remember, if the potential employer decides you've lied to him, you're not going to get the job anyway.

Another method is to create a highlights section in which you describe only those projects and accomplishments relative to the targeted job, and then later describe the rest of your work experience, as in the example beginning on p. 59.

■

With a little creativity, you will find that almost any special problem can be overcome without resorting to lying about your record or using a non-executive résumé style. Think, experiment, and don't be afraid to omit damaging information.

# General and Financial Management: VP to CEO

The last two chapters really serve as the introduction to this chapter. The following are classic general and financial management résumés, providing the information employers want in the order they want it. They are easy to skim, substantive, and provide a high "verifiability" factor.

In general, do not look for just the résumés in your own field. Look for styles that appeal to you, that you would want to represent you, and look for solutions others have used to any career challenges you may face. By careful reading, you'll find a lot of language you can use in your own presentations, even if many of the examples are from other industries. Pay particular attention to the varying use of profile and highlights sections, the balance between scope and accomplishments, and the mix of narrative paragraphs and bulleted items.

The résumés in this and the following chapters represent real people, so you'll find some odd career twists, education that is out of sync with the career, a permanent residence in one area and a full-time job in a distant state, and other peculiarities. I have retained these specifically to illustrate the wonderful variety of career patterns that can lead to success. Contrary to what many people believe, *at any time in your career* you can suddenly take off and achieve astounding success.

Be sure to check the index for résumés in other chapters that may apply to your particular case.

# Cordell Baker

5 Clam Beach Path
Bristol, Rhode Island 02809

Home Office: (401) 555-8928
cb.ceo@wan.net.com

## EXPERIENCE

**Equity Financial Group, Inc.,** Providence, Rhode Island, 1979–1996

**C.E.O. & Chairman**

Built financial services company from zero to NYSE company with 1500 employees, $4.5 billion under management, $95 million in sales, and pre-tax income of $19 million. R.O.E. ran 25-40% in last six years.

Company became a factor in money management ($2.5 billion), real estate ($2 billion), property management (25 billion feet), and equipment leasing ($200 million). Had 300,000 retail accounts, plus institutional and international operations.

Company known for consistently bringing out successful new financial products and new public financing strategies, and creation of an entrepreneurial work ethic inside the company. Personally initiated and guided joint ventures and subsidiary operations in Japan and Europe.

Other strengths of the company were a solid information sciences infrastructure that was well ahead of industry norms, and operational controls throughout that facilitated smooth operations during periods of rapid growth.

Company had a 16-year track history of consistent profitability and growth (guided company through the 1987 crash without significant losses). Sold company to Mid-Atlantic Investors Corp. in November 1995, at approximately 16 times earnings and 40% over market value, and completed the transition by February 1996.

Subsequently, owners installed entirely new management team, and the company's progress since that time has been guided by them.

**Capital Funding Corporation,** Providence, Rhode Island, 1974–1979

**Branch Manager**
**Sales Manager**

Took this office from second worst to the best (top grossing office in the nation out of 24 offices). Recruited and trained new sales team. Designed training and incentive systems that were copied company-wide. Personally ranked in top ten producers out of over 500 account executives nationwide.

**Kabor Accessories Company,** Providence, Rhode Island, 1968–1974
(subsidiary of Kabor International)

**Director of Marketing Research**
**Controller**
**Legal Department**

Earned rapid promotions by creating dramatic growth and profitability for the company. Profit went from zero to $2.8 million. Made strategic contributions to capitalization, marketing, advertising, and sales.

Developed sophisticated system to monitor and predict consumer trends, resulting in sales, growth and profit. Achieved ROS of 65%.

## EDUCATION

**B.S., Finance,** University of Massachusetts, 1968

ADDITIONAL INFORMATION PROVIDED ON REQUEST

# MARGARET ELLIS ARMSTRONG

14 Rock Lake Circle
Piedmont Hills, California 94612

Office/voice mail: (415) 555-2855
Residence/voice mail: (510) 555-1735
m.armstrong@is.tri.com

---

**EXPERTISE**

**Information Technology and Global Information Delivery Systems —
Consulting, Planning, Management, Marketing, Strategic Analysis, Alliances**

*Highlights*

Seeking a new challenge.

Over ten years CIO experience in state-of-the-art information technology in telecom, R&D, manufacturing, medical, financial and aerospace environments. Entire career history in developing applications based on emerging technologies.

Presided over the design and launch of a strategic, global information network linking staff, contractors, customers, and key industry organizations with full features (text search/retrieval, real-time interactive data sharing, catalog/order/fulfillment, file transfer, e-mail, BBS, news) *that was fully operational years before commercial acceptance of the Internet.*

Skills include strategic planning, budgeting and finance; recruiting visionary scientific and technical staff; setting protocol, goals, and missions for subordinate business units; ensuring IS integration into the larger organization.

**EXPERIENCE**

TELEDAT RESEARCH INSTITUTE (TRI), INC.      Palo Alto, CA

**Director (CIO), Advanced Information Technology Group**      1994–Present
**VP (CIO), Information Technology**      1984–1994

TRI is the largest industry-sponsored R&D organization in the world, a $600 million think tank and "idea engine" for the high-technology information industry.

*Honors*

1995 Chief Information Officer — Top 100 Company Award

1993 1st Place International Paper Competition: "GNOSIS: Leveraging Knowledge"

*Highlights*

Built a state-of-the-art information technology function from scratch, providing vision and executive direction, capitalization/funding/budgeting/organization, staffing, and integration/user relations with the larger organization.

Direct information technology core research program and electronic technology transfer to over 6000 IS engineers at hundreds of client companies. Manage 100+ staff and budgets of $15 to $20 million. Represent employer and department on a national level (see affiliations).

**Other contributions:** Designed and launched the new Advanced Information Technology Research and Consulting Services business unit.

Commissioned and managed landmark "NII Business Opportunities and Risk" report for the industry.

Conducted 26 recent briefings at national industry and government meetings, including collaboration/consultation/testimony before Economic Council, World Bank, Department of Energy, Department of Commerce, Electric Edison Institute, and similar.

Continue to manage, advance, and enhance state-of-the-art information services for TRI and supporting organizations.

STAGECOACH BANK      San Francisco, CA

**Vice President, Central Systems Division**

Analyzed and restructured Central Systems Division of Stagecoach Bank. Directed employees responsible for systems supporting 58 to 78 billion dollars per day of business. Developed strategic technology management plan. Repositioned the department to better anticipate the changing business environment.

FEDERAL RESERVE BANK      San Francisco, CA

**Vice President, Computer Systems**

Directed development, enhancement, and maintenance of computer information systems. Wrote Long-Range Automation Plan. Reorganized department to align with business functional areas. Responsible for design and implementation of state-of-the-art deposit reserve system for 400+ banks in western United States.

CUTTER LABORATORIES      Berkeley, CA
(a subsidiary of Bayer)

**Business Systems Development Manager**

Responsible for automation of all U.S. manufacturing plants. Oversaw manufacturing, cost accounting, quality assurance and scientific application systems development. Developed business systems and technology planning. Designed first online network supporting five geographically dispersed manufacturing plants and HQ.

U.S. DEPT. OF HEALTH, EDUCATION & WELFARE      Washington, D.C.

**Consultant** and **Technical Director, Bureau of Quality Assurance**

Directed resolution of interagency problems. Managed design, testing and implementation of National Medical Information System, a $500,000 development project. Designed standardized QA programs for medical care industry.

CALIFORNIA STATE DEPARTMENT OF HEALTH      Berkeley, CA
**Director** and **Statistician**

> Designed and implemented the first statewide dialysis and transplant information system in the nation. Developed statewide uniform cost reporting system. Designed, programmed, and implemented cancer incidence system. Conducted original research presented in papers and reports.

THE RAND CORPORATION      Santa Monica, CA
**Assistant Scientist**

> Assisted in analysis of decision-making theory, cost analysis, economic modeling, and foreign aid mission projects. Top secret clearance.

**EDUCATION**

**B.A.,** Dean's Scholar, University of Washington

Continuing Education:

> **Executive Management Program,** IBM
> **Executive Graduate Program,** UCLA Graduate School of Management

**AFFILIATIONS**

**Society for Information Management**

**U.S. Council on Competitiveness**
(21st Century Information Infrastructure Working Group)

**National Academy of Science**
(NII Working Group)

**American Management Association**
(Information Technology Advisory Committee)

**Information Management Executives**
(Conference Board)

**Cross Industry NII Standards Committee**
(Executive Committee)

# SARAH HOPKINS WATERMAN

4100 Park Border Drive
Cincinnati, Ohio 45241

Office: Direct line/voice mail: (513) 555-8983
Residence (message): (513) 555-8563

---

**PROFILE**

Background of senior line management positions with emphasis on strategic contributions. Strengths in the following areas:

- **Sales, Marketing & Merchandising**
- **Distribution**
- **Supplier Relations, Customer Relations**
- **Knowledge of the Marketplace**

Additional strengths: vision, team building, effective people management, management of technology planning.

**EXPERIENCE**

SPITZ-REITZ U.S.A. CORPORATION US HQ: Cincinnati, OH
HEALTH SYSTEMS DIVISION

**Vice President & General Manager**    1994–Present

Provide direction and daily management for an organization generating $2 billion in annual revenues. Delegate to staff through subordinate managers (vice president and department head level). Personally manage relationships with senior management of drug companies, group purchasing organizations, and integrated health care networks.

Report directly to the C.O.O. of Spitz-Reitz U.S.A. Member, executive team, the strategic planning group developing our approach to the rapidly changing U.S. managed care environment (involving a revolution away from selling products and toward becoming a true solutions provider).

*Contributions:*

Organized this new division, providing focus and top-to-bottom design (information flows, technology, integration, customer retention plan, new business development plan). Gave presentation to parent company officers in Switzerland to win endorsement of the new strategic plan.

Collaborated with line managers and re-evaluated operations throughout the company to make them more responsive to this customer segment.

Business process owner for potential alliances or acquisitions. Currently in initial stages of two potential agreements; recently completed a third.

Also currently working with customers and suppliers of Medicorp, our Canadian subsidiary, to improve product flow through Canadian drug wholesalers.

*Continued . . .*

**Vice President & General Manager**      1993–1994
P&L Phoenix/Salt Lake City, 1994
P&L California Central Valley, 1993–1994

Provided regional P&L management (distribution, sales, merchandising, operations, logistics), total staffs up to 200, two distribution centers in each assignment, and revenue responsibility close to $1 billion.

*Contributions:*

Personally oversaw relationships with all levels of management of drug companies, regional chain accounts, retail, and hospitals.

Strategized major restructuring projects, achieving cost savings and concurrent sales increases of approximately 10%.

Reengineered sales and distribution functions. Focused on quality improvement, enhanced process control, and implementation of cross-functional teams. Ensured training and development of employees.

**Vice President**      1986–1993
**Director**      1984–1986
Merchandising — National

Provided direction and daily management to national merchandising efforts, all product categories, all distribution channels, representing approximately $10 billion in annual business to the company. Supervised staff of 22 (merchandisers; managers, national accounts; support staff).

*Contributions:*

Improved market segmentation company-wide, developing several highly successful niche programs and improving focus of existing programs. *Increased profit by factor of eight.*

Improved relationships with major accounts (Wal-Mart, Longs, Mercy Hospital Group, and similar) and suppliers (Eli Lilly, Glaxo, Mylan — basically all the major pharmaceutical and health/beauty aid suppliers).

Integrated purchasing, merchandising, and marketing for merger of Rx-Rite and Mother's Healthcare Company into Spitz-Reitz.

Developed and installed LAN accounting system to invoice, track and deduct promotional monies, rebates and advertising allowances, generating a trackable $2 million in additional revenues in first year alone.

Introduced a series of efficiency measures, for example, designed supplier reporting process to reduce delivery lead time and cost of inventory.

Spearheaded introduction of Mother's Healthcare private label into Medicorp, our Canadian subsidiary.

Member of the Board, Spitz-Reitz Foundation. Chairwoman, Consumer Products Committee, National Retailers Association.

*Continued . . .*

**District Sales Manager**      1976–1984
Chicago

Managed sales for one of the company's largest distribution territories. Developed and motivated a staff of 16 sales professionals.

*Contributions:*

*Created a threefold increase in business* through new customer development and improved selling technique. Author, *New Customer Development Manual,* adapted later for use nationwide.

National sales award for increased sales.

National sales management award for successful implementation of Loc-Trac, one of the first fully computerized order management systems.

Regional sales award for best overall results.

*PRIOR:*

**Account Manager**
**Inventory Manager**
**Supervisor — Cartex**
**Account Manager — Cartex**
**Telephone Sales Representative**

EDUCATION

UNIVERSITY OF CHICAGO — EXECUTIVE DEVELOPMENT
**Finance Course**

UNIVERSITY OF CINCINNATI
**General Studies**

XEROX SALES TRAINING COURSE
**Personal Selling Skills**

ADDITIONAL

Public speaking skills. PC skilled (word processing, analysis, spreadsheets). Available for relocation as needed. Please keep this information confidential.

# ANNE LIVINGSTON

70 Waterville Place NW
Seattle, Washington 98147
Residence/message: (206) 555-9218

800 Tolkien Drive
Rochelle Park, New Jersey 07662
Nationwide direct office line: (800) 555-8000
Residence/message: (201) 555-0662

---

**PROFILE**

Senior executive with extensive P&L background in rapidly evolving high technology markets. Strengths include general management, vision, leadership, execution. Proven talent for change management, including leading the paradigm shift currently underway throughout Becker-McKenzie.

**EDUCATION**

**M.B.A., Finance,** The Wharton School, University of Pennsylvania, *with honors*
**B.A., History,** SUNY — Stony Brook, *with honors*
**B.S.E.E.,** Cornell University, *with honors*

**EXPERIENCE**

BECKER-MCKENZIE

**Vice President,** Business Process Reengineering, Becker-McKenzie Worldwide, 1995–Present
Hartford, Connecticut

*Worldwide Reengineering Project:*

Responsible for redesign of worldwide sales and services processes to ensure common, consistent execution on a global basis. Believed to be the largest single sales reengineering effort in the world in aggressiveness and scope.

Responsible for building business case, managing to it, and reporting to Becker-McKenzie's CFO and CEO on results. Manage teams responsible for effecting redesign, communications, education, application development and deployment in a matrix management system covering Becker-McKenzie's six geographic divisions: North America; Latin America; Asia-Pacific and Australia; E.C.-Western Europe; Middle East-Africa; Eastern Europe and former Soviet Bloc.

Redesign will impact approximately 100,000 personnel. Initial deployment began worldwide in 2Q '96.

Involves changes in processes, application systems, and tools, but more importantly, radical changes in management system and culture. Work with senior line executives to ensure changes take effect.

*North America responsibilities:*

Creation of business strategy for North America sales and service. Report to President of Becker-McKenzie North America, work with him and his executive team. Together, build a business strategy to be communicated to employees and customers.

Senior line executive for North America fulfillment (ordering, contracts, billing, A/R, facilities, and support operations). Approximately 4,000 staff.

**General Manager,** Business & Consumer Division, Southern California, 1992–1995
Los Angeles, California

Provided strategic direction and daily operations management for this business unit with 750 direct employees, 270 indirect, and annual revenues of approximately

$870 million. Responsible for products and service for large and small customers. Managed P&L, capital and operating budgets, real estate, strategic and tactical market planning, employee compensation and incentive structures, business unit IS, process management systems, and administration.

Supervised CFO; CIO; Director, Consulting and Services; Business Unit Executive; Product Marketing Executive; Real Estate Manager; Quality Manager; and other department heads. Reported to the Area General Manager and indirectly to the President of Becker-McKenzie U.S.

*Selected contributions:*

Created a transformation of this business unit that was later adopted by every other unit in the United States. This was in response to market intelligence that indicated Becker-McKenzie was no longer responsive to customer concerns. The restructuring was comprehensive, rapid, and revolutionary, from planning to implementation.

Repositioned the entire sales force from on-site generalists to floating specialists, improving service, reducing headcount, and regaining customer loyalty and respect. This required a top-to-bottom operations redesign, including state-of-the-art business concepts (360-degree evaluation, "hoteling," flatter, cross-pollinated work teams, lowest-possible-level decision-making authority, opportunity-based resource allocation, performance-based incentives, consultative selling). Created numerous new revenue streams by converting sales mentality from products and maintenance to solutions and availability guarantees.

Designed program to educate and sell a full paradigm shift to existing employees. Achieved 50% reduction in headcount with remarkably light press coverage and no pending legal actions, documented improved morale in retained employees. Fashioned new systems to encourage employees to take responsibility for career pathing and advancement.

Implemented end-to-end process management system in conjunction with reengineering the business.

Developed market management and segmentation studies for 22 different markets (brand, industry, service), with business and financial plan for each market.

Developed system to measure, analyze, and improve customer satisfaction by transaction type. Built criteria into compensation systems to foster ownership by employees.

Implemented a "troubled projects" process to identify negative cost potential on services / consulting engagements. Renegotiated several contracts to prevent loss with 100% customer retention and increased customer satisfaction.

Built a new type of teleservices center with inbound / outbound telephony designed to increase customer service and staff utilization, while simultaneously creating an IS database used to improve both sales and customer satisfaction. Won the "Best Use of Technology" award from the American Marketing Association, 1995.

Installed new mentoring program for managers and technical personnel, separating career pathing from daily / technical / team management.

Reversed negative revenue and profit trends. Doubled revenue in services business. Increased market share in large system processors, AB / 9000, SW, RS / 42s, and PCs.

This unit was a pilot center for numerous human resources, process, and go-to-market programs later slated for rollout nationwide. Had pricing authority for contracts placed through the business unit (deals go to $250 million). Also structured and negotiated joint-venture, enterprise agreement, and subcontracts with business partners.

With direct access to all members of top executive committee, continued to provide input on companywide review of Becker-McKenzie's marketing organization, employee compensation systems, software pricing, terms and conditions on domestic contracts, and the role of the geographic manager.

Earned Becker-McKenzie Leadership Award for outstanding performance.

**Staff Assistant to R. Michael Tollers,** SVP, 1991–1992
Cupertino, California

Special assignment as staff to R. Michael Tollers, SVP, one of the four members of Becker-McKenzie's senior management committee. Oversaw ongoing product development and manufacturing for worldwide and domestic sales. Gained expertise in manufacturing and development processes, domestic and offshore. Reviewed management and human resources changes for Becker-McKenzie worldwide.

Orchestrated worldwide planning for financial restructuring of sales, general, and administration expenses. Initiated numerous quality projects, including disseminating Malcolm Baldridge concepts to managers and creating process management systems.

**Director of Marketing & Support**, Government Marketing, 1989–1991
McLean, Virginia

Responsible for market analysis, development of strategy, and marketing programs for Becker-McKenzie's hardware, software, and services offering to all state and federal government customers. Identified federal product requirements and negotiated development plan changes with the product lines of business. Managed line product sales organization based in Washington, D.C., and active in all fifty states. Restructured SW sales. Strategized entire company approach in this multiyear, multimillion-dollar contracting environment. Achieved #1 sales growth in the nation for two years straight. Increased SW sales from last to first in the United States.

**Manager, S**ales Plan Operations, 1988–1989
Hartford, Connecticut

Responsible for the sales (commission) plan for U.S. marketing representatives, systems engineers, and management. Tasks included sales plan development, education, execution, administration, and management of the commission budget. Restructured budget process, allowing precise projections of expense and eliminating overruns. Refocused sales incentives to reward solution selling, now the paradigm companywide.

**Branch Manager**, 1986–1988
Seattle, Washington

Responsible for marketing and support activities in the state of Washington, revenue approximately $65 million, with staff of 180 marketing representatives, systems engineers, administrative personnel. Represented Becker-McKenzie in the community as location manager for Washington. Improved management approval rating from 6% to 94%. Broke every single sales record in branch history.

**Regional Marketing Manager**, 1984–1986
Detroit, Michigan

> Responsible for marketing programs and situation support for the company's large systems product line and financial offerings to branches supporting customers in Illinois, Indiana, Iowa, and Michigan. Tasks involved working with corporate pricing and product functions as well as Becker-McKenzie Credit Corporation to structure solutions for customer requirements. Achieved record-breaking large systems market share growth.

**Marketing Manager**, 1983–1984
Joliet, Illinois

> Managed 10 marketing representatives supporting a wide range of customers and selling Becker-McKenzie's entire product line. Customers included International Harvester, Inland Steel, and a number of intermediate-sized manufacturing, process, and service firms. Increased customer satisfaction and achieved record sales for 1984 calendar year.

**Financial Advisor**, Financial Information Center, 1982–1983
Hartford, Connecticut

> Responsibilities included providing financial marketing advice to the U.S. field force, analyzing purchase versus lease comparison, developing financial offerings, working with third-party leasing organizations, and delivering basic financial education. Facilitated launch of subsidiary leasing corporation, Becker-McKenzie Credit Corporation.

**Marketing Representative**, 1977–1982
Chicago, Illinois

> Responsible for marketing large systems product lines to large companies, including Amoco Oil and Commonwealth Edison. Hundred Percent Club every year (100+% quota).

*Prior*

Blue Diamond Scientific Instrumentation Corp.

Positions in training, market research, and customer service management.

**COMMUNITY SERVICE**

Lighthouse of Hope (Board)
Fiscal Advisory Committee, King County (appointed)
Salvation Army
Seattle Food Bank
Friends of the Elderly
Red Cross
YWCA Leader Luncheon
Bergen County Chamber of Commerce and Industry (Board)
Hospice of Hartford (Board)
United Way (Division Chair)
Recording for the Blind (Board)
Friends of New Jersey Parks (Board)

**REFERENCES**

References provided on request. Please keep this proposal confidential.

# Henry James Hudson, Jr.

1258 St. Charles Avenue
New Orleans, Louisiana 70112

Telephone/message: (504) 555-5387
hank.hudson@mailhost.bus.tulane.edu

---

## KNOWLEDGE

**Operations**
**Manufacturing**
**Food Manufacturing**
**General Management & Leadership**
**Process Improvement & Change Management Diversity**

## EXPERIENCE

KRAFT GENERAL FOODS — KRAFT USA, 1987–Present
    **Educational Leave** (see education, below), 1995–Present
    **Operations Manager (Staff)**, 1991-1995
    Grocery Products Division, Kraft USA HQ, Glenview, Illinois

Provided executive staff assistance, project management, reporting and analysis for division manufacturing $1 billion value/2 billion pounds goods per annum, up to $88 million annual period budget, up to $70 million annual capital budget, $494 million assets, over 4000 employees.

Reported to the Vice President of Grocery Operations. Served as his liaison and representative throughout the company. Supported major manufacturing facilities nationwide. Provided staff direction to 8 plant managers (directly) and entire division staff (indirectly).

This position is designed to groom future multiunit line managers. Postponed the promotion to pursue one-year executive program in organizational development.

*Significant contributions:*

Collaborated with V.P. Grocery Operations and others throughout the company to develop and integrate strategic vision for the division. Point person for budget mix between priorities (e.g.: cost reduction investment vs. operations and maintenance).

Participated in staff and strategic planning meetings with division General Manager, executives from R&D and Marketing, and Kraft corporate heads, e.g., S.V.P. Manufacturing, V.P. Finance, V.P. Systems, V.P. Strategy, V.P. Logistics, V.P. Engineering, V.P. Human Resources.

In charge of the investment portfolio for the division, $168 million over tenure, representing 41% of all Kraft Foods operations capital. Planned and analyzed budgets for division Manufacturing, R&D, Systems, Marketing, and Quality functions.

Facilitated profit enhancement and optimization projects across the board: capacity utilization, low-cost producer status, process reengineering, systems and technology evolution, diversity management, total quality, high-performance team development.

Spearheaded confidential ground-up cost rationalization of entire division. Identified $9 million in immediate income from reallocation of 300 million pounds of production. Integrated tax-advantaged equipment transfers throughout Philip Morris (international). Strategized legal, media, and communications resources to smooth transition.

Developed 200-page strategic document detailing cutting-edge thinking on change management, new organizational structures, and leadership principles, used as internal executive resource and management development tool.

Member, Kraft General Foods Diversity Council. Evaluated and funded local projects in education, culture, diversity, community health and nutrition.

### Business Unit Manager (Line), 1989–1991
Meat Enhancement and Foodservice, Kraft USA, Atlanta, Georgia

Managed manufacturing and company-wide integration of meat enhancement commercial and brand products, including Bulls-Eye Barbecue Sauce, McDonald's and Kentucky Fried Chicken portion-controlled sauces, and bulk product for commercial accounts, including 50% of Kraft's production in the meat enhancement product sector.

The business unit manager's position is cross-pollinated across organizational lines, facilitating rapid decision-making and bringing financial, production, quality, and personnel authority to the front-line management position.

Total staff of 93 employees and 6 managers, manufacturing $150 million value/80 million pounds goods per annum in 70 SKUs from 400 raw materials.

Supervised manufacturing teams running high-performance production lines, a proprietary technology unique in the United States.

Interacted with other divisions and functions on project basis, e.g., orchestrated manufacturing support of Bulls-Eye Labor Day cross-promotion integrated into a national Labor Day NASCAR event.

Originally brought in to reorganize a troubled plant operation, with purview over every aspect of the business unit. Established new training, procedures, performance and quality standards. Created over $1.4 million in cost savings through several innovative programs.

### Business Unit Manager, 1988–1989
Process Cheese & Foodservice, Kraft USA, Decatur, Georgia

Brought in to provide stability to de-unionized plant with entirely new management team. Priorities were to reduce costs, improve morale, raise quality, reengineer the lines, and establish formalized planning.

Applied Statistics Based Management and Total Quality Management principles to a plant with historically ad hoc management policies. Planned and emplaced a series of capacity utilization and cost structure revisions.

Coordinated Quality Control, Engineering, Human Resource, and Financial plans for the business unit.

Eliminated third production shift through first-ever flexible scheduling (10 hour day/4 day week). Retained third shift as training program. Solved mechanical, technical, logistics, and sanitation issues to create paradigm shift in production thinking.

### Production Supervisor, 1987–1988
Process Cheese Plant, Kraft USA, Champaign, Illinois

Managed 30 employees on the production floor, a multimillion-pound operation. Oversaw production, sanitation, quality, material, packaging, and daily planning.

Initiated Dr. Deming's Statistics Based Management within the department.

Hand-picked for high-potential management program.

## U.S. ARMY, 1985–1987

### Personnel Automation Officer, 1985–1987

Managed staff of up to 16 in fully computerized administrative management environment, controlling records for headquarters, U.S. Army 7th Corps, including thousands of military personnel and their dependents. Personnel Action Officer, including one-on-one counseling and employee relations, as well as personnel-related presentations to groups up to 200. Wrote *Automation Management,* a training and procedures document on systems management, systems analysis, and error resolution.

With full responsibility for training, leadership, equipment, and planning, led my battle task readiness team to #1 ranking in the command.

**Team Executive Leader**, 1985–1986

Managed a team of 60 persons, with full responsibility for the group's leadership, ethics, teamwork, commitment, task and physical training, and tactical/technical proficiency.

## EDUCATION

TULANE UNIVERSITY — GRADUATE SCHOOL OF BUSINESS
**Graduate Coursework** in **Organizational Development**, *currently*

UNIVERSITY OF CHICAGO — GRADUATE SCHOOL OF BUSINESS
**M.B.A.**, with emphasis on **International Business**

GEORGETOWN UNIVERSITY — SCHOOL OF BUSINESS
**B.S.B.A.** in **Management** with concentration in **Human Resources**

NORTHWESTERN UNIVERSITY — KELLOGG GRADUATE SCHOOL OF MANAGEMENT
**Graduate Courses** in **Corporate Finance** and **Total Quality**

CLARK ATLANTA UNIVERSITY — GRADUATE SCHOOL OF ARTS & SCIENCES
**International Affairs**

U.S. ARMY
**Human Resources Institute**
**Officers Basic Course**

**ALSO:**

Capital Appropriations
Communications Workshop
Team Dynamics
Reengineering Conference
Statistics Based Management
Managing and Appraising Performance
STEPS Problem Solving
Quality Seminars & Workshops (numerous)
Computer Applications Workshops (numerous)

## HONORS

KGF Finance Award for Asset/Facility Rationalization
Chicago Area Diversity Council, Task Force of the Year
KGF Achievement Award for Capital Appropriations Process Improvement Team
KGF Letter of Appreciation for Cash Flow Management

## REFERENCES

References and additional information gladly provided upon request.

# CLYDE L. SUTTON, PH.D.

Office direct line/voice mail: (415) 555-2855
132 Ransom Avenue
Los Altos Hills, California 94022

Residence/message: (415) 555-2965
clyde.dman@vesper.com

---

**PROFILE**

**Information Technology ▪ R&D Management ▪ Strategic Planning ▪ Consulting**

Expertise in new technology development, strategic planning re information technology, general strategic business planning, and ongoing information technology management.

Background emphasizes visionary technology projects, well ahead of the commercialization curve. Reputation as dynamic agent of change, with entrepreneurial nature and high energy level. Effective combination of engineering/research management talent and interpersonal sales, collaboration, and deal-making skills.

Seeking a new opportunity requiring a mix of technical, strategic, and leadership skills.

**EXPERIENCE**

VESPER, INC.      Palo Alto, CA
**Manager, Advanced Information Technology, Strategic Development Group**
    Dec. 1994–Present

VESPER is a $1 billion organization with principal focus on projects marketable to the aerospace and defense industries.

Charged with developing a new line of R&D in Information Systems and Telecommunications (IS&T), with the goal of devising technologies and strategic deployment plans to position those technologies for acceptance in a newly restructured defense environment. Drafted VESPER R&D target statement, essentially an outline for research into Information Systems Integration (ISI). Subsequently joined the Advanced Information Technology Group to work on a wide range of projects.

*Additional contributions:*

- Launched a protocol standard for wireless telecommunications technical services, adopted by all key defense telecom contractors.
- Collaborated on DoD Vendor Communications Infrastructure (DVCI) research project.
- Assisted in a study of Business Opportunities and Risks on the National Information Infrastructure (NII).
- Organized and delivered a workshop on Information and Telecommunications Technologies for U.S. Defense Contractors, co-sponsored by the NIST (U.S. Dept. of Commerce).
- Conceived idea for Information Science & Technology (IS&T) business unit and won approval for the first entirely new direction in R&D at VESPER in over 12 years.
- Designed and conducted market assessment to strategize formulation of new IS&T unit, including intensive sampling of DoD vendor CIOs and top executives.
- Developed R&D plan to create 24 new products within the mission of the unit.
- Organized IS&T R&D unit, identifying and recruiting talent from VESPER Advanced Information Technology, Customer Systems Group, Product Delivery Group, and outside.

- Established successful Wireless Telecommunications Technical Services team as prototype (structure / function / mission) for the new business unit.
- Obtained U.S. Department of Commerce co-sponsorship for "Information and Telecommunications Technologies for U.S. Contractors," Atlanta, Georgia, January 30–31, 1996, attended by top execs from vendors nationwide.
- Authored technical papers, e.g., "DoD Customer Communications Infrastructure," and "Operation and Management of Information Networks for Government Contractors."
- Co-developed and strategized R&D initiative, "Vision in Information as Power," aka VIP™, a $900,000 effort.
- Structured IS&T integration into VESPER, slated for $7 million ramp up in FY 1996–1997.

**Manager, Computer Products, Delivery Systems Office**      1991–1994

Spearheaded VESPER software quality initiative, and oversaw VESPERGEMS product line and the VESPER Computer Product Center. Principal architect and author, VESPER software quality guide series. Expanded VESPERGEMS product portfolio from 15 to 40 software products. Launched VESPER Bundled Workstation initiative. Designed the Computer Product Center, integrating over $600,000 in co-funded business from VESPER technical divisions. Established in-house capability for developing and delivering topical CD-ROMs. Oversaw development and industry evaluation of prototype multimedia technical information system. Mentored a commercial start-up, Electric Software Products, to complement in-house computer product activities and provide a needed outsourced technical capacity.

**Manager, VESPERGEMS Project**      1988–1991

Selected to direct a "skunkworks" project sponsored by the VESPER President's Office to develop a more innovative way to transfer VESPER technology to the DoD contractor industry. VESPERGEMS pioneered a range of standardized software-user interfaces, professional installation strategies, quality assurance processes, reusable software libraries and components, and contractor / developer qualification approaches. Achieved advanced product applications combining expert systems technology with traditional programming to make VESPER software user friendly.

Earned President's Certificate of Recognition for success of this project.

**Program Manager, Control and Diagnostics,**
**    Nuclear Power Support Division**      1983–1987

Investigated AI technologies for potential use in VESPER nuclear power applications. This work led to first practical use of expert systems in VESPER R&D products and subsequently by entire nuclear industry (power and weapons systems), e.g.: (1) Reactor Emergency Action Level Monitoring System (REALM), installed and used at Consolidated Edison's Indian Point 2 plant, and (2) Boiling Water Emergency Operating Procedures Tracking System (EOPTS), demonstrated at Taiwan Power's KuoSheng power plant. Also developed Lisp-based expert systems shell (SMART), later used in a number of VESPER expert system applications.

Earned Innovation / Creativity award for SMART and its application to a water chemistry expert system installed at PG&E's Ginna nuclear power plant.

**Principal Investigator, TMI-2 Core Damage Assessment Team,
Nuclear Safety Analysis Center** 1979–1980

Emergency assignment to Three Mile Island Accident Industry Advisory Group. Helped plant operations personnel interpret instrumentation readings and bring the plant into a stable shutdown condition. Collaborated with NSAC personnel to develop a water inventory and boil-off model used in sequence of events analyses and damage assessments of the TMI-2 accident.

*Prior*

**Project Manager, Nuclear Safety and Analysis Department,
Nuclear Power Support Division**

Developed advanced instrumentation for the nuclear power division. Initiated and managed projects to develop in-situ instrument response-time testing techniques, oversaw two-phase instrumentation projects used in thermal hydraulic testing, managed thermal-hydraulic code development and validation testing programs in the areas of nuclear safety and analysis. Established and managed a research program in aging prediction of safety-related instrumentation and electrical equipment used in nuclear power plants. Organized nuclear industry group pioneering environmental qualification of safety-grade, Class IE systems.

WESTINGHOUSE NAVAL REACTORS A1W FACILITY        Idaho Falls, ID
**Senior Plant Operations Engineer**

Plant Operations Engineer, Crew Supervisor, Engineering Officer of the Watch.

**EDUCATION**

**Ph.D., Electrical Engineering**, Stanford University

**M.S., Electrical Engineering**, University of Washington

**B.S., Electrical Engineering**, *cum laude*, University of California

**Operator's Certificate**, Westinghouse Nuclear Power School, Idaho

**ACADEMIC RESEARCH**

Under auspices of NIH-funded grant, investigated analog and digital image processing methods to detect and estimate signals transmitted through aberrant, noise-degraded X-ray or gamma imaging systems. Developed and experimentally evaluated optimum linear enhancement techniques applicable to a wide variety of imaging systems.

**AFFILIATIONS**

Member, IEEE

Member, Eta Kappa Nu engineering honor society

**PATENTS &
PUBLICATIONS**

List on request.

# Marshall Bender DuPont

12 West Frederick, 3rd Floor
New York, New York 10014
(212) 555-8776

---

## EMPLOYMENT

**Balfour Securities,** New York, New York 1992–Present
**Vice President,** Investment Research Department

## CURRENT SPECIALTY

**Infrastructure.** Initiated infrastructure group in 1994 to research and forecast infrastructure market fundamentals. Identified the 75 public companies established as the universe for ongoing analysis, including large and small capitalization companies which stand to be impacted by fluctuations in public and private sector infrastructure spending. 1994–Present.

Direct stock ideas to internal sales force, directly to Balfour clients, and indirectly through the financial press and participation in industry panels. Publish monthly *Infrastructure Perspectives* research product and company reports and updates. Initiate and participate in banking relationships related to infrastructure issues. Available to business press.

*Accomplishments:*
Research generated approximately $5.0 million in 1995 sales/trading commissions.
Completed three public offerings in 1995 with combined fees exceeding $3.1 million.
Ranked third in 1995 Greenwich Associates Institutional Research Survey after one year of industry coverage.

## PRIOR SPECIALTY

**Aerospace and Defense Electronics.** Research analyst on aerospace and defense companies and related special situations. Forecasted commercial aircraft demand and studied related industry trends, until drop in this market in early 90s.

Initiated new business relationships for corporate finance and M&A. Initiated and assisted in banking relationships and M&A transactions. Developed financial models and valuation methods as needed.

*Accomplishments:*
Created investment research product that generated $2.3 million in annual brokerage commissions.
Initiated several corporate finance relationships culminating in considerable fee income.
Ranked sixth nationally for aerospace/defense electronics grouping by Greenwich Associates survey.

**J.P. Morgan & Company,** New York, New York      1988–1992
**Research Analyst,** Aerospace and Defense Industries
Research analyst responsible for statistical analysis and stock selection in a universe of 125 aerospace, defense, and diversified companies. Completed bank management training program, a one-year program with in-class emphasis on financial accounting, corporate finance, and equity/credit analysis.

## EDUCATION

**Amherst College**, Amherst, Massachusetts
**B.A., Economics** and **History** (double major), *cum laude*      1988

**The Thatcher School,** Deer Meadow, Connecticut
**Diploma**, *cum laude*      1984

## PERSONAL

Have studied classical piano and harpsichord for twenty-five years. Perform solo recitals and in various music groups. Sports: city league basketball, long-distance running.

Fluent in French.

# ALISTAIR DOYLE

ali43@aol.com
Office: (212) 555-6815
Private line: (212) 555-4982
Private fax: (212) 555-1365

52 East 20th Street, #211F
New York, New York 10009

---

**EXPERIENCE**

GOURMAN, LTD.    New York, NY
**U.S. Treasury Coupon Broker**    1993–Present

Manage relationships with bond traders at major U.S. government primary dealers. Serve as a third-party broker, providing anonymity and liquidity. Build and maintain relationships with dealers; manage direct-wire and telephone communications; solicit bids and offerings; execute trades; ensure accuracy and compliance. Top ranked in office.

Achieved commissionable volume of up to $1.5 billion per month.

CHAPLIN & CO.    New York, NY
**U.S. Treasury Coupon Broker**    1988–1992

Recruited to revitalize and rebuild a Treasury department that had languished. Assigned 5 key accounts. Brought on board 4 new primary dealers as direct-wire customers.

In collaboration with a business systems analyst, redesigned broker interface screens to streamline and reorder information flow.

RJR SECURITIES    New York, NY
**U.S. Treasury Coupon Broker**    1985–1987

Assisted in all areas of Treasury coupon brokerage. In full charge of one account. Assisted other brokers on account management as needed.

MARTIN & TYNE    New York, NY
**Sales Assistant** 1984–1985

Assisted the firm's top institutional broker in presentations and client relations.

**EDUCATION**

MARIST COLLEGE    Poughkeepsie, NY
**B.S., Business Administration**  1982

*Areas of Concentration:*
Finance, Accounting, Economics, Marketing, Statistical Analysis.

**PERSONAL**

Seeking a new challenge using a combination of analytical and interpersonal skills. Ability to deliver accuracy and volume in a performance-critical environment.

References available upon request, but please keep this information confidential at this time.

# Paul Stuart Leach

913 Cherry Hill Lane
College Park, Maryland 20740

Private telephone:
(301) 555-0388

---

## EDUCATION

**Marquette University, School of Business**
**Bachelor of Science, Business Administration**

## HISTORY

**Merrill Lynch** (full-service brokerage)

*Current*

**Financial Consultant**

Ranked first in an office of 55 consultants in equity sales, fourth in annuities and insurance-related products, fifth in money management accounts. Manage $200 million in 132 aggressive and 1035 less-active investor accounts. Received numerous recognition awards for sales of investment products and services. Designed and proved a market timing approach that significantly enhanced clients' investment return. Qualified for All-American Team of the American Funds Group. Beat the market for all of last six years.

*Prior*

**Account Executive**

Opened 130 new accounts in first year of production. Led the office in opening IRA accounts. Earned special recognition award. Designed and presented public investment seminars.

**Investment Research Group** (investment advisors/financial planners)

**Consultant**

Conducted in-depth information and data gathering interviews and prepared a comprehensive financial plan for clients with specific recommendations in areas of investments, tax planning, and estate conservation.

**Crocker National Bank** (trust operations)

**Financial Planning Trust Officer**

Responsible for developing new trust business from 23-branch area. Worked closely with attorneys and gave trust seminars and workshops. Initiated a noon-hour estate planning seminar for corporate executives.

**Mansfield Mills Inc.** (investment counselors)

**Regional Manager** and **Senior Financial Planning Officer**

## CREDENTIALS

NASD Series 7
Index Futures & Options
Life & Disability
Annuity
Real Estate Brokers License

# Michael Dana Tilden-Thomas

4 White Street, 5B
New York, New York 10014

Office: (212) 555-2627
Residence: (212) 555-8776

---

**EXPERTISE**

**Investment Analysis / Industry Analysis**

**SECTOR SPECIALTY**

**Telecommunications and Networking**

**EDUCATION**

**GEORGETOWN UNIVERSITY**    Washington, D.C.
   **B.A., Economics** and **Public Policy**

**EXPERIENCE**

**SALOMON BROTHERS INC.**    New York, New York
   **Associate — Equity Research**    1995–Present

Co-analyst following universe of 20 telecom/networking stocks. Provide investment summary on stock recommendations to 60+ sales force and traders, as well as institutional equity managers/portfolio managers. Develop sources; seek and analyze raw data from top management, competitors, suppliers, and industry consultants. Develop analytical methodologies, provide industry trends analysis, write research reports, establish buy/sell recommendations.

*Highlights:*
   One of only two analysts with telecom and data/voice processing expertise for the top investment bank in telecom/ networking financings in 1995 (5 IPOs, $180 MM raised).
   Stock recommendations up 86% vs. 27% for S&P high-tech sector, 1995.
   Within Salomon, our sector is the technology trading volume leader, second only to biotechnology in number of equity offerings completed during 1995.
   Increased universe of coverage from 14 to 20 stocks.
   Wrote industry and specific stock reports distributed nationwide to clients and staff.

**ROBERT W. COWAN & ASSOCIATES**    Bergen, New Jersey
   **Associate**    1993–1995

Assisted the principal with venture capital and equity portfolio projects. Analyzed business plans, researched and investigated venture proposals. Analyzed potential equity investments, including trends analysis, fundamental analysis, market analysis, and assessment of top management teams.

*Sample project:*
   Structured terms and conditions of $3.2 million financing of plastic thermoforming company using mixed virgin and recycled plastics. Met with top individuals in plastics and plastic recycling industries. Represented the venture to other investors. Recommended new market in plastic sheeting. Company sold to Fortune 50 company.

**MONTGOMERY SECURITIES**    San Francisco, California
   **Corporate Finance Analyst**    1990–1993

Analyst with sector specialty in telecommunications industry, including regional holding companies, independent telephone companies, cellular service providers, and others. Developed and presented M&A and financial advisory analyses (debt/equity financing alternatives, stock repurchase, dividend).

*Highlights:*
   One of only two analysts in Corporate Finance in the number one bank in telephone company debt financing.
   Number one bank in telephone company cellular equity offerings (5 deals, $400 MM).
   Co-analyst on valuation of $6 billion telecom company (and numerous similar M&A projects).
   For 1½ years was the group Senior Analyst. Recommended for Third Year Analyst Program. Chosen to be a lead member of the Analyst Program Review Committee.

# PATRICK J. GALLAGHER

87 Beacon Street
Boston, Massachusetts 02215

Office: (617) 555-5837
Residence: (617) 555-0530

---

## EDUCATION

THE WHARTON SCHOOL, UNIVERSITY OF PENNSYLVANIA
**M.B.A., Finance**

SWARTHMORE COLLEGE
**B.A., Mathematics**

## HISTORY

HALLINAN & GRACE, INC., Boston
**Senior Vice President / Director of Research / Chief Financial Officer,** current

Key member of senior management team, assisting with development of strategic direction and company objectives. Manage all research and technical analysis of potential opportunities, providing detailed information concerning potential risks and rewards. Establish and implement all in-house financial controls, as well as maintaining comprehensive and current financial analyses.

BUSINESS REALTY SERVICES, Boston
**General Partner / Chief Financial Officer,** 1990–1994

Managed all administrative and financial aspects of highly successful consultancy servicing investment and commercial banking clientele. Instrumental in developing firm's overall direction and administrative / financial infrastructure.

*sample clients:*

McMORGAN & COMPANY
STONE HILL BANK
FIRST BOSTON MORTGAGE COMPANY

SECURITY PACIFIC BANK
FAR EAST NATIONAL BANK

*selected highlights:*

Managed $75 million of clients' construction projects, on-time and within budget.
Attained 16% return on investment to institutional lender through conception, set-up, and management of innovative computerized loan administration program.
Significantly increased financial performance of investment banking client by completing consulting contract addressing company's organization, management, compensation, and incentives.

FIRST SECURITY NATIONAL BANK, Boston
**Vice-President / Team Leader,** 1988–1990

Managed 7 employees in Boston Commercial Group. Eliminated potential loan losses by negotiating tightened term loan covenants. Improved control by recognizing and securing proper documentation of bank credit files, obtaining payoff or adequate guaranties on numerous insecure credits. Advised clients in safeguarding against poor investments by exposing false economies.

*selected highlights:*

Developed new business, more than doubling goal, and increased return on assets to 3.6%.
Created and implemented new business development program for United Way of Boston, achieving 170% of goal.

BANK OF COMMERCE, New York
**Vice President / Unit Manager**, 1976–1988

Evaluated and approved credits with personal unsecured lending authority of up to $1.5 million, and secured lending authority of up to $10 million in New York, Boston, Chicago, Hong Kong. Solicited and structured over $1 billion in new commercial loans and related deposits. Focused staff and improved employee morale by developing measurable, objective personnel evaluation system. Developed and taught PC programs for online managers to price loans, track collateral, and analyze financial statements.

*selected highlights:*
> Increased profits by $15 million by writing policy change for local Wall Street client loans. Authored policy guide, "Lending to Security Brokers and Dealers."
> Managed Hong Kong international credits during period of 30% compounded annual growth.
> Reclaimed key domestic relationship by co-leading HK$617 million project financing.
> Initiated concept of auctioning collateral on nonperforming loans through a bank subsidiary, significantly decreasing bank's exposure.
> Recovered $473,000 in compensating balance and service charge shortfalls.

MARINE MIDLAND BANK, New York
**Assistant Vice President**

UNITED STATES ARMY
**First Lieutenant / Company Commander**

# JONATHAN MULLINS PIERCE

500 Meadow Court
Santa Clara, California 95050

Telephone/voice mail/fax: (408) 555-5040
http://www.consult.com/ideafactory/custnet/sample.html

---

## EXPERTISE

**Business Information Systems and Technology Evolution Planning**

**Software Methodologies & Best Practices**

**Process Engineering & Reengineering**

**Turnaround Management**

**Change Management**

**Internal Education**

Extensive strategic IS background, including success in a series of systems development, consulting, turnaround, reengineering, and reorganization assignments. **Proven interim executive**, with business relationships lasting 6 months to 15 years. Strengths: analytical business planning and management, technology evolution, internal processes analysis/development, training, IS customer/user relations, and outreach to achieve acceptance of change.

Performance-oriented manager, driven by goals, time frames, and quantifiable benchmarks.

No restrictions on travel/relocation.

## HIGHLIGHTS

Reduced annual operating costs by $1.2 million by leading development and implementation of standardized software methodology and best practices, which improved productivity by 34%. **Emerson Electric**.

Led business redesign and strategic plan development resulting in 35% performance improvement while absorbing increased workload and 15% staff cut. **Apple Computer**.

Strategized organizational change and developed long-range plan i*n one day* by facilitating management meeting which identified 21 accomplishments and 53 operational deficiencies. **Apple Computer**.

Directed project team of 4 consultants whose efforts led to 25% gain in effectiveness of 490-person staff through decentralizing corporate data processing functions. **Bechtel Corp.**

Managed 4 sections of 10-week training program which cross-trained 580 engineers into software engineers, achieving measured level of 3 years of software experience at graduation. **General Dynamics**.

## EXPERIENCE

PIERCE & ASSOCIATES
**Principal Consultant**

Throughout my career, have performed consulting engagements on interim basis. For example: Coordinated CFO, VP Info Systems, MIS Manager, and analysts on project to assess requirements and specifications for a new computer system. Developed 110-page technology planning blueprint, **Oceanroutes**. Some of the following projects also performed under auspices of Pierce & Associates.

APPLE COMPUTER
**Consultant, Environmental Technologies & Strategies**, 1995

Assisted in brainstorming strategy and program for Apple to become a leader in developing environmentally compliant and friendly products. Designed 7 action plans.

**Consultant, Engineering Interface & Design**, 1994–1995

Developed business requirements and strategic plan for 175-person group, including 120 initiatives to reduce cost, improve services, and reengineer operations.

**Consultant, Worldwide Configuration Management**, 1990

Created long-range plan for the Director, and developed long-range planning skills in the Director.

**Consultant, Worldwide Product Documentation Control Group**, 1989

Reduced ECN cycle time from 129 days to 43 days by reengineering business processes and developing and directing implementation of online job support and training system.

INTERMEDIA

**Systems Development Consultant** (and **Co-Founder**), 1989–1992

Technical officer for this multimedia development pioneer. Built multimedia programs and marketing presentations for **Apple**, **Lawrence Livermore Laboratories**, and others. Listed *California Business* magazine as one of the top 50 multimedia companies in the Bay Area.

IDE

**Consultant, Training**, 1989

Created IDE's software product training program strategy for its CASE tool; provided methodologies for design of training programs in support of other software products.

CRI

**Associate Consultant**, 1987–1989

Developed and presented project management, software project management, and systems engineering courses for government and defense industry corporations, e.g., **ESL, TRW, NASA Ames** and classified government agencies.

EMERSON ELECTRIC

**Consultant, Software Development Processes**, 1987–1988

Brought in to troubleshoot a failed software operation. Provided situation assessment, turnaround plan, and manager advise and counsel. Retained to direct the development and specification of Emerson's corporate software development methodology. Also developed and delivered courseware and training.

INTELLIGENT BUILDING COMMUNICATIONS

**Director of Software**, 1986–1987

Part of the start-up team for this "think tank" industry consulting firm funded by **Pacific Telesis** to develop, apply, and promote intelligent building design methodology. Liaison to **Kajima Corp.** of Japan, the fourth largest construction company on the Pacific Rim.

INFO-SCI, INC.

**Trainer** and **Management Consultant**, 1974–1985 (part-time and full-time)

Developed computerized and platform presentation coursework, seminars, and workshops on SW development, programming, analysis, design, and management. Traveled throughout United States, Canada, and Europe. Active in **NCC, DPMA, IEEE, ASM**, and **ACM**.

Sample consulting engagement: Developed RFP and criteria for evaluating vendor software proposals for the **FAA** to procure automated test engineering software used to repair all FAA microchip-based equipment operating in the field, over 80 categories of electronic devices. Selected vendor.

CONTROL DATA CORPORATION

**Consultant, Training Program Development**, 1979

Developed courseware; recruited and trained trainers; planned and scheduled trainings; conducted and/or oversaw classes, presentations, seminars, and workshops.

## COMMUNITY SERVICE (recent only)

COMPUTER TECHNOLOGIES PROGRAM

**Member, Board of Directors** and **Business Advisory Council**, 1995–Present

Achieved a turnaround of this nonprofit training program teaching computer skills to disabled workers. Brought a management science mentality to the organization, wrote long-range plan, developed an officer-level industry symposium, enlisted practicing professionals as trainers and mentors, devised business community partnership/sponsorship program.

UNITED WAY

**Consultant, Technology and Training**, 1993–1994

Provided situation assessment, specifications, and recommendations for a user training program for UW's new campaign management system, a very large, functionally complex interactive system.

## MILITARY

UNITED STATES AIR FORCE

**Software Development** (four years active duty)

## EDUCATION

**Glendale College**

**El Camino College**

**University of Maryland, European Division**

**U.S. Department of Agriculture Graduate School**

**University of California, Santa Cruz**

**Cabrillo College**

**U.S. Air Force Training School**

State-of-the-art technology and process careerist; have developed and delivered over 20 graduate-level education programs in software management and technology subject areas.

## AFFILIATIONS

Bay Area Organizational Development Network

Technology Executives Roundtable

## ADDITIONAL SKILLSET

Joint application development, rapid prototyping, enterprise analysis, life cycle development methodologies, process modeling, business and technical project planning. Fully computer, PC, and multimedia skilled. Accomplished platform and public speaker (keynote).

## ADDITIONAL INFORMATION

Additional information gladly provided on request.

# REGINALD ANDREW GOODWIN IV, PE

12006 West Scottsdale Road
Phoenix, Arizona 85029

Telephone/Message: (602) 555-5433
Pager: (800) 555-1892

---

**EXPERTISE**

**Construction Management, Commercial, High-End Residential,** some **Industrial**

**Structural & Non-Structural Remodel & Rehab**

**Seismic Retrofit**

*Profile:*

Extensive experience in the construction field leading to responsibilities as **Executive Vice President** for Brownell Talbot Company of Los Angeles. Experience includes extensive seismic retrofit, mid-rise and high-rise rehab, and major commercial remodeling. Training in structural engineering and architecture. Professional Engineer, State of California.

Skills include contractor and subcontractor selection, contract negotiations, project management, design review, owner representation, and similar functions where depth of experience is required.

**EDUCATION**

California State Polytechnic Institute, San Luis Obispo, CA

**M.S., Architectural Engineering**
**B.S., Mechanical Engineering**

**EXPERIENCE**

Brownell Talbot Construction Company, Los Angeles, 1974–1992

**Executive Vice President & Manager**, Phoenix, 1982–1996
**Construction Manager**, Los Angeles, 1980–1981
**Estimator/Project Manager**, Los Angeles, 1977–1979
**Estimator**, Los Angeles, 1974–1976

Participated in a period of consistently strong growth for the company, as it furthered its reputation as a contractor capable of the more challenging retail, commercial, and high-end residential projects, including seismic upgrades, conversions, additions, and similar projects. Opened and operated the Phoenix office for the company, but was based out of Los Angeles for majority of tenure. Assignments throughout the United States.

*Sample projects:*
- Valentino, Christian Dior, Jessica McClintock, Cole-Haan, and Davidoff, Rodeo Drive, Beverly Hills. Tenant improvements.
- Union Square 100, 100 Potrero Avenue, 735 Battery Street, 394 Pacific Avenue, 1050 Battery Street, San Francisco. Seismic upgrade, conversion, and major commercial remodel.
- Delta Memorial Hospital, Phoenix. New wing. Mayo Clinic, Iowa. Major rehab.
- Hoover House at Stanford; Hotel Mark Twain, Cathedral Hill Hotel, San Francisco. Seismic bracing, complete renovation. Post-fire work on Cathedral.
- University High School, Dallas. Conversion, new construction, physical plant.
- Telegraph Hill Racquetball Club, San Francisco Bay Club, Gold's Gym, San Francisco. Conversion and remodel.

**Experience, continued:**

- Dolby Laboratories, San Francisco. Seismic reconstruction, office construction.
- Chanel Stores, New York, Los Angeles, Costa Mesa, Washington, D.C., Palm Beach. Remodel and new construction.
- Macy's West. Seismic upgrading of six stores in the greater Los Angeles metro area.
- Playland Arcade, Santa Monica Pier. Demolition, relocation and temporary housing, new construction.

*PRIOR:*

Bethlehem Steel Corporation, Richmond, California
Fabricated Steel Construction Division, Western Construction District

**Project Manager**
**Field Engineer**, Richmond Office
**Field Engineer**, Los Angeles Office
**Field Engineer**, Richmond Office

Field and office engineering in support of major steel-frame construction.

Gromme & Priestly, Architects, Los Angeles, California
**Intern**

**REFERENCES**      References and recommendations provided on request.

# Martin Quick

18972 Lakeview Drive
Highland Park, Illinois 60035

Office: (312) 555-8663
Residence: (847) 555-0549

## PROFILE

Regional/divisional line manager. Strengths include management team building and motivation, acquisition and integration of new branches and business units, turnaround management, expense control, automation, strategic business planning. Special skill: training front-line staff to sell.

## EXPERIENCE

MARBLE, FINCH, SPINNER & HATCH, INC.

**Regional Vice President**
Chicago, Illinois, 1993–Present

Provide executive direction to Midwest Region with 22 branches in 6 states, over 265,000 accounts, over $10 billion in cash and equities.

Oversee 164 FTEs, delegating through Regional Director, Regional Administrator, and 22 Branch Managers.

*Accomplishment:* Brought Midwest Region from average performance to first-place ranking out of 12 regions nationwide. Created and chaired task forces to review and restructure job responsibilities for branch staff; increased specialization and worker expertise, resulting in major increases in productivity.
- Ranked #1 for Asset Production.
- Ranked Top Tier for Customer Satisfaction.
- Exceeded Expense Control Accountability Targets.
- Opened two new Branch Offices, 1993–1994.

Improvements accomplished mostly by rejuvenation of existing staff, with minimal turnover and maximal remotivation.

Overall performance of this division is currently recognized as the best in its history.

CROCKER MASON NATIONAL BANK

**Executive Vice President & Division Manager, Golden State Division**
San Bernardino, California, 1990–1992

Provided executive direction to retail bank network of 120 branches throughout Southern California, $4.7 billion on deposit and over $1 billion per annum in new commercial, consumer, and real estate loans.

Oversaw 1450 FTEs (3350+ total employees), delegating through a management team of 11 (Senior Vice President, First Vice President, Corporate Vice President, Regional Vice Presidents, Market Area Manager, and Unit Heads).

*Accomplishment:* Turned retail division around from historically mediocre performance to first-place ranking (bankwide) in the following production and expense categories:
- Ranked #1 in Real Estate Loans.
- Ranked #1 in Consumer Loans.
- Ranked #1 in Transaction Account (DDA) Growth.
- Ranked #1 in Fee Income.
- Ranked #1 in Expense Control (including compensation).
- Ranked #1 in Customer Retention.

*Additional accomplishment:* Completed acquisition and assimilation into retail branch system of 35 former offices of Gibraltar S&L, Mercury S&OL, and Southland S&L, including related systems, automation, staff training projects. Exceeded average retention by 10%.

Overall performance of this division is currently recognized as the best in its history, with over twenty years of prior performance.

*Continued . . .*

**Senior Vice President & Division Administrator, Northern Division**
San Francisco, California, 1989–1990

In charge of 104 branches, 1175 FTEs (2500+ total employees), $4 billion in deposits, and approximately $1 billion in new outstandings per annum.

*Accomplishment:* Top Sales Leader (bankwide).
■ Ranked #1 in Overall Performance (out of 7 retail divisions).
■ Ranked #1 in Overall Loan Production.
■ Ranked #1 in Fee Production.
■ Ranked #1 in Expense Control (including compensation).

*Other accomplishments:*
■ Served on the ABA Small Business Committee in Washington, D.C.
■ Assimilated 31 new retail and commercial branches into the network.
■ Received Affirmative Action Award as Top Executive Sponsor.

**Senior Vice President & Division Administrator, Inland Division**
Riverside, California, 1988–1989

In charge of 96 branches, $3.5 billion in deposits, and $750 million in new outstandings per annum.

*Selected accomplishments:*
■ Ranked #1 bankwide in DDA Growth, Loan Generation, Fee Income, Expense Control (first time this division had performed at potential).
■ Conceptualized and developed system for control of operating losses and teller balancing. This system is now in place bankwide, reducing teller shortages by 60%.

**Regional Vice President & First Vice President**
Riverside, California, 1985–1988
■ Developed new sales processes, for example: pioneered indirect consumer lending to vehicle dealers.
■ Ranked #1 in Sales out of 32 Regional Managers. Became statewide mentor and then national sponsor of the bank's speakers' clubs, increasing membership 400% and club charters by 300%.

**Vice President & Branch Manager**
Beverly Hills, California, 1984–1985
■ Ranked #2 (bankwide) in Personal Lines of Credit.

**Vice President & Branch Manager**
Los Angeles, California, 1983–1984
■ Ranked Top 10 (bankwide) in most production areas.

**Regional Loan Supervisor**
Los Angeles, California, 1981–1983
■ Reduced S.A.C. Credits from 132 ($7.85 million) to 23 ($2.6 million).

**Prior:** promotions from Management Associate to Branch Manager, 1972–1980.

*Continued . . .*

## MILITARY

U.S. Army, 1965–1967
Vietnam veteran, decorated, honorable discharge.

## LICENSURE

NASD Series 7, 8, 63.

## EDUCATION

UNIVERSITY OF CALIFORNIA at LOS ANGELES
**B.S., Economics**

EXECUTIVE BANKING SCHOOL at GEORGETOWN UNIVERSITY
**Certificate, Banking**

## REFERENCES

References provided on request, but please keep this information confidential at this time.

# BARBARA JAËGEN

Dockside Village, Bldg. 1, #1205
New York, New York 10031

Residence/message: (212) 555-3879
Office/direct line: (212) 555-2480
24-hour private fax: (212) 555-3888

## PROFILE

*Strengths*: administrative management, strategic planning, operations, internal controls, budgeting, government/industry relations, facilities, risk management, human resources, staff development, technology planning, information systems, management studies.

*Highlights*: significant start-up, reorganization, and M&A experience; proven leader in both rapid expansion and consolidation business environments.

## EXPERIENCE

New Bank of Manhattan, New York, New York
**Executive Vice President**, 1993–Present

Promoted to EVP to assist the CEO in restructuring of this entrepreneurial private bank launched in 1965. Oversee strategic planning, information systems, operations, marketing, escrow, trust, internal audit, telecommunications, facilities management, risk management, and legal services.

Supervise SVP Operations, SVP Information Systems, VP Escrow, VP Trust, Marketing Officer, and 65 direct-reports. Plan and control administrative services budget of $10,100,000 per annum.

***Contributions***:

Orchestrated development of three-year strategic plan, achieved consensus on the vision of the turn-around effort, personally responsible for plan development and implementation throughout the bank.

Established criteria for reduction in force, oversaw structure and negotiation of outplacement contract for exempt and nonexempt staff, oversaw job redesign, developed communications plan (internal and external) to control media coverage and protect customer relationships. Result: Achieved 18% reduction in payroll expenses with zero loss of service delivery to customers.

Reorganized the Management Information Systems Department. Established goals and objectives, set standards for performance, recruited new VP MIS. Result: Achieved "superior" internal audit rating following reorganization.

Provided leadership to a comprehensive review of internal controls and a rewrite of policies and procedures.

Directed space planning and relocation of departments/functions to create 15,000 sq.ft. of financial district office space for sublet, creating a new revenue stream.

Set standards for legal services and established a legal expenses review process resulting in estimated 30% reduction in legal fees.

This strategic plan is now in its second year and has achieved its goal of reversing negative business trends at the bank. Available for a new challenge.

**Senior Vice President**, 1992–1993

Recruited to manage the opening of this private bank's first branch, the Scarsdale office. Involved from the earliest stages; member of executive team that planned the launch.

Oversaw demographic and market studies, strategic plan development, site selection, design, and construction. Personally designed operations, internal controls, and administrative procedures. Recruited, trained, and supervised operations staff. Oversaw marketing activities.

Directed development of a customer relationship profitability information system, implemented bankwide.

Collaborated on the development and implementation of a first-year strategic plan bringing in $80,000,000 in assets and achieving profitability—in the first year.

First Empire Bank, New York, New York
**Vice President, Manhattan Business Center**, 1990–1992

Chairperson of the acquisition team that planned and directed the merger of Harrison Private Bank Corp. into the First Empire system (retained by the acquiring bank to direct the integration, an unusual honor).

Oversaw integration of management information systems, policies, procedures, staff, and customer base. Designed the communications package resulting in 90%+ retention of accounts. Oversaw retraining and job redesign functions.

Also managed integration of another acquisition, absorbing Brown & Wilson Bank's commercial operations with similar success.

Spearheaded the statewide implementation of Harrison Private Bank Corp's business banking incentive program into the First Empire system.

Oversaw site development, established operations and service delivery systems for new business banking centers in Syracuse and Buffalo. Result: Exceeded objectives for First Empire's entry into business and private banking services.

Harrison Private Banking Corp., New York, New York
**Senior Vice President**, 1979–1990

Founding officer of this entrepreneurial business bank, still a relatively new concept at the time. Member of the executive team that built this bank into an institution with $375,000,000 in assets, 120 employees, and profits that were considered outstanding throughout the banking industry. Designated "Premier Performing" by Findley Reports, the independent banking analysts.

Co-chaired the development of comprehensive Director Policy Manual prior to opening the bank. Directed the development of management and Board of Directors information systems. Oversaw production of the bank's Strategic Plan annually.

Primarily responsible for coordinating the bank's relocation to its permanent site, including overseeing design process, working with architects and contractors, ensuring budgetary control, and meeting construction timelines for a new $6,000,000, 16,000 sq.ft. landmark building. Planned logistics for a one-weekend move; successful. The new building immediately won an architectural award for Best Commercial Design, 1983.

Recruited and retained an exceptional employee base, an integral contributor to the success of the institution.

Oversaw design and development of a customer relationship profitability system, employee incentive system, and other operating systems considered state-of-the-art in banking at the time.

Chemical Bank, New York, New York
**Vice President (Operations Manager)**, 1974–1979

Earned rapid promotions leading to officer-level responsibilities.

## EDUCATION

**The Executive Program in Commercial Banking, Harvard University**, 1981

**Financial Management of Commercial Banks, The Wharton School**, 1978

**Certificate, National School of Real Estate Finance, ABA**, 1977

**Cash Management for Bankers, AMA**, 1984

**Accounting, American College**, 1971

## SERVICE

Leadership Service Club — Charter Member, 1988 Alumni Chair

South Manhattan Business Association, 1980–1990
  President, 1990
  Board Member, 1980–1989
  Government Relations Committee, 1985–1989

Senior Service Center — Advisory Board Chair, 1990–1991

New York City Literacy Program — Tutor

New York Ballet
  Board Member
  Strategic Planning Committee Chair

YWCA — Board Member

Special Olympics

FreeWheelers

Private Bankers Association
  Operations Committee
  Executive Conference Committee

Toastmasters

Homeowners Association — Board of Directors

Easter Seals — Bankers Panel (fund-raising)

## REFERENCES

References provided on request. Please keep this information absolutely confidential.

# ANDREW BAXTER CLAY

15 East 55th Street
New York, New York 10031

Office: (212) 555-0399
Residence: (212) 555-5697

---

**EXPERIENCE**

**GARAVAN SECURITIES**   New York, New York
**Senior Vice President**   1994–Present

**MOORE, SCHLEY, CAMERON & CO.**   New York, New York
**Investment Banker**   1992–1994

**APPLE FINANCIAL**   New York, New York
**Investment Banker**   1989–1992

**R.B. DAYTON**   New York, New York
**Manager, Private Placements**   1987–1989

**EDWARDS, DODD, EDWARDS & WATKINS**   New York, New York
**Investment Banker — Trainee**   1986–1987

*Highlights*

Develop business relationships with CEOs and founders of public and private companies to provide capital services. Develop financial strategies, provide strategic financial planning, structure and manage public and private offerings of stock. Manage three revenue streams: trading (1/3), investment banking retainers (1/3), fees for raising capital (1/3).

Full responsibility for initiating relationships; structuring and negotiating transactions, retainers and other agreements; regulatory compliance; and problem solving. Increasingly involved in international placement, raising money with European investors under new SEC regulations governing sale of private stock to non-U.S. residents. Have placed stock with money managers in Milan, Lugano, Zurich, Geneva, London, and Paris.

Currently seeking a investment firm with greater resources, to support larger transactions and better serve the expanding needs of my clientele.

*Representative accomplishments:*

Retained by public biotechnology company to advise management on continuing financing for the company, $15,000/month retainer plus options on 100,000 shares. In separate action, completed a private placement of $2,000,000 with placement fees and options on additional 200,000 shares. Negotiated six-month extension on retainer.

Retained by public computer maintenance company to advise management on financial matters.

Retained by NYSE-listed company to raise capital in private placement, $6,000,000 to $10,000,000. Currently raising this money with European investors.

Obtained and structured venture capital financing for a private food technology company. Subsequently arranged IPO for $4,000,000.

Numerous other projects, details on request.

**EDUCATION**

**UNIVERSITY OF NOTRE DAME**   South Bend, Indiana
**B.A., Business Management**   1982

**LICENSE**

**NASD Series 7**

# Donald James Watkins

12 Ironwood Terrace
Sacramento, California 95817
(916) 555-3800

---

**PROFILE**

Senior financial executive with emphasis on turnaround management, REO and workout projects. Over 25 years outstanding experience in lending, savings, advertising, and business development for both stable and troubled financial institutions.

**BACKGROUND**

WATKINS FAMILY TRUST, Las Vegas, Nevada, 1992–Present
**President**

Currently managing a family trust valued in the high seven figures. Also provide consulting on commercial real estate loan workout negotiations and REO portfolio liquidation for:
- First Nevada Savings Bank
- Crocker National Bank
- Wells Fargo Bank
- Imperial Valley Savings Bank

GARDEN GROVE SAVINGS BANK, Stockton, California, 1989–1991
**President / CEO**

Recruited to Garden Grove Savings Bank as a turnaround manager, to maintain control of this troubled thrift, stabilize operations, eliminate non-prudent practices, and ensure profitability. My selection as President/CEO was reviewed and approved with the full endorsement of the Office of Supervision, FHLB, 11th District. Mother Lode Savings Bank had 3 offices, 45 staff, and $107 million in assets. I supervised all staff through the following officers: Senior V.P. Loans, V.P. Savings, V.P. Controller, V.P. Administration/Personnel, V.P. Branches/Compliance, V.P. Advertising/Marketing.

Immediate operating accomplishments included: (1) met all reserve requirements as mandated by FIRREA, (2) brought operational areas of the bank into full compliance with all state and federal regulations, (3) achieved operating ratios as specified by the business plan and the Board of Directors, (4) wrote a new business plan and budget and won approval of the Board and FHLB, (5) regained public confidence by implementing public relations campaign modeled after successful campaigns utilized in prior turnaround assignments (see next job listings), (6) established single-family residential home loan program with product salability in the secondary market, (7) expanded existing commercial loan department to become a stronger profit center and expand professional client base for the thrift. These accomplishments are particularly noteworthy in light of some of the problems left over from previous administrations.

Upon achieving stabilized and prudent operations, I initiated a comprehensive review of long-range planning for the institution, including (1) scenario modeling on multiple economic and financial variables, (2) hands-on evaluation and analysis of existing loans at the portfolio level, and (3) consideration of FHA, VA, FDIC, FHLB, and RTC regulations in effect at that time. Presented three options to the Board, with recommendations and analysis, including a liquidation scenario (not likely), a detailed plan to raise private sector capital and convert the thrift to a state-chartered bank, and a plan to explore potential for merger with a commercial bank, as permitted under FIRREA.

Initiated and engineered a cash offer of $27.59 a share from U.S. Shares Bank of Portland, Oregon, through its wholly owned subsidiary U.S. Shares Bank of California, with very few conditions of sale. Participated as a principal in the negotiating team that structured the terms of the sale/merger, and facilitated all regulatory approval.

Maintained the following ratios in accordance with terms of sale: annualized net income of not less than $325,000; reserves less than 4%; loss reserves not less than $800,000; nonperforming loans less than $1.5 million.

Earned merit performance bonus plus severance package. Excellent recommendations available.

GREAT WESTERN TIMBER BANK, Eureka, California, 1988–1989
**President / CEO**

Appointed by direction of the Supervisory Agent, Office of Supervision, FHLB, 11th District, to serve as temporary President/CEO of this troubled thrift until it could be formally placed in conservatorship by the FDIC in April of 1989. The thrift had 2 offices, a staff of 14, and assets of $46 million. Reported to the Board and the FHLB. Supervised all staff directly.

Initiated an immediate public relations campaign to regain depositor confidence. Initiated a detailed review of assets of the association, and developed an action plan for REO. Identified 3 serious REO problems, initiated aggressive marketing program including advertising but featuring personal, direct contacts to appropriate brokers.

Worked closely with FDIC officials during transition to conservatorship. Achieved goals of stabilizing the thrift and minimizing losses until the FDIC was able to complete its takeover, resulting in no loss of savings or public confidence in the institution.

The thrift was successfully incorporated into Central Stockton Savings one year later, in part due to my efforts in this interim period.

HIGHTOWER SAVINGS & LOAN, Santa Nella, California, 1985–1988
**President / CEO**, 1987–1988
**Executive Vice President** / COO, 1986–1987
**Senior Vice President**, Workout Officer, 1985–1986

Originally recruited as REO/loan workout specialist under the FHLB Management Consignment Program. Earned rapid increase in responsibilities leading to appointment as President/CEO during critical transition period and merger into Western Federal Savings on favorable terms. Supervised all subordinate staff through the following officers: Controller, S.V.P. Lending, S.V.P. Savings, S.V.P. House Counsel, V.P. Loan Servicing, V.P. Human Resources, V.P. Branch Administration, V.P. REO/Workout.

Hightower had 21 offices, 300+ staff, and assets of $1.3 billion (almost all of them nonperforming at time of hire). The organization was losing $7 million per month at time of hire. Personally engineered a major turnaround on behalf of the Board and the FHLB.

*Major accomplishment:*
- Turned $900 million of non-earning assets into earning assets for the FSLIC, in less than three years and at a cost *of less than 3% of book value*. Achieved this primarily by selling assets that realized $440 million in cash proceeds, and by restructuring non-earning loans into earning loans in the amount of $350 million.

*Selected details:*
- Originated and closed the largest cash land sale in the Santa Nella area, a $10 million transaction. Sold another REO for $22 million cash.
- As lead workout negotiator for five participants in a $62.3 million loan on 400,000 s.f. mixed-use project in Southern California. Successfully restructured loan to retain book value of $62.1 million rather than liquidate at $40 million value as REO, in effect saving a loss of over $22 million.

Reported directly to the Board, but worked closely with FHLB, 11th District. Earned FHLB trust. Was one of only two institutions to come out of the Management Consignment Program as independent management. Had highest in-house approval authority for real estate transactions (as set by the FHLB, 11th District), and had a 100% approval rating for transactions that did need FHLB review.

As Head, Work Out Department, worked with all non-earning assets, to include single-family real estate, commercial loans, joint ventures, and commercial real estate. Designed and managed advertising campaigns, initiated broker relationships, found creative solutions to problems and won approvals from the Board, FSLIC and other regulatory agencies.

**Other projects:** (1) hired full-time public relations representative and implemented public confidence campaign stressing new management, (2) developed single-family loan program, (3) replaced $300 million in brokerage funds with core deposit savings, (4) developed successful program to attract senior citizens investment and savings deposits.

Assisted and facilitated the merger of Hightower Savings into Western Federal at the request of the FHLB, 11th District.

HAWAII SAVINGS BANK, Honolulu, Hawaii, 1978–1985
**S.V.P. Administration** and
**Member, Board of Directors**
also
**Managing Director, Board of Directors**, Breeze Properties, Inc.
**Chairman of the Board**, Investors Life Insurance Company of Hawaii
**V.P.**, HF Corporation, a wholly owned subsidiary of Hawaii Savings

Reported to and served on the Board. Supervised the following officers: Supervisor of Property Management, Supervisor of Budgeting, Supervisor of Compliance, as well as others in subsidiary corporations. Duties consisted of 40% branch supervision, 30% budgeting and business planning, 15% special projects, and 15% public relations.

Represented the thrift as: President, Hawaiian Arts Council; President/Treasurer, Honolulu Theatre for Youth; Member, Honolulu Chamber of Commerce; Member, U.S. Navy League.

**Additional accomplishments:** (1) structured and facilitated merger with Hawaii Federal, (2) contributed $3.5 million cash reserves to parent company as result of merger, (3) negotiated purchase of life insurance company for $7 million and subsequent sale for $11 million, realizing $4 million medium-term gain, (4) designed state-of-the-art budgeting system allowing consistent 90+% budget to actual projections.

Joined this savings and loan in the year of its incorporation as the **Treasurer/Accountant** and earned advancement through the ranks to President and CEO. Knowledgeable in all aspects of operations, marketing, staffing, business planning.

## COMMUNITY & PROFESSIONAL SERVICE

**Member, Advisory Committee, Federal Home Loan Mortgage Corporation:** Served on the Advisory Committee in 1976 that first raised the issue of possible problems with capital adequacy for the Freddie Mac Corporation. Our recommendations at the time seem particularly pertinent in light of recent developments in this area.

**Expert Witness,** First Circuit Court, State of Hawaii: Lending practices and standards of care for industrial loan companies.

*also:*

Director, Federal Home Loan Bank, 12th District
Director, United States Savings & Loan League
President, Hawaii League of Savings Associations
President, Financial Managers Association, Hawaii Chapter
Member, National Association of Accountants
Member, Public Relations Society of America
Member, Advisory Committee, Federal Home Loan Mortgage Corporation

## EDUCATION & CREDENTIALS

University of California, Irvine
**M.B.A.**

University of Hawaii
Graduate Studies in Business and Economics

University of California, Irvine
**B.S.B.A.**

Continuing Education: Institute of the U.S. Savings & Loan League (annually)

**Certified Professional Accountant**
State of Hawaii
State of California

# JUDY TISDALE

13250 Deep Valley Drive
Dallas, Texas 75244

Office: (214) 555-4592, ext. 1200
Residence: (214) 555-7453
judy28@ix.netcom.com

## HIGHLIGHTS

- Designed an investment strategy that doubled a boutique bank's income at < 10% of total operating costs.

- Manager for $120 million investment portfolio, $650 million mortgage loan portfolio.

- Specialist in niche market development.

## EXPERIENCE

LONE STAR SAVINGS BANK, Dallas, Texas
**Vice President / Director, Secondary Marketing / Director, Capital Market Group**, 1994–Present

Invited by the CEO to reform the Capital Market Group into a small, innovative, entrepreneurial team, virtually unique among small commercial banks in America. Empowered to devise new profit-generating opportunities and manage across organizational lines in the following four areas:

*Loan Portfolio Arbitrage:*

Created new department specializing in the purchase and resale of loan portfolios with the sole objective of generating a profit on the transaction. The team is responsible for all steps from identifying acquisition opportunities through due diligence, closing, and resale.

- **Doubled** the institution's 1995 earnings through portfolio arbitrage; contributed over $11.5 million to net income.
- Pushed Lone Star Savings's earnings to record levels through loan acquisition / resale alone, the largest and by far the fastest-growing net revenue contributor in the bank.

*Portfolio Acquisitions:*

The goal of the portfolio acquisitions team is to identify and acquire loans for the bank's investment portfolio with rates and terms more favorable than the general market.

- Substantially lowered production costs; maintained efficient, cost-effective, three-member department compared to the bank's 45-member loan origination department.
- Yields on acquired loans were more than 50 basis points higher than general market yields, and the delinquencies were significantly lower than the general market.
- Diversified product type and credit location to meet the bank's needs.

*Secondary Marketing:*

This function is the typical secondary marketing function found in most savings and loans. Managed secondary marketing and product development, developed pricing and hedging strategies, managed closing and underwriting, initiated new business relationships.

- Established market-responsive loan packages which increased our capital turnover, primary and secondary market competitiveness, and new loan production.

*Continued . . .*

*Treasury:*

Analyzed and strategized daily cash investment and asset / liability mix, monitored cash investment performance, recommending strategies to maximize yield within the bank's regulatory / policy constraints; reported on market movements, initiated investment trades.

- Also specialize in restructuring a variety of mortgage-related investments including LSBO, REMIC, residual certificates, and private labels. Consolidated portfolio to generate profits and improve cost efficiencies.

**Manager & Chief Analyst, Secondary Marketing**, 1993–1994

Expanded secondary marketing department, set up new loan origination system; established and monitored lock-in procedures. Created secure hedging strategy for pipeline management. Developed profitable execution strategy for securities sales. Reviewed and monitored underwriting guidelines. Developed computer application to set daily loan pricing. Reported to VP of secondary marketing.

- Conceived of arbitrage acquisition operation, initiated market test program.
- Head, due diligence team, secondary marketing.
- Evaluated mortgage loan conduit programs. Priced loan offerings and mortgage-related investments.
- Promoted to V.P. after only six months as manager.

FIRST SECURITY BANK, Morgan Hill, Texas
**Manager, Secondary Marketing**, 1991–1992

Reported directly to the president of this $200 million savings bank. Oversaw secondary marketing, including pricing of loan sales and purchases, pipeline management, portfolio management, shipping, investor relations and development. Managed correspondent lending program.

- Reorganized procedures for origination of FHA-VA loans, which raised success rate in final loan sales from 65% to 100% over pilot test period.
- Originated loan acquisition division which generated over $200 million in production in its first year.
- Implemented hedging policies and procedures for the bank.
- Analyzed servicing value and servicing portfolio disposition.
- Analyzed and valued mortgage loan products for purchase and loan origination.

**Analyst, Investor Accounting**, 1988–1991

**Senior Accountant**, 1985–1987

## EDUCATION

UNIVERSITY OF ARKANSAS, Fayetteville, Arkansas
**B.A., Mathematics**, 1981

UNIVERSITY OF TEXAS, Austin, Texas
Studies in **Music** and **Latin**

# STANLEY DAVID STOKES

3200 Porter Avenue
Buffalo, New York 14201

Telephone/Message:
(716) 555-9326

---

## PROFILE

**Strengths:** tactical and strategic business planning, budgeting and cost controls, organizational development, and leadership. Managed stand-alone $64 million division to record profitability. Knowledge of retail, food, manufacturing, distribution and sales. Major accomplishments with every company.

## EXPERIENCE

**The Printing Company,** Buffalo, New York, 1994–1996
**Acting Chief Operating Officer**

Recruited by CEO to serve as Acting COO and strategic consultant to this entrepreneurial marketing and print brokerage company. Brought in to plan a business expansion into full manufacturing capabilities.

- Personally managed feasibility study—vendor analysis, market study, sales plan, and pro forma cash flow projections—on vertical integration of manufacturing operation. Forecasted subsequent market contraction, recommended company not go into manufacturing, which saved company at least $1.6 million.
- Concurrent operating accomplishments: negotiated new line of credit to facilitate faster production services and improved account servicing; developed company's first tactical planning and five-year strategic plan.

*Other major accomplishments:*
- Organized company's first "Good Manufacturing Practices Committee."
- Negotiated favorable plant and retail clerk union contracts.
- Identified five stores for closure; opened ten new stores in Washington, Utah, Colorado, California, and Hawaii.
- Launched new retail concept, opening three "combo" retail quantity-order shops.
- Appointed by CEO to the Board of Directors of the company's federally chartered Credit Union.

**See-Saw Candies, Inc.,** Rochester, New York, 1982–1994
**Vice President, General Manager, Northern Division,** 1990–1994

Full P&L responsibility for a $64 million division with 1300+ employees, a manufacturing plant, corporate organization, and 98 company-owned stores in six Eastern U.S. states and Quebec. Planned capital budget averaging $4 million per year. Supervised management and administration team of 32.

- Achieved highest percentage profit and highest dollar profit in the 65-year history of the company (1993), with concurrent reduction in cost-of-sales.
- Achieved 19% pre-tax profits for total division, sales increase every single year, and new stores sales as high as $750,000 on only 1100 sq.ft.
- Put in the first Quebec store, which became the highest-grossing store in the chain.

**Assistant General Manager, New York Metropolitan Division,** 1982–1990

In charge of daily operations management and implementing business plans for this division with $96 million in annual sales, up to 2300 employees at peak season, a manufacturing plant, and 113 company-owned stores in six Eastern states.

*Selected accomplishments:*
- Created the company's "cottage look" for in-line regional mall shops, now the company's trademark visual identity.
- Designed cost-containment programs for each operating department, increasing division profit margin by 18%.
- Established a training program reducing manufacturing re-work by 37%.
- Designed operations, reorganized jobs and work flow in collaboration with human resources.
- Created a plan and performance-to-plan work environment throughout the division.

*Continued . . .*

## PRIOR EXPERIENCE

**Hoffman Candy Company,** Brooklyn, New York
**General Manager**

Responsible for manufacturing and operations for $3.5 million company serving the wholesale grocery industry in New York and Long Island.

**Collins Foods International,** Newark, New Jersey
**Area Manager**

Corporate responsibility for 25 fast-food outlets with aggregate sales of $11.5 million. Established operations, set policies and procedures, ensured maximum profitability.

**MacFarlane's Candies of Southern California,** Los Angeles, California
**Executive Vice President, General Plant Manager**

Directed manufacturing, wholesale sales, and retail operations. Directed sales to major department store chains and built and implemented a franchise program.

## MILITARY

**Captain, Naval Aviator, U.S.M.C.**

## EDUCATION

**Graduate School of Management, University of California,** Los Angeles, California
**Certificate, Executive Management Program**

**California State University,** Los Angeles, California
**B.A., Business Administration** and **Marketing**

## ADDITIONAL

FAA Commercial Pilot's License and Commercial Pilot's Instructors License.

Think you could reach this man by phone? Also, note the billing sheet, p. 81.

# RICHARD PANINI

Headquarters Office / voice mail: (916) 555-5125
San Francisco Office / voice mail: (415) 555-0239
Mobile: (916) 555-1896
Fax: (916) 555-6109
Residence / message / emergency: (916) 555-2448

265 Nevada Avenue
South Lake Tahoe, California 96150

---

**PROFILE**
- Litigation & Mediation Services
- Estimates & Adjustments
- Expert Witness
- General Contracting
- Transport & Drayage

**LICENSURE**  **General Contractor, State of California, 641506 B-1**

**STRENGTHS**
- **Construction Defect / Malpractice**
- **Construction Accident / Personal Injury**
- **Estimating / Valuation Analysis**
- **Destructive Testing / Nondestructive Inspection**

**RELATED EXPERIENCE**

**PANINI & ASSOCIATES / RICHARD PANINI CONSTRUCTION**
South Lake Tahoe, California
**General Contractor,** 1990–Present

Hands-on contractor, providing bids, estimates, and repairs *currently and on an ongoing basis* in addition to consulting, testing, and expert witness engagements. Can provide objective, up-to-the-minute analysis based on standard industry practices.

Business includes a wide mix of projects, approximately 30% commercial, 60% residential, 5% institutional, and 5% industrial, ranging from simple room additions for private residences to stores and offices to 14,000 sq.ft., $2.5 million Acid Bath Facility with complex HVAC requirements. Plan, coordinate, and supervise multiple projects and multiple work crews.

Handle projects from initial concept through design-build stages to final acceptance by client. Knowledge of regional architects, designers, subcontractors, specialty contractors, suppliers.

Consultant on faulty craftsmanship, buyer / seller disputes, construction malpractice, contractual irregularities, and overexpenditure disputes. Private inspector for structural defect and plan and code violations. *Also:* Outside Inspector, City of South Lake Tahoe. Former Senior Building Inspector and Chief Building Inspector (see below).

**CONIFER CONSTRUCTION COMPANY**
Chino, California
**Foreman,** 1983–1985

Pre-job planning, permitting, code interpretation, and daily supervision of crews of up to 20 personnel, including subcontractors.

**AMERICANA VACATION RESORT**
South Lake Tahoe, California
**Senior Building Inspector**, 1981–1983

Planning, permitting, and daily supervision over up to 5 different multi-million-dollar projects and total staff up to 30.

**CITY OF SOUTH LAKE TAHOE**
South Lake Tahoe, California
**Senior Building Inspector**, 1981

Inspected commercial, highrise, multiunit residential, and SFD structures to insure that all construction, alteration, and maintenance work was done in compliance with building codes and other pertinent laws and regulations. Included structural, electrical, plumbing, mechanical, HVAC, fire and safety systems, as well as such matters as access, height, zoning, and similar concerns. Kept detailed records, wrote reports and findings, justified interpretation of codes. Maintained expertise on all federal, state and local laws, statutes, codes and ordinances.

**CITY OF SEAL BEACH**
Seal Beach, California
**Chief Building Inspector**, 1980–1981
**Building Inspector/Plan Checker**, 1979–1980

Same as above, with added responsibility of reviewing and issuing building permits. Also rewrote Chapter 5, City Code, Building Division.

**MARE ISLAND SHIPYARD**
Vallejo, California
**Building Inspector,** 1975–1979

**WESTWARD BUILDERS**
San Pablo, California
**Superintendent,** 1970–1975

**U.S. NAVY / SEA BEES**
**Heavy Equipment Operator,** 1968–1969

*also*

**DEL WEBB HIGH SIERRA**, Stateline, Nevada, 1984–1986
**Security Officer** (including OSHA compliance)

**CALZONA TANKWAYS,** Richmond, California, 1986–1988
**Tanker Driver** (including Haz Mat Certification)

**SHELL OIL COMPANY,** Martinez, California, 1988–1989
**Tanker Driver** (including Haz Mat Certification)

**EDUCATION**

UNIVERSITY OF CALIFORNIA at BERKELEY — **Construction**

U.S. NAVAL SCHOOL — **Inspection**

ICBO (International Conference of Building Officials) — **Plan Check School, Inspection School**

CONTRA COSTA COLLEGE — **Carpentry Journeyman**

**CONSULTANT**

Numerous cases, both *plaintiff and defense*, on behalf of the following firms and companies:

Law Offices of Berding and Weil, Alamo, California
Law Offices of Gibson and Thomas, Novato, California
Law Offices of Sedgwick, Detert, Moran and Arnold, San Fran., Cal.
Law Offices of Richter, Senn, and Palumbo, San Francisco, California
Law Offices of Brown and Wood, San Francisco, California
Law Offices of David W. Herrick, Lakeport, California
Law Offices of Michael J. Flynn, San Francisco, California
Sapirstein Law Offices, San Francisco, California
Forward Star Corporation, Red Bluff, California
Tuscan Properties, Inc., Red Bluff, California
Teicheira Construction, Inc., Vallejo, California
Vintage Hills Homeowners Association, Pleasanton, California
Creekview Associates L.P., El Sobrante, California
C&W Electric, Vacaville, California
(and others, list on request)

# RICHARD PANINI

Headquarters Office/voice mail: (916) 555-5125
San Francisco Office/voice mail: (415) 555-0239
Mobile: (916) 555-1896
Fax: (916) 555-6109
Residence/message/emergency: (916) 555-2448

265 Nevada Avenue
South Lake Tahoe, California 96150

## Fee Schedule
## effective March 1996

Consultation, portal-to-portal ..................................................................... by contract, or $100.00/hr

Project management ...................................................................................... by contract, or $110.00/hr

Estimate review, evaluation, and recommendation ............................................................. $100.00/hr

Estimate preparation ................................................................................................................. $100.00/hr

Photo log or videotape documentation ................................................. $100.00 minimum per project

Deposition ............................................................................................. $150.00/hr plus expenses

Destructive investigation .......................................................................... $100.00/hr plus L.M. & OH.

Travel: Travel and per diem expenses billed at cost plus 15% (but no less than $75.00/day outside the Bay Area).

# Arthur M. Louis

Chestnut Hill — Cowell at College
Philadelphia, Pennsylvania 19118

Office/main line: (800) 555-3208
Residence/message/fax/pager: (215) 555-7469

## EXPERTISE

**Marketing / New Business Development / Franchise Consulting**

*Strengths:*

- Consistently proven ability to design and direct marketing campaigns leading to increased gross sales, increased market share, and reduced cost-of-sales.
- Consultant on operations design and internal policies and procedures development to ensure success of marketing efforts through appropriate organizational support.
- Expertise spans (a) feasibility planning, demographic research, site selection, (b) paid and free media planning, (c) promotions, premiums, direct response efforts, (d) cooperative, industry and trade programs, (e) signage, catalog, identity and collaterals development.
- Former PepsiCo executive with full P&L responsibility. Qualified for general management consulting on finance, capitalization, operations, competitive analysis, and other areas.

## EDUCATION

Pennsylvania State University, State College, Pennsylvania
**B.S., Marketing**

## EXPERIENCE

**Marketing Design Group**, Philadelphia, Pennsylvania          1995 – Present
**Managing Director**

Initiated, structured, and conducted marketing consulting projects, including all phases of business analysis, market analysis, media planning, staff training, and organizational development in support of marketing efforts. Designed marketing campaigns for two existing companies; designed entire marketing function (staff, policies, operations) for two start-up companies. Examples:

- New Faces, Education Division — Providing organizational consulting and marketing plans for a cosmetic surgery spin-off company. Working directly with the founder of the company to develop realistic marketing budgets and plans for various business launch scenarios. Ongoing.
- Eastern Colleges of Applied Technology — Revamped marketing and advertising functions for this educational non-profit with 15 campuses. Restructured $3 million annual ad/marketing budget. Solicited, reviewed, and selected an advertising agency. Consolidated and standardized marketing, advertising, and media planning for all campuses. Achieved 41% increase in fall class with no increase in ad/marketing budget. 1995.
- Charlottesville Star Restaurants, Inc. — Planned and conducted comprehensive review of marketing plans for five restaurants in suburban Washington, D.C./Virginia area. Wrote the company's first formal media plan. Achieved 13% increase in business with minimal increase in marketing budget. Also consulted on some operational areas to improve company image. 1995–1996.
- Papyrus, Inc. — Retained to establish structure and internal marketing function for newly formed franchise/real estate department for an aggressive new retail chain. Provided competitive analysis, consulted on site selection, collaborated on business plan development and strategic plan for franchisee development. 1995.

**The Sharper Image,** San Francisco, California          1991 – 1994
**Director of Real Estate**

Recruited to organize, consolidate, and standardize real estate and property management functions for this national retailer. Directed administration, planning, negotiations, policy development.

- Opened 15 new stores in 30 months.
- Reduced store build-out costs from $101 per square foot to less than $64 per square foot.

**Pizza Huts of Columbia**, Missouri      1988 – 1991
  **Owner/Operator**

Bought three units which had been performing well below potential as an entrepreneurial challenge. With full P&L responsibility, built a fourth unit and introduced delivery, achieved turnaround and sold out in just three years. Built company to 105 employees, $2.7 million annual sales, from an anemic $1.8 million. Directed personnel, advertising, marketing, budgeting, financial controls, legal and government relations. Heavily involved in local store marketing and community relations activities.

- Reversed negative revenue trends; achieved 17–27% increases in same-store sales.

**Pizza Hut, Inc.**, Wichita, Kansas
  **Vice President, Restaurant Franchising**

Responsible for 2600 franchised Pizza Hut restaurants nationwide. One of seven top officers of the corporation, member of the strategic management team. Guided policy development and direction of company. Developed and/or reviewed long- and short-term plans, specific expansion strategies, new product proposals, and similar projects.

- Responsible for a department contributing $56 million per annum to Pizza Hut's bottom line.
- Presided over period of increased cooperation and harmony between franchisees and corporate offices.

  **Divisional Vice President, Operations**

Directly responsible for 630 company-owned units, indirectly responsible for 570 franchised units. Delegated through four Regional Vice Presidents of Operations and Division Directors of Finance, Human Resources, and Marketing.

- Managed a division with annual sales of $280 million.
- Achieved the best P&L results in the history of the division. Also recognized for improving personnel relations and reducing turnover to new company-wide lows.

  **Prior**

Supervised 25 restaurants to 175 restaurants in various corporate positions over a six-year span.

- Responsibilities included market development, P&L improvements, and human resource maximization.

## REFERENCES

Provided on request. Please keep this application confidential at this time.

# FRANCISCO PARÉS CANTO

*Curriculum Vitae*

*Mailing Address:*
Tetuán Nº 5275, bajos 1º B
08190 Sant Cugat del Vallès
Barcelona
SPAIN

*Telephone:*
34.3.648 1255

---

**PROFILE**

Senior executive involved in:

- **International Trade / International Marketing**
- **Product Development**
- **New Business Development and Launch**
- **General Business and Marketing Consulting**
- **Turnaround Management**
- **Joint Venture Development**

**PERSONAL**

Born in Barcelona, Spain, April 30, 1942.

Married, four children.

Languages: Catalan and Spanish (native tongues), English (superior), French (good), Italian (some).

**EDUCATION**

UNIVERSITY OF NAVARRA, Barcelona, Spain
PADE, IESE

UNIVERSITY OF BARCELONA, Barcelona, Spain
Perito y Profesor Mercantil, School of Higher Commercial Studies

ESCUELAS PÍAS DE SARRIÀ, Barcelona, Spain
Diploma

**PROFESSIONAL HISTORY**

INTERSECT, S.A., Barcelona, Spain, 1994–Present
**Managing Director** and **Partner**

Provide management and marketing consulting to a range of companies, with emphasis on international trade issues. Services encompass strategic planning, business development, and problem solving throughout Europe and the United States.

Sample engagements:

- **Sogeoil, S.A.**, high technology industrial oil recycling service provider, a joint-venture with a Chicago-based company. Sogeoil recycles industrial oils on customer premises via a state-of-the-art mobile processing plant. The target market is users of industrial oils with a high degree of technical development, who can better relate to this innovative technology outsource company. Contributions:
  - Researched project.
  - Negotiated joint-venture agreement with the U.S. partner.
  - Raised capital.
  - Established Sogeoil, S.A.
  - Initiated and structured involvement of Instituto Quimico de Sarria (I.Q.S.) in the venture. (I.Q.S. is the preeminent chemical laboratory in Spain.)
  - Designed the company's technical department and hired a technical manager.
  - Developed a marketing, sales, and business plans for business launch.

- **F & O Management**, a new investment fund established to trade in futures and options. Currently in start-up phase, trading capital invested by the principals.
  - Positioned the company to gain approval for managing third-party funds (individual and institutional) and providing management services to banks and savings banks.
  - Set up Reuters link to CBOT futures.
  - Created analysis tools to facilitate company goals.
  - Provided successful investment strategies for commodities.

- **Spainsko**, exclusive Spanish agent for a Danish manufacturer of specialty shoes. Spainsko is the first mail order company to target the Spanish market with a line of footwear.
  - Negotiated exclusive rights with the Danish manufacturer.
  - Developed the mail order marketing and business plan.
  - Created a complete set of sales and catalog materials, including concept development, image development, design, production.
  - Developed psychographic and demographic profiles of target customers.
  - Identified and procured specialty mailing lists to build a direct marketing database.

- **Personal Script**, purveyor of high-quality writing instruments.
  - Negotiated exclusive distribution rights for the Spanish market for the Daniel Hechter of Paris line of writing instruments.
  - Developed sales and business plans to reach an upscale market. Established company and hired personnel. Identified and initiated relationships with suppliers of affinity products, for example, Sanford of USA.

Also structured and completed consulting projects for the following:

- **Vincke, S.A.**, a first-tier supplier to the automotive industry in Europe. Provided strategic plan to the year 2000.

- **Instituto de Comercio Exterior (ICEX)**, Spain's official government export agency. Analyzed history and current status of export intermediary companies in Spain, with policy recommendations.

- **Syster Informatique, S.A. (France)**, developers of software for manufacturing systems. Feasibility studies and business plan for establishing a company office in Spain.

- **Vins Font, S.A.**, a winery. Created business plan to take the company out of Chapter 11, including repositioning the company's product offerings and direct negotiations with creditor banks.

ASSIS OFIMUEBLE, S.A., Valls, Tarragona, Spain, 1991–1993
**Managing Director**

Brought in as turnaround manager for this manufacturer of office furniture, a distressed family-owned business needing transition to a more corporate management approach to remain competitive. (Assis Ofimueble was bought by BAMSA, which was itself later acquired by Grand Tibidabo.)

- Developed plan to reshape and relaunch Assis Ofimueble, including new management team, new sales team, new corporate image.
- Restructured manufacturing processes and reduced production staff from 146 to 100.
- Updated technology utilization (e.g., implemented CAD company-wide).
- Developed five new product lines in collaboration with professional designers (Oscar Tusquets, Vicens Martínez, Lola Castelló, Ramon Bigas, Toni Clariana, and others).
- Took control of Assis Lusa, S.A.; set up Assis France, S.L., Assis UK, Ltd.

GDS — COMERCIO INTERNACIONAL, S.A., Barcelona, Spain, 1984–1991
(a subsidiary of GDS Corp., owned by Caixa de Barcelona)
**General Manager**

Provided *internal and external* consulting and management services in the areas of export and multinational business operations. GDS — Comercio Internacional, S.A. (GDS — CI), was an innovative group of 11 employees. GDS Corp. as a whole had over 400 employees, annual revenues of 40,000 million pesetas.

Served as a principal in the creation and start-up of the following export consortia:

- **Comercio Internacional para el Habitat, S.A. (CIH)**, acted as **Promoter** and **President** for this export consortium of manufacturers of contemporary design furniture (Perobell, Disform, Grup T, Punt Mobles). Took sales to 400 million pesetas in two years.

- **Comerç Internacional Ramader de Catalunya (CIRC)**, acted as **Managing Director** for this export society of one hundred cattle growers jointly importing feedstuffs and supplies and exporting meat. Took the society to trade in excess of 1000 million pesetas.

- **Comercio Internacional del Vino, S.A. (CIV)**, acted as **Promoter** and **President** for this export consortium established by GDS — CI and Bodegas Martínez Bujanda (Conde de Valdemar — Rioja), Bodegas y Destilerías Pedro Rovira (Tarragona), and Cavas Roger Goulart (Agrolimen Corporation). Took the consortium to close to 400 million pesetas in export sales volume.

- **CIV USA Inc.**, acted as **Promoter** and **President** for this United States subsidiary of CIV. Established the company and hired local employees in Napa Valley, California, to sell CIV wines in the United States.

Also conducted feasibility and marketing studies to evaluate the potential market for export consortia in the following categories:

- Automobile parts
- Books
- Fresh fruits
- Alabaster sculptures
- Consumer goods for children

In addition to exploring and/or setting up the above trading concerns, also provided outside consulting for other organizations, including:

- **The European Community**. Conducted a study to establish a framework for economic cooperation between Argentina and the EC. Developed a curriculum in international trade for the Peruvian Diplomatic Academy. Completed trade study assignments involving Costa Rica and Venezuela.

- **Irish Export Board**. Developed plan to promote commercial relationships between Ireland and Catalonia.

- **INFE — ICEX (Instituto Español de Comercio Exterior)**. Evaluated ICEX efforts to promote export consortia in Spain.

- **Valle del Ebro Trading Co.** Conducted special study on behalf of 15 savings banks, 20 chambers of commerce, and several development societies on the topic of trading companies (Spain and worldwide), with related feasibility study on proposed new company.

- **Government of Navarra**. Designed center for dissemination of commercial and industrial opportunities and contacts.

- **COPCA**. Prepared analysis and briefings for the President of the Generalitat of Catalonia on trade issues.
- **Fomento del Trabajo Nacional**. Developed plan to promote foreign trade and export consortia.

PARÉS HERMANOS, S.A., Barcelona, Spain, 1961–1984
**President** and **General Manager** (final rank)

Executive manager of this family business importing agricultural, construction, and industrial transportation machinery, sole distributors in Spain for Ford Tractors, Ford Building and Construction Machinery, Ford Indupro, New Holland, and others. The company had five branches, 200 employees, and total revenues in excess of 3500 million pesetas.

Brought a corporate management philosophy to a traditional, family-owned business, including building a new management team. Structured and closed sale of 25% interest to a British investment group. Managed day-to-day operations. Also initiated a diversification strategy, including setting up the following ventures:

- **Parés Implementos, S.A.,** popularly known as **PIMSA**. Acting as **Promoter** and **President**, built this new business to 25 employees and 500 million pesetas in revenues. Structured and negotiated joint-venture agreement with three European agricultural implements manufacturers:
  - **Hartvig Jensen & Co.** of Denmark, the world's second leading and Europe's leading purveyor of spraying equipment.
  - **Kverneland A/S** of Norway, the world's second leading and Europe's leading purveyor of ploughs.
  - **Antonio Carraro di G.** of Italy, a manufacturer of specialty tractors.
- **Lansing Parés, S.A.** Acted as **Promoter** and **President** in this joint venture with Lansing Bagnall of Switzerland, one of Europe's leading manufacturers of industrial machinery for automated warehousing and internal transportation.

**ADDITIONAL ACTIVITIES**

University of Navarra, Barcelona, Spain

IESE (Instituto de Estudios Superiores de la Empresa)
**Assistant Professor-Lecturer, Marketing Department** (part-time)

Co-teacher, with Prof. Renart: "Export and Multinational Marketing."

Co-author with Prof. Renart on some 25 cases describing export market development efforts by Spanish companies. Many of these cases are published in business books internationally, and one of them won the first prize in Europe, 1991, European Foundation for Management Development (EFMD).

Centre HEC-ISA, Juoy-en-Josas, Paris, France, 1990
AESE, Lisbon, Portugal, 1985–1992
IAE, Buenos Aires, Argentina, 1992
**Visiting Professor**

ESADE, Barcelona, Spain, 1989
Bi-Annual World Marketing Congress, 1987
**Presenter & Speaker**

Member, Board of Directors, Sabat Selección, S.A., 1988–1995

Member, Board of Directors, EURESA (a subsidiary of BEPCO UK), 1992–1994

# KENNETH MASON WILSON

75 College Avenue, Suite 1
Annapolis, Maryland 21401
U.S.A.

Telephone: (410) 555-7759
Fax: (410) 555-7760
km.wilson@consult.com

---

## HISTORY

**Gesellschaft für Wirthschafts Strategie, A.G. (GfWS),** Frankfurt, Germany, 1992 – Present
**Permanent Advisor**

Provide ongoing strategic consulting and tactical assistance to the co-founder of one of the most profitable financial services companies in the world. With a minimum account requirement of US$1 billion, GfWS provides investment advisory services exclusively to multinational corporations, central banks, and government agencies typically at the CEO or finance minister level. The core of GfWS's highly secretive technical modeling methodology is the largest commercially owned supercomputer array in the world, 18 CyberPlus Control Data Corporation supercomputers in parallel. Recent projects include:

Identified U.S. acquisition candidate, a money management firm using proprietary quantitative computer processes to predict directional movements within the world's major financial markets. Provided rationale for the successful acquisition, a US$100+ million transaction.

Initiated and directed confidential discussions with CEOs of the leading supercomputer firms to explore major enhancements to GfWS's computing capacity and related enabling technologies.

**The World Econometrics Group (WEG),** Philadelphia, Pennsylvania, 1991 – Present
**Permanent Advisor**

As special project counsel to the acquiring Chairman & CEO, assisted in the purchase, merger and reorganization of Haas Econometric Forecasting Associates and Mellon Econometrics into WEG, a world leader in economic research and financial data, with offices worldwide and clients in 45 countries. Continue to advise WEG on business development and strategic planning. Currently facilitating joint ventures between WEG and one of the world's largest database software vendors, an international publishing conglomerate, an electronic financial data company, and the leading supercomputer manufacturer, working directly with the Chairmen of all five organizations, to jointly develop proprietary data management projects.

**Wilson & Woodward, Inc.,** Los Angeles, California, 1988 – Present
**Managing Director**

Direct client development and research activities as senior consultant of this management consulting organization, founded in 1940 by my grandfather, and a charter member of the Association of Management Consulting Firms. The firm counsels industrial companies in financial, marketing, and new product commercialization strategies. Clients have included American Brands, Inc., Dow Corning Corporation, EG&G, Inc., General Foods Corporation, Gestetner Corporation, Johnson Controls, Inc., TRW, Union Carbide, and similar. In recent years Wilson & Woodward has undertaken a number of projects for major European and Arab Gulf companies, particularly in the area of international trade and investment.

Brought several engagements to the firm, for example:

On behalf of Internation Exchange Inc., a wholly owned subsidiary of Wilson & Woodward, initiated discussions with the CEOs of six of the world's top 20 non-U.S. commercial banks to manage foreign currency exposures, and to structure an automated network to distribute U.S. money market investments to non-U.S. entities.

On behalf of the primary venture capital investor in an emerging biotechnology company, advised the board of directors on virtually all management issues, and collaborated with the CEO to write the business plan to jump from R&D to full commercialization for four proprietary vaccine products. The company has completed critical joint ventures with two of the largest pharmaceutical companies in the world.

On behalf of both the CEO and CFO of a major West Coast pipe fabricating concern, provided market studies and financial analyses for the establishment of a US$100 million large-diameter pipe bending and fabricating facility in the eastern United States. As part of the study, met with 24 CEOs of East Coast-based public utilities, petroleum and chemical companies, scrubber manufacturers, and engineering and design firms, all potential users of specialty pipe. Initiated key new business relationships throughout the region even before the plant reached the design stage.

On behalf of the primary investor, the family trust of a blue chip company founder, collaborated with the senior management of an entrepreneurial software engineering firm to create a business plan for a proprietary product to "internationalize" English-based off-the-shelf software for immediate application.

Details from similar projects provided on request.

**Emerald Scientific Corporation,** Menlo Park, California, 1987 – 1991
**Managing Director**

Principal in a "think tank" entrepreneurial company with domestic and overseas holdings in commercial banking, financial services, manufacturing, electronic publishing, and scientific companies. Involved in several projects, including launch and spin off of subsidiary companies. Selected projects:

Acquired a bloc of shares in Bank Institute Zurich, a well respected banking, investment advisory, and portfolio management organization founded in 1689. Guided Swiss-based management in the process of establishing business development activities in the United States.

Designed and launched Blackout Inc., a manufacturing company, to produce OEM laser printer toner units in response to the worldwide monopoly quietly established by Canon of Japan. Orchestrated organizational development, recruited President & CEO, COO, CFO and other top management, coordinated house and outside counsel, and solved problems as an acting line manager wherever necessary. Successfully competing with and outperforming Canon, generated company-wide purchase orders at the CEO level at several hundred companies, including Clorox, Ford Motor Company, Hewlett Packard, Unysis and similar. Operated plants in the United States and Switzerland (Inter Printing, A.G., a joint venture with Intercountry Management Corporation). Sold company in 1989 to investor group led by the founder of Compaq.

Served as interim EVP in charge of client engagements, strategic planning and business development for HK Survey Corporation, which provided senior management of large industrial concerns with extremely confidential quantitative data for making decisions regarding current and emerging problems in the handling of hazardous process materials and the systematic elimination of hazardous waste.

**Garden State Micro Relay, Inc.**, Jenkintown, Pennsylvania, 1985 – 1989
**Consultant**

Served as primary advisor to the CEO of this terrestrial microwave common carrier from purchase to sale. Initiated and directed MBO negotiations with Warner Communications, Inc. (now Time-Warner). Arranged third-party capital participation with a single telecommunications industry silent partner. Advised management during period of increase in market value from US$2.7 million to US$42.3 million. Directed sale and merger of company in 1989 (now known as MicroNet, Inc.).

**Kenneth M. Wilson & Company, Inc.**, Annapolis, Maryland, 1983 – 1987
**President**

Founded this firm to provide strategic consulting and act as venture partner on selected projects. Areas of emphasis included pioneering application of advanced computer, communication, and database management technology to financial markets (Money Instruments Technology), as well as marketing and new product commercialization areas. Sample Projects:

Developed market for a unique retail-oriented cash-management product, attracting over US$200 million in new assets for a consortium of multibillion-dollar money fund organizations. This concept was copied by other large money fund groups generating new assets under management in excess of US$5 billion.

Organized and managed a national deposit acquisition division for a group of banking institutions owned by First Deposit Corporation, the financial services subsidiary of Capital Holding Corporation. This project generated over US$2 billion in retail and institutional deposits, which were in turn profitably utilized to fund receivables for the *FirstSelect*™ VISA program.

Advised members of the U.S. Congress and other government officials on matters pertaining to banking and financial services industry legislation.

Additional projects described on request.

**Robbins Financial Corporation,** Washington, D.C.
**Consultant — Acting Chief Marketing Officer**, 1984 – 1986
**National Director**, 1982 – 1983

Developed the market for CD*x*™, the world's first multidimensional real-time computerized exchange for negotiable certificates of deposit. This company's trading volume reached US$1 billion in its first nine months of operation, increasing to US$7 billion in annualized trading volume within three years. The achievements of CD*x*™ were covered in every major newspaper and magazine in America (reprints of representative articles available upon request).

Clients consisted of 600 depository institutions and 3500 institutional investors. Assisted in the market analysis of ED*x*™ for Euro certificates of deposit. Introduced the idea of a nationwide distribution network, which was utilized by a subsequently developed clone operation called *Basis Point*, a division of Reich & Tang, L.P., generating over US$20 billion in annualized trading volume.

**Bankers Finance Corporation,** Arlington, Virginia, 1981 – 1982
**Senior Investment Officer**

On behalf of the firm's mutual fund group, Government Investors Trust (GIT), worked with senior executives of 160 U.S. commercial banks to perform detailed credit analyses of their institutions and negotiate multimillion-dollar deposit terms. Managed a fixed income portfolio of US$24 million.

## EDUCATION

**Harvard University,** Cambridge, Massachusetts
**Major: Economics**

## HONORS

National Forensic League — Degree of Distinction

American Legion Gold Oratory Medal

domestic and overseas references available upon request

# Barbara Nolan

2375 Haystack Hill Road
Richmond, Virginia 23225

Office/direct: (804) 555-2882
Office/switchboard: (804) 555-2800
Residence/message: (804) 555-4715

## STRENGTHS

- **Administrative Management**
- **Accounting Operations Management**
- **Accounts Receivable & Collections**

Designing/managing accounting and administrative operations, policies, and procedures; selecting/motivating/retaining accounting and HQ administrative staff; directing programming, systems development/administration specialists; contributing to strategic decision-making process.

## EXPERIENCE

**Baylor & Carter Insurance,** Richmond, Virginia
**V.P., Chief Administrative Officer**      1993 – Present

Manage administrative function for a major branch and 2 subsidiary offices, with a total staff of 18 direct-reports and administrative authority over additional staff of 102. Report directly to the General Manager/Resident Vice President. In charge of policies and procedures, productivity, real estate, fleet program, travel, computing, supplies, furniture, equipment, and budgeting. Plan and manage budgets totaling $5+ million per annum, including all reports and analyses. Participate in national meetings of Admin/HR managers (including committees and national/regional task forces).

*Major accomplishment:*
- Assigned to turn around branch service levels. Developed action plan, reduced expenses, implemented cross training, restructured job descriptions to incorporate quantitative standards and accountability for every position, eliminated staff with concurrent *increase* in service provision.

*Also:*
- Identified and reassigned 30,000 sq.ft. excess real estate, achieving $750,000 expense charge savings for the branch.
- Discovered and disputed a 35% service charge from corporate to branch-level for forms and supplies, winning complete elimination of this charge for branches nationwide.
- Consistently achieve one of the highest service levels in the business:
    New Business:     80% in 30 days/100% in 45 days
    Renewals:         95% in 30 days/100% in 45 days
    Endorsements:     95% in 30 days
- Increased electronic policy issuance from 50% to 85% by retraining existing staff, reducing error rate and increasing productivity.
- Co-prepare the Unified Plan with the rest of the management team, including projections for premiums, growth, commission ratio, loss ratio, and monthly pro forma cash flows.
- Organized party celebrating 140 years of business in Richmond (with Office of the Mayor).
- **Brought 1995 budget in at 91% of projections; brought 1994 budget in at 95% of projections; currently running under budget for 1996.**

**Territorial Accountant**      1985 – 1993

Supervised up to 32 Accounting Clerks and 4 Supervisors in managing cash flow, accounts receivable, and collections for 13 Western States. Provided accounting function for profit center branches in the region. Oversaw collection and processing of $375 million per annum, including legal collection efforts. Coordinated with the national organization. Reported to the Manager, California Operations.

*Continued . . .*

*Contributions:*
- Made major contributions to the organization of the accounting function and the integrity and efficiency of the data flow. Won approval from corporate office for national Territorial Accountants Meetings to improve standardization.
- Worked closely with systems development specialists on upgrades and conversions.
- Created "Service Representative" program copied nationally.
- Directed collections from customers and from affiliates. Redesigned the collections procedure. **Succeeded in reducing nonadmitted assets from 60% to 7%.**
- Directed accounting portion of territorial consolidation projects, including branch audits. Discovered $1 million in nonaccounted production and alerted home office.
- Selected to train all accounting staff in newly acquired regional company in Milbank, South Dakota. Brought 16 staff in compliance with company norms. Oversaw MIS conversion.
- Routinely traveled as needed for audits, training, and problem solving.

**Associate Regional Accountant** (staff of 27)     1983

**Assistant Regional Accountant** (staff of 24)     1979 – 1982

## PRIOR

**Collections Accountant II**, **Kemper Insurance,** McLean, Virginia
**Bookkeeper**, **Strong & Company,** Roanoke, Virginia

## EDUCATION

**Duke University**
Business, Accounting, Finance

**International Business Machines (IBM)**
The IBM Executive Seminar

**Xerox Management Training**
Interpersonal Management Skills
Focused Selection Interviewing

**Reimer & Associates**
The Art & Practice of Supervision
Time Management for Supervisors & Managers

**Insurance Personnel Management Association**
Managing for Productivity

**Federated Employers**
Effective Management of the Culturally Diverse Workforce
How to Make Quality Improvement Work

**Battle & Carter Insurance**
Managing With Respect
Performance Appraisal — Managing the Process
Salary Administration Program
Design & Administration of On-the-job Training
Personnel Workshop for Managers & Supervisors

# John A. Yamada

170 Chatham Drive
Atherton, California 94027
(415) 555-5364

## HISTORY

### Current

**Partner, Myers & Dodd,** San Francisco and Menlo Park, California, 1969–Present

Partner in charge of administrative and tax matters for the firm's two offices, San Francisco and Menlo Park; co-manage with other partners the firm's diversified portfolio of $4.5 billion invested in all types of standard domestic and foreign financial instruments as well as VC endeavors.

### Sample activities:
- Investigate all types of domestic and international investments and companies, with an eye to optimum ROI.
- Serve as director and/or interim officer for emerging technology-based companies in which our firm has an investment.
- Represent firm to IRS and SEC, as well as any other local, state, federal, and foreign national regulatory entities.
- Manage relations with McKenzie & Stearn; strategize and oversee firm legal matters.
- Coordinate tax planning, reporting, and compliance for a matrix of individuals, trusts, estates, and partnerships.
- Coordinate with UK accountants and attorneys re six individuals I represent, who are "names" for Lloyd's of London.

### Prior

**Manager/Tax Specialist, Haskins & Sells** (now part of a "Big 6" firm), Los Angeles, California

Expert in probate, estate, gift tax, and foreign income matters. Performed in-depth accounting and legal research, devised case-specific tax strategies for estate and fiduciary tax filings, supported legal counsel in some litigated matters. Also created staff training materials, served as instructor at national training conferences.

**Accounting Instructor, University of Colorado,** Boulder, Colorado

**Member, U.S. Army Counter Intelligence Corps**

## OFFICER-DIRECTORSHIPS/TRUSTEESHIPS

### Business and Professional

Brisbane International Travel, 1975–Present
**Director**

Brisbane is the largest corporate/commercial travel company in the region comprised of Los Angeles/Metro Southern California, Southern Arizona, Southern Nevada.

CBMT, Inc., 1990–Present
**Chairman, Chief Financial Officer,** and **Director**

Provided key organizational and business development advice during the formation of this small financial services company, which has increased from a $200,000 start-up to more than $170 million under management today.

Western Service Corporation, Inc., 1979–Present
**Chairman** and **Director**

Provided leadership for growth of this computer service company, one of the first of its kind. Guided firm through mainframe-mini/server-micro evolution with steadily increasing revenues, from $1.5 million at acquisition in 1979 to $25 million revenue with net income in excess of industry standards.

20-20 Engineering, Inc., 1990–Present
**Director** (20-20 is an R&D company with a robot "vision" solution)

Western Association of Venture Capitalists, 1973–Present
**Treasurer** (awarded Certificate of Special Distinction, 1988)

Zymon Family Trust, 1971–Present
**Trustee**

*Charitable and Nonprofit Organizations*

Wabash College, 1982–Present
**Regent, Board Chair** 1990–Present
Vice-Chair
Member, Executive Committee
Chair, Development Committee, Finance Committee, College Investment Policies Committee

Chaired a fund-raising program which proved to be the largest in the history of the college to that time. This program generated the first-ever $1 million gift for the college.

The Brisbane Foundation, 1974–Present
The Myers & Dodd Foundation, 1978–Present
**Treasurer** and **Trustee** (tax-exempt charitable organizations)

San Francisco Boys Chorus, 1979–1984
**President, Chairman, Director**

Directed and promoted the chorus's rise to national prominence. Established proper administrative and financial tracking systems. Assisted in sponsoring album recording and supervised chorus tours, including the White House Christmas Tree Lighting Ceremony in 1982.

## EDUCATION & CERTIFICATION

**C.P.A,** State of California

**M.S., Accounting,** University of Colorado
Graduate Scholarship Award

**A.B., Economics,** Wabash College
Recipient, Distinguished Service Award, 1980

## PROFESSIONAL AFFILIATIONS

Western Association of Venture Capitalists
American Institute of CPAs
California Society of CPAs
Beta Alpha Psi, Honorary Accounting Fraternity

## ACADEMIC POSITIONS

**Faculty Member**
**Accounting, Economics** and **Taxation**
University of California, Extension
California CPA Foundation
University of Colorado
Trinity University (Texas)
Wabash College

## SOCIAL ORGANIZATIONS

The Family
Menlo Circus Club
Merchants Exchange Club
Laurel Oaks Swim & Tennis Club
The Olympic Club of San Francisco

# NANCY RUBIN

1740 Broadway, #503
San Francisco, California 94109

Telephone/Message:
(415) 555-6776

**PROFILE**

**Integrated Marketing ▪ Publishing ▪ Event Merchandising ▪ Sales Promotion**

Intimate knowledge of the international tourism, epicurean, and fashion world. Senior management strengths in marketing, strategic positioning, product development, public relations, event promotions, sponsorship, and joint-venture arrangements.

Top level contacts worldwide: tourism, wine, food, fashion, media, and entertainment industries.

**HIGHLIGHTS**

**Ritz-Carlton Hotels' World of Wines**

Co-Founder, coordinator, co-producer/co-promoter of this event, the largest consumer-paid wine and food event in the country, drawing an international crowd of wine and food celebrities. Brought on board key sponsorships: Italian Ministry of Tourism, Italian Wine & Food Center, BMW, Ministry of Foods & Wines of Spain, Spanish Board of Tourism, Tiffany & Co., Calvin Klein Cosmetics. Signed Julia Child to the event, along with her sponsors: Braun, Farberware, and others. Also involved, annually for eight years, in launching a new line of crystal designed by Archduke Dominic of Austria, in conjunction with Gump's. Similar involvement in the **Napa Valley Wine Auction** — Co-Founder, brought in American Airlines, Tiffany & Co., and Romendin as sponsors, also annually for eight years.

**Fairmont Hotels — I. Magnin — Moet et Chandon**

Created integrated marketing program for the above clients to capitalize on the exclusive wedding market. Designed/produced brochure featuring I. Magnin's bridal department, Moet et Chandon champagne, and Fairmont San Francisco's renowned penthouse suite. Distributed 100,000 brochures to bridal planners and market influencers worldwide. Designed cross-promotion for the month of June 1993. Similar involvement in an integrated marketing project with Meadowood Resort, Neiman Marcus, and Range Rover as co-sponsors.

**Gump's Treasures of Asia — Asian Art Museum — Mandarin Oriental Hotels, Hong Kong**

Designed and created a complex, integrated marketing program involving Gump's, San Francisco Asian Art Museum, Hong Kong Tourism Board, Mandarin Oriental Hotels, Wedgwood, Orrefors, Georg Jensen, Spode, Ginori, Baccarat, and world-renowned artisans and experts on Asian art and antiques. Launched and managed a month-long cross promotion of lectures, presentations, and events, coordinated with a dedicated issue of *Epi Scene* magazine. Fall 1992.

**7th on Sale**

Liaison and co-promoter/co-producer, acting as direct assistant to Nicole Miller and Donna Karan in the creation of the nation's fashion industry's premier benefit for AIDS research. Biannual event, West Coast launch in 1992.

*Continued . . .*

**Hayman Island's International Epicurean Festival**

Co-Founder of this upcoming event held on a private island off Australia's Great Barrier Reef, owned by Rupert Murdock's News Corporation. This event is designed to bring together the world's renowned chefs and vintners to provide a global spotlight on the corporate sponsors. First annual scheduled for 1996.

**HISTORY**

**Premier Publishing, Inc. /** *Epi Scene* **Magazine**
**President & Publisher**, 1991–Present

Launched *Epi Scene* magazine, an acclaimed epicurean publication with a current national circulation of 302,000, average household income of $95,000+. Provide creative and strategic direction to this custom marketing and publishing company. Manage staff of 15 FTE, and over 35 contract employees. Developed business and marketing plans, established publishing operations, negotiated contracts, established major advertiser relationships, managed finance and cash flow.

**Sample contributions:**

- Developed innovative circulation strategy, working directly with heads of numerous exclusive hotel and retail companies, and the world's leading newsstand distribution company.
- Established national network of advertising sales offices.
- Developed full-service integrated marketing department to devise, sell, and manage innovative sales support and merchandising programs.
- Developed subsidiary custom publishing and design operation serving fashion and retail accounts worldwide.
- Personally provide creative direction on photo shoots, layout, look, and image. Personally provided creative direction to concept development and integrated marketing concepts. Personally manage key relationships.

*Wine Country International* **Magazine**
**Publisher**, 1980–1991

Provided strategic direction and daily operational control for all publishing operations. Led this publication through a period of expansion and redefinition, leading to recognition as one of the nation's leading consumer wine and food publications.

**Sample contributions:**

- Developed strategy to reposition the magazine from a local Napa Valley publication to a leading international publication focusing on wine, food, travel, and leisure industries.
- Successfully redefined, redirected, redesigned, and reformatted every aspect of the publication, including both art and editorial aspects.
- Increased ad revenue from $125,000 to over $4,500,000 per annum.
- Negotiated national newsstand distribution agreement with the country's leading distribution company.
- Collaborated with targeted advertisers to create forward-looking integrated promotional and merchandising programs to meet their needs.

*Continued . . .*

**Foote, Cone, Belding & Honig** and **J. Walter Thompson**
**Advertising Art Director**, 1978–1980

Provided creative and production services in print and television media for two premier San Francisco ad agencies.

Accounts:
- Eddie Bauer
- California Raisins
- Clorox
- C&H Sugar
- Dole Pineapple
- Levi Strauss & Co.

**EDUCATION**

**San Francisco Academy of Arts College**
**M.F.A., Advertising Art**, 1978

**Linfield College, College of Business**
**B.A.,** dual major: **Business** and **Art Direction**, 1976

**World Campus Afloat**, 1976–1977

**AFFILIATIONS**

American Institute of Wine and Food

Magazine Publishers Association

San Francisco Advertising Club

Chaíne des Rôtisseurs

# ROGER D. WOODWARD

21 Prince Court
Albany, California 94706

Office/voice mail: (408) 555-4277
Residence/message: (510) 555-8548
roger.wood@sj.gov

| | |
|---|---|
| **PROFILE** | **Expertise in guiding major public projects through all stages,** from initial concept through legal/financial/political/legislative review, design, construction, and grand opening. Strengths include demonstrated ability in moving projects forward in a difficult public-private matrix; identifying and developing relationships with individuals and organizations with the potential to contribute to the project; negotiating complex joint-venture development and operating arrangements with involved parties; and managing project scope, cost, schedule and quality. Outstanding record for results in complex, politicized arenas. Prior history in project control with Bechtel. Collaborative management style; effective in a variety of organizational structures.<br><br>Recent projects total in excess of $500 million, including the *SAN JOSE COMMUNITY ARENA* and the *TECH MUSEUM OF INNOVATION.* |
| **EDUCATION** | **HARVARD UNIVERSITY**   Cambridge, MA<br>**Bachelor of Arts**, *cum laude*   1976 |
| **EXPERIENCE** | **SAN JOSE REDEVELOPMENT AGENCY**   San Jose, CA<br>Program Development Office<br>**Senior Negotiations Officer**   1993–Present<br>Chief negotiator on major projects. Supervise redevelopment teams of up to 20 staff, plus up to 10 consultants (legal, environmental, economic, financial, design, etc.). Report to the Director of Program Development. Sample projects:<br><br>**Tech Museum of Innovation** — an $80 million, 120,000 sf science and technology museum; currently in design stage; architect: Ricardo Legoretta.<br><br>Led negotiations on Disposition and Development Agreement (DDA) and Operations and Management (O&M) Agreement among San Jose Redevelopment Agency, City of San Jose, and the Board of the private nonprofit Tech Museum of Innovation. Presented final agreement for approval. Also strategized negotiations with IMAX Corporation for inclusion of specialty OMNIMAX theatre. Oversaw design, estimating, budgeting, scheduling, and design of project controls. Monitored museum's compliance to mission statements.<br><br>**Mexican Heritage Gardens** — a $24 million mixed-use project with outdoor plaza, classrooms, studios, theatre, and parking; currently in design stage.<br><br>Negotiated Letter of Intent among City, Agency, and Mexican Heritage Corporation. Coordinated process leading to acceptance of project EIR. Oversaw acquisition of 9 site properties. Coordinated application for capital grants from HUD, CDBG, and Santa Clara County. Facilitated site delivery for adjacent 60-unit senior housing project.<br><br>**Jose Theater** — a $13 million, 700-seat theater with state-of-the-art multimedia and broadcast technologies.<br><br>Conceptualized business plan for Jose Theater reuse. Coordinated feasibility explorations with private nonprofit partner, El Teatro Campesino. |

San Jose Community Arena
**Negotiations Officer**     1989–1993

Instrumental in creating the **San Jose Community Arena**, one of the most successful redevelopment projects on the West Coast, a joint venture with the City of San Jose and the San Jose Sharks for a $165 million, 18,000-seat state-of-the-art multipurpose arena with associated parking and infrastructure; architect: Sink, Combs, Dethleffs. Served on team that landed the NHL hockey franchise. Supervised consultant studies on arena economics, market for luxury box leasing, and parking projections. Negotiated Letter of Intent and Development/Management Agreements; monitored design/build phase for compliance with agreements. Strategized final Settlement Agreement with NHL Sharks, and City/Agency Cooperation Agreement to ensure smooth turnover of completed facility.

San Antonio Plaza Project Area
**Project Manager**     1986–1989

Supervised teams up to 12 (construction managers, architects, attorneys, consultants) and collaborated with venture partners to bring major public and private works from concept to completion (hands-on management of scope, schedule, cost, quality). Samples:

> **San Jose Museum of Art** — a $12 million addition; architects: SOM/RMW
> **Plaza Park** — a new 3-acre city park; architects: Hargreaves & Associates
> **Paseo Plaza Condominiums** — $20 million, 200-unit luxury condos; architects: BAR
> **Pavilion Shops** — $35 million, 100,000 sf specialty retail mall; architect: Jon Jerde
> **Fairmont Hotel** — $110 million, 580-room luxury hotel; architects: HOK
> **Fairmont Plaza Office Building** — 17 story office tower; architects: SOM
> **City Infrastructure** — roads, parking and other public projects

**BECHTEL CIVIL & MINERALS, INC.**     San Francisco, CA
Measure "A" Highway Improvements Program (San Jose)
**Project Controls Manager**     1986

Prepared and presented proposal for Santa Clara County Traffic Authority resulting in program management consultancy for $800 million highway project. Developed project management controls and processes.

South Station Renovation Project (Boston)
**Project Schedule Engineer**     1985–1986

Provided scheduling systems for this highly successful reconstruction of Boston's South Station rail terminal into an office and retail complex.

Pakistan Airports Project (Karachi)
**Project Schedule Engineer**     1983–1985

Developed and implemented computerized project cost and schedule control system for $80 million airport renovation program for Pakistan's Civil Aviation Authority. Set up local office; trained foreign national staff.

Strategic & Operating Plans (HQ)
**Assistant to the Director of the Technical Services Division**    1980–1982

Provided analysis and projections for 5-year strategic plan and annual operating plan for division with $3 billion per year in design and construction projects.

Publications Division (HQ)
**Technical Editor**    1979–1980

**TRAINING**    Continuing education in **finance, negotiations, construction, scheduling, estimating, cost engineering**. Details on request.

**SKILLSET**    Advanced PC skills: project management, database, word processing, and spreadsheet applications; worldwide research on Internet.

# KEVIN R. DUNCAN

3201 Wilshire Blvd., #1212
Los Angeles, California 90036
(213) 555-8521

## PROFILE

- **Financial Executive** — international and domestic financial management.
- Experience in manufacturing, distribution, retail.
- Expertise in treasury, control, planning, taxes, MIS.

## EXPERIENCE

MITSUI ELECTRONICS COMPANY U.S.A        1990 to Present
**CFO, Vice President-Finance, Treasurer**

CFO of $3 billion stand-alone office automation and consumer electronics groups within one of the world's largest manufacturer/distributors of electronics products. Directed financial management of four Far East manufacturing plants. Supervised 16 financial controllers. Directed all treasury functions of Western Hemisphere, an additional $16 billion sales/distribution operation.

Managed financing, banking, accounting, auditing, taxes, credit and collections, strategic planning, acquisitions/divestments, insurance and pensions, HR, MIS. Coordinated with clients and vendors including IBM, Tandy, Sears, Penney's, CompUSA, The Good Guys, and many, many others.

*Sample contributions:*
- Directed financing for growth from $8 billion to $16 billion.
- Arranged $800 million in Eurobond offering/private placement/acquisition financing.
- Negotiated financing for and participated in ten company start-ups.
- Developed/implemented automated systems and centralized finance projects.
- Instituted online cash management systems, global order entry system.
- Designed and implemented automated Swiss-based reinvoicing center.
- Centralized foreign exchange and global cash management.

BUSINESS COMPUTERS, INC.        1987 to 1989
**Vice President/Controller**

Directed financial controls of six-year-old, $1.2 billion NYSE-listed company. Managed $4 million budget; supervised treasurer, four assistant controllers. Oversaw 125 microcomputer sales and service centers nationwide.

Functioned as corporate officer, reporting to SVP Financial/Corporate Operations. Managed banking, treasury, accounting, credit and collections, taxes, planning.

Coordinated with MIS, HR, international, field sales and leasing operations. Worked with major vendors including IBM, Apple, Compaq, Hewlett-Packard.

*Sample contributions:*
- Raised credibility/utility of finance function; upgraded staff and systems.
- Reduced outside auditor's management control letter comments from 16 to zero.
- Developed systems that enabled revenue growth from $450 million to $1.2 billion.
- Facilitated acquisitions in the United Kingdom, Canada, Europe, and the United States.
- Converted financial and operating systems of newly acquired companies.
- Implemented an integrated cash-management system for safety/security of retail operations.
- Obtained $90 million in long-term subordinated debentures.
- Negotiated $50 million unsecured credit facility.

CAPITAL INTERNATIONAL      1979 to 1980
**Director of Treasury Services/International Treasurer**

Treasurer of international division of NYSE, Fortune 100 diversified manufacturer. Directed operations of European reinvoicing center.

*Sample contributions:*
- Arranged $400 million in financing through Eurobonds/private placements/credit facilities.
- Implemented online worldwide cash management, foreign exchange and financing system.
- Expanded foreign exchange exposure system to include all international affiliates.
- Developed multicurrency financial reports and treasury manuals.

FAIRCHILD INSTRUMENTS CORP. (Schlumberger)      1975 to 1979
**Assistant Treasurer/Director of Banking**      (1977 to 1979)

Managed treasury operations of $700 million semiconductor manufacturer. Responsible for acquisition of funds, credit/collection, capital budgeting, leasing. Directed M&A's, investments, strategic planning, project financing, SEC reporting. Coordinated global cash management and tax planning, expatriate financing.

*Sample contributions:*
- Completed/implemented international cash mobilization, intracountry cash studies.
- Developed transfer price system in compliance with tax authorities worldwide.
- Developed standardized foreign exchange accounting and exposure procedures.
- Participated in securing $30 million Eurobond and $30 million private placement.
- Arranged $60 million multicurrency line of credit.

**Controller, International Manufacturing Operations**      (1975 to 1977)

Managed financial controls, accounting, profitability, planning, budgets. Responsible for transfer pricing, managerial/financial reporting, financial analysis.

AMERICAN BRANDS
**Group Controller**

Directed financial management for six operating companies and six holding companies. Coordinated SEC registration, liaised with investment bankers in public offerings.

*Sample contributions:*
- Directed conversion from direct-costing inventory system to full absorption system.
- Upgraded financial reporting, cost accounting, budgeting, profit planning systems.
- Implemented comparative reporting of foreign and domestic operations.

**Divisional Controller, Europe**

Controlled London-based European sales and manufacturing operations.

## EDUCATION

**MBA-Accounting & Finance**, Stanford University

**BA-Accounting & Management**, San Francisco State University

# Deborah Goldberg

4118 East Sylvan Hills Lane
St. Louis, Missouri 63119

Residence/message/fax/pager: (314) 555-8318
gold.girl@risknarm.com

**PROFILE**

**Chief Financial Officer & Accounting Manager**

*Strengths:*

- Experience with two start-up companies, including designing financial systems and procedures from the ground up.
- Design and preparation of all statements and reports; cash management and treasury; budgeting and projections; business planning, business research, feasibility studies.
- Design of integrated financial systems, including systems analysis and documentation, procedures design, information flows.

**EXPERIENCE**

CALLAHAN & BARTHOLOMEW INSURANCE SERVICES, INC.     St. Louis, MO
**Chief Financial Officer**     1994–1996
**Director**     1995–1996
**Chief Accountant**     1989–1994

Directed every aspect of financial management and operations for this wholesale insurance brokerage (surplus lines) with annual premium sales in the range of $22–$45 million. The company serves a national clientele of insurance retailers, specializing in the placement of executive risk, professional and employment-related liability coverages.

Involved from the inception of the company, with primary responsibility for setting up and maintaining the accounting, personnel, and administrative systems. Ensured compliance with state and federal employment and insurance regulations. Managed out-of-state licensing process. Served as IS officer for the firm.

Reported to the president and the board. Prepared annual budgets, coordinated annual audit by CPA, prepared all statements and reports, provided cash management and treasury, handled all tax filings, analyzed financial impact of proposed changes in business practices, provided direction to the strategic planning process. Managed financial reporting and correspondence with London-based 50% owner. Established policies and procedures; supervised staff of four.

As **Corporate Secretary & Treasurer**, maintained all corporate records (prepared resolutions and minutes, issued stock certificates, amended articles of incorporation, ensured compliance with corporate by-laws).

Controlled trustee accounts (collection, payment, investment) in accordance with strict guidelines. Reviewed all contracts, directed licensing renewals with the state, monitored compliance with multistate departments of insurance regulations, monitored pending legislation for impact on operations, integrated changes as needed.

Also directed special projects related to strategic changes in the direction of the company, e.g.:

- Established policy issuance procedure in compliance with Lloyd's of London regulations as authorized "facility" for directors and officers liability coverage.
- Contributed to new corporate identity, including logo and brochures.
- Planned and directed one office build-out and three office moves.
- Handled rollout for a new product (employment termination and discrimination coverage).

DIVERSIFIED RISK INSURANCE BROKERS   Chicago, IL
**Accounting Manager**   1980–1988

Managed all accounting functions through financial statements. Prepared budget and monitored variance. Managed trust funds, with daily cash management (investing successfully enough to cover the accounting department's salaries with interest income alone). Planned and conducted management projects, e.g.: Converted manual accounting systems to outside batch computer services to in-house computer system. Co-chaired restoration and build-out for office relation. Coordinated license filings. Administered the company's pension/profit-sharing plan. Structured and administered capital leases on behalf of an affiliated holding company.

INDUSTRIAL INDEMNITY   Chicago, IL
**Technical**   1977–1980

Provided general accounting for the cash management department, including bank reconciliations and account management. Reconciled accounts with up to $10 million in/out flow per month per account. Developed daily monitoring systems to assist controller with investment decisions. Researched and resolved account problems caused by computer coding mistakes.

*Prior*

**Accounts Payable** and **Payroll**, Andros Inc.   Chicago, IL

**Accounts Receivable**, General Steamship Corp.   Milwaukee, WI

**Payroll**, Roos Atkins, Inc.   Carbondale, IL

**EDUCATION**   UNIVERSITY OF ILLINOIS at URBANA-CHAMPAIGN   Champaign, IL
**Bachelor of Science, Business Administration** 1974

**REFERENCES**   References provided on request, but please keep this information confidential at this time.

# John James "Jay" Johnson

118 Gardenia Street
Cambridge, Massachusetts 02138

Office: (617) 555-1546
Residence: (617) 555-1824
jay.jay3@aol.com

---

## EXPERTISE

### Training & Development Management

Effective combination of strengths: technical expertise in training and corporate education, management experience, business acumen, organizational skill. Experience in needs assessment, design, implementation and evaluation of (a) employee training, (b) management development programs, (c) customer/client training. Includes documentation and collateral materials design. Have trained all subjects, but specialties are management training, technical training, sales and customer service training, quality program training. Consultant on related organizational development.

Additional strength: general human resources management background prior to specialization in training, education and development. Skills: staff forecasting, job design/redesign, salary/benefits, EAP, recruiting, and other areas.

Computer skilled with instructional technology packages CAN-DO, MindPack, PILOT, Auto-PILOT, SkillCheck, and others.

Member, ASTD. Workshop Panelist, ASTD National Conference 1996.

## EDUCATION

**M.A.** (ABT), **Education — Instructional Technology**, 1994
Brandeis University

**Executive Program in Training & Development** (including Instructional Technology), 1987
Stanford University

**B.A., Economics**, 1981
Northeastern University

## HISTORY

InterPlay Med Systems (an AutoDidact, Inc., company)
Cambridge, Massachusetts
**Director of Education and Training**, 1994–present

Recruited to develop a training program for users of a new software product, a fully integrated, fully automated online medical records system for large HMO applications. Developed training programs targeting five different user groups. Consult as a performance analyst in the design of software-user interface. Full responsibility for methodology, module and materials development, collaboration with programming specialists, and training-related project planning and management. Departmental staff of four, with collaborative authority company-wide. Report to the C.O.O.

Special challenge: developing training for non-computer-oriented doctors to orient them to software/hardware/information processing environment to ensure acceptance of product. Developed strategy and materials for successful train-the-trainer program. Directed the development of all user documentation. Implemented training at the beta test site, a joint venture between Harvard Community Health Plan in Massachusetts and E.D.S. of Texas. Currently working with programming specialists to put all training online. Travel up to 50%.

Recent project: Designed and implemented the company's Quality Program, ensuring employee participation in problem identification and resolution. Incorporated issues in management-staff communications, empowerment, financial accounting, system life cycle, among others.

Available for new challenges with appropriate notice to current employer.

SkyFreight Systems, Inc., Boston, Massachusetts, 1990–1993
**Director of Education**

Reported directly to the CEO; coordinate with Human Resources Department. Recruited to provide strategic direction and daily oversight to training programs, to reorganize training and development to support overall business strategies, and to revitalize employee performance at every level. Hired and trained Instructional Designer, Documentation Specialist, Field Training Coordinator. Established procedures, methodologies and documentation. Integrated training function back into the Human Resources Department.

Selected projects: Designed and implemented training programs for 500 employees in 13 locations. Designed sales training program with guides and manuals, achieving 17% to 42% increase in individual performance. Supervised the documentation and training related to major software conversion. Developed train-the-trainer program for each facility. Gained certification in Zinger-Miller Management Training. Implemented new management training modules on hiring skills, performance appraisal, team building, supervisory, and communication skills. Instituted videotape newsletter and videotape QA training to increase management presence in remote locations.

Marshall Hale Memorial Hospital, San Francisco, California, 1983–1986
**Vice President, Human Resources & Communications**

Managed HR functions for over 500 union and non-union personnel. Reported to the President and CEO; oversaw five department heads. Developed, coordinated, and managed training and in-service programs. Personally supervised management training program. Served on multiemployer/union Committee on Retraining. Chaired multiemployer Task Force on Education.

Reviewed job creation and revision. Managed EDP conversion. Developed pay-for-performance at management level. Initiated employee newsletter. Revamped the Safety Training Program, accomplishing a 75% reduction in incidents. Designed volunteer recruiting program increasing number of volunteers by 35%. Designed an attendance control program resulting in a 20% reduction in leave time. Reorganized the housekeeping department, saving $45,000 in first year.

As **Director of Communications,** developed, implemented, and coordinated advertising and marketing programs with an ad agency and in-house staff. Identified target markets and service niche opportunities. Evaluated creative proposals. Maximized return on ad budget.

Seton Medical Center, Daly City, California, March-April 1983
**Consultant**

Organized, developed, and managed the dedication program and media coverage for the inauguration of a new hospital facility and the name change. Rated an outstanding success.

Seton Medical Center, Daly City, California, 1975–1983
**Training Coordinator**

Developed and directed training and employee development programs for a staff of 1500. Supervised professional staff of five Instructors and Trainers. Managed $400,000 annual capital and operating budget. Included medical, safety, and financial subject matters.

Note "Knowledge"
section on p. 2.

# MARK SCOTT THOMAS

88 Ashton Alley
New York, New York 10014

Personal telephone/message/fax: (212) 555-9664
Personal home page: http://www.empire.com:8080/3first.html

---

**EXPERTISE**

**Fashion, Retailing, Concept Development**

*Strengths:*

- Effective combination of management skills and ability to create excitement and enthusiasm for fashion.
- Domestic and international product and private label development; negotiated key international agreements.
- Close contacts throughout the industry.

*Honors & Awards:*

- Awarded the Uomo Moda award by the Italian Trade Commission for promoting Italian fashion in the United States, 1995.
- Honored by *W* magazine's bellwether "What's in Store" issue, 1993–1994.
- Named "Best Men's Store" twice in *M* magazine, 1993, 1995.
- Store featured in *Interior Design* magazine, 1991.
- Comme des Garçons featured in *Progressive Architecture* magazine, 1989.

**EXPERIENCE**

**Mark Scott Thomas Men & Women**, New York, 1991–1996
**President & CEO** (continue to the present as **Consultant**)

Conceived, designed, and launched this store to serve cutting-edge fashion to a sophisticated clientele. Shopped worldwide to bring unique designs to the store. Maintained relations with designers. Created a private label program, 3first, generating 15% of total store volume. Maintained high markups and high turn by providing exclusivity and a forward-thinking look.

Trained staff in retail sales technique. Used theatre background to teach the "velvet hammer" of personalized attention. Directed advertising, promotions, events. Obtained considerable press coverage.

Managed all business aspects: budgeting, cash flow, staffing, seasonal planning, O.T.B., negotiations, supplier relations, store design, facilities, real estate.

Sold the store and concept in 1996 to a high-end Japanese retailer; retained rights to the 3first label. Currently on retainer but available upon notice.

**Comme des Garçons**, San Francisco, 1986–1990
**President**

Opened Comme des Garçons San Francisco. Worked with the Japanese designer and architect, Hero Ko, to understand her vision and to create the proper image for this international design house.

Assisted Hero Ko in developing commercial product for our market. Spent a month in Tokyo annually. Bought for both the New York and the San Francisco stores.

Created a market for Japanese fashion in San Francisco. Recruited the right sales staff and trained them how to sell our image and product.

Reported sales to New York and Tokyo. Collaborated with Japanese press office in Tokyo to develop distinctive advertising for the United States.

**Comme des Garçons**, New York, 1983–1985
**Vice President**

Opened the first Comme des Garçons in the United States. Worked with Dianne Benson and Hero Ko to translate Japanese image to Soho environment. Served as U.S. liaison for the U.S. market.

**Dianne B.**, New York, 1982–1983
**Executive Trainee**

Introduced Men's line for Dianne Benson.

**KNOWLEDGE**

*Men:* Jean-Paul Gaultier, Comme des Garçons, Issey Miyake, Yohji Yamamoto, Matsuda, Romeo Gigli, Gorgio Armani, Verri, Claude Montana, Thierry Mugler, Byblos, Paul Smith, Katharine Hamnett, Donna Karan, Calvin Klein, Karl-Lagerfeld, and others.

*Women:* Jean-Paul Gaultier, Comme des Garçons, Issey Miyake, Yohji Yamamoto, Matsuda, Romeo Gigli, Katharine Hamnett, Claude Montana, Thierry Mugler, Jil Sander, Norma Kamali, Stephen Sprouse, Byblos, Chantal Thomass, Jean-Charles de Castelbajac, Moschino, Dolce Gabanna, Mizrahi, Giorgio di sant Angelo, Emanuelle, Michael Kors, G- Gigli, and others.

**EDUCATION**

Boston University

Lee Strasberg Theatre Institute

Stella Adler School

The Cate School

The Fessenden School

**PERSONAL**

No restrictions on relocation or travel for the right opportunity.

Professional and personal references provided on request.

# HEATHER MCGUINESS

15 North Ruby Circle _ Chicago, Illinois _ 60637
Residence: (312) 555-4381 _ Fax (312) 555-4381

## PROFILE

Agricultural commodities broker with established relationships with (a) worldwide importers and brokers, foreign wholesalers and governments, and (b) major packers and canners worldwide. Emphasis on large-scale international trades. Worldwide travel.

Fluent in Spanish; proficient in German, French, Italian; basic greetings in Arabic, Polish, Russian, Japanese, Mandarin, Korean, Hungarian, Swahili.

## EDUCATION

**B.Sc., Agricultural Business/Agricultural Economics**
Montana State University, Bozeman, Montana

**A.Sc., Agricultural Economics**
State University of New York, Cobleskill, New York

## LICENSURE

**Agricultural Commodities License, U.S.D.A.**

## EXPERIENCE

**Parker Brothers International,** Chicago, Illinois      1990–1996
**Vice President**

Initiated and processed trades of agricultural commodities on world markets (legumes, popcorn, birdseed, and dried fruits and nuts). Annual export sales exceeding $90 million, with smaller import emphasis. Knowledge of financial procedures (LOCs, drafts, terms, contingencies). Territory: EC, Eastern Europe-Russia, Canada-United States and all Latin America, all Asia, Africa. Conducted major $20 million with Japanese trading houses (Mitsui & Co., Toshoku, Mitsubishi, etc.). Coordinated trading and support staff of 35–45 in collaboration with the president/C.O.O. Trained and developed promising subordinate staff.

Achievements:
- Managed joint venture with a Chilean company to grow, transport, and sell beans. Devised complex financial matrix of bank warrants to borrow against crop purchases.
- Created incentive program to control and enhance joint venture productivity.
- Negotiated ship charters and freight contracts for container movement.
- Achieved status as largest legume exporter in Chile, 1994–95, 30,000 metric tons.

*Continued . . .*

**H. McGuiness & Company,** Chicago, Illinois      1984–1990
**President**

Founded, managed, and operated international and domestic agricultural commodity brokerage. Specialties included dry edible beans, peas, lentils, popcorn, birdseed, and dried fruits and nuts.

### Achievements:
- Established first international brokerage in these commodities in the United States.
- Brokered $17 million trade in lentils between Canada and Algeria.
- Brokered $6.5 million trade in Great Northern beans between the United States and Bulgaria.
- Averaged $12 million to 38 million in trades per annum.

Merged this business with Parker Brothers International, 1990.

**Berger & Plate Company,** Chicago, Illinois      1979–1983
**Trade & Export Manager, Bean Department**

Planned, coordinated, and executed field purchases of agricultural commodities from farmers. Traded goods through company offices worldwide.

### Achievements:
- Obtained cross-training in spices, dried fruits and nuts, bird seed, and legumes at the request of the C.E.O., to facilitate understanding of complete company product line.
- Youngest associate ever made export manager.

## AFFILIATIONS

### Member, Gafta, London, United Kingdom
- International Association of Pulse/Grain Trading Companies

### Member, Board of Directors, American Dry Pea & Lentil Association
- Chair, Foreign Marketing Committee

### Member, United States of America Dry Pea & Lentil Council

### Member, California Bean Shippers Association

### Member, Michigan Bean Shippers Association

### Member, Rocky Mountain Bean Dealers Association

## REFERENCES

References and recommendations provided upon request.

# DONALD C. MARTIN

1948 Cambridge Drive
San Carlos, California 94070

24-hour telephone/message/fax/pager: (800) 555-0591
secure e-mail: dmartin@bus.berkeley.edu

---

**PROFILE**

**Financial Officer / Financial Manager** with a twenty-year track record of success in **telecommunications, computers, biotech,** and **software** environments.

*Strengths:*
- Talent for working with high-energy entrepreneurs and company founders with technical and scientific backgrounds. Experience in both high growth and restructuring environments. International expertise, working closely with overseas customers/vendors/investors/venture partners.
- Significant accomplishments in corporate partnering, fund-raising, negotiations, and improvement/enhancement of financial controls.

**EDUCATION**

**M.B.A., Finance**, University of California at Berkeley
**Instructor,** "Venture Capital," UCB Haas School of Business, 1992–present

**B.S., Accounting**, Wharton School of Business at the University of Pennsylvania

**C.P.A.**, State of California/**C.P.A.**, State of Pennsylvania (inactive)

**EXPERIENCE**

**Donald C. Martin**     San Carlos, California, 1994–Present
**Financial Consultant** and **Interim Financial Officer**

Provide comprehensive financial and administrative management functions to client companies on a project and/or extended basis. Excellent recommendations.

*Sample engagements:*

– **Togai InfraLogic**, a software development company. Interim president and CEO. Brought in by Canon, Inc., a major shareholder, to design and install management controls and revitalize sales for this $2.5 million start-up with facilities in Munich, Houston, Tokyo. Sample contributions:
  - Negotiated joint development agreement with Siemens, A.G.
  - Renegotiated contract with largest customer, Hitachi America, achieving 40% increase in revenues.
  - Doubled the number of distributors in U.S.A., Western Europe, Asia.
  - Oversaw launch of the world's first fuzzy logic CASE tool, TilShell 3.0, winning *Control Engineering*'s "Editors' Choice Award."
  - Formulated long-term strategic plan for a pioneer company in an emerging industry.

– **FaxNet, Inc.** Negotiated two spin-offs of FaxNet, a former employer (see job description below). Successfully consummated sale of manufacturing division to Canadian Marconi ($9 million transaction) and network division to KDD, Japan ($1.5 million transaction). Negotiated with shareholders (buyer and seller), creditors, suppliers, including terms, conditions, and tax ramifications.

– **R.W. Lynch**, a $10 million advertising agency serving the legal profession. Interim CFO, including review of controls, systems, procedures.

– **Canon, Inc.**, a $20 billion electronics firm with 30% stake in FaxNet and 40% in Togai InfraLogic (see below). Represented Canon in difficult negotiations for sale of FaxNet ATM division to Connectware (a division of AMP, Inc.), resulting in consummation of $5.7 million sale.

- **Avanti Systems**, a software development company specializing in serving the worldwide aircraft remanufacturing industry. Strategic business development plan (product evolution, marketing, sales, financing requirements), used to obtain funding from Unisys Corp.

- **Bay Alarm**, a $36 million security system company with $50 million real estate portfolio and majority interest in $12 million telecommunications firm. Transition CFO, including historical and industry financial analysis and design of new MIS.

- **Peninsula Labs**, $8 million biotech manufacturer with operations in California, United Kingdom, Germany. Negotiated buyout of minority shareholders and new capital infusion to the company from Itoham, a Japanese food conglomerate ($2 million buyout and $1 million new funding). Negotiations were successful in an environment of open hostility between majority and minority shareholders.

- **Bob Mann Sports**, a $10 million supplier of golf videos and equipment. Successfully restructured debt with creditors, reopening supply lines.

**FaxNet, Inc.**    Foster City, California, 1984–1993
**Vice President, Chief Financial Officer**

Directed financial systems, reporting, planning, financial controls, manufacturing systems, human resources, facilities management, risk management, legal services, and strategic planning processes for this $25 million communications company. Administrative, R&D, and manufacturing facilities on West Coast, sales offices in London and New Jersey, technical facility in Washington, D.C. Reported to the Chairman and founder.

FaxNet manufactures and distributes proprietary data communications systems and provides related consulting services. Products include fax server networks, software development, and turnkey equipment installations. Customers were worldwide, with emphasis on U.K., Canada, Korea, P.R.C., Brazil, Japan, Denmark, Germany, Philippines, Mexico.

*Contributions:*
- Provided strategic and operational financial management during period of growth from $4 million annual sales to $25 million annual sales, 180 employees (100 engineers), and record profits.
- Negotiated creative agreement with a major communications equipment supplier to develop a state-of-the-art ATM switch platform, generating $20 million in fee revenue up front, potential $20 million in royalties, and *retaining proprietary rights to the developed technology*. Principal negotiator.
- Negotiated $30 million in new capitalization (debt and equity financing) with two foreign-based companies (Canon and DHL) as venture partners on R&D and international launch of a pioneering telecommunications service product. Structured legal and financial relationships, finalized negotiations. Maintained successful investor relations continuously for eight years.
- Negotiated reassignment of expenses for a costly technical support center to a venture partner, creating $5 million in revenues and contribution to profit.
- Structured and negotiated complex conversion of $23 million in debt funding into equity, resulting in an annual savings of more than $1.8 million.
- Negotiated $5 million commercial line of credit and $10 million in equipment lease facilities for a company with negative net worth.
- Designed complex employee benefit programs including equity compensation plans, 401K plans, and group health insurance packages.
- Directed MIS program to effect timely billing of network services involving 300,000+ records per month.

- Continued to manage financial forecasting, reporting and control systems, project accounting, manufacturing cost control systems, facilities changes, and other operational areas.

**Stellar Computers, Inc.**     San Leandro, California, 1982–1984
**Vice President, Chief Financial Officer**, promoted from **Treasurer/Controller**

Presided over two years of 100% growth per annum for this manufacturer of multi-user microcomputers with worldwide distribution and OEM relationships. Supervised staff of 35 involved in financial, administrative, MIS, human resources, and legal functions. Reported to the Chairman and founder.

*Contributions:*
- Coordinated and completed S-1 registration for IPO.
- Negotiated $20 million unsecured bank credit facility.
- Created credit administration programs with distributors worldwide to optimize balance of sales volume and credit exposure. Reduced delinquency from $3 million to $400K in six months. Reduced DSO from 70 to 45 days.
- Directed inventory control and liquidation projects. Achieved inventory turn of 150% of industry average. Generated $2.5 million (cash) from excess inventory.
- Facilitated setup of Ireland manufacturing plant utilizing free government grants, long-term loans, and a ten-year tax holiday.
- Designed and emplaced financial and administrative systems to control and contribute to rapid growth from $10 million annual sales to $40 million, with particular attention to MIS, manufacturing controls, materials planning, cost accounting, credit administration, tax planning, and cash flow.

**Donald C. Martin**     San Francisco, California, 1980–1982
**Financial Consultant**

Negotiated successful debt and equity placements, developed and created business plans to obtain funding for emerging businesses, provided feasibility and M&A consulting.

*Sample engagements:*
- Negotiated and coordinated financial aspects of the acquisition of a private medical imaging company by a major publicly held OEM.
- Completed SEC registration for successful public offering of debt securities; compiled and presented long-term financial forecast for rating agency.

**Boole & Babbage, Inc.**     Sunnyvale, California, 1979–1980
**Corporate Controller**

Provided reporting and control for $20 million software company. Reported to the CFO. Boole & Babbage is now a $100 million publicly held company.

**Bio-Rad Laboratories**     Hercules, California
**Manager, Financial Planning & Analysis**, promoted from
**Assistant Controller, Accounting Manager**

Key participant during phase of rapid growth, from $4 million to $50 million. Bio-Rad is now a $300 million biotech manufacturer and an established industry leader.

**Max Epstein & Company, CPAs**     Philadelphia, Pennsylvania
**Senior Auditor** (regional CPA firm)

**REFERENCES**     References and additional information gladly provided on request.

# Michael Newberry

13814 Crescent Drive
San Jose, California 95125

Office: (415) 555-3145
Cellular: (408) 555-7843
Residence/Message: (408) 555-1924
ideas@sin.mgmt.xtel.com

---

**BACKGROUND**

Senior **operations manager** with expertise in **manufacturing,** test engineering, materials, engineering services, warehouse/shipping, export administration, hardware and software release control, agency certification, budgeting, scheduling, facilities, off-shore manufacturing, vendor negotiations, international distribution, domestic and Far East materials sourcing, ISO 9000.

Background includes **general management** and **finance** duties. Experience in both high technology and traditional manufacturing environments, staffs up to 60. Seasoned executive—track record of success with companies facing **rapid expansion**, **reorganization**, and **turnaround** challenges.

**EDUCATION**

**M.B.A.**, University of California, Berkeley, 1982
**B.S.B.A.**, University of California, Berkeley, 1977

**EXPERIENCE**

**NuvoCOM, Inc.**, Cupertino, California, 1992–Present
(an affiliate of Federal Express and Panasonic-Japan)
**Vice President, Operations**

Direct manufacturing, test engineering, materials management, procurement, traffic, export administration, budgeting, compliance certification, and daily operations for this $25 million entrepreneurial technology and communications company. Recruited to this then four-year-old R&D company to design and launch a manufacturing function to build facsimile and advanced telecommunications equipment for the world PTT market. NuvoCOM was founded by Dr. Robert Lawrence, a world-renowned telecommunications pioneer. My role was to bring a product manufacturing focus to what had been an engineering-driven company.

Designed system-level assembly and test manufacturing process to control costs and maximize flexibility. Specified computer system for control of manufacturing. Established scheduling, designed communications protocol for interaction with customers, designed jobs and information flows, recruited internally and externally to build the manufacturing team, and integrated manufacturing into every aspect of the existing organization.

Continue to manage manufacturing for FSUs, fax networking systems enabling simultaneous single-sender transmission to as many as 5000 recipients, involving Group 3 to Group 4 signal conversion to allow super-high-speed transmission, proprietary hardware and software, third-party software licensing, agency and international telecom certification, and telecom, computer and laser technology export issues. Also oversee sourcing, procurement and prototyping for ongoing R&D efforts and for-fee engineering services, including a state-of-the-art ATM multimedia switch platform.

*Selected contributions:*
- Critical member of a four-person executive team that transformed this company from an unprofitable development organization to a product-oriented, profitable, self-sustaining corporation.

*Continued . . .*

- Built a manufacturing organization generating $10 million per annum in customized high-technology products with 100% customer acceptance rate.
- Facilitated migration from R&D to full commercialization of four major product lines, enabling this previously unprofitable company to achieve four years of continuous profitability.
- Developed system test specifications and procedures which have resulted in consistently greater than 99% hardware reliability.
- Performed audit of past export activity resulting in identification of 16 infractions. Negotiated resolution with DOC and DOD. Won approval for 20 more export licenses with revised procedures. (80% of company's products are exported, so export licensing is critical.)
- Implemented computer-based production, inventory control systems, and online purchasing.
- Oversaw corporate relocation, including design of new manufacturing, development laboratory, and office space. Planned and orchestrated a one-weekend relocation with zero interruption of production schedule.
- Completely revamped order scheduling resulting in a rise in service levels to over 95%.
- Served as **Interim CFO** for four months at the request of the Chairman.
- Personally oversaw agency certifications for FCC, UL, CSA, JATE, EN60-950, CISPR 22, VDE, and Austel approvals.

**Nav-Star Computers, Inc.**, San Leandro, California, 1982–1992
**Vice President, Operations**, 1988–1992

Brought into this pioneer microcomputer manufacturer to manage procurement and materials during a period of phenomenal growth. Designed sourcing and procurement systems to facilitate rapid growth in sales from $10 million per annum to over $42 million per annum with high level of flexibility. Involved in most of the major innovations of the early PC revolution (see below).

During period as **Vice President, Operations**, was in charge of 60 employees. Negotiated all supplier agreements for both hardware and software. Coordinated material requirements and shipments for California and Ireland facilities. Determined and managed entire production process.

*Selected contributions:*
- As part of the executive management team, provided crisis management during period of rapid contraction in sales. Devised methods to conserve cash and cut expenses across the board.
- Developed and orchestrated strategic staff reductions to cut staffing costs and maintain viability of the company. Initiated downsizing of physical plant, including company relocation and sub-lease of excess facilities. Achieved major contribution to cash flow.
- Liquidated excess inventory by opening up new revenue streams (competitors, gray market, direct consumers sales). Forced vendors to accept return of excess materials and components. Renegotiated vendor/creditor payment plans. Established prudent inventory levels. Achieved major readjustment to balance sheet.

*Continued . . .*

- Continued to move the company forward: Implemented extended final test program resulting in increased product reliability and reduced customer returns. Negotiated third-party maintenance agreement with Honeywell for Canadian market. Developed program for tracking customer returns resulting in increased perceived quality and a reduction in RMAs.

**Materials Director**, 1984–1988

Responsible for corporate materials function, facilities, and MIS during initial period of contraction. Supervised approximately 30 employees.

*Selected contributions:*
- Implemented radical scheduling techniques resulting in reduced domestic inventory levels from $10.5 to $4.5 million in just ten months, matching declining sales in spite of overstated sales forecasts.
- Supervised closing of auxiliary office and warehouse, spearheaded liquidation of capital equipment.
- Disposed of over $1 million of excess inventories over a 90-day period at greater then 90% of standard cost.
- Negotiated turnkey manufacturing agreements with Japanese suppliers resulting in lower cost and higher quality sub-assemblies.
- Jointly, with CFO, negotiated an extended payment plan with 80 suppliers covering $3.5 million.
- Sharply reduced material receipts from $2 million/month to $200,000 in just four months.
- Implemented FIFO system in warehouse to minimize exposure to obsolescence.

**Purchasing Manager**, 1982–1983

Responsible for corporate purchasing, contract negotiations, and material procurement for all aspects of manufacturing process during period of rapid growth from $10 million to $42 million per annum. Responsible for the organization and function of the department. At the peak, purchased $25 million annually with a department never exceeding six members.

*Selected contributions:*
- Negotiated software contracts with industry leaders such as Microsoft, Ashton-Tate, and MicroPro.
- Negotiated OEM peripheral contracts with Tandon, Shugart Associates, Seagate, Miniscribe, Archive, and Rodime.
- Implemented the purchasing sub-system of the NCA manufacturing software system.

**Prescolite**, San Leandro, California, 1977–1981
(a division of U.S. Industries)
**Purchasing Agent**

Progressive positions of responsibility culminating in **Purchasing Agent** for this $45 million manufacturer of lighting equipment. Responsible for the management of corporate purchasing function. Derived budgets for quarterly purchasing allocations.

**REFERENCES**

References furnished upon request. Please keep this information confidential at this time.

# Qi Pi Ling

15 Noble Road
Stamford, Connecticut 06904

Private Line (message/fax/pager): (203) 555-6398
Office: (203) 555-2783
E-mail: pling@ucon.edu

---

## STRENGTHS

### Human Resources — Generalist / Consultant / Special Projects Manager

Senior human resources generalist with strong international business orientation and experience in recruiting, staffing, TQM, communications, HRIS, benefits, organizational development and profit and loss. Successful hands-on management experience with international and domestic staffs. Developed and managed HR functions. Key participant in business and strategic decision-making. Multidisciplinary experience: human resources, operations, financials. Native fluency in English and Mandarin Chinese; conversationally fluent in French, Japanese, and several Chinese dialects.

## EDUCATION

**M.B.A.,** The Wharton School, University of Pennsylvania, Philadelphia, Pennsylvania
**B.A.,** Mathematics-Economics (double major), Reed College, Portland, Oregon

## EXPERIENCE

**WHALEN-MASTERS INTERNATIONAL**, *Stamford, Connecticut*
**International Human Resources Consultant**, 1995–Present

Engaged by director of international human resources to provide full-scope generalist support to 10 international joint ventures in start-up to fully operational status, $48 million total seed monies, 32 interlocked business partners, initial staffing targets of 600+.

- Improved customer service to clients by developing "single point of contact" structure.
- Established recruiting and staffing processes, identified new sources for technical contractors, and designed and implemented new tracking and reporting methods.
- Redesigned international programs by benchmarking best practices, evaluating vendors, and identifying productivity enhancements.
- Structured short- and long-term employment packages for international assignees.

**MORROW TECHNOLABS, INC.**, *Boston, Massachusetts*
**Human Resources Consultant,** Taiwan, 1994

As the only human resources expert on a technical team of 36, designed and installed a DB2 Human Resource system for a national company with 12 regional offices and 40,000 employee records.

- Developed business statement and detailed conversion plan; assisted client in designing HR programs.
- Extensive formal and informal knowledge transfer/training to client and United Nations consultants involved with project.

**MIEJING USA**, *Los Angeles, California*
(formerly The Harmony Companies, see below)
**VP & Merger Team Member, Human Resources,** M-USA HQ, 1993

Consulted closely with country managers to resolve issues related to merger of Asian operations with a US-based acquisition, The Harmony Companies, comprised of 24 US and offshore facilities and 4300 affected staff in 12 countries. This was a fast-paced project, with heavy load of daily communications as project parameters, specifications and objectives evolved.

- Created process framework for post-merger staff selection and successfully represented the process to country managers. Managed process; provided counsel regarding contracts and staffing issues.

- Project managed the integration of key human-resource related activities by country to ensure resolution of critical issues by merger date.
- Developed reporting method for senior management to determine country-specific human resource support, staffing, and expense levels pre- and post-merger.
- Highest ranking officer of The Harmony Companies offered a permanent position after reorganization.

**THE HARMONY COMPANIES**, *Los Angeles, California*
**VP of Human Resources**, 1989–1992

Administered centralized human resources function for 4300 employees, 600 retirees, and 150 inactives, including international assignees. Managed staff of 16, planned and administered $2.8 million annual HR budget (aggregate), controlled $950,000 in US-based assets.

- Developed and successfully implemented TQM practices which proved value added to top management; built credibility for human resources by linking HR strategies to business strategies and financial measurements.
- Managed proposed and actualized M & A integration involving businesses from 100 to 2,000 employees.
- Project managed the introduction of flexible benefits corporatewide in 10 months and within budget.
- Merged four departments, decreased staff by 23%, decreased total operating expense by 17%.
- Served on Human Resource Information System (HRIS) Steering Committee.

**CHEMEX BANK NT & SA**, *New York, New York*
**VP & Manager, Training, Asia Division, Human Resources,** Regional HQ, Tokyo, Japan/ Training HQ, Singapore, 1985–1989

Provided strategic direction and interpreted policy in human resources development relative to country-specific business plans, budgets and organizational development issues. In Singapore, supervised a core staff of 10 with diverse responsibility for instructional design, training, IS, and administration. Functionally responsible for development of training/personnel officers in all 15 division countries.

- Created new revenue stream of more than $1 million over four-year period by designing, negotiating contracts and delivering fee-based training services to Korean correspondent banks, financial institutions, and government entities through Singapore center.
- Migrated corporate programs to 15 countries in the division as part of fundamental change in culture/strategy.
- Implemented corporatewide performance planning, coaching and evaluation process in Asia Division as part of move to standardize world practices.
- Engineered downsizing of eight full-time employees and trained local continuation successor, upon completion of change project.
- Managed design, development and piloting of standardized global Credit Training Program.

PRIOR
**Management Development Instructor, Corporate Human Resources**
**AVP & Head of Credit, Consumer Credit Card Center**
**Training Officer, Chemex New York**

**CONTINUING EDUCATION / PROFESSIONAL AFFILIATIONS**
American Compensation Association Certification, *in progress*
Senior Professional in Human Resources (SPHR),
Human Resource Certification Institute
Society for Human Resource Management
Institute for International Human Resources

**AWARDS**
Executive Incentive Plan Award, Restricted Stock Awards, Exceptional Performance Awards

# Roberta Rovner

22146 West Hillsdale Avenue
Sandy, Utah 84092
Office: (800) 562-9532
Residence: (801) 555-02850
rr@hardon.com

---

## EXPERTISE

- **Compensation / Benefits**
- **Productivity Engineering**
- **HR Generalist**

## SUMMARY

Career HR professional, author of corporate- and division-level people solutions for multinational, $3+ billion computer company. Possess leadership, business acumen, creativity, and concern for people. Excel in strategic organizational goal-setting, reward and recognition systems, and morale improvement planning.

## HISTORY

HARDON COMPUTERS INCORPORATED, Salt Lake City, Utah, 1982–Present
**Vice President, Compensation and Benefits, Worldwide**, 1995–Present

Currently lead a team of 14 analysts responsible for designing and implementing competitive compensation and benefits programs. *Approx. 12,000 employees worldwide.*

- Launched new total cash compensation and contribution management system to achieve business plan objectives: quantify and benchmark performance, reward and retain key talent, increase employee productivity, meet earnings-per-share target.

- Managed $50 million domestic health and welfare budget balancing positive employee perception of programs with opportunities for fixed-cost reduction; improved financial management and tracking system, set performance measures for vendors, rewrote communications plan.

- Developed manager tools for planning, reporting and measuring cash compensation; implemented automatic stock grants, redesigned data analysis and report distribution.

- Other programs: deferred compensation plan for high-income earners, outside directors compensation plan, new ESOP, modified vacation accrual policy, new disability and workers' compensation claims system, and enhancements to 401k.

Just completed compensation recentralization and restructuring as part of reorganization of HR function: compensation and benefits staff reduced from 24 to 14, 4 management positions eliminated.

**Director, Human Resources, Headquarters Administration**, 1992–1994

Provided full-service HR support, including organizational development, employee relations, guidance to executive team. *Approx. 4000 employees in corporate and field locations (Utah, California, Texas), staff of 15 HR professionals.*

- Chief, design team, for Hardon's largest reduction in workforce. Directed HQ pilot implementation team. (This project completed in next position, above.)

- Teamed with organizational development function to design/introduce high-performance work-team concepts to accelerate the new product development cycle.
- Developed human resources, communications and community relations plan for new factory start-up operation near Dublin, Ireland.
- Developed human resources plan for sale of manufacturing operation (*approx. 450 employees*) and two field business subsidiaries (*approx. 60 employees*).

**Director, Human Resources, Hardon Affiliated Companies Group**, 1990–1992

Managed HR activities for Hardon's independent business units and wholly owned subsidiaries. *Approx. 1000 employees, staff of 12 HR professionals.*

- Designed HR plan to support conversion of Austin, Texas, personal computer manufacturing plant to R&D center. *Approx. 160 employees, 80% RIF.*
- Articulated the HR support philosophy and integration model for wholly owned operating units.
- HR officer on M&A team. Performed HR due diligence, designed integration programs, comp/benefits assimilation plans, retention/exit packages.

**Manager, Corporate Staffing, Headquarters Administration**, 1988–1990

Managed corporate employment and staffing function during period of rapid growth, hiring targets of 750–1000 new hires per year. *Staff of 15 permanent HR professionals, 10 contract recruiters.*

- Met corporate hiring objectives and established cost/hire evaluation process.
- Passed contested EEO audit, Austin, Texas.
- Revised policies regarding temporary employment, employee referral, and internal transfers.
- Negotiated recruitment advertising contract at 20% reduction in fees.

**Manager, Human Resources, Sales & Marketing Organization**, 1985–1988

HR generalist for Headquarters Marketing and Western Region Sales offices. *Approx. 450 employees in client group.*

- Redesigned succession plan on merit and performance models.
- Articulated Hardon's corporate "Philosophy and Values Program." Instructor, management and employee development programs: performance management, hiring, time management, workplace communications, team building.
- External HR consultant to Hardon business partner (total HR revamp: staffing plan, employee handbook, orientation program, compensation, ESOP). Directed assimilation when partner was acquired. *Approx. 200 employees.*

**Human Resources Generalist**, 1983–1985

Assignments in Manufacturing, Sales and Marketing, Development, Finance, MIS departments.

**Recruiter**, 1982–1983

## EDUCATION

**The Executive Program in Human Resources**, Stanford University
**MA, Organizational Psychology**, Brigham Young University
**BA, Journalism**, University of Utah
Continuing education: list on request.

# JOYCE WEISEL

25 Woodcutter's Court
Cincinnati, Ohio 45242
(513) 555-0826
j.weisel@hrr-assoc.net.com

---

**EXPERIENCE**

**CARMICHAEL'S**
(an operating company of **Disston-Travis Corporation**)
45,000 employees, 15 states
$3.9 billion sales, 221 stores

**Vice President, Human Resources**, 1990–1996
Human Resource Division: 100 people
Budget: $60 million
Reported to CEO
Member, Executive Committee

Provided executive leadership to total human resource function, corporate and field, including recruitment/placement, college relations, employee relations, compensation & benefits, human resource development, internal communications, E.E.O., A.D.A., A.A., OSHA, etc.

**Highlights:**
- Strong partnership with the CEO and management team in building environment with high performance standards, high value on human capital, long-range vision re policy development.
- Designed $40 million self-insured health insurance plan, saving estimated $10 million per annum over previous ad hoc/external systems.
- Installed pay-for-performance environment, top to bottom, including implementation of a broad-scope gainsharing plan.
- Promoted employee involvement and leadership; maintained union-free headquarters environment; beat three union challenges at stores level.
- Improved the senior management succession plan, achieving 83% backup at the officer level.
- Pioneered automated employee-information systems, including automated telephone FAQs, job hotline, benefits hotline, and first-of-a-kind employees-only home page with 5th generation security access protection.
- Leadership in successful organization change and major organization redesign, recentralization and downsizing.
- Developed corporatewide supervisory and management development training program — Carmichael's University — modeled on McDonald's.
- Banned external recruiting below executive level, reestablished in-house recruiting function, cut recruiting expense by 38%.
- Appropriated the internal communications function from corporate communications department; improved print and video offerings, implemented real-time corporate meeting and training narrowcasting.

Provided strong leadership and forward-looking management to an HR function selected by Harvard B School as "a model of innovation." Position eliminated in cost-cutting program, September 1996, and responsibilities down-migrated. Outstanding recommendation available from the president of Carmichael's citing contributions to the company.

Prior positions at Carmichael's:

> **Divisional VP, Executive Recruitment, Placement, Development**, 1988–1990
> **Director, Executive Staffing**, 1987–1988
> **Director, Staff Development**, 1986–1987

**BULLOCK'S CALIFORNIA**
(a division of **Federated Department Stores**)
2,000 employees, 7 locations
Departmental: 36 (24 FTEs + 12 shared)

**Director, Training, & Development**, 1984–1986

Management development, organization development, systems and operations training.

**SOUTHLAND YWCA**
Program Participants: 20,000
Volunteers: 800

**Director, Community and Public Relations**, 1981–1984
**Director, Volunteer Management & Services**, 1980–1981
**Director, Youth & Teen Programs**, 1977–1980

Including staff and volunteer recruitment, development, allocation; funding development; program development and administration; benefactor, government, and VIP liaison; development of marketing, public relations and multicultural programs.

**EDUCATION**

**Harvard Executive Program on Organizational Change**

**BA, Sociology, Miami University of Ohio**

**Graduate Studies in Education, UCLA**

# ANTON RUBENSTEIN

Falcon's Lair, Apt. 43-B
Castle Point on Hudson
Hoboken, New Jersey 07030

Office (discreet): (201) 555-6438
Residence (message): (201) 555-2441
ar45@delphi.com

## PROFILE

### Operations Management ■ Distribution Management

Strengths include all aspects of operations management: distribution, plant operations, quality assurance, facilities; technology management, labor relations, general administration. Greatest strength: finding a simple answer to a complex question.

*Track record of taking existing companies to record profits.* Can work closely with executive management team to revitalize operations, remotivate staff, maximize productivity.

Successful management experience with rapid growth and turnaround situations. Hands-on manager; lead by example; able to get staff "buy in" for organizational change.

## HISTORY

POWER-TRAC ENTERPRISES, Jersey City, New Jersey, 1992–Present
**General Manager / Operations & Distribution**

*Highlight:* Achieved almost 100% increase in productivity without increasing headcount. Net margins improved from 1¢ on the dollar to 20¢ on the dollar.

Power-Trac is a manufacturer of nutritional supplements for the health food industry, annual sales of $30,000,000, 200 employees, one processing plant. Recruited by the company's outside accountancy firm to improve operating controls. Worked directly with the founding president of this sixteen-year-old company to increase profitability, standardize operating procedures, and plan for growth. Orchestrated a comprehensive review of company practices. Continue to handle day-to-day operations management.

*Primary contribution:* Brought a whole new attitude of accountability to the company, where every worker, every process, and every practice was tested against objectives. Brought a renewed negotiating/problem solving effort to relationships with vendors, suppliers, customers, and employees. Improved cost and management accounting functions to get timely and useful financial data to the executive team. Also:

- Revised jobs and work flows to improve efficiency. Motivated and redirected staff to almost double output.
- Identified credit restrictions as out of line with industry standards and revised them to take advantage of rapidly growing market. Simultaneously reduced outstandings (over 90 days) from $300,000 to $50,000.
- Documented company officer embezzling $1,200,000 (liaison to FBI on this case).
- Expanded private label program. Renegotiated contracts with distributors. Improved relations with all business partners by improving on-time deliveries.
- Improved space utilization and product handling areas.
- Wrote new business plan and negotiated expanded credit line with bank (at _ of one point over prime).
- Planned company's technology evolution for the immediate future (mainframe based).

Above contributions made without major staff changes. All key projects have been implemented successfully. Currently interested in seeking a new challenge.

*Continued . . .*

HAPPY COW FARMS, INC., Brooklyn, New York, 1989–1992
**Plant Manager**

*Highlight:* Improved efficiency to achieve record profits.

In charge of the company's main production/distribution plant, 100 employees, fully unionized (Teamsters), turning out $50,000,000 per year in product. Reported directly to the General Manager and indirectly to the senior executive team. Sunnydale is a high-volume milk and dairy products company serving the New York metropolitan area. Dairy products are FDA and NYC Health Department-inspected; milk is a highly perishable material requiring quick handling and leaving little margin for error.

*Contributions:*
- Set daily production goals to maximize plant output and keep two processing lines, one blow-mold operation, and five production lines running at full capacity. Restructured daily work flow to minimize plant turnaround through an ever-changing set of circumstances (staff, equipment, raw material, inspectors, dock schedule).
- Delegated through foremen and shift managers, oversaw nightly operations to load 135 trucks per night (out of 22-bay dock).
- Designed "No Double Handling" and "Platform Rotation" programs to increase efficiency. Redesigned product handling areas. Team leader for redesign of factory line. Selected new equipment.
- Reduced overtime from 14% to 8% with simultaneous 20% increase in production volume, while *maintaining excellent relations with a powerful union.*

OLÉ FOOD PRODUCTS, Brooklyn, New York, 1982–1989
**General Manager**

*Highlight:* Reduced materials costs by 28% by improved procurement on commodities markets.

Managed production plant manufacturing snack foods, 45 employees. Reported directly to the president.

*Contributions:*
- Spearheaded successful management response to unionization attempt (Teamsters).
- Increased productivity to meet increasing sales demand without increasing staff (sales increased by 40%).
- Developed procurement strategies that beat all prior practices for purchasing raw materials (see Highlight above).
- Established more cooperative environment with USDA Inspectors reducing downtime by 20%.
- Reduced paper costs by 10% by renegotiating contract with long-time supplier.
- Installed new factory line machines to reduce labor costs by 35%.

## EDUCATION

NORTHEASTERN UNIVERSITY, Boston, Massachusetts
**Chemical Engineering**

## REFERENCES

References and additional information provided on request, but please keep this information confidential at this time.

# PETER ALLEN FALK III

*Curriculum Vitae*

3200 West Busch Gardens Drive
Tampa, Florida 33618

paf.iii@risk.ufsys.edu
Office: (813) 555-7445
Residence: (813) 555-7822

## PROFILE

Executive expertise in public entity risk management, self-insurance and risk management through the Joint Powers Authority. Additional public administration background. Comfortable with extensive authority and responsibility. Combination of interpersonal, analytical, organizational, and leadership skills. Greatest talent: orchestrating diverse others to focus on a common goal.

## EDUCATION

**J.D.,** Law, Southeast Texas State University School of Law, Houston, Texas
  Allstate Insurance Scholarship (one of four selected out of 120 applicants nationwide)

**B.A.,** History, University of Florida, Gainesville, Florida

Graduate Studies in Public Administration, Rice University, Houston, Texas

## EXPERIENCE

Florida Schools Insurance Pool, Tampa, Florida
Florida Medical Insurance Group, Tampa, Florida
  **Executive Director**, 1993–Present

Provide strategic planning, financial, operations, and administrative management to a risk management organization representing 37 school districts, 2700 employees (2 major unions), and 22,000 students. Report directly to two Boards of Directors (one for property and general liability, one for medical) and indirectly to the Boards of all 37 represented school districts. Supervise administrative support staff. Use law background to collaborate closely with legal counsel and reduce legal expenses.

Liaison on daily basis to School Superintendents and District Business Managers on risk management issues. Provide a custom-designed, comprehensive, self-funded insurance program covering health, workers' compensation, property, and general liability areas. Constantly analyze operations to identify and enact cost-saving measures.

Selected contributions: Initiated and completed a comprehensive review of the mission and the operations of the entire organization. Drafted and won approval for a new mission statement. Standardized policies and procedures throughout the organization.

Negotiated recapture of unauthorized expenditure of $274,000 released by Blue Cross of Florida as third-party administrator.

Reorganized health screening program to improve constituency targeting, achieving 42% reduction in costs with concurrent increase in service provision to at-risk constituents.

Restructured rating and reevaluated plans in medical area to eliminate deficit revenue trends.

Analyzed mix of internal and external service provision to optimize efficiency, resulting in increased service offering without increase in either staff or expense budgets.

Improved information flow to the governing Boards resulting in increased acceptance of change and smoother overall operations.

Won respect of union negotiators in a difficult political environment. Regained overall confidence of members that this organization should serve their needs and represent them well to their constituencies and communities.

Gavilan County Community College District, Tarpac, Florida
**Campus & Business Services Manager**, 1983–1993

Chief business official for the college, reporting directly to the President and indirectly to the Board. In charge of all noninstructional operations, including financial, procurement, personnel, facilities, physical plant and other operational areas. Major contributions include:

Designed and won faculty-Board-community acceptance for a strategic financial plan that redirected the college from near bankruptcy to a consistent and sustainable solvency.

Served as chief negotiator for the district, including all major procurement projects and numerous agreements on salary, benefits, and human resources policy matters. (Also developed good employee relations to avoid numerous legal disputes.)

Served as compliance officer and de facto house counsel for the district, including assessment of various legal risks and control of outside legal expenses.

Developed strategic plans for improvement of college-owned lands. Initiated strategic development plan, including a main campus Cultural Center project.

President, Community College Insurance Pool for Workers' Compensation. Board Member, Property and Liability Group.

**Personnel Director / Affirmative Action Officer**, 1977–1983

Presided over comprehensive redesign of personnel policies, including developing the institution's first Affirmative Action Policy and Plan. Redesigned benefits plans, providing more options and minimizing adverse selection. Undertook several compensation studies on both rates and potential new pay structures.

*also*

Gavilan Community College, Tarpac, Florida
**Instructor**

"Business Law," "Management," "Supervision."

Business Institute of Tampa, Tampa, Florida
**Instructor**

"Business Funding," "The Regulatory Environment."

*prior*

San Pedro Unified School District, San Pedro, Florida
**Assistant to the Operations Superintendent**

Responsible for specific operational issues; for example, developed first-ever comprehensive risk management program, facilitated employee collective bargaining process, leased various school sites, managed school attendance (both records and truancy-elimination efforts).

San Pedro County Office of Education, San Pedro, Florida
**Personnel Analyst**

Provided employee relations and counseling concerning benefits and medical claim issues. Conducted class, position, and wage surveys for classified positions in an established civil service system. Interviewed and evaluated candidates. Designed and administered pre-employment tests. Set benchmarks and standards.

## ADDITIONAL CREDENTIALS & PROFESSIONAL ACTIVITIES

Certified Mediator, University of Miami

Certified Rehabilitation Counselor, American Society of Rehabilitation Counselors

Expert Witness and Consultant, San Pedro County, involving charges of race discrimination and improper personnel practices.

Consultant and Court-Accepted Expert, Graham Consulting Group, involving charges of wrongful discharge.

President, Joint Powers Authority, for three community colleges, in the area of workers' compensation.

## AFFILIATIONS

Public Agency Risk Management Association (PARMA)

Florida Association of Joint Powers Agencies

Schools Excess Liability Fund (S.E.L.F.), Alternate Member of the Board

Regional Excess Liability Insurance Fund (R.E.L.I.F.), Alternate Member of the Board

State Bar of Florida, Employment Section

American Association of Rehabilitation Counselors

Association of Florida School Administrators

Florida Association of School Business Officials

College and University Personnel Association

## REFERENCES

Additional information of any kind gladly provided upon request. Please keep this information confidential at this time. Availability limited to appropriate notice to current employer.

# ROSE STEEL

*Curriculum Vitae*

26 Wildwood Canyon                                        Office direct line: (805) 555-8497
Ventura, California 93004                              Residence/message: (805) 555-7342

---

## PROFILE

**Medical Administration • Marketing • Program Development**

Strengths include program development, marketing, and ongoing management of complex, diversified-service delivery organizations. Skills include negotiating contracts and memorandums of understanding with clinical and business partners, recruiting/retaining/motivating qualified credentialed and management staff, directing budgeting, accounting and finance, directing public relations and advertising, and serving as a collaborative leader and a key representative of the employing organization.

Significant experience in strategic planning, staff training, initiating/controlling organizational change, directing the MIS and automation technology functions, improving administrative controls, and other cost/profit matters.

## EXPERIENCE

**Carol Burnett Foundation Hospital**      Burbank, CA
**Director, Network Development**      1994–Present
**Director, Ambulatory Care Center**      1992–1994

Direct Burnett's network development efforts with major public and private partners to expand primary care market share in the Southland. Negotiate affiliations, working closely with Senior Vice President of Finance and Business Development. Proactively explore physician and health care delivery group relationships and practice opportunities, initiating action and mediating potential conflicts. Involves demographic assessments, volume forecasts, and site analyses; start-up and relocation processes; operations and ongoing practice management and monitoring systems. Technical knowledge of physician and facility payment issues and managed care concepts.

Initially recruited to oversee a consolidated executive position for the Ambulatory Care Center formerly held by a Vice President and a Director. Directed a primary care clinic and 33 subspecialty clinics currently generating 50,000 annual visits, total staff of 205 FTEs, including 75 direct reports (nursing and administrative) and collaborative relationship with 130 physicians (70 faculty and 60 residents and fellows). Recommended consolidation of five positions into one physician director and one administrative manager for the Center; retained 6-month consultant to assist in overseeing this transition.

Member of Operations Team responsible for developing the operating budget for the entire hospital, a $110,000,000 strategic budget as of FY1994. Team leader in creating process to generate, evaluate, incorporate efficiency measures proposed by staff from the bottom level up. Result: created 6% budget reduction overall, 12% budget reduction in area of authority.

Negotiate and monitor affiliate contracts; structure and supervise monitoring of expenses. Current network consists of 7 entities. Recent example: Blue Cross Prudent Buyers Preventive Screening Clinics Arrangement, a joint venture of UCLA and Burnett.

In conjunction with California Children's Hospital Association, currently developing a pilot capitated managed care program for Burnett and California Children's Services. Includes extensive financial analysis and scenario modeling.

Full authority over departmental operating budget and program policies. Also involved in a comprehensive review of all clinic financial matters: direct revenue, indirect revenue from clinic and ancillary services, direct and indirect overhead, margins, profit and loss by revenue stream, visit volumes, payor mix, reimbursement, billing and collection systems. Oversaw compliance with JCAHO and other regulatory authorities. Initiated a new quarterly reporting mechanism for improved clinic management.

*Continued . . .*

Wrote White Paper on future of Ambulatory Care at Burnett, including strategic plans for hospital-based and satellite clinics and assessment of various scenarios under possible managed care environments resulting from health care reform.

Member of executive management team creating the Physician Hospital Organization. Member, Strategic Planning Committee (hospitalwide, with recent work emphasis on physician networking, MSO, ambulatory surgery, ER/urgent care, satellite development). Additional committee service: approximately 15 internal strategic, QA, UR, TQM, and operating committees, and external committees such as the Tri-Institutional Total Quality Improvement Team on Registration Process. Full list of appointments on request.

**CDP Primary Care /**
**San Diego Addiction Research & Treatment (SDART) /**
**California Detoxification Program /**
**Family Addiction Center for Education & Treatment (FACET)**    San Diego and Orange County, California
**Vice President, Health Service Programs**    1990–1992

Directed 4 separate medical programs, a total staff of 280, and an aggregate budget of $7 million. In charge of 4 regional service areas (San Diego, Orange County, San Bernardino, Laguna/Newport Beach) serving over 4000 clients per day. Staff were primarily management, professional and credentialed personnel: clinic managers, physicians, psychologists, physicians' assistants, nurse practitioners, RNs, and counselors. Responsible for all aspects of medical programs for substance abuse populations, including primary care, HIV/AIDS, TB, hepatitis, STDs, pregnancy, and clinical support of recovery.

Developed and administered budgeting. Wrote grants and proposals and represented organization to funding sources. Represented organization to hospitals, insurance carriers, public health departments, MediCal, MediCare, and other local/county/state agencies.

Negotiated agreements and contracts. Oversaw and conducted program design, implementation and evolution. Set policy and procedure. Ensured organizational compliance to executive direction.

Reported to the Executive Director and the Board. Collaborated on every aspect of strategic management.

Special accomplishments: Widened the targeted focus beyond substance abuse issues to overall community health and well being. Designed and launched the CDP Primary Care Program from scratch, including designing the organization and negotiating memorandums of understanding with public health departments, private physicians, hospitals, third-party insurers. Wrote system specifications and managed bid/vendor selection/negotiations process for new computer system, a $250,000 procurement project. Improved audit trail and increased administrative control of medical transactions.

*Program profiles:*

**CDP Primary Care** — Designed and implemented this entirely new program, providing general primary care to same clients as above, their significant others, and their offspring, $2 million budget, 11 sites, rapid growth.

**SDART** — Methadone maintenance programs on county and state contracts through 11 sites in/near Los Angeles, Fresno, San Bernardino, San Diego, $3 million budget, serving 3200 clients/day.

**Cal Detox** — 21-day outpatient opiate detox programs on fee-for-service, MediCal, third-party insurance, and private pay, 10 sites in/near Los Angeles, Fresno, San Bernardino, San Diego, $1.5 million budget, serving 500 clients/day.

**FACET** — Enhanced and upgraded this existing program, providing on-site OB/GYN services for high-risk women, pediatric services for their children, $500,000 budget, 3 sites in Los Angeles, serving 170 clients/day.

*Continued . . .*

**Department of Health Services,**
**Public Health Division,**
**County of San Mateo**     San Mateo, California
**Supervisor**     1986–1990

Directed 75 staff employed in 6 program areas: Child Health Disability Prevention Program, Child Protective Services/Natural Parent Program, Family Outreach Project, California Children Services HIV Program, County Educator/Training Program, County Family Nurse Practitioning Program. Staff were nurse practitioners, public health nurses, social workers, LVNs.

Projected staffing budgets for the separate programs, and collaborated on capital and operating portions, $4.5 million aggregate annual budget. Represented programs and public health staff to area departments of social service, mental health, and law enforcement. Wrote grants and proposals. Acted as liaison and representative.

Highlights: Developed 25 foster care homes and provided advanced training to parents to decrease hospital days for certain categories of high-risk infants. Managed relations with Zellerbach Foundation resulting in two years of continued funding at $72,000 per annum. Designed the program for identifying HIV and substance exposed pediatric cases in collaboration with Stanford and San Francisco General Hospital. Provided in-service to MDs, NPs, PAs and PHNs in physical assessment and identification of substance abuse, high-risk, HIV, TB, STDs and home care problems for all patient populations (pediatric, adult, geriatric).

**Community Health Educator** (Independent Contractor)     1983–1986

Designed and taught family health education classes in pre-natal, post-natal, and parenting issues. Designed advertising and program collaterals.

**Mills Peninsula Hospital**     San Mateo, California
**Registered Nurse**     1980–1984

*Prior*:
**Family Nurse Practitioner/Private Practice**

*Avocations*:
**Real Estate Investor**
**Partner, Steel Ranch**

## EDUCATION

**Stanford University/University of California (UCD)**     Stanford/Davis, California
**M.H.S.** (Health Services)     1977

**University of California (UCSF)**     San Francisco, California
**Biodysfunction** and **Statistics**     1975

**University of San Francisco (USF)**     San Francisco, California
**B.S.** (Nursing)     1974

*Continuing Education*
**List on Request**

Continued . . .

**LICENSURE**

Registered Nurse, State of California     *current*
Board Certified Family Nurse Practitioner     *current*
Licensed Real Estate Salesperson, State of California     *inactive*

**AFFILIATIONS**

Member, Society of Ambulatory Care Professionals
Member, Outpatient Care Institute
Member, California Hospital Association
Member, California Health Care Executives
Associate, California Women Health Care Executives
Member, Board of Directors, Institute for the Advancement of Human Behavior
Past-President, Past-Publicity Chair, California Association for Neurologically Handicapped
Children and the Association for Children and Adults with Learning Disabilities, San Diego Chapter
Past-Executive Secretary, PTA, Baywood Unified School District
Member, Women's Advisory Board, County of San Diego
Member, California Nurses' Association

**REFERENCES**

References and additional information gladly provided on request, but please keep this information confidential at this time.

# Mellory A. Smith

734 Beacon Hill Terrace
Pittsburgh, Pennsylvania 15221
Office: (412) 555-2241
Home: (412) 555-8351

---

**PROFILE**

Administrative and financial manager with wide-ranging skills: design of office and administrative procedures, training and development of subordinate staff, design of administrative information flows, design of accounting and financial information systems, collaboration with IS officers and programmers, direction of all client relations functions.

**EXPERIENCE**

**National Sundries & Supply Company**     Pittsburgh, Pennsylvania
**Vice President & Director, Credit & Accounts Administration**     1988–Present
**Assistant Vice President, Credit Administration**     1986–1988
**Accounts Manager**     1985

Administer credit and accounts for well-established sundries distributor with 25,000 domestic and international accounts ranging from small drugstores and mom 'n' pop groceries to all the top chains, approximate annual A/R of $164 million, total staff 400+. Company sells to distributors in approximately 50 countries, wholesale through 44 company-owned sites, and through several private label programs (Bristol-Meyers, J.C. Penney, Supercuts, etc.). Report to the CFO, supervise department of 8 (credit specialist, credit coordinator, credit analysts).

*Selected contributions:*

Designed the entire credit department, including policies, procedures, information, and staffing. Researched credit-related law, competitor practices, and efficacy of existing practices to design a credit department that would facilitate rapid growth. Collaborated on redesign of credit-accounting-sales matrix relationships. Put maximum emphasis on account retention through numerous company changes. **Key contributor to 600%+ growth.**

Member, M&A Management Task Force, along with CEO, CFO, and accounting manager. Researched A/R portfolio for proposed $20 million acquisition, with valuation and risk analysis, action plan (if acquired), and recommendations to management. Integrated the acquired company; **reduced DSO from 150 days to 36, collected 98% of outstanding receivables.**

*Also:*

- Researched, wrote, and delivered fraud prevention seminars to credit administration staff. Also wrote module on fraud prevention for the company manual.
- Reduced bad debt loss to <1% of sales while maximizing sales and distribution.
- Reduced DSO in parent company by more than 16 days.
- Lowered bank discount rate by >3%.
- Designed and implemented staff and departmental incentive programs, and adjusted sales commission based on A/R aging period.
- Collaborated with IS manager and programmer on systems design and enhancements to proprietary platform and PC-mainframe link.
- Trained staff in technology evolution. Standardized software applications companywide.

**Specialty Brands, Inc.**     Pittsburgh, Pennsylvania
**Department Manager, A/R & Credit**     1983–1985

Directed A/R and credit administration for this well-established wholesale food distributor, approximate annual sales of $150+ million, over 1500 domestic and international accounts, including every major grocery chain (Kroger, Safeway, Lucky, Cost Plus, etc.), as well as specialty and regional chains and independents. Reported to controller. Supervised staff of 7 (credit analysts, accounts receivable specialists). Operations included large volume and very complex allowances, discounting, co-op and promotional programs. Negotiated directly with accounts on credit and account issues.

*Major contribution:*

Redesigned the department from the ground up: procedures, information flows, relations with other parts of the company, staffing. Reduced DSO by 5 days. Earned a letter from president of Specialty Brands, Inc., citing the **best A/R aging in the history of the company.**

**Levi Strauss & Company**     San Francisco, California
**Management Development Program**     1981–1982

First non-MBA candidate accepted into this 12-month rotation program designed to advance achievers through middle to upper management. Intensive focus on 4 key areas: Marketing, Finance, Business Planning, Operations & Sales.

**District Administrator, Credit**     1980–1981

Managed A/R for U.S. Group operating divisions, $40–$50 million per month, 4,000+ accounts. Reported to Regional Credit Manager. Supervised staff of 4 (major account representative, account representatives).

*Sample contributions:*

- Improved morale by leadership and direct employee relations.
- Improved DSO, customer relations, and profit contribution.

**Motorola Communications & Electronics, Inc.**     San Mateo, California
**Credit Analyst**     1979–1980

Managed large consumer/commercial/industrial/government accounts, average A/R $30–40 million monthly. Reported to credit manager.

**EDUCATION**

**Levi Strauss & Company**     San Francisco, California
**Graduate, Management Development Program** (see above)     1981–1982

**University of Florida**     Gainesville, Florida
**B.S.** candidate, **Business Administration**     1975–1977

**PERSONAL**

Please keep this information confidential.

# Mark Silvers

1208 Pilgrim Court, House 3
Lexington, Massachusetts 02173

hiho.silvers@zippy.com
Office: (617) 555-4639
Residence: (617) 555-5490

**PROFILE**

Proven executive manager with expertise in bringing high-technology product lines from R&D to release and full commercialization. Background features consistent series of accomplishments in new line/new division start-up. Expertise: working on cutting-edge technologies that are just breaking from late development stage to universal market acceptance. Combination of talents: technology and product development; sales and market development; budgeting, team building, operations design. Directed business units in recent past that are currently creating in excess of $350 million in annual sales.

Seeking a new challenge with a company committed to being a market or market segment leader.

**EXPERIENCE**

DIGITAL MASTERS, INC.

**Director**    1994–Present
**Mobile and Wireless Communications Division**, Lexington, Massachusetts

Selected by the Communications Group Vice President and the President of DIGITAL to launch a new business unit, including full responsibility for strategic plan and implementation. Selected unit management team, recruited outside talent with expertise in specific technologies, oversaw formulation of total staff of 45. Manage rapidly increasing multimillion-dollar budget, provide operational and financial projections, track P&L, and report to GVP. In charge of marketing, IC, and system engineering.

Assignment: devise strategy for market dominance in wireless voice and data LAN/WAN into the next decade and beyond, with focus on comprehensive product line, business, and market development.

Sample contributions:
- Strategized unit R&D in wireless LAN, ISDN, modems, CDPD, DECT, GSM, CT2, TDMA/CDMA, low-end PCs. Targeted overall IC-based, system-level solutions to bring to market (multibillion-dollar market potential).
- Structured and managed customer partnerships to develop market-driven emerging technologies.
- Engineered the company's first internal RF silicon design and development capability.
- Designed engineering, marketing, and administrative management functions to handle rapid expansion.
- Identified resources throughout Digital family of companies to contribute to success of unit; achieved cooperation and support across all organizational lines.

**Director**    1991–1994
**Desktop Networking**, Lexington, Massachusetts

Directed product development for desktop networking market, the fastest growing market in the company at the time, with sales in 1994 in excess of $150 million. Supervised total staff of 76, delegating through 6 managers. Comprehensive IC, HW, SW, solution and market development.

Strategized and oversaw development of IC-based system solutions for the desktop networking market (100 Meg technologies, Ethernet, VG/AnyLAN, wireless LAN, and other programs).

Sample contributions:
- Developed family of "single chip" Ethernet products targeting adaptor card and motherboard markets, new revenue streams for the company.
- Negotiated contract with Xircom for licensing Netwave wireless technologies.
- Negotiated agreement with Compaq for Ethernet and SCSI chip to go into every DeskPro motherboard. (This contributed to winning the processor contract for Compaq's 486 line.)
- Brought a phenomenal number of products to market under compressed development/release structures.

**Director**     1989–1991
**Ethernet Products**, Sunnyvale, California

Created and released Ethernet products (all responsibilities of this position rolled into expanded role of position listed above). Developed PCnet family of products. Managed total staff of 75 through 6 managers.

Selected contributions:
- Developed PCnet-ISA, which was first fully integrated Ethernet adaptor solution in the market, named "New Product of the Year," *PC Week* magazine.
- Co-negotiated agreement with Apple for combined Ethernet, SCSI, SCC, ISDN chip, standard on all Power PCs.
- Directed the IMR Ethernet repeater program, a co-development effort with Hewlett-Packard, which has since grown into an $80 million business.

**Product Line Manager**     1987–1989
**Network Controller Products**, Sunnyvale, California

Designed entry into the 100 Meg standard market, involving FDDI controller and fiber optic technologies. Managed total staff of 50 through 4 managers.

Selected contributions:
- Oversaw design/development of company's first internally generated integrated Ethernet chip.
- Developed FDDI product family, which led to current dominance with 50% market share.

**Product Line Manager**     1985–1987
**Telecom Products**, Austin, Texas

Directed all product-line engineering on telecom products targeting the line card/PBX markets. Managed total staff of 40 through 4 managers.

Selected contributions:
- Directed product and test engineering for entry to ISDN markets. Created products based on new DSP-based CMOS circuits. Directed packaging development in PDIP, PLCC, LCC areas.
- Developed cost, yield, and financial planning for product line shipping 3 to 4 million units/year.
- Designed and launched computer-aided manufacturing (CAM) group.
- Personally handled customer relations with Siemens, Plessey/GEC, and Ericsson on joint design projects.

**Product and Test Engineering Manager**        1983–1985
**Telecom Products**, Austin, Texas

Directed product, test, and CAD engineering on MOS telecom products.

Selected contributions:
- Designed and launched this start-up group, including recruiting 30+ qualified engineers and managers.
- Developed testing philosophy, product characterization requirements, lab set-ups, and methodologies.
- Provided technology evolution planning for state-of-the-art testing facility.

**Product Engineering Supervisor**        1981–1983
**Telecom and Microprocessor Products**, Sunnyvale, California

Directed development of product engineering for proprietary NMOS telecom and microprocessor products. Staff of 10.

**Senior Product Engineer**        1980–1981
**Telecom and Microprocessor Products**, Sunnyvale, California

Provided product engineering on SLAC and MODEM telecom products and an arithmetic coprocessor.

SILICONIX, INC.

**Product Engineer (Team Leader)**        1978–1980
**Telecom and General Products**, Santa Clara, California

Directed product engineering on industry's first CODEC chip set. Team of 6.

**EDUCATION**    CORNELL UNIVERSITY    Ithaca, NY
**B.S.E.E.**    1978

CONTINUING EDUCATION:  list on request.

**REFERENCES**    Provided on request. Please keep this information confidential at this time.

# JOHN C. PERKINS

2118 Ridgewood Drive
Syracuse, New York 13206

Telephone/Message:
(315) 555-8525

---

## PROFILE

**Operations Development & Management / Corporate Restaurants / Franchise Management**

Background of proven success in entrepreneurial restaurant endeavors. Combination of franchise, financial/analytical, marketing, staffing, training, and operations expertise.

## EXPERIENCE

**Chicago's World Famous Franchise Corporation**     Syracuse, New York, 1989–Present
- The 2nd largest pizza chain in the world, 1565 locations, annual sales of $730 million.

**Director of Operational Development**

Guide product and service development efforts; ensure close relations between corporate office and franchisees; report directly to the president; in charge of total staff of 245 in four key areas:

- **Delivery** — Recognized expert on delivery systems, representing $172 million in business revenues. Guide implementation, analyze demographics, develop methodologies to quantify service levels, strategize insurance coverages, provide technical support to franchisees. This is perhaps the most competitive area in pizza restaurant operations today.
- **Research and Development** — Formulate new product and procedural development systems. Set up and continue to manage in-house test kitchen. Also review projects and reports from an outside research and development company and other consultants.
- **Training** — Collaborate with Corporate Resources Department to develop and implement operational training materials, videos, and manual revisions.
- **Marketing Interface** — Provide "internal consulting" on operational perspective to marketing programs and concepts. Ensure operational support to marketing efforts.

Member, executive team, involved in all corporate aspects of real estate, advertising, government relations, labor relations, as well as finance and long-range planning.

Serve on joint franchisee/franchisor committees: Product Review and Development Committee, Delivery Committee, Operations/Training Advisory Group, Systems Standards Committee, The Delivery 2000 Project.

Prior positions: **Director of Operations** (in charge of 250 units and 3 Operations Consultants), **Director of Delivery Services** (increased delivery services from 32% to 84% of locations), and **Operations Consultant** (for Southern California-Southern Nevada-Arizona).

**Red Lobster, Inc.**     San Diego, California, 1986–1988
- Largest dinnerhouse chain in the United States, 400 locations, annual sales over $1 billion.

**Concept Development Consultant / General Manager**

Hired to develop and design a "California" concept for Red Lobster's expansion into the California market. Team leader for operational and conceptual development. Generalist on concept, operations and menu development; specialist on wine and spirits presentation. Managed team of internal consultants. Opening team for the first unit in Oceanside. General manager for second unit in La Jolla (5 managers, 4 trainers, 120 total staff).

- Many aspects of this development project were implemented at units nationwide, and were incorporated in redefining the Red Lobster chain for the 90s.

**San Diego Culinary Concepts, Inc. (SDCC)**     San Diego, California, 1985–1986
- The leading independent dinnerhouse chain in San Diego, 5 locations (all white tablecloth), annual sales in excess of $13 million.

**Opening Coordinator / General Manager**

Hired to open a European-concept white tablecloth dinnerhouse with three separate menus, French-Continental, British Pub/Carvery, and Italian Dinnerhouse. Assisted in final stages of concept development and build-out. Collaborated on complex menu development incorporating Italian, French, and English cuisines. Oversaw opening, hiring, and training of staff of 150, including 4 managers and 5 trainers. Reported to the V.P. and principal investors.

- Achieved monthly sales of $250,000. Earned media coverage of new restaurant concept.

**Diversified Concepts, Inc.**     Dallas, Texas, 1983–1985
- Regional chain of diversified concepts ranging from gourmet hamburger chains to full-service seafood dinnerhouses.

**Operations Consultant / General Partner** (subsidiary)

Originally hired to improve operations in owned units. Reported directly to the president. Provided site selection and demographic analysis for proposed projects in Albuquerque and San Diego. Assisted in opening gourmet hamburger concept in Denver, including grinding our own fresh hamburger and baking our own buns daily. Brought in as General Partner of the gourmet hamburger subsidiary.

**El Torito-La Fiesta Restaurants, Inc.**     Irvine, California, 1980–1983
- Largest Mexican restaurant chain in the United States, average annual unit volume of $2.5 million.

**District Operator / General Manager**

Assigned to serve on the development team for a new Mexican restaurant concept, featuring singing and dancing waitstaff and over 15 choreographed scripts. Promoted to General Manager of $3+ million unit; *achieved highest unit sales in the history of the company to that time, with consistent 13% to 20% profit contribution.* Promoted to oversee 4 units in Texas and Arizona, combined annual sales in excess of $7.5 million. Later assigned to concept team in specialty restaurants division; served as the opening Coordinator for a white tablecloth Continental restaurant in New Orleans.

**Adam's Rib Restaurant / Moby's Deck Oyster Bar**     San Diego, California, 1979
- Full service.

**Opening Coordinator / General Manager**

**Sea Thief Restaurant**     La Jolla, California, 1974–1978
- Full service.

**Opening Team / Manager**

## EDUCATION

**University of Arizona at Tucson**
**Business Administration**

# Lavinia D'Arby

2201 South Gilbert
Anaheim, California 92804

Residence/message/fax: (714) 555-2482
74130.3470@compuserve.com

## PROFILE

Skills encompass financial analysis, forecasting, financial management, cash management, accounting and control, policy development and implementation. Experience in start-up environments involving rapid growth and ongoing systems design and refinement. Prior diversified experience with a major accounting firm. C.P.A., State of California.

## EXPERIENCE

**Australia New Zealand Direct Line U.S.A.,** Long Beach, California, 1993–1996

**Vice President, Finance & Administration**, Corporate Headquarters

CFO for the U.S. headquarters of this Australian company. Prepared the financial and management reports for this start-up with annual revenues in excess of $110 million. Coordinated three country controllers in Australia, New Zealand, and North America, as well as the corporate controller and the operations accountant in the headquarters office. Reported to the president, U.S. operations, and indirectly to the S.V.P. finance and administration in Sydney. Worked directly with the president in drafting analyses for the monthly management report. Interfaced with V.P. operations and V.P. information systems on report generation.

Prepared weekly consolidated cash flow report, with projections and recommendations. Consolidated four independent general ledgers (Australia, New Zealand, Long Beach, San Francisco). Prepared the monthly comprehensive management report, including income statement and balance sheet. Controlled internal cash transfers to meet funding requirements and minimize exposure to foreign currency fluctuations. Prepared financial reporting to foreign parent company.

- Designed system used in all four operating locations to prorate voyage revenues and expenses by month, facilitating timely voyage accounting and integration into regular corporate financial reporting.
- Analyzed, standardized, and improved the financial reporting system at all levels to generate timely reports in formats immediately useful to executive management.
- Identified and corrected errors in the general ledger consolidation and foreign exchange programs, resulting in more accurate reporting of financial information.
- Designed and implemented cash transfer procedures to increase efficiency and maximize cash position.

**Accounting Manager**, Corporate Headquarters

Managed all general ledger accounting functions: payroll, accounts payable, accounts receivable, fixed asset system, travel and entertainment, and all subsidiary ledgers and statements. Supervised staff accountants and clerks. De facto senior accounting/financial officer in the United States, reporting to Sydney-based comptroller and coordinating with local accountancy. Analyzed accounting data and produced wide range of reports, including budget variance report and cash flow projections.

- Developed and conducted a comprehensive review of actual versus budgeted administration expenses for one full year ($4.6 million), by category, vendor, and nature (start-up, recurring, nonrecurring). Analyzed results and presented recommendations to executive management. Developed comprehensive plan to tighten budgetary control and reduce costs. Contributed fundamental cost control policies for implementation companywide.
- Generated the operational procedures to accomplish goals set forth above. Standardized account coding procedures for 25 departments. Initiated overhaul of travel and entertainment policies. Pursued related projects such as development of Lotus-based model to allocate overhead expenses to third-party operating units.
- Also had responsibility for accounting systems development and software review.

**Deloitte Haskins & Sells,** Los Angeles, California, 1986–1993

**Senior Accountant**

Planned and executed audit engagements, with full responsibility for accounting practices and client interaction. Also provided business and financial consulting to clients. Trained and supervised staff accountants. Clients ranged from start-ups to Fortune 500 companies, with exposure to the following industries: real estate development and management, transportation, telecommunications, utilities, hospitals, private schools, and banking.

- Demonstrated talent for working with small companies, including performing audits for new clients when there was no prior work to follow.
- Consistently demonstrated ability to isolate areas of increased audit risk. Thereby reduced total audit engagement hours and increased net collection rate.
- Selected to perform due diligence procedures for a client acquisition of a downtown office building.

**Staff Accountant**

- Selected to conduct a detailed assessment and valuation of loan packages for a major savings and loan being held in receivership by the FSLIC.

## EDUCATION

**B.S., Business Administration**, University of California, Berkeley

**Personnel Practices & Employment Law**, Graham & James

**Continuing Education** (list on request)

# KENT BALDWIN

180 Bedford Street
Lexington, Massachusetts 02173-4418

superkent@zippy.com
Office: (617) 555-4749
Residence: (617) 555-2821

## PROFILE

Senior executive with proven track record in *both* technical and managerial domains. Entrepreneurial, market driven, experience managing business and product development in a rapidly evolving industry.

Knowledge of all aspects of IC development and manufacturing (design, production, testing, systems, and applications engineering). Twenty-two U.S. and international patents.

## EXPERIENCE

DIGITAL MASTERS, INC., HQ: Lexington, Massachusetts        1988–Present
**Product Line Director**        1993–Present
**I/O and Network Products Division**

Selected by division V.P. to organize and direct this start-up business. Oversaw the merger of two separate organizations and successfully integrated the peripheral and the I/O product lines. Recruited eight extremely entrepreneurial, technically skilled engineering managers and built a cohesive management team. Developed strategic direction and implemented operational plan. Supervised department staff of 45–70 indirectly.

General management responsibilities included the definition and development of integrated circuits that support the I/O channels of PCs. Developed and supported I.C. products including SCSI, Serial, and Multifunction I/O controllers, generating over $50 million in sales in 1995.

In pursuit of strategic goal of building a sustainable business in semicustom PC I/O products, created a technology base and methodology that facilitated the manufacture of I/O chips with development costs and schedules competitive with ASICS. Instrumental in the development of the corporate logic design system, integrating numerous OEM design tool types into a single methodology, as well as creating innovative improvements to existing and new tools.

Managed an annual operating budget of $8 million. Interacted and developed relationships with customers, suppliers, industry members, and with others throughout the Digital Masters family of companies. Chosen to chair design engineering and design methodology sections of annual company technology conference with over 1,000 attendees.

**Product Line Manager**        1990–1993
**Standard Product Division**

Primary focus of the engineering organization was on supporting manufacturing for a $60 million/year business running 4 million units/quarter. Oversaw product management for three different product families including over two dozen individual products. Managed staff of 25 and an annual operating budget of $2.5–$4 million. Interacted with customers, vendors, and factories to resolve manufacturing issues.

Lowered wafer costs by 15% and resolved service and quality issues through negotiation and collaboration with overseas foundry supplier. Continuously provided cost improvements through yield and productivity enhancements. Consolidated manufacturing tester platforms for memory and bus interface products, which lowered costs and reduced cycle time. Effectively managed end-of-life products by streamlining product family to maximize production efficiency while maintaining revenue. Conducted in-depth market analysis, managed selection of manufacturing environments, and oversaw customer conversion.

Achieved goal of building business through new product development. Designed two products in memory-controller family which generated over $15 million/year in sales. Built technology-base for supporting SCSI products which later evolved into the I/O product line. Led development of SRAM-based FPGAs that was shelved by executive management during major corporate restructuring in 1992.

**Design Manager**      1987–1989
**Specialty Memory Products**

Managed design team of 10–15 engineers and layout designers in the development of specialty memory products (principally CMOS FIFO memories). Administered annual budget of $1.2 million. Interacted with factory, division management, and external foundry.

Built a cohesive, well-trained team of engineers and design support staff which developed an industry-competitive family of 10 products in two separate process technologies. Products generated over $25 million/year in revenue and achieved 35% to 40% market share. Received multiple patents for cost- and performance-leading architecture.

Developed relationship with Japanese silicon foundry and established manufacturing capability for $25 million/year business.

MEGA-MEMORY, INC., Santa Clara, California      1980–1987

**Design Engineering Supervisor**      1984–1987

Directed four contributing engineers and two technicians in the design of integrated circuits. Full schedule and technical responsibility. Project management included skill alignment and work partition, resource acquisition and allocation, risk management, and interdepartmental interface. Generated multiple U.S. and international patents, including patent for world's first ECL PAL. Developed first CMOS memories in corporation and pioneered adoption of CAD tools in integrated circuit design.

**Design Engineer**      1980–1984

Chosen by director of advanced technology development to serve as project leader. Guided four engineers and layout designers in the development of digital bipolar integrated circuits. Managed process from design through introduction. All projects were executed on schedule and surpassed project objectives. Generated multiple U.S. and international patents and led design team in the development of the world's highest performance bipolar FIFO memories.

## EDUCATION

MASSACHUSETTS INSTITUTE OF TECHNOLOGY      Boston, Massachusetts
**M.S., Computer Science**      1980
**B.S.E.E.**      1978
**B.S., Physics**      1977

STANFORD UNIVERSITY      Palo Alto, California
**Graduate Coursework in Mathematics and Electrical Engineering**      1980–1983

*Additional:* Management Development Seminars

## REFERENCES

Provided on request. Please keep this information confidential at this time.

# Julia Cross

11 Hanover Court
Mount Laurel, New Jersey 08054

Office direct line: (609) 555-5356
Residence/message/private fax: (609) 555-2771
Unsecured E-mail: julia.cross@ir.flange.com

---

**EXPERTISE**

**Corporate Communications — Investor / Public / Media Relations**

Strengths include communications project management, written and oral communication skills, and organizational follow-through. Special strength: writing persuasive copy. Effective combination of management, financial, analytical, and sales skills.

**EXPERIENCE**

**Flange Corporation,** Mount Laurel, New Jersey, 1992–Present
(formerly **Eastern Piping & Supply Mfg. Co. Inc.**)
**Manager, Investor Relations, Public Affairs, Government Relations**

Strategize and direct all contact with shareholders, analysts, and financial and business media. Design and control production of corporate publications, annual reports, factsheets, corporate profile, proxy statements, press releases, and other materials for general release. Serve as key media contact and spokesperson to any and all external audiences. Collaborate with senior officers on speech-making and public appearances. Prepare briefings for senior managers. Direct report to the CFO; indirect to the Chairman and CEO. Supervise support staff. Plan and manage procurement and departmental operating budget in excess of $1,000,000.

Manage and protect the corporation's public image. Monitor community and civic trends, serve on the board of the local chamber of commerce, represent the company to area nonprofit and civic organizations of every type. Chair, Contributions Committee, generating and disbursing $2,300,000 per year. Liaison for grant process. Coordinate volunteer program and manage the volunteer database.

Also manage government relations, including monitoring state and federal legislative trends with potential to impact the corporation, developing scenarios and options for action based on potential legislative outcomes.

Recent contributions:
- Completed annual report on time and under budget.
- Designed and put in place an action plan to increase public awareness of Flange and its contributions to the local and statewide community. Developed a more formalized public affairs plan to institutionalize a more active stance.
- Increased analyst coverage on the company.
- Diversified and increased shareholder base.
- Increased local and national media coverage.
- Developed a more formalized investor relations plan.
- Directed all public communications for a major acquisition.
- Participated in the "Leadership Tomorrow" program sponsored by the Greater New Jersey Chamber of Commerce.

**Corporate Research Services,** Princeton, New Jersey, 1984–1992
**Senior Regional Director**

Developed and managed investor relations materials and full programs. Initiated client relationships and serviced major accounts in a six-state territory. Collaborated with top officers from client public companies. Developed proposals and negotiated agreements for investor relations programs ranging from $1000 to $100,000 per project. Developed custom publications and high-level telemarketing campaigns to enhance the visibility and diversify the ownership of public company stock. Executed, tested, and reported on the impact of investor relations programs. Supervised regional manager and marketing assistant.

Monitored trends in investor relations and continually developed financial communications ahead of market. Guided copywriting and creative development of telemarketing scripts and all print materials. Directed projects at all organizational levels to ensure contract success. Designed the company's own marketing and direct mail materials. Also planned and managed key social functions.

One of the top account executives in the company, generating over $700,000 per annum in fee income.

Initiated and developed the following new business:

- Trans-Star Corp.
- Sun Microsystems
- Citibank
- Oryx Energy Corporation
- Genentech, Inc.
- NYNEX
- Quest Corp.
- Applied Materials
- Oracle Systems
- Many, many others.

**Bozell & Jacobs** (public relations), Palo Alto, California, 1982–1983
**Assistant Account Executive**

Wrote press releases, designed and compiled press kits, organized travel and trade shows, researched and compiled targeted mailing lists, maintained stock, scheduled and controlled work flow.

Accounts:

- Digital Microwave
- Qume Corp.
- Ampex

EDUCATION

**Graduate Course in Financial Analysis**
University of California, Berkeley

**B.A., Public Relations**
San Jose State University

PROFESSIONAL
ACTIVITIES

**National Investor Relations Institute**
State Chapter President, New Jersey
Chapter Vice President of Programs, Princeton
National Planning Committee for Annual Conference

ADDITIONAL

Available for unlimited travel.

# JUNE LEE WONG

**United States:**
220 - 15th Avenue
San Francisco, California 94116 U.S.A.
Telephone/Message: (415) 555-2731
Fax: (415) 555-2975

**Taiwan:**
No. 17 Minsheng East Road
Section 5, 5th Floor
Taipei, TAIWAN
Telephone: (02) 476-7933
Fax: (02) 679-3418

## EXPERTISE

Track record of executive, managerial, and marketing success, with major contributions in every position. Consistently increase sales, improve positioning, lower cost of sales.

*Strengths:*
- Thorough knowledge of what motivates the retail customer, including considerable international business experience. Understanding of retail as entertainment. Success positioning stores as a "product" themselves; launching private label lines; differentiating stores, labels, and lines.
- Establishing and maintaining strategic partnerships, including innovative alliances with media, government, vendors, and even other stores.
- Fluent in English, Mandarin, Fookien, Tagalog. Proficient in Cantonese, French. Expertise in pan-Asian business protocols and practices in general, and Japanese and Chinese in particular.

## EXPERIENCE

ASIAWORLD INTERNATIONALE GROUP, 1984–1996
**Asia World Department Store, Inc.**, 1992–1996

**GENERAL MANAGER, TAIPEI (MAIN) BRANCH**, 1995–1996

Initiated complete, US$20 million renovation and re-positioning of this US$150 million, 330,000 square foot, rapid growth full-line store located in sixteen-story building in the center of Taipei's financial district. Store contained fashion clothing and accessories, supermarket, food court, movie houses, as well as normal department store product lines. Reported directly to CEO of Asiaworld Internationale Group, a privately held, diversified, multibillion-dollar, multinational corporation. Directly responsible for both this store and Chung Hsiao branch.

Managed in-house staff of over 1,000 employees, and over 2,000 concessionaires (including supermarket). Established concessionary and business relationships, merchandising agreements, negotiated rates and terms of payment and occupancy and physical improvements. Proposed and established partnership agreements for department store division and other subsidiaries with major international corporations (e.g., Itoki Company Ltd., the largest furniture company in Japan). Traveled considerably throughout Asia, especially Japan and Hong Kong, for market and competitive research, and to explore new opportunities.

Developed, communicated, implemented corporate image, vision and mission. Ensured optimal product mix. Oversaw all aspects of marketing, customer service, administration, finance, employee training and development.
- Store sales *increased 40%*, January-August 1996 versus January-August 1995, to projected annual rate of US$150 million.

**GENERAL MANAGER, CHUNG HSIAO BRANCH**, Taipei, 1991–1995

Managed the largest fashion and accessories store (over 170,000 square feet) in downtown Taipei, from conception, through construction, to store opening and beyond. Refocused store on target market of 16–35 year-olds, repositioning product lines accordingly. Provided design specifications, planned space utilization, recruited tenants and managed relations, promoted store, oversaw contractors. Supervised 500 staff along with 300 tenants/concessionaires. Developed and ensured store identity, maintaining desired image among target clientele.
- First-year sales were US$43 million, *increasing 20% or more every year*. Market share continues to increase annually. *Gross margins consistently average 2.5 points above industry average* for Taiwan.
- Established leasing agreement with Sega Japan, Limited, leasing entire floor of store space for amusement center.

**Asia World Plaza Hotel**, Taipei, Taiwan
**DEPUTY GENERAL MANAGER**, 1988–1991

Conceived and managed renovation/construction of 23,000 square foot lounge into 45-tenant shopping arcade for this 1057-room, 5-star property. Assisted with design, selected and managed relations with vendors/contractors, established tenant leasing policies, procedures and lease agreements, ensuring proper tenant mix; coordinated with other hotel departments to guarantee minimum of disruption. Also coordinated design and managed construction of 70,000 square foot, private membership club and coffee shop.

Served as manager of purchasing and administration departments. Purchased all supplies for hotel. Oversaw financial controls, regulatory and legal compliance, general quality control.

- *Arcade renovation increased overall first-year cash flow by US$7.9 million and immediately increased monthly rental income over 300%.* This project was completed in only six months.

**Asia World Department Store, Inc.**
**BRANCH MANAGER, TAINAN BRANCH**, 1986–1988

Managed US$4.5 million, 100,000+ square foot full-line store (including supermarket). Supervised staff of 300. Managed all aspects of "soft" renovation: store concept, tenant mix, product mix.

- Recruited to serve as **Deputy General Manager**, **Main Branch** for 3 months. Was then recruited out of retail division to improve leasing situation at hotel.

**MANAGER, MERCHANDISING DIVISION, TAIPEI (MAIN) BRANCH**, 1985–1986

First manager for newly established department due to rapid growth. Established all policies and procedures concerning merchandising and product mix: fashion clothing and accessories, household products, electronics, cosmetics, lingerie, children's clothing, books. Directed all domestic and import operations. Worked with suppliers/manufacturers regarding space design, sales staff, advertising (including copywriters and art departments). Supervised staff of 200.

**ASSISTANT MANAGER, SUPERMARKET OPERATIONS**, 1984–1985

**SUPERVISOR, FOOD & HOUSEHOLD ITEMS/CONSUMER PRODUCTS**, 1983–1984

**BUYER, SUPERMARKET DIVISION**, 1982–1983

## EDUCATION

UNIVERSITY OF SAN FRANCISCO, San Francisco, California
**BACHELOR OF SCIENCE, FINANCE**, 1982

COLLEGE DU LEMAN, Geneva, Switzerland
**BACCALAUREATE**, 1977

## ADDITIONAL

- Significant travel throughout Asia: Japan, Hong Kong, Philippines, Southeast Asia.
- **Vice President**, INTERNATIONAL COUNCIL OF SHOPPING CENTERS.
- Excellent personal and professional references upon request.
- Available for assignment worldwide.

# David McCloskey

Office: (505) 555-1458
Residence: (505) 555-2541

22689 Manuel Cordoba Boulevard NE
Albuquerque, New Mexico 87111

---

## EXPERTISE

**Finance**
- Construction emphasis
- Transportation specialty

## PROFILE

Entire professional career in transportation industry. Experience developing financial systems, guidelines and controls for cost containment, materials management, project status tracking and reporting for rail and related construction projects. Effective liaison with Federal Railroad Administration, auditors and representatives of other modes. Strong knowledge of information sciences in transportation field.

Proven vision required for the modern worldwide/intermodal environment.

## EXPERIENCE

**Southwestern Rail Transport Company,** Albuquerque, New Mexico, 1990–present
**Capital Budget Manager**      1993 – present
Assigned by executive management to establish Capital Budget Department, including all polices and procedures fully integrated with existing departments' policies, procedures, and information systems.

Currently manage $360 million capital budget for transportation construction projects throughout a 13-state system. Monitor more than 400 projects per year, individual project budgets up to $5 million.

Provide financial and accounting support to Assistant Chief Engineer of Design and Construction. Generate monthly financial status reports, conduct cost studies, and conduct/supervise field audits of selected projects. Oversee estimating, project control and related information systems. Liaison with Accounting Department and all auditors.

*Highlights:*
- Member of management task force responsible for selection of $3 million automated cost system for integration of Accounting, Engineering, Purchasing, and Estimating Departments with Transportation Distribution Services. Primary liaison to consultant for engineering portion of project.
- Developed capital budget cost tracking system. Instituted new policies and procedures for Engineering Department, which provide for increased contract and project control.
- Standardized forms and procedures for handling of capital contracts throughout the 13-state system.
- Wrote company's first-ever inspection and contract administration manual, 200 pages, distributed to 450 officer-status engineering personnel system wide.
- Planned and conducted comprehensive 2-day inspector training program for Eastern Region. Trained two classes with 75 participants in each module.

**Project Engineer**      1991 – 1993
Managed scheduling and estimating for environmental waste and geotechnical projects ranging from $100 thousand to $2 million in a 13-state area. Traveled extensively to conduct on-site reviews and provide project guidance. Initiated design changes in the field and authorized issuance of change orders.

### Construction Superintendent     1990 – 1991
Supervised construction of a $12 million railroad yard project; included utility, rail, and bridge structures. Managed construction track and engineering survey crews.

### Project Accountant     1989 – 1990
Created a PC-based, online system for cost and material accounting, which provided for timely collection and distribution of critical data. Also originated systems for accountability of contract payments and change orders. Interpreted contract specs.

### System Coordinator     1987 – 1989
Controlled and allocated federal funds totalling $35 million for major construction project. Developed cost control and collection systems in accordance with Federal Railroad Administration requirements.

### Cost and Material Manager     1984 – 1987
Administered and audited all aspects of cost control, reporting, and cost management for $197 million railroad construction project from initial phase through completion.

### Chicago Rock Island & Pacific Railroad, Chicago, Illinois, 1980–1984
### Cost Engineer
Devised and implemented a production reporting system for program maintenance ($275 million annual budget). Prepared Federal Rail Administration loan applications. Reviewed and approved invoices, time records, and personal expense accounts.

## MILITARY

**United States Army**, E-5

## EDUCATION

**UNIVERSITY OF PHOENIX, ARIZONA**
Bachelor of Science
**Business Administration**

**Additional:**
Heavy PC user (finance, report development, Internet)
Track Foreman Training School
Licensed Inspector, American Concrete Institute

Please maintain utmost confidentiality with respect to this document and employment inquiry.

References provided upon request.

# PAUL MORRISSEY

1152 West Carnie Terrace
Kansas City, Missouri 64114

moneman@finelines.com
Office/message: (816) 555-7729
Residence/message: (816) 555-9693

---

**EDUCATION**

UNIVERSITY OF CHICAGO     Chicago, IL
**M.B.A., Finance**     1991

LONDON SCHOOL OF ECONOMICS     London, England, UK
**M.S., Economics**     1989

UNIVERSITY OF CALIFORNIA     Berkeley, CA
**B.S., Business Administration**     1985

**EXPERIENCE**

JOHNEE-BOY ACCESSORIES     Kansas City, Missouri
**Financial Consultant**     1992–1993
**Acting Chief Financial Officer**     1993–Present

Brought in on an interim basis to assist the entrepreneurial founder of this manufacturer of patented beauty accessories. Retained continuously due to outstanding performance. Report directly to the president. Supervise up to 25 employees (direct and indirect). Annual sales of $3.4 million.

In full charge of financial and administrative management of the company. Involved in every aspect of company operations. Includes finance, budgeting, accounting, statements and reports, credit, factoring, banking relations, human resources, telecom, and business computing; and to a lesser degree, operations, logistics, and production.

Advised president through periods of rapid growth and contraction, modeled business scenarios, analyzed consequences of proposed business activities, assessed risk/benefit, analyzed industry and company trends.

Identified sale of company as greatest potential ROI. Packaged the company for sale, including preparing all financials, identifying and evaluating brokers and direct avenues for sale. Hired attorney and tax advisor to facilitate negotiations and transfer. Served as lead negotiator with two suitors. Currently in negotiations with $200 million manufacturer/distributor for sale of the company, with major return for founder.

Other contributions include:

- Quadrupled cash in first six months through improved margins and reduced overhead and receivables. Managed large portfolio of cash and securities to protect business liquidity and safety and facilitate long-term growth.
- Structured a reduction in force and outsource program, reducing fixed overhead and risk without reducing capacity.
- Identified and implemented a continuous stream of cost control projects.
- Served as IS officer for the company, providing technology planning, hardware, network and software evaluation, and troubleshooting.
- Designed financial and administrative procedures to handle rapid growth.
- Installed "quick response" electronic data interchange (EDI) program with key customers. Negotiated with major customers and suppliers to improve company cash flow during critical financial period.
- Established 401k / PS plan and directed its investment portfolio.

CRESAP/TOWERS PERRIN CONSULTING     Chicago, IL
**Management Consultant**     1991–1992

Completed two major projects and contributed to a number of others. Major contributions:

Analyzed the organizational structure of the information systems group in a leading U.S. oil company; assisted the internal team that restructured this group.

Developed strategic profiles of the major competitors of a large consumer products company, including developing information sources for primary data, devising the analytical methodologies, and drafting final reports.

WELLS FARGO BANK, N.A.     San Francisco, CA
**Loan Examiner**     1986–1987

Analyzed bank assets ranging from traditional unsecured and asset-backed loans to construction lending and trade finance. Examined and reviewed bank assets totaling over $2.2 billion.

Evaluated borrowers ranging from multinational corporations to partnerships and sole-proprietorships in most sectors of the economy, including high-technology, manufacturing, retail, real estate, construction, agriculture, and numerous service industries. Traveled up to 85%.

**Loan Officer Development Program**     1985

Rotated through each of the three main examination groups: Corporate, Commercial, and Real Estate. Mastered the fundamentals of lending and credit evaluation. Graduated to examiner appointment six months ahead of class.

**ALSO**

Editor and business writer, *Chicago Business* newspaper, U. Chicago.

Honor student, U.C. Berkeley.

Graduated with honors, London School of Economics.

Dean's list, U. Chicago.

Traveled extensively in Western and Eastern Europe and the former Soviet Union.

**TECHNICAL**

Advanced PC user: spreadsheet, accounting, word processing, database, Internet. Qualified systems consultant: specification, configuration, LAN.

# MICHAEL HOLMES

168 Monte Cristo
Chicago, Illinois 60611
Office: (312) 555-4398 / Residence: (312) 555-9259

## PROFILE

### FINANCIAL MANAGEMENT

with expertise in the Hospitality Industry

Comprehensive experience directing all facets of finance, accounting, and administration management. Hands-on management style. Proven ability to deliver positive results in economic periods of growth or contraction. Particular expertise in:

- Operational Accounting Supervision
- Budgeting and Forecasting
- Statements Preparation and Analysis
- Systems Development

- Capital Expenditures
- External Audit Supervision
- Accounting Office Start-Ups
- Staff Development

## EXPERIENCE

### PARK PLACE HOTELS INTERNATIONAL

Chicago, Illinois

1991–Present

**Corporate Controller, North America**

Direct all aspects of finance and accounting, including reporting, internal controls, information systems, risk management, facilities management, and strategic planning processes for six hotel properties with annual budgets of $65 million.

- Managed complete operational conversions of five hotel accounting offices in a period of five years. Set up banking relationships, all accounting and report procedures, installed/converted/upgraded systems as necessary.

- Standardized budgeting and financial reporting procedures.

- Negotiate national contracts with telephone carriers, credit card processors, property management, and point-of-sale systems. Oversee installation and ongoing maintenance.

- Recruit, train, and motivate property controllers and assistants.

- Conduct quarterly property visits/internal audits and year-end property reviews in preparation for external audits.

*– Continued –*

### PARC FIFTY HOTEL

San Francisco, California

1988–1991

**Controller**

- Restructured problem accounting office.
- Improved internal controls and information accuracy.
- Implemented new Lanmark computer system.
- Established new collections procedures and attained set targets.
- Streamlined operations with staff reductions in all areas.

### INNCO HOSPITALITY, INC.

Wichita, Kansas

1984–1988

**Corporate Controller**

- Standardized accounting procedures for seven hotels.
- Established centralized accounting procedures for Clubhouse Inns of America.
- Recruited, trained, and motivated property controllers and staff.
- Conducted property internal audits.
- Initially recruited from college into Assistant Controller Development Program. Earned a series of promotions to Corporate Controller in 1984.

### PRIOR

Controller, Hilton Inn East, Wichita Airport Hilton and Executive Conference Center,
Wichita, Kansas (Innco Hotels)

Controller, Casper Hilton Inn, Casper, Wyoming (Innco Hotel)

Assistant Controller, Embassy-on-the-Park, Kansas City, Missouri (Innco Hotel)

## EDUCATION

University of Nevada, Las Vegas

**B.S., Hotel Administration**

1981

Additional professional seminars and training in various areas of management, including internal controls, POS systems (NCR, Tec, Remanco), PC packages (accounting, spreadsheets, stock control systems), and property management systems (Logistix, H.I.S., C.L.S.). Also completed Innco Hotels Assistant Controller Development Program.

## ADDITIONAL

Willing to travel and relocate as necessary. References and additional information gladly provided upon request.

Note international data at bottom of this résumé.

# ABRAHIM HELLES

179 Shattuck Avenue #32
Berkeley, California 94709 U.S.A.
(510) 555-8486

---

**SKILLS**
**Administrative Management / Project Management / Construction Management**
**Budgeting & Financial Management / Foreign Government Relations**
**Global Purchasing & Procurement / Contract Administration**

**LANGUAGES**
Fluent in **English, Spanish, Hebrew**. Basic **French**.

**EXPERIENCE**
RAMADA RENAISSANCE    Barcelona, Spain
(on contract through GURBEE LTD. NV, see below)
**Acting Hotel General Manager (Owner's Representative)**    1994–1996

Originally charged with turning over the hotel to a management company upon completion of project, a turnkey architectural and interior design-build-equip project including every last detail (furniture, art, linens, crystal, tableware, lighting, etc.) down to the designs on the matchboxes.

Retained by the owners to serve as the hotel's **Acting General Manager** after the management company failed to meet the owners' objectives (employed under contract through Gurbee, the internationally renowned design-build-project management firm based in Amsterdam). Built the new Ramada Renaissance Barcelona into the premier hotel in Barcelona, the first choice of visiting celebrities and heads of state (207 rooms and suites, 2 restaurants, 1 bar, 212 employees, US$10+ million annual revenues).

Responsible for every aspect of operations, staffing, sales, quality control, financial control, strategic and tactical planning. Delegated through the **Resident Manager**, who was a Spanish national.

*Contributions:*
- Repositioned and relaunched the hotel, designed and implemented new sales and marketing strategy, increased average room rates from US$140 to US$215 while maintaining the occupancy rate. Created vast improvement in net cash flow.
- Reorganized all departments, including recruiting new department heads. Restructured the staff training program to meet higher benchmarks for service and quality. Earned increase in the property's rating from 4-Star to 5-Star. Also reorganized jobs, work flows, and areas of responsibility to improve efficiency.
- Hired computer programmer and directed development of proprietary software for management/control/analysis of the hotel's sales and maintenance areas.
- Declined offer to become permanent **General Manager**. Assisted the owners with the transition and in selection and orientation of new manager.

GURBEE LTD. NV    HQ: Amsterdam, The Netherlands
**Project Manager, Interiors/Equipage/Government Relations** and
**Assistant Project Manager, Construction**    1993–1994

Second in command for a US$20 million renovation (turnkey design-build-equip) of an older hotel property in Barcelona, Spain. Reported to the CEO of Gurbee on nonconstruction matters (equipment specification and procurement, interior design, financial reporting, local taxation and government relations). Reported to the Project Manager on site concerning construction matters. Second in command over staff and subcontractors numbering up to 400. *Achieved complete renovation from closure of old hotel to opening of the new Ramada in under six months,* perhaps a record for a US$20 million project.

Negotiated constantly between owners, designers, and vendors worldwide on specification and final design details for this luxury hotel. Collaborated with management on local taxation strategies for the development. Selected and managed contracts with 47 separate subcontractors. Purchased and imported construction materials, mechanical and electrical systems. Evaluated and selected hotel MIS computer systems, including worldwide vendor review. Utilized Gurbee's global computerized project control program. Frequent travel as needed.

**GUR CORPORATION, LTD.**      HQ: Zurich, Switzerland
**Project Assistant to the CEO / Business Development**      1992

Evaluated new business opportunities under the direct supervision of the CEO of Gur Corporation, a major multinational design-build-equip firm specializing in major turnkey development projects. Surveyed hotel/resort projects in Europe. Provided feasibility analysis for projects under consideration. Assisted in bid and proposal development.

Also supervised renovation of luxury residential property in London.

**Assistant Project Manager**      1990–1991

Established company operations in Ciskei, South Africa, for a rapid-track design-build-equip contract for a 200-bed rural hospital and 1000-pupil school using specialized, light-weight construction and involving substantial grade work. Completed project within one calendar year, from design to placement of scalpels in the Operating Room supplies drawers. Earned second contract for 250-bed hospital and 1000-pupil school. Both projects completed and company local office closed within two years. Staff and subcontractors totaling up to 1000 workers on site.

Established purchasing office, local vendor contacts, and operating procedures for procurement of materials. These projects were in remote areas, involving orders for substantial quantities and adjustment to nonstandard construction materials. Negotiated and managed contracts with local subcontractors. Managed distribution and materials control; supervised company stores at all sites. Purchased medical equipment to specifications.

This project was managed by a state-of-the-art project control program housed at the largest IBM service centre in the country. Produced progress reports, budgets, and analysis with this program. Communicated directly with the CEO in Zurich, and locally with the client.

*Prior:*

Military obligation fulfilled.

**EDUCATION**      UNIVERSITY OF CALIFORNIA at BERKELEY      Berkeley, CA, U.S.A.
**Bachelor of Arts, Pure Mathematics**      1990
  Secondary concentration: **Political Science**

DE SHALIT ACADEMY      Rehovot, Israel
**Baccalaureate**      1980
  Concentration: **Sciences**

**PERSONAL**      Marital status: single. Date of birth: July 21, 1961. Place of birth: Rehovot, Israel. Citizenship: Israeli. Passport: Israeli (current). Available for assignment: May 1996. No restrictions on travel or relocation worldwide for the right opportunity.

Note "Highlights" and
treatment of no-fault
"demotion" in latest job.

# MADISON ANN FARROW

*mailing address:*
120 Legion Court, Top Rear
Lexington, Massachusetts 02173

Office/voice mail: (212) 555-0695
Residence/message: (617) 555-0861

## PROFILE

**Financial executive/manager** with significant regional/divisional line management success. Strengths include management team building and motivation, turnaround management, cost control, quality programming, new systems development, strategic business planning. Thorough knowledge of both sales and operations. Consistent record of innovation and accomplishment.

Greatest strength: leading, motivating, and setting example for front-line staff and management to produce results.

## HISTORY

EVANS, FAUQUET, HORGAN & ALLEN, INC.    HQ: New York, New York

**Group Support Manager - HQ Group**
Headquarters, New York, New York, 1996–Present

*Highlights:*
Coordinated pilot of "Service Sells" and "Market Intelligence" programs.
"Top-Rated Group in Active Trading"

As part of the top-down reorganization, selected for staff role providing executive sales skill development and troubleshooting branches throughout the Northeast. Only regional director retained after reorganization.

**Regional Director - Northeast Region**
Regional Office, Boston, Massachusetts, 1995

*Highlights:*
"Long Term Incentive Award for Extraordinary Leadership"
"Cited for 'Creating the Model for Successful Branch-Region Teamwork'"
"Chairman's Inner Circle"

Provided direction in competitive region with 11 branches in 7 states, a total of over $4 billion in customer assets. Direct responsibility for 3 regional investment specialists, 2 investor service centers, and indirect responsibility for 100 employees and 2 retail business centers. Assisted with turnaround in employee morale and performance. Cited for success in developing subordinate managers. Delivered sales training throughout the region. Provided personal example and commitment to excellence.

Also involved in developing/reviewing companywide pilot programs, incentive schemes and contests, operations manuals, customer promotions, technology changes, and sales-service-follow through procedures and materials. Performance rating: "Outstanding," the highest possible ranking.

*Continued . . .*

### Vice President & Branch Manager
Boston, Massachusetts, 1991–1994

*Highlights:*

"Long Term Incentive Award for Extraordinary Performance"
"Service — Top 10% in the Country"
"Chairman's Club"
"Above Target Asset Performance"
"Chair, Branch Manager Advisory Council"
"Branch Manager of the Year"

In full charge of branch with 23 brokers and supervisors. Branch served as support center for offices with smaller teams, with specialized business in-house: operations centralization, financial advisor marketing, regional investment specialist team. Also had many HR contributions during this assignment: developed 7 employees that later became branch managers, and 2 that became regional investment specialists; also created intern program to hire and train college students. Performance Rating: "Outstanding."

### Vice President & Branch Manager
Southfield, Michigan, 1990

*Highlights:*

"Rookie Manager of the Year"
"Chairman's Club"
"Most Improved Branch"
"Best Operating Performance"
"Best Asset Growth"
"Service — Top 10% in the Country"

In full charge of branch trading, operations, and sales: staffing, trading operations, administrative operations, reporting, risk management, compliance, interpretation of company policies, account relations, and problem solving on every aspect of the business. Performance rating: "Outstanding."

### Branch Career Development Program (management training)
New York, New York, 1989

### Operations Supervisor
Orange, California, 1986–1988

*Highlights:*

"Audit Coordinator — Rating 'Excellent'"
"Acting Manager — 1987 IPO"
"Acting Manager — Oct. 19, 1987"
Branch won "IRA Sales Award"
Branch won "Branch Sales Award"
Branch won "Chairman's Club"

Participated in hiring, training, and motivating staff; directed branch operations. Proved talent for operations control as well as sales and business development. Ensured that staff credentials were in order (Series 7) and that all staff were cross-trained. Helped manage risk and audit issues. Managed new account process, daily operations.

*Continued . . .*

### Registered Representative
Sunnyvale, California, 1985–1986

Initiated 300+ calls per day. Gained thorough knowledge of sales and trading procedures and policies, trading strategies, and regulatory policies. Possessed thorough knowledge of firm's products, services, and accounts.

*PRIOR:*

MERRILL LYNCH, PIERCE, FENNER & SMITH, INC.
**Broker's Assistant**, Napa, California, 1984–1985
**Wire Operator**, Napa, California, 1983–1984

JIM HAYHOE DEVELOPMENT, St. Helena, California

CHARTER NATIONAL BANK, Austin, Texas

WELLS FARGO BANK, San Francisco, California

## EDUCATION & CREDENTIALS

NASD
**Series 7, 8, 63**

PROFESSIONAL SELLING SKILLS - LEARNING INTERNATIONAL
**Certified Trainer**

BUSINESS ADMINISTRATION & MANAGEMENT

**Michigan State University**
Santa Barbara City College
Santa Clara University
Northwestern Michigan College
University of Texas at Austin

# RUBY R. KRAMER

205 East Huron Street
Chicago, Illinois 60611
Office: (312) 555-4664
Residence: (312) 555-3664

## PROFILE

Consumer marketing professional at national/international VP/Director level in financial services and packaged goods. Skills encompass P&L management, strategic business planning, new product development, advertising, promotions, direct response, customer service, events management, and corporate identity development.

**Highlight:** Pioneered almost every innovation in consumer credit cards in last decade: existing balance conversion, affinity cards, loss leader introductory rates, credit card "checking," prime-variable interest, bank debit cards, and college campus marketing.

## EXPERIENCE

**MEMBER MARKETING SYSTEMS,** Chicago, Illinois

**Senior Vice President & GM, Bank Card Division,** 1992–Present
**Vice President & GM, Bank Card Division,** 1988–1992

Design revenue programs for the largest credit card companies in the nation, bank and nonbank. Manage the largest and most profitable division in the company, currently representing 38% of revenues at only 23% of costs. Report directly to the president; have 3 division marketing VPs as direct reports and a matrix relationship with 3 regional VPs and 9 marketing managers. Manage multiple revenue streams/projects.

Sample recent projects:

- Directed a market segmentation process which established a database of 3 million Visa/MasterCard cardmembers as targets for conversion. Direct response programs acquired over $450 million in new credits for client at cost *of less than $10 million.*

- Designed a national customer service program for a client company, now recognized as one of the best in the industry. Coordinated delivery through 500 branches nationwide for such services as: lost wallet assistance, emergency cash, 24-hour card replacement and payment access. Marketing programs resulted in 5 *straight months of record sales.*

- Tested Visa/MasterCard product enhancements which figure prominently in client's strategy to combat competition from nonbanks. Increased cardmember spending by 7% and profitability by 4%; *reduced attrition rate by more than 80%.*

- Consistently exceeded all new customer acquisition goals on every single engagement.

**CITIBANK TRAVEL & ENTERTAINMENT DIVISION,**
**GLOBAL PAYMENT PRODUCTS GROUP,** Chicago, Illinois

**Vice President & Senior Director, Financial & Electronic Products,** 1986–1988

Managed a major group of products with $20 million in after-tax profits. Reported to SVP; managed a staff of 10. Introduced new products to enter a $1 billion market.

- Among high-risk customers in the S&L industry, managed pricing and credit strategies which maintained $2 million in revenue with *zero credit losses.*

- Introduced the division's first totally electronic payment product. Test market gained new accounts in 3 key growth segments and grew sales by 25%.

*Continued . . .*

### VP & North America Marketing Director, Travelers Checks, 1984–1986

Managed the P&L of a business with $1.8 billion in sales. Implemented marketing programs with a $5 million marketing budget. Supported sales through 3000 institutional accounts.

- Launched the industry's first consumer benefit package. Managed worldwide program delivery of interpreter services in 20 languages, and medical and legal referrals to English-speaking providers in 100 countries. Introduction of service exceeded new business sales goal by 70%.
- Launched an expert spokesperson program to promote awareness of benefit package. Coordinated a national media/PR campaign, including corporate and consumer events which featured Arthur Frommer, noted travel author (e.g., *Europe on $25 a Day*). Sales grew by 30%.

### LOWRY MANAGEMENT CONSULTANTS, Chicago, Illinois, 1979–1983

### Senior Engagement Manager

Managed the delivery of consulting services to Fortune 500 and mid-size corporate clients. Maintained 100% billable hours.

- Brought in BankAmerica as a new client. Conducted research among hundreds of commercial accounts which was designed to identify strategies to avoid customer attrition related to statewide branch closings.
- Managed a multimedia campaign for the San Francisco Convention and Visitors Bureau to increase awareness of the $1 billion financial contribution of tourism to the city's economy. Worked with hotel and restaurant industry and corporate and civic groups. Improved awareness by 37%.

### HEUBLEIN, INC., San Francisco, California, 1976–1979

### Product Manager, United Vintners Wine Division

Managed marketing strategies for Inglenook Wines, a $70 million product line in the premium category. Designed consumer and trade programs with a $9 million budget.

- Repositioned the Napa Valley winery property away from a mere production facility to a showcase for participation in the growing "Wine Country" tourism. Executed plans which orchestrated guest arrivals, multimedia presentations, winery tours, VIP tastings with head wine maker, and retail sales strategies. Increased sales by 40%.

### THE CLOROX COMPANY, Oakland, California, 1974–1976

### Brand Associate, Formula 409 Cleaner

Designed and implemented promotions for a $25 million product line.

- Developed a national sales promotion around the sponsorship of a racing car in the Formula 1 U.S. Tour. Coordinated VIP trackside trade events and "greeting" occasions with Jim Hunt, a champion race car driver. Achieved 100% promotion sell-in among major chain accounts.

## EDUCATION

UNIVERSITY OF ILLINOIS

### Master of Business Administration, International Marketing, 1974
### Bachelor of Science, Marketing, 1973

- Ford Foundation Scholar. Former faculty member, School of Business & Economics, Purdue University. Have lived in Europe and Africa. Extensive travel in Asia. No restrictions on business travel or relocation for the right opportunity.

# OTTO H. HERMANN

747 Marbreak Court
Sausalito, California 94965

Telephone/Message:
(415) 555-7033

## EXPERTISE

**Shipping / International Marketing / International Trade / Project Development**

Involved in many of the chief innovations of the shipping industry, including containerization, house-house transportation, intermodal pricing, and increasingly complex joint-venture and joint-service arrangements between carriers. Future-oriented, bottom-line oriented, with aggressive, entrepreneurial approach.

Combination of international marketing and client relations skills, knowledge of finance, operations management experience, expertise with logistics and systems for business control, new business development and strategic planning experience.

Seeking continued career challenge.

## TRANSPORTATION EXPERIENCE

**Heim-Linie U.S.A., Inc.**, San Francisco, California, 1987–
**President**
Recruited by Chairman/Founder to launch U.S.-based round-the-world container service for this new German shipping line. Headquarters staff of 20, division staff of 300, budget responsibility of US$300 million.

Established San Francisco headquarters, staff of 20, on-site MIS, and worldwide communications network. Guided creation of affiliated U.S. general agency, a separate company with 300 employees. Designed this company, built infrastructure, trained all levels of staff. Traveled constantly to train staff and solve problems.

Negotiated operational contracts with ports, stevedores, terminals, and surface carriers. Developed pricing and marketing strategy and provided guidance and support to sales force. Filed tariffs and applications, ensured regulatory compliance, and solved all problems with U.S. Federal Maritime Commission.

*Accomplishments:*
- In less than four months, provided first sailing with cargo.
- In ten months, was shipping 60% utilization of capacity outgoing; 100% incoming.
- Established service at optimal cost levels, in excess of 20% below industry standards.
- Engaged in executive sales, building relationships with top customers in the United States.
- Achieved these accomplishments in the face of negative industry trends.

**Hapag-Lloyd**, HQ: Hamburg, Germany, 1967–1987
**Managing Director, Transpacific Service**, San Francisco, 1985–1987
Directed managerial staff of 50, divisional staff of 500, annual budget of US$300 million. Managed reorganization effort during rate-war conditions. Developed plan to put the pacific service back into the positive revenues.

- Operated within first-ever joint-service agreement with Sealand (largest U.S. carrier), tripling available sailing dates.
- Implemented sales-support database system tracking competitors' cargo share, customers, and rates, a highly effective sales management tool.

**Managing Director, North Atlantic Service,** Hamburg, 1980–1984
Directed managerial staff of 65, divisional staff of 500, annual budget of US$500 million. Formerly, there were two co-directors, one in charge of pricing/operations, one in charge of marketing/sales. These positions were consolidated for me.

- Reversed the largest loss in history of this service and turned it into solid profit source during intermodal rate war conditions.
- Integrated pricing and marketing/sales to greater competitive advantage of the company.
- Created strategy of systematically gathering and reporting intelligence on competitors customer base, market share, and pricing using U.S. customs data. Developed business profiles on targeted customers and succeeded in converting their business to Hapag-Lloyd.
- Implemented statistical analysis of sales staff performance.
- Renegotiated almost every contract in our budget to lower costs by an average of 30% to 50% on each contract. Increased contract administration, resulting in *increase* in service performance with concurrent *decrease* in overhead cost.

**Senior Vice President, Intermodal Service,** New York, 1978–1980
Co-founder of Hapag-Lloyd America, Inc.; in full charge of the new Intermodal Division. Directed management staff of 12, division staff of 120, annual budget of US$120 million. Logistics and operational control for all land transportation in North America, including carrier agreements, equipment control, maintenance and repair, leasing and purchasing. Initiated variable pricing to reduce equipment imbalances.

**Deputy Managing Director, Director of Operations, Transpacific Services,** 1977–1978
Launched new Hapag-Lloyd transpacific service. Established business relations and presence in San Francisco. Built operational groundwork and directed six-vessel intermodal liner service connecting Far East with North America.

PRIOR:

**Owner's Representative, European Service,** 1977
**Container Coordinator, North America,** 1976
**Deputy Managing Director, Australia-New Zealand Service,** 1973–1975
**Coordinator, Consortia Australia-Europe Container Service,** 1970–1973
**Marketing Manager, Far East Service,** 1969
**Management Apprentice, Australia,** 1967–1969

## FINANCE EXPERIENCE

Self-Employed, San Francisco, California, 1988–1990
**Commodities Trader**
Traded a portfolio of commodities, stocks, and options. Performed fundamental research on companies, including constant financial analysis on computer. Researched industry trends. Communicated daily with institutional investors, brokers, other traders.

## EDUCATION

**B.S.B.A., International Transport, Logistics & Trade**    (credentials equivalency)
Business School for International Trade, Hamburg, Germany
**Management Apprentice,** North German Lloyd Bremen
**Management Apprentice,** Hapag-Lloyd

# DIANA EAST

46 Nicollet Circle South
Minneapolis, Minnesota 55420

Telephone/Message:
(612) 555-9241

## PROFILE

Strengths include technology planning and management, organizational control, organizational development, strategic planning, team development, R&D and product development, financial management. Multifaceted, participatory manager.

Expertise with service-based businesses, especially those with complex technical, logistical, communications challenges. Project-oriented; successful turnaround, consolidation, and reorganization experience.

## EXPERIENCE

**National Scholarship Assessment Testing Corp (NSAT)**      Minneapolis, Minnesota
**Executive Director, Operations**      1993–Present

Direct operations and logistics for the largest NSAT center in the United States, the flagship test design/sales/processing center (out of 16 worldwide), a stand-alone operation with revenues of $32 million, 325 regular employees and up to 180 agency and consulting staff. Full bottom-line responsibility: technology, administration, capital and operating budgets, cash flow planning, facilities, staffing, warehousing/transport/traffic, R&D, new business development, and interface with other satellite centers and corporate, also in Minneapolis.

NSAT (1) administers national and international educational tests to pre-college populations, including skills attainment by grade or subject matter, English and foreign language proficiency, and a battery of learning disability diagnostics, (2) provides financial aid and admissions processing services to private schools throughout the United States and internationally through satellite offices in Zurich, Paris, London, Hong Kong, and Sydney, and (3) designs, administers, and grades professional certifications for state, local, and foreign governments.

Staff include wide range of personnel, from Ph.D. specialists in psychometrics and test design to blue-collar personnel working in a high-tech, factory-floor environment.

Recruited to modernize and automate this operation, which had invested considerably in technology without achieving increased productivity and efficiency.

*Sample contributions:*
- Reviewed enterprise agreement with NSAT's main technology vendor; rejected the direction of development, broke the contract costing $250,000 up front and saving millions of dollars later on.
- Hired specialists on an ad hoc basis to integrate current systems for testing data capture, analysis, reporting. Implemented new technology evolution plan designed to skip at least one cycle of technology investment.
- Initiated internal R&D on the future of paperless testing.
- Implemented satellite data-link allowing the center to serve as a work overload service provider for 15 other centers (for-fee basis; each is a profit center).
- Renegotiated workload balance between testing center and corporate, achieving greater utilization of corporate assets and improving our bottom line.
- Emplaced numerous work flow measurement and performance standards, increasing administrative and operational control.
- Decreased expenses 11.6% with increased workload of 14.2%.

In short, I eliminated a complacent, reactive organizational environment and replaced it with a future-oriented approach embracing and planning for change.

**First Commercial of Canada**      Vancouver, British Columbia
**Vice President & Director, Project Management Department**      1989–1993

Recruited to establish the Project Management Department under the umbrella of the Systems Engineering Division, an organization with 5000 employees worldwide, $1 billion annual budget. Charged with identifying and removing redundant technologies and systems in MIS project planning and productivity enhancement across divisional lines, serving all corporate and subsidiary entities.

*Sample projects:*
- Consolidated decentralized function into a group of 75 highly skilled professionals in four sub-departments: Methodology & Standards, Project Management, Corporate Information Security, Systems Development & Programming.
- Established policies, procedures, goals, project and operating plans. Wrote and managed $10 million annual budget.
- Standardized systems and service offerings; established Consulting Services Group to promote utilization. Reduced staff functions by 50% with simultaneous 60% increase in user base.
- Eliminated nine redundant computer systems, resulting in a $600,000 savings in the first year and annually thereafter.
- Lobbied both state and federal government agencies on behalf of the bank. Provided leadership on matters of data and information security.
- Directed the MIS and systems integration for two major acquisitions, FirstWest (fully integrated) and Charles Schwab Canada (reporting functions).

**Levi Strauss & Company**    San Francisco, California
**Planning Manager**    1985–1989

Directed planning for a $22 million Corporate Data Processing Department serving all domestic MIS needs. Chair of separate committee reviewing technology acquisition plans worldwide. Directed all stages from assessment through implementation and integration, with emphasis on top-end IBM computers and peripherals.

*Sample projects:*
- Devised nationwide MIS equipment cost-reduction program. Reduced annual costs by $800,000 by aggressively renegotiating existing hardware and information services contracts.
- Identified and implemented cross-divisional cost-reduction programs. Commissioned work flow and data flow studies.
- Designed corporate MIS complex; directed relocation of corporate data center with zero service loss.

**Manager, Quality Assurance & Performance Measurement**    1983–1985

Established new departments in corporate and subsidiary entities to develop and implement standards, improve service levels, identify and enhance resource utilization, and develop advanced management tools (computer modeling programs).

**Manager, Corporate Computer Operations**    1982–1983

Directed processing functions at corporate EDP center. Promoted and assigned the task of turning around performance of $9 million department with staff of 100.

**Manager, Special Projects**    1980–1982

**Electronic Data Systems**    Dallas, Texas
**Team Project Leader, Special Projects**

Managed special projects for Lester Alberthal, now President of EDS.

**Western Region Administrative Analyst**
**Programmer/Analyst**

## EDUCATION

University of California, Berkeley, Graduate School of Business
**Executive M.B.A.**
A night program with the same professors and classload as the nationally ranked Berkeley day program.

California State University, Long Beach
**B.S., Industrial Technology**

*ADDITIONAL INFORMATION PROVIDED ON REQUEST*

# Karen Westcott Young

56 Whipple Drive Off: (800) 555-7335 or (203) 555-4310 / Res: (203) 555-7913 Ridgefield, Conn. 06877

## PROFILE

Executive with a combination of financial, sales/marketing, and organizational talents. Strengths include identifying niche markets, development and commercialization of new products, and initiating successful business partnerships and alliances. Proven ability to create and exploit market opportunity. Top-level officer and liaison between technology companies.

## EXPERIENCE

**HRA Computer Services, Inc.**     1995 – Present
(an independent subsidiary of IBM)
**President**

Recruited by IBM senior management team to turn around negative revenue trend at this wholly owned subsidiary, a $14 million company with 44 employees. Developed new business plan and marketing strategy. Wrote company's first mission statement and marketing plan. Restructured company's operational system (accounting, finance and budgeting process, procurement/distribution, etc.). Set standards for performance.

- Completely reorganized and repositioned company, achieving highest profit in history of the company after just seven months, currently projected at $675,000 on $16 million revenue plan (after loss of $890,000 in 1995).

*Sample contributions:*

Repositioned company from value-added remarketer to put more emphasis on systems integration, turnkey migration/conversion services, and joint ventures with other computer services companies.

Restructured financial agreements with lender. Regained lender confidence and increased borrowing from $1 million to $3 million to allow implementation of new business plan.

Identified $2 billion market potential for a project in R&D, an IBM Series 1 to Unix conversion and migration product allowing same "look and feel" for the 120,000 worldwide users of the old IBM Series 1 systems. Brought product line to full commercialization six months ahead of plan.

Obtained commitment from IBM to use HRA as their Series 1 to AIX migration strategy.

Negotiated business partnership and capital participation with IBM on another project, with initial capitalization of $150,000 and highly favorable royalty (IBM's 15,000 representatives market the product, and HRA receives 95% of net revenues).

Negotiated first international agreements in history of the company, closing contracts with both European and Asia/Pacific client companies.

Reorganized key positions and staff. Increased cash-on-hand from $12,000 to $750,000 by eliminating expenses, increasing margins, reducing inventory.

Restructured vendor contracts. Eliminated inventory and carrying charges by negotiating distribution and warehousing costs back onto our major supplier.

*Continued . . .*

**IBM Corp**     1983 – 1995
**Manager, Software Market Development   1995**

Hand-picked to launch a new marketing approach for IBM, a strategic shift in IBM's positioning and distribution philosophy. Created project strategy, signed up business partners, and implemented a Software Integration Laboratory for the Office Vision line. Negotiated agreements with venture partners.

Exceeded all project objectives. (Was originally assigned to "generate interest," achieved 24 partnership agreements in less than one year.) Increased Office Vision penetration by 48%, with concurrent reduction in real distribution costs.

**Account Executive,** Aetna Life & Casualty Account     1992 – 1995

Worldwide responsibility for a top-20 account, Aetna Life & Casualty. Directed sales, marketing, engineering, services and distribution. Managed organization of 50.

Created revenue growth from $50 million to $120 million per annum in less than three years. Won the award for Aetna's Gemini II Project for agency automation, a single agreement worth $150 million to IBM.

Developed financial analysis to support development of an "Aetna unique" workstation. Gained senior management approval, developed product, and won $20 million award. This product went on to become a highly profitable standard in the IBM product line.

**Marketing Manager,** New York City, Industrial Sector     1989 – 1992

Recruited and trained a dynamic sales team. Achieved highest revenue production for this sector in the history of the New York City branch.

*PRIOR:*

IBM, Executive Assistant, White Plains, Industrial Sector     1987 – 1989

IBM, Marketing Representative, Pittsburgh, Process Industries     1983 – 1987

Roadway Services, Sales Manager, Pittsburgh, Pennsylvania     1981 – 1983

## EDUCATION

**Advanced Insurance Institute, Georgia State University**     1992

**IBM President's Course, Harvard University**     1986

**B.S., University of Cincinnati**     1980

## REFERENCES

References and additional information provided on request, but please keep this information confidential.

# Marvin Hoskins

# Professional Profile

Office: (713) 555-3125
310 Parkland Draw
Houston, Texas 77040

Home office: (713) 555-2876
Private e-mail: go.rangers1996@aol.com

## EXPERTISE

P&L responsibility for companies and divisions with up to $100 million in gross revenues: creating rapid growth in start-ups and entrepreneurial companies, financial management and capitalization of critical growth phases, bridging R&D to full commercialization, building staff and designing operational systems to control growth.

Extensive M&A and joint venture experience, including international trade and venture agreements, licensing, technology transfer (Japan, Russia, Europe, East Bloc).

Proven team builder and catalyst, creating new business opportunities, exploiting new market niches, establishing strategic business relationships, overcoming regulatory barriers.

## HISTORY

**Bios-Futura, Inc.**, Houston, Texas, 1993–1996
**President** and **C.E.O.**

Brought company from R&D stage into commercialization, releasing proprietary instrumentation applicable to the biotechnology research market. Introduced a market orientation to an engineering-driven firm. Solved production and capitalization problems. Created a sales function, including worldwide distribution network.

Selected accomplishments: (1) located and negotiated venture capital funding to assist company at critical juncture in its development, (2) created the company's strategic marketing plan, (3) initiated relations with Japanese and European companies as strategic partners for international licensing and distribution, (4) designed the company's operational system (accounting, purchasing/procurement, management and financial planning and variance analysis, budget process, etc.), (5) achieved sales of $400,000 in 1995, on track for $3.5 million by end of 1996 calendar year.

Secured the sale of this start-up to a larger company, obtaining a strong return for the stockholders. Initiated a joint-venture, discovered and developed interest in a merger, structured and negotiated the deal.

**DATAX Instruments**, San Jose, California, 1989–1993
**President** and **C.E.O.**

Revitalized this engineering-driven, factory-floor workstation company with stagnant sales by implementing a vigorous marketing orientation. Took sales from $300,000 per annum to $7.2 million per annum, with ROS improving from $600K loss to 20% pretax profit on $6.5 million sales FY 1992. Developed the business plan and strategy; attracted venture capital; negotiated capital infusion. Hired and directed a dynamic management team. Established international distribution, with 20% sales in Australia, Canada, Far East. Online to open up Western Europe and East Bloc.

Selected Accomplishments: (1) identified and pursued niche markets, (2) streamlined product development and improved manufacturability of designs, (3) created national sales force and international distributor network, (4) put entire company on incentive pay, (5) increased gross sales, margins, and ROI.

*Continued . . .*

**National Instrumentation Labs, Inc.**, Richmond, California, 1985–1989
**Group Vice President**, Medical Diagnostics Group

> Reported to C.O.O. Responsible for daily operations, P&L, 200 employees. In charge of three Division Managers, V.P. Marketing, Director of Finance, and FDA Administrator. Led rapid growth: Sales increased from $13 million to $25 million, ROS jumped from 6% to 16% in less than three years.

> Strategic accomplishment: Designed and set up an internal system to evaluate products still on the drawing board to assess potential markets, potential share, and market needs. Other accomplishments: (1) removed cap on sales force and improved incentives, (2) increased international sales to 40%.

**Nux-Gold Inc.**, Chicago, Illinois, 1976–1985
**Group Vice President**, New Business, 1983–1985

> Managed internal development and worldwide M&A, coordinated joint ventures, and directed licensing of related corporate businesses. Member of Operating Committee, providing strategic direction to this $2 billion corporation. Reported to E.V.P., interfaced with C.E.O.

**President & G.M.**, Foil Division, 1980–1983

> Full P&L. Managed division during period of high growth from $8 million to $85 million in sales over a three year period.

> Accomplishments: (1) Number one division in profitability at 38% ROS, (2) dominated worldwide market niche for thin foil used in high-tech hardware manufacture, 40% market share worldwide, 40% sales international, including heavy increase in trade to Japan, West Germany, East Bloc and Russia, (3) initiated negotiations for joint venture to manufacture in Japan, built new manufacturing plant in Phoenix, (4) developed marketing team, revitalized R&D, managed $45 million in fixed assets.

**General Manager**, Emissions Control Division, 1978–1980

**Sales & Marketing Manager**, 1976–1978

**Materials Technology, Inc.**, Somerset, New Jersey, 1971–1975
**V.P., Sales & Marketing** and **V.P., Operations**

**EDUCATION:**

**M.B.A.**, Rutgers, The State University of New Jersey

**B.S.**, Chemical Engineering, Massachusetts Institute of Technology

# Clinton Eckert

381 Tsing Court
San Jose, California 95113

cman@lazrfast.com
Office: (415) 555-1358
Cellular: (408) 555-3751
Residence/Message: (408) 555-1924

## PROFILE

Senior strategic and technical executive with a strong engineering background — expertise in global telecommunications, engineering management, R&D, commercialization of R&D, market assessment, and strategic modeling of business variables. Strengths include technology development, relationship management with customers and venture partners (domestic and international), engineering and R&D team building, negotiations, and project management from (a) proposal to sign off or (b) concept to product release.

## EXPERIENCE

**GigaWave, Inc.**, Milpitas, California, 1993–Present
**Senior Vice President of Development**

Manage the engineering and development of next-generation ATM switch for the corporate marketplace at RDS systems, a division of ConnectCOM, a wholly owned subsidiary of GigaWave, Inc. (ConnectCOM purchased a part of FaxNet December 1993; see below.) Provide all project management and technical leadership for 28 engineers, both hardware and software, including oversight of $5 million annual budget.

Developing switch utilizes high-performance, low-cost ASICs, designed in-house, and supports full Q93b protocols, SNMP protocols, LAN emulation, classical IP, and numerous other features. This switch will be capable of handling voice, video, and data at speeds far exceeding all other products currently in the marketplace.

Serve as **General Manager** of **AfX-sys** engineering group of 10 in Salem, Oregon, with $1.4 million budget, in development of high-end Token Ring Bridges and Routers—products that are number one in performance in their respective marketplaces. Travel 50%.

**FaxNet, Inc.**, HQ: Santa Clara, California, 1982–1993
**Senior Vice President**, 1988–1993

First manager hired by FaxNet, an entrepreneurial start-up launched by former executives of AMD (see below). Recruited to assist in the start-up due to technical expertise and reputation for building successful engineering and administrative teams.

Part of the executive team during rapid expansion from zero to $30 million in gross revenues—administrative, R&D, and manufacturing facilities on West Coast, sales offices in Washington, D.C., and New Jersey, and technical facility in Washington, D.C.

Reported directly to the CEO, indirectly to the founder. Participated in all areas of strategic planning. Directed engineering services, delegating through two vice presidents to manage a total of 110 direct reports out of a total company staff of 170 employees.

Directed all research, development, and manufacturing activities for the company's two main revenue streams, equipment sales and contract engineering of products destined for the international PTT market.

Technological challenges include design and build of high-reliability and fault-tolerant systems which can meet a wide range of international certifications and international standards. Very knowledgeable on data communications protocols, especially facsimile and ATM, including T.series, X.25, X.400, SMDS, Frame Relay, and ATM UNI.

*Continued . . .*

Created the company's main product, a facsimile server unit to provide value-added facsimile networking. Equipment sales customers include AT&T, British Telecom, MCI, Korea Telecom, Embratel (Brazil), and Denmark Telephone. This represents approximately $20 million per annum in gross revenues. Was in full charge of engineering; some customer relations role.

The company's other primary activity is the sale of large R&D projects to other corporations on a contract engineering basis. In this business, provided extensive sales support, structuring and/or negotiating major for-fee development efforts, in addition to directing engineering. This business represents average $10 million in annual revenues.

*Sample projects included:*
(1) For 18 months, FaxNet was engaged in the design and development of large ATM switch for DSC Communications Corporation for release to the PTT market. The project was a multiyear contract for more than $20 million. This ATM switch represents the foundation of DSC's next generation switching product line.

(2) Ongoing management of R&D new business development efforts, including R&D contract proposals with Canon and FastNet, Tokyo, Japan, representing $3.6 million in potential business, and LANNET, Tel Aviv, Israel, representing $1.5 million in potential business.

(3) Directed design and development of large, 2000 node, distributed networking system for use by the Italian Postal System. Personally responsible for the overall design and detailed designs of many of the system modules.

**Director, Vice President, Development**, 1982–1987

Assigned on a seconded basis to the company's majority owner, DHL Worldwide, holding the position of **Director of Global Development**. Managed FaxNet staff in Virginia, DHL Airways staff in California, and DHL Systems staff in London, UK. Responsible for the development of all MIS systems to DHL, including financial systems, tracing and tracking systems, customer service systems, electronic mail systems, and on-site customer systems. DHL is the largest international courier company in the world.

**Director of Development** for FaxNet in the development of Satellite Express (SATX), the DHL equivalent program to Federal Express's ZAP MAIL. The SATX system was based on development of a very high-quality imaging terminal for scanning, transmission, and printing of documents overnight around the world using a digital packet network. Lead designer on the project, which achieved technical success but did not capture projected market potential due to widespread introduction of low-cost Group 3 terminals in the general business environment.

Also designed and implemented a number of smaller communications systems for DHL, almost all of which are still in operation today, using the original software that I designed to withstand rapid increase in capacity; examples: communications portion of the highly distributed DHL Airways tracing and tracking system, the DHL electronic mail system, and the Telex interface system.

**AMD,** Regional HQ: Stamford, Connecticut, 1979–1982
**Director, Product Planning, AMD Business Communications Systems**, 1981–1982

Directed enhancement of existing PBX product lines to meet competitive pressures, including one project to create a large, highly advanced PBX system, a ultra-high-speed packet switch capable of carrying voice, data, and video—a precursor to current ATM.

After this group was up and running, temporarily assigned to headquarters **Senior Planning Task Force**, established by the President of AMD to review, evaluate, and make recommendations regarding the AMD customer premise equipment business. Served as principle investigator and analyst of all aspects of AMD business, directing financial modeling, market and product line analysis, over 1000 sales calls and customer focus interviews, compensation planning, competitive analysis, AMD development evaluations, and field support reviews.

*Continued . . .*

Also directed the **Advanced Systems Planning Group**, 43 professional staff, developing all system requirements and planning specifications companywide for development programs ranging from PBX upgrades to design of new ergonomic telephone handsets.

**Director, AMD Telenet Communications Corporation**, 1979–1981

Joined Telenet just prior to its being acquired by AMD Telecom, then an independent subsidiary of AMD.

Served as **Director of Network Architecture Design**, responsible for research and product specifications on all new network products. Created the private networks product support group, supporting the Private Network Sales and Marketing Department. Established the documentation and training department for the company. Finally, guided Telenet participation in international standards activities, including service on ANSI and CCITT committees.

**NCR Comten**, HQ: St. Paul, Minnesota, 1978–1979
**Systems Analyst**

Senior computer analyst on a state-of-the-art development project to design an X.25 packet interface for NCR Comten's front-end communications system.

**Santa Clara State University**, Santa Clara, California, 1974–1978
**Senior Programmer / Instructor**

Instructor for computer programming classes. Key member of the instructional computing staff, providing expertise to the faculty at large. Designed applications to support academic research; collaborated with professors to develop research methodologies to capitalize on computerized data analysis. Participated in the design and implementation of a pioneer campus network for UNIX and Digital computers.

## EDUCATION

**California State University**, Fullerton, California
**B.A., Business Administration**, 1974
Concentration: **Statistics & Operations Research**

# William C. Howard

16 Brattle Way
Chestnut Hill, Massachusetts 02167

Residence: (617) 555-8283
Office: (203) 555-0978

---

## EXPERTISE

Financial executive with a broad record of accomplishments in all levels of corporate taxation. Background includes progressively increasing levels of responsibility in financial management and auditing. Proven ability to establish and direct an efficient tax department. Record of consistent savings in compliance and planning. Demonstrated talent for research and problem solving and successful completion of audits.

## EXPERIENCE

**THE HARTFORD GROUP, INC.**     Hartford, Connecticut
**Corporate Tax Director**     1990–Present

Established in-house tax department to handle compliance, planning, research, and audits for one of the largest international transportation and integrated logistics services companies. Direct filing of federal consolidated return involving 28 domestic companies and information reporting on 97 foreign-controlled corporations. Coordinate filing of returns for offices in 32 states.

*Selected Contributions:*

Currently finalizing settlement with IRS to reduce $7.9 million proposed deficiency to agreed refund of $300,000 for 1986–1987 tax years.

Reduced IRS tax assessment from $9.7 million to $543,000 for 1984–1985 tax years.

Used IRS Advanced Issue Resolution (AIR) procedure to save company a minimum of $500,000 in processing costs, and expedite a $4 million claim for refund.

Computerized federal and state income tax preparation using an efficient internally developed system which enabled tax filings to be handled by only 1 compliance person with no out-sourcing.

Developed and instituted completely computerized domestic and international tax provision system, enabling tighter earnings forecasting and facilitating rapid calculation of minimum estimated tax payments.

Initiated intercompany service agreements on a worldwide basis which allow domestic and overseas companies to allocate charges between them without adjustments or disallowances by tax authorities.

Collaborated on a cash management system which resulted in greater efficiency and higher investment yields.

Implemented record retention policy and procedure program to facilitate future audits and ensure avoidance of penalty assessments.

**GEORGIA-ATLANTIC CORPORATION**     Atlanta, Georgia
**Director, Tax Services Department**     1986–1988

Directed transition team during phase-over of tax services resulting from takeover by James River Corporation. Managed full-service tax function with staff of 23, interacting with senior corporate and group management on all tax matters. Advised senior management on potential tax impact of proposed legislation and assisted in the formulation of corporate positions on such issues.

Represented company in contact with various tax authorities, controlled all audits and appeals, and monitored tax compliance to ensure implementation of corporate tax policy. Represented company at industry group meetings having tax considerations.

*Selected Contributions:*

Initiated actions which resulted in reduction of several IRS audit assessments totalling $34 million to settlements of $6 million.

Conducted tax analysis and planning for acquisition and disposition of corporate assets.

**Assistant Director, Tax Services Department**    1983–1986

Handled extensive tax planning for 4,700 corporate returns involving federal and state income tax reporting, employment, sales and use, and specialized areas. Assisted in formation of corporate tax policy, developed responses to management tax incentive inquiries, and tracked legislative regulatory issues with subsequent reporting to management. Central control of all tax audits with federal, state, and local examiners. Directed development of data for appeals and protests.

Responsible for extensive departmental administration; hiring, training, motivating, evaluating, and scheduling work flow for a staff of 13. Developed systems and procedures for tax reporting and directed complex revisions to Controller's tax manual.

*Selected Contributions*:

Developed administrative system with computerization of functions and elimination of redundancies to enable the same staff to handle consistently increasing workloads.

Created tax allocation strategies on recent acquisitions which yielded $3 million savings.

Provided extensive support for numerous acquisitions ranging from $4 million to $100 million.

**Manager, Tax Accounting — Compliance**    1972–1983

Responsible for preparation, review, and filing of all tax returns and payments of liabilities for the corporation, its domestic subsidiaries, and international affiliates.

*Selected Contributions*:

Implemented strategy to enable consolidated tax return filing yielding $10 million tax savings in the first year.

Developed and instituted rapid calculation approach for key tax return provisions enabling tighter earnings forecasting.

Computerized federal and state income tax preparation using newly formed company system that has subsequently been adopted by a high percentage of Fortune 150 taxpayers.

**Manager, Financial Accounting**    1970–1972

Administered corporate accounting function, handled all financial statements to management, and supervised all operational areas.

**Senior Analyst, Federal Income Taxes**    1969–1970

Provided tax research and preparation of all subsidiary federal income tax returns, including Georgia-Atlantic International, Inc.

**INTERNAL REVENUE SERVICE**    San Francisco, California
**Internal Revenue Agent / Team Audit Coordinator**

Acted as team coordinator for Large Case Examination Group. Examinations included Foremost-McKesson, Stauffer Chemical, Sherman Clay & Company, and Spreckels Sugar.

**EDUCATION / CERTIFICATION**

**B.A., Business**, Babson College, with emphases in Finance and Accounting
**Certified Public Accountant**, Connecticut, Georgia, New York

**AFFILIATIONS**

Tax Executives' Institute, **Former President, Member Board of Directors**
American Society of Certified Public Accountants, **Member**
Connecticut Society of Certified Public Accountants, **Member**
*prior*
Georgia Manufacturers' Association, **Tax Committee Member**
Georgia Taxpayers' Association, **Member**

Cf. this résumé with
the academic ones in
chapter 10, and legal
ones in chapter 8.

# Clive Scott Gilbert

*Business:*
c/o 2500 Cottonwood Park Boulevard, Suite 100-120
Dallas, Texas 75207
Nonsecure fax line: (214) 555-3627
Business: (214) 555-3410

*Residence:*
7845 Claiborne Way
Dallas, Texas 75246
Residence/message/private fax: (214) 555-1734
Car: (214) 555-8854

**PROFILE**

Senior executive/attorney with extensive legal, legislative, and fiscal management background in financial services, higher education, and state government. Strengths include strategic analysis and planning, general management, vision, leadership, execution. Proven talent for change management including leading reorganizations, turnarounds, and conducting complex negotiations.

**EXPERIENCE**

TREVOR FINANCIAL SERVICES GROUP       1987 – 1995
**Consultant**, *to present*       Dallas, TX
**Executive Vice President,** 1994 – 1995
**Senior Vice President and General Counsel**, 1987 – 1994

Recruited by the chairman and chief executive officer of Trevor in December 1987 to assume responsibility as senior vice president and general counsel for restructuring the legal services delivery system within the Trevor Financial Services Group of companies with $6+ billion in assets, 5,000 employees, annual revenues of approximately $1.2 billion, and seven operating divisions: mortgage banking, information systems, credit card, life insurance, commercial leasing, short-term construction lending, and real estate development. Served as secretary/assistant secretary to each of the corporate entities within the Trevor Financial Services Group, including Trevor Financial Corporation and four other affiliated companies listed on the New York Stock Exchange.

Restructured the legal services delivery system in such a way as to save the consolidated Trevor Financial Services Group $8+ million per year.

Chosen by the chairman and chief executive officer to be a member of the Lomas team which attempted to negotiate an out-of-court arrangement with Trevor's creditors during 1988 and 1989 when the real estate market crash of the 1980s precipitated a liquidity crisis for the group.

- Concurrently with workout negotiations, participated in the successful negotiations to sell the credit card division for aggregate consideration of $600+ million and the elimination of $1.8 billion in debt.

- Assumed direct responsibility for steering Trevor Financial Corporation and its real estate companies through Chapter 11 process after a September 1989 filing for protection under the U.S. Bankruptcy Code.

- Successfully led a team of Trevor personnel and outside professionals in negotiating the reorganization of the filed companies in 28 months, a near record time for a Chapter 11 of Trevor's magnitude, consummating the reorganization plan on January 31, 1992. Relocated to New York during the reorganization period.

- Headed negotiating teams which successfully sold the commercial leasing and life insurance divisions, as part of and during the reorganization process, for aggregate consideration of $310+ million and the elimination of $1+ billion in debt.

Promoted in January 1994 to executive vice president; continued to provide overall leadership and direction for the Office of the General Counsel and risk management unit; expanded responsibilities to include providing overall leadership and direction for:

- Information systems division with $38.5 million gross annual revenue in the process of being tendered for sale; led the negotiations resulting in the successful disposition of this business unit with 448 employees to a unit of The Prudential in December 1994.

- Short-term lending division which, as a discontinued operation of Trevor, emerged from Chapter 11 holding $365 million in assets pending payment of $240 million principal amount of debt due in October 1996; prepaid the full amount of debt a full two years ahead of schedule.

- Real estate investment banking unit arranging financial solutions related to real estate on a fee-for-service basis.

- Insurance-related operations, increasing net income from a base of $8+ million in FY 93 to $10+ in fiscal year 1995.

- Field services unit in the process of being downsized and readied for sale; unit provides property preservation and inspection services to Lomas's mortgage banking division and approximately 40 other leading mortgage servicers nationwide.

Served on parent and subsidiary boards of directors and management committees.

**THE UNIVERSITY OF TENNESSEE SYSTEM**     1970 – 1987
**Vice Chancellor and General Counsel**, 1980 – 1987     Knoxville, TN

Recruited by the chancellor and former chairman of the Board of Regents to come to the U.T. System in Knoxville from the University of Texas at Dallas in 1980 to lead the System's Office of General Counsel.

Directed legal affairs with extensive involvement in strategic decision-making processes for fourteen institutions within the university system, the system administration, the university's $4+ billion endowment fund, and the Board of Regents.

Developed and drafted bills for legislative programs to be considered by state and federal legislative bodies. Cultivated and maintained political contacts to champion legislative programs through the state legislature and federal congress jointly with the vice chancellor for Governmental Affairs. Represented the system and all component institutions before federal, state and local agencies.

Supervised 21 internal legal and administrative professionals, and all outside counsel including intellectual property, federal tax, medical malpractice, and bond counsel. Supervised legal counsel for a broad range of personnel issues including workers' compensation, equal employment opportunity laws, civil rights laws, and employment grievances.

Administered $30+ million self-insured medical malpractice fund insuring 3,800+ professionals. Supervised outside counsel for medical malpractice suits and coordinated litigation.

Administrator for fiscal and legal aspects of systemwide trademark licensing program.

Counseled, advised, and supervised internal and outside counsel for a broad range of complex real estate matters, issues related to oil and gas production on 2+ million acres of endowment lands established by the state constitution as well as other endowment properties, and issues related to the investment of $4+ billion in endowment funds managed by The University of Tennessee System.

**The University of Texas at Dallas**     1971 – 1980
**Executive Vice President,** 1977 – 1980     Dallas, TX
**Vice President,** 1974 – 1977
**Assistant to the President,** 1971 – 1974
**Professor, Political Economy**
**Lecturer, Environmental Law**

Recruited by the newly installed president of The University of Texas at Dallas to move in 1971 from U.T Austin to U.T. Dallas to assist in the start-up of this newly created state university.

Provided strategic direction and planning for start-up of new campus of The University of Texas System created by the Texas legislature in 1969. Oversaw all aspects of financial planning, operating budget development and submissions to the legislature. Served as acting vice president of Business Affairs, and acting vice president of Academic Affairs during vacancies in these positions.

Represented The University of Texas at Dallas before the state legislature.

Worked with the president in maintaining relationships with the officers of the foundation that established the private research and graduate education institute that formed the basis for the new state university; these efforts resulted in U.T. Dallas becoming the most richly endowed state-supported university of its type nationwide.

Prepared academic degree program submittals and orchestrated their approval by The University of Texas System Board of Regents and the Coordinating Board, Texas College and University System resulting in implementation of 25 bachelors, 16 masters, and 8 doctoral programs.

Recruited students and 130+ faculty members traveling nationwide with the vice president of Academic Affairs for the admission of the university's first undergraduate students in the fall of 1975.

**The University of Texas at Austin**
**Assistant to the President,** 1971     Austin, TX

Selected by the director of the U.T. System Law Office and assigned by the chancellor and chairman of the Board of Regents of the U.T. System to the U.T. Austin campus to closely observe and provide legal assistance related to the at times tumultuous Vietnam War demonstrations.

In addition to advising on campus disorder situations, performed a wide range of administrative duties on the behalf of the president.

**The University of Texas System Law Office**
**(Office of General Counsel)**
**University Attorney,** 1970

Recruited from the Texas Water Quality Board by the director of the U.T System Law Office to join the law offices of this rapidly growing university system which had been assigned the task of building and operating several new educational institutions as a result of the expansion and reorganization of higher education by the Texas legislature in 1969.

**STATE OF TEXAS**     1966 – 1970
Texas Water Quality Board     Austin, TX
**Director of Hearings and Enforcement,** 1969 – 1970
**Chief Legal Officer**

Charged by the Board and the chief executive officer with the responsibilities of ensuring appropriate permitting of discharges into the waters of the state and enforcing compliance with the terms of waste permits granted.

Texas Senate Committee on Youth Affairs
**Counsel**, 1969

"Loaned" to this special committee of the Texas Senate by the Texas Water Quality Board at the request of the committee's chairperson.

Conducted a study and investigation of juvenile offender facilities and programs in Texas.

Office of the Governor of Texas
**Administrative Assistant**, 1968 – 1969

On leave of absence from the Texas Water Quality Board under arrangements worked out between Governor John Connally's chief of staff and the chief executive officer of the Texas Water Quality Board.

Texas Water Quality Board
**Director of Hearings,** 1967 – 1968
**Chief Legal Officer**

Recruited from the Texas Legislative Council by the initial chief executive officer of the Texas Water Quality Board. Provided the rare opportunity to implement legislation authored while at the Legislative Council.

Established and supervised the rules, regulations, and administrative law procedures for granting or denying and enforcing waste discharge permits by the Board.

Texas Legislative Council
**Legislative Counsel,** 1966 – 1967

Authored legislation creating the first comprehensively empowered Texas state agency to deal with water pollution problems along with numerous other pieces of water- and environment-related legislation including the first comprehensive air pollution control legislation.

Conducted extensive research and worked on the codification of the state's laws related to water in the development of a Texas Water Code.

**SELECTED BOARDS AND COMMITTEES**

Higher Education Legislative Political Action Committee
**Secretary**

Texas Foundation For Higher Education
**Secretary**

School of Management/The University of Texas at Dallas
**Member, Advisory Council**

Vista Properties, Inc.
**Member, Board of Directors**

Alliance for Higher Education of North Texas
**Member, Board of Trustees**

Southwest Public Affairs Task Force/U.S. Chamber of Commerce
**Member, Education, Employment, and Training Committees**

Mortgage Bankers Association of America
**Member, Legal and Legislative Issues Committees**

**EDUCATION**

SOUTHERN METHODIST UNIVERSITY      Dallas, TX
**LL.B.**
UNIVERSITY OF OKLAHOMA      Norman, OK
**B.A.**

**ADMISSIONS**

Member, State Bar of Texas
Member, State Bar of Tennessee

# ANTHONY L. CARBONEAU

Residence: (501) 555-7509
Office: (501) 555-5836

2801 West Cabot Street
Little Rock, Arkansas 72201

---

## PROFESSIONAL EXPERIENCE

HARVEST TRUST COMPANY       Little Rock, AR
**Chief Investment Officer / Portfolio Manager**       1992 to Present

Chief investment officer of $300 million trust department of one of the largest banks in Arkansas. Personally manage 93 trust and institutional portfolios, total market value of $184 million, client base of high-net-worth individual, business, and institutional clients.

Develop investment strategies and policy guidelines.

- Assist clients in establishing investment objectives and rate of return expectations.
- Responsible for asset allocation.
- Conduct proactive client servicing program.

Responsible for administration, research, and trading.

- Direct the activities of two portfolio managers.
- Responsible for equity and bond research.
- Supervise trading of bonds and stock.
- Personally handle the trading of all taxable bonds for managed accounts.

Active in new business development.

- Work actively with three regional trust managers and new business officer to develop and close new business.
- Make presentations to individuals, investment committees, and trustees.
- Conduct business development through brokers, attorneys, and pension administrators.

*Contributions*:

- Implemented a sophisticated client contact/lead management program.
- Selected PNC and Harris Trust as investment research correspondents.
- Installed Bloomberg terminals in three regional investment offices.
- Developed $104,000 in new fee income during 1st year with bank.
- Achieved 10.37% three-year annualized return in ITC Equity Common Trust Fund to March 31, 1995.
- Produced 5.42% three-year annualized rate of return in ITC Fixed Income Common Trust Fund to March 31, 1995.

LECREAUX FINANCIAL GROUP, INC.       New Orleans, LA
**Vice President / Portfolio Manager**       1989 to 1992

Managed 53 accounts with $156 million market value for $300 million investment management and venture capital firm.

Asset base included 22 employee benefit plans up to $13 million, three corporate accounts, and 31 individual accounts.

*Contributions*:

- Achieved a twelve-year annualized equity return of 22.6% versus 16.6% for S&P 500.
- Added seventeen new clients with market value of $8 million.

*Continued . . .*

TEXAS MIDLAND STATE BANK, ASSET MANAGEMENT DIVISION    Houston, TX
**Vice President / Portfolio Manager**    1987 to 1989

Managed 117 trusts, pension accounts, profit sharing, and agency accounts with market value of $132 million with responsibilities for portfolio management, new business development, and research. Member of Equity Strategy Committee.

*Contributions*:
- Generated $68,000 in annual fees in first three months with the bank.
- Achieved two-year annualized equity return of 11.2% versus 10.5% for S&P 500.
- Achieved 8.4% equity return in 1987 versus 5.3% for S&P 500.

DAVIS SKINNER INVESTMENT MANAGEMENT    Houston, TX
**Vice President / Portfolio Manager**    1982 to 1987

Directed $52 million in assets for 33 institutional pension fund accounts in the $400 million institutional division of investment counseling firm with a 60-year history. Supervised marketing rep, research associate, and administrative assistant.

Managed corporate, union, and individual pension and profit sharing plans.
- Asset base included 24 employee benefit plans, two foundation accounts, and seven individual accounts.

*Contributions*:
- Attained 21.3% overall rate of return in seven-year period.
- Achieved audited performance record 60% better than S&P 500.
- Increased portfolio from six to 33 accounts, $12 to $52 million, 1982–1987.

TRANSAMERICA INVESTMENT SERVICES, INC.    Los Angeles, CA
**Vice President / Portfolio Manager**    1976 to 1982

Portfolio Manager for 31 nontaxable institutional accounts with $97 million value of $250 million Transamerica investment subsidiary. Member of Transamerica Investment Policy Committee.

U.S. TRUST COMPANY    New York, NY
**Portfolio Manager**    1974 to 1976

Portfolio Manager for 171 individual, corporate and trust accounts with $202 million value of $12 billion investment management firm.

## EDUCATION

GEORGE WASHINGTON UNIVERSITY    Washington, D.C.
**Masters of Business Administration** (ABT)

WAKE FOREST UNIVERSITY    Winston-Salem, NC
**Bachelor of Science, Business Administration**

TULANE UNIVERSITY    New Orleans, LA

NEW YORK UNIVERSITY    New York, NY

NEW YORK INSTITUTE OF FINANCE    New York, NY

## AFFILIATIONS

Member, Society of Security Analysts, Greater Southland Chapter

Member, Arkansas Governor's Council on Economic Prosperity

# JOELLYN C. GREENBERG

68 Warren Avenue
Millbrae, California 94030

Telephone/Message:
(415) 555-9472

---

**PROFILE**

**Club Management**

Dedicated manager with a history of innovation and rapid professional advancement. Full knowledge of all facets of the industry based on an extremely integrated background involving hands-on experience at every level. Seeking a new challenge. Available for relocation.

*Strengths:*
- Leadership, team building, training, management, and motivation.
- Budget projection and administration.
- Image development and positioning/PR management/customer relations.
- Strategic planning, decision making, and problem solving.

**EXPERIENCE**

PRESIDIO ARMY GOLF COURSE     San Francisco, CA
**Manager**     1987–1995

Oversaw all facets of operation for this eighteen-hole course, serving 1,200 military members and 400 country club members and their guests. Reported directly to commanding general of the post. Supervised twenty-four employees and seven volunteers including course superintendent, starters, office staff, greenskeepers, and range attendants. Formulated and presented short- and long-range plans involving capital expenditures, construction/renovation, and regular operations. Oversaw annual operating budget of $1 million. Conducted monthly informational briefings with board of directors, commanding general, and post commanders to define objectives and ensure teamwork.

*Contributions:*
- **Increased net profits by 17% within four years** by advertising in trade journals and expanding promotional efforts.
- **Increased Northern California Golf Association rating for Presidio course from 61.9 to 74.4** by working closely with course superintendent to redesign tees, bunkers, and greens.
- **Saved club over $30,000/year** by recruiting and training senior volunteer player assistants.
- Established and maintained excellent rapport with personnel; **encouraged 100% of staff to remain with club with closure imminent**.
- Orchestrated closure of facility; coordinated equipment removal, sale of fixed assets, and 1001 details for a smooth closing. Solved equipment crisis caused by zero capital expenditures due to closure by "testing" new turf grass equipment to keep course operational until the last day.
- Received highest commendation from commanding general on professionalism, leadership ability, tact, and diplomacy at all levels of command.

*Continued . . .*

**Assistant Manager**     1980–1987

Planned and organized tournaments and directed golf outings. Analyzed club performance and wrote comprehensive manuals covering policies, rules, and regulations to improve operations. Selected, trained, supervised, and motivated key employees. Interacted with club manager, board of directors, and committee heads to elevate club's overall standards. Acted resourcefully to anticipate and resolve operational problems and maximize productivity. Attended Presidio Golf Club functions and acted as ambassador and liaison between military and private sector.

*Contributions:*

- Identified previously unexplored source of income and successfully campaigned to have Presidio host major charity tournaments. Built strong tournament business of fifty-two nonmember tournaments / year **generating an additional $150,000 annually for the club**.
- Created and implemented club image improvement project. Upgraded course, initiated fairway contouring and landscaping, and replaced military score card with four-color country club-style design.
- **Reduced employee attrition rate by 90%** by developing rapport with staff at all levels, and writing performance standards for eight different positions to increase employee understanding of requirements and expectations.
- **Increased guest play by 30%** by coordinating publicity with charity tournament directors and stepping up public relations efforts.
- **Increased driving range usage by 25%** by instructing starters to promote its use among golfers waiting for tee time.
- Earned outstanding performance reviews each year; promoted to manager based on performance.

**Office Manager**     1978–1980

Established scope and range of work program and arranged schedules for busy and off seasons to meet the overall club goals while increasing efficiency. Administered annual operating budget of $50,000 and capital expenditure budget of $100,000. Reviewed club activity reports, made cost analyses, and purchased equipment and supplies. Determined office personnel requirements, and hired, trained, and supervised staff of nine. Acted as liaison between department heads and management.

*Contributions:*

- **Pioneered Hospitality Training Program** for front office and starter personnel. Conducted weekly training meetings covering subjects including telephone etiquette, courtesy, handling cash, and anticipating customer needs.
- **Saved club 23% in starter costs** by hiring flex employees.
- Oversaw successful computerization of office systems.
- Earned highest possible performance rating on every review and received promotion to assistant manager due to success of personal initiatives.

**Club Secretary**     1977–1978

In addition to providing all general office services, worked closely with public affairs office to coordinate public relations for the club. Attended board of directors and committee meetings to participate in discussions and present proposals for innovative projects.

*Continued . . .*

*Contributions:*

- **Personally developed proposal to expand club services to include all branches of the military.** New categories of membership were subsequently created, contributing to club exposure and generating an additional $4,000/ month in revenue.
- Earned highest performance rating possible each year in position.
- Received promotion to office manager.

**Club Clerk**     1977

Provided all general secretarial services for manager and board of directors and handled club customer relations.
- Promoted to club secretary after four months.

*Prior*

ROTC DEPARTMENT, GEORGIA MILITARY COLLEGE, Milledgeville, GA
**Assistant to the Professor of Military Science**

Full administrative responsibility for cadet commissioning process. Interacted with students, their parents, faculty, government officials, and dignitaries to answer inquiries and provide information on all aspects of the program. Oversaw daily function of the four sections of the military department.

*Contributions:*

- **Created and directed internship program** within the ROTC department to provide cadets with hands-on administrative experience.
- Taught Army administration courses twice daily to classes of thirty ROTC junior college cadets.
- Consistently received Army's highest performance rating throughout tenure.

**EDUCATION**

GEORGIA COLLEGE     Milledgeville, GA
**B.A., Business Administration,** *Emphasis:* **Management**

*Additional Training*
SKYLINE COLLEGE     San Bruno, CA
**Studies in Hotel/Restaurant Management**

*Areas of Special Study:*
- Dining Room Management
- Purchasing
- Sanitation
- Cost Analysis

CLUB MANAGER ASSOCIATION OF AMERICA     HQ: Alexandria, VA
398 Continuing Education Units

*Special Studies Include:*
- F & B Profitability
- Marketing Alcohol
- Menu Management
- Quality Food Service
- Food & Beverage Sales

**AFFILIATIONS**

Club Managers Association of America, Member, Local Board Member 1994

National Association of Female Executives, Board Member 1991

**REFERENCES**

References, recommendations, news clippings presented on request.

# ROYCE DAVID CASSADY

1200 Polk Street, #2
San Francisco, California 94115, U.S.A.

24-Hour Telephone/Message: 415-555-1533
Kitchen: 415-555-6363

---

**PROFESSION**

**Executive Chef**

*Strengths:*

- Demonstrated mastery of food styles. Skilled at menu development, recipe creation, staff training in culinary arts, image, and concept.
- Start-up experience. Opening team for several units. Effective manager, including costing, sales and profit analysis, aggressive negotiations with suppliers, control of kitchen operations.
- Experience with international kitchen and work crews.

*Awards:*

- Five Star — Double Bay, NSW Australia
- Five Diamond — Buckhead, Georgia
- Malcolm Baldridge Quality Award — Washington, D.C.

**EXPERIENCE**

St. Francis Yacht Club on the Marina      San Francisco, CA
**Executive Chef**      1994–1996
(volume $5.2 million)

This world renowned yacht club has two restaurants, one cafe style and one fine dining room. Banquet functions ranged from 30 to 1000.

In addition, the club owns an island north of San Francisco. Six holiday functions were held there annually, with attendance from 350 to 650.

In full charge of creating the culinary function: Developed menus, trained and managed a brigade of 25 chefs and cooks, managed purchasing.

Also, responsible for costing, analysis, and reporting to General Manager.

Achieved increases in profitability as high as 8.5%, with food quality comparable to any fine restaurant in this region famous for its restaurants.

Letter of appreciation from the Japanese Consul for outstanding service to Their Royal Highnesses Prince and Princess Hitachi of Japan.

Guest Artist, ice sculpture for 100,000 attendees of the U.S.-Japan Expo '95 in Anaheim, California.

Guest chef, The Plaza San Antonio for Fortune magazine's Forum 500, with Texas Governor Ann Richards and CEOs from top U.S. corporations.

San Diego Convention Center      San Diego, CA
**Executive Chef**      1992–1994
(volume $20 million)

Executive chef in charge of 12 concessions throughout the Convention Center, including 4500-seat ballroom, 4500-capacity outdoor sail loft, and over 40 meeting rooms. This was strictly a banquet facility, planned meals for 10 to 6000, from fine dining to trays of hors d'oeuvres.

*Continued . . .*

Position required strong planning, management and interpersonal skills, meeting with event representatives and coordinating closely with other departments to orchestrate high-quality events. Supervised large staffs in multiple locations.

Also required skill with a wide range of foods, including intensive and constantly changing menu planning. Also: purchasing, vendor relations, costing, negotiations, food and payroll budgeting, operations management.

Contributions: Improved quality of food, increased menu options, developed fine dining menus within tight budgets, brought a reputation for higher quality to the Center. Through tighter operations all around, reduced food costs from 26% to 23%, labor costs from 16% to 11%.

The Ritz Carlton Hotel at Double Bay     NSW Australia
**Executive Chef, Opening Team**     1991–1992
(volume $6 million)

Executive chef on the pre-opening team. Hired a crew of 35 chefs and cooks to staff four restaurant kitchens. Prepared initial menus. Established and wrote culinary procedures.

This five-star hotel has 120 rooms, 24 club level suites, and two presidential apartments.

Food service in seven outlets, ranging from fine dining, banquet for up to 700, daily high tea, and champagne bar.

Our first guests were President George Bush, Prime Minister Heath, and seven U.S. Senators.

The Ritz Carlton Hotel at Pentagon City     Arlington, VA
**Executive Sous Chef, Opening Team**     1990–1991
(volume $5 million)

Assisted the Executive Committee in interviewing and hiring staff. This four-star hotel has 215 rooms, 30 suites, and two restaurants. One is a fine dining room with a three-star Michelin chef, the other a grill restaurant. Banquets up to 750 at private club level of service.

My daily responsibilities included the physical operation of the kitchen and staff of 37 chefs and cooks. Assisted the Executive Chef in corporate training programs and professional certification of the culinary staff.

During this time, we had two presidential visits and many Pentagon and other U.S. government officials as guests. Foreign dignitaries also frequent this property.

The Ritz Carlton Hotel at Rancho Mirage     Rancho Mirage, CA
**Executive Sous Chef**     1989–1990
(volume $5.5 million)

Joined this destination four-star hotel shortly after opening. Assisted the Executive Chef. Provided daily supervision of a brigade of 40 chefs and cooks, one fine dining restaurant, one cafe restaurant, banquet functions for up to 650, poolside restaurant, club level, and daily high tea.

My responsibilities also included purchasing, training, scheduling sous chefs, new menu development, and company-sponsored quality management programs.

Hosted several Chaine de Rotisseurs dinners, presidential visits, Ritz Carlton corporate meetings, and visiting Michelin chefs.

*Continued . . .*

The Ritz Carlton at Buckhead    Atlanta, GA
**Tournant Sous Chef**    1988–1989
(volume $7.5 million)

Assisted the Executive Chef in the operation of all culinary outlets in this 540-room hotel. Responsibilities ranged from developing new menu items, theme menu development, corporate dining room promotions, and full responsibility for kitchens in absence of the Executive Chef.

Outlets included one fine dining restaurant, one cafe restaurant, espresso bar, club level, and daily high tea.

Numerous culinary events, including Babette's Feast, Chaine de Rotisseurs dinners, Meals-on-Wheels, visiting Michelin chefs.

*also*

The Ritz Carlton at Sydney, Australia

The Ritz Carlton on Amelia Island

The Ritz Carlton at New York (implemented Quality Vision Program)

The Ritz Carlton at Kansas City (opened the grill restaurant)

The Ritz Carlton at Cleveland (opening team)

**TRAINING**

Continuing Chef's Training, 140 hours annually on diverse subjects including: Technique, Vision, Quality Management, Union Avoidance, Target Selection Hiring Practices, Leadership, Business Issues.

**Diploma, Food & Beverage Management**
**Johnson & Wales College**, Providence

*Honors:*
- Ice Sculptures — Concept & Design
- Tallow/Butter Sculptures
- Vegetable and Fruit Carvings
- Hotel Culinary Art Demonstration
- Styrofoam/Papier-Mâché Sculptures

Member, The National Ice Carving Association

Member, American Culinary Federation

**PERSONAL**

References, photo portfolio, and/or video presentation provided on request. Available for assignment worldwide.

Date of birth: November 6, 1954.
Place of birth: Sydney, Australia.
Dual citizenship: Australia, U.S.A.
Marital status: single.

Please keep this information confidential at this time.

*Continued . . .*

# ROYCE DAVID CASSADY

1200 Polk Street, #2
San Francisco, California 94115, U.S.A.

24-Hour Telephone/Message: 415-555-1533
Kitchen: 415-555-6363

---

**CHRONOLOGY**

St. Francis Yacht Club on the Marina    San Diego, CA
**Executive Chef**    1994–1996

San Diego Convention Center    San Francisco, CA
**Executive Chef**    1992–1994

The Ritz Carlton Hotel at Double Bay    NSW Australia
**Executive Chef, Opening Team**    1991–1992

The Ritz Carlton Hotel at Pentagon City    Arlington, VA
**Executive Sous Chef, Opening Team**    1990–1991

The Ritz Carlton Hotel at Rancho Mirage    Rancho Mirage, CA
**Executive Sous Chef**    1989–1990

The Ritz Carlton at Buckhead    Atlanta, GA
**Tournant Sous Chef**    1988–1989

Omni International Hotel    Atlanta, GA
**Executive Sous Chef**    1986–1987

Omni International Hotel    Hampton, NH
**Executive Sous Chef**    1985–1986

Cutwater Incorporated    Portsmouth, NH
**Consulting Executive Chef**    1983–1985

Preakness Hills Country Club    Wayne, NJ
**Executive Sous Chef**    1982–1983

Fairview Country Club    Greenwich, CT
**Executive Sous Chef**    1980–1982

Stouffer's Inn of Westchester    White Plains, NY
**(Acting) Executive Chef / Executive Sous Chef**    1978–1980

Waldorf Astoria Hotel    New York, NY
**Second Sous Chef**    1977–1978

Capitol Hilton Hotel    Washington, D.C.
**Executive Sous Chef**    1975–1977

# PAUL J. ROONEY

1155 Hammond Drive
Atlanta, Georgia 30328

Office: (770) 555-2321
Residence: (404) 555-4605
Private Fax: (404) 555-4610

---

**PROFILE**

**General Management — Operations, Sales, Marketing, Distribution**

Effective combination of analytical and leadership skills, with expertise in the following operational areas:

- **Production / Inventory Management**
- **Transportation / Distribution / Logistics**
- **Import / Export**
- **Coordinating and Management of Broker — Dealer Organizations**

Background of accomplishment as the manager in charge under the company's executive operating officer. Available for business travel and / or relocation as needed for continued career advancement.

Member, American Production and Inventory Control Society.

**EXPERIENCE**

SHOWMAN DISTRIBUTING COMPANY, INC.      Norcross, GA
**Director of Operations**      1990–Present

Report directly to the President. Forecast and manage product flow from 16 suppliers through company warehousing system to countywide point-of-sale distribution points. Supervise staff of warehouse managers and data clerk. **Relief General Manager**, with responsibility for sales and finance.

Forecast, track, and analyze 2.5 million cases ($35 million) in annual sales, with emphasis on planning product flow for perishable product lines (beers, wines, sodas, water beverages). Also: pricing administration, promotion planning, warehouse allocation, traffic management, transportation management, freight cost control. Sample contribution:

Designed an order forecasting system that sets a new industry standard, used as a model for two major software development vendors. This system allows for greater accuracy than ever achieved in the history of the company, lowering inventory capital expense, improving flow-through, and virtually eliminating spoilage.

Participate in strategic decision-making process for this family owned and operated company.

**Marketing & Operations Consultant**      1988

Designed, conducted, and integrated the results of a series of special projects in **marketing, inventory control,** and **human resources**, for example:

- Designed sales incentive programs.
- Developed shipping/receiving procedures to reduce computer input errors to an absolute minimum.
- Compiled and wrote a new *Company Policy Manual*.

MORELAND LIGHTING SERVICES     Marietta, GA
**Branch Manager**     1988–1990

Reported to the Regional Manager; supervised branch staff of 35, including sales manager, sales staff, operations manager, service manager, and operations and service technicians. The company maintains large-scale commercial lighting systems for corporate and government accounts, for example:

- Safeway
- MARTA
- Bank of Georgia

Directly responsible for this $3 million business, part of a $428 million parent company (ABM Industries). Sample contributions:

- Brought this branch from negative revenue trends to solid profitability in just 18 months through attention to business fundamentals.
- Designed a computer program to automate the bidding process, allowing faster response and eliminating underbidding/misbidding.
- Increased service crew training to reduce job costs, allowing more competitive bidding on new contracts.
- Computerized vehicle maintenance records and other branch expenses to better track and control overhead.

MARINER DISTRIBUTION COMPANY     Marietta, GA
**Vice President, Operations**     1980–1987

Reported directly to the President and General Manager. Supervised the sales department, office, and warehouse operations. Forecast and ordered product. Budgeted, tracked, and controlled expenses. Scheduled the fleet maintenance program. Analyzed company's operations to identify projects for improvement in efficiency and/or economy. Equity position; member of executive team.

*prior*

*Sales* management experience (set up a sub-wholesaler network over the entire South) and military service with Georgia Army National Guard.

**EDUCATION**

GEORGIA STATE UNIVERSITY     Atlanta, GA
**B.A., Business (General Management)**     1986

Additional studies in **mathematics** and **physical sciences**.

# John D. "Jack" Davis

26 Northeast Fountain Square, Bldg. D, No. 1
Sunrise, Florida 33322

Telephone/Message: (954) 555-3437
73287.13204@compuserve.com

## PROFILE

Track record of accomplishment in sales, marketing, and strategic management. Heavy involvement in emerging technologies and start-up situations under diverse and complex circumstances. Ability to design operations, provide strategic planning and direction, and build teamwork within an organization. Consistently able to access and build relationships with top decisionmakers in business, government, and industry.

Areas of knowledge include high technology, electronics, data telecommunications, finance, nuclear physics, instrumentation, and all aspects of training and instruction.

*HIGHLIGHTS:*

- National experience as marketing consultant for technology-based companies.
- Recruited to be regional manager of start-up OEM sales group for Paradyne Corp. Created sales organization that took sales from zero to $50,000,000, establishing exclusive relationships with AMD, Intel, DEC, and other major OEMs.
- As regional manager for the Atlantic Seaboard, took sales from $500,000 to $7,000,000, for Universal Data Systems, a Motorola subsidiary.
- As district manager for New York City, increased district sales from $200,000 to $5,000,000 for Codex Corp., a Motorola subsidiary.
- Co-founder and director of marketing for a biotech start-up; directed feasibility studies, collaborated with R&D, engineered highly profitable sell-out to V.C. group.
- Gave seminars and symposia on nuclear and infrared devices to Ph.D.-level audiences throughout the United States. and internationally on behalf of Beckman Instruments, Inc.
- Lab chief, Hanford Atomic Works, Richland, Washington, while in U.S. Army.

## RECENT HISTORY

**Merrill Lynch**     Miami Beach, Florida
**Financial Consultant**     1993–Present

Represented investment products to high-net-worth individuals, mainly 150 key investors, top-level active and retired corporate officers. Developed and presented my own investment strategies to investors. Took this position to manage personal portfolio and maintain contacts with top industrialists nationwide. In spite of financial success, am currently interested in more challenging employment.

**Timeplex Inc. (a Unisys company)**     Woodcliff Lakes, New Jersey
**Manager, Distributor Sales**     1990–1993

Hired, trained, and motivated wholesale representatives. Recruited, evaluated, and negotiated agreements with 22 distributor organizations. Administered sales/marketing department. Exceeded management goals by 225%, taking sales to over $100,000,000.

**General Data-Com**     Danbury, Connecticut
**OEM Sales Manager**     1988–1990

Designed a sales/marketing strategy to penetrate major OEMs and VARs with new modem product lines.

**Teneron Corp.**     Portland, Oregon
**Regional Manager**     1986–1988

Directed all sales and marketing west of the Mississippi for this V.C.-funded start-up selling data security software for PC applications.

**Paradyne Corp.**    Largo, Florida
**OEM Regional Manager**    1982–1986

**Motorola Corp.** (via the following two subsidiaries)    1975–1982
**Regional Manager, Universal Data Systems**    1977–1982
**Regional Manager, Codex Corp.**    1975–1977

## EDUCATION

**Boston College,** Boston, Massachusetts

**B.S., Economics-Physics**

## ADDITIONAL

NASD Series 7, 23 Licenses. Additional knowledge of commercial real estate. Intellectual interests include history, philosophy, and theological studies.

Continuing education—list on request. Social affiliations and community involvement—list on request. References—list on request.

# Stanford Rappaport

1046 North Salinda Avenue
Los Angeles, California 90049
(213) 555-4716

---

## PROFILE

Strengths include financial and management analysis, with accomplishments in (1) developing strategic and operational plans; (2) evaluating, structuring, and negotiating mergers and acquisitions; and (3) providing internal management consulting, with emphasis on reengineering and effective management practices.

## EXPERIENCE

THE INTERNATIONAL FASHION NEWS GROUP, 1990–1996
**Associate Publisher** and **Chief Financial Officer**, 1995–1996

- Ensured the profitable operation of this $6 million company publishing seven separate trade publications, 80 permanent staff, offices in Los Angeles, New York, Dallas, Atlanta, Chicago, Germany, Hong Kong, and Australia.

Developed the strategic positioning for continued growth and profitability of the company. Worked directly with the president to set both strategic and operational goals and objectives. Oversaw development of operating plans and budgets. Directed a multidisciplinary team of upper-level executives in day-to-day management.

Personally guided the marketing research department in ongoing economic forecasting and analysis of our environment. Primary force behind expanding international endeavors. Spearheaded launch stage of new products and new revenue streams.

Also served as the company's legal liaison, represented the company at various industry functions, met with presidents of our top advertisers (companies with up to $100 million annual gross revenues), and established strategic business relationships.

**Chief Financial Officer** and **Chief Operations Officer**, 1994–1995

- Engineered a turnaround resulting in promotion to associate publisher. Developed strategic plan responding to changing market environment. Conducted complete competitive and market analysis, domestic and international, leading to decision to divest some products, launch others, and restructure internal operations to better manage debt.

Developed definitive operational plans covering each period of the year, each year, and projected out for a four-year period as preparation for M&A activities. Also established corporate standards for performance in all departments.

Directed the acquisition team in gathering data on four targets. Engineered the purchase of our major competitor in our fastest growing market, negotiating 90% seller financing.

Supervised department managers and assured their support of changes in organizational structure. Maintained continued high morale throughout the company during changes.

*Continued . . .*

**Controller**, 1992–1994

- Directed accounting, budgeting, profit planning, and performance reporting of the organization. Prepared the pro forma budget. Reported to the C.F.O./C.O.O. Assessed and recommended purchase of new publishing and information technologies.

Part of the team that packaged and marketed the company to potential suitors. Developed evaluation analysis to set pricing. Analyzed LBO offer to assess viability. Retained by new management as C.F.O.

**Financial Analyst and Operations Analyst**, 1990–1992

- Reported to the C.F.O. Major accomplishment: recommended and won approval for a restructuring of operations and reporting systems, leading to the gradual reorganization of this company to a focus on operational and strategic planning.

*Prior*

GREENSPAN VENTURE CAPITAL GROUP, 1982–1989
**Associate** (equity), 1986–1989
**Chief Analyst**, 1984–1986
**Analyst**, 1982–1984

- Analyzed venture proposals for financial viability. Recommended promising projects to the principal for further investigation. Assisted in negotiations and deal structuring.

Identified the International Fashion News Group as a promising venture, and engineered assignment leading to eventual line management responsibilities listed above.

## EDUCATION

**M.B.A. Candidate**, Executive M.B.A. Program, *ongoing*
University of Southern California, Los Angeles

**B.A., Finance**, 1982
University of California, Irvine

## ACTIVITIES

Executive Financial Board, Association of Business Publishers. Member, Western Publishers Association. Member, Advertising Club of Los Angeles. Fund-raiser, Cedars Sinai Hospital, City of Hope, AIDS Project/LA. Member, LA County Museum. Member, National Debate Team (UCI). House Manager, Sigma Alpha Mu.

## PERSONAL

Excellent recommendation can be obtained from current employer, but please keep this application confidential at this time.

# EDIE RAPP

75 Essex House Court, No. 1
Danbury, Connecticut 06811

24-hour private voice mail: (203) 555-9056
Office line: (203) 555-4698
Residence: (203) 555-8332
rapp@aol.com

## STRENGTHS

**Public Relations ▪ Media ▪ Special Events ▪ Promotions ▪ New Business Development**

Background of high profile positions in publishing and television requiring sales and negotiating ability, tact, diplomacy, creativity, event/project management skills, and consistent ability *to make things happen* in a fast-paced environment. Entire career has involved direct interaction with VIPs from government, culture, and business. Proven ability in both operational and strategic management roles. Seeking a new challenge.

## EXPERIENCE

**Answer Magazine**    New York, New York
**Publisher/President/Member of the Board**   1992–1996

Recruited to revitalize this 50-year-old tourist guide magazine with a solid niche identity but lagging financial, sales, and organizational management. Directed sales, production, circulation, collections, cash flow control, staff of 15. Contributions:

- Regained creditor confidence, renegotiated terms on long overdue payables, reopened key supplier channels to keep the magazine publishing on schedule.
- Personally represented the magazine to agencies and key advertisers, resolving problem outstandings and improving advertiser relations. Brought in major new accounts.
- Implemented standards, policies, and procedures in a company that had allowed management controls to lapse.
- Redesigned entire publication, updated maps, developed our most popular feature ("Celebrity Scene"), initiated new editorial policies.
- Due to successful turnaround performance, was appointed to **Board of Directors, Answer Magazine, Inc.**, the parent franchisor of 22 markets, 1994–1996.

**Answer Net Publishing, Inc.**    New York, New York
**President**    1990–1991

Designed and launched a corporation to serve as a cooperative national sales organization for a consortium of East Coast Answer Magazine franchises: Maine, Boston, Nantucket/MV, New York, Pittsburgh, Carolinas Coast, Daytona, Miami.

- Created media kit, national rate cards, and sales strategies.
- Promoted advertising sales workshops and seminars attended by franchisees and affiliates.

**ABC Television**    New York, New York
**Director, Special Events, ABC News & Sports**    1980–1990
**Manager, Special Events, ABC News & Sports**    1977–1980
**Client Relations Representative, ABC Sports**    1975–1977

Created and orchestrated special events to serve as a foundation to advertising sales and other business objectives of ABC Television. Planned and managed every aspect of major events, for example:

- 1984 Winter Olympics, Sarajevo — Traveled fourteen times to Sarajevo for site surveys. Selected venues and orchestrated three five-day itineraries for groups of 200 people (telecast sponsors, ABC VIPs, government officials, and guests). Interviewed and hired local hostesses/interpreters/drivers. Arranged air travel, Olympic credentials, hospitality lounges, hotels, private dining, gifts, side trips to Dubrovnik (by air), and every detail.

- 1983 Bureau Chief meeting, Rome — Orchestrated global executive meetings in Rome. The President of ABC News & Sports decided to provide Superbowl telecast at the meetings, but no satellites were available. Served as liaison to the U.S. Army to share a satellite feed. Then, we needed programs to the game, which had to be hand-carried around the world in less than 24 hours. Finally, the hotel refused to cater the event (after midnight on a Sunday in Italy). Invited high-level Vatican priests to the event, which motivated the hotel to provide an outrageously sumptuous buffet for the game.
- Wide World of Sports 20th Anniversary Extravaganza — Coordinated a black-tie evening at the Waldorf Astoria in New York for 1000 guests. Located 20 years of famous athletes in all corners of the world. Arranged visas and travel from many countries. Orchestrated seating for A list and B list guests. Arranged tuxedos for the American Hockey Team in three hours. Specified Tiffany ice buckets for all guests. Opened florists all over Manhattan to redesign centerpieces for entire ballroom to ensure clear headshots for the telecast.
- Voting for Democracy — Arranged this event for the President of Harvard University and the Chairman of the Board of ABC to explore the reasons for decline in voting among American citizens. Planned meetings to be held in the Senate chambers. Brought in two ex-presidents as speakers, coordinating with the Secret Service. Planned two main black-tie dinners, ancillary dining events and parties, side trips for spouses and guests (including private tours of White House). Conducted three food tastings to select caterer and plan menus. Arranged all travel, accommodations, security, every detail.
- Also orchestrated numerous other press trips, executive and Board of Directors meetings: ABC News VIP Retreats & Events, ABC News Strategic Planning Meetings, Summer and Winter Olympics, NFL, MLB, Monday Night Football, Monday Night Baseball, British Open, ABC News Bureau Chief Meetings, PGA, US Open, Leonard Goldenson's Annual Golf Outings, ABC Affiliate Meetings, Heavyweight Fights, Rodeo, Indianapolis 500, Daytona 500, Kentucky Derby, Preakness Stakes, and numerous large and small meetings.

PRIOR:

**WFIA News**       Bloomington, Indiana
**Newswriter, Newscaster**       1975

**WTIU Television**       Bloomington, Indiana
**Production Assistant**       1974

**EDUCATION**

**Indiana University**       Bloomington, Indiana
**B.A., Radio & Television Arts**       1975

# CAROL L. COX

9412 East San Salvador Drive
Scottsdale, Arizona 85258

Office: (602) 555-1213
Home/Car/Message: (602) 555-0385
Home Fax: (602) 555-0386

---

## PROFILE

Strengths in multistate/multiproject planning, development and construction management. Unusual breadth of experience, with knowledge of every phase of real estate development: due diligence, acquisition of raw land, all phases of entitlement to final map, processing to lots, off-site construction, and homebuilding.

Recent accomplishments feature success in gaining entitlement for 1250 lots on large, controversial and difficult project in Northern California. Politically astute. Also have constructed over 3000 lots in a single five-year period.

Technical skills encompass real estate law and all aspects of EIR process and permitting from Desert Conservation Commission, U.S. Army Corps of Engineers, Regional Water Quality Control Board, State Lands Commission, and similar.

## EXPERIENCE

**Southwest Diversified, Inc.,** Phoenix, Arizona, 1992–Present
**Vice President, Planning & Processing**

In charge of planning, entitlement, and processing for projects in Arizona, New Mexico, and California for this major developer with a total of almost 10,000 acres under development. Report to the corporate senior vice president, supervise support staff and consultants.

*Highlights:*

- Highly productive. Have obtained discretionary approvals for 1250 lots in last seven years in politically sensitive areas of California and Arizona. (Southwest Diversified specializes in geologically, environmentally, and politically difficult properties.)

- Northeast Ridge, San Bruno Mountain — As the technical specialist in a three-person processing team, coordinated 21 consultants and represented company through 19 public hearings resulting in vesting tentative map for 578 units on 92 acres in return for 135 acres designated for a Habitat Conservation Program with 10(a) permit under the federal Endangered Species Act of 1973. This is possibly one of the most complicated residential developments in the Bay Area, involving litigation to appellate court level, heavily overlapping federal, state and local jurisdiction, mediation, and multiple property owners and complex options. After 13 years, civil construction began July 1996.

- Rush Creek — Generated neighborhood support for a 390-acre, $60 million project, resulting in an amicus *curiae* lawsuit by neighbors in favor of the development, the first ever in Marin County, California. Dedicated 319 acres to Marin County Open Space District and 53 acres of marshland to California Department of Fish and Game to crystalize community support. Initiated a lawsuit and won a settlement agreement that overturned a 6–0 zoning defeat and reversed a 3–2 Board of Supervisors defeat to win final approval for development of 89 single family homes.

*Continued . . .*

- Marine Lagoon — Won approvals and permits from U.S. Department of Fish and Wildlife, U.S. Army Corps of Engineers, California Department of Fish and Game, Regional Water Quality Control Board, and City of San Diego. Processed 224 for sale units from master plan through vesting tentative map and final subdivision map recordation in ten months without losing a single unit.

- Sandpiper Lagoon — Processed approvals and permits for 134 single family homes located on Steinberger Slough in the master planned community of Redwood Shores. BCDC staff used our landscape plan, plant palette, and public access program as a model for future developments.

- Numerous other projects — details on request.

**Kaufman & Broad of Northern California,** Dublin, California, 1986–1992
**Project Manager**

In charge of off-site construction, subcontractor and technical consultants, and tract superintendents. Developed over 3000 lots from raw land to finished building sites in Contra Costa and Solano Counties.

**Crockett Building Company, Inc.,** Tulsa and Oklahoma City, Oklahoma, 1984–1986
**Project Manager**

Directed all phases from acquisition and processing through construction for subdivisions in the two largest cities in Oklahoma.

**First Service Corporation,** Oklahoma City, Oklahoma, 1983–1985
(a wholly owned subsidiary of a major regional savings and loan)
**Vice President**

Provided planning and processing for thousands of acres of REO bailouts that had been deeded back in lieu of foreclosure during early 80s recession. Planned, processed and sold 25% of the portfolio in just two years. Designed disposition procedures adopted as policy by the company.

## ADDITIONAL

**Planning Assistant, City Planning Department**

**Owner/Developer** (residential — spec and custom)

**Consultant** (planning and processing)

**Community Service** (list on request)

## EDUCATION

**Vanderbilt University,** Nashville, Tennessee

**B.S., Management Science / Business**

# John Cochran

16533 Sky Ranch Road
San Diego, California 92138

Office: (619) 555-6974
Residence: (619) 555-3284

---

## EXPERTISE

- **Creating Property Value**
- **Directing the Entitlement Process**
- **Resolving "Difficult Properties"**

## PROFILE

Expert at moving the real estate entitlement process forward on politically sensitive properties. Strengths include creating community support for major development projects, developing and motivating key political resources, evaluating environmental and market conditions, and orchestrating land acquisition, site preparation, design, preconstruction and construction phases. Strong mixed-use product background encompassing office, retail, light industrial, and housing components.

Special skills include technical expertise with EIRs, traffic analysis, appraisals, inverse condemnation, wetlands problems, toxics assessment, and geotechnical analysis. Significant experience with CALTRANS, redevelopment agencies, U.S. Army Corps of Engineers, Air Quality, Water Quality, State Lands Commission, B.C.D.C., and similar regulatory agencies.

Persuasive in written and oral presentations. Demonstrated talent for complex and difficult projects.

## EXPERIENCE

**Southern Pacific Realty,** San Diego, California, 1991–Present
**Director of Development**

Provide strategic direction to all predevelopment phases for major projects currently totalling 5.2 million square feet of mixed-use product in 3 cities. Supervise a staff of project managers; utilize an additional staff of 15–20 consultants (attorneys, architects, planners, engineers, economists, political advisors). Plan and administrate $2.0 million annual operating budget. Contribute to both the value and the caliber of assets.

Projects:

- *Emery Racetrack Project.* Created plan for 1.5 million square foot mixed-use project on 40-acre parcel overlapping two cities. Negotiated and signed Owner Participation Agreement in a 90-day period. Devised strategy to settle a lawsuit against City of Emeryville necessary to ensure project advance. Generated favorable climate by trading separate 2-acre parcel as new city park. Conducted largest public meeting on a development project in Emeryville history. Initiated EIR process. Established master schedule. Currently negotiating with tenant for 1 million square foot build-to-suit.

- *Sparks Industrial Park*, Sparks, Nevada. Established new contacts in totally new area. Analyzed political, regulatory, market and economic constraints on 300-acre parcel. Hired consultants and created new master plan for property. Secured city council approval for re-zoning into several new land-use categories, allowing immediate sale/development. Doubled current property value from $25 million to $50 million in just six months.

*Continued . . .*

- *Albany Waterfront Project*. Directed conception of 3.7 million square foot mixed-use development project on 142-acre parcel of land. Researched constraints, planned and implemented entitlement strategy. Made over 100 public presentations to community groups up to 300. Created successful constituency development program. Established close working relationship with city staff and council members. Established media relations; published regular community newsletter. Negotiated lease settlement with existing tenant (Golden Gate Fields) to vacate, securing Phase I and Phase II. Created $500,000 information center, project and pre-sales office, currently under construction.
- *Richmond Shoreline Holdings*. Assessed market and political constraints affecting development potential of 5 parcels of land totalling 80 acres. Secured appointment by Mayor of Richmond to the Citizens' Committee to Plan the Richmond Shoreline. Gained favorable land-use designation for several parcels ensuring development potential. Defeated attempts for open-space designation.
- *Berkeley Waterfront*. Processed applications for 4.1 million square feet of mixed use product on 174 acres. Citizens initiated successful open-space zoning. Countered with inverse condemnation suit against City of Berkeley and pursued to U.S. Supreme Court. Supported voter initiative resulting in $40 million appropriation to purchase this property as public lands. Currently negotiating sale.
- Many similar projects and accomplishments.

**Office of Economic Development and Employment**
City of San Diego, San Diego, California, 1983–1991
**Supervisor of Projects Development and Management**

Directed project planning and day-to-day operation of all public commercial and industrial real estate development in the City of San Diego. Supervised staff of 25 (project managers, planners and architects). Responsible for approval process, financing, land acquisition, site preparation, design and construction. Also directed media relations and served as representative to major developers and state and federal regulatory agencies.

Projects:

- Supervised TransPacific Centre Phase I ($70 million), City Center (4 million square feet), Coliseum Business Park (250,000 square feet), 16-structure historic preservation district, San Diego Convention Center (including 500-room Hyatt Regency Hotel).
- Negotiated city position on Foreign Trade Zone project (13 acres), Acorn Shopping Center (50,000 square feet), and Victorian Row Project ($33 million commercial).
- Represented department on city's negotiating team for the Southern Gateway Redevelopment Project, including trips to Hong Kong to negotiate directly with the developer.
- Demonstrated financial and contractual expertise with HUD, EDA, SBA and UDAG.

**Prior:**

**Project Manager,** San Diego Redevelopment Agency

**Architectural Officer,** San Diego Housing Development Division

**EDUCATION**

**Executive Institute for Business, Economics, Management,** 1994
University of Southern California, Los Angeles, California

**Bachelor of Architecture,** *cum laude*, 1973
University of California, Berkeley, California

# RORY DALY

1527 Bartlett Road
Memphis, Tennessee 38134

Office: (901) 555-9226
Residence/message: (901) 555-6424
Cellular: (901) 555-1783

## PROFILE

**Income Property Management**

Specialist in regional management of residential holdings with full P&L responsibility. Expertise includes business planning, budget controls, pro forma studies, cost analysis, and acquisition analysis. Strength: selection, motivation, and skills development of subordinate personnel.

Talent for sales and marketing ventures including strategic conceptualization, client contact, presentation approach, deal structuring, and contract negotiations. Background includes developing corporate leasing business.

History of successful dealings with general and subcontractor groups; have optimized company position in this area based on industry analysis and multilocation property coverage. Reliable in market-sensitive policy making.

## EXPERIENCE

**House of Windsor Property Corporation**, Memphis, Tennessee          1993–Present
**Regional Manager**

Full P&L responsibility for 2500 apartment units in 13 locations, producing over $20 million in annual revenues. Supervise 13 managers and on-site staff, for a total of 75 employees. Prepare all operating budgets with full responsibility for achievement of budget goals. Direct and control the marketing and operational activities for the entire portfolio.

Source and obtain competitive subcontractor and vendor contracts. Authorize capital expenditures, monitor and direct all on-site operational expenses. Hire, train, motivate, and evaluate on-site management personnel; oversee hiring of all nonmanagement personnel. Example: Recently developed a manager to be promoted to assistant regional manager.

Review and approve all operating statements. Meet monthly with site managers to evaluate and direct expenditure of operating funds.

Select advertising media, compose advertising text, plan and manage ad budget, pre-approve all marketing expenses. Example: Selected and monitored a vendor to provide sales training for all leasing personnel, leading to improved sales techniques and results.

Other projects:

- Developed and implemented a corporate housing program in select areas resulting in a stabilization of occupancy and a revenue increase of 15%.

- Developed and implemented quality control standards, including Action Line Program (resident feedback) and Move In Program (thank-you letter, comment card, and opportunity to review customer service performance).

- Developed and implemented a Net Operating Income (NOI) bonus program for on-site management and staff to reward same for exceeding NOI goals.

- Staffed and directed new construction from lease up through stabilization and sale of one property. Directed three other properties through marketing and sales. Directed rehabs of 390-unit property and 590-unit property. Implemented cost-effective trash compactor for 722-unit property. Proposed water conservation program for 590-unit property to achieve 40% reduction in water bill. Negotiated cable television contracts.

- Met monthly with vice president and quarterly with owner and CEO to review operating results and map strategies to meet company's goals. Convene quarterly manager meetings and training seminars to translate senior management objectives into concrete action.

*Consistently maintain expense ratios at 30–35%.*

**Home Sweet Home**, Las Vegas, Nevada     1992
**Consultant**

Designed business plan and marketing approach for this apartment referral start-up. Produced feasibility studies, pro forma, and property surveys. Assembled operations and marketing staff. Acquired permits and licenses.

**Lincoln Property Co., Inc.**, Westlake, California     1991–1992
**Assistant Vice President, Business Development**

Recruited to independently originate company marketing plan and sales strategies. Initiated contact with real estate owners and developers leading to an accumulated base portfolio of 1,000 new units in less than 12 months. Designed presentation package and marketing approach still used by company today.

**Monarch Properties, Inc.**, Newport Beach, California     1989–1991
**Director of Property Management**

Full P&L responsibility for 15 apartment properties producing $25 million in annual revenues. Directed both operations and marketing areas. Prepared budgets and related pro forma analysis; instituted company policy, internal controls, and financial management strategies. Recruited and controlled the business affairs and leasing activities of four regional managers in California and Kansas. Indirectly responsible for the performance of 250 employees.

Sourced and obtained competitive subcontractors and vendor agreements. Directed the rehabilitation of several properties which increased marketability of more than 1,600 units. Increased the rental income by 17% during tenure. Accumulated new management contracts incorporating 2500 units. Devised management incentive programs and sales competitions to boost company edge and occupancy drive. Authored operations manual to establish continuity between regional operations.

Originated corporate housing program; controlled marketing and sales contact with the business community. Acquired accounts with several Fortune 500 clients. Program led to a 10% income increase and a 7% occupancy increase. Hired and trained professional sales staff to absorb responsibility for this area. Assisted CFO in regional audit engagements.

**R&B Enterprises**, Los Angeles, California     1983–1989
**Regional Manager**, promoted from **Property Manager**, promoted from **Leasing Manager**

Managed portfolio of 3000 units located throughout the Greater Los Angeles Area. Units generated in excess of $30 million annually. Administered a site rehabilitation plan among four apartment locations which led to a 12% increase in revenues. Recruited and directed 12 managers responsible for a combined maintenance and administrative staff of 170 employees.

Led company negotiations with vendors and developers in subcontractor agreements. Expanded into on-location specialty services: dry cleaners, salons, and minimarkets. Generated marketing analysis through on-site inspections and "best use" studies.

Provided a specialized business package and established leasing contracts with the United States Olympic Committee and the federal government. Package incorporated more than 400 units and led to a net gain of 17% in less than nine months. Reviewed facility audits performed by professional groups (general contractors, lawyers, designers) to ensure compliance with city codes.

**Topps & Trowsers — The Bank Stores**, Denver, Colorado     1978–1983
**Regional Vice President**

Coordinated six store openings and simultaneously managed 13 additional retail operations throughout a seven-state region. Promoted to California territory. Increased annual sales 20% and reduced shrinkage levels to < 1%.

## EDUCATION

**Graduate Studies, Business**, University of Northern Colorado, Greeley, Colorado     1973–1974

**Bachelor of Arts, Sociology**, Western State College, Gunnison, Colorado     1972

# MARTIN P. BUCKLAND

Box 1E Comp 10
Tulameen BC V0X 2L0
CANADA

Office: (604) 555-3445
Residence/Message: (604) 555-0045
bucky@boma.com

## PROFILE

### Facilities Management / Operations Management / Engineering Management

Engineering management over portfolios of properties, including acquisitions analysis, project management, and all aspects of ongoing operations management. Effective package of skills spanning engineering, estimating/budgeting/finance, business planning, staff selection and development, tenant and public relations, and ability to manage a very large load of diverse, simultaneous, and critical responsibilities.

PC skills: advanced spreadsheet, financial analysis, pro forma, and financial modeling skills. Qualified HW engineer at modular level for both PCs and control systems.

## EXPERIENCE

ENVIRO ENGINEERING, Victoria, British Columbia, 1990–Present
(a subsidiary of Johnson Controls)

**Vice President, Senior District Manager, Engineering**, 1994–Present

Plan and direct engineering services for a portfolio of 16,000,000 sq.ft. of properties, including high-rise office, mixed-use, retail, and light industrial properties. Supervise a total engineering staff of 80, delegating through 2 district managers and 10 chief engineers. Report to the executive vice president, regional manager, in charge of company operations in all Canada west of Quebec.

Direct site engineering for owned and managed properties, both union and nonunion. Prepare engineering reports on acquisitions candidates. Develop budgets, business plans, and detailed action plans to achieve company goals for individual properties. Serve on executive teams, committees, task forces. Travel up to 40%.

Represent company in marketing efforts, attend BOMA conferences and events in Canada and the United States, initiate relationships with owners and managers, conduct building surveys and property reviews, prepare reports for owners and managers, give presentations to managers and investors, negotiate contracts and agreements, maintain contacts for the life of the relationship.

Hire and train engineers and engineering managers. Set employment standards. Ensure training and certification of staff. Set operating policies and procedures. Negotiate union contracts for existing properties and for acquisitions. Review all construction plans for engineering component.

Selected recent projects:

- Conducted acquisitions review for Queensland Galleria and Apartments, approximately 1,500,000 sq.ft. retail, 900 residential units, and 100,000 sq.ft. office building.
- Rewrote all job classifications to comply with employment law in collaboration with employment law firm in Ottawa, including negotiation/renegotiation of union contracts.
- Wrote, produced, and gained acceptance for the company's first Union Employees' Handbook.
- Wrote new Emergency Procedures Program for all properties.
- Wrote new Fire Safety Program for all properties.
- Designed and launched Energy Audit Program resulting in average reduction in utility expenses of 17%, saving $1,262,043 per annum.
- Established Preventive Maintenance Scheduling for all properties.
- Launched Mobile Engineer Program to serve smaller clients; wrote first contracts for this new service.
- Obtained asbestos credential and brought asbestos abatement projects in-house, saving as much as $50,000 per property on outside contractors.

**District Manager,** 1992–1994

Same as above, with responsibility for a 6,000,000 sq.ft. portfolio of properties.

Major contribution:

- Orchestrated company response to the Western Blizzard of 1993. Enlisted company engineers from the Northwestern United States to assist in ensuring fire, safety, and human environmental conditions in owned and managed buildings throughout British Columbia. This involved logistical challenges getting transportation for engineers, crews, and parts when air and road travel were practically impossible.

**Chief Engineer**, 1990–1992

Similar to above, with closer responsibility for an individual property, 615,000 sq.ft., mostly high-rise office.

Sample contribution:

- Reduced energy expenses up to $250,000 per building.

SPARTAN HOSPITAL, Chicago, Illinois, 1986–1989
**Stationary Engineer / Assistant Chief Engineer** (1,750,000 sq.ft., mixed use)

GENERAL ELECTRIC COMPANY, Chicago, Illinois, 1980–1986
**Industrial Electrician**

## EDUCATION & AFFILIATIONS

**Credential — Asbestos Abatement Engineering**
U.C. Berkeley — Extension, Berkeley, California

**E.P.A. Certificate — Asbestos**
U.S. Environmental Protection Agency

**Certified Fire Safety Director — High-rise**
State of California

**HVAC, Electronic Troubleshooting, Control Systems, Remote Sensing**
Holy Pines College, Sacramento, California

**Administration of Justice, Labor Law**
Merritt College, Oakland, California

**Continuing Education**, constantly taking seminars and training classes in the United States and Canada, recent examples:

Employment Law Update, annually
Sales & Marketing, annually
Hazardous Materials Seminar, annually
Bloodborne Pathogens Seminar, 1996
U.S. ADA Compliance, 1995
Indoor Air Quality Seminar, 1994
CFC Seminar, 1994
Water Treatment Seminar, 1993
Safety Seminar, 1992
Air Balance Seminar, 1992
Fire Alarm Maintenance Seminar, 1990
Pneumatic Temperature Control Seminar, 1990
PRIOR — list on request.

**Member, Association of Energy Engineers (AEE)**

**Member, American Society of Heating, Refrigeration, & Air Conditioning Engineers (ASHRAE)**

# GEORGE FENWICK GRUBER

151 West Passaic Street
Rochelle Park, New Jersey 07662

Office: (201) 555-7622
Car: (201) 555-0552
Residence: (201) 555-1466

**PROFILE**

Diversified real estate professional with expertise in commercial and residential development, affordable housing, land development, with emphasis on the entitlement and approval process, financial and political packaging, work-out strategies for distressed properties, feasibility studies, pro forma analysis, and direct sales and marketing of individual properties or whole portfolios. Licensed New Jersey Real Estate Broker.

**EDUCATION**

**Pratt Institute,** New York, New York
**M.S., City Planning (Housing Finance & Development),** 1981

**S.U.N.Y. Purchase College,** Purchase, New York
**B.A., Political Economy,** *with honors,* 1977

**University of London,** London, U.K.
**Urban Policy & Environmental Design,** 1976–1977

**N.Y.U. Real Estate Institute,** New York, New York
**Finance, Development, Investment Analysis,** 1980–1981

**EXPERIENCE**

**George Fenwick Gruber,** Rochelle Park, 1991–Present
**Real Estate Consultant**

Provide political/financial/proposal consulting on low-income housing projects. Provide financial modeling and economic and political feasibility studies of wide range of proposed projects. Strengths include loan blending, creative finance, and development strategy coordination to succeed in declining markets and problematic political climates.

*Sample projects:*

- Packaged and represented 20 low-income housing tax credit applications on behalf of 9 different developers, 1996. All 20 applications were approved as submitted; accruing $40 million in federal and state tax credits.

- Equity Lenders, Walnut Creek, 1993–1995: Formulated a work-out strategy for 87-unit low-income apartment building located in North Sacramento. Analyzed the deal, presented a finance solution with $2.6 MM in Prop. 77 monies, found a buyer, handled complex, multilayered negotiations, gaining write-down concessions from the existing lenders to facilitate the transaction.

- Tom Lam Associates, Oakland, 1995: Conducted feasibility study on 57-unit artists' loft industrial conversion project. Structured the deal as developer's representative.

- Tom Lam Associates, Oakland, 1992: Provided economic and financial feasibility analysis for turning vacant hotel into a low-income senior citizen housing development. Projected serious cash flow difficulties and recommended decline of the project.

- RAF Investments, Berkeley, 1991: Conducted feasibility analysis on proposed 30-lot subdivision in Visalia, including local market survey. Developed multiple scenario work outs for the principals.

- Ace Construction & Development, Oakland, 1991: Formulated complex loan-blending and tax credit financing strategy for 20-unit low-income senior housing project.

**RAF Investments,** Bergen, 1990–1991
**Loan Broker — Investment Property Specialist**

Served as loan packager and underwriter on commercial and residential income developments. Prepared loan documentation, prepared cash flow and pro forma analyses, underwrote loans under FHA, FNMA and Freddie Mac guidelines.

**Burt & Dulay,** Parsippany, 1986–1989
**Site Analyst**

Conducted site selections surveys with all attendant analysis (zoning, market and location analyses, client requirements) for major retailers and fast-food franchisees. Also negotiated with property owners.

**Abeles and Schwartz,** New York, 1985–1986
**Staff Planner (Analyst)**

Prepared zoning studies, development strategy analyses, economic feasibility studies, market evaluations, and input to environmental impact reports for residential and commercial projects.

*Special project:*

- Assigned to prepare the opposition response to the EIR for the 42nd Street Redevelopment Plan, one of the largest in modern New York history.

**St. Nicholas Neighborhood Development Corp.,** New York, 1983–1985
**Project Manager**

Managed pre-construction for 25,000 s.f. neighborhood commercial project. Prepared funding applications from commercial and civic sources, negotiated approval process, supervised consultants (engineers, architects, marketing research).

**South Bronx Development Office,** New York, 1982–1983
**Special Projects Manager**

Served as Team Leader, Team Member, and Team Planner for diverse housing and economic development projects: 150 units new apartments, 25 single family homes, 300 units rehab, 100,000 s.f. Bathgate Industrial Park, Woolworth Building industrial conversion, 100-unit commercial district parking garage.

Managed the public approval and multiagency compliance process, with authority to motivate city bureaucracy and reorder the priorities of city agencies to keep projects on track.

Prepared and packaged financing applications, served on Interagency Project Task Force, drafted memorandums to the mayor, and assisted the White House liaison to the South Bronx.

**REFERENCES**    References provided on request, but please keep this information confidential at this time.

# Wallace Levine, A.I.C.P.

2318 West J Street
Sacramento, California 95817

Office: (916) 555-5687
Residence: (916) 555-8677

---

**INTERESTS**

**Corporate Real Estate Planning**
**Economic Development Analysis**
**Portfolio Management**

**EXPERIENCE**

**Pacific Gas & Electric (PG&E)**    1985–Present
**Senior Planner (Corporate Economic Development Representative)**
1994–Present

Provide industrial siting assistance and economic development consulting to nonPG&E corporate entities in order to obtain plant sitings in PG&E's service territory (Northern and Central California). This service is free of charge to the corporate client, and is provided either directly to the corporate entity or through the corporate client's own local real estate consulting organization.

As part of the PG&E team that developed this innovative program, have cataloged and databased all major industrial development sites in Northern and Central California, established close working relationships with real estate brokers throughout the state, and built ties with local government representatives.

Also collaborated on the marketing and promotion of this service, through direct contacts, through existing real estate and planning organizations, and through presentations at industry and trade shows. Requires frequent travel.

Interface directly with top management of client companies (domestic and international). Evaluate client requirements and match with appropriate sites and communities. Provide confidential introductions to local officials and real estate professionals. Generate project-specific analysis in a confidential and time-sensitive environment. Supervise project specialists as needed.

Sample of clients served directly:
- Birmingham Steel
- Kagome Co. Ltd.
- Centex Cement Enterprises
- Litton Applied Technology
- Market Wholesale
- Fuller-O'Brien Paints
- American Brass & Iron Foundry
- California State Dept. of Commerce
- Advance Remediation Technologies, Inc.
- M.G. Industries

Sample of consulting firms utilizing our services:
- Bechtel Corporation
- Pilko & Associates
- Runzheimer International Inc.
- Reese Wilson & Associates

**Land Use Planner**    1989–1994

Compiled and prepared land development forecasts of residential/commercial/industrial development for specific sub-regional areas in Northern and Central California. These forecasts were incorporated into PG&E's long-range capacity and facilities planning processes. Project team leader over planners, specialists and consultants.

These forecasts included extensive generation of original data and development and cross-checking against secondary and tertiary data. Planned and coordinated research projects involving on-site interviews and inspection of local government documents. Compiled and analyzed data, wrote reports on findings, gave oral presentations to utility management and other planning groups.

Also conducted socio-economic impact analysis of company construction projects and coordinated the legislative review process for PG&E's Land Planning Section.

Sample areas studied:
- Downtown high-rise office development in San Francisco, Oakland, San Jose, and throughout San Mateo County.
- Industrial development in Newark, Fremont, Union City.
- Residential development in specific areas of the Sacramento and San Joaquin Valleys.

**Loaned Economic Development Executive, City of East Palo Alto**     1993–1994

PG&E *pro bono* assignment for the City of East Palo Alto. Performed a community economic-demographic analysis, prepared a state enterprise zone application and a preliminary redevelopment plan. Worked closely with the city's Economic Development Director and the City Manager.

Earned commendation and resolution of appreciation for PG&E from the City Council.

**Planning Analyst**     1987–1989

Represented company to scores of local, state, and federal agencies to obtain land-use and environmental permits related to new construction and maintenance projects for major gas/electric transmission and power generation facilities. Reviewed and ensured regulatory compliance. Trained in state and federal environmental law. Coordinated between authorities and company engineers. Negotiated terms and conditions of permits.

Gave presentations before open and closed public meetings of all kinds. Arranged and led frequent tours and official site visits.

Sample projects:
- Humboldt Bay Power Plant Low-Level Radioactive Waste Storage Facility (permit process to the Nuclear Regulatory Commission level).
- Diablo Canyon Nuclear Power Plant Ocean Intake Structure Reconstruction Project (permit process including California Coastal Commission and NRC).

**Assistant Land Technician**     1985–1987

Produced maps from field survey data; performed title searches and legal documentation research as assigned.

**Curtis & Turk, Inc.**     1984–1985
**Land Surveyor**

**EDUCATION**

**M.B.A., Finance,** *in progress,* Golden Gate University
**Certificate, Land Use & Development Planning,** U.C. Berkeley — Extension
**A.S. (equiv.), Civil Engineering Technology,** City College of San Francisco
**B.A., English,** *with honors,* University of Wisconsin, Madison
**Certificate, Basic Economic Development,** University of Massachusetts, Amherst
**Certificate, Industrial Real Estate I,** Society of Industrial and Office Realtors

**AFFILIATIONS**

American Institute of Certified Planners, Member
American Planning Association, Member
California Association for Local Economic Development, PG&E Representative
National Association of Industrial and Office Parks, PG&E Representative
San Francisco Planning and Urban Research Association, PG&E Representative
Society of Industrial and Office Realtors, PG&E Representative
Industrial Development Research Council, Delegate, 1995 Convention

# WILLIAM H. WATKINS II

c/o 150 Broad Street
New York, New York 10004

Office/direct line: (212) 555-3604
Residence/message: (212) 555-9672
landman1@peabody.com

## PROFILE

Significant business success leading to position as president and chief operating officer of $130 million company. Strengths include creation of a premiere sales organization with concurrent tight control of operations and overhead. Strategic skills include extensive background managing expansions, mergers, and consolidations of operations.

## EXPERIENCE

FERRIS PEABODY

**President,** Northeast Regional Operations, New York        1995–Present

Chief operating officer of one of the largest and most profitable real estate brokerage companies in America, a stand-alone company with 162 offices, 5000 sales associates, 35,000 transactions per annum, $130 million in gross revenues, $18 million in profit in 1995.

Direct residential sales, marketing, training, relocation, personnel and human resources, administrative staff of 65, and 5 house counsel.

- Reorganized company in merger with company-owned operations from Illinois, Missouri, Colorado, and Texas.
- Analyzed fringe districts and found greater profit in selling company-owned operations to franchisees in Detroit, Salt Lake City, and Portland. Negotiated sale of $16 million company (5 offices), $12 million company (7 offices), and $5.5 million company (2 offices). Maintained market presence and increased cash flow to the parent company.
- Shaved $4 million from fixed expenses (from $30 million to $26 million) in 1995.
- Reduced senior management team by almost half with no reduction in efficiency.
- Maintained legal liability budget at less than $1 million (for both settlements and administration) on $130 million in sales.
- Maintained profitability in a challenging and variable market. Increased market share (last three quarters).

**President,** New York        1991–1994

Chief operating officer for the largest and most profitable residential real estate brokerage company in New York State.

- Opened 15 new offices (from 31 offices to 46 offices) with consistent profitability.
- Increased revenues from $32 million to $60 million.

**Senior Vice President** and **Regional Manager,** Syracuse        1989–1991

Part of the management team that structured the new Ferris Peabody subsidiary, involving a merger with Empire State Realty, Inc. Selected to serve as General Sales Manager over the newly created region. Provided training and leadership to a total of 100 sales associates.

- Increased region from 4 sales offices to 8 sales offices, from 100 sales associates to 250 sales associates.
- Created an organization that continues to rank #1 or #2 for market share in the region. Maintained consistent profitability throughout expansion.

**District Manager,** Buffalo        1988–1989

Coordinated merger of operations between Ferris Peabody and Smith, Johnson & Hills, Inc., active throughout New York, Pennsylvania, and Ohio.

*Continued . . .*

## PRIOR

SMITH, JOHNSON & HILLS, INC., HQ: Buffalo
**General Sales Manager**
**Branch Sales Manager** (two branches)
**Sales Manager**
**Associate**

## EDUCATION

CALIFORNIA STATE UNIVERSITY, Sacramento
**Business Administration**

## ORGANIZATIONS

NEW YORK ASSOCIATION OF REALTORS      current
**Director**      1988–1992

NEW YORK CITY BOARD OF REALTORS      current
**Director, Treasurer, Vice President**      1992–1994
**President**      1995

## REFERENCES

References provided on request, but please keep this material confidential at this time.

# Ramon G. Garza

14807 Outer Line Road
Austin, Texas 78766

Day/Night/Home/Office: (800) 555-1203
http://www.arrow.com/future.html

---

## EXPERIENCE

ARROW ELECTRONICS, INC., HQ: Austin, Texas       1990–Present
**Director of Marketing, Corporate**       1993–Present
**Director of Sales, Voice/Data Sales Group**       1995–Present
**Sales Manager Representative, Genie Group**       1991–Present
**General Sales Director, Corporate**       1992–1993
**General Manager, Sales & Distribution, Headquarters Branch**       1990–1992

Part of a complete reexamination and reorganization of this 75-year-old company, creating a key transition from a reactive proprietorship to a proactive, competitive corporation with a clear identity and mission. Arrow Electronics is a supplier of passive electronic components, mainly wire, cable, and connectors, to four key markets, annual sales of approximately $21 million. Revenues currently running 5% ahead of plan.

Central contribution: Orchestrated the operational and cultural transformation of this company from reactive top-down management into an employee-empowered customer-first sales organization with a collaborative management style. Sold the reorganization and new strategies to all levels of management and staff to ensure buy-in and successful evolution.

Strategic and operational contributions:

- Spearheaded efforts to identify the company's four key markets: MRO Broadcast, MRO Voice/Data, MRO General, OEM. Fostered niche market mentality to replace "all things to all people" approach that had suffered market share erosion from all sides.

- Identified voice/data market as high potential. Created first company focus on this market which includes electrical contractors, systems contractors, and end-user accounts. Surveyed market, established new vendor relations, wrote marketing plan and sales strategies, hired expert staff. Currently 17% of total gross revenues for the company — market segment with maximum growth in the last fiscal year. Also co-planned entry into the voice/data market by the Aladin Group, an affiliated national buying co-op.

- Worked closely with existing sales organization to engineer refocus of sales effort companywide from low volume, low potential accounts to high volume, high potential accounts. Introduced time and territory management, account forecasting, and other cost-benefit analyses to the sales force. Increased efforts to work closely with accounts to specify our products.

- Analyzed product flow and existing customer requirements to streamline our product offerings. Reduced vendor relationships from 287 lines to 86 lines, improving supplier relations and focusing the efforts of the company on its strengths. Liaison between customer needs and suppliers, including product development. Direct interface to manufacturers reps, directors of sales, and application engineering departments of supplier companies.

- Participated in reduction-of-overhead projects, including selling one branch and consolidating two others.

- At the department level, standardized operations and established written departmental and interdepartmental procedures. Designed and implemented problem analysis program to create accountability and achieve structural solutions to structural problems. Example of ancillary program: Brought in consultants to provide telephone sales/service/communications training for all levels from warehouse to executive suite.

- Initiated headquarters staff meeting to discuss sales, open quotations, bookings, and shipments comprehensively. Increased collaboration, coordination, and collective purpose.

- At branch level, reduced negative sales trends to achieve increases of 10.3% first full fiscal year, and 11% second year, in a down market. Earned "Best of Arrow" honors twice.

TRANSWORLD CABLING, INC., HQ: Houston, Texas    1988–1990
**General Manager**

Provided strategic direction, long-range planning and oversight of daily operations for this rapidly growing high-tech start-up company. Recruited to provide executive management for the co-founders, a group of technicians with limited business background. Full title: V.P., G.M., Corporate Secretary/Treasurer. Company designs and implements on-site solutions to data/voice cabling and network problems.

Implemented standard business management practices. Clarified areas of responsibility within the company. Created a shift in corporate culture from a technical to a market-driven orientation. Revitalized stalled sales efforts. Implemented customer service as a top priority.

Financial duties included: projected cash flow, provided detailed profit planning, prepared and administered annual budgets, coordinated CPA and in-house bookkeeping. Represented company to bankers, investors, insurance, and regulatory entities.

Accomplishments:

- Increased both margins and gross revenues (tripled corporate revenues).
- Took company from routine sales in the $2500 to $7500 range and built new base of contracts in the $40,000 to $100,000 range.
- Engineered and maintained a 50% growth rate.
- Directed materials planning to reverse upward trend and reduce shelf stock by 33%.
- Increased productivity by 17% over six-month trial period.
- Created and oversaw relationships with major customers such as Nordstrom, Texas Instruments, Hewlett-Packard, Digital Equipment Corporation, various Texas city governments, and many others.

R.M.B. ENTERPRISES, HQ: San Francisco, California    1988
**Consultant**

Negotiated purchase of entire product line from Darome, Inc. Closed an agreement for all engineering, production, administrative and marketing records, open orders, finished goods, work in progress, component inventory, manufacturing/testing facilities, tools and fixtures. Followed through to create new product logo and marketing direction. Sold interest to A.T. Products, Inc., of Harvard, Illinois.

DAROME INC., HQ: Chicago, Illinois    1985–1987
**Regional Manager**, San Francisco

Upon completion of major operational project at HQ, was selected to take over marketing/sales on the West Coast. Prepared annual budget and sales plan. Had just developed business/operational plan for a potential southeastern office when company went through hostile takeover and reorganization.

**Corporate Systems Manager**, Chicago Headquarters

Developed and implemented standards, policies, procedures, and multilevel corporate planning for this corporation offering teleconferencing engineering and services. Had free hand to achieve objectives of President and CEO. Created systems to achieve interdepartmental cooperation and communication for geographically separated offices for engineering, manufacturing, sales, and HQ. Designed training and staff development program. Standardized process for opening new regional offices. Oversaw preparation of manuals, written policies, and other documentation.

Also managed a project to develop and package new products and technologies to pitch to key accounts; e.g., coordinated a $200,000 effort involving engineering, sales, and manufacturing to develop a proposal for a $4 million contract with E.F. Hutton.

**Acting Director of Purchasing**, Harvard (Illinois)

Recruited to design and implement a modern Materials Control Department.

PAN-TECH MARKETING, HQ: Mexico City      1982–1984
**Co-Founder**

Partner in an intensive two-year start up effort to import American electrical/electronic materials into Mexico. Performed product and marketing research, developed business and marketing plan, established government relations, developed one new product through prototype, explored U.S. parts/Mexican assembly opportunities. Obtained and sold U.S. patent on prototype.

SCHULHOF COMPANY, HQ: Woodstock, Illinois      1979–1982
**Assistant Branch Manager**
**Outside Sales Representative**

DAROME, INC., HQ: Harvard, Illinois      1974–1978
**Controller**
**Office Manager**

## EDUCATION

**B.S., Industrial Technology**      1972
Southern Illinois University, Carbondale, Illinois

**Professional Selling Skills PSSIII**      1990

## REFERENCES

References provided on request, but please keep this application confidential at this time.

# DANA BUCHANAN

2737 Pine Court NE
Seattle, Washington 98124

Office: (206) 555-5763
Car: (206) 555-1700
Residence: (206) 555-6713

## PROFILE

M.B.A.-educated financial officer with knowledge and skills encompassing diverse areas: commercial credit analysis and credit-related issues, commercial real estate lending and development, investment banking services for Fortune 500 companies. Additional experience in new business development and high-level customer services. Special expertise: toxic and environmental issues impacting commercial real property credits.

Advanced quantitative skills including financial analysis, pro forma development, design of computer models to analyze business scenarios, all types of spreadsheet analysis. Languages: French and German.

*Highlights:*

- With current employer, ranked #1 in the bank for loan production, 1995. Also restructured all nonconforming loans in a $55 million portfolio (underwrote, restructured, documented, closed) to meet year-end deadline.
- Contributed to successful turnaround of segments of First Bank's domestic commercial loan portfolio through identification of problem loan originators and increased loan standards.
- Successfully presented $13.5 million construction loan to credit committee through improved analysis of borrower cash flow and fundamentals.

## EXPERIENCE

**First Bank**      Seattle, WA
**Vice President**      1994–Present

Manage $55 million commercial real estate loan portfolio, one-third of the bank's total real estate exposure. Renegotiate and restructure troubled loans. Originate, document, and underwrite new credits, with attention to risk management. Analyze credits and assess risk of loans in the portfolio; prepare and present reports to the president, chief credit officer, and the board. Represent the Real Estate Division to federal regulators. Cross-sell all bank services and participate in DDA origination/retention efforts. Supervise loan officer and administrative staff.

*Contributions:*

- Originated $5 million in the first three months in position, generating loan fees in excess of prior year's annual salary.
- Successfully restructured and booked packet of troubled loans to meet year-end deadline, the only account officer to meet the deadline 100%.
- Designed and implemented a more accurate system for computing Allowance for Loan and Lease Losses, achieving a 10% increase in accuracy.
- Member, Loan Policy Task Force, incorporating recent federal regulations and developments in appraisal and environmental issues into the bank's lending policies.
- Designed and implemented system for reporting on criticized assets in the Real Estate Division to the Office of the Comptroller of the Currency, achieving a 75% decrease in time required for report production process, and a 50% increase in efficiency.
- Have been instrumental in retaining long-time customers in a difficult banking environment.

**Bank of America/Security Pacific National Bank**    San Francisco, CA
**Account Officer, Real Estate Industries Group**    1990–1994

In full charge of $70 million loan portfolio, providing credit analysis, monitoring, reporting, and related proposal development. Also had secondary responsibility for a separate $100 million portfolio. Facilitated quick approval of successful and profitable projects, and resolved problem loans by gaining senior management trust with thorough due diligence.

*Contributions:*

- Averted a problem loan by identifying cash flow deficiencies and potential toxic problems with a $15 million loan request from a $100 million relationship top-tier developer.
- Developed a new account earning a 2.45% return on assets, with a small developer who successfully weathered the recent downturn. The loan was repaid as scheduled through intensive strategy of due diligence, credit checks, financial analysis, loan structuring, and review of development plan.

**Bank of America**    Los Angeles, CA
**Credit Examination Officer**    1988–1990

Project leader for two credit examinations of major commercial portfolios, approximately $750 million each. Delegated assignments and controlled a staff of 20. Reviewed examinations on loan-by-loan basis. Developed recommendations to the Examining and Auditing Committee on the inherent risk and rating of each portfolio, and on the performance of bank managers contributing to the portfolios.

*Contributions:*

- Successfully recommended more sophisticated monitoring of loan portfolio concentrations to lessen the bank's susceptibility to industry downturns.
- Due to real estate knowledge, was invited to serve as guest examiner of two major real estate offices involving loans to very large developers.

**Goldman, Sachs & Co.**    Los Angeles, CA
**Administrative Assistant, Investment Banking Services**    1984–1987

Coordinated executive coverage of over two hundred Fortune 500 corporations, including interfacing with clients' top management, outside legal counsel, and regulatory agencies.

## EDUCATION

**University of California**    Los Angeles, CA
**Postgraduate Studies in Real Estate**    1989–1990

**University of Southern California**    Los Angeles, CA
**M.B.A., Finance & Accounting,** *with honors*    1988

**University of California**    Los Angeles, CA
**B.S., Languages,** *cum laude*    1980

## AFFILIATION

Commercial Real Estate Women
  Board of Directors; Director, Special Projects

## ADDITIONAL

No restrictions on business travel. References on request, but please keep this information confidential at this time.

# ANDRA C. BRUBAKER, C.P.A.

3904 Flagstone Terrace
Alexandria, Virginia 22306

Telephone/Message: (703) 555-2710
abrubaker@aol.com

## STRENGTHS

Reducing costs while improving efficiency, designing reports and analyses; improving executive team access to timely financial data; design of data capture and automated reporting systems; technology evolution planning.

## EDUCATION / CREDENTIALS

**M.B.A., Finance,** University of California, Berkeley, 1991
**B.S.B.A., Accounting,** University of Denver, 1979
**C.P.A.,** State of California, 197281
**Adjunct Professor, Accounting,** Golden Gate University, 1995–1996

## HISTORY

STANLEY BROS., INC., Alameda, California, 1990–1996
**Controller** and **Chief Financial Officer** — Managed all financial functions for retail chain with 16 locations and annual sales of $25 million. In charge of budgeting, taxes, fixed asset acquisitions, insurance and banking relationships, credit and data processing. Restructured collection procedures and credit/sales authorization guidelines; achieved 34% decrease in accounts receivable outstanding over 60 days. Developed a computerized monthly gross margin and reporting system to provide timely management information and an expense control system. Developed specifications for updates to financial data processing systems. Managed staff of 24.

CBS SPECIALTY STORES, Roanoke, Virginia, 1988–1990
**Assistant Controller** — Responsible for central accounting functions for a chain of 89 stores. Oversaw payroll, accounts payable, general accounting, sales audit, inventory control, and co-op advertising. Prepared cash flow analysis and forecasts. Performed comprehensive work flow analysis resulting in a 33% reduction in staff and conversion to a cyclical physical inventory system. Consolidated multistate and profit-center reporting with manufacturing facility. Supervised staff of 50.

JOSEPH'S, INC., New York, New York, 1986–1988
**Director of Accounting** — Managed staff of 20 in general accounting, payroll and credit for 50 store retail chain. Utilized sophisticated cash management system and fully interfaced general ledger system. Planned and implemented changes in computerized management reporting systems: designed and converted to an automated gross margin system.

HOOD & STRONG, CPA'S, San Francisco, California, 1981–1986
**Senior Accountant** — Planned audits, performed field work, produced reports, prepared SEC reports and tax returns. Clients included privately held companies, governmental entities, a local bank and various manufacturers.

PRICE WATERHOUSE & CO., CPA'S, San Jose, CA, 1980–1981
**Staff Accountant** — Completed field work in all asset and liability captions of the balance sheet. Performed complex earnings per share calculations, audited payroll-based job-costing system.

# Joseph R. "Butch" Bortocci

98 Pacific Crest Heights
Tiburon, California 94920

Telephone/Message:
(415) 555-2835

---

**EXPERTISE**

Receivables Management — Commercial / Consumer / Industrial

Collections — Collections Management — Credit Management

*Strengths:*
- Entire career history in credit and collections. Outstanding track record for managing receivables. Detailed knowledge of federal credit and collections regulations (Fair Debt Collection Practices) and bankruptcy law. Technical understanding of commercial and consumer credit, credit analysis, receivables analysis, and all related accounting and analysis. Computer skilled. Ability to train and motivate a professional and productive collections team.
- Fluent in Spanish, Italian; proficient in German.

**EDUCATION**

University of Southern California, Los Angeles, California
**M.B.A., Finance,** 1982
**B.B.A., Management,** 1980

**EXPERIENCE**

Golden Gate Recovery, San Francisco, California, 1994–Present
**Recovery Manager — Consumer**

Manage a professional team of up to eight skip tracers and collections representative managing a $6+ million portfolio of nonperforming accounts, *all over nine months delinquent,* the most difficult credits in the company's total accounts receivable portfolio. Report directly to General Manager. Coordinate with field collection staff as needed.

*Contributions:*
- Cited by the General Manager for running "the most productive department in the history of the company" on a cost-revenue basis.
- Oversee and/or conduct national skip tracing. Coach collections staff on defining customer financial situations and credit counseling (restructuring, refinancing, PMA, referral for litigation).
- Manage complex accounts involving all types of third-party payments (reassignment, insurance coverages, entitlement incomes).
- Extensive bankruptcy/reaffirmation experience, including knowledge of legal procedures, documentation, and follow-up.
- Reduced outstandings steadily for each of the last 20 months. Productivity standards in this department are higher than they have ever been before.

Aerofund, Inc., dba All County Collections Bureau, San Jose, California, 1991
**General Manager — Consumer & Commercial**

Recruited to launch this start-up collections agency, primarily receivables referred from the parent company ($200,000 initial portfolio) but also receivables solicited from medical clinics, hospitals, and small independent retailers throughout the Bay Area.

Established operating procedures, wrote scripts and letters, strategized mix of telemarketing, correspondence, and field collections efforts, trained and motivated staff of four professional collections associates.

Also conducted telemarketing campaigns to generate new business for the agency.

First Gibraltar Bank, San Antonio, Texas, 1987–1991
**Assistant Vice President — Consumer**

Hired to launch this retail consumer lending division for First Gibraltar Bank. Managed $360 million portfolio of cars, trucks, boats, and airplanes used for collateral. Directed collection, repossession, refinancing, collateral substitution, loan restructuring, and insurance settlement issues for the bank. Reviewed and analyzed all late accounts. Counseled customers, identified and negotiated solutions to financial difficulties, made asset repossession/liquidation decisions, dealt with repossession contractors and insurance companies nationwide.

Maintained delinquency rate under 1.25%, well in excess of management objectives.

ITT Financial Services Co., San Antonio, Texas, 1986–1987
**Collections & Accounts Manager — Commercial & Consumer**

Managed multimillion-dollar portfolio of consumer and commercial loans, including solicitation, credit analysis, financial analysis, loan origination and documentation, and collections. Telemarketing and field officer for collection, refinancing, restructuring, reassignment, and collateral repossession.

Chemical Express Corp., Dallas, Texas, 1985–1986
**Credit & Collections Manager — Commercial & Industrial**

Managed credit and collections activities up to $80 million per annum for a trucking firm specializing in liquid and dry chemical transport. Supervised staff of four. Investigated credit-worthiness of new accounts, set credit limits, analyzed receivables aging, identified and worked with problem accounts, traveled on-site to resolve billing disputes and negotiate settlements, documented and referred accounts to litigation with outside counsel when necessary.

Datapoint Corporation, San Antonio, Texas, 1980–1985
**Senior Credit Analyst — Commercial**

Managed all receivables, credit and collections issues for accounts comprising a $50 million portfolio. Set lines of credit based on financial analysis of income statements and balance sheets, contributed to companywide Corporate Credit Policy and Procedures, traveled nationwide to negotiate resolution to nonperforming receivables and to perform site inspections for credit analysis. Gained legal understanding of escrow accounts, letters of credit, personal guarantees, corporate guarantees, co-signator instruments, unsecured lines of credit, company/individual net worth analysis, asset collateralization, and similar.

Selected by senior management for participation in developing the General Electric Credit Corporation Vendor Finance Program.

**REFERENCES**        References and recommendations provided on request, *but please keep this information confidential at this time.*

# MARIAN GESSLER, Ph.D.

964 Branch Drive
McLean, Virginia 22102

Telephone: 703/555-5612
worldsup@inside.com

## SYNOPSIS

Nationally recognized as a visionary leader in the field of interior design, Marian Gessler consistently pursues her own design theories, with an emphasis on bringing humanism and aesthetics of comfort into interior space planning and design. Her firm provides commercial, residential, and theoretical/academic design services.

As a specialist in cross-cultural design, Dr. Gessler has aggressively researched and recorded living spaces around the world, emphasizing primitive and native structures, textures, and colors. With intensive travel and study in Alaska, India, Tibet, Nepal, Kashmir, the Philippines, China, Japan, Scandinavia, Mexico, and rural Europe, she brings a fresh eye to a design aesthetic that has become overly cold, linear, and sterile.

Dr. Gessler is an expert on the history and symbology of color and on the balance of color and texture. She has developed a theoretical framework to design artificial space divisions, personal territories, and related psychological divisions through the use of color selection, coordination, and application of color on texture.

Well known to major designers throughout the United States, Dr. Gessler's work is influential far beyond her own practice, clients, writings, and classes.

## HISTORY

### President, The Marian Gessler Collection, Washington, D.C., 1982–Present

After traveling throughout the world to develop and prepare her own design theories emphasizing the introduction of nature-evoking textures and colors into human living, Dr. Gessler designs for a worldwide private clientele. Her creative genius is behind a line of handmade rugs in finer showrooms in New York, Los Angeles, Dallas, Seattle, and Washington, D.C. She is represented internationally by Shyam Ahuja in Paris, London, Frankfurt, Lisbon, Rome, Kuwait, Tokyo, Hong Kong, and Sydney.

### Team Member, Interior Color and Habitability Team, U.S. Space Station, 1992–Present

In collaboration with Dr. Yvonne Clarendon, NASA, Ames Research Center, Dr. Gessler serves on the team designing a humanized and liveable interior for the U.S. Space Station. Her design theories have been adopted into NASA's long-range policy documents for space exploration human habitation environments.

### Adjunct Professor, Interior Design Department, New York University, 1982–Present

"Materials and Sources for Interior Designers," "Decorative Textiles," "Presentation Techniques," "Worldwide Custom Manufacturing," "The Anthropology of Interior Spaces."

### Interior Scout, Consultant, Home Magazine, Los Angeles, California, 1995

"African Influences in Scarsdale," June 1985, "Hale House," July 1985. (Also see publications, below.)

### President, Virtu Design, New York, New York, 1983–1985

Dr. Gessler provided creative direction to this firm renowned for its designs of homes and professional offices. She currently holds the title of Designer Emeritus, and still owns an interest in the firm.

### Designer, Communication Art, Inc., Boulder, Colorado, 1981–1982

As one of the first designers hired by this firm, Marian Gessler provided the theoretical bridge between graphic and environmental arts that is its trademark.

### Designer, Victoria Degette & Associates, Denver and Vale, Colorado, 1979–1981

Working directly with Ms. Degette, then President of ASID and a specialist in social design, Marian Gessler advanced her conceptual design theories.

### Designer, Cooke Construction & Home Design, Los Angeles, California

### Designer, Department Manager, Staff Consultant, FB Design, Boulder, Colorado

## CREDENTIALS

**Professional Member**, American Society of Interior Designers

**Member, Advisory Council**, New York Academy of Arts

**Member**, New York Museum of Modern Art

**Board Member**, U.S. Historic Preservation Society

**Ph.D., Anthropology**
Yale University, New Haven, Connecticut
Dissertation: *Mine/Yours/Ours: One Room into Many: Bantu Boundaries of Color and Texture*

**B.F.A., Studio Art & Art History**
University of Colorado, Boulder, Colorado

**A.S., Studio Art**
Pine Manor Junior College, Chestnut Hill, Massachusetts

**Photography**
Center of the Eye Photography Studio, Aspen, Colorado
(with Leland Rice)

**Art History**, Rome, Italy

**Art History**, Brussels, Belgium

**Art History**, Lausanne, Switzerland

**Art History**, Paris, France

## RECENT PUBLICATIONS

*Art and Antiques*, November 1996
*New York Magazine*, September 1996
*Architectural Digest*, June 1996
*Metropolitan Home*, October 1995
*Los Angeles Magazine*, October 1995
*Interiors Magazine*, May 1995
*Texas Monthly*, December 1994
*Home Magazine*, February 1994
*California Magazine*, November 1993
*Image Magazine, San Francisco Chronicle*, October 1993
*Home Magazine*, February 1993
*Glamour Magazine*, February 1993

Additional publications: full bibliography on request.

## SAMPLE EVENTS & ENGAGEMENTS

**Keynote Speaker**, California Builders Council
**Co-Chair**, Opening Night Committee, AIA National Convention
**Co-Chair**, ASID National Convention
**Professional Liaison**, Southern California, ASID
**Chair**, ASID Career Day
**Lecturer**, California Textiles Market

## REFERENCES

Professional references, media kit, portfolio samples available upon written request.

# Marianne Castille Farrow

590 Fifth Avenue, Penthouse Rear
New York, New York 10036

Residence/Message:
(212) 555-6926

---

## PROFILE

Full P&L responsibility in charge of major stores and multiple stores, aggregate sales up to approximately $30 million. Career emphasis on high levels of customer service, and effective control of operations and expense. Significant expansion and downsizing experience. Exemplary record of consistent performance.

## EXPERIENCE

**PALACE MANAGEMENT CORPORATION**, HQ: Fifth Avenue, Manhattan, 1985–Present
**THE PALACE NEW YORK**
**Executive Director**, 1992–Present

Executive director of The Palace's flagship store, 590 Fifth Avenue, 156 employees storeline, approximately $35 million in annual sales, expense budget (occupancy) approximately $3.5 million per annum, expense budget (payroll) approximately $6.7 million, and 50,000+ s.f. of selling floor. Also collaborate on management of 18,000 s.f. warehousing and distribution center in New Jersey, supporting stores in eight states. Also responsible for the position of group vice president, retail, during his absences.

The Palace offers a unique mix of high-end hard lines, including proprietary lines of fine jewelry; Continental antiques and antiquities; contemporary American art gallery; full-line interior design service and fine home furnishings; tabletop china, crystal, and silver (extensive collection of Baccarat, Lalique, Steuben, Buccellati, Christofle, Puiforcat); fine stationery and related select gift collectibles; gift gallery (European, Traditional, Contemporary, Asian).

*Highlights:*

- Negotiated two union contracts with Retail Clerks Union and Display Workers Union. Also deal daily with Teamsters Union for warehousemen and Teamsters Union for drivers.
- Instituted a quantitative performance review system for floor sales associates resulting in identification and elimination of nonproductive staff and increases in sales of up to 22% in certain long-term employees. Created a profit-center mentality in each sales department.
- Oversaw ten-month remodeling/renovation project to increase store from 35,000 s.f. to 50,000+ s.f. of sales floor. Relocated executive and financial offices to new corporate location. Managed to keep sales space open during entire project, maintaining cash flow and Fifth Avenue identity and presence.
- Assumed responsibility for corporate gifts division (New York, Boston, Beverly Hills, approximately $3.5 million annual sales) and special events department (New York, Boston, approximately 150 events per year). Saved corporate parent two group vice president-level positions, saving well over $200,000 per annum on a pro-rated basis. Continue to oversee bridal registry and personal shopping services with national and international clients. Also, launched a new gift catalog.
- Lecture as often as possible to interested groups on topics related to The Palace's product lines, e.g., antiquities, 165-year history of The Palace, tabletop etiquette and service, weddings and special family events.
- Serve on the Executive Committee. Integral member of the management team that packaged The Palace for sale, successfully completing the sale in 1995 (*New York Times* and *Wall Street Journal*, February 10, 1995). Continue to serve as liaison to the incoming transition team, developing multiple scenario plans and assisting in writing the store's new strategic plan.

*Continued . . .*

*Community Involvement:*
- New York Academy of Science (1996 Academy Ball)
- New York Opera (1995 Opening)
- New York Ballet (1992 and 1993 Opening)
- The Museum of Natural History (Origin of Birds, 1994)

**The Palace New York**
**The Palace Beverly Hills**
**Palace Distribution Center**
**Executive Director**, 1991–1992

During period of transition, was in charge of two major stores and the distribution center, total staff of 214, approximate store sales of $29 million, approximate total distribution responsibility for $60 million in product for four stores. Traveled constantly to manage stores on both coasts.

**The Palace Beverly Hills**
**Executive Director**, 1986–1991

Executive director of store with annual sales of approximately $7.5 million, 35 employees, 12,000 s.f. of selling floor.

*Highlights:*
- Increased sales by almost exactly 50% in less than five years through increased coordination of buying with the needs of our unique clients and through increased community involvement.
- Executed a personal sale of corporate gift program to Citibank worth over $550,000 per annum.
- Collaborated with jewelry buyer to acquire stones and designs for private clientele that brought in over $400,000 per annum in addition to regular jewelry department sales of approximately $2 million.
- Created close relationships with interior designers worth millions of dollars in exclusive sales. Ensured follow through and attention to these sales.
- Opening manager for The Palace Beverly Hills. Hired and trained opening staff, assisted in store layout, merchandise planning, space planning, operations design.

*Community Involvement:*
- Board of Directors, New York Museum of Natural History
  Chairman, Dinosaur Ball; Assistant Chairman, Dinosaur Ball
- Sponsor, Achievement Rewards for College Scientists Ball
- Assistance League of New York, Mannequins Division Fashion Show
- Beverly Hills Chamber of Commerce
  Sponsor, Beverly Hills Diamond Jubilee Celebration
- New York Orphanage Guild
- Celebrity Committee, Hands Across America

**The Palace Miami**
**Executive Director**, 1985–1986
**Assistant Store Manager**, 1981–1985

Opening assistant store manager for The Palace Miami.

*Continued . . .*

**NEIMAN MARCUS**, HQ: Dallas, Texas, 1977–1981

**Neiman Marcus Dallas** (flagship store)
**Assistant Buyer** and **Executive Trainee**, 1980–1981

**Neiman Marcus Houston**
**Director of Men's Division**, 1979–1980
**Department Manager**, 1978–1979
**Merchandise Coordinator** and **Assistant Department Manager**, 1978
**Sales Associate**, 1977–1978

**HARROD'S**, HQ: London, England, 1975–1976
**Sales Associate**

## EDUCATION

Birmingham College, Birmingham, England

**N.N.E.B.** *with honors*, a hotel and business management degree offered in conjunction with the internship program of the Cambridge House, London.

## REFERENCES

References and additional information provided on request, but please keep this information completely confidential at this time.

# Geoffrey Parker

10 Downing Street, 135R
New York, New York 10014

Store line: (212) 555-7319
Residence line: (212) 555-1789

---

## EXPERIENCE

**Brooks Brothers,** Manhattan, 1995–present

### GENERAL MANAGER

Manage high-end retail specialty store, supervising selling staff of 35, nonselling staff of 13, and three assistant managers. In charge of budgets, operating costs, personnel, daily management. Track record of success in key areas: training and motivating a professional staff, controlling operating costs, and designing effective targeted marketing programs.

- Took over the Manhattan store after a period of lackluster performance. Restocked and remerchandised entire store; replaced and/or remotivated sales staff; revitalized local marketing; designed stock control system virtually eliminating shrinkage; took store back to its ranking as the #1 Brooks Brothers store in the nation.
- Came in $1 million over plan in first nine months alone; designed a new public relations posture with Wall Street seminars, product placement on local television, hotel displays, foreign tourist outreach program, and similar promotions.
- Hired and trained women sales associates with sales 38% higher on average than men of comparable experience. Designed sales incentives to improve in-store experience of customers.
- Currently running an average of 30% over prior year for the second year in a row.

Other contributions: Developed a pilot management development program based in the Manhattan store. Selected to troubleshoot underperforming units, with emphasis on training and motivating sales associates and devising local marketing strategies.

**The Broadmoor Stores Company**, New York-New Jersey metropolitan areas, 1988–1995

### STORE SALES MANAGER

Maximized sales and productivity for a department store generating $22.5 million annually. Supervised staff of 15 area sales managers in daily store operations, merchandise presentation, and purchasing. Analyzed and planned staffing, budget, and advertising programs.

- Analyzed and defined customer profile to refine buying, merchandising, and advertising strategies; created 8.5% annual sales increase in a down market.

### OPERATIONS MANAGER

Developed annual budgets and supervised store maintenance and payroll, rotating through four stores in one year.

- Created and implemented inventory and cash shortage controls to take one store from the worst out of 23 stores to the best, with 0.43% loss record.

### RECRUITMENT & TRAINING COORDINATOR

Recruited staff in management, selling, and nonselling areas, serving as human resource specialist for the chain. Trained staff members in customer service and advanced selling skills.

- Designed and implemented successful area sales manager development program.

### AREA SALES MANAGER

Managed multiple selling areas (women's apparel/RTW, men's sportswear, fashion accessories, and home divisions) with responsibility for up to $4 million in annual revenue. Increased sales and productivity by understanding sales trends, analyzing business needs, and emphasizing customer service.

**Aurora Restaurant Corporation**, Landsdown, Rhode Island, 1982–1988

**REGIONAL MANAGER**

Supervised six restaurants, one restaurant/nightclub, a 180-room hotel, and a busy catering/banquet facility in Rhode Island and Massachusetts.

PRIOR

Additional experience in hospitality and tourism businesses where service and tight management control are the keys to success and profitability.

**EDUCATION:**

**Fashion Merchandising**, Long Island College

**Art**, The Pratt Institute

**ADDITIONAL:**

Community activities (extensive; list on request).

Media appearances (extensive; list on request).

Publication: "Male Shoppers: Gender Differences that Matter," chapter 22 in *Retail as a Science*, Houghton Mifflin, pp. 312–325.

Fluent in French and German, basic proficiency in Arabic and Japanese.

# DEBORAH A. SHEEHAN

511 Commonwealth Avenue, No. 2
Boston, Massachusetts 02116

Telephone/Message:
(617) 555-2237

---

**EXPERTISE**

**Apparel Manufacturing**

- **Manufacturing**
- **Product Development**
- **Merchandising**
- **Licensing**

Strong managerial, human relations, and quantitative skills. Greatest strength is achieving that delicate balance between design and manufacturing technique that allows a company to offer unique lines at an attractive pricepoint. Totally career committed. No restrictions on business travel.

Computer skilled: Apparel Pro, AIMS, MAI, Paragon, Excel, Lotus, WordPerfect, and others as needed.

Ready for a new challenge.

**EXPERIENCE**

**CORY CLOTHES, INC.**, Boston, Massachusetts, 1995–1996

**Operations Manager / Acting C.O.O. (on contract)**

Recruited for consulting contract; retained for one year until C.O.O. could be hired to take over my functional responsibilities. Cory Clothes is a 14-year-old company managed by the founder/designer, annual sales of approximately $8 million, 90% wholesale, 10% retail.

Brought on board to design and emplace cash flow and inventory controls. Worked closely with controller to improve management reports, budgeting, and planning. Reduced capital expenses through staged production and inventory liquidation. Provided analysis used to renegotiated agreements with factors.

In charge of six departments: Design, Production, Sampling, Customer Service, Distribution, and Retail. Set company goals and priorities, prepared budgets and operations plans, set design and production calendars, led executive management meetings.

Full responsibility for the business during owner's maternity leave. Excellent recommendation available.

**TOM TOM'S,** Boston, Massachusetts, 1991–1995

Contributed to massive growth in this company, from $2 million to $25 million in core product and $26 million in licensed product sales. Reported directly to owner/president. Held three concurrent positions. Highly productive (was replaced by three managers).

**Director of Licensing**

Created the licensing department, which eventually accounted for $26 million in annual sales for the company. Managed 10 domestic and three international licensees, including merchandising to their individual market needs. Worked closely with legal counsel to develop approval systems and procedures to protect the Tom Tom's trademark and copyrights. Ensured integrity of quality, concept and design. Supervised production manager, design assistant; orchestrated art projects with Graphic Arts Department.

### Director of Product Development

Actualized owner's design concepts with attention to fabric, cost, and fit. Sketched flats; directed assistant designer, patternmaker, sample sewer, sample coordinator; orchestrated art projects with Graphic Arts Department. Approved fits and patterns from muslins through sales samples. Prepared budgets, merchandised core product and international licensed product. Developed a women's loungewear line (licensed). Established calendars, deadlines, and internal control procedures.

### Manufacturing Director

Oversaw all aspects of manufacturing from sales samples through finished goods. Directed production managers, assistant production manager, trim purchaser, driver. Reorganized the department to handle rapid growth. Sourced facilities in England, China, Hong Kong. Improved costing, renegotiated contracts, implemented new computer system, assisted CFO in negotiating through cash flow difficulties.

**TWO WAY**, San Francisco, California, 1989–1991
### Designer / Operations Manager

Designed and developed open-line and couture hats from first patterns through finished product. Researched markets, sourced piece goods, trims, and domestic and offshore factories. Orchestrated gallery showings and fashion shows.

**JAN MICHAELS**, San Francisco, California, 1987–1989
### Assistant Designer and Production Manager

Worked directly with the designer on all collections from first samples through production. Directed production and ensured quality control standards were met. Coordinated and represented at trade shows. Assisted in direct sales.

**RED PEPPERS**, Boston, Massachusetts, 1982–1987
### Buyer / Manager

Buyer, merchandiser, manager, and display director for a specialty retailer with six stores. Oversaw concept, store design and build out, staffing, accounting and operational controls.

**DEBORAH A. SHEEHAN**, Boston, Massachusetts
### Consultant, 1984, 1988

**Chihuahua,** women's sportswear, wholesale with retail outlet. Assisted owner / designer with design and merchandising of all lines. Contributed critical analysis to positioning and identity development. Designed and directed displays and advertising for wholesale and retail divisions. Represented the company at sales shows, generating largest orders in company history.

**Penyelux,** Turkish-produced junior sportswear. Designed and merchandised three collections. Produced flats, specs, storyboards. Approved patterns, samples, and fits. Directed merchandising meetings and provided direction to match market trends.

*PRIOR:*

**Top Sales Associate** and award-winning **Display Artist** for **Casual Corner**.

**EDUCATION**

Bucks County Community College, Newtown, Pennsylvania

**Associate of Arts** in **Illustration/Photography**

# ANDREA WOLFSON

76 Coal Alley
New York, New York, 10021

Residence/message:
(212) 555-6539

---

## PRODUCTION MANAGEMENT / BUSINESS DEVELOPMENT / QUALITY CONTROL MANAGEMENT

---

### PROFILE

Successful developer of business lines/units within large retail organizations. Effective combination of technical expertise, organizational talent, and analytical skills. Have traveled extensively to source and develop new agents, suppliers and manufacturers. Skilled in product development, sundry development, merchandising, and production planning.

**Comprehensive, high-level management skills; ready for a new challenge.**

### EXPERIENCE

SPIRIT    New York, NY
**Director of Production and Sourcing (temporary executive)**    1995

Sourced new agents and maintained existing accounts through the conversion of one apparel line and the phasing out of another. Developed procedures, improved communication flow, and performed cost and time analyses.

Coordinated the sampling and costing of 1996 spring line of Susie Tompkins originals (women's contemporary upper-end garments). Gained expertise in better apparel; coordinated with manufacturers of single-needle-construction garments in France, Italy, Hong Kong, and British Columbia. Successfully closed down this division: found buyers for excess inventory of piece goods and yarns, resolved payment issues with vendors, and gained vendors' support through transition period.

Converted Spirit's Dr. Seuss Division (an exclusive licensee reproducing images of Dr. Seuss characters on children's clothes sold exclusively through J.C. Penney's) to a sweatshirt and t-shirt line. Investigated new production sources and developed a vendor base. Negotiated standards with Penney's labs; raised levels of quality and quality controls in all aspects to Penney's standards. Communicated Penney's product standards to Spirit's production team; maximized sales of remaining inventory.

MARVYNS    Newark, NJ
**Sourcing Manager**    1991–1994

Sourced, investigated, and evaluated new agents and manufacturers for apparel and hard lines. Managed process from initial survey of country to test order for production. Represented new sources of manufacturing to product development teams within Marvyns. Also troubleshot existing company programs as part of overall travel responsibilities.

Conveyed policies, procedures, and specifications to worldwide manufacturers. Investigated and resolved any difficulties with quotas, local government relations, banking, labor markets, infrastructure, transport, etc.

Traveled 30% to Canada, Israel, Turkey, Egypt, Spain, Portugal, Germany, Bangladesh, El Salvador, Dominican Republic, Honduras, Guatemala, Brazil, Philippines, Thailand, Singapore, Hong Kong, Malaysia, Indonesia and the United States.

Identified and developed 75 new supplier relationships, representing $100,000,000 in potential annual contracted relationship, **at an estimated cost savings of 20% over existing/prior suppliers and reduced lead times of 1 to 2 months per cycle**.

**Product Manager**    1990–1991

Sourced, negotiated, and managed programs with domestic manufacturers of knit apparel, approximately $50,000,000 per annum. Presented costings to management, placed production, monitored vendor from order through delivery, including all problem solving and contract modifications.

**Assistant Buyer**      1987–1990

Planned and bought sleepwear. Increased volume from $6,600,000 to $25,000,000. Increased gross margin from 33.2% to 38.7%.

DILLARDS, formerly JOSKES      Phoenix, AZ
**Buyer**      1986–1987

Bought $5,000,000 in sleepwear for 19 stores.

**Buyer**      1985–1986

Bought $4,000,000 in budget junior dresses for 27 stores.

**Buyer**      1984–1985

Bought $2,000,000 in budget and better junior dresses and swimwear for 10 stores.

**Assistant Buyer**      1983–1984

**Area Manager**      1981–1983

## EDUCATION

**Fashion Merchandising**, Long Island College

**History**, East Bruinswick College

**Liberal Arts**, Phoenix Community College

**References and additional information provided on request.**

# ELIZABETH PRATT SAWYER

9023 Haliday Avenue
Los Angeles, California 90047

Residence: (213) 555-6330
http://www.fashion.net/users/rudegirl.html

---

## PROFILE

### Financial Management / Analysis / Planning

Apparel manufacturing financial manager with additional expertise in contract negotiations and operations planning. Strengths include finance problem solving, cash control, and strategies to achieve rapid cash turnaround. Also financial projections, financial analysis, worldwide purchasing, profitability analysis, and liaison with offshore operations.

## EXPERIENCE

**BLUE CALIFORNIA, THE APPAREL GROUP,** Los Angeles, California
*Vice President of Production*, 1995–1996

Directed all phases of financial and contract management, as well as production operations, for Blue California, a $6 million division of The Apparel Group. Negotiated production contracts on a daily basis with manufacturers in the United States and Hong Kong. Head buyer for fabric and sundries. Worked closely with designers to determine marketability of proposed products. Interacted with customs officials to determine quota categories and duty rates. Created detailed costing sheets for individual garments and generated projections for each product produced. Analyzed purchase order information from seasonal New York shows and determined sales line; placed orders with manufacturers in Hong Kong. Managed all production and shipping from placement of cut ticket through delivery to stores; issued cuts, and oversaw quality control. Full responsibility for catalog production requiring unique labeling, packaging, shipping, and invoicing.

*Contributions:*
- Compiled extensive vendor lists for fabrics, sundries, and trims and aggressively negotiated deals with new vendor contacts which decreased materials' costs by $15,000 to $20,000/year.
- Decreased errors in fabrication by 75% by creating garment design forms.
- Set up L/C microtrade system for Hong Kong with B of A. Connected system directly with B of A saving Blue California an average of $15,000/year in interest.
- Established computerized flow system to anticipate fabric needs. Saved approximately 20% per garment by purchasing materials at favorable market conditions.
- Saved over $10,000 in production costs by implementing design request forms which required approval prior to placing order.
- Initiated commercial invoice forms, purchase order forms, care label forms, and sundry forms to clarify ordering process.
- Designed forms to organize packaging and care instructions, extra buttons, thread, or zippers for each individual product.

*Continued . . .*

*Controller, 1994–1995*

Directed all accounting systems and procedures; prepared financial statements, audits, A/P, A/R. Shut down Willis Garment Company; handled buy-out statements involving inventory, A/R, A/P, and company assets.

### *Highlights:*
- Converted all Willis accounting systems into Blue California's systems for organizational transition.
- Promoted to Vice President of Production.

**WILLIS GARMENT COMPANY**, Los Angeles, California
*Vice President / CFO, 1990–1994*

Reported directly to the president of this garment company with $6 to $11 million annual sales. Oversaw design, production, operations, and administrative staff of 25. Controller; treasurer; risk management officer. Handled all banking responsibilities. Prepared and supplied financial information to factors and outside accountancy. Coordinated accounts receivables with Manufacturers Hanover. Assembled OSHA risk control materials and conducted informational meetings to ensure company compliance. Established pension and profit sharing programs and arranged related insurance and tax requirements. Reviewed and approved cost sheets and accounts payable vouchers.

### *Contributions:*
- Saved company $15,000 by successfully handling IRS audit.
- Saved company over $100,000 by rightsizing production and merchandizing staff.
- Created budget analysis plan and negotiated new payback program for line of credit with bank. Set up A/P payment plan with all vendors.
- Implemented cost controls for all company expenses which cut unnecessary expenses by 20%.
- Exposed Hong Kong agent who was tried on 19 counts of fraud in Hong Kong. Interacted with Hong Kong police and courts and personally handled all case-related company information.

*Controller, 1986–1990*

Provided timely and accurate financial data to support the senior management strategic decision-making process. Handled financial reporting, letters of credit, A/P, A/R, general ledger, outside payroll, and purchased all computers, machines, and equipment for company. Interacted with bank and factory on a daily basis.

### *Contributions:*
- Saved company $100,000 by establishing general ledger and accounts payable systems.
- Saved company $50,000 on first turn-around. Assumed invoice preparation duties of two employees, and assisted shipping department on weekends.
- Promoted to Vice President.

*Continued . . .*

*Prior*

**LEVI STRAUSS & CO.**, San Francisco, California
*General Accounting Manager*

Supervised 19 contractor accountants and cost accountants for this $2 billion company. Managed cash disbursements, factory audits, travel accounts and advances, freight, fabric accounts, financial analysis of cost accounts, and divisional asset accounts.

*Financial Systems Project Manager*

Selected and implemented new general ledger system for Levi Strauss & Co.. Brought project in on time and under budget. Hired as full-time general manager.

*Budget Analyst, Financial Analyst*

Handled all budgets for company. Financial analyst for all four Levi Strauss divisions. Chosen to head financial reporting project team to create new general ledger system.

## EDUCATION

LOS ANGELES CITY COLLEGE, Los Angeles, California
**A.A., Accounting**

# ARDEN TERRELL, CAE

45 East 45th Street
New York, New York 10021

Office: (212) 555-6318
Residence: (212) 555-7411

---

## HISTORY

**Senior association executive** with track record of success.

*Strengths:*

- Establishing and implementing overall vision and organizational strategy to guarantee both the health of the organization and service to members.
- Creating innovative revenue streams based on services for members and customers, and lessening dependence on dues and fundraising efforts.
- Increasing organizational efficiency, streamlining procedures and improving controls.
- Recruiting and building effective teams; bringing together and motivating talented individuals (volunteers, staff, members, vendors) to accomplish organizational objectives.
- Providing positive, highly visible organizational presence.

## PROFESSIONAL HISTORY

**National Association of Real Estate Professionals** (NAREP), New York, New York
**President and Executive Director**, 1991–Present
**Senior Vice President**, 1990–1991

Ranking executive for this professional association with $4.5 million budget and 16,000 members nationally; report directly to the board; supervise senior vice president, vice president, marketing director, information services manager, foundation manager. Provide vision and direction to membership development, information services, leadership development activities, awards programs, and the NAREP Foundation. Serve as the key media and public spokesperson for NAREP.

*Major contributions:*

Reengineered planning, marketing, and budgeting functions, integrating them into all levels of NAREP's membership and program functions. Spearheaded automation projects, including updating platform/infrastructure. Created 15% staff cut with concurrent increase in productivity.

Directed a $280,000 study as a member service and to be used as a foundation for all future association planning: "Excellence in Real Estate: People, Technology, Finance."

*Also:*

- Initiated processes and organized team that redefined NAREP's mission/vision.
- **Instrumental in NAREP's $1+ million financial turnaround**, from a deficit of $700,000, to reserves in excess of $300,000.
- Increased membership from 9,000 to 16,000, despite raising member dues and a real-estate recession of over five years.
- Created comprehensive membership recruitment and retention system, as well as a database with more than 60,000 prospective and actual members.
- Achieved highest retention rate (85%) in NAREP history, 1994–1995.
- Established Canadian branch office; increased Canadian membership by 600% in three-year period.
- Established nonvoting "Associate" corporate and individual memberships, creating a new revenue stream and pool of potential new venture partners.
- Designed the organization's response to criticism re the lack of diversity in the ranks, including a media response kit and a minority recruitment kit.
- More than quadrupled information services revenues, from $45,000 to $195,000.
- Tripled Foundation funding revenue by soliciting for-fee research projects.

**International Association of Hospital Administrators** (IAHA), Washington, D.C.
**Vice President, Chapter & District Relations**, 1987–1990
**Director, Chapter & District Relations**, 1983–1987

Managed IAHA's relationships with 115 chapters in 11 districts/regions internationally. Coordinated and supported volunteer recruitment and retention programs.

*Sample contributions:*
• Quadrupled revenue of annual international awards program.
• Increased membership approximately 80%.
• Established a formal leadership development program and an auxiliary credential system.

**Blanket Industries, Ltd.**, Syracuse, New York
**Communications Manager**, 1980–1983

Established and managed employee communication programs, including a bilingual newsletter, for holding company with real estate management, nursing home, legal support services, construction, maintenance, and employment agency subsidiaries (3200 total employees). Provided advice and counseling to subsidiaries on public relations issues and challenges. Assisted with media planning and customer relations policies for eight interlocking corporations. Reported directly to the holding company president and indirectly to the vice president of operations.

Promoted from **Information Coordinator**, 1978–1980, preparing media kits, writing promotional materials, and coordinating advertising campaigns.

## CONSULTING PROJECTS

**American Association of Medical Transcriptionists**

**National Academy of Water Sanitation Specialists — Credentialing Committee**

## PROFESSIONAL MEMBERSHIPS/VOLUNTEER LEADERSHIP

**Greater New York Society of Association Executives**
**Chair, Nominating Committee**, 1993–1995
**Member, Board of Directors**, 1993–1995
*Association Executive of the Year*, 1993
**Chair, Scholarship and Awards Committee**, 1992–1993
**President**, 1991–1992
**Secretary/Treasurer**, 1989–1990
**Chair, Executive Education Committee**, 1988–1989
**Chair, Awards Committee**, 1987–1988

**American Society of Association Executives**
**Chair, Eastern Regional Advisory Committee**, designate, 1997–1998
**Council Member, International Section**, 1996–1998
**Council Member, Membership/Marketing Section**, 1986–1990

**Eastern Conference of Association Executives**
**Chair, Executive Council**, 1991–1992

**Joint Allied Societies of Association Executives**
**Chair**, 1992

**East Side Building Owners Association**
**Steering Committee, Founding Member**, 1985
**Chair, Nominating Committee**, 1987–1988
**Member, Board of Directors/Membership Chair**, 1986–1987

## PRESENTATIONS/SELECTED SPEAKING ENGAGEMENTS

American Society of Association Executives

Association of New Jersey School Administrators

Rutgers University — Communications Week

New York-New Jersey Association of Life Underwriters

Texas Cattlemen's Association

Metropolitan Funeral Directors Association

New Jersey Nurses Association

New York Pharmacists Association

Canadian Cooperative Credit Society

American Productivity and Quality Center

American Association of Medical Transcriptionists

International League of Electrical Associations

Coro Foundation

Professional Insurance Agents of New York and New Jersey

Columbia University

The Eye-Bank for Sight Restoration, Inc.

SUNY, Binghamton

## CERTIFICATIONS

**American Society of Association Executives**
**Certified Association Executive**, 1988

## EDUCATION

**University of Southern California**, Los Angeles, California
**Master of Arts**, Communications, 1978

**Southern Methodist University**, Dallas, Texas
**Bachelor of Arts,** English, 1976

# Kenomweh Miwatu (Ms.)

51089 Rolling Hills Drive
Dallas, Texas 75230
(214) 555-8078

---

**EXPERTISE**

**Operations / Administration / General Management**

- Experienced COO with fiscal responsibility for budgets over $45 million.
- Full administrative management experience, including planning, budgeting, human resources, facilities management, operations, public relations, and publications.
- Proven team builder and catalyst, effectively revitalizing workplace procedures and repositioning business strategies to maximize goals.
- Extensive experience in highly visible and political roles.

**EDUCATION**

**HARVARD LAW SCHOOL**, Cambridge, Massachusetts
**J.D.**
*Member, State Bar of New York, admitted 1974*
*Member, State Bar of Texas, admitted 1974*

**UNIVERSITY OF TEXAS,** Austin, Texas
**M.A.,** Sociology
**B.A.,** Social Sciences

**EXPERIENCE**

**STATE BAR OF TEXAS**, Dallas, Texas      1993–present
**Deputy Executive Director (Chief Operating Officer)**

Chief Operating Officer to this 70,000 member association with 350 employees and four office locations. Fiscal responsibility for general fund budget of $35 million, with an additional $10 million special fund budget.

Lead all activities of senior executive team in all areas of operations, including communications, public relations, human resources, policy management, facilities, security, disaster planning, and document management.

*Selected accomplishments:*
- Directed the development and production of new official member publication (distribution of 85,000), *Texas Bar Journal.* Defined editorial content. Recruited project team. Wrote budget and leveraged negotiations with major vendors. Oversaw research and design of advertising campaign strategy. Publication revenues of $165,000 projected for FY 1996.
- Managed the office of human resources for two years through a reorganization. Designed clear policies and procedures. Later recruited a senior executive to direct the office.
- Spearheaded the design, writing, and implementation of a revitalized and highly visible affirmative action function. Pioneered family work initiatives. Won monitoring groups' praise for effectiveness.
- Improved communications among management and staff involving direct and indirect methods (e.g., blind suggestion channels). Led meetings with management, program groups, committees, and employees. Sponsor of new employee activities. Founder and editor of employee newsletter.
- Member of management's labor negotiations team.
- Directly responsible for outreach activities and management's responses to operational audits.

**MAYOR'S OFFICE, CITY OF AUSTIN**, Austin, Texas      1989–1993
**Chief of Staff** (General Manager)

Managed all aspects of office administration. Established priorities and direction to staff. Developed and managed annual budgets. Prepared written reports, press releases, correspondence, statements, and speeches. Coordinated programs.

Made recommendations and coordinated appointments to boards, commissions, and committees. Assisted in policy development. Liaison with city attorney, city manager, numerous agencies, community and business groups and leaders, and the general public. Represented the office to the press and at events. Highest ranking manager in the office, reporting directly to the mayor.

**GARBON & BECKMAN**, Houston, Texas      1987–1989
**Managing Attorney**

Managed the start-up of this branch office of a Denver-based firm specializing in energy and utility law. Recruited, trained, and motivated 15 attorneys and support staff. Set policies and procedures. Personal emphasis: municipal law and state/local regulations impacting energy exploration and production.

**CITY ATTORNEY'S OFFICE, CITY OF AUSTIN**, Austin, Texas      1982–1987
**Director of Litigation / Assistant City Attorney**

Directed all of the City of Austin's litigation. Supervised a staff of trial attorneys and coordinated outside counsel. Litigation issues consisted of tort defense as well as workers compensation, land use issues, administrative hearings, and wrongful death actions involving the police department. Advised City Council on potential settlement and posture on cases.

Implemented automated programs for case management. Developed computerized pleadings and a pleading bank. These automated functions greatly improved office's efficiency.

Additionally managed a personal case load of major liability tort defense cases, including wrongful death cases in state and federal courts and Civil Service Board hearings on employee actions.

**AUSTIN PUBLIC SCHOOLS**, Austin, Texas      1981–1982
**Legal Advisor,** Austin Public Schools

Directed legal department of the school district. Served as general counsel on all legal issues, as well as pending and current litigation. Hired outside counsel. Managed administrative hearings and appeals. Advised the board, superintendent, administrators, principals, and teachers on a daily basis.

**LAW OFFICES OF KENOMWEH MIWATU**, Austin, Texas      1976–1981
**Attorney-at-Law**

Managed active private practice.

**RECOGNITIONS/**
**AWARDS**

National Bar Association, National Convention Honoree, 1994

Woman of the Year, Texas Black Leaders Council, 1992

Who's Who of Professional and Business Women

American Biographical Institute

Who's Who Among Black Americans

Frequent keynote speaker, panelist, and honorary chairperson at numerous conferences, events, and university functions.

**APPOINTMENTS/**
**AFFILIATIONS**

Chair, Board of Directors, The Unity Council, 1993–1995

Chair, Board of Directors, Austin Convention Center, 1990–1993

Member, American Bar Association, 1986–present

Member, National Bar Association, 1990–present

Nominating Committee, National Association of Bar Executives, 1995–present

Member, National Association of Bar Executives, 1993–present

Founder and first President, 1981–1983, Ex-Officio Member of the Board, 1983–1984, Secretary 1984–1985, Texas Women of the Law

Member, Lawyers Club of Austin, 1992–Present

Citizens' Review Board, City of Austin (one of the first police review boards of its kind in the country), 1982

Executive Committee, Holy Names College Business Symposium, 1986–1988

Advisory Board, Texas Black Chambers of Commerce, 1989–1991

Also: UNCF Advisory Board, Centro Legal de la Raza, Aztlan Cultural, United Way of Texas, State Bar of Texas Committee on Legal Training, Celebrate Austin Committee, Texas Rangers Serving Texans, Narcotics Education League, and National Historically Black Colleges Foundation.

Bar Grader, State Bar of Texas, 1980

# RICHARD BAXTER WAINRIGHT

16 Mount Blanc Circle
Highland Park, Illinois 60035

Office direct line: (847) 555-1212
Residence/message: (847) 555-3453

**PROFILE**

Senior financial and general management officer with wide-ranging skills: portfolio management, financial statements, financial analysis, design of procedures, accounting management, asset management, risk analysis, taxation, finance.

Greatest strengths: (1) deal evaluation, structuring, funding (2) contributing to profitable business endeavors through analysis and counsel to top operating management, (3) ensuring tight financial controls, (4) designing controls and procedures to handle rapid growth.

Experience in fast-paced and rapidly changing endeavors. Comfortable with major responsibility in a complex business environment.

**EDUCATION**

**M.B.A.,** Cornell University, Ithaca, New York

**B.S.**, Management, Georgetown University, Washington, D.C.

**EXPERIENCE**

Wainwright Consulting, Chicago, Illinois
**Financial Consultant**, 1996–present

Provide financial analysis, valuation studies, pro formas, and recommendations to investors and real estate companies.

*Sample projects:*

- Provided investment modeling and consulting on strategic issues for proposed 1200-unit residential subdivision.
- Consolidated and refinanced three commercial properties, $28 million, including packaging and lender relations through closing.
- Reconciled construction budget and advised principle on negotiating strategies to resolve outstanding issues with general contractor.

Chicago Mercantile Bank, Chicago, Illinois
**Vice President, Credit Risk Management Group**, 1994–1996

Determined current credit risk and future loss exposure of the bank's commercial real estate portfolio, a $10 billion portfolio. Individual deals typically ranged from $5 million to $50 million, and included construction loans, OREO, mortgages, mortgage revenue bonds, residential subdivisions, and derivative products such as interest rate swaps. Also served as **Chief Monitoring Officer** for mortgage warehousing unit, which was under the umbrella of the commercial real estate group.

Traveled up to 26 weeks/year to investigate deals. Responsible for reporting on the quality of individual deals, identifying trends and influencing commercial real estate policy based on research. Supervised staff of seven on a special project.

Conducted on-site examinations. Analyzed partnership and corporate financial statements, operating statements, cash flow forecasts. Evaluated management team, regional/national economic trends, local government and regulatory environments impacting credits. Researched FASB and GAAP as needed to verify quality of financial information.

*Continued . . .*

*Sample contributions:*

- Analyzed, identified, and proposed action plans to correct deficiencies in the bank's $10 billion commercial real estate portfolio.
- Evaluated over 100 deals in one year.
- Developed the procedures for risk evaluation in residential mortgage warehousing, a little understood unit in the bank.
- Brought in to design and conduct a special assessment of residential mortgage warehousing unit after market went sour in 1994. In spite of well publicized industry trends, credit quality improved and no losses were recorded while I was serving as the monitoring officer.

Trower, Kiesel & Co., Inc., Chicago, Illinois
**Vice President**, 1991–1994

Member, executive team, for this entrepreneurial independent commercial mortgage banker, founded 1981, 15 employees, $2 billion servicing portfolio. Key contributor during period of rapid growth (see below), involving enhancements in technology utilization, and strengthening of service offerings. As vice president, had primary responsibility for asset management, as well as some restructurings and new loan production. Designed and oversaw reporting to institutional investors (Teachers Insurance and Annuity Association, CIGNA Investments, Inc., Allstate Insurance, etc.).

*Sample contributions:*

- Supervised integration of Allstate portfolio ($100 million) and Latimer & Buck portfolio ($25 million), including all systems, servicing, and reporting aspects.
- Set up all systems for asset management, monitoring restructured loans.
- Developed accounting and management procedures for expansion into construction loan administration which enabled the firm to place $200 million in new construction loans.
- Restructured deals totalling $100 million.
- Team leader for creation of an investor-specific portfolio risk profile. Involved annual review and analysis of operating statements, reconciliation to pro forma, cash flow projections, and physical property inspections.
- Added $50,000 first-year annual revenues through 10 properties under management.
- Directed TI buildouts for investor controlled assets.
- Consulted with investors and borrowers on a continuing basis.

**Manager, Loan Servicing and Closing**, 1989–1991
Department manager duties concurrent with the above, staff of four.

*Continued . . .*

*Sample contributions:*

- Supervised acquisition and integration CIGNA portfolio ($300 million), including all systems, servicing, and reporting aspects.
- Initiated and implemented a fully computerized loan servicing system to facilitate rapid growth (servicing portfolio grew from $300 million to more than $2 billion). Worked directly with programmers on proprietary application development.
- Established standard procedures for monthly investor accounting.
- Negotiated cash management services.
- Prepared the company's internal financial reports for management decision-making.
- Hired and trained new company officers and administrators.

**Chief Closing Officer**, 1986–1994

Continued to have Chief Closing Officer responsibilities for entire tenure described above.

*Selected contributions:*

- Closed over 100 commercial real estate transactions, representing the placement of $1.8 billion for institutional investors, including joint ventures, participating loans, construction loans, leasehold mortgages and credit enhancements.
- Researched and selected office automation and communications equipment acting as the administrative officer for the company.

*also*

Five years experience in title insurance industry.
Five years as sole proprietor of retail business.

# KHALID N. KHORGIAN, PH.D.

| *U.S.A. / permanent address:* | *U.K. address:* | *Swiss family address:* |
|---|---|---|
| 800 Pacific Heights Avenue | "The Cedar" | "Chalet Lisabeth" |
| Penthouse | 16 Copse Hill | Champ de Moulin |
| Laguna Beach, California 92651 | London SW20 ONL | 1296 Charmey |
| U.S.A. | England, U.K. | Switzerland |
| (714) 555-1381 | 44.81.568.6385 or 44.81.568.5816 | 41.29.75820 |

## PROFESSIONAL HISTORY

**Vice President and Manager, Credit and Marketing**     1993–present

Al Arabian Bank, Offshore Unit, Manama, Bahrain, based through London Office, U.K.

Direct and administer commercial lending and marketing activities (exact monetary figures proprietary, but quite large, typically in the hundreds of millions of dollars U.S.), working directly with private and semi-governmental entities in the Middle East, Pakistan, South Korea, Hong Kong, Taiwan, Singapore. Member, Loan Committee, reviewing commercial and industrial loan requests. Evaluate financial analysis; set credit policies and strategies; identify strategic problems within the bank's structure. Monitor exposure; set lending limits; assess and report on portfolio performance; review asset pricing and vulnerability to credit loss.

- Expanded loan portfolio by 35% with concurrent increase in performance (return and reliability).
- Averted potential credit losses despite financial cutbacks at the bank and two large-volume bankruptcies by customers.

**Associate Economist**     1989–1992

Citibank World Headquarters, Economics Policy Research Department

Advised senior management and clients of economic shifts and their implications. Researched and analyzed world economic environment and macroeconomic changes and their effect on international capital markets and banking. Prepared country risk studies/analysis and balance-of-payments forecasts. Developed computerized country risk-rating system (with auto updating methodologies) to assess exposure and lending limits on a country-by-country basis. Met with U.S. federal examiners periodically to present bank's position.

- Persuaded management to reduce exposure and lending limits to certain countries in Latin America and Middle East. Experience of other institutions proved prudence of these policies.

**Assistant Economist**     1988–1989

Citibank World Headquarters, Economics Policy Research Department

Advised senior management and made recommendations on country exposure and investment opportunities. Analyzed the economies and forecasted balance-of-payment posture of countries in Asia, Africa, and Middle East. Forecasted foreign exchange and interest rate fluctuation and effect on external finance position of 35 countries. Established country risk ratings and lending limits on a country-by-country basis.

**Associate Mathematician**     Summer 1988

Credit Lyonnais, London, U.K.

Assistant to the Senior Analyst, world currencies markets, on project to develop new analytical methodologies with better predictive capacities.

**Research Assistant**     Spring 1988

Prof. M. B. Lehrbach, Economics, Wharton School of Business, University of Pennsylvania

Researched contemporary European industrial policy for a book-length scholarly work under development (later released as *The Impossible Dream: The Historical, Political, and Monetary Obstacles to a Unified European Industrial Policy*, Oxford University Press, 1991).

**Management Intern**      1986–1987
Emirates Petroleum Products Company, Dubai, United Arab Emirates

Rotated through refining, marketing, personnel, retail, and finance departments.

**Intern**      Summer 1985
Association of Civil Engineers, London, U.K.

Public relations intern, providing daily reports of press coverage and managing a public relations campaign promoting civil engineering as a career.

**Secretary General of the Model Arab League**      Spring 1984, 1985
National Council on U.S.-Arab Relations, Washington, D.C.

Recruited 17 universities to participate in model Arab League; coordinated the event hosted jointly by National Council on U.S.-Arab Relations and Georgetown University, 250+ student and faculty guests. Participated as **Delegate** in Spring 1984; elected Secretary General by 1984 participating faculty.

## EDUCATION

**Banking Education Program,** Wharton School of Business, University of Pennsylvania      1989

**Econometrics**, Wharton School of Business, University of Pennsylvania      1988

**Econometrics**, London School of Economics, London, U.K.      1985

**Ph.D., Economics**, University of California at Los Angeles      1982–1986, 1987

Dissertation: *European Industrial Policy and Arbitrary EMUs: Problems with Modeling* (May 12, 1991)

**B.A., Economics-Mathematics**, Reed College, Portland, Oregon      1982

Thesis: *The Function and Activities of 'Save the Children': An Economist's Model* (May 2, 1982)

**Economics**, City University, London, U.K.      1980–1981

**Baccalaureate**, The Hobson School, Briarcliff, U.K.      1977

## PUBLICATIONS

"Islamic Law and International Banking: Why European Banks Win and American Banks Fail," in *Journal of International Finance*, October 1993

"Brazil: The Negative Effects of FDI," in *Banking Journal* (U.K.), September 1993

"War Brings Death Throes to Ailing OPEC Unity" (jointly published with Michael B. Lehrbach, Ph.D.), *Wall Street Journal*, September 21, 1992

"Evolution of Economics after John Maynard Keynes," op-ed, *New York Times*, June 10, 1991

Doctoral dissertation: see above.

Undergraduate thesis: see above.

## ADDITIONAL

Languages: English, American English, Arabic, German (fluent); French (conversational). Dual citizen, U.S.A. and U.K. Currently valid U.S. and British passports. Qualified for assignment throughout U.S. and E.C. Please keep this information confidential.

# MAX MILLAN

Office direct line: (908) 555-6200
2418 Diamond Circle
North Brunswick, New Jersey 19716

Residence/message: (908) 555-5234
Private fax: (908) 555-5235

## PROFILE

Top performer with twenty years of progressively responsible experience leading to executive responsibility over administration, operations, accounting, finance, sales, and strategic planning.

*Areas of expertise:*

- Sales, marketing, new business development, key account relations.
- Fixed and variable expense control, corporate cash management.
- Inventory control and distribution systems.
- Management and sales team building.
- Market-driven product development.
- Operations troubleshooting.
- Merchandising.

Entrepreneurial by nature. Background includes success in turnaround management, business expansion, and new business launch.

## EXPERIENCE

National Lock, Briarton, New York, 1994–1997
**General Manager / C.O.O.**

Selected by the Chairman of the Board of Waterman Industries to turn around negative trends at National Lock, a recently acquired subsidiary. National Lock was a $17 million company with 85 employees. The company had an excellent reputation for quality, but had failed to adjust to the exit of the founder and changing market conditions.

*Contributions:*

- Reversed dramatic sales and gross margin slide in an industry experiencing 30% sales losses overall. Increased gross sales to $20 million per annum in a down-trending market. Improved morale and remotivated key staff.
- Increased gross margins from 24.8% to 30.1%, decreased operating expenses from 24% to 19%, increased after-tax profits from 3.2% to 4.8%.
- Opened three branch operations nationally; developed the plans for five more.
- Created electronic lock development program to position company to regain competitive advantage over other old-line lock manufacturers.
- Developed annual budgets and long-range strategic plans to bring company under control and keep it on track.

*Continued . . .*

Sara Knight's, New York, New York, 1989–1994
**V.P., Senior Merchandise Manager — Hardlines**

Total purchasing, merchandising, and gross profit responsibilities for hardlines in a 50-store chain of discount department stores. Area of responsibility comprised $75 million in sales, approximately 30% of the total volume of the chain.

*Contributions:*

- Recruited to turn around a troubled department. Exceeded all objectives; made it into a highly productive and smoothly coordinated operation with high morale.
- Converted three departments from private label to national brand and private brand. Developed resources and programs in the Orient, Europe, India, including product and package design.
- Improved and standardized business planning. Prepared one-, three-, and five-year budgets.

The Cambridge Associates, San Francisco, California, 1986–1989
**General Manager / Sales Manager**

Founded this project management and consulting company to design, sell, and distribute general merchandise programs to food and drug store chains, and to advise manufacturers and distributors on packaging and selling programs to chain buyers.

*Contributions:*

- Represented Aloe Creme Labs in introducing a skin care and suntan lotion program to the West Coast via Whitelock Distributors, a $3 million relationship. Also opened Long's Drugs to a direct buying relationship with Aloe Labs.
- Designed and placed a Royal Tools program with Long's Drugs, opening a critical relationship for Royal Tools and generating first-year sales of $1,400,000.
- Achieved acceptance of a test program for Qualco Basic in four Food 4 Less stores in Oregon, with potential for full-chain rollout.

Montgomery Ward, Miami, Florida, 1983–1986
**Merchandise Manager — Hardware, Paint, Home Improvement**

Managed merchandising, advertising, co-op programs, pricing, sales, item and program selection.

*PRIOR:*

**Buyer, Hardware & Automotive**, Zeeman's Corp., Framingham, Massachusetts

**Group Operations Manager**, Topps Discount Stores, New York, New York

**Manager**, Robert Hall, New York, New York

## EDUCATION

**B.S., Marketing & Economics**, Long Island University, New York

## REFERENCES

References provided on request, but please keep this information confidential at this time.

# David O. Gallagher II

185 Pacific Ocean Avenue
San Francisco, California 94109

Private line: (415) 555-6570
E-mail: dogmanfun@aol.com

## STRENGTHS

**Sales & Customer Service Training • Sales Consulting**

**Financial Research & Analysis • Industry Analysis • Strategic Consulting**

## CONSULTING

**Gallagher & Associates, Consultants**, 1994–Present
**Principal**

Sales and motivational trainer in retail and wholesale sales environments. Specialist in consultative and relationship selling in inside/outside sales environments.

*Excellent references:*

- FanSport — importers/distributors/manufacturers of sporting equipment, a $6 million entrepreneurial company. Designed sales program, developed training program, reduced cost-of-sales. Created retailer support program to lock in preseason orders and ensure sell-through of product. Reviewed trade show sales program. Provide ongoing strategic consulting on sales and product lines to senior management. (1994–present)

- In The Running — small retail chain of specialty and high-end sports equipment and clothing, a mature company seeking a second growth phase. Collaborated on competitive analysis and plans to revitalize sales. Designed commission incentive program. Reviewed operations and merchandising. Delivered motivational sales clinics; taught sales reps to build relationships and create repeat customers. Reduced cost-of-sales. (1994–present)

- Nouvo Pasta Arts — fresh pasta manufacturer, direct wholesaler to restaurants. Provided financial consulting on equity/debt financing options and business analysis related to retail/wholesale/diversification growth options. (1995)

- Sailaway — retail and catalog sporting equipment sales organization, a $3 million entrepreneurial company. Provide ongoing strategic consulting and sales training and motivational clinics. On retainer. (1995–present)

## ENTREPRENEURIAL

**Sailaway, Inc.**, 1990–1995
**C.E.O. / C.O.O. / Director of Sales**

Officer of start-up sporting equipment company, with responsibility for sales and strategic planning, staffing, finance, franchising, real estate, and administration.

*Highlights:*

- Took company from one store with $280,000 annual sales to two company-owned stores, five franchise stores, two windsurfing/sailing schools, national catalog sales, and related warehousing/distribution/ administration infrastructure, sales of $3.5 million.

*Key contributions:*

- Designed inventory control system that allowed tight control of inventory-related capital expenses and provided prompt SKU sales analysis for prudent buying.

- Personally shopped all competition and markets to maintain optimum up-and-coming products in a very trendy, image-conscious market.

- Analyzed sporting equipment retailing industry in Europe to glean new strategies.

- Designed and launched franchise program, including legal, financial, franchise sales, and franchisee training/support aspects.

- Designed and launched catalog and mail-order business. Built 80,000 mailing list of watersports enthusiasts. Achieved mail-order response as high as 9%.
- Designed/opened/merchandised/moved numerous retail stores, including large urban locations and smaller specialty stores in destination resorts.
- Designed and managed boat show sales program.
- Negotiated collaborative ventures with resorts in Southampton, Nantucket, Aruba, and Puerto Rico.
- Negotiated contracts with suppliers in Milford (Conn.), Los Angeles, Santa Barbara, Maui, Elmsford (New York), Hood River (Ore.), Stevenson (Wash.), Seattle, Boston.
- Strategized and created capital infusion to finance rapid growth of the company, including presentations to private investors and commercial credit officers. Also represented the company in credit relationships with suppliers. Won $350,000 LOC from banks, $600,000 LOC from suppliers, and $305,000 real property mortgages.
- Negotiated sale of business to outside investor, retained as consultant (see listing above).

## PRIOR

**First Boston Corporation**
**Fixed-Income and Equities Departments**

**Not To Worry**
**Charter Captain**

**Windsurfing International**
**Television Series, Windsurfing Instructor**

**Offshore Sailing School**
**Director, Windsurfing Department**
**Sailing Instructor**

**Sail New Haven**
**Manager**

## EDUCATION

**Columbia University**
Architectural History, School of Architecture

**Oberlin College**
**Bachelor of Arts**

Major: Economics
Minors: Art History, East Asian Studies

# Geri Bond

65 West 56th Street
New York, New York 10019

Private telephone:
(212) 555-7832

## INTEREST

To explore opportunities with a major dance company that would utilize my multifaceted experience in business and my dance background to ultimately further the goals of the company.

*Strengths:*
- Highly effective combination of sales, financial, and organizational skills. Full profit-and-loss responsibility for a service business — marketing and promotions, client relations, design of operating procedures, accounting and control, budgeting and cash flow management, staff hiring and motivation, logistics and details, and high quality delivery of a service product.
- Proven performer. Entrepreneurial by nature.

## BUSINESS EXPERIENCE

**Top Tier Travel, Ltd.**     New York, New York
**President**     1993–Present

Designed and launched this corporate travel agency serving the needs of corporate clients in specific industry sectors:

- Advertising
- Fashion
- Politics/Foreign Governments
- Investment Banking
- Securities Industry
- Real Estate

Established relationships with key accounts, focusing on our understanding of their travel needs and our role as specialist travel consultants. Created and zealously protected our reputation for accuracy, extreme thoroughness, and flexibility.

Also hired, trained and motivated staff, designed office, accounting and administrative procedures, oversaw computer systems, and otherwise managed small business.

- Customized travel programs for each client, with extreme attention to details and individual preferences.
- Acted as a travel consultant, working directly with client company officers (CFOs/COOs). Reorganized client travel policies to reduce their travel costs and increase efficiency.
- Negotiated bulk rate contracts with domestic and international airlines and resold to our client base. Also negotiated preferred rates with hotel and car rentals.
- Developed sales and marketing strategies that capitalized on our strengths.

Just completed sale of this company to a national competitor as the first unit of their planned entry into the high-end market. Currently serving as consultant to the acquiring company's management team. Ready for a new challenge.

**Top Drawer Relocation**     New York, New York
**Sales Manager**     1992–1993
**Senior Account Executive**     1990–1992
**Account Executive**     1989–1990

Relocated Fortune 500 senior-level management (and their families) into the New York metro area. Hired, trained, and motivated a sales team qualified to interact with top corporate officers and high-net-worth individuals. Prepared relocation plans, with budget projections, time line, and detailed integration into local schools and communities. Negotiated lease agreements with landlords and property owners. Devised new business development campaigns. Ensured satisfaction of each and every client.

- Part of the original team that established Top Drawer as the premiere residential real estate company specializing in relocating wealthy families and top corporate clients to New York.
- Developed a cost-savings plan achieving 50% reduction in costs for clients relocating to New York on short-term basis.
- Contributed to strategic planning for the company.

## MODELING EXPERIENCE

**Foster-Fell Modeling Agency**     New York, New York
**Fashion Model**

**Perry Ellis**
- One of two women selected for House and Fit modeling.
- Runway model.

**Goldin-Feldman Furs**
- Fashion show model.

## DANCE EXPERIENCE

**Chicago Dance Ensemble**     Chicago, Illinois
**Member**
- Director: Loryce Vegh

**San Francisco Ballet**     San Francisco, California
**Member**
**Student**
- Director: Marlia Houlton

## EDUCATION

**Dominican College**     San Rafael, California
**Dance** (minor in **English**)
- *Dean's Honors*

## PROFESSIONAL LICENSE

**Registered Real Estate Broker** current
State of New York

# Rhetta D'Amato

Office: (707) 555-0808
6001 Connolly Lane
Napa, California 94558

Car: (707) 555-1608
Residence / Message: (707) 555-1343

---

## STRENGTHS:

### Staff & Administrative Management / Customer & Client Relations / Marketing

Effective combination of analytical, interpersonal, organizational, and communication skills. Track record of strong contributions in different environments. Solid command of technical business skills: accounting management, financial analysis, business writing, business planning, work flow control.

Dedicated, energetic, ready for new challenges.

## EXPERIENCE:

**George S. Kalibare,** dba
**Wine World Imports,** San Francisco and Napa, California      1994–Present
**General Manager**

Recruited by the owners to revitalize marketing and reorganize administrative controls for this retail wine store with one central store/warehouse location, mail order business, and outlet in San Francisco, $2,987,000 combined annual sales, sales/stock staff of 25, office staff of five. Store's target market is the sophisticated wine buyer (retail) and smaller restaurants seeking European labels (wholesale); most sales are by the case. Full P&L responsibility for operations, capital and operating budgets, staffing, marketing, policies and procedures. Report directly to the owners.

- Reorganized and redesigned office and administrative systems. Created job descriptions, personnel policies, and operations manual. Converted accounting and inventory systems to computer. Reviewed and renegotiated insurance coverages. Eliminated two positions. Reduced expenses by 20%.
- Audited all prior records, identifying and recovering $28,000 in uncollected A/R, cataloging $21,000 in missing fixed assets, and discovering $82,000 in shrinkage. Brought all company records in line with actuality.
- Designed inventory accounting system, cash control procedures, A/R aging and collections system, and stock control procedures to minimize these types of losses.
- Added onto rental cellar, creating potential for $60,000 increased annual revenues, already 75% occupied.
- Discovered that 65% of total business came from the 6000 households on the store's mailing list. Redesigned the newsletter from an "informational" letter into a "direct response" piece, creating a 18% increase in sales.

Reorganization is now complete, with all new systems up and running smoothly.

**Spirit of the West,** Salt Lake City, Utah      1993–1994
**Leasing Manager**

Leased, tracked, and managed 1218 properties in 32 states, primarily small retail and office-retail strip malls. Negotiated leases and subleases with large and small tenants. Negotiated agreements with local leasing agents, maintenance, and contracting firms. Oversaw A/P, A/R, and analysis for properties with complex interlocking corporate and partnership ownership and expense/profit-sharing agreements. Supervised Accounting Manager and office staff of six.

- Revised and streamlined procedures; designed spreadsheets to computerize journal entries; identified and researched unusual expenses to recapture dollars from property owners.

*Continued . . .*

**Nan Taylor,** Los Angeles, California       1991–1993
**Store Manager**

Trained and motivated sales associates. Prepared sales plans and analyzed store performance *in detail.* Coordinated community fashion shows. Taught in the company's management training program. Selected for opening team of two new stores.

- Achieved fastest rise from Associate to Manager in Western Region history.

**Whispering Pines Coffee Shop,** Flagstaff, Arizona       Summers, 1988–1990
**General Manager/Lessee**

For three straight summers, entrusted with full P&L responsibility over a small coffee shop in a resort area, staff up to six. Expanded the menu, improved service and image.

- Prepared business plan and won concession in open bidding.
- Increased profits by 60% over prior best records.

**EDUCATION:**

**B.A., Economics**       1991

University of California, Los Angeles
- Concentration in **Management Science**
- Minor in **Psychology**

# Headhunter Résumés, Business, Principal, and Company Profiles

Narrative, third-person presentations like the ones in this chapter are usually written by some third party—a headhunter, a public relations firm, the better résumé-writing firms, or the public affairs or marketing department within a company. They show up in all types of business proposals and plans, press releases and media kits, commercial loan applications, and even some annual reports; they also commonly play a part in senior executive placements. When written about a company as a whole, they are called a company résumé, a company profile, or a corporate résumé. When written about an individual, they are called a narrative profile or, incorrectly, a vita.

Consultants can make good use of this style, using all kinds of accolades about their company (even if they are the whole company) that would seem inappropriate on a regular résumé. Although not as flashy as a company brochure, they can be as effective, are vastly cheaper to produce, and can be changed for every proposed engagement.

Some high-end headhunters favor this style, packaging all their finalists for a placement in a format like this. For a candidate to submit this style on her own in a job-search setting can appear awkward, as the presumed third-party sponsor is lacking. However, to be fair, this style is not that uncommon among executives with the highest salaries.

This is a versatile style, as often written in chronological order as in reverse chronological order, and quite broad in what it can contain. It is also worth mentioning again that this style is capable of omitting or glossing over the most inconvenient data without drawing attention to that fact.

As mentioned in chapter 1, this style is difficult to write well, especially about oneself. Part story and part information, bragging yet at the same time understated, it can be a challenge. On the other hand, once you have a presentation like this, you will find that the occasion to use it will come up often, especially if you deal with the media or the public at all.

Note that the first example below is the narrative version of a résumé from chapter 1 (many executives prefer to have both; cf. p. 11). Also compare these profiles with the resume from the last chapter starting on p. 216, which is written in third-person but is not in a narrative format. Finally, be sure to notice the extensive project addenda following the example starting on p. 259. If you decide to prepare one of these for yourself or your company, check the index for résumés in other chapters, in addition to the examples presented here, that may have language you can modify.

Cf. the "vita" style presentation for the same person, p. 11.

# C. PARKER CLEMMONS

## PROFILE

C. Parker Clemmons is chairman of **Wilson & Woodward**, a management consulting firm founded in 1958. Wilson & Woodward is a charter member of ACME, the Association of Management Consulting Firms, and provides counsel to industrial and financial companies in marketing, technology, and new business development. Clients have included American Brands, Dow Corning Corp., EG&G, General Foods, Johnson Controls, TRW, Union Carbide, Hewlett-Packard, and similar. Wilson & Woodward management consulting services can smooth entry into new markets and revitalize stagnant growth.

In addition to consulting on ongoing and proposed business ventures, Wilson & Woodward provides policy-level economic research and analysis to companies and governments. Wilson & Woodward has undertaken research and policy study projects on behalf of major Arab Gulf and European companies, and the U.S. government has sought Mr. Clemmons's assistance in formulating its Middle East policy. Currently, Mr. Clemmons is president of the Northeastern Chapter of the National Association of Business Economists. He is known for pioneering economic research methodologies to solve long-range planning problems, such as long-term forecasts of economic growth and power consumption used by capital equipment suppliers to the power generation industry.

Some of Mr. Clemmons's other activities include development of innovative financial products, such as an international automated market system allowing foreign firms to invest and trade in U.S. certificates of deposit, and short-term cash investment instruments used by Arab investors to comply with the sharia, the code of Islamic law which bans interest on loans. Mr. Clemmons has served as director and interim senior corporate executive for public and private companies, and has held elective office in local government.

As a firm, Wilson & Woodward oversees the development and commercialization of technology applications for financial companies, including systems for banks, pension funds, and other institutional investors. The firm brings technology purveyors and clients together, advises R&D firms on commercialization of new technologies, and shepherds the development process as a third-party advisor and project overseer. W&W advises companies in general on currency hedging, investments, new markets, strategic acquisitions, operations, and management structures.

Prior to his association with Wilson & Woodward, Mr. Clemmons was president of Reed Securities, the management consulting branch of **Montrose Securities**, a New York-based investment banking firm. He was involved in investment banking with Montrose and with **White Weld & Co.**, providing such services as underwriting, bridge financing, and design of new investment instruments and products. Montrose Securities provided counsel to foreign national governments on access to U.S. technology and capital markets, and this sparked Mr. Clemmons's interest in multinational business-government ventures.

Mr. Clemmons launched his career with **Douglas Aircraft**'s corporate-planning department, and with the **U.S. Department of Commerce**'s International Investment Office. Mr. Clemmons holds a graduate business degree from **Harvard University** and an undergraduate degree from **Dartmouth College**. Mr. Clemmons has close and ongoing relations with the current Harvard Business School faculty, and is a well known speaker, seminar presenter, and a frequently quoted authority in the business press.

With a background of representation of the most sensitive types of projects, Mr. Clemmons has the contacts and the experience to meet any corporation or government's financial and management consulting goals.

Asher Associates, updated 2/96

# W. Biswell "Mac" McCall

58 Santa Clarita Court
West Hollywood, California 90069

Telephone:
(213) 555-3109

## PROFILE

Mac McCall is a veteran of 54 years of factory and R&D experience within the aerospace and airplane component manufacturing industries. For 31 years he was a Director of Quality Control, in charge of up to 300 engineering and technical personnel. He is a contemporary of Jack Northrop, Clifford Garrett, and Walker Brownlee, revolutionaries in the field of aeronautics. He was a part of the start-up team for Garrett's Airesearch Manufacturing Company, now a part of Allied Signal. He has been a participant in several start-ups, contributing to troubleshooting both mechanical designs and manufacturing processes.

As a lifetime avocation, Mr. McCall has devoted himself to studying pure rotary devices. He holds three U.S. patents and five foreign patents for rotary positive displacement devices. His lifetime of applied, "factory-floor," and R&D engineering experience have allowed him to combine disciplines without prejudice or conceptual limitation. The result is a series of three unique rotary designs with potential applications as very high output engines or pumps.

Mr. McCall's genius is the conceptual development of rotary devices, with emphasis on revolutionary geometric designs that require an absolute minimum of moving parts. With the advent of modern materials and numerical control machines, these designs overcome the loss of efficiency and durability that have plagued other rotary designs.

Having retired from his quality control career, Mac McCall is now seeking association with a larger organization that may be able to develop full commercialization of his designs. Interested parties will find a clear and concise presentation of truly innovative rotary designs.

## SKINNY BOY

( Skinny Boy ) is the brainchild of design team Carlino Vernace and Michelle "Angel" Vernace. She's a costume designer from Club Med, he's an award-winning clothing designer from New York and Milan. Their company became a volume shipper from almost the moment it came into existence in 1993. Currently it ships four collections a year to the majors, including Nordstrom, Saks, Bloomingdale's, Macy's, as well as numerous specialty stores. A recently introduced men's collection is gaining rapid recognition with the same retailers. Skinny Boy has earned its national reputation with quality, price, timely delivery, and consistent newness.

In just three years the company has grown to over 170 accounts across the United States and Europe. Ai-Lin Huang is the West Coast representative, and East Lines is the showroom in New York. Carlino Vernace has managed to cement a close marriage between the New York and L.A. representatives, and Angel works with individual retailers as needed. Skinny Boy manufactures in the Los Angeles area, close to home, where Carlino and Angel can keep a tight rein on the quality and scheduling.

Carlino and Angel Vernace have been called "the rising stars of LA-based fashion designers." In just three years, they've been feted by the major trade magazines covering West Coast apparel manufacturing. Their designs have won feature photo and editorial coverage in California Apparel News, CA Market, and L.A. Style. Their full-page ads can be seen in fashion publications nationwide.

Skinny Boy is producing an outstanding collection of contemporary better women's sportswear. One of the trademark features of the line is the use of leather and the innovative mix of materials. This is the result of Carlino's design background in leather and Angel's costume design experience. The line appeals to a wide range of customers. Because of the fashion forward shapes and sophisticated use of fabrics, the look is more for lifestyle than age-related dressing. The unusual design, moderate pricing, and all-around versatility make the collection a hit in both bridge and contemporary departments. Both the men's and the women's lines have earned a reputation for consistent sell-through.

Skilled merchandising and design talent have worked together to make it possible for Skinny Boy to become a very solid better-sportswear company in just three years. Skinny Boy is a name to remember. Phenomenal growth from a small company like this can only mean one thing: Watch for more from this hot new label!

899 SAN JUAN SUITE 101
LOS ANGELES
CALIFORNIA 90014
(213) 555-4622

**SKINNY BOY**

# SKINNY BOY

## Carlino Vernace

Carlino Vernace grew up in the milieu of New York City. Although he was drawn to New York's fashion industry, he decided to pursue a career in medicine. After two years of success in pre-medical studies at York College in New York City, Carlino realized that his vitality and creativity could never be fulfilled in such an institutionalized career, so he followed his design interests to Brooks College in California.

There he earned the associate degree in fashion design in 1989. During his last year he studied volume manufacturing and served as an apprentice to Michelle Laurent, a Los Angeles manufacturer. He was selected top of his class by the design department and earned the prestigious Fashion Explosion Award. Carlino went immediately to his first position as assistant designer at Johnathan's, the largest apparel manufacturer on the West Coast.

At Johnathan's, Carlino was quickly promoted to designer and placed in charge of the Naturals collection, a $60 million subdivision. He directed a staff of nine. He stylized the line, developed costing, ordered sample yardage, and oversaw sample production. Here Carlino Vernace demonstrated a true talent for production pattern making; he solved fabric and yardage problems resulting in huge savings for the company. Trilingual in English, -French, and Italian, Carlino was able to serve as interpreter to facilitate difficult import agreements for European fabrics. In this large design and manufacturing environment, Carlino demonstrated the initiative and expertise that would ensure his success as CEO of a rapidly growing apparel manufacturer.

During this time, Carlino began to feel the need to create his own company. With his wife Angel as a collaborator in both life and design, he started Skinny Boy in 1993. The result is one of the most up-and-coming apparel manufacturers in Los Angeles. Through design talent and attention to business detail, Skinny Boy has grown exponentially every year. In addition to the four collections of contemporary better women's sportswear that Carlino and Angel design together, Carlino produces two collections of

men's wear yearly. Carlino has a hands-on approach; he continues to design his own production patterns; he personally selects fabrics in Italy, New York, and Los Angeles; he even sews his men's line samples through a Los Angeles tailor. Carlino negotiates and coordinates CMT through 10 local contractors, with close attention at every step to producing a quality and timely product.

Carlino and Skinny Boy have earned a reputation for strong distribution. Due to fast sell-through in both men's and women's lines, Carlino has had to develop and maintain systems for quick response in the areas of manufacturing and distribution. Every area of the business bears Carlino Vernace's distinctive stamp of strong creativity and management. Carlino Vernace has demonstrated that he knows both the design and business ends of the fashion industry.

899 SAN JUAN SUITE 101
LOS ANGELES
CALIFORNIA 90014
(213) 555-4622

**SKINNY BOY**

Principal's profile, a
useful media and venture
partner handout.

## SKINNY BOY

## Michelle "Angel" Vernace

Angel Vernace earned an associate degree in fashion design in 1989 from Brooks College in Long Beach, California. Her studies included the design and the operations side of the apparel industry. While at Brooks she earned two awards for her innovative designs, including the "Reflections" first-place bridal design award.

Angel served her apprenticeship with Teddi's of California, a major women's wear manufacturer based in Los Angeles. There she learned volume production and sample room management.

After completing her apprenticeship, Angel Vernace decided to explore the business side of the industry. She served as a sales representative for the West Coast division of Avalon International. In this capacity she traveled constantly between New York and West Coast markets. She developed the strong sales and account relations skills which she uses today to manage accounts for her current company, Skinny Boy.

After Avalon, Angel was assistant designer for Le Entourage for one year, in which capacity she oversaw development of production patterns and samples for a better women's sportswear collection.

In the interest of expanding her horizons, Angel decided to accept an offer of a position with Club Med to design costumes for their elaborate musical and stage shows. This was a liberating experience for Angel, as it allowed her a great deal of design freedom. She was costume designer for three installations, including a complete redo of Club Med's showcase club at Paradise Island, Nassau, Bahamas.

As costumier, Angel designed and oversaw production of elaborate costuming for Las Vegas-style reviews, for French cabarets, for Mardi Gras, and for productions of popular Broadway shows. She shopped for fabric and trim in Miami and Nassau, designed a large volume of costumes under deadline, and to a lesser degree, assisted with stage, lighting and set design. At the same time, Angel continued to create award-winning bridalwear, influenced by the designs of the 18th and 19th centuries.

With her husband, Carlino, Angel Vernace started Skinny Boy in 1993. As a design partner for the women's wear collections, her creative influence is felt in every piece. Her critical role in the business, however, is merchandising and marketing. As such, she is a major influence on the strategic success of the company. Angel designs ad campaigns, serves as key liaison to representatives, oversees trade shows, and is the company liaison to major accounts. Her strength is responding to the needs of representatives and buyers. She does extensive pre-line work with key accounts, and is known to go to great lengths to do specialty work and design modifications to meet a client's needs. This type of service has gained the trust of her accounts, and along with solid sell-through, has contributed to the rapid growth of Skinny Boy.

899 SAN JUAN SUITE 101
LOS ANGELES
CALIFORNIA 90014
(213) 555-4622

**SKINNY BOY**

Another corporate résumé, with management profiles as addenda.

# Corporate Resume

Modern Mythology is a Hollywood success story. This television commercial production company, started in 1990 by the convergence of three entertainment veterans, skyrocketed to prominence by providing top talent at the best price. Technically impeccable and creatively fresh, the company's rate of repeat business is the envy of the industry. Agencies and advertisers alike are drawn to its mix of proven performers and its commitment to developing bright new directors. The company has enjoyed that most powerful of ingredients: the right mix of people.

The result has been the kind of phenomenal growth that is only possible when a dynamic creative team is matched to outstanding management. The company beat all its own projections to turn a profit in the first year. Annual growth since then has been as high as 340%. Revenues last year exceeded $20 million, which is very respectable for a company with only 17 employees.

Modern Mythology has produced national-release commercials for every major agency on behalf of such clients as:

- American Airlines
- AT&T
- Black & Decker
- Burger King
- Chevrolet
- Citicorp
- Coke
- Coors
- Eastern Airlines
- Eastern/Continental
- Ford
- Jordache Jeans
- Kodak
- Miller Genuine
- Mountain Dew
- Nestle's
- Pepsi
- 7-11
- Sony
- Toyota
- Visa Gold
- *and many, many others.*

Already an award-winning commercial production company with offices in Hollywood, Chicago and New York, Modern Mythology recently formed a motion picture division, Modern Mythology Films, to capitalize on its exceptional talent pool. Modern Mythology Films expects to draw from the background of its commercial directors and to build the same kind of magnetic team that has exemplified its commercial productions.

**Executive Team**

Modern Mythology is headed up by Gibbons, Gould, and Strike. **Jim Gibbons** broke into commercial directing in Hong Kong, after he gained a strong editing and postproduction background. After a stint with Dragon Films in the early 80s, Gibbons put together a reel that was so compelling that he jumped straight into stateside commercial production. After directing many big-budget projects for The Film Group of Los Angeles, he became one-third of Modern Mythology in 1990.

Gibbons attributes a great deal of his directorial skill to his background as an editor. "I think it's wonderful to go on a set and know how it's all going to cut together," he says. "It gives you a lot of confidence." Gibbons won a Mobius for his Chevrolet commercial "Heartbeat of America" with Aretha Franklin.

**John Gould** is Gibbons's line producer and a behind-the-scenes administrator for Modern Mythology. Gould also worked for The Film Group, where he budgeted and produced commercials. He is a former UPM/AD and worked as such on the 1990 movie *Wrongful Discharge,* with Melanie Griffith and Tippi Hedren. He was line producer for the "Heartbeat of America" campaign mentioned above.

**Harley Strike** began his professional career as an auditor with the CPA firm of Arthur Young and Company. He quickly decided to apply his talents in the entertainment field, enlisting with Wakeford-Orloff for six years. He produced commercials and worked on two features, *Executive Action* and *The Brothers Karamazov.* Strike joined The Film Group as executive producer in 1981, and in the following ten years he produced hundreds of national-release commercials. In 1988 he took a one-year sabbatical to produce *Flashpoint* starring Kris Kristopherson and Treat Williams. Harley Strike provides Modern Mythology with a solid fiscal perspective that is essential for success in any creative, but highly competitive, environment.

**Marc Derkatsch** is president of Modern Mythology's new motion picture division, Modern Mythology Films. Derkatsch began his career at 23 years of age as a production executive for Paramount Pictures, overseeing the development and production of motion pictures, including the phenomenally successful *Ducks over Manhattan.* He went on to produce numerous award-winning television productions including ABC TV's 1989 *A Streetcar Named Desire,* which won several Emmys. Derkatsch later became vice president of Motion Pictures and Television for Taft/Barish Productions, which produced such well-known pictures as *Sophie's Choice, 9½ Weeks,* and *Big Trouble in Little China,* among others. Most recently, Derkatsch executive produced *Summer School,* directed by Carl Reiner for Paramount Pictures.

Other key business executives include **Robin Devlin**, executive producer, **Harrison Balz**, executive producer of Modern Mythology's New York office, and **Jack Antigos**, the company's Chicago representative.

### Additional Talent

Modern Mythology has a large stable of directors and associated talent, including **Colin Powers**. Powers directed Michael Jackson's comeback video "Street Criminal." He won an Academy Award for Best Special Effects Director for his work on *Superman VI: The Final Ending.* He directed the first episode of *War of the Worlds* and directed the first two episodes of *Superboy.* His background is particularly strong in special effects, and his reel features spots for *Newsday,* Chevrolet, Zest, 7-11 and Toshiba.

**Peter Hart** became part of the Modern Mythology team two years ago and brought with him seven years of directing experience including a successful tenure with Capital Records and advertising agencies Young & Rubicon and Lintas. A veteran of music video production, Hart has contributed his creative savvy to performing artists, Man in Power, directing the band's "Some Like It" video. Hart was also awarded a Clio for his work on Toshiba's "Movie Star" commercial.

Modern Mythology prides itself on finding and launching new talent. Two of these are **Scott Hains** and **Daniel Milsont**. Hains, a director/cameraman, shot his first commercial footage at five years of age (his father is Warren Hains of skiing fame, who shot over 375 skiing movies over a 36-year period). He went around the world as director of photography for Jean Claude Killy's TV series, *The Killy Challenge.* After earning a nomination for an Oscar for a student film, he worked on several mainstream and cult features: *A Change of Seasons, Hollyweird, Talking Walls, Lords of Flatbush,* and others. Hains signed with Modern Mythology and immediately distinguished himself as a hot property, directing spots for Kodak, Citicorp, Nestle's, Audi, Miller, and many others.

**Daniel Milsont** is another talent that took off under Modern Mythology's guidance. Milsont gained a name for himself as a talented cinematographer, and in his first quarter as a commercial director he completed eight projects. Agency staff reported being stunned by his imagery, and he is now in hot demand. He also has written three screenplays currently under development.

Modern Mythology prides itself on cross-pollination of ideas. It has tremendous resources for advanced technical skill, without a "technician's approach." Modern Mythology is clearly poised to continue its outstanding growth in television commercials and feature films.

Cf. the medical
CVs in chapter 7.

# SARA NEUMAN, Ph.D.

## PROFILE

Sara Neuman, Ph.D., is a licensed clinical psychologist with expertise in workplace psychological issues, including conflict resolution, crisis intervention, workplace violence, and trauma. Dr. Neuman specializes in the development of effective management structures, organizational growth, and program formation and implementation to support an organization's strategic goals. She has worked with individuals, corporations and nonprofits across the country as a consultant, advisor, and presenter.

Dr. Neuman is a vice president and senior associate of Dr. Barbara Hermann, managing director of Hermann and Associates of Chicago, Illinois, the leading experts in workplace psychological issues. Currently, she is engaged in projects including on-site management of stress, change, trauma, and violence. In addition, Hermann and Associates performs workplace mediation to resolve interpersonal and business conflicts, provides trainings to promote organizational/personnel alignment, and leads executive development programs in the emerging field of human potential/high performance.

Possessing a wide range of clinical experience with high-functioning patient populations, Dr. Neuman is conversant with issues including workplace and domestic violence, substance abuse, and post-traumatic stress disorder. In addition, she has worked with severely disturbed and psychotic patient populations, providing diagnostic depth useful even in a high-functioning environment.

Special strengths include ability to perform crisis intervention; organizational needs assessment; counseling in emergency, brief, and ongoing scenarios; appraisal and development of treatment plans for impulse control disorders; and design corporate emergency response teams.

Dr. Neuman has consulted with the Chicago police and public health departments, has performed interventions with adolescent gang members in the Chicago schools, and has been involved with the Psychological Services Office of the Chicago Free Clinic. She is an on-call hostage negotiations specialist for the FBI and numerous Midwestern state and municipal SWAT teams.

Dr. Neuman received her Ph.D. from the Wright Institute in Los Angeles. She possesses an M.A. in developmental psychology and a B.A. in child development. She has performed research at the University of Chicago and Harvard University, and has taught and given presentations at Antioch University on such subjects as adult development, organizational philosophy, clinical techniques, and assessment of violence potential. She is a frequently quoted consultant to the media on workplace violence and other matters.

Adroit in the design, implementation, documentation, and launch of clinical, safety, and performance enhancement programs, she is able to link new systems and controls to existing structures. Any company interested in workplace psychological issues would benefit from association with Dr. Neuman, a leader in the field.

# Kenneth Jackson

## PROFILE

Kenneth Jackson is a financial services specialist with advanced knowledge of Estate Planning, Portfolio Management and Health Care Finance. He is the principal of Kenneth Jackson & Associates, a financial consulting firm, and an associate with Ty Debright & Associates of Miami, Florida, Member NASD-SIPC.

In recent years, Mr. Jackson has specialized in estate planning services in association with several Florida law firms. The major thrust of this business is to (1) minimize taxation on transfer of pension monies to heirs, and (2) manage pension funds for maximum accrual.

A related area of interest is the design and implementation of charitable remainder trusts. Mr. Jackson is a noted pro bono speaker on this topic. He is an expert at maximizing estate benefits for the client's family, while ensuring full support for the charitable organization.

Mr. Jackson is also an acknowledged expert in two specialized areas, (1) strategic management of assets held by individuals and private pension funds, and (2) financial and health care planning for seniors.

Clients include high-net-worth individuals; owners of closely held corporations; independent surgeons, physicians and medical corporations; and legal and other professional corporations. Mr. Jackson's company has developed a computer program to model pension fund strategies for funds in excess of $1 million. These programs account for labyrinthine state, federal, transfer, and estate taxes to graphically demonstrate a client's options. His clients have reported tax savings in excess of $1 million and accrual beyond their most ambitious expectations.

As specialists in financial and health care planning for seniors, Mr. Jackson and his associates serve as guest speakers before such organizations as AARP, SIRS, and Alliance on Aging. Jackson & Associates has developed a comprehensive, comparative database on insurance policies of interest to seniors, including long-term care, medicare supplementary, life, whole life, and related programs. A related service is the selection of very low risk investments to meet the projected needs of his clients.

Not content with the products available on the market, Mr. Jackson has identified new market needs ahead of the major financial service companies. When it has been necessary, he has developed new products and then secured the vendors to support them.

Mr. Jackson's firm was profiled in a September 1996 Inc. magazine article titled, "The Champion Wealth Savers, What You Need to Know Before You Die Rich." For a copy of the article, call 800-555-1234, ext. 16.

Mr. Jackson is licensed by the NASD (Series 7 and 21), the SEC, and the Florida Department of Consumer Affairs Insurance Council. All fees are disclosed and explained in detail, in advance. There is never a charge for an initial consultation.

Asher Associates, updated January 1997

# Joshua C. Kellerman III

45 Del Mar Court
Marina del Rey, California 90292
Residence: (310) 555-6750
Office: (310) 555-0421

---

## *Profile*

Joshua C. Kellerman III is chairman and principal of First Western Mortgage Corporation, principal and director of United Bank, and president of JCK Interests, a holding company for Arlington Development Group, Midwestern Industrial Properties, Kellerman Investments, and a number of investment and development partnerships. His entire career has revolved around real estate investment, development, capital formation, cooperative ventures, and banking. As a principal, he has structured and executed in excess of a billion dollars in real estate transactions over the years. He holds a current California real estate brokerage license.

United Bank of Watkins Glen, New York, was acquired by Mr. Kellerman and a partner in 1985. At the time of acquisition, this financial institution had footings of only $25 million and had been cited for inadequacy of capital compliance. Currently, footings exceed $260 million and the bank's capital position is 6%.

Arlington Development, of which Mr. Kellerman was chairman and principal, was one of the largest developers of residential subdivisions in the Chicago area, having built in excess of 2000 residential units.

Midwestern Industrial Properties, with Mr. Kellerman as controlling partner, has developed and invested in over 3,000,000 SF of industrial distribution facilities and two (2) major industrial office parks. Thornton Center for Commerce and Industry, comprised of over 400 acres, is one of Chicago's largest and most successful office and research parks.

Mr. Kellerman has owned a number of office, industrial, apartment, and retail buildings throughout the United States and Canada, and has been a partner with a variety of institutions such as Trans Union, Illinois Central Railroad, New England Life Insurance, Twin City Financial, and Homart. Mr. Kellerman has been involved as a principal in the investment and development of four regional shopping centers comprising in excess of 3,000,000 SF. Furthermore, the company has owned and leased numerous neighborhood shopping centers nationwide.

Significant family holdings have been managed by Mr. Kellerman for the past 32 years, including eleven leased J.C. Penney stores throughout the Northeast and Midwest, Skyharbor Airport, Norton, Nebraska, multiple Learjet regional distributorships, and numerous real estate investments throughout the United States.

## CIVIC ACTIVITIES/AFFILIATIONS

Mr. Kellerman serves as president of the Kellerman Educational Foundation, former vice chairman of the Major Gifts and Sustaining Fellows of the Art Institute of Chicago, is a member of the National Advisory Board of the Hazel Foundation, and is a member-designate of the Mayor's Council of Chicago. Kellerman Educational Foundation has donated the largest women's residence on the campus of the University of Southern California, and is the largest single contributor to the Alliance for American Women's Colleges.

## EDUCATION

Mr. Kellerman has been the author of numerous professional articles, one of which has been used as course material at the Harvard Graduate School of Business.

He received an A.B. from Stanford University and participated in the M.B.A. program at Kellogg Graduate School of Management at Northwestern University. Mr. Kellerman currently resides in Marina del Rey with his wife and son.

**Kern & Brighton, updated 4/94**

## INDUSTRIAL

S.S.T. Transport
Bridgeview, Illinois
90,000 SF
Project: distribution center

Armitage Building
Chicago, Illinois
1,000,000 SF
Project: building for Admiral Corporation

135 Mt. Prospect Road
Mt. Prospect, Illinois
450,000 SF
Project: distribution center leased to Rockwell
Corporation

Toys-R-Us
Benton, Illinois
120,000 SF
Project: distribution center

1010 Foster Avenue
Benton, Illinois
380,000 SF
Project: Midwestern distribution center for
Montgomery Ward

450 Lombard
Addison, Illinois
40,000 SF
Project: warehouse

Thorton Center for Commerce and Industry
Woodacre, Illinois
400 acres
Project: office and research park

Schaumberg Park
Schaumberg, Illinois
50 acres
Project: office and industrial park
Major tenant: Motorola

Louisville Industrial
Louisville, Kentucky
300,000 SF
Project: public warehouse and business incubator
site

LaGrange Building
Bensenville, Illinois
340,000 SF
Project: build to suit

## RESIDENTIAL

Arlington at Itasca
150 single-family units in Minneapolis, Minnesota

Pheasant Walk
80 single-family units in Hoffman Estates, Illinois

Highland Woods
128 single-family units in Bligh, Illinois

Highland Meadows
130 single-family units in Rolling Meadows,
Illinois

Twin Lakes
523 single-family units in Las Vegas, Nevada

Arlington Lakes
44 single-family units in Springfield, Massachusetts

Maryknoll
160 townhouse/single-family units in Madison,
Wisconsin

Atrium
430 condominium/townhouse units in Glen Ellyn,
Illinois

Colonial Heights
114 townhouse units in Richmond, Virginia

## *OFFICE BUILDINGS*

Longhorn Towers
Greenway Plaza, Houston, Texas
160,000 SF

Regency Office Park
Regency Square, Louisville, Kentucky
72,000 SF

Beaumont Plaza
Beaumont, Texas
100,000 SF

Fincastle Building
Houston, Texas
93,000 SF

Provident Bank Building
Cincinnati, Ohio
250,000 SF

## *SHOPPING CENTERS*

K-MART
Seattle, Washington
Freeport, Illinois
Grand Rapids, Michigan
Ft. Wayne, Indiana
each project approximately 110,000 SF

J.C. Penney
11 sites nationwide (leased)

Sunrise Mall
Brownsville, Texas
450,000 SF

Richland Fashion Mall
Waco, Texas
750,000 SF

Centennial Mall
Amarillo, Texas
1,200,000 SF

College Grove Shopping Center
San Diego, California
900,000 SF

Holiday Manor Shopping Center
Louisville, Kentucky
375,000 SF

# D.D. Martin

## PROFILE

The story of D.D. Martin reads like a modern novel. She began her fashion career as a model at the age of fourteen. She went on to become president of John Casablanca's Elite, one of the world's largest model agencies. Along the way she taught dance with Stanley Kahn, produced and directed musical reviews, designed and opened several top nightclubs, and founded two fashion design/manufacturing houses. Currently she is a highly regarded couturier, and as the *Dallas Morning News* put it, "a custom designer whose clothes are favored by the city's social elect."

D.D. Martin, a third-generation Texan who has designed for such clients as Danielle Starr and Marla Trump, makes the woman look as long and lean as possible. Bright, energetic, and still trim and pretty enough to model her own clothes, D.D. says, "I can make a woman look divine—make her tall, strong, sultry, however she wants. That's what the magic of couture is all about."

D.D.'s forte is flirty cocktail attire, fine evening wear, and grand-occasion dresses, which she calls "table-top" dresses. Her style is heavily influenced by the golden age of feminine attire, as seen in classic films from the 40s and 50s. D.D.'s approach is strictly sensual. "I choose fabrics for the sensations they evoke. I love the sound of taffeta, the mystery of velvet, and the way a perfume's fragrance lingers on silk." D.D.'s dresses are flamboyant and sexy, and her interpretations of classic styles always look brand new.

Her studio also offers a range of custom-made garments from daytime linen suits and dresses to handsome theater suits, debutante gowns, and wedding dresses. She has fabric sources all over the world, and she is known for designing her own print fabrics and making her own buttons and trim; so she can produce hats, belts, evening bags, trimmed evening shoes, and costume jewelry to complete her ensembles to the last detail.

Although as a couturier she has shared the society columns with the likes of Oscar de la Renta, Mary McFadden, and Bill Blass, she is better known nationally for her prêt-à-porter label, D'D'Martin. Although D.D. licensed out her label in 1993, up until then her own designs were seen in Neiman Marcus, Saks Fifth Avenue, Bloomingdale's, Macy's and over 120 other department and specialty stores nationwide.

D.D. Martin created her ready-to-wear line almost by accident. "After I won the Golden Shears Award for the second time, an agent called from New York and said she wanted to represent me," D.D. recalls. So with a couture client along as a companion, D.D. went off to meet her. D.D. took one look at the agent's selection of $100 dresses and was willing to bag the whole thing and go shopping; then her client said, "D.D., we're here already. Let's go see some of the other agencies."

D.D. and her client went to five agencies, and all five wanted to rep her. D.D. particularly liked the mother-daughter team doing business as Whodunnit. The owner said, "We've been trying to find someone like you for 2½ years. Can you have a 15-piece collection ready in ten days?" D.D. said, "Of course!" without hesitation and without a clue as to how she would get it done.

Back in Dallas she tracked down a friend with a dormant factory building and borrowed it for two weeks. "I called everybody I knew to get some help on this," she says. She sequestered herself in this basement for a week, came out with the collection, and shipped it off to New York. As the boxes were opened in the showroom, buyers started buying the collection before the dresses could be hung. Saks, who never buys a new designer, bought her line within a week. She rented a real manufacturing facility, the couture client who had accompanied her to New York financed her tool-up to full production, and the D'D'Martin label was launched.

As a testament to her management skills, in addition to her design sense, D.D. went from making two or three dresses per week to making hundreds without a hitch, and the D'D'Martin label built a reputation for on-time quality. This was, after all, her second full design/manufacturing concern; she had been the designer and production manager who launched private label ready-to-wear for the exclusive Jean Paul Deux chain of 18 stores, but that is another story.

In addition to designing, D.D. is an accomplished public speaker on fashion and beauty, speaking before business groups as diverse as University of Texas graduate school of business and meetings of the Trilateral Commission. She has been a frequent guest on radio and television and is a highly sought director, producer, choreographer of stage shows. While she was president of John Casablanca's Elite, she built the annual presentation of models into an internationally attended event. She also wrote the curriculum for 35 weeks of model and TV commercial training, launched an exclusive line of house cosmetics, and presided over the fastest growth in the history of the agency.

Whatever she does next, you can bet that D.D. Martin's touch will ensure success.

For more information, call her studio at 214-555-4929. If you don't reach D.D. herself, ask for David Carr. Press book available.

Kemper Communications, Dallas

# JAQUELINE M. BOUVIER

## *Profile*

Jaqueline M. Bouvier is president of Sophia Academy, a Catholic women's high school in suburban Chicago, Illinois. Sophia Academy became classified as a college-preparatory institution in 1987, following withdrawal of sponsorship by the religious organization that had founded it in 1963. Sophia Academy offers the advantages of a traditional prep school: a small-school learning environment that provides personal attention (student to teacher ratio is 17 to 1), a highly challenging curriculum, and education that directly promotes and develops individual leadership. In keeping with the increasing interdependence of world society, Sophia Academy also places emphasis on cultural diversity along with personal self-empowerment.

Ms. Bouvier has devoted the energies of nine years of service to the development of Sophia Academy into the thriving school it is today. She had the honor of being the academy's first lay principal, and then its first president, and has focused much of the development of the academy on taking advantage of the single-gender setting. Young women at Sophia Academy are not isolated; rather, they are encouraged to identify and develop their unique talents and learning potential. To this objective, Ms. Bouvier brings enthusiasm and extensive skills in teaching, administration, public relations, and fund-raising. She brings her proven experience and accomplishments in these areas to her present position, along with a commitment to enhancing the positive role of women in building a culturally rich, equitable society through development of leadership in the nonprofit/ education sector.

She has demonstrated her abilities in crisis management and team building, having lifted Sophia Academy, a school given only a 1% chance of survival when she accepted responsibilities as president, to a consistently growing and stable student population which is integrated into the larger community. Ms. Bouvier was raised in a family of educators. Having begun her career in teaching herself, she believes it to be the most transformative of professions. She is widely published and has consulted and spoken to many deserving organizations.

Ms. Bouvier founded and is the president of Women's Schools Forever, a consortium of single-gender Catholic high schools like Sophia Academy. She has chaired the Special Education Program Committee of the Arlington, Virginia, public school system, has served as Associate Professor at the School of Education and Human Services of Marymount College, and has served as project director of both a private/public collaborative ventures at Arlington and Marymount and for the National Association of State Boards of Education in Washington, D.C.

Additionally, she has been a national policy fellow at George Washington University, and has successfully held developmental and directorial positions in the state of Wisconsin, in cognitive science research and special education, with consistent development of curriculum in close coordination with development of teachers' skills and parental training and involvement.

With a background that continually establishes her strengths in finding and implementing new ideas that revitalize, challenge, and build educational institutions at the most personal levels, Ms. Bouvier has the experience to meet the particular challenges of any school or nonprofit organization of any size, and lead it to a brighter future.

Asher Associates, updated 6/96

# Danaelle Kerlyn Watkins Bell

West Coast 25 President Street Sausalito California 94965 415 555 9677
East Coast 433 West Broadway New York New York 10015 212 555 1864

Danaelle Bell is an art dealer with a phenomenal ability to bring the right patrons and artists together for the benefit of everyone involved. Currently she is an independent art consultant for private collectors and corporations internationally. She has an extensive network of artists, agents, and collectors spreading from Paris to Tokyo, Tokyo to Paris.

After studying art history at Sarah Lawrence College, Ms. Bell began her career as an art consultant with the Kahala Fine Art Gallery in the Kahala Hilton Hotel in Honolulu, Hawaii. She was promoted to assistant director and director based on her phenomenal success developing Japanese patrons for living Western artists. She developed relationships with Japanese media, promoted individual artists, and featured "invitation only" openings with bilingual associates on hand to facilitate communication between artists and Japanese corporate and private collectors. These and other measures created a 400% increase in art transactions at the gallery and a 900% increase in the average value of the art changing hands.

At the same time, she developed an agency relationship with Tamar Max, then living in Hawaii and well known as the creative inspiration for the Mundane School of painting. When Max had a retrospective at So So Harris in New York, he had Ms. Bell design the show's layout and design, lighting, display walls, show composition and positioning, as reviewed in "So So not So So for Max," New York Times, November 16, 1989. Ms. Bell then joined Euro Scene in Manhattan as director. In that capacity she provided total aesthetic direction to the gallery. Ms. Bell demonstrated her ability to attract artists of national and international prominence, and established relations with leading art dealers and consultants worldwide. Articles about Euro Scene shows have appeared in *Style, Home, Architectural Digest, Art World, Museum, Scene, Art & Antiques, The New Yorker, Deco, Epi Scene,* and *Entertaining* magazines, as well as similar publications worldwide (France and Japan, in particular).

In 1995, Danaelle Bell was recruited to open a chain of galleries in luxury hotels worldwide for an investment group with no prior art background. After opening in Paris, Milan, San Francisco, and Monaco, she experienced aesthetic differences with the board and turned the project over to others.

She is currently offering her services as an art consultant to individuals, museums, foundations, and corporations with a desire to select art that is both exquisite to behold and an investment vehicle of uncommon return, an asset in every sense of the word. During her tenure at Euro Scene, Ms. Bell served as an art consultant to an anonymous collector, directing procurement of some $16 million in art now valued at $36 million. She revived the reputation of Hollis Underwood, as his paintings increased in value from $36,000 (Babe in the Woods, resold 1986) to $1.8 million (Woman in Confusion, resold 1996). She advised Donald Trump on public art for the Emperor's Village Complex, which won the AIA Award Golden Palm for Art Integration into Edifice Design.

Ms. Bell may be contacted through her New York and San Francisco offices.

# Sales, Marketing, New Business Development

Sales and marketing résumés can be a little flashier and a little bolder than other top-level presentations. In the following examples you will find stronger language and grander claims than in prior chapters. If there's ever a place to put your best foot forward, to make your best claim first, a sales and marketing résumé is it. Anyone who has ever hired sales professionals has been faced with a mountain of people, all of whom claim to be able to out-wrestle Superman.

Nevertheless, sales and marketing résumés are driven by hard data. No amount of flowery language will gloss over a lack of quantifiable accomplishments, and a sales and marketing résumé lacking in hard data *will not attract attention.*

Data, however, can be represented in many forms. As Mark Twain says, "There's lies, damned lies, and statistics." As a professional in the persuasion industry, it is your job to discover the most impressive way to present your information. Your performance can be measured on gross, margin, share, comparison to plan, comparison to last year, comparison to a specific other competitor, comparison to other regions/departments/divisions/branches/product lines within your own company, or even cost of sales. Data can be presented in dollars, units, volume, weight, or percentages. *Verbum sapienti.*

Go for it. And remember, check the index for résumés in other chapters that may apply to your particular case.

# DAN SCHICKMAN

*East Coast:*
c/o D.B. Brubaker
2322 Queen River Drive
Lexington, Massachusetts 02173
Message: (617) 555-4969

*West Coast:*
67 Sacred Woods Lane
Holly Grove, California 94078
Office: (818) 555-3330
Residence: (796) 555-3203

---

## EXPERTISE

### Sales & Operations Management

*Highlights:*

Eight years of P&L responsibility. Sales *and* budgeting *and* operations *and* marketing management background. Proven track record on both coasts. Talent for motivating staff and meeting marketplace needs in both market environments.

Track record of continuous growth in highly competitive and mature markets. Consistently beat all company and market trends.

Structured merger of acquired company, solving pricing and service issues for nonoriginal equipment and smoothing transition to retain new customers.

**Top performer; ready for a new challenge.**

## HISTORY

WORLDWIDE OFFICE CORP., HQ: Lexington, Massachusetts
**Western Region Manager**, 1993–Present
**Eastern Region Manager**, 1992

Full P&L responsibility for $28 million division of $125 million company, VAR for a full line of office equipment. Report directly to the C.O.O. Manage 12 branch offices; staff of 123 sales, technical and operations personnel; 9000 accounts. Member, Senior Management Team, with the president and the CEO. Member, National Sales Council, setting sales policies nationwide, including incentive structures, goals, and sales development programs. Contribute to ad hoc committees and task groups as needed.

Provide leadership and direction to the regional sales force, including overseeing sales training, motivational programs, special speakers, and incentive meetings. Ensure regional compliance with national policies. Work closely with branch managers to ensure all sales and operating goals are met.

Manage region resources, including premises and capital equipment in branch offices, automotive fleet, and $5 million in inventory (machines/parts/supplies). Direct region human resources and office administration, and region-based accounting and reporting.

**Achieved highest sales in the record of the Western Region while in charge.**
**Achieved highest sales in the record of the Eastern Region while in charge.**

**Director, Printing & Duplication**, Company Headquarters, 1991

Appointed by the president to serve as the company's senior marketing manager, with specific responsibility for a $43 million product group. Reported to the president; coordinated directly with Worldwide international in London and OEMs. Developed group budget, sales, and operations plans. Managed purchasing, vendor relations, and wholesaler relations for this core business line.

First director of marketing assigned to the Senior Management Team, involved in all company sales, marketing, and strategic decisions. Spearheaded revision of compensation and incentive plans, attracting higher caliber of sales professional.

Orchestrated six new nationwide product launches. Created new sales literature and collaterals for domestic markets. Coordinated marketing effort with our own sales function and with dealer channels.

**Boosted sales 20% year-to-year. Maintained market share while increasing margins 10%.**

**District Manager**, Northern California, 1988–1991

P&L responsibility for $12 million business, 5 branch offices, staff of 120. Involved in acquiring a $6 million competitor.

**Selected by the president to structure the merger and integration, including operations, staff, policies, and customer retention program.**

**District Manager**, San Francisco, 1986–1988

P&L responsibility for owned branches prior to the merger. Selected by v.p. sales to be the marketing team program leader, troubleshooting branches nationwide, improving branch and district manager skills, and implementing new sales programs.

**Achieved record sales for the district.**

**Branch Manager**, San Jose, 1982–1986 — Number One Branch, Nationwide
**Sales Manager**, San Francisco, 1979–1982 — Number One Sales Representative, Nationwide

## EDUCATION

STATE UNIVERSITY OF NEW YORK, Farmingdale, New York
**Business Administration**

STATE UNIVERSITY OF NEW YORK, Brockport, New York
**Business Administration**

CONTINUOUS TRAINING IN MANAGEMENT, SALES, AND PRODUCT AREAS

## REFERENCES

References and additional information gladly provided on request, but please keep this information confidential at this time.

# JUDITH FRIEMAN

800 West Aurora Street
New York, New York 10014

Office: (212) 555-8215
Residence: (212) 555-7270
Personal e-mail: judge.gogo@metro-net.com

## PROFILE

### Marketing & Communications

Strengths include full P&L responsibility for market, product, and image management. Background in major corporate environments, with some start-up/entrepreneurial experience. Comfortable with full or collaborative responsibility for strategic direction of organization's public image and/or product/service lines. Special strength: significant involvement with emerging communication and media technologies.

## EXPERIENCE

HILL & KNOWLTON, New York, New York, 1993–1996
### Vice President & Group Director, Marketing Communications

Full P&L responsibility for 12-person business unit with annual revenues of $12.5 million. Created and implemented marketing communications programs for key accounts:

- Bayer Aspirin
- NetScore Services Co.
- State Bar of New York
- Revlon
- *Ladies Home Journal*
- Mary Kay Cosmetics
- Shaklee Corp.
- ABC News

*Selected accomplishments:*

- Created $2+ million in new business, bringing on board State Bar of New York and NetScore Services, the largest commercial Web site designer in the United States. Also spearheaded Web-site design services within H&K, creating a major new revenue stream for the company, and designing services, technical teams, and contractual standards adopted companywide.

- Created revenue-stream mentality for the State Bar's communications functions, e.g., planned tabloid-style, advertiser-supported newspaper for members; developed strategy to market publications to members as client-development tools, resulting in 50% increase in revenues.

- Received "John Hill Award for Excellence – 1994" for "It's no joke!" State Bar legal education program that demonstrably improved image of attorneys in New York state.

STATE BAR OF NEW YORK, New York, New York, 1988–1992
### Senior Executive, Professional and Public Services
### Senior Executive, Communications and Public Education

Managed communications, continuing legal education for attorneys, meeting services, legal services for the poor, law-related education for the public, and local bar relations for the State Bar and its 185,000 members. In charge of five sub-departments and a total staff of 70; planned and managed $9 million budget; generated large volume of internal business plans, feasibility studies, and proposals. Reported directly to the Executive Director; collaborated on strategic decisions affecting the organization as a whole (personnel, legislation, operations, finance, politics, technology).

Promoted from responsibility for communications and media relations unit, serving as chief public relations strategist, editor-in-chief for Bar publications, and media spokesperson.

*Selected management contributions and special projects:*

- Served as catalyst for new revenue-generating technology applications, e.g., developed business plan for interactive, fax- and PC-based referral and information services.
- Created and orchestrated "Legal Basics" public education campaign gaining media recognition and earning ABA award (national). Oversaw design of Legal Service Corps to expand legal services for the poor. Established joint venture with State Library to establish legal literacy centers in immigrant neighborhoods and communities.
- Successful turnaround manager: Converted dispirited and risk-aversive communications staff into "can do," idea-generating team producing more and better marketing-oriented communications products.

TELACTION CORPORATION, New York, New York, 1986–1987
(a venture subsidiary of JCPenney Company, Inc.)
**Director of International Development**

Developed international licensing strategy for interactive, cable-based, home-shopping technology in Europe and Canada. Successfully negotiated first sale of license to Canadian retailer.

TELEDATA SERVICES CO., White Plains, New York, 1984–1986
**Manager of Market Development for Merchandising**
**Consumer Marketing Manager**

Developed online home-shopping, grocery shopping, and event-ticketing services. Analyzed market research and prepared initial market requirements for product/system design. Brought on board major retail and grocery clients. Received "Outstanding Achievement Award – 1985" for client acquisition.

WARNER COMMUNICATIONS, New York, New York, and Washington, D.C., 1979–1984
**Director of Market Development**
**Franchise Coordinator**

Researched and planned pioneering cable-based interactive service. Acquired major clients. Formulated market roll-out strategy. Orchestrated cable television franchising campaigns in three counties. Led staff of political consultants in developing political, public relations, and community outreach strategies. Served as primary writer/editor for multivolume proposal for interactive cable system using QUBE technology.

U.S. DEPARTMENT OF COMMERCE, Washington, D.C., 1977–1979
**Special Assistant to the Assistant Secretary for Trade & Industry**

Advised and represented Assistant Secretary Frank Weil on policy issues: export development, trade regulation, trade policy.

U.S. SUPREME COURT, Washington, D.C., 1975–1976
**Law Clerk to Justice Tom C. Clark**

Assisted Justice Tom C. Clark in preparation of judicial opinions (U.S. Court of Appeals). Drafted speeches for the Justice.

U.S. DEPARTMENT OF STATE and U.S. CONGRESS, Washington, D.C., 1970, 1973, 1974–1975
**Intern**

General Counsel, Agency for International Development. Senator Birch Bayh. Congressman John Brademas.

## EDUCATION

**J.D., The William Jefferson Blythe School of Law,** Yale University, New Haven, Conn., 1975

**B.A., Brown University,** Providence, Rhode Island, 1972

**London School of Economics,** London, England, 1969–1970

# Jens "Jocko" Sörensen

office
2400 Wilshire Boulevard, Suite 100
Los Angeles, California 90057
**Office:** (310) 555-7391

residence
200 South Edge Way, E-415
Raleigh, North Carolina 27612
**Home:** (919) 555-0346

---

## EXPERTISE

### Sales & Marketing / Account Relations / New Business Development

Strengths are aggressive new account development, relationship sales, consultative sales, regional office management, strategic and tactical sales planning, integrating priorities between sales, engineering, corporate and client issues.

• Proven ability to create business opportunity.

Sales experience includes target identification, prospecting, trade shows, proposal development and RFP responses, demonstrations, follow-through and closing, contract negotiations, follow-up with customer and implementation teams, wellness calls.

Related skill is relationship building with business partners (technology vendors).

Technical sales skills include regional forecasting, feasibility analysis, P&L accountability, and information management. Available as needed for travel or relocation.

## EXPERIENCE

**Security Solutions Group, Inc.**
HQ: Rochester, New York
**Western Regional Account Manager**      1993–Present

Created West Coast presence for SSG, the leading purveyor of identification and privilege control systems for colleges, universities, hospitals, airports, and other large government and industrial accounts. Represent custom turnkey integrated hardware/software systems, average order of $80,000, including configuration, installation, testing, training, and support. Typical sale cycle is 10 to 20+ months. Continue to build and maintain relationships after the sale to ensure orders for upgrades, peripherals, extensions, and enhancements.

• Created $1,850,000 business from scratch. Full P&L responsibility for 11 Western States, Alaska, Hawaii, British Columbia, and Alberta. Travel 70%. Gross profit contribution to corporate as high as $485,000.

Personally opened and continue to serve West Coast accounts. *Sample accounts:*

| | | |
|---|---|---|
| • Reed College | • U. of Alberta | • U. of Victoria |
| • Stanford | • U. of Calgary | • U. of Hawaii |
| • Marriott Corp. | • St. Marys College | • U. of British Columbia |
| • Santa Clara U. | • Lewis & Clark | • Harborview Medical Center |
| • Loyola Marymount | • U. of Portland | • San Jose State University |
| • Cal Poly | • Whittier College | • The Colorado College |
| • U. of New Mexico | • Humboldt State U. | • Albertson College |
| • Seattle Pacific U. | • U. of the Pacific | • Sacramento State U. |
| • Kaiser Permanente | • U.C., Santa Cruz | • Cal State San Bernardino |

Have exceeded all management objectives for West Coast business: gross sales, share, penetration, repeat/referral sales, speaking and PR activities, overhead control.
• Exceeded 1994 quota by 49%.
• Exceeded 1995 quota by 25%.
• Exceeded 1996 quota by 68%.
• Named "1995–1996 Salesman of the Year" (National).

**The Gillette Company**
HQ: Boston, Massachusetts
**Account Representative**     1991–1993

Serviced more than 300 retail accounts along coastal North Carolina, from major chains to single-unit operations. Responsible for merchandising strategies, marketing tools, brand visibility, product distribution, and Gillette's inventory control system. Introduced aggressive clerk education and retail assessment programs.

**Wright Brokerage**
HQ: Richmond, Virginia
**Independent Account Sales Representative**     1989–1991

Sold frozen food lines to second-largest retail grocery chain in the state of Virginia and two other leading grocery chains. Handled buyer relations, major program presentations, promotional co-op advertising. Forecasted/analyzed budgets to plan slotting allowances and advertising dollars for each account.

Facilitated integration of acquired nonfoods company. Oriented and trained staff. Established company-standard forms, policies, procedures. Earned rapid promotion from **Chain Store Representative**.

Prior: outside sales to the construction equipment, materials, and supplies industry.

## EDUCATION

**Purdue University,** West Lafayette, Indiana
**Master of Business Administration** (a top-20 ranked program)     1989

**North Carolina State University**, Raleigh, North Carolina
**Bachelor of Science, Sociology**     1984

## REFERENCES

Customer and employer references provided upon request. Please keep this application confidential at this time.

# LARRY FRAPP

800 Fildell Avenue
Villanova, Pennsylvania 19085

NY Office: (212) 555-2967
PA Office: (215) 555-2524
Residence: (610) 555-8836
Company E-mail: l.frapp@report.com

---

**EXPERTISE**

**New Business Specialist**

Strengths include (1) managing client relationships, working directly with client company top officers (CEO, COO, Pres, GM, Owner), (2) business planning, sales planning, market planning, product development and management, (3) advertising, marketing materials, image development, collaterals, (4) identifying and developing potential venture partners, (5) capitalization.

Consistent series of accomplishments in new business/new market development.

*Highlights:*
- Founding member of software start-up achieving positive cash flow and real profits in the first year.
- Founding partner in high technology vendor of point-of-sale systems, generating positive cash flow and real profits in first year.
- Proven ability representing both tangible and intangible products/channel and direct sales/Fortune 500, small business, DoD, government accounts.
- Consistent series of sales accomplishments, e.g.: Achieved highest profit and largest volume in company history for 52-year-old company.

**EXPERIENCE**

REPORT TECHNOLOGIES, INC.    Philadelphia, PA
**E.V.P. / Director of Marketing and Alliance Management**    1993–Present

Founding member of this commercial software development corporation serving the financial services industry. Track record of major strategic contributions *and* ongoing sales achievement. Travel up to 80%, including trade shows, site demos, and distributor product and sales training.

*Sample contributions:*

Wrote the company's sales and marketing plans, contributed to company's strategic plan. Member, executive team, involved in all decision-making. Sourced legal and accountancy services for the company.

Lead negotiator, structuring a development and distribution agreement with TTI Financial for $971,000 cash, $250,000 per annum maintenance, and up to 25% of gross sales, for our Pro Active application, a PC-based banking application used to monitor and report compliance to the federal Community Reinvestment Act.

Personally oversaw first installations and customer training cycle. Set standards and monitoring system for our distributor/partner.

Negotiated fee-for-services engineering development contract with GeoReference for GIS application to track seismic and environmental concerns impacting construction lending nationwide. Won approval for $70,000 WIP payment based on acceptance of prototype.

Developed and delivered company presentations to key industry players: Office of the Comptroller of the Currency (OCC), Bank of America, Barnett Bank, M&I Mortgage. Speaker/presenter at national conventions and trade shows.

RETAIL SYSTEMS      Swarthmore, PA
(div. of Eastern Cash Register)      1986–1993
**Partner / New Business Development Officer / Account Executive**

Founding partner in new venture to represent dedicated point-of-sale systems to retail and restaurant accounts throughout the Philadelphia-South Jersey area. Created market presence and account base from scratch. Turnkey solutions selling environment: HW, SW, installation, training, support. Featured one-entry fully integrated sales, inventory, ordering, and staff performance measuring systems, ranging from $15,000 to $75,000 for initial order, plus support.

Hired and trained sales professionals. Ensured cooperating / collaboration with the service office in Camden. Set up office procedures, including accounting, credit, collections, personnel, facilities.

Sourced new vendors, evaluated new products, strategized product mix and positioning.

*prior*

BJM DIRECTORY PUBLICATIONS      Newark, NJ
**Account Executive** (trade advertising)

ENSIGN MAGAZINE      Boston, MA
**Marketing Director / Managing Editor** (increased ad pages 15% per month)

NEW GLASGOW DAILY NEWS      New Glasgow, Nova Scotia, Canada
**Newspaper Reporter** (features and breaking news)

**EDUCATION**      WAYNE STATE UNIVERSITY      Detroit, MI
**Bachelor of Arts, History**

CONTINUING EDUCATION:
**Sales, Marketing, Finance, Accounting, Computers**

**TECHNICAL**      Heavy PC user: word processing, spreadsheets (accounting and analysis), GIS, database / project / contact management applications, etc.

Strong technical aptitude. Able to learn new applications / technologies quickly and easily. Able to communicate technical info to technical and nontechnical managers.

# EDWARD D. WHETSTONE

c/o Mailboxes, Etc.                                         #30 Asahi Ambision Ebisu
Box 1640                                                      3-29-13 Ebisu Minami
2269 Chestnut Street                                                    Shibuya-Ku
San Francisco, California 94123                                         Tokyo 150
**U.S.A.**                                                               **JAPAN**
Message: (203) 555-7438, Ridgefield, Connecticut, U.S.A.       Office: (81-3) 3234-5586
                                                            Residence: (81-3) 3791-0252

---

## PROFILE

**Sales • Sales Management • Product Development/Marketing — International & U.S.A.**

Proven top performer, gaining rapid promotion from Marketing Engineer to Sales Engineer to Senior Sales Engineer to District Supervisor to Manager-Japan in less than five years. Advanced skills in relationship building, direct outside sales, product development, PR, sales management. Significant international experience. Fluent French; proficient Japanese. Proven talent for technical products. PC skilled (spreadsheets, word processing, CAD).

## EXPERIENCE

**Luxor Acutrac Japan K.K.**, Tokyo, Japan          1995–Present
**Manager-Japan, Technical Support**

Only American representative in the new Tokyo office of this lighting controls manufacturer. Responsibilities in three interwoven areas: (1) establish Luxor as a player in the Japanese market, which entails developing strategic business relationships and paving the way for future Luxor executives in Japan; (2) redesign U.S. domestic products to meet Japanese government standards and market requirements; and (3) establish local business operations, including the design of internal office procedures, quotation/order systems, information systems, and communication with parent company in the United States. Also involved in Luxor activities throughout Asian markets. Luxor provides a complete range of commercial and consumer lighting control products (see next listing for complete description of Luxor U.S.A.).

*Highlights*:
- Provided critical interface between Japanese director, Japanese distributor, and parent company to achieve market penetration in excess of company objectives.
- Instrumental in evaluating product requirements for Japanese market and coordinating with U.S.-based engineering team.
- Established Tokyo office in collaboration with the Japanese director.
- Trained Japanese distributor's engineering and sales staff on Luxor products and applications.
- Helped close $500,000 order to supply equipment for the tallest building in Japan, 70-story Yokohama Landmark Tower, *owned by the parent company of a Japanese competitor*.
- Assistant to the Vice President, International Sales & Marketing, collaborating on plans for business expansion in Hong Kong, Malaysia, Singapore, Thailand, South Korea.
- Interviewed and recommended appointment of new Agent for Hong Kong marketplace.

**Luxor Electric Co., Inc.**, Cardinal, Pennsylvania       1990–1994
**District Supervisor, Western United States**

District supervisor, representing three major product divisions with over 5000 individual products. Managed 15 distributor sales and specification sales representatives throughout Western United States, Alaska, and Pacific Rim.

*Highlights*:
- Established West Coast office in Los Angeles.
- Achieved aggregate of $4.5 million in annual sales revenues with margins in excess of company targets.

- Reversed prior negative growth trend and achieved solid 20% sales growth for two straight years.
- Regained 50% of shelf space taken by competitors under prior territory management.
- Improved penetration into the design community, resulting in 40% increase in specification-generated sales.

Position required advanced skill in two distinct sales areas: (1) creating demand in the architectural and design community to specify our products in commercial and residential applications, and (2) gaining shelf and merchandising space in wholesale and retail electrical/lighting distributor outlets.

*Additional:*
- Tripled business with the largest single lighting design account, to $400,000 per annum.
- Closed first computerized lighting system and largest order in history of this territory, a $150,000 invoice.
- Closed largest single retail account in Washington, $50,000 initial stock order.
- Designed job tracking "tickler" system, increasing hit rate in jobs by 30% (quotations-to-orders ratio).
- Realigned California wholesale and retail distribution, reducing account base from 120 to 60 authorized dealers, with concurrent 30% *increase* in total gross sales to distributor accounts.
- Recruited, selected, and signed on three new manufacturer's representatives in Oregon, Nevada, and Idaho.
- Doubled sales in Korea by supporting company agent in Seoul.
- Served as product manager to launch two new major product lines, Graphix Line and Nova Luna Line, including coordinating engineering, production, marketing, and sales.

**Cornell University**, Ithaca, New York      1984
**Research Assistant**

Prepared silicon and gallium arsenide samples for research using transmission electron microscopy. Operated and maintained sophisticated laboratory equipment.

**Photo Verbaine**, Geneva, Switzerland      1983
**Sales Associate**

Sold consumer audio-visual and electronic goods in both French and English.

## EDUCATION

**Sony Language School**, Tokyo, Japan      1995
**Japanese Writing and Language (series of 4 courses)**

**University of California — Extension**, Los Angeles, California      1993–1994
**International Marketing & Management, Strategic Marketing, Japanese Language & Culture**

**Cornell University**, Ithaca, New York      1989
**B.S., Materials Science & Engineering**, with concentration in **Electronics & Electronic Materials**

**International School of Geneva**, Switzerland      1985
Baccalaureate Diploma

## AFFILIATIONS

American Chamber of Commerce — Tokyo
   Member, Construction Subcommittee

Far East Society of Architects and Engineers

Illuminating Engineering Society of North America

Cornell Club of Japan
   Active committee member

## REFERENCES

References available upon request.

# DAVID HAGEN

190 Linda Mar Boulevard
San Gabriel, California 91770
Message: (213) 555-2355
d.hagen@haku.com

4-3-5-341 Kamisoshigaya
Setagaya-ku, Tokyo 177, Japan
Phone: 81-3-3494-2456
Fax: 81-3-3484-3592

## SUMMARY

International trade expertise, especially EC and Japan, with emphasis on market development, sales, technical customer support. Strengths: designing country-specific sales strategy, recruiting in-country sales professionals, solving key account problems. Fluent in English, German; business proficiency in Spanish, French, Russian, and Swedish; some ability in Japanese.

## EXPERIENCE

**Shimatsu (TrialTest) Corporation,** Tokyo, Japan      1993–Present
**New Business Officer, International**

Created sales strategies for the world's largest manufacturer of automatic test equipment for integrated circuits, opening untapped markets and increasing worldwide share. Initiated new broker/dealer/support relationships in target countries, initiated and closed direct sales, controlled product flow and inventory, generated sales and management reports; typical sales $1.8 to $10+ million, with maintenance/operation agreements running $500,000+ per unit. Trained and directed international sales staff of 18.

*Sample contributions:*
- Increased sales in target areas from $0 to $220 million in less than two years.
- Launched corporate sales efforts in Latin America, Australia, India; *in all three we are now the market leader.*
- Penetrated Chile market, leading to the first corporate service facility and labor agreement to import permanent in-country employees from TrialTest Japan.
- Prospected contacts in government service in India, leading to contract financed through the World Bank.

**Alexander The Great, Inc.,** Jersey City, New Jersey      1991–1992
**Manager**

Launched sales accounts with large specialty store chains and smaller retail outlets. Imported leather goods from Spain to locations throughout the United States. Established wholesale pricing strategy, sales systems and procedures, sourcing, and effective distribution system. Recruited independent field sales professionals for California, Texas, and the Mountain States. Sold business to New York-based Diversified Wholesalers, Inc.

*Continued . . .*

**Thompson Aircraft Tire**, LAX, Los Angeles, California      1988–1991
**Service Manager**

Scheduled time and action calendar to control retread work on leased tires, ensuring adequate supply and high quality product for airlines flying routes including the West Coast, Mexico, and Central America. Arranged inventory exchanges with other company branches internationally to meet customer needs. Built business relations with head-office purchasing agents for domestic and international airlines.

*Sample contributions:*
- Signature authority for FAA quality assurance documents at LAX.
- Negotiated "first choice" vendor relationships with the top three LAX airlines, worth $8 million to the company (only service manager to sell more than $1 million).

**Traskofabriken,** Stockholm, Sweden      1983–1988
**Export Manager**

Created, implemented, and maintained export and marketing policies for popular shoe manufacturer. Implemented policies through managing directors of subsidiaries in all EC member countries. Provided analysis of sales and marketing data, strategized optimum trade routes, duty controls, and pricing.

## EDUCATION

**B.A., International Trade**

Kungliga Tekniska Hogskolan (The Royal Institute of Technology), Stockholm, Sweden

# KEVIN W. HALL

9911 Davidian Drive
Menlo Park, California 94025

Private line/message/fax/pager: (415) 555-9681
Santa Clara office/voice mail: (408) 555-4748

---

## STRENGTHS

**Sales Management** ▪ **Account Management** ▪ **HW/SW Solution Selling**
**Joint Venturing / Relationship Partners** ▪ **Project Management**

### Track Record:

Over seven straight years of beating all sales goals with Fortune 500 companies:

| 1995 | 1994 | 1993 | 1992 | 1991 | 1990 | 1989 | 1988 |
|------|------|------|------|------|------|------|------|
| 171% | 130% | 142% | 123% | 157% | 103% | 125% | 118% |

Above performance delivered in highly competitive markets with a variety of product lines, some new and some mature. Absolutely committed to continued excellence.

### Sales Method:

Ability to access top officers of target companies — president, CEO, directors, CIO, CFO, v.p. engineering, etc. Ability to train sales professionals to access these top officers, as well. Talent for assembling project teams with complementary strengths — sales, engineering, support. Additional strength: distributor development.

### Technologies:

Total business solutions (manufacturing, financial, engineering, etc.), unusual combination of strengths in hardware *and* applications *and* networking *and* solution consulting. Current experience in RISC, UNIX, CISC, mainframe and PC environments. Quick study.

## EXPERIENCE

DARWIN DIGITAL CORPORATION, HQ: Massaqua, Massachusetts
**Account Manager**, Commercial/Manufacturing Division, Northern California, 1994–Present

Provide business solutions to major international corporations based in Northern California. Maintain intimate knowledge of business operations and key executives within target client companies. Conceive of potential business solutions projects. Assemble and supervise project teams of internal and external specialists. Direct the project from initial concept to proposal and acceptance and all the way through service provision. Keys to success: access to key target company executives, team building and management skill, attention to every last detail.

### Sample projects:

Re-engineering of worldwide manufacturing and financial systems for Seagate Technology, a $3.5 billion high-technology manufacturing company. Initiated project talks with Seagate. Negotiated participation of Ernst & Young consultants (Seagate's external auditors), retaining Darwin as prime contractor. Structured relationship with Oracle as venture partners. *Created a three-year $20 million project from the ground up.*

Structured the consolidation of IS infrastructure for the merger of Synops and Wellfleet, now Bay Networks, the largest networking company in the world. Direct liaison to CFO, CIO. Structured relationship with SAP, the software solutions provider. *Instrumental in winning approval of Darwin standard over HP on West Coast.* This was a $4 million project.

Approached Specialized Housewares, a $150 million manufacturer and worldwide distributor, to win approval to upgrade existing VAX mainframe environment to run DEC-developed manufacturing and financial solutions. This was a $500,000 project.

Solicited Varian, a specialty instrument/scientific/high technology manufacturing company, to adopt Darwin digital components for integration into their product lines. Structured $1 million relationship (first year alone).

Also concurrently oversee distributor relations with five key business partners in Northern California selling workstations, mid-size servers, high-end servers, software, PCs, and storage systems. (See below.)

**Distribution Sales Specialist**, Commercial/Manufacturing Division, Northern California, 1993

Managed relationships with 25 distributors and VARs throughout Silicon Valley region. Planned and sold to targeted discrete manufacturing accounts. Produced $2.6 million in sales revenue, including $500,000 in services, to win several sales awards.

UNISYS CORPORATION, HQ: Bluebell, Pennsylvania
**Account Team Leader**, Commercial Division, Northern California, 1988–1992

Position structurally similar to current duties (at Darwin). Initiated business solutions projects with targeted client companies in Northern California. Assembled account teams of internal and external specialists on a project-by-project basis. Managed the account relationship from initial contact through approval and service provision.

*Sample projects:*

Initiated, sold, implemented and integrated a UNISYS HW/SW/services solution to National Aeromotive, a jet engine remanufacturer. Project included shop-floor control, manufacturing, and financial solution, *a $5 million relationship including services.*

Initiated, sold, and implemented a nationwide manufacturing, financial, and shop-floor system for Oliver Rubber. Sold add-on integration of acquired Goodyear subsidiary. *Instrumental in winning UNISYS as standard over IBM.* Total project value of $2.5 million.

**Senior Account Representative**, Bay Area, 1987–1988
**Associate Sales Representative**, Operation Bright Star, Princeton, New Jersey, 1985–1986

## EDUCATION

CALIFORNIA STATE UNIVERSITY, Chico, California
**Bachelor of Arts, Public Administration**

BABSON SCHOOL OF EXECUTIVE EDUCATION, Wellesley, Massachusetts
**Certificate in Management**

UNIVERSITY OF CALIFORNIA—EXTENSION, Berkeley, California
**Certificate in Management** (ongoing)

CAMBRIDGE TECHNOLOGY (associated with HARVARD BUSINESS SCHOOL)
**Certificate in Sales Training / Open Systems Strategies**

PRODUCT TRAINING SEMINARS (numerous)

# J. SAM MITCHELL

1982 Shallots Run
San Jose, California 95120

Office/voice mail: (415) 555-7855
Residence/message: (408) 555-8927
Internet: sam.mitchell@power-net.com

---

**PROFILE**

**High Technology Marketing — Emerging Technologies**

Expertise: executive management of the marketing function in a high technology marketplace. Background emphasizes visionary technology projects, serving as the catalyst for (1) market acceptance of new commercializations and (2) pioneering use of emerging information delivery systems in the sales/marketing/customer support role.

Includes market research, customer research, market-driven input to product design, market/product/business planning, positioning, competitive analysis, training and development, design of research methodologies.

**EXPERIENCE**

POWER NET, INC.     Palo Alto, CA
**Marketing Manager, Global PrivateNet**     1993–Present

Power Net is a technology purveyor providing *private* and *secure* commercial communications networks to industry sectors, governments, and very large corporations worldwide, annual revenues $800 million.

Provide effective marketing programs for Global PrivateNet, a proprietary, subscription-based, online service serving customers in six targeted industry sectors: retail, trucking, financial services, health care, energy, public safety (police). Manage staff of 16, operating budget $2.6 million, as well as outside vendors, consultants, contractors.

Design market planning and analysis projects, involving original research and culminating in strategic and action plans. Contribute key elements of the Power Net Master Business Plan, including:
• Global PrivateNet Product Strategy
• Market Analysis by Industry Sector, United States and Canada
• Marketing Plan by Industry Sector

Conduct and manage actionable market and customer research focused on technology assessment, customer needs assessment, usage patterns, and competitive/alternate market analysis. Collaborate with sales function.

Manage delivery of customer support activities, including account management, help desk, and order fulfillment functions.

Design and produce internal and external marketing communication vehicles.

Plan and produce Global PrivateNet User Conference.

Develop presentations at industry events, including business sector meetings and high technology gatherings.

Achieved 600% growth in spite of stiff competition from the Internet itself.

APPLE COMPUTER, INC.     Cupertino, CA
**Market Development Manager, PIC Division**     1992–1993

Managed $400,000 research budget for introduction, positioning, and forecasting of new personal computing product. Designed and developed research objectives, screening, and survey instruments. Sourced, structured, and managed relationship with external research supplier. Reported results to over 40 Apple internal/external groups. Collaborated in the definition, creation, and refinement of marketing plans for product positioning.

**Planning and Analysis Manager, Enterprise Markets Division**     1992

Coordinated FY93 business planning process for $400 million division. Analyzed input from 6 contributing groups. Developed and initiated $200,000 research program to assess and measure effectiveness of individual marketing programs. Created effective presentations for use by division VP/general manager and others. Strengthened marketplace perception of Apple as viable supplier of business computers.

**Planning and Analysis Manager, Federal Systems Group**     1991–1992

Coordinated FY91–92 business planning process for $125 million division. Developed Federal Solutions Model as the basis for the FY91 plan. Functioned as corporate liaison for Washington, D.C.-based organization.

**Technical Solutions Manager, Federal Systems Group**     1988–1991

Defined and shaped key solutions for the federal market. Developed *Federal Solutions Guide* used by AFSG sales force. Identified and funded development of new Mac-based data products by federal agency developers, including NASA, NOAA, and USGS. Provided field sales organization with technical training and expertise for solutions through seminars, training events, and "go alongs" on sales calls. Created and managed "Proof-of-Concept" program to penetrate new government agency accounts, used successfully to open 8 new business relationships.

DATAQUEST, INC.     San Jose, Ca
**Senior Industry Analyst, CAD/CAM Industry Service**     1987–1988

Provided all aspects of subscription-based service to clients in GIS/Mapping, AEC, and PC-CAD markets. Developed and published 5-year forecasts of industry performance. Designed, developed, and wrote new revenue generating product (PC-CAD). Researched, wrote, and published incisive and timely newsletters. Exceeded company revenue targets for all 3 solution areas of responsibility.

*prior*

GE CALMA CO.     Milpitas, CA
**Industry Marketing Manager**
**Senior Sales Representative**
**National Account Manager**
**Product Manager**

Selected contributions: Devised innovative national account sales strategies focused on achieving initial sales at Bechtel and Chevron, resulting in opening new multimillion-dollar relationships. Product Manager/Team Leader over product specification, pricing, sales support, engineering liaison, competitive analysis, life cycle planning, product delivery for $5 million in sales.

**EDUCATION**     **Ph.D.,** Duke University

**M.S.,** University of Wisconsin, Madison

**B.S.,** University of Wisconsin, Madison

# MARY K. THURMOND

28 Desoto Court
Charleston, South Carolina 29406

Office/voice mail: (803) 555-6391
Residence/message/fax/pager: (803) 555-8563

## PROFILE

**Mortgage Banking — Commercial & Residential — Construction & Permanent Lending**

*Strengths:*

- Proven ability to originate, process, close, and service real estate lending, including renegotiations and work outs, management of REOs, troubleshooting of portfolios. Expertise in documentation, pro forma and credit analysis, and underwriting. Existing contacts throughout the real estate industry in South Carolina.

## EDUCATION

**M.B.A.,** Finance/Real Estate, University of South Carolina, 1977

**B.S.,** Business Administration, University of Georgia, 1972

## EXPERIENCE

FINEMAN & SONS (F&S), Charleston, 1991–Present
**V.P., Mortgage Services**

**Leading revenue producer** in mortgage services. Originate, place, process, and close commercial and industrial mortgage loans, typically in the range of $1 million to $15 million, but occasionally much larger. Work directly with real estate lending institutions and major direct investors to provide full-service structuring, packaging, placement, and closing.

Borrowers include individuals, partnerships, corporations, joint ventures, and institutions. Lenders include insurance companies, pension funds, banks, thrifts, credit companies. Structure and arrange multilender participation if necessary. Identify and resolve documentation problems, negotiate resolution to borrower/lender impediments, ensure compliance to regulatory requirements.

Personally handle financial analysis and drafting of agreement proposals. Strengths: Wide range of existing contacts throughout the industry, ability to qualify borrowers accurately, and ability to create solutions to lending difficulties.

Strategic contributions: **Obtain and review approximately 125 bona fide deals per annum, more than any officer in the company.** Improved relations with lenders, including establishing F&S as an approved/preferred mortgage broker with 15 of our largest lenders. Also maintain relationships with an additional 200 lenders for potential utilization as needed.

MAXIMA INVESTMENTS, INC., Charleston, 1988–1991
**V.P., Real Estate Finance/Mortgage Brokerage**

Originated and placed debt and equity requirements for commercial/residential property client base, working with diversified institutional sources. Coordinated financings for in-house real estate developments for the general contracting and development departments of the company. Serviced $20 million portfolio, including monitoring all areas of leasing, marketing, and property management.

Sample projects: Structured and placed financing for 20,000 sq.ft. retail and office and 25,000 sq.ft. condominium properties (construction loan, permanent/take out loan). Arranged construction loans for residential tract transactions. Arranged and managed successful sale and disposition of company's finished projects.

Strategic contributions: Diversified banking relationships for construction financing to eliminate dependency on a primary construction lender; achieved more competitive bidding and increased company stability. Enhanced project quality to improve institutional acceptance.

PIONEER FINANCIAL CORP., Columbia, 1984–1988
(a subsidiary of PIONEER SAVINGS BANK, FSB)
**V.P./Co-Manager, Income Property Financing**

Originated construction and permanent loans for parent bank, including processing, closing, and managing the administration of average outstandings of $150 million. Also placed loans with other institutions on an as needed basis. Approximately 75% mortgage banking and 25% brokerage.

COLONIAL MORTGAGE SERVICE CO., Charleston, 1982–1984
(a subsidiary of PHILADELPHIA NATIONAL BANK)
**A.V.P./Manager, Income Property Financing**

Originated income property and construction loans, as above. Approximately 80% mortgage banking and 20% brokerage.

IMPERIAL BANK, Los Angeles, 1980–1982
**V.P., Real Estate Department**

Originated, structured and processed construction loans, providing uncovered commercial and residential lending.

JACK DYMOND ASSOCIATES, Mountain City (Cal.), 1979–1980
**Developer** and **Property Manager**

Developed office buildings, light industrial warehousing, and strip retail projects. Managed land acquisition. Approximately 1,000,000 sq.ft. in total portfolio.

CORNISH & CAREY, Palo Alto (Cal.), 1978–1979
**Broker, Commercial Sales & Leasing**

COLDWELL BANKER COMMERCIAL BROKERAGE, San Jose (Cal.), 1977–1978
**Broker, Commercial Sales & Leasing**

CALIFORNIA CANADIAN BANK, Los Angeles/Orange County, 1975–1977
**A.V.P./Real Estate Loan Officer**

UNION BANK, Los Angeles/Beverly Hills, 1972–1975
**Loan Analyst, Credit Manager**

**MILITARY**

U.S. NAVY, 1965–1971

Vietnam veteran (medical technician), honorable discharge.

**CREDENTIAL**

Licensed Real Estate Broker, State of South Carolina, current

# FRANK C. GALLO

32 Hanover Plaza, #1800
New York, New York 10026

Office (voice mail): (800) 555-8545, x7932
Office (voice mail): (212) 555-9238
Residence (message): (212) 555-4835

**PROFILE**

**Sales & Account Management ▪ New Business Development ▪ Sales Training**

*Highlights:*

- Top producer in sales and sales management, with records for new account development, account retention, increase in sales to existing accounts. *Extensive* staff training and development background. Proven performer with dealer/distributor networks *and* with direct sales roles. Greatest strength: motivating others to excel.
- Eager for a new challenge.

**EXPERIENCE**

COSMAIR, INC. HQ: New York, NY
**L'Oréal Technique Professionnelle**
*V.P. Sales, Domestic*     1993–Present

Direct the sales of L'Oréal's exclusive professional line to distributors, beauty salons and beauty products wholesalers throughout the United States. Develop sales plan and operating budget. Hire and manage staff (total 185/300 seasonal). Analyze trends. Administer human resources and expensing. Report directly to the president. Member, Executive Team. Travel 70%.

Personally manage relationships with four major distributors, representing approximately $12 million in wholesale business. Coordinate with corporate marketing department to implement promotions. Independently develop territory promotions to maximize flow through. Plan and produce monthly sales meetings for 600+ people.

Supervise staff of regional and district sales managers, educational managers, and technical partners who sell to and train salon sales associates and professional stylists throughout the country. Delegate assignments, plan education, forecast budgets, administrate expense reports, motivate educators to maximum results.

*Contributions:*

- Plan and produce the largest beauty show in North America, including orchestrating guest appearances, venue, staging, models, wardrobe, and trade promotions and publicity, up to 60,000 attendees. Produce five shows/year.
- Manage the largest distributor relationship in the country, a critical business relationship.
- Currently achieving revenue plan with cost-of-sales 25% *under* budget.
- Identified and developed two new distributors, now contributing almost $1,000,000 in new revenue streams.
- Motivational speaker before groups up to 1000.

Position requires top organizational skills, sales talent, ability to motivate others, analytical skills, and high level of energy and commitment.

*Continued . . .*

**Keralogie L'Oréal Technique Professionnelle**
*Regional Manager*     1991–1993

Responsible for sales in 11 Western States, with 3 **Technical Advisors** and 16 **Field Training Associates**. Developed promotions, incentives, and bonus programs. Personally served as troubleshooter on key accounts. Prepared business plans and forecasts. Reported to VP-sales.

*Contributions:*
- Developed the first part-time field associates program in the country, now an industry standard.
- Planned and produced one of the largest trade shows in the country.
- Motivational speaker over groups up to 400.
- Achieved 100% sales *growth* in a downtrending market.

**L'Oréal Keralogie**
*Regional Technical Trainer*     1990–1991

Trained and developed the skills of sales force, directly responsible for train-the-trainer programs for field training staff of 22 and indirectly in charge of sales/product training for every distributor sales representative and store sales associate, over 200 salespeople.

*Contributions:*
- Rewrote all sales scripts for use in the region, adopted companywide.
- Brought conceptual rigor to sales.
- Wrote an innovative sales manual, *How to Sell Color.*
- Motivational speaker over groups up to 200.

**L'Oréal Professional Division**
*Technical Sales Consultant*     1989–1990

*Contributions:*
- Technical Sales Consultant of the Year (for top sales).
- Trained at L'Oréal in Paris, *four times* selected for this honor (one out of all 500 consultants).

**L'Oréal Professional Division**
*Technical Advisor*     1987–1989

*Contributions:*
- New business development specialist. Opened 450 new accounts in one year. Held the highest retention rate in the territory to date.

**EDUCATION & CREDENTIALS**

THE HOBSON SCHOOL     Darien, CT
**Diploma**

# DONNIE GILBERT

2455 Titan Avenue
Saratoga, California 95070

Residence/message/fax: (408) 555-0257
Personal e-mail: donnie.girl@navi.com

---

**EXPERTISE**

**Sales ▪ Marketing ▪ New Business Development ▪ Product Management**

*Strengths:*
- Strategic planning of sales and marketing activities, market and competitive analysis, staff motivation, commercialization of new products. Experience spans sales, marketing, trade advertising, promotions, materials development, and supervision of sales, engineering, and support functions.
- Effective combination of analytical and interpersonal skills.
- Ready and eager for new challenges.

**EXPERIENCE**

**MITSUKA OPTICAL SYSTEMS, INC.**   Los Gatos, CA
(subsidiary of **Mitsuka Photo Optical, Ltd.**, Japan, and **Mitsuka Film**)
*Director of Sales and Marketing*   1994–1996
*Worldwide Marketing Manager*   1992–1993

Directed domestic and international sales for this $9 million high-technology dental products company, a subsidiary of Mitsuka Japan. Prepared all objectives, budgets, and forecasts. Managed $1.5 million sales and marketing budget. Member, executive team, involved in all strategic management decision-making for the company. Collaborated daily with the president.

Supervised headquarters team of sales professionals, applications engineers, customer service representatives, and product specialists. Oversaw all direct and indirect sales and marketing activities. Established sales quotas, led motivational sales team meetings, established customer service performance benchmarks, planned and oversaw trade show representation, strategized market and competitive intelligence, traveled domestically and internationally as needed.

Contributed ideas for new product development, resolved product issues between customers and U.S. Mitsuka engineers, provided critical information to the parent company in Japan concerning U.S. and worldwide market trends, coordinated with Mitsuka Europe on some product lines.

Hands-on leader and manager. Comfortable with all levels and types of technical, financial, and management contacts internally and in client companies.

*Selected contributions:*
- Built worldwide exclusive dealer network from scratch, including extensive training in sales, promotions, competitive analysis, and pricing techniques. Initiated relationships creating $12 million in new revenues.
- Worked closely with the president to co-develop the dental imaging business (intraoral television imaging devices), a new $60 million market.
- Introduced product to Mitsuka Europe, including a market roll out in Cologne, Amsterdam, London. Created immediate sales.
- Represented company to beta test sites for clinical evaluations. Orchestrated FDA and OSHA product approvals.
- **Chairperson**, American Dental Association, Construction & Safety Committee for ADA Standards on Clinical Devices, 1996.

*Continued . . .*

Mitsuka Optical Systems, Inc., continued:

- Improved internal sales and product support operations, for example: reduced order shipping to 5 working days or less, implemented no-charge loaner program for repairs, reduced repair turnaround (+ numerous similar projects).
- Troubleshot the internal engineering-sales relationship to ensure cooperation and effective interface with customers and markets.

*Product Marketing Manager*     1991–1992
*Dental Product Manager*     1989–1991

*Contributions:*
- Arranged exclusive partnership with one of the largest domestic dental dealers.
- Developed new exclusive arrangement with the largest Canadian dental dealer.
- Provided extensive training for over 500 sales and equipment specialists.
- Developed all new marketing and sales materials (from concept through printing and dissemination).
- Improved competitive analysis and sales support.
- Pioneered commercialization of new technologies.
- Achieved record sales of $7 million.

*PRIOR*

**APPLE COMPUTER**     Fremont, CA
*Macintosh Communications*

Writer/editor/coordinator. Managed internal communications and public relations for one of the most automated factories in the world. Attended and reported on trade shows and special events. MarCom division representative. Also prepared minutes and agendas for staff, and managed special assignments for Steve Jobs.

**NEW PRODUCT DEVELOPMENT**     San Francisco, CA
*Office Manager*

Researched and analyzed competitor product information, collaborated on developing sales and marketing plans.

**ENHANCE CORPORATION**     San Jose, CA
*Office Manager*

Critical link between senior management and $12 million direct sales organization. Assisted in marketing projects such as packaging design.

**EDUCATION**     UNIVERSITY OF SAN FRANCISCO     San Francisco, CA
**M.S., Organizational Development**

SAN JOSE STATE UNIVERSITY     San Jose, CA
**B.S., Marketing**

UNIVERSITY OF WISCONSIN     Madison, WI
**American Marketing Association, School of Marketing**

**REFERENCES**     Provided on request, but please keep this information confidential at this time.

# JILL SANDERS

3917 Orchard Drive
Mountain View, California 94043

Residence/message: (415) 555-2592
js33@top-solutions.com

**EXPERTISE**

**Sales & Sales Management**

**Relationship Management**

**International New Business Development**

**Distributor Development**

**HIGHLIGHTS**

- "**Sales Manager of the Year**" for major software company targeting Fortune 1000 companies.
- "**President's Club**" for nine out of eleven possible years in both sales management and direct sales roles. Ran as high as **240% of quota** in direct sales.
- "**New Business Expert**," with *consistent* series of sales and sales management accomplishments.

**EXPERIENCE**

**SMART Software International**     Santa Clara, CA

Provider of SLICE client-server enterprisewide software and services solutions across mainframe, UNIX, VAX, and PC environments to major corporations worldwide. Typical sale of $150,000 to $250,000 corporate, $500,000 to multimillion-dollar agreements with distributors.

**Vice President of International Sales**, 1993–Present

Selected by the president to spearhead the company's first market push into Asia-Pacific, Mexico, and Canada markets. Developed sales strategies, business plan, budget, and objectives. Frequent travel (Japan, Australia, Mexico, Canada, Hong Kong, Singapore, Malaysia). Continue to be involved in strategic decision-making companywide; report directly to the president; member, Product Planning Committee.

Identified and evaluated top quality distributors in targeted regions. Negotiated long-term exclusive agreements in **Canada**, **Mexico, Australia**. Created sales and technical training programs for distributor sales professionals. Act as the **Sales Manager** for the distributor sales force, providing strategies, supporting negotiations, and approving any departure from standardized deals.

**Relationship Manager** for Suntory, Ltd., a $6,000,000 relationship, the largest client in the company's history. Successfully negotiated $1,300,000 in 1995 revenue.

**Director of Sales, Western Region**, 1990–1993

Sales manager for five sales offices covering the western two-thirds of the United States. Provided sales strategies to develop new business with Fortune 1000 companies, a complex multiuser sales cycle involving IS executives and nontechnical managers. Motivated three Branch Managers, 12 Sales Representatives, 12 Technical Specialists, and support staff. Wrote 1992/1993 U.S. field compensation plan. Reported directly to the V.P. Sales; collaborated with the President on pricing and product development.

**Exceeded region quota of up to $5,000,000** and P&L targets each and every year. Named "**MVP of U.S. Field**," 1990. Developed the "**Branch Manager of the Year**" and "**Sales Representative of the Year**." **Grew central area revenue by 250%.**

*Continued . . .*

Managed sales cycle for the company's first Japanese account; developed the client relationship. Co-**Negotiator** on agreement which generated $6,000,000 in software, development, and royalty revenues.

Consistently prevailed over industry leaders with more technical and sales resources. Personally assisted sales staff throughout new account sales cycle. Achieved 90% win rate on competitive trials.

**Western District Manager**, 1987–1990

Managed total staff of 15 Sales Representatives and Technical Specialists in Los Angeles, San Francisco, and Seattle. Oversaw four of the company's five largest clients and negotiated enterprise software agreements. Designed sales training workshop for company sales meetings.

Exceeded quota each and every year, running as high as **136% of quota**. Named **"Sales Manager of the Year."** Developed **"Sales Representative of the Year."** Achieved customer conversion from a major competitor. Ranked top revenue district in the United States. Awarded **"Continued Excellence in Sales Management."**

**Dun & Bradstreet Computing Services**      San Mateo, CA
Provider of 4GL/RDBMS software and services to Fortune 1000 companies.

**Sales Manager, Northwest District**, 1984–1987

Managed sales staff and offices serving western United States. Wrote and implemented 1985, 1986, 1987 sales plans. Designed Customer Focus program. **Relationship Manager** for Boeing, one of the five largest customers worldwide, generating new revenue and thwarting a major competitor's acceptance.

**Achieved 101% and 105% of quota. Top Revenue District** and **Top Profit District**, 1986. Motivated two Sales Representatives to **"President's Club."**

**Marketing Representative**, 1981–1985

**Achieved 240% of quota, 155% of quota, 181% of quota**. Achieved highest revenue booked in the history of the company (240% of quota). Earned region "Top Producer" award for consulting sales.

**NCR Corporation**      Los Angeles, CA

In a division providing turnkey computer systems (minis and proprietary applications software) to government, education, and commercial markets.

**Account Manager**, 1978–1980

**Achieved 168% of quota, 100% of quota.**

**EDUCATION**      **California State University**      Northridge, CA
**B.S., Business Administration** and **Marketing**
Graduated *magna cum laude*

**REFERENCES**      Excellent references and recommendations available upon request, but please keep all information confidential at this time.

# Preston Taggart, CTC

600 Marina Point Plaza, Apt. F53½
Marina Del Rey, California 90292

Telephone: (310) 555-4577
Private fax: (310) 555-4579

## PROFESSION

### Director of Sales & Marketing — Hotels

**Results-oriented high-achiever able to engineer major increases in sales, revitalize staff and operations, and turn around negative-performing properties.**

*Strengths:*

- Directed hotel sales and marketing for upscale properties in San Jose, Washington, D.C., Chicago, San Diego, Los Angeles. Specialist in corporate and travel industry sales, domestic and international markets. Extensive experience with Europe, Latin America, U.S.A., Asia markets.

- Skilled in account relations and new business development. Extensive experience in planning, directing, and conducting professional sales campaigns incorporating major trade shows: NTA, Pow Wow, ITX, World Travel Market, NBTA, ITB, and major consumer shows.

- Expertise in multiproperty sales management, in-house systems, yield management advertising, public relations campaigns. Member, Executive Committee, involved in strategic planning. Acting General Manager, in full charge in absence of the G.M. CHA candidate (completion by January 1997).

- General management skills, including input to operations design and quality control issues. Have developed budgets to $49 million sales and $5 million gross revenue. Special strength: significant experience with high-end, world-class business and leisure properties.

## HISTORY

TOP FLIGHT HOTEL, Los Angeles Airport, California    1994–Present
**Director of Sales and Marketing**

Provide strategic direction and daily management of the sales, marketing, and catering functions for Top Flight Hotel Los Angeles International Airport (owned and operated by a division of Grosvenor Properties, Inc., one of the largest hotel companies in the world). This property is a 615-room, business-class, full-service hotel. Report directly to the general manager. Responsible for promoting business with national corporate accounts, large travel agencies, consortiums, retail agencies, incentive companies, wholesalers, airlines, and car rental companies.

Revitalized the entire sales and marketing function. Developed new marketing and sales plans. Recruited and trained new sales team. Oversaw design and production of new brochures, fliers, sales kits, and marketing collaterals. Represented the hotel at major trade shows and conventions.

Created the "LA's Business Hotel" campaign, repositioned the hotel to better meet current business needs, achieved 17% increase in occupancy.

SO-CAL HOTEL MANAGEMENT, INC., San Diego, California    1992–1994
**Director of Sales and Catering**

Managed sales for two owned properties; provided sales and market analysis and planning for potential new properties. Provided strategic sales planning, seasonal to daily sales management, and detailed training and motivation to sales professionals at two properties, the Hotel Old Town and the Western Shores Inn, 386 rooms/suites total. The Hotel Old Town is an award-winning deluxe hotel, a very successful property, with the top occupancy rate in the local business region.

Directed sales to domestic and international markets, corporate accounts, travel industry, and associations. Oversaw sales, catering, and marketing departments. Developed and implemented sales strategies, market segment analyses, advertising/promotions/public relations campaigns, and travel package development with venture partners. Member, ASTA, ICTA, MPI, HSMA.

*Continued . . .*

FAIRVIEW CREST HOTEL, Chicago, Illinois    1991–1992
**Director, Travel Industry Sales**

Managed and coordinated development of business from national corporate accounts, large travel agencies, consortiums, retail agencies, incentive companies, wholesalers, airlines, and car rental companies for this 700-room luxury hotel with an international reputation. Negotiated rates and packages. Represented the hotel to major trade shows and conventions.

POTOMAC HOTELS, INC., Washington, D.C.    1990–1991
**Corporate Director, Travel Industry Sales**

Complete charge of Travel Industry Sales for 13 properties (3500+ rooms) in the Washington, D.C., Philadelphia, and Baltimore metropolitan areas. Renegotiated contracts and initiated contacts with accounts generating $1.5 million in new business.

RADISSON PLAZA HOTEL, San Jose Airport, California    1989–1990
**Director of Sales and Marketing**

Full responsibility for planning and executing all sales, marketing and advertising activities for this 200-room luxury hotel. Managed all pricing and negotiations. Handled media, vendor, and travel industry relations.

Redirected marketing strategy to target upscale market, promoting luxury hospitality services. Achieved a sustained 10% increase in occupancy and a 30% increase YTD in average daily rate. Called on corporate accounts and intermediary markets. Heavy involvement in rate negotiations.

THOMAS COOK TRAVEL, USA, San Francisco, California    1977–1989
**Regional Manager**    1985–1989

Directed activities of over 80 in customer service, sales, and operations in the Northern California Region. Handled strategic planning, budgeting, cost control. Select, supervise, and motivate management and staff. Emphasis on developing new business and providing top quality service. Extensive sales and service involvement, especially proposal reviews and contract negotiations with key clients/vendors.

Hotel sales responsibilities involved extensive corporate account management, including business development and client servicing. Administered preferred vendor programs. Quality Management Program Participant. Operations Committee Member.

Prior positions: **City Manager**, San Francisco, 1984–1985, **Branch Manager**, 1980–1984, **Assistant Manager**, 1977–1980.

## EDUCATION

University of California at San Diego
**M.A. in Sociology, B.A. in Social Sciences**

American Hotel and Motel Association
**CHA** Candidate

Institute of Certified Travel Agents, Wellesley, Massachusetts
**CTC**, **Executive Travel Management**

Aarhus University, Aarhus, Denmark
**Danish**

*Continued . . .*

## TRAINING

Dun and Bradstreet — **Quality Management**

Massachusetts Institute of Technology — **Operations Management in Service Industries**

Thomas Cook Management Development Program, U.K. — **Financial Management** and **Interpersonal Management Skills**

Xerox Corporation — **Professional Selling Skills**

American Airlines — **SABRE Reservations System**

Fairview Hotels — **Managing Sales People**

Radisson Hotels — **Yield Management**

Cornell University — **Hospitality Executive Management Training**

American Hotel and Motel Association — **Annual Seminar for Hotel Management Executives**

# JACK PIERCE

2800 – 10th Street, No. 2
Santa Monica, California 90404

Business/voice mail: (310) 555-9396
Residence/message: (310) 555-6399
http://www.ccmarket.com

---

**EXPERTISE**

**Retail Marketing & Promotions ▪ Licensing ▪ New Product Launch**

*Strengths:*

Demonstrated ability to generate a large volume of creative strategies for retail marketing, promotions, licensing and sponsorship sales, free and bartered media—including collaborative alliances of similar and dissimilar business partners—to generate exposure well beyond the reach of simple marketing efforts.

Persuasive ability as a company representative to media, the public, and co-op/collaborative business partners. Consistently proven ability to gain participation of others to benefit company projects.

Entrepreneurial and action oriented. Entire career history has emphasized building marketing efforts from zero to create new revenues with new products, new alliances, and new distribution channels.

Comfortable with high-profile assignments; effective speaker, trainer, spokesperson, coach. Comfortable with rapidly evolving technology. Extensive background managing agency and consulting business partners.

Successful background: variety of fields, products, marketing roles.

**DIRECTLY RELATED EXPERIENCE**

CATALINA CORP.    Los Angeles, CA

**Vice President, Director, Consumer Marketing**    1994–Present

Brought on board to design and launch a totally new kind of agency, one that uses the most sophisticated forms of databasing, direct mail, computer modeling, and traditional marketing to provide a vertically integrated retail shopping center promotions service. The division was based on the radical concept that a shopping center's value was based not on its tenants but on its ability to attract customers. We adapted five massive databases of purchase information on 40,000 households tested for 8000 products and services and tied to a digitized street map of America. No program had ever been created to do this before. R&D budget $500,000/total budget responsibility $1.5 million/staff of 13.

Part of the senior management team that identified and developed $6 million in potential additional funding. Secured financial involvement of Fortune 500 companies, including Pac Bell, The Good Guys, Safeway, Von's, Taco Bell, McDonald's, Pier 1, Strouds, Hallmark, etc.

*Additional contributions:*
* Test mailings generated 11% returns, nearly three times the national average.
* Market survey completed to determine merchants' marketing needs, experience, and financial commitments to marketing and promotions.
* Identified test markets and designed test phase.
* Hired and trained sales personnel to represent agency to merchants, national chains, major centers. Instrumental member of senior management team on acquisition of new clients worth $500,000+ each.
* Created first-ever bar-coded premium tracking system, tracking each redeemed promotion back to the *specific* customer and marketing effort.
* Generated net operating profit after first mailing.
* Oversaw acquisition of 11 new accounts representing $2.5 million in fee revenues per year.

TOGA GLOBAL TRADING COMPANY   Los Angeles, Hong Kong, Manila, Foochow
**Vice President, Marketing**   1979–1986

Provided strategic and tactical management in fast-paced consumer products company. Coordinated 25 new product sourcing agents in Asian locales, identifying and developing artisans and products for distribution throughout United States markets. Supervised 50 consumer products representative organizations in United States markets, coast-to-coast. Traded East-West and West-East, but with emphasis on development of offshore sources and domestic markets.

*Selected contributions:*
- Developed, produced, and distributed over 100 new consumer products.
- **Doubled revenue every year for five straight years** to solid seven-figure sales.
- Conceived, produced, and procured underwriting for year-long promotion tour of Chinese national artists, coordinating with Neiman Marcus, Garfinkle's, Woodward-Lothrop, and the Chinese national government.
- Opened new accounts with major American department stores: Neiman Marcus, Sakowitz, Bullocks Wilshire, Carson Pirie Scott, Garfinkle's, The Broadway, Saks Fifth Avenue, and others.
- Opened new accounts with major consumer and affinity catalog retailers, including American Express, Pacific Telephone, Willoughby & Taylor, Applause, Kaplan's Ben Hur, Sunset, Hunt's, Chris Craft, and others.

**ADDITIONAL RELATED EXPERIENCE**

INDEPENDENT CONSULTING   Santa Monica, CA
**Marketing Consultant**   1993–Present

*Sample engagements:*
- **GolfGame CD-Rom** (created unique coalition of sponsors and product placements in support of most successful golf-based PC game).
- **The World Ride Against Cancer** (raised $1,250,000 in funds for research for International Jaycees).
- **The Ultra-America** (packaged $26 million project, a cross-country footrace).
- **Greater L.A. Zoo**.
- **Caltrans Grand Reopening I-105**.

CINCH DYNAMICS   Santa Monica, CA
**Senior Director, Marketing**   1991–1993

Provided new business development, sponsorship packaging, sales and fulfillment for highly regarded 25-year-old sports/entertainment marketing company.

*Selected contributions:*
- Negotiated and sold six-figure national promotion to M&M Mars, which distributed 1.5 million product samples at 750 live events in 37 states.
- Doubled Santa Barbara Jazz Festival sponsor revenue, bringing in Jim Beam, Pepsi, Amex, GTE, and others.
- Co-developed Youth Cup International, first-ever national youth soccer championships, sponsored by divisions of Walt Disney Co.

UNITED STATES OLYMPIC FESTIVAL-'91     Los Angeles, CA
**Vice President, Marketing**     1990–1991

Directed all sponsor procurement and fulfillment, advertising, and promotions for this ten-day, $15 million pre-Olympic event. Built the marketing function from scratch with minimal resources, short notice, and record-breaking results.

*Selected contributions:*

- Team leader on signing record $10 million in sponsorships from 107 corporations, including Coca-Cola, 3M, Bristol-Myers Squibb, Kodak, Bausch & Lomb, M&M Mars, AT&T, Kelloggs, GTE, and others.
- Saved $3 million by negotiating bartered media; leveraged this media into additional sponsorship exposure.
- Managed multiproduct licensing for $500,000 revenues.
- Interfaced with Fortune 500 senior management, agencies, media, USOF-'91 board, U.S. Olympic Committee.
- Personally signed many of the major sponsors.

SPRING GAMES USA     Los Angeles, CA
**Vice President, Marketing**     1988–1990

Secured venture capital, overall marketing, executive recruitment, sponsorship sales and management, fulfillment, for nationally televised college sporting event. This was the first organization the cities of Daytona and Palm Springs ever partnered with, providing sponsorship of events for college students during spring break.

*Sample contributions:*

- Personally raised $300,000 to finance first-year start-up phase.
- Increased sponsorship 525% in second year.
- Increased entrants to 10,000+ in second year.
- Produced highly effective promotional video as sales tool.

**EDUCATION**

UCLA - EXTENSION
**Certificate Program in Marketing** *(one-third complete)*

WHITWORTH COLLEGE
**B.A., English / History** *Dean's List*

CONTINUING EDUCATION
**U.S.P.S. Seminar on Direct Marketing**
**Seminar Leader's Program**

# Spencer Carlisle

19906 Foothills Boulevard, #1205
Ft. Collins, Colorado 80525

Telephone/fax/message/pager: (970) 555-4567
sc3@sales.phoenix.com

| | |
|---|---|
| **EXPERTISE** | **Sales & Sales Management**<br>**Key Relationships Management**<br>**New Business Development** |

Award-winning sales executive with I.B.M. and Moore. Entire career history targeting Fortune 500 and other major domestic and multinational corporate clients. Expert at customer-focused solution selling. Able to gain market acceptance for cutting-edge technology products.

Special strengths: ability to identify market opportunity, make strategic adjustments in products and sales efforts to exploit market opportunity, access and build working relationships with top officers of any corporation worldwide, achieve exclusive agreements in highly competitive markets. Bilingual, French-English.

Dynamic top producer, seeking product and company committed to rapid sales expansion and new market development.

**HIGHLIGHTS**

- Provided sales strategies and market-driven product refinements for entrepreneurial **High-Technology Start-up Company**.
- Senior account representative in **National Account Group** — co-built sales team that generated 27% of company revenues with less than 7% of cost-of-sales.
- **Top Salesman in the Nation** for two straight years while with I.B.M. Canada.

**EXPERIENCE**

PHOENIX L.A., 1995–1996
**Account Manager**, Ft. Collins, Colorado

Identified applications and markets for document engineering programs, an advanced print-on-demand system based on a Xerox Docutech engine. Phoenix's main service product allows zero inventory, daily revision, and simultaneous worldwide distribution for manuals, forms, and books.

The Print-on-Demand and Just-in-Time printed materials management systems reduce book-length printed materials production time from two weeks to a couple hours, with up to 15% reduction in cost. These systems also allow overnight worldwide release of larger documents with *total security*, a capacity not previously available at any price.

Recruited to strategize and design new market penetration efforts, refine ancillary product offerings, launch sales campaigns, and contribute to companywide sales planning efforts. Phoenix is a three-year-old start-up.

Identified over 700 qualified customers for Phoenix applications. Codeveloped the prototype contractual agreement for this new market. Expanded the service line to exploit vertical markets. Identified and targeted software development and high-technology manufacturing companies as major new market (product manuals).

Closed twenty-two accounts before company engineering officers revealed product release schedule would be delayed by months, possibly even a year.

Sample accounts: A major European automobile manufacturer — training manuals and owner's manuals for all car models sold in the United States for last ten years. A major grocery chain — operations manuals and weekly price lists for 160 stores.

MOORE BUSINESS FORMS AND SYSTEMS, 1979–1994

**Special Account Group Account Executive,** Omaha, Nebraska, 1986–1993

On the opening team for the newly formed Special Account Group, targeting major national and multinational corporations with $500,000 minimum annual relationships. Moore provides forms management systems (hardware, software, distribution, warehousing, reporting and information control services) to major corporations.

Identified, developed and closed new national accounts for Moore, with emphasis on three-year exclusive agreements. Developed creative solutions using internal and external resources and new technologies. Acted as internal consultant for client companies, identifying needs and designing solutions on a major scale.

Also structured and provided experimental services never before offered by Moore, e.g., conducted purchasing for client companies.

Designed forms systems for companies experiencing rapid expansion. Solved forms and information control problems, e.g., Homebase (63 stores / 700 info originators) and Mary's Diners (215 stores / 92 info originators).

Developed a $9 million program with Eastman, Inc., the largest office supplies distributor in the western United States.

Introduced Electronic Data Interchange (EDI) to a major account, a single-entry data / form / information management system.

Salesman of the Year, 1989, Top Sales Bonus, 1992.

**Senior Account Manager**, Minneapolis, Minnesota, 1982–1986

Developed two national accounts, one a $2 million relationships and one a $450,000 relationship.

Introduced bar code technology (hardware and software) for chart, document, and patient test control in the Nuclear Medicine Dept. of a hospital, achieving 22% cost savings over manual methods. Identified need and worked with client to design custom application; Moore then adopted the product nationwide.

**Account Manager**, Montreal Financial District, Canada, 1979–1982

Recruited to elite group targeting financial companies in Montreal. Opened three major new accounts: Greenshields, the largest broker in Canada; B.N.P. (Banque de Nationale Paris), the North American headquarters for this French bank; Fiducie du Quebec, the pension plan for provincial employees.

Wrote exclusive three-year contractual agreements with first-time accounts. First person in Canada to sell Compurite, a pioneer selectronic data-to-form publishing system.

Top Salesman in Eastern Region, Top Five Award (nationwide).

INTERNATIONAL BUSINESS MACHINES (I.B.M.), 1975–1979

**Sales Representative**, Montreal, Canada

Sold office automation systems to major corporations. Ran 186% of quota. Ranked #1 in the nation two years in a row. Provided operations analysis and solution configuration. Gave presentations to top management.

**EDUCATION**

**Sir George William University: B.A., Commerce**
**C.E.G.E.P. du Vieux Montreal: Honors in Marketing**
**Advertising Sales Executive Club of Montreal: Honors**

**PERSONAL**

Dual citizenship, United States and Canada.

# Jennifer S. Turner

103 Leaning Pines Street
Austin, Texas 78758

Telephone / message:
(512) 555-3837

---

**PROFILE**

**Sales ▪ Marketing ▪ New Business Development ▪ Account Relations**

Strengths include direct sales and account management, design and management of sales / marketing / advertising campaigns, and quantitative skills for business budgeting / planning / analysis. Entrepreneurial by nature.

**EDUCATION**

STANFORD UNIVERSITY, Stanford, California
**B.A., Economics**
**B.A., Sociology**

**EXPERIENCE**

TEXAS INSTRUMENTS, Austin, Texas
**Marketing Director** (three years)

Recruited to design and manage marketing programs for a new vertical marketing strategy targeting the medical industry with dedicated SW / HW systems. Supervised staff of three marketing administrators. Reported directly to the V.P. of marketing. Traveled up to 50%.

Conceptualized and developed marketing plan to introduce TI as a SW vendor to medical markets. Developed national product rollout plan, including image development, media mix, PR programs, promotional events, trade show representation, and all related sales tools, schedules, and budgets.

*Contributions:*
- Increased distribution channels from 1 to 600.
- Personally served as TI ambassador, demonstrator, and key speaker at conventions, seminars, and trade shows nationwide.
- Designed and produced national **direct mail** campaigns targeting medical professionals.
- Designed **print media** campaigns and set media mix for magazine and trade publications.
- Created a **telemarketing** function, including staffing, scripts, and lead management systems.
- Published **newsletter** and created steady stream of materials / collaterals for sales force (supported 150 sales professionals nationwide), for example, designed a second newsletter specifically for clients who were considering the purchase but had not signed on yet.
- Brought a much needed market awareness to the engineering process.
- Dealt directly with national **key accounts** such as Blue Cross to ensure account loyalty.

This was a pilot program, so all strategies, administration, analysis, and reporting had to be designed from the ground up. Achieved successful product launch; perhaps most significantly, was able to overcome engineering delays and sustain market interest until product was ready for application.

This program was used within the TI organization as a model of successful niche marketing.

CROWN ZELLERBACH CORPORATION, Los Angeles and San Francisco
**District Sales Representative** (four years)

Sold industrial papers to distributors and major end-users of paper bags, freezer paper, napkins, towels, tissues, tapes. These were primarily major accounts (routine orders were for car load or truck load units of a single product) but did include some small accounts (approx. 5%). Also originated some sales direct to smaller end-users that were channeled through the most appropriate distributor. Accounts included all major paper distributors in territory, as well as major retail and department store chains, aerospace, medical, high-technology, and military customers.

In full charge of sales planning and all sales activities. Targeted and developed new accounts, accessed and sold to client company top officers (usually president or C.O.O.). Also troubleshot all accounts, coordinating with all internal Zellerbach departments (credit, shipping, production) on behalf of accounts.

*Contributions:*
- Built excellent reputation for service on accounts.
- Ranked #1 in the entire Western Region (out of 20 peers).
- Grew territory from $5 to $8 million.
- Consistently proved ability to close headquarters sales.
- Created promotional programs for distributor sales.
- Trained and motivated distributor sales force.
- Represented Zellerbach in industrial trade shows.

CROWN ZELLERBACH CORPORATION, San Francisco
**Human Resources Administrator (Recruiter)** (two years)

Recruited professionals in engineering, finance, data processing, marketing, sales, and management. Interviewed and recruited college applicants nationwide. Strategized use of classified advertising, search firms, and employment agencies. Designed computer systems for candidate data management.

SCOTT PAPER COMPANY, San Francisco
**Sales Representative** (two years)

Managed 125 accounts in Northern California, with full responsibility for sales, account relations, merchandising, and promotions. Graduate of one of the best corporate sales training programs in the country.

**AFFILIATIONS**          Stanford Professional Women

# JAY ROBERT SPRINGER

22 Kent Drive, #25
San Mateo, California 94401

Telephone/message: (415) 555-3257
jrs33@telnet.com

---

**STRENGTHS**

**Sales / Marketing / Sales Management**

Ability to identify and develop market opportunities, both as a **sales executive** and as a **sales/marketing manager**. Entire career background in high-tech environments, including software, hardware, turnkey systems, and emerging technologies. Successful turnaround manager.

Contributions:
- Developed and closed multimillion-dollar OEM and distribution contracts.
- Built two national sales organizations from nothing to solid profitability.
- Consistently able to build rapport with top officers of targeted companies (CEO, Pres., CFO, EVP, etc.).

**EXPERIENCE**

**VAST Systems Software U.S.A.**
Burlingame, California / Frankfurt, Germany
**Sales Manager, North & South America**, 1993–1996

Recruited to reorganize and revitalize a sales organization in the third year of a start-up phase, the U.S. subsidiary of a major German corporation. Company's expansion plans had stalled due to poorly structured incentives and failure to carve its niche out of a potential market of 4200 mainframe data centers in the United States. Products: a line of MVS applications for prep, QA and job management functions, $15,000 to $100,000 in cost.

Highlights:
- Prior sales organization had developed only 18 accounts in three years. Personally brought on board 15 new accounts in less than one year, for example MCI, AT&T, New York Life, Bank of Boston, Reebok, Marriott, Manufacturers Life Insurance, Royal Bank of Canada, Moore Business Forms.
- Eliminated 13 sales positions and reversed extravagant spending on advertising, travel, and entertainment. Performance:
  - $2,000,000 expenses on $300,000 revenue (prior to taking control)
  - $500,000 expenses on $1,400,000 revenue (first full year in charge)
  - $900,000 expenses on $2,500,000 revenue (second full year in charge)
- Revised pricing strategy, adding service and support. Sold products for $100,000 that prior sales force had been unable to sell for $25,000.
- Created first sustained cash flow, doubled company revenues, eliminated $400,000 short-term debt, generated $250,000 surplus operating capital.

Identified synergistic opportunity for spin-off/merger/JV with Altai Software of Arlington, Texas. Initiated relations with Altai resulting in merger of product lines, technology transfer, and exchange of markets. Result:
- Engineered a profitable retreat from U.S. markets for the parent company, VAST Systems Software AG, turning a $1,500,000+ loss into a projected $1,000,000 gain. Additionally, the parent company is projected to achieve a 24% increase in net profit from benefits of Altai's European business.

*Continued . . .*

**SDI Financial (now Vanguard Systems)**
Cambridge, Massachusetts / London, England, U.K.
**Vice President, Sales**, 1989–1992

Represented securities trading and accounting software to the top 100 banks and financial services companies in America, closing sales agreements for $600,000 to $2,500,000 per product installation. Targeted buyer: client company Treasurer, CFO, VP Trading, EVP Operations, and similar. Supervised a sales department with staff of 25 (sales and tech support). Featured speaker at industry and trade conferences.

Highlights:
- Created a sales and account management organization, including job descriptions, workload analysis, performance standards, and budget. Revised sales strategies, retrained staff, reduced the sales cycle by 50%.
- Personally closed the largest sale in the company's 15-year history, a $2,500,000 contract.
- Personally closed the largest annual volume for personal sales in the 15-year history of the company.
- Recovered lost client worth $500,000 per annum in recurring revenues.
- Specified and launched new product, an international, multicurrency securities accounting product, generating $5,000,000 in first-year licensing fees alone.
- Avoided long-term sales with certain major bank customers, each of which failed within 12 months, saving millions of dollars in uncollectible receivables.
- Brought on board Chase Manhattan, First Chicago, European American Bank, Harvard Management, American Insurance Group.
- Negotiated resale and co-marketing agreements with third-party vendors, for example: IBM. Wrote contracts and designed contract control system.

**EXXON Technolabs** (a division of **EXXON Company, USA**)
Boston, Massachusetts
**National Sales Manager, U.S. and Canada**, 1986–1989

Built national sales force from nothing to staff of 25 (sales and tech support) in 9 sales offices. Introduced new products and technology to industrial markets and DoD contractors. Negotiated master distributor contract with Canadian General Electric Company. Featured speaker at industry conferences.

Contributions:
- Achieved $6,000,000+ in revenues in first six months of start-up.
- Brought on board Federal Express, Boeing, General Electric, U.S. Navy, Westinghouse, FMC, Rockwell.

**Product Marketing Manager, Office Automation Systems**, 1981–1982

Built training program and sales strategy for national rollout. Responsible for plans, budgets, staff. Managed a first-year pilot team of 42 sales professionals. Directed second-year rollout to the organization's total sales force, 2500 sales professionals, ad budget of $2,500,000.
- Ran 167% of sales plan in first year.
- Achieved second-year revenues in excess of $45,000,000, also exceeding sales plan.

**Program Manager, Major Accounts, Office Automation Systems**, 1977–1980

Developed and managed major accounts programs targeting Fortune 100 companies. Initiated the company's largest contract through creative sales strategy.
- Consistently ran 200+% of sales plans.

*Continued . . .*

**Deltak, Inc.**
Schiller Park, Illinois
**District Sales Manager, New England**, 1977–1980

Opened New England for this start-up company.
- Personally closed a three-year, $5,000,000 contract with GTE.
- Developed marketing aid (which is an industry standard today) that directly increased average contract size by 1000%.

**Datasaab Systems**
New York, New York / Malmo, Sweden
**Branch Manager, New York**, 1975–1977

Represented workstations for data entry to IBM mainframes.
- Top sales office out of 10.
- Managed sales, service, support for New York, New Jersey, Connecticut.

**Singer Business Machines**
New York, New York
**National Accounts Manager**

Represented data processing systems and IBM mainframe-compatible peripherals.
- Consistently ranked in the top 10% out of sales force of 3000.
- Accounts included General Foods, Nestle, CIBA / Geigy.

**EDUCATION**

**B.A., Hobart College,** Geneva, New York

**Harvard Business School**, Executive Series in **Financial Management**

**Boston University** and **Northeastern University**, studies in **Sales & Marketing**

**S.P.I.N. Selling System**

**XEROX PSS II**

**REFERENCES**

References and additional information provided on request. Please keep this information confidential at this time.

# Roy Sossa

1565 Vista Court • Denver, Colorado 80217 • (303) 555-1395

---

## SUMMARY

Sales and marketing professional with strengths in revenue production, innovation, brand development, staff maturation. Demonstrated capacity to move organizations from zero revenue to multimillion-dollar sales production quickly. Prior successful P&L management, including financial analysis, budget control, revenue forecasting.

## EXPERIENCE

**Fantastic Products,** Denver, Colorado     1993–1996
**Vice President, Sales and Marketing**

Managed national and international sales and marketing for all types of handheld electronic games, PC-based games and peripherals, and amusing doodads and gadgets. Reported to C.E.O. and C.F.O. Recruited and supervised three domestic sales reps, one international rep. Restrategized sales effort to build distributor/broker relations with independent consumer electronics sales reps, gift showrooms, premium/incentive reps, and rep specializing in military exchanges. Planned product introductions, with rollout schedule, media plan, market studies. Traveled 70% (United States, Canada, France, Hong Kong). Positioned firm as being innovative, design-intensive, product-oriented.

*Accomplishments:*
- Cited by C.E.O. as main reason the firm won Ernst and Young Entrepreneur of the Year Award, 1994.
- Increased sales from $4.1 million in 1993 to $8.4 million in 1995.
- Developed $2 million sales program with membership club.
- Established $1.2 million L/C plan with Texas department store chain.
- Increased net margins from 12% to over 25% in one year.
- Changed terms of sale for 90% of accounts from NET 90 to NET 30, reducing receivables from 100+ days to 45 days.
- Reduced inventories to 45 day supply, maintaining key items in stock.
- Cut trade show expenses by 40%, yet increased number of shows attended.
- Opened international markets in the EC accounting for $800,000 in 1994, growing to $1.5 million in 1995.

**Bondwell Industrial Co., Inc.,** Boulder, Colorado     1989–1993
**Vice President, Sales and Marketing**

Revamped product lines of U.S. branch of Hong Kong-based computer and electronic toy firm, converting it into a $15 million supplier of IBM-compatible PCs, toys, and computer/video game controllers. Created all sales programs and policies, including complete development of systems and procedures, sales terms, and pricing. Controlled sales and marketing programs in United States, Canada, Mexico, and South America. Managed advertising budget in excess of $650,000. Staffed offices in Canada and United Kingdom, resulting in first year sales of $2.5 million and $4.0 million respectively. Recruited, trained, and managed staff of 14 heading national sales, marketing, technical service, purchasing, and warehouse services.

*Continued . . .*

*Accomplishments*:

- Increased sales from $0 in 1984 to $15+ million in 1989.
- Developed 20 independent sales representatives specialists for consumer electronics division, 10 specialists for the toy market.
- Generated exclusive distributorship agreements in Canada and South America which accounted for 10% of total company revenues.
- Established QuickShot as the #1 selling joystick in the United States.
- Planned and implemented production of OEM infrared controller for Worlds of Wonder, Inc., and collected receivables prior to bankruptcy.
- Introduced licensed Ferrari and Nintendo products into product mix.

**Atari, Inc.,** Sunnyvale, CA          1985–1989
**Director of Sales**

Produced short- and long-range sales forecasts for home computer/video game company with $500+ million in U.S. market sales. Directed all product roll outs, successfully adhering to a stringent schedule. Established distribution in grocery chains, convenience, book, and video rental stores. Planned and executed complex matrix of sales contests, involving national, and regional promotions. Integrated and coordinated sales and marketing policies to compliment manufacturing capacity, credit requirements, distribution center needs, and national advertising commitments.

*Accomplishments*:

- Developed new channels of distribution accounting for $6 million of sales.
- Created stock balancing programs with major accounts, allowing them to return slow sell goods and continue as Atari Retailers.

**EDUCATION**

**Juris Doctor**
    American College of Law, Anaheim, CA

**Bachelor of Arts, Political Science**
    California State University Fullerton, Fullerton, CA

# CHRISTINE HELLMAN

160½ North Flat Street
Wausau, Wisconsin 54403

Office: (715) 555-2882
Residence/message: (715) 555-4495

---

**PROFILE**

- **Territory Management**
- **Marketing**
- **Branch Management**
- **Consulting**
- **Presentations**

Senior marketing, operations, and administrative manager with a track record of outstanding contributions. Background includes (a) multiple business unit management, (b) new business growth and retention, (c) new program development, target marketing, niche marketing, (d) industry relations, business partner relations, (e) design of policies, procedures, goals, objectives, and methodologies, (f) staffing, (g) budgeting, control, reporting, (h) event planning, (i) newsletters. Seeking a new challenge.

**EDUCATION**

**M.B.A., Boston University**, Boston, Massachusetts

**B.A.,** *cum laude,* **Bridgewater State University**, Bridgewater, Massachusetts

**EXPERIENCE**

**REGENCY INSURANCE COMPANY**, Wausau, Wisconsin
**Marketing Manager — Central States**, 1992–Present

In charge of all marketing for 22 central states representing one-third of all U.S. revenues for Regency Insurance, a worldwide insurance company based in London. Position encompasses 60 agencies generating $29,000,000 per annum in premium revenues (98% commercial). Report to vice president in U.S. HQ.

Responsible for profitable new business growth and renewal premium retention, with emphasis on branch strategic planning and sales/business development with agency business partners. Negotiate contracts, growth incentives, and profit sharing agreements and actively work to increase corporate visibility through advertising and promotional events. Provide sales and marketing training and development for commercial lines underwriters. Coordinate and deliver marketing presentations to independent agents. Identify market potential for new programs; create sector marketing campaigns. Personally represent Royal at affinity group meetings, trade shows, and insurance industry association events. Travel 40%.

Solicit new agency relationships and discipline/terminate/rehabilitate existing relationships as necessary.

*Sample projects and contributions:*

- Created large account and key account strategies to penetrate national brokers. Consistently achieve average 15% growth pattern overall, outperforming 90% of other Regency branches nationwide, in spite of localized downturns in Rust Belt. Currently running 124% of new business objective and 105% of written premium objective for 1995. Earned Company Recognition Award in 1993 and $12,000 performance bonus in 1995.
- Promotional Events: IIAA Chicago dinner reception for top Regency producers ($35,000 budget); IIAA Hawaii formal dinner for 100 ($50,000 budget); 140th Anniversary "Faith in Wausau" Celebration ($30,000 budget, attended by the governor and mayor, local media coverage); "Rock 'n' Roll with Regency" dance party ($7,000 budget, 150 persons in attendance).

- Continue to develop producer business plans that result in exceeding *all* of corporate's objectives for the region.
- Create and edit bimonthly newsletter distributed to all active producers.

**TRAVELERS INSURANCE COMPANY**, Hartford, Connecticut
**Manager, Agency Operations**, San Diego, 1988–1991

Branch manager in charge of sales/marketing, underwriting, and operations; annual operating budget of $2,000,000. Managed branch staff of 21 and relationships with 28 independent agents in San Diego and Imperial Counties. Responsible for revenue growth and profit margins in three major lines: commercial, personal, and financial services (investments). Reported to Regional Vice President.

In addition to full strategic responsibility for branch, operated as a consultant to key independent agents providing overall agency strategic planning, as well as specific marketing and operational business plans.

*Sample projects and contributions:*

- Managed $18,000,000 commercial lines volume, $4,000,000 personal lines volume, $3,000,000 financial services sales. Achieved 115% of Financial Services objective, ranking Number One in the Western Region, despite challenging business climate.
- Engineered company response to California Proposition 103, designing 25% reduction in commercial and personal lines production while retaining positive business relationships with existing customers. Collaborated with corporate counsel. Identified and eliminated unprofitable products and relationships and retained profitable ones. Designed program to keep agents loyal to Travelers.
- Introduced "Star of the Moment," "The Distinguished Service Award," and other staff performance incentives resulting in high morale. Had minimal turnover and a staff attendance rate four times higher than state average.

**Territory Manager, Agency Operations**, Boston, 1985–1988

Liaison between the carrier and 22 agencies generating $8,000,000 in business. With sales skills and underwriting authority, participated in direct business development of commercial lines, personal lines, and financial services business with agency business partners. Provided other services ranging from sales and operations consulting to business automation plans.

**Assistant Manager, Commercial Lines**, Boston, 1979–1985

Trained and developed staff; monitored underwriting results; had full underwriting authority for the branch; key liaison for the branch's two largest producers.

**CREDENTIALS & AFFILIATIONS**

NASD Series 7 License, Wisconsin and Illinois LA&H and Casualty/Property insurance sales licenses.

Continuing Education (CLU/CHFC classes).

Member, NAFE, AMA.

**PERSONAL**

References and recommendations available upon request, *but please keep this information confidential at this time.*

# JOHN H. (JACK) PELTIER

(513) 555-0981
155 Lakeside Parkway
Cincinnati, Ohio 45207

## SALES — MARKETING — ENTREPRENEURIAL PRODUCT DEVELOPMENT

### AREAS OF EXPERTISE:

Over 20 years of executive experience in new business development, working within both rapidly expanding and mature markets, new and mature technologies. Encompasses directing existing sales and marketing organizations and managing all phases of start-up, new product development, and new market penetration.

Ability to create a marketing strategy from product concept to money in the bank; proven success taking sales from nothing to $1.5 million in one year on costs of less than $150,000.

Full budget, accounting, and systems responsibility; extensive contract negotiation and administration; demonstrated ability to design systems and procedures to withstand success.

### PROFESSIONAL HISTORY:

INTERNATIONAL DEVELOPMENT ASSOCIATES, Cincinnati, Ohio, 1994–Present

**Director of Business Development**. Technical liaison and marketing/sales consultant during development and investment/manufacturing stages for diverse products, from industrial desalination units to laser-disk memory systems. Consultant/broker/intermediary between private VC sources (high-net-worth individuals and small pension fund managers) and entrepreneurs/inventors. Source and evaluate 100+ bona fide deals per annum, develop only one to three, serving as the sales/marketing force for the endeavor.

Define target markets, devise marketing stance and image, write sales literature and news releases, design direct mail campaigns. Also provide VIP, protocol, and public relations services for investors and engineers from Japan and throughout the United States. Develop worldwide licensing agreements and assist in contract negotiations. Liaison to targeted key accounts, national and international.

*Sample project:*

- Martell Desalination Technologies, Ventura, California — assisted the ex-chief scientist from a defunct military contractor in the commercial production of portable purification/desalination plants that fit into a standard 60' truck trailer, ready for instant worldwide placement wherever pure water is needed, a $600,000 prototype project. *Achieved orders for 22 units in first six months,* with projected ROI for investors of 28% per annum with cashout in less than three years.

PHOTOMASTER, U.S.A., Lima, Ohio, 1991–1993

**Northeast Regional Manager**. Hired directly by the President to open new vertical territories for Photomaster. Created sales strategy and implemented the campaign to market equipment, installation, and training. Sales range: $18,000 to $72,000; average sale: $50,000.

Defined primary target market of government agencies, insurance companies, and banks. Wrote sales literature and comprehensive set of form letters. Created a direct sales strategy that achieved a 30% referral rate within the first six months. Also revitalized our network of independent dealer organizations to promote equipment under $10,000.

CONSOLIDATED MICROGRAPHICS, Dayton, Ohio, 1980–1990

**Director of Sales**, 1990–1992. Full profit and loss responsibility for over $12 million in revenues for the world's leading manufacturer of large-scale microfiche duplicators (engineering, warehouse, library applications). Directed eight sales managers and 80 sales and support staff. Personally handled key national accounts. Set sales/service policy and coordinated marketing and operations to maximize sales, customer satisfaction, and continued growth. Full line of products, services, and supplies. Increased profit margins, reduced discounting, and increased activity throughout the account base.

**Director of Field Service Operations**, 1989–1990. Created an independent nationwide service organization. Designed service order systems, accounting/record-keeping, and support operations. Recruited and trained 16 service managers and 160 technicians and dispatchers.

Included extensive negotiations with independent maintenance engineers. Also negotiated contracts and agreements with national accounts. Completed mandated assignment in 100 days. Subsequently increased sales by increasing customer confidence in service and support.

**Director of Product Management**, 1984–1989. Brought in on the ground floor as part of a management team to design a $30 million business focused on commercial micrographics. Complete product line responsibility including pricing structures, vendor negotiations, quality assurance measures, production cost analysis, market and competition analysis, sales and support, as well as lawsuit management, defense and countersuit.

Participated in the development and production of the OP microfiche duplicator line, still the first choice of heavy-volume users worldwide.

**Regional Sales & Systems Support Supervisor**, 1980–1983.

DIETZGEN COMPANY, HQ: Berlin, Germany / US HQ: Akron, Ohio, 1978–1980

**Branch Manager**. Managed a sales and support organization marketing a full line of engineering supply products: office equipment, scientific calculators, and large reprographic and microfilm systems for engineering and surveying. Streamlined all operations: increased sales 10% while reducing expenses 12%. Reduced discounting and shortened A/R by 42%.

MOSLER INFORMATION SYSTEMS, Akron, Ohio, 1976–1978

**Account Executive/Sales Engineer**. Outside sales of computers peripherals and various storage/retrieval systems, combined with specialized operating systems. Included corporate, educational and governmental sales, finance, training, and support. Successfully introduced our products into a market still skeptical of computer applications.

## PRIOR HISTORY:

Engineering, product development, sales, and management in R&D of computer-based micrographics, aerospace and aviation simulators, instrumentation, and related technological products.

## EDUCATION:

**B.E.E., Electrical Engineering,** Manhattan College, New York City

**Finance/Accounting,** The Wharton School, University of Pennsylvania

**Sales Training,** PSSII

REFERENCES & RECOMMENDATIONS PROVIDED ON REQUEST

# HEATHER BELLAMY

résumé

permanent mailing address:
East 1677 - 22nd Avenue
Spokane, Washington 99204
Sales office in **Oakland**: (510) 555-2577
Residence/message in **San Francisco**: (415) 555-6345
Residence/message in **Spokane**: (509) 555-7448

---

**PROFILE**

**Sales ▪ Account Management ▪ New Business Development ▪ Marketing**

*Strengths:*

- Ability to access decision-makers and build vital relationships to maximize revenues. Skilled with Fortune 500 corporate accounts, major institutional and government accounts. Creative and successful negotiator.
- Proven talent for planning independent sales/marketing campaigns, from media to contract negotiations.
- Ready for a new challenge using advanced sales and account development skills.

**EXPERIENCE**

UNITED AIRLINES, HUB: San Francisco
**Corporate Sales Manager — San Francisco Bay Area**       1994–Present

Represent United Shuttle to 400+ corporate accounts in San Francisco Bay Area, from Silicon Valley to Marin. Direct advertising, promotions, incentive programs, contract negotiations, and account relations. Supervise support staff. Responsible for generating and troubleshooting $10 million in corporate travel sales. Active participant in industry trade associations.

*Contributions:*

- Brought major new accounts on board, for example: "preferred carrier" agreement with Oracle software, "exclusive carrier" agreement with Crowley Maritime, renewed "preferred carrier" agreement with Hewlett-Packard, an existing major account.
- Developed PC-based account database system as a sales tool, with exhaustive account detail down to client company flow charts, revenue analysis, destination data, location data.
- Accounts: Bank of America, Bechtel, American President Lines, Stanford University, Apple, IBM, Intel Corp., and similar. Direct interface to travel managers and top company officers.

**Top performer** — retained through two reorganizations. In full charge of territory sales planning and reporting. Achieved major account growth in accounts under management.

Recommendation available at the appropriate time, but please keep this information confidential at this time.

*Continued . . .*

**District Sales Manager — Eastern Washington**     1990–1993

Same as above, but with responsibility for corporate and agency sales in a multistate territory, a total of $30 million in air travel sales.

*Contributions:*
- District Sales Manager of the Quarter, 1991.
- Achieved consistent sales increases of 8% to 10% per annum.
- Designed and promoted 50 escorted travel agency and corporate account "get acquainted" tours, a major marketing vehicle for the district.
- Devised participation in trade shows, corporate incentive programs, and community affairs organizations, generating favorable exposure, free publicity, and key new business relationships.
- Earned rapid promotion to corporate accounts position, considered the top travel sales position in the company. Assigned immediately to the #2 district over many same-level sales professionals.

**Sales Representative — Los Angeles**     1986–1990

Major accomplishments in one of United's most contested territories.

*Contributions:*
- Sales Representative of the Year, 1989.
- Coordinator, United Way Campaign, involving over 400 company and outside contacts.

**Passenger Service Trainer/Coordinator — Seattle**     1984–1986

**Customer Service Agent — Orange County (John Wayne Airport)**     1983–1984

CONTINENTAL AIRLINES, HQ: Houston, Texas
**Customer Service Agent — Seattle**     1979–1983

*PRIOR*

BRITISH AIRWAYS, HQ: London

THAI AIRWAYS INTERNATIONAL, HQ: Bangkok

**EDUCATION**

Highline Community College, Des Moines, Washington
**Associate of Applied Sciences in Transportation Business**
*Including coursework in:*
- MIS in Travel & Transportation
- Airline Operations
- Hotel/Motel Operations
- Marketing

**Xerox PSS Sales Skills**

**Dale Carnegie Strategy Presentation Workshop**

**AFFILIATIONS**

**Silicon Valley Business Travel Association**

**Bay Area Business Travel Association**

# Herbert D. "Bud" Palmes II

53 Asbury Circle
Atlanta, Georgia 30322

Office: (404) 555-9535
Home: (404) 555-3587
bud.palmes@alumni.emory.edu

## STRENGTH

Highly effective combination of marketing, financial, technical skills.

## EDUCATION

**M.B.A.**, Management, Emory University, 1996

Completed while working full time.

**B.S.**, United States Military Academy at West Point, 1979

Concentrations in Math, Engineering, and Science.

## HISTORY

BANK OF THE SOUTH, 1993–Present

**Vice President**, Group Marketing Manager, Business Services Division. Responsible for product development and enhancement of service bureau software products. Products include payroll, personnel, tax accounting and reporting services for businesses with 30 to 10,000 employees. Manage five departments with line of command over a staff of 92. In charge of Product Management, Marketing Research, Advertising, Training, and Documentation Departments. Generate $131 million per annum in revenues.

Initiated departmental restructuring: (1) reevaluated all technology utilization, with goal to fully integrated data collection/flow, (2) reengineered work to eliminate redundancies and bottlenecks, (3) reduced staff 30% while achieving increase in productivity, (4) analyzed product line and discontinued four services. **Improved gross (8%) and profits (23%)** in a downtrending market.

Other accomplishments include:

Presently developing the bank's internal personnel/payroll system, to be implemented on a nationwide basis centralized to our offices in Atlanta.

Recommended purchase of a $2 million vendor software company, now under negotiation, to monopolize a highly competitive technology.

Solved security problems to release Internet-access personnel package and Internet-access payroll product, eliminating human interaction on account service.

SCHLUMBERGER LIMITED, 1987–1993

**Controller**. Involved in a start-up venture in Computer Integrated Manufacturing, financed by Schlumberger Limited. Acted as V.P. of Administrative Services. Provided financial planning and systems design for the venture. Set up systems and procedures to handle rapid expansion. Established accounting and treasury functions in a highly decentralized environment, interfaced with financial institutions, performed real estate functions such as site location, modification, and lease negotiation. Developed close relationships with Bank of America and Morgan Guaranty.

**Financial Manager,** Linear Division, Fairchild Camera and Instrument (a subsidiary of Schlumberger Limited). Responsible for all areas of accounting, fiscal, and management reporting for this division producing $100 million per annum in revenues. Revised all fiscal policies and procedures; supervised staff of 38.

Decentralized all accounting functions from their former highly centralized state; simultaneously improved quality control. Corrected numerous audit deficiencies while reducing staff.

**Controller,** Schlumberger Well Services. Responsible for financial planning and control for an Engineering Group of 537 employees, annual operating budget of $44.5 million, capital budget of $20 million. Decentralized Accounting and Controller functions; improved quality control.

Managed a project including site selection and development for a second Engineering Center near Austin, Texas. Negotiated close on 221 acres of industrial property for $5 million; negotiated lease of 33,000 sf temporary site with extensive leasehold improvements (total value: $2 million). Also managed relocation of Schlumberger equipment and the families of the Austin Engineering personnel.

INTERNATIONAL BUSINESS MACHINES, 1985–1987

**Marketing Representative.** Responsible for business-to-business technical marketing of IBM mainframes and software. Direct interface to financial and educational institutions.

UNITED STATES ARMY, 1979–1985

**Aide-de-Camp** to a Major General, the Assistant Surgeon General, U.S. Army, in charge of all U.S. Army medical, dental, and veterinary facilities and operations throughout the Continental United States, Hawaii, Puerto Rico, and Panama.

**Controller.** Planned and directed fiscal and management functions for a command consisting of four general hospitals, operating budget in excess of $100 million.

## PROFESSIONAL AFFILIATIONS:

Member, Institute of Management Accounting
Member, National Association of Accountants
Member, American Management Association
Past President, IBM Employee Club
Member, International Visitors Center
Member, United States Army Reserve
Controller, St. Francis Episcopal Church

# William J. Strickland

221 - 19th Avenue South
Minneapolis, Minnesota 55455

Telephone/message/fax: (612) 555-4415
73287.12834@compuserve.com

## PROFILE

### Sales / Marketing / New Business Development

Strengths include direct, high-level sales, developing relationships with corporate buyers, senior corporate officers, sophisticated investors, and others. Marketing skills include telemarketing and direct mail operations in support of new account development. Proven in diverse environments: Wall Street-trained, international business experience, sales management experience.

Skilled with sophisticated sales techniques incorporating presentation of financial, intangible and technical product benefits.

## EXPERIENCE

**Torch Resources, Ltd.,** Manila, Philippines, 1994–1996
### Director of Marketing

In full charge of launching a sales function for a new product line, imported polyethylene- and polypropylene-laminated packaging foils. Provided marketing, sales, and administrative business aspects in collaboration with the company founder, a technical and financial manager with no knowledge of sales. Co-managed office and sales staff. Researched potential factories in Singapore, Hong Kong, Japan, Korea, and Taiwan. Negotiated pricing, shipping, delivery, and other details of supply. Wrote product literature. Hired and trained sales representatives. Opened accounts. This is a marketing and trade company only, with no warehousing and transport aspects of its own.

Penetrated highly competitive market in the Philippines, gaining market share against long-established companies. Position required constant socializing with top corporate officers of target company. This is a sophisticated sale on Asian protocol, requiring lead time and the patient building of social relationships before business is discussed.

Technical knowledge areas include complex letters of credit, strength testing, full-color printing and color separations, shipping, and government relations.

Created business relationships worth up to US$2.5 million per annum each. *Sample accounts:*
- RFM Corporation, second largest food conglomerate in the Philippines.
- Birch Tree Corporation, the Holland-based multinational.
- General Foods, Philippine subsidiary of U.S.-based multinational.

**Kettler Investments,** Basle, Switzerland, 1990–1993
### Sales & Marketing Manager, English-Speaking Europe

Recruited to create a New York-style marketing organization for an old-line European investment house. Reorganized the direct mail operation, telemarketing operation, and investment advisor function. Recruited heavy hitters from New York and London to be account executives. Trained and coached all levels of staff. Coordinated with operations specialists on database, accounting, and trading matters.

Bought and mailed to lists of English-speaking households in Europe. Wrote and designed the direct response cards used in direct mail campaigns, achieving response up to 7% (highest in history of the company). Coordinated printing, mailing, and logistics for international direct mailing projects budgeted at US$40,000+. Recruited, coached, and supervised the cold-calling staff known as "openers," and the account executives who serviced all accounts thereafter.

Originally assigned to one office. Created a ten-fold increase in fee income. Was reassigned to implement program companywide. Restructured and supported offices in Cypress, Athens, Barcelona, Manila, Amsterdam, Rotterdam, and Geneva.

*Continued . . .*

**Citiwide Capital Corporation,** New York, New York, 1986–1990
   **Registered Representative (equities and fixed-income)**

Retail stockbroker for this firm during phase of rapid growth and media exposure. Firm specialized in IPOs and private placements. Participated in 15 new issues. Sold complete range of investment products. Responsible for own research and analysis.

**D.S. Meyers & Co.,** New York, New York, 1984–1986
   **Registered Representative (options)**

Worked directly with the owner of this "boutique" brokerage, one of the first Wall Street firms to develop an effective automatic trading system for options. Developed private book of clients, all sophisticated investors, high-net-worth individuals who were qualified for speculative investment.

**Marsan Securities,** New York, New York, 1982–1984
   **Registered Representative (equities and fixed-income)**

One of the youngest account executives in the history of this firm. Promoted from operations clerk to trading assistant to registered representative.

## EDUCATION

**New York Institute of Finance**
Licensing Examination Preparation

**S.U.N.Y. Brockport**
Pre-Medical Studies

**Dale Carnegie**
Sales Training

## REFERENCES

Provided on request.

# Technical, Engineering, and Scientific

Technical, engineering, and scientific résumés and CVs are frequently project-based. Like consultants, scientists and engineers must tie their experience to discrete projects that have certain internal challenges, time frames, and budgets. For this reason, you will frequently see engineers and other technical professionals list a purview of their job, that is, a scope statement, followed by descriptions of their projects in place of a list of accomplishments per se.

You will note that these résumés are a little more schematic, with less description and detail and a lot more baldly presented data. They also tend to be less self-congratulatory in nature, trusting the reader to know which of these accomplishments are a big deal and which are just part of technical routine.

As stated in chapter 2, the order in which the projects are presented need not be chronologically based, but should be based on the order of desired impact on the reader. If an older project is more likely to interest your targeted reader, then by all means list it first.

It is a good idea to take a management point of view in presenting technical projects, providing budget data even if that did not personally interest you and showing some understanding of how your task fit into the company's overall goals. For example, perhaps you made some perfectly routine adjustment to the software used to track and manage $100 million in goods. The task may even have been boring, but be sure to point out such bigger-picture consequences as this: "Resulted in 5% reduction in inventory due to more efficient logistics, representing a one-time $5,000,000 savings to the company." Any time you can tie your contribution to the bottom line, your contribution will seem more essential. This is something that many engineers, too oriented only on the technical aspects of their jobs, miss.

Also, in engineering, and especially in scientific, résumés you will find a lot of addenda and headings not found on other résumés, such as "technical skillset," "publications," "teaching," "patents," "licensure," "certifications," and "credentials." Scientific résumés can be very long, sometimes over a dozen pages, as every article, book, and presentation is delineated.

Some of these examples are technologically obsolete, but stylistically current. They are included for format and style purposes. Note the functional résumés, pp. 333–340, and the résumé for the engineer with no degree who studied psychology, p. 329. (He told me he's been working on cutting-edge technology all his life, and you can't go to school for that, so he studied psychology.) For medical résumés and CVs, closely related in style to some of these, see the next chapter. As mentioned earlier, there is really a smooth continuum of style between a true academic/scientific/medical CV and a basic business-oriented, accomplishment-based chronological résumé. You simply need to find a style that looks right to you and that is commonly used by others in your situation.

WARNING: If you are looking here for general and financial management résumés for individuals running technical companies, you are looking in the wrong place; see chapter 3, above. This chapter has résumés for people whose skills are primarily technical in nature, not primarily managerial or financial.

Of course, be sure to check the index for résumés in all the other chapters that may apply to your particular case.

# Dion van den Bosch

Voortseweg 34
Eersel, (N-B), 5211 J.D.
The Netherlands

24-hour message telephone: 011.31.4970.13671
Telephone: 011.31.4970.12536
24-hour fax: 011.31.4977.65607
NONSECURE E-mail: dion.vdb@eng.offshore.com

## PROFILE

### Civil / Structural Engineer

Eight years of structural steel experience as field engineer, one year experience with reinforced concrete, additional engineering time in home office. Main experience is fabricating/installing offshore oil platforms, 24-hour-day construction schedule, often in harsh conditions. Specialist on steel fabrication, installation, and work safety. Strong experience in supervising and motivating crews. Qualified for many heavy construction positions requiring expertise in civil/structural engineering.

Completely fluent in English. All engineering work conducted in English as, by international convention, English is the international language of offshore engineering. Can also supervise work crews in Spanish and German, and speak some Portuguese.

Stable and reliable employee, perfect record on all jobs. References on request.

## EXPERIENCE

**Harmony International, N.V.**
**Harmony Marine Contractors, S.A.**
**Harmony Engineering Services, B.V.**
Engineering HQ: Leiden, The Netherlands

**Vice President, Field Operations** and **Civil / Structural Engineer**     1981–Present

Harmony is a world leader in offshore structure construction, building traditional steel platforms and experimental designs. This is a quality-oriented company with an outstanding record for safety and engineering innovation, annual revenues up to US$600,000,000, and contracts with major oil companies worldwide.

Field engineering manager in charge, offshore platform installation projects. Project planning, offshore fabrication, local labor and vendor selection and oversight, client liaison. Responsible for writing and following detailed engineering, job safety, and cost control procedures. Typically coordinate, oversee, and directly supervise approximately 50 field personnel.

Sample projects:

- **Field Engineer** on Jolliet TLWP floating platform for Conoco, installed in 1712 feet of water in the Gulf of Mexico. This was a first-of-its-kind installation. Supervised and coordinated 60 welders, riggers, divers, surveyors, tugboat captains, and marine crane operators. Developed classes and trained actual crews (foremen, engineers, winch drivers, mates, etc.) every day for two weeks. Successfully applied never-before-tried engineering plans.

- **Field Engineer** and **Construction Supervisor** on upgrade and refit of Crane Vessel Hermod from 5000 tons to 9000 tons lift capacity, Port of Rotterdam. Kept project on schedule. Up to 1000 personnel per day contributed to project. Ensured build-out to plans. Made inspections with Certifier from Lloyd's. Controlled material flow. Completed project in just six months. (Bidding shipyards had estimated in excess of 1 year.) Total project cost US$80,000,000.

- **Company Representative** at the fabrication facility, Gulf Marine Fabricators, Aransas Pass, Texas. Verified compliance with design provided by our engineering department. Updated scheduling and filed progress reports with home office. Modified rigging layout, reducing costs by improving over 1 mile of heavy installation. Supervised during jacket load out (24,000 tons).

- **Field Engineer** on Crane Vessel Balder in Gulf of Mexico. Supervised riggers and welders during installation of jacket (24,000 tons) and topsides (5000 tons). Designed caisson installation aids. Changed crane operation organization saving 12 hours spreadtime (US$150,000 daily rate). Designed and surveyed installation guides for platform modules.

- **Project Engineer,** Mobil Green Canyon Platform, Gulf of Mexico. Designed installation procedures for skirtpiles and caissons, and prepared the offshore installation manual. Supervised a project team of 8. Modified existing antitwist device for 550-ton underwater block to make it applicable to other crane vessels.

- **Field Engineer** and **Construction Supervisor** for launch and pile barges for ULA platforms for British Petroleum in the North Sea. Supervised up to 80 welders, riggers, foremen, and inspectors under extremely harsh weather conditions.

- **Field Engineer** for Pat III off the Brazilian coast for Petrobas. Designed and fabricated a gripper to recover stabilizers from bottom of drilled pile hole, where they were preventing project progress. Also Surveyor for fabrication yard in Rio.

- **Field Engineer** and **Company Representative** to Hyundai subcontractor on installation of 12 pipeline risers to a platform for India's National Oil Company, Arabian Gulf. Supervised 30 Korean welders/riggers and English divers.

**Dutch Railroad Company, N.S.,** Zwyndrecht, The Netherlands      1980–1981
**Engineer-in-Training**

Completed supervised training period with the national railroad. Major assignment was as field engineer for six-month viaduct project, steel-reinforced concrete construction. Built viaduct on double track railroad operating daily, the Rotterdam-Dordrecht line, one of the busiest in the Netherlands, approximately US$4,000,000 project.

## EDUCATION

**Bachelor of Civil Engineering**      1980
Technische Hogeschool Tilburg
Tilburg, (Noord-Brabant), The Netherlands

**Diploma,** Rythovious College      1975
Eersel, (Noord-Brabant), The Netherlands

## PERSONAL

Hobbies include travel, camping, hiking, and martial arts (karate, jiujitsu, judo). Also read and train self during off time (technical, financial, political, management, historical, and similar subjects).

# TIMOTHY J. KAMAHASALAN

tjk@hk.dwi.com

mailing address
1887 Wade Avenue
Santa Clara, California 95051

message phones
Office: (408) 555-3645
Residence: (408) 555-9387

---

## EXPERTISE

**Technical Systems Architecture • International Markets Development • Technology Transfer**

## SUMMARY

Background in large-scale information systems. Effective combination of *technical/engineering* expertise and *sales/marketing* skills. Significant experience as architect/consultant/representative for international markets. Prior history of rapid promotions leading to full responsibility for development, implementation, operation, and support of mission-critical systems in banking and financial services for major multinational companies.

## HISTORY

**Digital Wave, Inc. (DWI)**, Hong Kong and Santa Clara, California        1993–Present
**Senior Consulting Architect, Transaction Processing Systems Group**

Assist customers in architecting, refining, and rightsizing online transaction processing (OLTP) legacy systems incorporating client/server paradigms. Promote DEI-tp (DWI Transaction Processing) family of products for mission-critical enterprise computing to customers and potential customers in Singapore, Hong Kong, Thailand, Malaysia, Taiwan, the Philippines, and Japan. Develop detailed action plans to achieve DWI's strategic penetration of SE Asian markets. **Based primarily in Hong Kong**. Travel 80%.

Apply expertise to (a) address interoperability and portability issues across heterogeneous platforms using de jure/de facto standards to achieve Open Systems, (b) present the new MultiVendor Integration Architecture to DWI Asia and key customers at Information Technology conventions in SE Asia, (c) achieve high availability through distributed computing technology for mission-critical computing requiring seamless failover systems and using software fault tolerance for high reliability, and (d) provide technology transfer from corporate to sales/support personnel in the field.

Manage cross-cultural relationships, with interface to all levels of client company (CEO, IS Director, engineering staff). Plan and stage marketing/technical development road shows tailored to individual cultures/markets to access clients in banking, insurance, brewing, governments, securities, telecommunications, petrochemicals, steel, and utilities. Represent company in local media interviews. **Fluent in Malay, Tamil, Sinhalese; conversational in French; basic Japanese.**

Also take special assignments worldwide, e.g., developing DWI-tp demo for DWI's new 64-bit ALPHA machines, Valbonne, France; or developing a benchmark for a major banking institution simulating 10,000 users, Los Angeles.

*Contributions:*
- Conceived of international product support infrastructure: Field Readiness Program, Pre-sales Support, Customer Presentations, Benchmark SWAT Team, and supporting education and mentorship program.
- Instrumental in spearheading DWI-Japan's efforts to design and implement OLTP Field Readiness Program. Organized focus group to synergize available resources. Provided critical customer visits in Japan, helping close pending sales. Presented DWI-tp direction personally and coached account teams presenting to NTT/DNCS, NTT Architecture Group, HALC, KDD, Nomura Securities, Tokyo Gas, KAO, and others.
- Similar contributions in Malaysia targeting Syarikat Telekom Malaysia, Tenaga Nasional, Malaysian French Bank, Bank Bumiputra, and others.
- In the Philippines, with Far East Bank, National Computer Centre, Bank of the Philippine Islands, Bureau of Internal Revenue, Department of Transportation and Communication, and others.

*Continued . . .*

- In Hong Kong, with Computasia, Standard Chartered Bank, and others.
- In Singapore, with IIPL, National Computer Board, and others.
- In Taiwan with China Petrochem, China Steel, Taiwan Power, and others.
- In Thailand with Telecom Asia, Phatra, Bank of Asia, Stock Exchange of Thailand, and others.
- Involved in strategic planning concerning Pacific Rim markets. Key liaison between DWI engineers and Pacific Rim markets, ensuring competitive technological stance and forward-direction product design efforts.
- Brought in to revitalize market entry efforts as needed, e.g., key player in assisting acceptance of DWI's DART program in SE Asia, earning letter of commendation from DART program office.

**Independent Consultant**, San Francisco, California      1992–1993
**Management Consultant**, Visa International, San Mateo, California

Developed architecture and functional requirements for the new standard Terminal Management System for this international financial services organization.

**Management Consultant**, The Application Group, San Francisco, California

Reported directly to the CEO of this major consulting firm serving Fortune 100 clients. Selected to conduct a complete review and reorganization of in-house procedures for systems development projects.
- Authored *Systems Development Life Cycle,* based on state-of-the-art software engineering disciplines, *Effective Project Management Guidelines,* framework to measure and control software development projects, and *People Management,* guidelines designed to manage people in a technical environment.

**Tesseract Corporation**, San Francisco, California      1991–1992
**Project Manager**

Led select group of senior analysts with full responsibility for product development, from conceptual design through implementation. Key application: 401(K) Loans, supporting multiple online screens and interface to a payroll application. Modeled functional specifications and design blueprint using the Yourdon Structured Analysis/Design Techniques. Prepared and presented base models to users and senior technicians. Monitored ongoing software construction in ASSEMBLER.

**Bank of America**, San Francisco, California      1988–1991
**Systems Manager**, Capital Markets Group

Full responsibility for implementation and management of highly visible, strategic Securities Trading System consisting of some 12,000 different programs. System utilized 4GL technology and was designed for both online and batch operation nationally. Supervised professional and technical staff of 22.
- Designed implementation of a Change Tracking and Library Management System to facilitate the Software Development Life Cycle.
- Directed core group of seven in design and implementation of the Interest Rate Swaps System (4GL technology).
- Provided technical support to Futures and Options subsidiary conversion effort.
- Personally conducted national and international personnel searches.

**Systems Architect**, World Banking Systems

Principally responsible for international strategic systems architecture projects for development staff of over 1500.
- Developed the architecture for a Strategic Change Control System to ensure synchronized global software releases for the International Banking System, containing over 4 million lines of IMS/COBOL source code.
- Presented completed system model in Europe and in the United States.
- Created a Strategic Planning Model utilizing Foreign Exchange product as a prototype; derived an architectural blueprint applicable to several banking products.

*Continued . . .*

**Independent Consultant**, San Francisco, California      1984–1988
**Systems Development Consultant**

Contracted with the following companies in development, execution, and training of systems projects, with an emphasis on the Yourdon structured development tools.

- **Design Consultant**, Pacific Bell, San Francisco, California, 10/83–3/85. Participated in the design of an online/batch Customer Service Order System. Led a four-person design team in developing a forecasting prototype application. Provided hands-on guidance to several MIS groups in the use of structured software engineering techniques.
- **Staff Consultant**, Esprit de Corp, San Francisco, California, 12/82–8/83. Introduced state-of-the-art software engineering systems development tools and techniques. Provided in-house training and consulting in application development methodologies and project management. Wrote and published a formal development life-cycle for use with future application development projects.
- **Senior Consultant**, Bank of America, Toronto, Canada, 5/82–10/82.
- **Senior Consultant**, Bank of America, San Francisco, California, 4/81–5/82. Instrumental in providing a migration strategy to automate a manual foreign exchange office. Trained staff. For the North America Division, consulted in structured modeling tools. Improved long-range effectiveness of automated systems. Modeled Foreign Exchange, Money Market, DDA, and Cash Management Products.

**Fireman's Fund Insurance Companies**, San Rafael, California      1983–1984
**Senior Systems Analyst / Team Leader**

Resident expert in structured development concepts. Led a design team to restructure portions of the CIS System (IMS/COBOL), analyzing user requirements. Provided a framework to prototype software modules.

**Bank of Montreal**, Montreal, Canada      1976–1983
**Project Leader**, **Senior Systems Analyst**, **Systems Analyst**, **Programmer Analyst**

Managed teams, performed analysis and design, coded and implemented systems (CICS/ASSEMBLER/PL1). Participated in pioneering the use of structured development techniques. Trained users and co-workers.

## EDUCATION

Wesley College, Colombo, Sri Lanka
  **Baccalaureate, with distinction in mathematics**

Additional Professional Seminars and Training:

Numerous courses in management, strategic and tactical planning, human resources, public speaking, project management, systems analysis; as well as hardware, software, and telecommunications applications on multiple platforms (IBM, DEC, and others). Can self-train on any technical matter.

## ADDITIONAL

Willing to travel as needed and/or relocate for the right opportunity. Currently a Canadian citizen based legally in the United States while assigned to Hong Kong office.

Excellent references and additional information provided upon request, *but please keep this application confidential until the appropriate time.*

# Kirsten T. "Katie" Olson

1850 Washington Street, #10
San Francisco, California 94109

Residence office/message/fax: (415) 555-0431
katie@org.ucsf.edu

---

## PROFILE

Consultant to and executive manager of scientific programs, seeking rapid growth opportunities in business-oriented settings. Unusual combination of skills, including proven scientific/technical capacity; management and program development ability; team building, joint-venture and networking skills; and a strong facility for marketing, capitalization, promotions and public relations.

Highly energetic. Seeking a challenge and opportunity commensurate with abilities.

## EXPERIENCE

**K.T. Olson,** San Francisco, California
**Consultant**, 1994–Present

Consultant on project viability, commercialization strategies, clinical trial design, marketing strategies, and related issues in for-profit biomedical areas.

*Selected Projects:*

- **Marketing & Biomedical Consultant** — Hologic, Inc., Waltham, Massachusetts. Conducted competitive analysis to improve company's own understanding of their place in the market. Recommended slight repositioning of company's product. Developed external publication for clients of bone density diagnostic equipment. Provided editorial assistance on all materials for release concerning the company's technology.

- **Biomedical Consultant** — Chiron Corporation, Emeryville, California. Developed strategic plan for use of newly developed bone growth factors in the diagnosis of osteoporosis. Designed diagnostic studies for $9 million bone growth factor program. Initiated and facilitated joint clinical studies with Norwich Eaton and Sandoz. Identified and created collaborative relationships with key university investigators.

- **Biomedical Consultant** — Norian Corporation, Mountain View, California. Developed strategic plan for the commercialization of proprietary biomaterials for orthopedic applications. Designed pre-clinical and clinical trials. Identified and initiated relations with potential funding sources (venture capital, governmental, private). Initiated joint venture business with Chiron, Norwich Eaton, and others.

**University of California,** San Francisco, California
**Associate Director (Clinical), Osteoporosis Research Group,** 1992–1994

Co-founder of this research group. Provided strategic direction and hands-on management of research programs. Oversaw a staff of 20, including M.D./Ph.D. researchers, various technicians and nurses, and administrative staff. Initiated, developed, and negotiated research projects in partnership with pharmaceutical companies. Projected and administered budgeting. Reviewed outside literature; investigated new research avenues. Collaborated with researchers in medicine, orthopedics, geriatrics, and epidemiology in designing and conducting clinical trials.

Acted as liaison between U.C.S.F. and diverse research and financial partners. Served as health care consultant to National Aeronautics and Space Administration, Sandoz Pharmaceuticals, Parke-Davis Pharmaceuticals, Siemens, Schering-Plough Pharmaceuticals, Medical Imaging Centers of America, Hospital Corporation of America, and others. Board Member, Center for the Study of Aging. Group Member, Exercise and Osteoporosis Working Group, American College of Sports Medicine.

*Selected Accomplishments:*

- After founding this group as a separate entity, tripled the size of the research staff and quadrupled the funding.
- Built new business relationships with private sector as funding sources for synergistic research efforts.
- Achieved national and international recognition for research output. Requested to speak at over 20 engagements at national and international meetings.
- Appointed primary reviewer for four major medical journals, including JAMA.
- Appointed special study section reviewer for U.S. National Institutes of Health and National Health Research and Development Program of Canada.
- Expanded and redefined research and policy efforts into the study of exercise, physical fitness, osteoporosis, and frailty in the elderly.

**Specialist, Department of Radiology,** 1990–1994 (concurrent with the above)

Provided strategic direction and daily oversight to staff of 5, including radiologic technicians, research associates, and administrative staff. Developed methodology, personnel requirements, policies and procedures, but primary responsibility was the solicitation and procurement of funding for research projects.

*Selected Accomplishments:*

- Coordinated or authored 20 major clinical research grant submissions. Achieved an outstanding 60% funding rate (NIH average is 10%).
- Brought a total of $7,302,502 in research monies to the department.
- Conducted clinical projects for Sandoz, Schering, Norwich Eaton, Abbott, Meade-Johnson, Parke-Davis, Ciba-Geigy, Syntex, Squibb, and others.
- Designed and developed the first large exercise/calcium intervention program for young women, an NIH/NASA cooperative venture.
- Authored or co-authored over 60 publications.

**Assistant Specialist, Department of Radiology,** 1989

Published a major manuscript on the relationship between exercise and osteoporosis. Presented research at the "International Conference on Physical Activity, Aging, and Sports," West Point, New York, 1989.

**Staff Research Associate, Department of Radiology,** 1988

**Research Assistant, Department of Radiology,** 1987–1988

## ADDITIONAL

**Ancillary Specialist,** U.C.S.F. Institute for Health and Aging, 1992–Present
**Teaching, Public Speaking, Lectures** and **Seminars** related to areas of expertise.
Flexible and adaptable. Rapid learning curve. Comfortable with major responsibility.

## EDUCATION

**Ph.D.,** Anthropology, International Institute for Advanced Studies, Hilo, Hawaii, 1990
**A.B.,** Anthropology, Washington University, St. Louis, Missouri, *cum laude*, 1986
Graduate Studies, Human Development & Aging Program, U.C.S.F., California
Graduate Studies, Anthropology, Washington University, St. Louis, Missouri

## REFERENCES

Provided on request.

## PUBLICATIONS

List on request.

# KEVIN P. MURPHY

## *Consulting*

175 Suki Place, Suite H1
Sunnyvale, California 94087

Telephone/message/fax/pager: (408) 555-8245
k.murphy@techtalent.com

---

**STRENGTHS**

**Programming in C or LISP for scientific, engineering, and research applications**.

**CONSULTING COMPANY**

**Peter Hendrickson & Associates**, Sunnyvale, California
**Principal Consultant**

*Skillset:*
- Development environments: C, LISP/CLOS, LISP Machines, VMS, UNIX, SCO UNIX, Saber C, Microsoft C Compiler, Turbo C. Experience with object-oriented programming since 1982.
- Hardware: Mac and IBM PCs, VAX, LISP Machines, Symbolic LISP Machines, Sun 3, Sequent S81, Apollo, Sun 386, compatibles, Thinking Machines CM-1.
- Currently developing expertise in Microsoft Windows and C++.

*Applications:*
- Development and utilization of new software technologies, object-oriented programming, applications development, software "repair," upgrades, and enhancements in entrepreneurial, technical, and financial environments.
- Internal development projects: (1) "smart" bookkeeping program with complex time value of money application, (2) solitaire strategy analysis system and interface, (3) Mac-based critical path project management system.

**PRIOR HISTORY**

**Bitstream, Inc.**, Cambridge, Massachusetts
**Consultant**, 1988–1989

- UNIX and network administration in a diverse environment including Apollo and Sun Workstations, Sequent S81, Apple Macintoshes, IBM compatibles for this large-scale start-up company. Utility programming with Awk, shell scripts, C.

**Aware, Inc. (Novon L.P.)**, Cambridge, Massachusetts
**Technical Staff**, 1987–1988

- Aware is a start-up company established to apply novel mathematical methods for engineering computations and signal processing. Created software modules for exploring wavelets, a class of mathematical functions used in signal processing and other fields. Sun workstations, SunView window system, Sun compiler, Saber C, as well as IBM ATs, Microsoft C Compiler. Produced graphics package for Turbo C on IBM AT. Ported programs from LISP to C. Programmed Symbolics LISP Machines.

**Thermo-Therapy Devices Corp. (Novon L.P.)**, Cambridge, Massachusetts
**Engineering Technician**, 1987

- First employee of this medical technology start-up developing ultrasound-based cancer treatment system. Liaison for technology transfer with MIT Lab which had developed the prototype. Architected overall design. Assisted with SBIR proposal. Surveyed market for real time OS and high reliability equipment.

**Boston Technology, Inc.**, Cambridge, Massachusetts
**Research Scientist**, 1986–1987

- Second engineering employee and early stockholder at this early voice mail company. On-site liaison to out-of-state merger candidate. Created course in SCO UNIX and our own software. Installed prototype warning system at large nuclear facility. Evaluated and procured equipment to build into our product.

**Pomerleau Computing Systems**, Chicago, Illinois
**Technical Staff**, 1985–1986

- Provided technical expertise in a retail computing business serving an academic and entrepreneurial business community. Consulted in Chicago area on medical practice administration program.

**University of Chicago**, Chicago, Illinois
**Microcomputer Laboratory Manager**, 1984–1985

- Formulated policy. Hired and trained six supervisors. Provided support to faculty and student end users.

**MIT Artificial Intelligence Laboratory**, Cambridge, Massachusetts
**Technical Staff**, 1982–1983, Summers 1984, 1985

- Diagnosis, repair, maintenance, technical support to end users. LISP Machines, Thinking Machines CM-1, DEC VAX.

**EDUCATION**     **The University of Chicago**, Chicago, Illinois
**Physics**

**REFERENCES**     References and recommendations available on request.

# RAMON GONZAGA

6633 South Serpentine Road
Sacramento, California 95817
(916) 555-3339

---

**EDUCATION**

**MASSACHUSETTS INSTITUTE of TECHNOLOGY**
**Master of Architecture**, 1982

**UNIVERSITY OF CALIFORNIA at BERKELEY**
**Bachelor of Architecture**, 1979

**PROFESSIONAL EXPERIENCE**

**ESHERICK HOMSEY DODGE and DAVIS**
**Staff Architect**, 1988–1996

Design assistant to the principals, Messrs. Esherick, Homsey, and Davis. Team member on several of the most significant projects the firm has had in recent years (see below).

Versatile, high level of technical proficiency in addition to design background. Experience in programming, schematics, design, construction documents.

- Offices of the Secretary of State and the State of California Archives, $80 million project, one full city block in the Capital Mall district of Sacramento. Design assistant to Messrs. Homsey (directly) and Esherick (less directly). Brought in specifically for design development through working drawings of the lobby, entranceway, and public spaces.
- Medical Library, University of California at San Francisco, $22 million project, 120,000 GSF, integrated into an established neighborhood. Core team member under Mr. Davis (directly) and Messrs. Esherick and Homsey (indirectly) for all stages from programming through specialty interiors construction documents.
- University Center Building and Campus Infrastructure, Arizona State University, Phoenix, 120,000 GSF. Team member under Mr. Davis for schematics and design services only. Also contributed to conceptual development of exterior spaces.
- Housing and Mess Facilities, United States Coast Guard Training Center, Petaluma, California. Selected to prepare working drawings and details for exterior stairs under supervision of senior staff architect (design by Mr. Homsey).
- Additional Projects: Library, Mills College; Deer Valley Ski Resort, Utah; Art Center, Mills College.

Personal recommendations available from Messrs. Esherick and Homsey.

**PERSONAL WORK**

**RAMON GONZAGA**
**Architect**, 1992–Present

Following two independent projects in collaboration with Mr. Donald P. Reay, Architect, AIA, FRIBA, Prof. of Architecture, University of California at Berkeley:

- Contemplative Center and Chapel, Franciscan Order, Tonala, Oaxaca, Mexico. Schematics and design development. Project includes leading and coordinating regional, community, and church leaders in Oaxaca region to keep project moving forward.
- Carmelite Monastery, Oakville, California. Master plan design, proposal for redesign and expansion of existing monastery. Personally presented to the General Father of the Carmelite Order in the Vatican, Rome.

**APPRENTICE EXPERIENCE**

**NEIMI ASSOCIATES**
**Apprentice Architect**, 1988
- Godwin Residence. Working drawings and design details.

**REFERENCES**

References and portfolio presented upon request.

# MARK MacQUIN EASTWOOD

25 W. Grandview Road
Phoenix, Arizona 85023
(602) 555-3292

## PROFILE

**Consulting Engineer**

- Skilled at unifying marketing, sales, engineering, and manufacturing efforts. Unusual dual strength in *both* hardware and software. Significant strategic consulting experience. On-site, user support, and installation background. Skilled at third-party representation.

- Technical expertise in electrical/electronic engineering and in manufacturing areas: producing project specifications, hardware/software design, process automation, mechanical engineering, control systems, data acquisition, instrumentation systems, audio/video technologies, plastics, systems packaging, and custom manufacture of turnkey systems.

- Diversified background featuring **generalist** marketing, turnaround and troubleshooting experience, **specialist** engineering and project management assignments.

- Full financial skills: budgeting, costing/pricing/profit planning, value engineering. Also: feasibility and market studies, client surveys, technology surveys, vendor assessment.

## EXPERIENCE

**Forward Motion Consultants**     San Francisco, CA
**Chief Engineer / Principal**     1992–Present

Plan and conduct consulting engagements to meet client needs. Projects include:

- **Control Manufacturing Company** — Project Engineer for major engagements including:
  - **Matson Navigation** — Container Crane Automation System, a $2.5 million project, Long Beach: system design and specification, SW and HW engineering, 2nd vendor supervision (GE), installation supervision, acceptance testing, maintenance and user training, documentation.
  - **Space Station** and **Intelsat** — $1.3 million battery power testing system: project manager coordinating with Ford Aerospace, Loral Space Systems, Rocketdyne, Rockwell International, and NASA: system design, specifications, contract negotiations, HW and SW design and integration, installation, debug and start-up, user training schools, documentation.
- **Mayer Laboratories** — Proposed Latex Manufacturing Facility, Kiev, Ukraine and St. Petersburg, Russia: business plans, feasibility studies, site surveys, manufacturing plant design, foreign government regulatory negotiations, technology transfer issues.
- **Matson Navigation** — Special projects: (a) analysis of auxiliary power supply systems for containerships (fleetwide installation); (b) "as built" survey of vessel electrical systems for retrofit planning; (c) acceptance testing of electrical and control systems on new vessel.
- **Star Delta Elevator Co.** — Product development: design, prototyping, testing, production engineering of Overspeed Safety Monitor and Elevator Door Motion Drive products for new and retrofit applications, including operating, service, assembly, and engineering documentation.
- **Orthotech** — Strategic consulting to President of this $15 million company: (a) review of sales, customer support, and manufacturing integration; (b) reorganization of select departments, including job redesign; (c) overview report of company positioning, market, and challenges.
- **ArtLux Light Artists** — Product engineering: design of Multivault Fiberoptic Display System Controller for Japanese amusement park, later adopted in all ArtLux products (provided engineering documentation sufficient to allow company engineers to build variants to suit).
- **Tesla** — Disney Studios and special projects: design, prototyping and production engineering for film and video post-production industry: Video Streamer System for Orchestral Scoring, MIDI-based Time Reference and Click Generator, Digital Editing Suite, and synchronization products. PC board design, circuit design, component-level engineering.
- **California Pellet Mill Co.** (see below) — process automation projects: (a) continuous process automation; (b) turnkey system installation and start-up; (c) on-site company representative and troubleshooter.

**CPM Company — an Ingersoll-Rand Company**    San Francisco, CA
**Marketing Manager, Controls Products**    1988–1992

CPM is a major international supplier of mechanical equipment to the agricultural and chemical industries. Realigned product development for a family of microprocessor-based continuous-process automation systems. Achieved a cultural reorientation to market-driven product development from engineering-driven design. Bridged gap between sales and engineering. Improved coordination with CPM UK and CPM Europe. Created 5-year plan for new product family featuring increased access to worldwide markets, repositioning of market image, sequenced product introductions, improved opportunities for follow-on sales. Structured organizational systems to support plan. Earned highly positive reviews and merit raise.

**TAK Automation**    Burlingame, CA
**Director, Materials Handling Products**    1983–1988

Supervised development and marketing of microprocessor-based industrial process automation technology and turnkey systems to the heavy-industrial material-handling and primary metals industries, European and domestic markets. Engineering staff of 20.

**Record Plant Studios**    Sausalito/Los Angeles, CA
**Technical Director**    1975–1982

Managed budget of $150K, engineering and technical staff of 10. Designed analog and digital circuits, wrote specifications, managed consulting engineers. Advised recording engineers on use of state-of-the-art systems. Developed design modifications that became industry standards.

**FM Productions/Bill Graham Presents**    San Francisco, CA
**Chief Sound Engineer**    1974–1975

Engineer for more than 100 concert productions and touring shows. Audio and other electronic equipment design, construction, and maintenance. Test engineering.

## ADDITIONAL

Co-designed and directed the construction of the microprocessor-based broadcast audio system for Lincoln Center for the Performing Arts, New York City.

Designed and supervised production of a remote programmable hydraulic stage display controller system for a Broadway musical.

Extensive commercial broadcast production experience (TV and radio) and theatrical lighting design.

## EDUCATION

**Psychology**, New College of California, San Francisco, California

# DOROTHY A. ROLLINS, P.E., S.E.

24 South Fifty-Seventh Avenue
Arcadia, California 91006

Office: (818) 555-0359
Residence: (818) 555-4447
Private fax: (818) 555-6359

## EXPERTISE

### Engineering / Project Management

Skills encompass engineering management, team leadership, and field and home office project management. Background in industrial, commercial, petrochemical, and residential projects, with involvement from concept development and initial client presentations through design/build to acceptance and preparation of "as built" drawings. Extensive experience working with consultants (architectural, environmental, legal, government). Available for travel as needed.

## EXPERIENCE

### RANÉ M. PETERS, Pasadena, California          1990–1994, 1995, 1996–Present
### Principal Engineer

*Selected projects:*

Conducted damage inspections for ERMST (Earthquake Recovery Management Support Team) following the Northridge earthquake. Wrote reports for county authorizing residential buildings to receive funds for reconstruction.

Field Engineer at Tooele, Utah U.S. Army munitions storage plant. Resolved conflicts with design drawings and coordinated final design requirements. Provided detail for 100+ specially designed embedded wall plates that facilitated easy placement of concrete and expedited project.

Field Engineer at Shell Martinez refinery in charge of restoring main pipeway structure after major fire. Specified and sourced materials; completed project within 2½ months including field modifications for new material installation and coordination with electrical and mechanical group.

Conducted structural analysis using 3-D computer model of module for ARCO GHX-1 and GHX-2 steel frame structures.

### FLUOR-DANIEL/TRS, Hayward, California          1995–1996
### Civil/Structural Engineer

Managed FAA Golden Gate Airway Sector refurbishment project. Analyzed refurbishment needs for coming year, and created and implemented site-specific solutions. Monitored annual budget of $80,000. Acted as communications link traveling between field offices, sector office, and throughout region. Prepared budgets and cost estimates for projects and oversaw construction.

*Selected contributions:*

- Solved important logistical problem within a month that had plagued company for over a year. Saved client over $14,000 in construction costs and satisfied all parties including end-user and local officials.
- Preserved crucial air field operation at Port of Oakland by arranging runway project approval directly with Port and eliminating the need for time-consuming wetlands approval.
- Initiated cost-effective preventative maintenance program to protect vulnerable company equipment.
- Successfully identified and addressed problems at under-represented facilities before they became emergencies.

### J.R. MILLER & ASSOCIATES, Brea, California          1988–1990
### Lead Engineer

Designed 6 commercial and 4 major manufacturing facilities for accounts including Kal-Kans, PC Industries, and Anheuser-Busch. Worked closely with contractor on all projects. Coordinated changes with local

building officials to ensure code compliance. Supervised 2 junior engineers, an architectural designer, and a structural designer.
- Completed platform design for major account in under a week, earning commendation bonus and raise.
- Trained assistant designers on wood design and structural steel connection details.

**HNTB,** Kansas City, Missouri      1986–1988
*Project Engineer*

Lead structural engineer for creation of chapel facility and office building complex. Supervised structural design team of 2 designers and an engineer. Met with lead architect and electrical/mechanical engineers to develop design criteria.
- Directed careful on-site coordination of new structure with pre-existing buildings.

**VARCO-PRUDEN**, Turlock, California      1986
*Design Engineer*

Designed pre-engineered metal buildings for public, private, and commercial use.
- Developed construction details that allowed metal roof framing to accommodate masonry and tilt-up panel walls, significantly expanding product market and increasing sales.

**BROWN & LINDSEY**, San Francisco, California      1984–1986
*Chief Engineer*

Reported directly to owner and assumed full technical responsibility in his absence. Successfully designed hospitals, schools, office buildings, light industrial facilities, and commercial and residential structures. Supervised design staff of 2 designers and an engineer. Reviewed project plans with the Office of the State Architect and local building departments. Coordinated details and layouts with project architects, electrical/mechanical engineers, and clients.
- Earned 20% raise based on performance after less than 6 months with the firm.
- Applied specialized knowledge of seismic safety requirements to various institutional projects including schools and hospitals.
- Served on disaster preparedness committee of SEAONC and State Office of Emergency Services (OES).

**BECHTEL PETROLEUM, INC.**, San Francisco, California      1978–1984
*Design Engineer*

Served as field, construction, and resident engineer designing concrete and steel structures for refinery and chemical plants. Oversaw 4 engineers in pipe support group. Constructed 3-D computer models to analyze various structures. Designed grass-roots plant facilities and modification of existing facilities.
- Petrochemical projects: ARAMCO refinery, ARCO STP barge, UNOCAL Rodeo refinery coker unit expansion, SOHIO (BP) WPM modules, Mobile New Zealand GTG grassroots refinery.
- Power Plant projects: Farley power plant, Midland power plant.
- Manufacturing processing: Philip Morris, Proctor & Gamble, Urea Fertilizer plants.

## EDUCATION

UNIVERSITY OF KENTUCKY, Lexington, Kentucky
**Bachelor of Science**, **Civil Engineering**

## CREDENTIALS

State of California Civil Engineer No. C0393839
State of California Structural Engineer No. S088622

## AFFILIATION

Member, Structural Engineers Association of California

# Arthur R. Siegel, P.E.

1888 First Street, #200
San Leandro, California 94577

Telephone:
(510) 555-2564

## PROFESSION

Registered Mechanical Engineer

*Strengths:*

| | |
|---|---|
| **Facility Design** | • HVAC • Fire Protection • Site Work • Piping and Plumbing • Space Layouts |
| **Energy Systems** | • Power Generation • Cogeneration • Energy Recovery |
| **Material Handling** | • Cranes • Hoists • Conveyors |
| **Machine Design** | • Bridge Machines • Power Transmission |
| **Value Engineering** | • Studies |

## HIGHLIGHTS

### Transportation Maintenance Facilities — Mechanical Design

- AC Transit Richmond and Emeryville. Bus Maintenance Facilities.
- Golden Gate Bridge, Highway and Transportation District, San Rafael. Bus Maintenance Facility Expansion.
- Sacramento Light Rail Maintenance Shop.

### Transportation Maintenance Facilities — Studies

- San Francisco MUNI's New Metro East Maintenance Yard, Mission Bay, San Francisco.
- BART Vehicle Maintenance & Storage Analysis for Expansion Service Plan Study.
- Generic Planning Requirements for New Pullman Way Rail Fleet Maintenance Facility, San Jose.

### Facilities — Mechanical Design

- Renovation of Effie Street Pump Station, Oakland, California.
- Highway 101/237 Interchange Pump Station, California.
- Highway 880 Newark Pump Station, California.
- Bank of America, South San Francisco Branch, Linden Avenue.
- Pacific Telephone Building, TSPS, Pacifica, Crespy Drive.
- U.S. Naval Hospital (Old) at San Diego. Modified heating, plumbing and fire protection systems.
- Sandia's Livermore Laboratories. New HVAC systems and modified fire sprinkler system to major portion of Building #913.
- Somarco Project at Point Ubo, Brazil. Site utilities, water supplies, fuel oil facilities, and pier arrangements.

### Energy Systems — Mechanical Design

- Itaipu Project. 12,600 MW hydroelectric development for Brazil and Paraguay on the Prana River. Chief Mechanical Engineer and Project Coordinator of the Generation Facilities Group.
- Middle Fork American River Project. Hydroelectric project in Placer County, CA. Designed gate, hoist, and butterfly valve installation. Responsible for the mechanical and electrical equipment during construction.
- U.S. Naval Hospital at San Diego, CA. New 700 HP steam plant with underground distribution system.
- Central Marin Sanitation Agency, Treatment Plant, San Rafael, CA. Energy study and design of energy recovery and cogeneration system.
- Sandia's Livermore Laboratories. Economizer cooling of underground computer center using a cooling tower.
- U.S. Navy Installation, Pillar Point, CA. Economizer heating using a solar system.
- Coalstrip Fossil Fuel Plants, Numbers One and Two, Coalstrip, Montana. Developed an in-plant hydrogen generation and storing facility.

– continued –

### Material Handling

- U.S. Marine Corps Recruiting Depot, San Diego, CA. Developed material handling and storage facilities for the Exchange Warehouse.
- Various hydroelectrical and other projects. Developed equipment handling schemes, cranes, hoists, and aerial tramway designs.
- California Packing Corporation. Food handling and packaging equipment and facilities.

### Machine Design

- Miller-Sweeney Highway Bridge, bascule bridge between Oakland and Alameda, CA. Designed the machinery that won two awards for movable bridges in 1974.
- Design power transmission equipment utilizing gearing, hydraulic, and pneumatic components.
- Conceptual Report for Rehabilitation of Park Street Bridge, Oakland & Alameda, California.

### Value Engineering

- Attended a 40-hour Value Engineering course at University of California at Berkeley Extension. Participated in numerous value engineering studies on facilities and transportation installations.

### Shipbuilding

- San Francisco Naval Shipyard. Marine and Mechanical Engineer on shop and shipboard, including submarines, machinery, and ventilation installations. General Engineer coordinating work between design and production. Also visited universities to recruit engineers for the shipyard.

## EMPLOYMENT

**Morrow Consultants, Inc.**, San Francisco, CA, 1992–Present
**Sverdrup Corporation**, Walnut Creek, CA, 1989–1992
**Foster Engineering, Inc.**, San Francisco, CA, 1982–1989
**Kennedy/Jenks Engineers, Inc.**, San Francisco, CA, 1979–1982
**Koretsky King Division, Anderson-Nichols & Co., Inc.**, Richmond, CA, 1978–1979
**International Engineering Company, Inc.**, Rio de Janeiro, Brazil, 1975–1977
**International Engineering Company, Inc.**, San Francisco, CA, 1974–1975
**Bechtel Power Corporation**, San Francisco, CA, 1973–1974

*ALSO, employment and project experience with:*
**Simpson Stratta and Associates**, San Francisco, CA
**McCreary-Koretsky Engineers**, San Francisco, CA
**Western Gear Corporation**, Belmont, CA
**International Engineering Company, Inc.**, San Francisco, CA
**U.S. Naval Shipyard**, San Francisco, CA
**California Packing Corporation**, San Francisco, CA
**Magna Engineering Corporation**, San Francisco, CA

## EDUCATION & CREDENTIAL

**Registered Mechanical Engineer, States of California and Oregon**
**B.S., Mechanical Engineering, University of California at Berkeley**

## AFFILIATIONS

**Member, American Society of Heating, Refrigeration and Air Conditioning Engineers**
**Life Member, American Society of Mechanical Engineers**

## REFERENCES

Excellent references available from *all* former employers. Please keep this information confidential at this time.

# MELVIN A. HOPKINS

62 Clarissa Avenue
San Mateo, California 94402

Telephone/message/24-hour pager: (415) 555-9564
m.hopkins@pge.com

## STRENGTHS

- **Facilities Management (multisite)**
- **Environmental Management (certified)**
- **Project Management (int/ext)**

## CREDENTIALS

- **Facilities Management Administrator, B.O.M.A. International**
  Part I passed; Part II pending.
- **EPA Certificate, Hazardous Materials Management**
- **Environmental Management Certificate Program, U.C.B., Extension**
  Building Inspection and Management Planning for Asbestos
  Practices and Procedures in Asbestos Control
  Developing an Asbestos Operations and Maintenance Program

## PROFILE

Management knowledge encompasses lease and sale/purchase negotiations, labor relations, computerized data and financial management, business planning, report writing, comparative cost analysis, staff selection and motivation.

Technical knowledge encompasses building codes, abatement, environmental hazards, H.V.A.C., plumbing, electrical, roofs/exteriors, elevators, T.I., subcontracting, contract administration.

Computer skilled for project management, construction management, scheduling, budgeting.

## CAREER

Pacific Bell / San Mateo, California

**Facility Engineer (Management),** 58 Facilities, 2,500,000 sq.ft., 1991–Present
**Building Maintenance Supervisor (Management),** 1,000,000 sq.ft., 1989–1991
**House Service Supervisor (Management),** 1986–1989
**Building Mechanic (Technician),** 1981–1986
**Circuit Design & Special Services (Technician),** 1978–1980

## SKILLS & ACCOMPLISHMENTS

| | |
|---|---|
| H.V.A.C. | Large-scale HVAC retrofit construction, project budgets to $700,000, including specifications, contract negotiations, project oversight. H.V.A.C. for computer rooms, equipment buildings, office space. |
| Construction | T.I. from studs to turnkey build-outs, exterior maintenance projects, retrofit/refit up to 60,000 sq.ft., budgets to $650,000 per project. Includes permitting, contract negotiations, contract administration, etc. |

| | |
|---|---|
| Environmental | Member of two statewide task forces on hazardous materials, one for asbestos and one for underground storage tanks. Co-designer of five-year hazardous materials / site management plans encompassing company policy and standards, budgeting, regulatory compliance issues. Includes small remediation projects to full-scale abatement of occupied and evacuated spaces. Knowledge of federal / state / local regulations and requirements. |
| Life Safety | Completed high-rise conversion, 300,000 sq.ft., $750,000, from high voltage to low voltage multiplex system. Also includes earthquake preparedness and response plans. Restored 45 buildings to service after '89 Loma Prieta earthquake: civil engineering inspections, epoxy injection, seismic upgrades, cosmetic patching. |
| Electrical | Designed switchgear maintenance program. Managed many special projects such as installation of standby generators and large scale U.P.S. systems. Knowledge of large electrical distribution systems. |
| Maintenance | Preventive maintenance programs, elevators, asbestos O&M programs, hazardous materials compliance, quality assurance planning, worker safety, housekeeping, troubleshooting. |
| Plumbing | Suction, gravity, pneumatic tank systems, sanitary systems, storm drainage, fire protection and suppression. |
| Security | Direct hire and contract security staff, remote surveillance and multirisk console control, high-rise security. |
| Labor Relations | Proven talent for motivating highly skilled crafts, skilled technicians, union workers, nonskilled janitorial staff. Effective manager. |

## ADDITIONAL EDUCATION

Pacific Telephone Management Enhancement Training
- H.V.A.C. Optimization Seminar
- First Aid II & III / CPR
- Asbestos / Underground Storage Tanks
- Hazardous Materials and Waste Management
- Project Management
- Centrifugal Air Conditioning
- Refrigeration and Air Conditioning Technology
- Building Engineering & Management
- Information Management
- H.V.A.C. Control Systems
- Elevator Maintenance & Evaluation
- Labor Relations Management
- EEO and Management
- Quality Assurance Training
- Alarm Systems Inspection, Testing, Maintenance
- Building Operation & Management
- Plus many other courses.

# Travis Thompson

*office*
82 Central Avenue, #16
New Brunswick, New Jersey 08901
**Office/direct line voice mail: (908) 555-7474**

*residence*
2218 Monsanto Street
New Brunswick, New Jersey 08921
**Residence/message: (908) 555-2774**

---

## ENVIRONMENTAL SCIENTIST

---

### STRENGTHS

**Multidisciplinary Environmental Management**

Hazard Ranking System • EPA Projects

Remedial Investigations • Feasibility Studies • Multimedia Contaminant Assessments

Remedial Action Planning • Sampling & Analysis Plan Development • Health & Safety Plan Development

Forestry • Landfill Investigations • AST/UST Systems Management • Compliance Audits

Watershed Management • RCRA Waste Minimization Projects • Habitat Improvement

Asbestos & Lead-Based Paint Surveys • Emergency Response • Air Quality Assessments

Expert Testimony

### LICENSURE

| | |
|---|---|
| NJ/NY | Registered Environmental Assessor |
| US EPA | Asbestos Building Inspector and Management Planner |
| PADI | Open Water Diver |

### EMPLOYMENT

MYERS & SHEEHAN ENGINEERING CONSULTANTS, INC.      HQ: Brooklyn, NY
Environmental Operations Division      Branch: New Brunswick, NJ
**Senior Environmental Scientist**      1994 – Present

EARTH SCIENCES ENGINEERING CONSULTANTS, INC.      HQ: San Francisco, CA
Environmental and Remediation Services Division      Branch: Honolulu, HI
**Senior Environmental Scientist / Manager, Hawaii Field Office**      1988 – 1994

U.S. ENVIRONMENTAL PROTECTION AGENCY      Region: Houston, TX
Technical Assistance Team (with Ray Easten/E&E)      1985 – 1988
**Senior Environmental Scientist / Assistant TAT Leader**

U.S. DEPARTMENT OF ENERGY      Livermore, CA
LAWRENCE LIVERMORE NATIONAL LABORATORY      1984 – 1985
Environmental Sciences Division
**Environmental Scientist**

U.S. DEPARTMENT OF AGRICULTURE, FOREST SERVICE      Amboy, WA
Mount Saint Helens National Volcanic Monument      1983 – 1984
Silviculture, Watershed, and Wildlife Departments
**Soils Scientist**

– continued –

## PROJECTS

### Remedial Investigations/Feasibility Studies

*Palmyra Atoll Naval Aviation Station RI/FS*

U.S. DoD-requested senior member of remedial investigation team assessing WWII impact on deserted 600-acre atoll. Addressed USTs, AGSTs, ACM, uncontrolled hazardous waste. Developed RAP.

*Diamond Head Volcano/Fort Ruger Landfill RI/FS*

Managed media-sensitive RI/FS aimed at characterizing a 3.7-acre WWII era landfill in Diamond Head volcano. Project involved GPR survey, soil borings, soil test pits, and soil gas survey.

*U.S. DoD Defense Environmental Restoration Program* — Formerly Used Defense Sites

FSs addressed flora, fauna, UXO, EXO, hydrology, cultural resources, climatology, geology, hazardous wastes, land use, and real estate records. Reports followed strict DoD INPR format.

### Environmental Audits

*U.S. Army and U.S. Air Force Environmental Audits*

Group Manager for $16M, 4-year ECAS project at CONUS/OCONUS bases. ECAS/ECAMP audits done in accord with 10 to 17 protocol Federal, State, local and DoD regulations. Typically responsible for water quality, pesticides, hazardous materials, PCBs, and hazardous waste protocol.

*Spill Prevention Control and Countermeasure (SPCC) Audits*

Performed 70+ audits of on-shore petroleum storage facilities. Identified engineering deficiencies and suggested corrective action alternatives.

### AST/UST Systems Management

*United States Postal Service Western Region UST Program*

Project Manager of $500K, 3-year oversight contract to manage and upgrade 700 USTs in accordance with complex, multiple-agency guidelines. Technical oversight of removals through retrofits.

*Andersen Air Force Base, Guam, M.I., AST System Design*

Project Manager of joint venture team involving civil, mechanical, electrical, and environmental engineers and architects. Coordinated plans, specs, and cost estimates.

*Lawrence Berkeley Laboratory UST and AGST Closure Projects*

Project Manager requested by LBL to provide technical peer review for closure of acid, cyanide, and sodium hydroxide ASTs. Developed and executed UST closure plan. Assisted with NPDES permit.

### Sampling and Analysis Plan Development and Implementation

*MUNI Metro Hazardous Materials Sampling and Analysis Plan*

Senior Environmental Scientist for Bechtel, Inc.'s MUNI Light Rail Extension Project. Developed innovative, economical SAP incorporating hydropunch technology and drilling safety measures.

*SFDPW SE Waste Water Treatment Plant Sampling and Analysis Plan*

Project Manager for development and implementation of comprehensive, cost effective soil and groundwater investigation of a full city block proposed for the construction of a WWTP.

*MUNI/Islais Transit Facility Sampling and Analysis Plan*

Sole author of innovative SAP for field project involving on-site RCRA waste characterization of contents of 300 containers at former coconut refinery. Successfully implemented plan and prepared technical bid specs.

– continued –

## AFFILIATIONS

Professional Environmental Marketing Assn., Guest Lecture Committee    Director
Assn. of Ground Water Scientists and Engineers    Member
Academy of Certified Hazardous Materials Managers    Member
Assn. of Environmental Compliance Professionals    Member
American Society for Photogrammetry and Remote Sensing    Member
Assn. of Environmental Professionals, Education Committee    Member
University of San Francisco Environmental Alumni Network    Member
Society of American Foresters    Member
Professional Environmental Marketing Assn., Public Relations Committee    Member

## CERTIFICATIONS

Health and Safety Training, 40-Hour, OSHA    Level "B" PPE
Hazardous Material Incident Response Operations, 70-Hour, EPA    Level "A" PPE
Site Access Clearance, U.S. Department of Energy    P - Approval
S-130, Fire Suppression, USDA Forest Service    Red Card
S-190, Fire Behavior, USDA Forest Service    Red Card
Cardiopulmonary Resuscitation, American Red Cross    CPR Certified
Multimedia Standard First Aid, American Red Cross    First Aid Certified

## SPECIALIZED TRAINING

*Environmental Due Diligence,* Dunn & Bradstreet    1996
*EPA Hazard Ranking System Package Preparation,* EPA    1995
*Lead Contamination: A Public Policy Conference,* NYU    1994
*DoD ECAS Environmental Compliance Training,* U.S. Army    1993
*DoD ECAMP Environmental Compliance Training,* U.S. Air Force    1992
*COE DERP-FUDS/INPR Workshop,* ASEE    1991
*Site Assessments and Environmental Audits,* ASCE    1990
*Inspecting Underground Storage Tanks,* ABAG    1988
*Inspecting Hazardous Waste Generators,* ABAG    1988
*RCRA/CERCLA Alternative Technology,* ASEE    1988

## TEACHING

Environmental Technology, City College of New York    Faculty (part-time)
Advanced Environmental Management, Rutgers-Extension    Faculty (part-time)
Environmental Compliance Assessment Survey (ECAS) Training, DoD    Instructor
OSHA Health and Safety Training (29 CFR 1910.120; 8,24,40-hour training)    Instructor
Instrumentation, PPE, Field Methodologies: Monthly In-House Training    Instructor

## PUBLICATIONS AND PRESENTATIONS

*Site Characterization, Sampling and Analysis in New York City: A Handbook for Compliance,* New York Engineering Society Press, 328 pp., 1996

*Advanced Environmental Management: Environmental Assessments and Environmental Audits,* in the *Proceedings* of the Northeastern Conference on Hazardous Materials Management, Philadelphia, Pennsylvania, 1995.

*Environmental Asbestos: Forensic Correlation of Soil Contamination to Establish Probable Air Concentrations Over Specified Periods of Time,* a graduate thesis, Glenellen Engineering Library, The Graduate School of the Armed Forces, Wilmington, Delaware, 1987.

*RCRA Quantification of EPA Enforcement Samples Collected at the Aero Quality Plating Facility Stabilization Effort,* U.S. Environmental Protection Agency Document T96705-108, 1987, referenced in Hazardous Materials Control Research Institute SUPERFUND *Proceedings,* 1989, Washington, D.C.

– continued –

## MEDIA APPEARANCES

"Saving the Earth 101," *New York Times — Educational Supplement,* August 1994. Interviewed regarding environmental education and careers.

"Toxic Post Office Dirt Piles Up," *Honolulu Star Bulletin,* January 29, 1993. Interviewed on behalf of USPS regarding stockpiled soil generated during UST excavations on Oahu (front page headline).

"Nogales Landfill Fire," KMSB TV Channel 11, Nogales, Arizona, August 16, 1987, evening news. Interviewed on behalf of U.S. EPA regarding the physical and chemical nature of the landfill and subsurface anoxic fires.

## EDUCATION

**M.S., Environmental Management (Toxics and Waste Management)**
THE GRADUATE SCHOOL OF THE ARMED FORCES      1989

**B.S., Natural Resources Management (Silviculture/Business Management)**
OHIO STATE UNIVERSITY      1983

## MILITARY

U.S. ARMY RESERVE (1980–present)

# Elizabeth Udelhöfen, P.E.

1300 South Survey Platt
Golden, Colorado 80401

e.udel@trans.colo.gov
Engineering Office: (303) 555-4923
Residence: (303) 555-9386

---

## PROFESSION

**Transportation Engineer**

## EXPERTISE

- Knowledgeable on large civil engineering projects: feasibility studies, design, estimating, scheduling, site management.

- Background includes presentations and testimony on behalf of public projects before legislative, regulatory, and public forums.

- Advanced computer skills for engineering applications, including programming project-specific applications and training others (CADD, HIGHways, CURVO, STRESS, RM22, and E-TIKT).

## EXPERIENCE

**COLORADO DEPARTMENT OF TRANSPORTATION**, Denver, Colorado, 1990–Present
**Senior Transportation Engineer (Lead Project Engineer)**, 1992–Present

- Project engineer for transportation projects ranging from $2 million to $100 million in size. Involved in all phases of projects, from feasibility studies through design, planning, and scheduling, with emphasis on Measure A projects. Manage division staff of 22 transportation engineers and civil engineers, $2.4–$4.5 million annual engineering budget (80% expensed to projects).

- Represent projects to a wide range of public and regional groups. Write official correspondence to inquiries concerning specific projects. Develop and deliver presentations to city, county, state, federal, and community agencies and organizations. Attend community and government meetings as state representative.

- Direct staff in preparing design alternatives based on legal and political developments. Anticipate evolution of the project review process.

*Ongoing Projects*

- Preparing estimates, schedules, and ongoing design modifications for $20 million Measure A project to complete the Route 113/24 interchange in Bristol. Developing multiple solutions to jurisdictional and right-of-way problems. Creating complex geometrics to meet transportation objectives within financial and political constraints.

- Developing preliminary design proposal with schedules and cost development for Route 85 along the Western Slope, a proposed new freeway and interchange between the Mountain Freeway and 88/286 interchange. Directing engineering and estimating process reflecting constantly changing community priorities.

- Managing the design stage of $2 million soundwalls for freeway ramp areas adjacent residential areas in Denver. Wrote project report expected to be approved as written.

*Continued . . .*

**CALTRANS**, Sacramento, California, 1987–1992
**Transportation Engineer (Supervisory)**, Hydraulics Branch, 1988–1992

- Trained new staff in principles of highway drainage engineering. Performed drainage analysis, flood-plain analysis, hydrology studies. Team leader for staff of assistant transportation engineers and civil engineers. Wrote computer program to model drainage behavior. Prepared reports and proposals related to drainage and hydraulics.
- Special project: In charge of drainage design for $2 million Terra Bay project in South San Francisco involving retention basins below mean tide level and requiring tidal routing and pumps.

**Assistant Transportation Engineer**, Hydraulics Branch, 1987–1988

- Performed duties similar to above under supervision of senior engineers. Special project: Performed watershed analysis for $50 million Devil's Slide Bypass project on Hwy 1 near Pacifica.

**PARKER & JOHNS DESIGN ENGINEERS, INC.**, Danville, Colorado, 1984–1987
**Civil Engineer II**, 1986–1987

- Inspected construction on $1 million to $3 million highway rehabilitation projects. Special project: collaborated with airport civil engineering team to perform epoxy strength calculations and studies on Stapleton Airport/Interstate 70 overpass deck replacement project to determine best temperature versus epoxy thickness for temporary riding surface.

**Civil Engineer I**, 1984–1985

- Drafted project reports, made quantity estimates, performed engineering studies as assigned. Special projects: Developed traffic projections for Ralston Avenue Interchange on Hwy 270; designed building foundation for Arden Maintenance Station (wrote plans, specifications, and estimate for 6-month project).

## EDUCATION & CREDENTIALS

**B.S., Civil Engineering**, Colorado School of Mines, Golden, Colorado, 1982

**Hydrology**, U.C. Berkeley, 1988

**Value Engineering**, FHWA, 1989

**Professional Engineer**, State of California, License #19433, 1992

**Member**, ASCE

## ADDITIONAL

References and recommendations on request, but please keep this application confidential at this time.

No restrictions on business travel, field assignments, or permanent relocation.

# MICHAEL KELLEY

1750 Arrowhead Way
Fayetteville, Arkansas 72701

Telephone/message: (501) 555-1389
m.kelley@agri.uaf.edu

---

**PROFILE**

**Engineering and General Business Manager** with over twenty years of experience in the design, prototyping, testing, manufacture, and operation of mechanical equipment, custom agricultural equipment, industrial systems, commercial vending machines, conveyor systems, light-duty factory lines, aerospace systems, and oil and gas field drilling and production equipment.

Related skills in management of entrepreneurial businesses, assessment of markets and marketability of equipment under design, and full financial and strategic management of business operations.

Seed-to-store background in agriculture, with some knowledge or experience in all phases of farming, harvesting, packing, processing, distribution.

U.S. patent holder on two designs of specialized agricultural equipment.

**EDUCATION**

UNIVERSITY OF CALIFORNIA AT LOS ANGELES (UCLA)
**Master of Engineering**, *summa cum laude*

UNIVERSITY OF NOTRE DAME
**Bachelor of Science in Mechanical Engineering**, *magna cum laude*

**ENGINEERING EXPERIENCE**

GREAT WESTERN FARM EQUIPMENT        HQ: Stuttgart, AR
**Chief Engineer**        1989–Present

Design and fabricate custom farm equipment. Main project over last few years has been the design and prototyping of a machine to chop strawberry plants at the end of the season to prepare them for the next season's growth. This device performs this farming task at less than half the cost of traditional hand methods.

Also currently assisting an inventor in developing a new reeling bicycle lock from concept through prototyping, patent search, and pre-commercialization stages. This device has worldwide market potential in the hundreds of millions of units.

KELLEY DEVELOPMENT CORP.        HQ: Fayetteville, AR
**Chief Engineer**        1984–1992

Designed, packaged, prototyped, tested, and specified the manufacture of a new vending machine with radio remote control (carrier current radio transmission) for water and air dispensing. This machine was installed at eighty 7-11 stores in California.

Devised vibration isolation compressor mounts for vending machines, virtually eliminating sound and vibration problems and allowing for vending machine placement in areas where noise could not be tolerated.

Worked on long-term project to armor vending machines against break-ins and to improve locking mechanisms. After considerable experimentation, designed a cost-effective, burglar-resistant locking system.

*Continued . . .*

HI-GEAR HARVESTER COMPANY    St. Louis, MO
**Chief Engineer**    1970–1984

Designed, prototyped, and tested the first commercially successful celery harvester. These were large, self-contained machines capable of doing the work of a field crew of 40+. We manufactured ten of these machines at an average cost of $50,000 each and contracted them with our own trained operators to packers and growers. Supervised a crew of ten: mechanic, technicians, operators, and office person.

Developed a mechanical engineering work-study program in association with the Texas A&M University, providing Hi-Gear with smart, motivated technicians.

Completely redesigned and rebuilt a pepper harvester for a client, obtaining a patent for the new design (retained by the company).

Designed and built a turnip harvester eliminating 80% of retrimming labor cost typically required at the packing shed.

Designed and built an automated celery packing line to unload, de-leaf, wash, chill, orient, cut to length, and package celery sticks for wholesale and commercial accounts.

*prior*

PULSATION CONTROLS CORP.
**General Manager** (fluid dynamics)

HUGHES AIRCRAFT COMPANY — UCLA Master's Fellowship
**Reliability Engineer** (Phoenix missile systems)

DELTA TANK AND SUPPLY
**Field Engineer** (natural gas dehydrator)

**TEACHING EXPERIENCE**

UNIVERSITY OF ARKANSAS    Fayetteville, AR
**Instructor, Schools of Agriculture and Engineering**    (part-time) 1984–Present

SOUTHERN METHODIST UNIVERSITY    Dallas, TX
**Instructor, Mechanical Engineering**    prior

**FARMING EXPERIENCE**

BOB RAYMOND FARMS    Pine Bluff, AR
**Consultant, Partner**    1984–Present

CAL-TURF, INC. (sod farms)    San Juan Bautista, CA
**Farm Manager**    prior

**PERSONAL INTERESTS**

Music (singing, opera, musical theatre), woodworking, personal computing, developing engineering computer applications, researching agricultural practices of antiquity, including travel to Egypt, Israel, and prehistoric sites in the Americas.

# VICTORIA MUKERJI, Ph.D.

*Curriculum Vitae*

mukerji@corolabs.com
94452 East 62 Place, D-101
Indianapolis, Indiana 46220

Office: (317) 555-3481
Residence: (317) 555-0490

---

**EXPERIENCE**

**SENIOR CHEMIST**     1989–Present
Coro Labs, Inc.     Indianapolis, IN

Extensive work in several adhesive areas: Analytical, Hot-Melt, Polymer, Thermoset, Water Base, and New Product Ventures.

**Analytical**

Analytical method development and modifications in chromatography and wet analysis. Working knowledge of various analytical instruments, including UV-VIS, IR, TGA, DSC, GC, HPLC, GPC, and IC.

**Hot-Melt**

Developed and modified hot-melt adhesive formulations for various applications. Designed, synthesized, and characterized specialty polymers.

**Polymer**

Synthesized aqueous polymer products for various adhesives and coatings. Developed appropriate application procedures.

**Thermoset**

Formulation and scale-up of insulation window sealant.

**Water Base**

Formulated adhesives for paper converting and packaging, automotive, graphic arts, and woodworking applications. Modified adhesives for laminating substrate.

**New Product Ventures**

Coordinated surface analysis work with Surface Science labs. Developed specialty polymers for hot-melt and thermoset applications.

*prior*

**ANALYTICAL TECHNICIAN**     1989
Harding Analytic Laboratory     St. Louis, MO

**TEACHING & RESEARCH ASSISTANT**     1986–1989
Baylor University     Waco, Texas

**TEACHING ASSISTANT**     1983–1985
University of Texas — Austin     Austin, Texas

*Continued . . .*

**EDUCATION**

*chemistry*

**Ph.D. — CHEMISTRY**   1989
Baylor University     Waco, Texas

**M.S. — CHEMISTRY**   1983
Texas Southern University      Houston, Texas

**B.S. — CHEMISTRY**   1982
Texas Southern University

Graduated *magna cum laude*. Minor in Biology.

*legal*

**J.D. — LAW**   1995
Indianapolis College of the Law     St. Paul, Minnesota

Obtained J.D. at night in order to improve knowledge of patent process.

**AFFILIATIONS**

American Chemical Society

American Institute of Chemists

Graduate Women in Science

National Organization of Women Chemists and Chemical Engineers

**ACTIVITIES**

**Chair**, Coro Labs Day Center Project, 1990–1992

**Chair**, Varsity Heights — Coro Labs Community Affairs Council, 1992–1993

**Appointed Member**, Performance Planning and Appraisal (ad hoc committee), Coro Labs, Inc., 1995

**Appointed Member**, Professional Development Program (ad hoc committee), National Organization of Women Chemists and Chemical Engineers, 1995–1996 Also served as **Forum Moderator**.

**PERSONAL**

Willing to travel and/or relocate as needed.

# Kimberly Robertson, Ph.D.

12 Santa Monica Court
Santa Monica, California 90401
(310) 555-9462

---

**BACKGROUND**

- **Biochemistry, Molecular Biology, Medicine**
- **Neuroscience, Immunology, Retrovirology**

Full range of skills in laboratory research: combination of research and clinical knowledge, proven talent for setting direction of research, lab management skills (supplies, scheduling, costing), numerous publications.

*Specialties*

Gene expression regulation, gene therapy/viral vectors, transgenic mouse/knockout experiments.

*Laboratory*

Molecular: DNA cloning, PCR, Sequencing, Northern and Southern hybridization, HPLC.

Cellular: tissue culture. Dissections: particularly rat brain.

*Medicine*

Basic and clinical medical skills, including physiological, pathological, diagnostic, surgical.

*Computer*

Tools: nucleic acid and protein search and analysis, computer literature search, statistical analysis, word processing, graphics. All platforms (Mac, IBM, Unix).

**EDUCATION**

University of Southern California School of Medicine, Los Angeles, California
**Ph.D.** (ABD), **Biochemistry and Molecular Biology**, 1996

University of Southern California, Los Angeles, California
**M.S., Molecular Biology**, 1992
    Thesis: *Molecular Biology of Aging and Neurodegenerative Diseases*

Beijing Medical University School of Medicine, Beijing, China
**B.Med.** (Bachelor of Medicine), 1990

**RESEARCH EXPERIENCE**

University of Southern California, Los Angeles, California
**Graduate Research Assistant,** 1991–Present
*Molecular and Cellular Biology of Aging and Neurodegenerative Diseases*

Microglia Immunopathogenesis
- Found that the balance status between the protective and destructive roles of immune reaction in the brain might be the key to aging and neurodegenerative diseases, through theoretical studies.

*Continued . . .*

- Developed dissertation project that explored how neuroendocrine and neurotrophic factors might affect the balance status mentioned above, thus providing therapeutic clues for age-related neuronal disorders; specifically studied effects of glucocorticoid and Transforming Growth Factor b1 (TGFb1) on immunopathogenesis in the brain by activated brain-resident macrophages-microglia, through cell culture experiments.

GFAP Gene Expression Regulation
- Designed a viral vector, a plasmid-based defective Herpes Simplex Virus vector, for direct in vivo gene transfer of the fusion gene of GFAP promoter fragments and LacZ reporter gene into rat brain in the in vivo study of GFAP gene regulation, thus overcame the necessity of cell transplantation.
- Participate in the in vitro study of GFAP gene regulation by Northern hybridization experiments and chloramphenicol acetyl-transferase (CAT assay, leading to the finding that GFAP mRNA as well as its promoter activities were modulated, in a time- and dose-dependent fashion, by corticosterone, TGFb1, and cAMP in rat C6 glioma cells. Resulted in publication.

Other
- Participated in PCR cloning of human and rat probe templates of the complement component C1q-B chain, for the study of complement expression in aged and Alzheimer's brains.

*Molecular Basis of Retroviral Oncogenesis*
- Found a unified recombination site between exogenous FeLV genome and endogenous proviral elements by PCR and sequencing of multiple clones of experimentally induced lymphoma samples, as well as other tissue samples. Resulted in publication.
- Explored the integration site of exogenous FeLV into host genome by Southern Hybridization, subgenomic library studies, and inverse PCR.

*Molecular Genetics of Mammalian Central Nervous System Development*
- Performed theoretical studies of genes that have implicated roles in mammalian brain, especially forebrain, development, including Homeobox genes and related gene families such as Pox, POU, and Pax. (Review available upon request.)
- Designed a theoretical project which conducts functional analysis, by targeted gene disruption of the mouse homeobox genes Emx1/Emx2, whose embryonic temporal-spatial expression patterns highly correlate to cerebral cortex development. (Project proposal outline available upon request.)

*Human Genetics*
- Participated in the search for hot spot, recombination potentiating sequences(s), by molecular screening, enrichment, and PCR cloning.

*Prokaryotic Molecular Biology*
- Constructed a recombinant plasmid.

*Continued . . .*

Institute of Basic Medical Sciences, Chinese Academy of Medical Sciences, Beijing
**Undergraduate Research Assistant**, 1989

*Immunology*
- Participated in the purification of a low molecular weight B cell growth factor (BCGF) by high performance liquid chromatography (HPLC) for the study of expression and regulation of BCGF receptor(s) on human B cells in normal and abnormal states.

**TEACHING EXPERIENCE**

University of Southern California, Los Angeles, California
**Teaching Assistant**, 1991–Present

Developed instruction plan and taught undergraduate level laboratory courses as follows:
- BISC 450, Immunology
- BISC 312, Human Anatomy
- BISC 300L / 310, Microbiology

**PUBLICATIONS**

- *Association of Chimeric Feline Leukemia Viruses in Experimentally Induced Thymic Lymphosarcomas*, K. Robertson, R. Pandey, L.E. Mathes, and P. Roy-Burman, 1995.
- "Corticosterone Modulates the Expression of the Rat Glial Fibrillary Acidic Protein and Its Promoter Activity in the C6 Glioma," Abstracts for Society for Neuroscience 562.13, 22nd Annual Meeting, October 1993, Anaheim, California, C.J. Huang, N.J. Laping, K. Robertson, D. Morgan, C.E. Finch, 1993.

**REFERENCES**

References and additional information provided upon request.

# VICTOR KRESCHINSKI, Ph.D.

*temporary office*
94452 East County Road C, Bldg. A
St. Paul, Minnesota 55109 U.S.A.
Office/voice mail: (612) 555-3481
Residence: (612) 555-0490

---

**EXPERTISE**

**Welding Technology Engineering / Research**

Molecular-level welding chemistry and materials physics, composites and new materials development, inductive and deductive stress analysis and environmental testing, subordinate scientist development.

**EDUCATION**

Ukraine Academy of Sciences at Kiev
Paton Institute of Electrical Welding
**Ph.D, Materials Science,** 1988

Kiev Polytechnic Institute
**M.S., Materials Science,** 1983

Cornell University
**B.S., Materials Science,** 1981

**EXPERIENCE**

**Laboratory of Welding & Brazing of Composite and Dissimilar Materials**
Paton Institute of Electrical Welding
Ukraine Academy of Sciences at Kiev
1983–Present

The Institute employs 6,000 specialists and provides for the development of new methods of construction material welding, including the use of ceramics and polymers and production of new welding equipment and materials.

Since 1990, have led a research team of 12 scientists, chemists, engineers, and technicians in applied research. Design experiments, manage staff assignments, supervise laboratories, insure data integrity, write papers on findings.

**SENIOR SCIENTIST,** 1990–Present

- Developed a new system of filler metals for aluminum-based composite materials welding (brazing) between themselves and in combination with stainless steel, titanium, and ceramics.

- Developed models and programs for determining time-temperature parameters when arc and plasma welding, connecting spot welding, and brazing the above materials.

- Researched and developed new assembly-welding technologies to get inseparable constructions detailed and grouped for use in aviation and space technologies, as well as shipbuilding, medical equipment, and bicycles.

*Continued . . .*

**SENIOR RESEARCH ENGINEER,** 1988–1990
**RESEARCH ENGINEER,** 1985–1988

- Developed new, high-strength aluminum alloys, composites, and dispersive materials technologies.

- Investigated metal structure exchanges and their influence on high and cryogenic temperatures and mechanical deformations.

- Researched methods of surface treating materials to increase abrasion and corrosion resistance.

**WELDING ENGINEER,** 1983 – 1985

- Developed new equipment for the mechanization and robotization of welding processes.

- Prepared technological maps for assembly and welding operations, details, and operational groups of aircraft.

**PUBLICATIONS**

*Welding Aluminum and Magnesium Alloys* (the standard textbook used throughout former U.S.S.R.), Kiev, 1989

62 publications in Soviet and international scientific journals (approximately ⅓ in English, ¼ in German), full bibliography on request.

**ADDITIONAL**

Holder of 30 patents in the welding technology area, list on request.

Featured guest speaker, International Conference on Welding Technology and Methods of Joining New Construction Materials, Tokyo, Japan, December 1994.

Consultant, Braunschweig Technische Universität and Aachen Hochschule, Germany.

# Medical: Administration and Licensed, CVs and Résumés

Medical résumés run a smooth continuum between the general management styles in chapter 3 (see the medical administrative example there, p. 128 and ff.) to the purely schematic CV style—dates, places, and credentials—exemplified by the first example following. Unfortunately, in a medical setting, administrator résumés are frequently called CVs or curricula vitae, even though stylistically they are nothing more nor less than résumés. In general, if the candidate is a primary care provider, whether doctor, nurse, or specialist, the true CV style will most likely be appropriate; if the person is an administrator with all the classic strategic and business concerns, the standard business résumé style will be appropriate, whether you call it a curriculum vitae or not. Again, the best guide to which style is right for you is the style used by your most successful peers.

You will note that true CVs are practically devoid of accomplishments and any hint of a self-congratulatory tone. They are credentials-based, not performance-based. As in the technical/scientific examples from the last chapter, they may be loaded with addenda and special categories, such as "licensure," "laboratory skills," "honors and awards," "committees," "publications," "teaching," and so on. It is pertinent to note that these CVs can be very long, sometimes a dozen pages or more, as every book, article, and presentation is listed. Traditionally, in medical and academic circles, one never culls early listings from bibliographies; one simply adds to the list, putting new material at the top in reverse chronological order. Be sure to follow the appropriate style for bibliographies. Your reference librarian should be able to help you if you have any questions.

The administrator examples should be familiar to you from earlier in the book. However, be sure to compare the primary care provider examples with the scientific presentations from the last chapter and the academic ones from chapter 10. Of course, check the index for résumés from all the other chapters that may apply to your particular case.

# STANTON I. SCHAUNBAUM, M.D.
*Curriculum Vitae*

433 Fox Hills
Oakland, California 94605

(510) 632-0324
(510) 357-8665

---

**SPECIALTY**

**General Surgery**

**CREDENTIALS**

**Board Certified, American Board of Surgery**
**Fellow, American College of Surgeons**
**Medical License, State of California, #C5381**

**EDUCATION**

**University of Nebraska**, Omaha, Nebraska
**M.D.**, 1960
**M.Sc.** (Pathology), 1960
    Internship — University of Nebraska, 1960–1961
    Residency (Surgery) —
        City Hospital, Cleveland, Ohio, 1961–1962
        V.A. Hospital, San Francisco, California, 1967–1968
        V.A. Hospital, Oakland, California, 1970–1971
**B.Sc.** (Biology), 1952

**APPOINTMENTS**

**Humana Hospital**, San Leandro, California — Active Staff
*current*

**V.A. Hospital**, Livermore, California — Staff Surgeon (part-time)
**Eden Hospital**, Castro Valley, California — Courtesy Staff
**Physicians Community Hospital**, San Leandro, California — Courtesy Staff
**Alameda-Contra Costa County Medical Association (ACCMA)**, Oakland, California
    **Mediation Committee**, 1982–Present
**National Medical Audit, Inc.**, San Francisco, California
    **Surgical Audit** (peer review consultant), 1990–Present

*prior*

**St. Joan's Hospital**, San Leandro, California
    **Chief of Staff**, 1981–1982
    **Chief of Surgery**, 1976–1978
    **Highland Park Hospital**, Oakland, California
    **Teaching Staff**, 1971–1988
    **V.A. Hospital**, Oakland, California
    **Assistant Chief of Surgery**, 1971–1976

**ADDITIONAL EXPERIENCE**

**Private Practice** (general surgery), San Leandro, California, 1962–1989
**Eden Hospital**, Castro Valley, California
    **Trauma Surgeon**, 1986–1987
**Caterpillar Tractor Company**, San Leandro, California
    **Medical Director**, 1972–1984
**V.A. Regional Office**, San Francisco, California
    **Disability Evaluator**, 1969–1970

**ORGANIZATIONS**

East Bay Surgical Society
Southern Alameda Surgical Society
California Academy of Medicine

# VLADIMIR KHANTOROVICH, M.D., Ph.D.

*Curriculum Vitae*

580 Boylston Street, #2
Boston, Massachusetts 02116

Residence/pager: (617) 555-1476
vlad.khant@med.harvard.edu

---

**INTERESTS**   Orthopaedic Surgery, Ilizarov Technique

**CREDENTIALS**   ECFMG Certificate   June 1993

USMLE (step 1) (84th percentile)   September 1992
USMLE (step 2) (85th percentile)   March 1993

FLEX   June 1993

**EDUCATION**   Gorky Scientific and Research Institute of Orthopaedic and Trauma Surgery
**Ph.D., Orthopaedic Surgery**   Gorky, USSR, 1990
Dissertation: "Antiischemic prophylactics for pedicle skin flaps."

Abuali ibn Sino Tadzhik State Medical Institute   Dushanbe, USSR
**M.D.,** *cum laude* (six-year medical program)   1985

High School #1   Dushanbe, USSR
**Baccalaureate Diploma, General Education,** *with honors*   1979

**TRAINING**   Harvard University School of Medicine   Boston, Massachusetts
**Intern — General Surgery Residency Program**   1994–Present

Shriners Hospital for Crippled Children   Boston, Massachusetts
**Clinical Orthopaedic Observer**   1993–1994
At the invitation of Dr. Robert J. McWain, Chairman, Orthopaedic Surgery.

Abuali ibn Sino Tadzhik State Medical Institute   Dushanbe, USSR
**Resident — Orthopaedic and Trauma Surgery**   1985–1987
Including Ilizarov technique.

**PUBLICATIONS**   See attached bibliography.

**EXPERIENCE**   Harvard University School of Medicine   Boston, Massachusetts
**Research Associate — Orthopaedic Bioengineering Laboratory**   1994

Shriners Hospital for Crippled Children   Boston, Massachusetts
**Research Assistant (Volunteer)**   1993–Present
Assist Dr. K.W. Hanchak with research, including reviewing charts and researching
outcomes of Ilizarov method.

Department of Orthopaedic and Trauma Surgery of Tadzhik State Medical Institute
**Assistant Professor, Attending, Orthopaedics**   Dushanbe, USSR, 1990–1991
Instructor, researcher, and physician.

Gorky Scientific Research Institute of Orthopaedic and Trauma Surgery,
**Research Fellow**   Gorky, USSR, 1987–1990
Instructor, researcher, and physician.

Trauma Center — Level I   Dushanbe, USSR
**Staff Nurse** and **Cast Technician**   1984–1985

**HONORS & AWARDS**

Official Reward from the administration of Gorky Scientific Research Institute of Orthopaedic and Trauma Surgery for the treatment of victims of the natural gas explosion in Bashkiria, 1990.

Award and Honorable Gift from the Union of Medical Workers of Gorky Scientific Research Institute of Orthopaedic and Trauma Surgery for organizing a "Best Nurse" competition, 1990.

Medical diploma awarded *cum laude*, 1985. Dean's Scholar, 1980, 1981, 1982, 1983, 1984, 1985.

Awards of Student Scientific Society, Tadzhik State Medical Institute, 1983, 1984.

Award of the Dean of the Tadzhik State Medical Institute for coaching the "Convivial and Clever Club," an equivalent of a college bowl team for medical students, 1982.

Award of Championship in Handball, Sports Committee of Tadzhik State Medical Institute, 1980.

One patent in USSR; additional one pending.

**PERSONAL**

Permanent U.S. Resident, valid "Green Card," qualified for immediate employment.

**PUBLICATIONS**

Bueff, H.U., J.C. Lotz, O.K. Colliou, V. Khantorovich, F. Ashford, S. Hu, D.S. Bradford. "Instrumentation of the Cervico-Thoracic Junction After Destabilization." *Abstracts*. North American Spine Society's Ninth Annual Meeting, October 19–22, 1994, Minneapolis (accepted).

Lotz, J.C., J.S. Hariharan, V. Khantorovich, M. Doulek. "The Influence of Harvest Technique on Measures of Disc Hydration." *Abstracts*. 41st Annual Meeting, Orthopaedic Research Society, February 13–16, 1995, Orlando, Florida (submitted).

Khantorovich, V., and S. Muzafarov. "Pharmacologic Prophylactics in Non-Free Tissue Transfer." *Contemporary Methods of Prophylactics and Treatment in Practice*. April, 1991, 188–189.

Khantorovich, V. "Antiischemic Prophylactics for Pedicle Skin Flaps." Ph.D. diss. Gorky Scientific and Research Institute of Orthopaedic and Trauma Surgery, 118 p., 1990.

Khantorovich, V. "Effect of Reopolyglukin on Pedicle Skin Flap Survival." *Actual Questions of Traumatology and Orthopaedics*. 1990, 295–298.

Khantorovich, V. "Prevention of Ischemic Necrosis in Skin Plastics with Skin Flaps." *Abstracts of VI Republic Conference on the Problems of Thermal Injuries*. 1990, 166–167.

Levin, G., and V. Khantorovich. "Effect of Troxevasin on Survival of Pedicle Skin Flaps." *Skin Plastics in Purulent Surgery*. Fedorov, V., and U. Amirazanov, eds. 1990, 42–43.

Khantorovich, V. "Complex Approach in Prevention of Skin Flap Necrosis. *Abstracts of Interregional Conference on Skin Plastics in Traumatology and Orthopaedics*. Nov. 1989.

Azolov, V. V., S. Petrov, N. Aleksandrov, V. Khantorovich. "The Ways of Correction of Venous Flow in Reconstructive Hand Surgery." *Abstracts*. Proc. of IV Allunion Symposium on Venous and Lymphatic Flow. 10–11 Oct. 1989.

Khantorovich, V., and S. Koshechkin. "Termovision Criteria of the Viability of the Skin Flap under Reduced Blood Flow." *Materials of the Conference of Young Scientist*. 1989, 8.

Khantorovich, V., and G. Levin. "Effect of Tocoferol on Pedicle Skin Flap Survival." *Abstracts*. Proc. of Allunion Meeting on Transport of Oxygen and the Antioxidant Systems. Sep. 1989.

Razzakov, A., V. Khantorovich, A. Abdukhalilov. "Analysis of Prehospital Aid in High Speed Accidents." *The Motor Transport Injuries*. Nurulla-Khodzhaev, T. F., ed. 1988, 9–15.

Abdukhalilov, A., and V. Khantorovich. "Role of External Osteosynthesis in Management of Acute Trauma Patients." *Actual Questions of Traumatology and Orthopaedics*. 1987, 114–119.

Khantorovich, V. "Analysis of Disability After Motor Transport Injuries." *Annual Readings of Student Scientific Society*. Tadzhik State Medical Institute. 1984.

Khantorovich, V. "Dupuitren's Contracture: Etiology, Pathogenesis and Treatment Modalities." *Annual Readings of Student Scientific Society*. Tadzhik State Medical Institute. 1983.

**PRESENTATIONS**

Khantorovich, V. "Model of Axial Skin Flap on the Rat." #1625. Gorky Scientific Research Institute of Orthopaedic and Trauma Surgery. 05.30.89. Gorky, USSR.

Khantorovich, V. "Prophylactics of Ischemic Necrosis in Pedicle Skin Flap: Use of Low Molecular Dextran and Heparin." #1690. Gorky Scientific Research Institute of Orthopaedic and Trauma Surgery. 01.15.90.

Khantorovich, V. "Prophylactics of Ischemic Necrosis in Pedicle Skin Flap: Use of Tocopherol." #1691. Gorky Scientific Research Institute of Orthopaedic and Trauma Surgery. 01.15.90. Gorky, USSR.

Khantorovich, V., S. Koshechkin. "Prediction of Critical Pedicle Skin Flap Survival by Means of Termovision." #1692. Gorky Scientific Research Institute of Orthopaedic and Trauma Surgery. 01.15.90. Gorky, USSR.

Khantorovich V., G. Levin. "Prophylactics of Ischemic Necrosis in Pedicle Skin Flap: Use of Aspirin." #1693. Gorky Scientific Research Institute of Orthopaedic and Trauma Surgery. 01.15.90. Gorky, USSR.

Khantorovich, V., S. Petrov, N. Korotkova. "Variant #1 of Treatment of Hemangioma by Polymers Composition." #1707. Gorky Scientific Research Institute of Orthopaedic and Trauma Surgery. 02.26.90. Gorky, USSR.

Khantorovich, V. "Model of Critical Dorsal Pedicle Skin Flap on the Rabbit." #1711. Gorky ScientificResearch Institute of Orthopaedic and Trauma Surgery. 02.26.90. Gorky, USSR.

**PATENT**

Levin, G., V. Khantorovich. "The Protocol of Pedicle Skin Flap Necrosis Prophylactics." *USSR Patent #4828048/14 (03855)*. 06.03.91. Moscow, USSR.

# YOLANDA POLLER, M.D.

**Pathologist**

3360 South State Street
Chicago, Illinois 60616

Office: (312) 555-4929
Residence: (312) 555-3465

## EDUCATION

**Graduate**, Executive Management Program, 1992–1993 (6 Weeks FTE)
University of Chicago—Kaiser Permanente

**Pathology Residency Training**, 1979–1983
Kaiser Foundation Hospital, Chicago, Illinois, 1981–1983
Rush-Presbyterian-St Luke's Medical Center, Chicago, Illinois, 1979–1981

**M.D.**, University of Illinois, Chicago, Illinois, 1975–1979

**B.S.**, University of Illinois, Champaign, Illinois, 1971–1975

## CREDENTIALS

**Board Certified**, Anatomical and Clinical Pathology, 1983
**Licensed**, State of Illinois, 1980

## APPOINTMENTS

**Physician-in-Chief**, 1994–Present
Kaiser Permanente Medical Care Program, Chicago, Illinois

**Member**, Board of Directors, 1994–Present
The Permanente Medical Group, Inc., Chicago, Illinois

**Chief-of-Staff**, 1994–Present
**Attending Pathologist**, Surgical, Autopsy, and Clinical Pathology, 1983–Present
**Clinical Instructor**, Pathology Residency Training Program, 1983–Present
Kaiser Foundation Hospital, Chicago, Illinois

## PRIOR

**Assistant Physician-in-Chief**, 1988–1994
Kaiser Permanente Medical Care Program, Chicago, Illinois

**Assistant Director**, 1987–1988
Kaiser Permanente Regional Laboratory, Skokie, Illinois

**Director**, Blood Bank (AABB Approved), 1983–1994
**Director**, Hematology (CAP Approved), 1983–1993
**Director**, Clinical Pathology Program, 1983–1987
**Clinical Instructor**, School of Medical Technology, 1982–1985
Kaiser Foundation Hospital, Chicago, Illinois

**Inspector**, 1983–1987
College of American Pathologists

## ADDITIONAL

Committee assignments, professional affiliations, references and any additional information needed
will be provided on request.

# YOLANDA POLLER, M.D.

### Pathologist

3360 South State Street
Chicago, Illinois 60616

Office: (312) 555-4929
Residence: (312) 555-3465

## ADDENDUM

### COMMITTEES

Chairman, Ethics Committee, 1995–Present
Member, Regional Nurse Advisory Committee, 1995–Present
Chairman, Staff Executive Committee, 1994–Present
Member, Credentials and Privileges Committee, 1988–Present
Member, Interdisciplinary AIDS Task Force, 1991–1994
Chairman, Interdisciplinary Practice Committee, 1988–1994
Chairman, Investigative Drug Subcommittee, 1988–1994
Chairman, Quality Assurance Program, Pathology, 1988–1994
Chairman and Member, Tissue and Transfusion Committee, 1983–1994
Member, Regional Laboratory Equipment Committee, 1987–1988
Member, Laboratory Utilization Committee, 1985–1988
Member, Technical Committee, Memorial Blood Bank, 1984–1988
Vice President, Medical Staff Executive Committee, 1984–1986

### AFFILIATIONS

Member, Illinois Medical Association, 1989–Present
Member, Chicago Medical Society, 1989–Present
Former Member, College of American Pathologists
Former Member, American Society of Clinical Pathologists
Former Member, International Academy of Pathologists
Former Member, American Association of Blood Banks

# Clarissa Schick Howison, Ph.D.

*Curriculum Vitae*

2100 Chestnut Street
San Francisco, California 94123

Telephone/message: (415) 555-6346
claris@well.com

## PROFILE

**Licensed Clinical Psychologist,** PSY45061, State of California

**Certified Employee Assistance Professional,** Employee Assistance Professional Association

- Clinical skills include brief and long-term psychotherapy (group or individual), crisis intervention, telephone counseling, diagnosis and referral. Extensive EAP experience with employees of all levels, organizational problem solving, career issues. Experienced with multicultural/multiethnic populations.

- Expertise on workplace alcohol and chemical dependency problems, and cost-effective solutions.

- Program development skills include needs assessment, policies/procedures/methodologies, budget development, staffing, training and teaching, and organizational interface. Computer skilled for administration, records, and report generation.

- Effective interface and liaison between employees and inpatient/outpatient services, families, insurers, and the employer.

## EDUCATION

**Ph.D., Clinical Psychology,** California School of Professional Psychology

**M.S., Organizational Psychology,** San Francisco State University

**B.A., American Literature,** Stanford University

## TEACHING EXPERIENCE

California School of Integrative Studies
**Instructor,** 1990–Present
Graduate Seminar: DSM IIIR Personality Disorders.

## CLINICAL EXPERIENCE

Performance Enhancement, Inc.
**Consulting Psychologist** (on-site at Sylvax, Menlo Park), 1992–Present

Provide EAP services: crisis intervention, brief psychotherapy, treatment planning, and referral to appropriate continuation services. Involved with diverse issues, levels, and types of employees. Conducted workshops and consulted with the company's Occupational Health Service on specific issues and/or cases.

Office of Melvin M. Linten, M.D., I.M.E.
**Consulting Psychologist,** 1990–1994

Evaluated long-standing workers' compensation cases. Assessed and/or developed treatment plans. (Dr. Linten was the Director of WA&A, listed below.)

Worker Assessment & Assistance (WA&A), Inc.
**Staff Psychologist** and **EAP Coordinator,** 1989–1992

Coordinated EAP services for 2000 employees: telephone crisis intervention, diagnosis and referral, counseling, follow-up. Clinical supervisor for two on-site therapists. Tracked and analyzed statistics, monitored utilization review data, maintained records, reported on EAP trends and concerns. Trained supervisors, consulted with departments, organized health education program.

For long-standing workers' compensation cases: Provided assessment, psychotherapy, treatment planning, and case management.

Human Resources Group, Inc.
**Program Administrator,** 1987–1989

Provided telephone crisis intervention and counseling, evaluation, pre-therapy, referral, and follow-up in an external EAP. Consulted with workers, supervisors, and management. Conducted substance abuse confrontations. Group leader for sessions on traumatic stress.

Oakland Community Counseling
**Staff Psychotherapist,** 1984–1987

Individual psychotherapy with adult outpatients and group work with substance abusers. Clinical supervisor for interns. Administered EAP, including program development. Participated in agency administration: direct interface to businesses, agencies, schools and community at large. Member, Executive Director Search Committee.

San Francisco City College Health Services
**Intern,** 1981–1983

Individual brief psychotherapy with adult and late adolescent outpatients. Participated in research project to evaluate brief therapies.

San Francisco Mental Health District V
**Intern,** 1980–1981

Intake, crisis intervention, individual and group psychotherapy.

Wells Fargo Bank EAP
**Intern Counselor,** 1979–1980

Provided telephone counseling, crisis intervention, evaluation, referral, treatment planning. Provided initial drafts of new cross-cultural training and stress management programs for an EAP program serving over 18,000 employees. Collaborated with supervisors and line managers on EAP organizational issues, health education programs, and problem trends.

Oakland Community Counseling
**Schools Coordinator,** 1976–1979

Provided psychotherapy for children, adolescents, and adults. Developed and administered counseling program for up to 12 schools. Full charge of clinical protocols, policies, procedures, and clinical supervision of up to 8 interns. Represented the program to and coordinated with administrators, parents, and other social service providers. Included components for students, teachers, staff, and parents. Oversaw organizational and financial management, statistics, correspondence, files, evaluations, and records. Ultimately responsible for compliance to school board policy and applicable state/federal laws.

Alcohol Evaluation and Treatment Center
**Intern,** 1975–1976

Individual and group psychotherapy with alcohol inpatients.

## ADDITIONAL

Knowledge of public and private referral resources throughout Northern California. Effective speaking and presentation skills for training and inservice. Avocation: renovating residential buildings, including financial analysis, contract negotiations, and related management functions. Available for travel.

# Ruth D. Whitfield, MSW

2301 J Street NW
Washington, D.C. 20037

Office: (202) 555-5665
Residence: (202) 555-1589

---

## PROFILE

**Licensed Clinical Social Worker**

Areas of clinical expertise:
- **Counseling**
- **Alcohol & Chemical Dependency, Addiction, EAP**
- **Intake, Assessment, Testing**
- **Advocacy & Referral**

Additional skills in program administration, special events, training, retreats, budgeting. Strength: relational skills; able to make others feel valuable and comfortable; able to focus the efforts of diverse parties onto a common goal.

Knowledge of Capital-area social and psychotherapy services, public and private.

## CREDENTIALS

**Licensed Clinical Social Worker, State of Virginia**

**Hypnosis Certification, Board of Behavioral Science Examiners**

## EDUCATION

**M.S.W., Counseling**, University of Virginia

**B.A., Humanities**, Russell College

## EXPERIENCE

**Clinical Division of Catholic Charities**, 1990–Present

**STAFF THERAPIST** (approx. 50% of duties)

Provide a wide range of therapy to children, adults, and couples, including crisis intervention, brief therapy, advocacy, and referral to Capital-area social services. Handle all phases of screening, intake, triage, treatment planning. Specialize in dependency, addiction, and ACA issues; survivors of sexual/physical abuse; grief counseling (death, divorce, job loss, and other issues). Patient population includes individuals from diverse cultural/ethnic backgrounds.

Supervisory/coordinating duties: Supervise three interns; delegate cases, oversee caseload. Collaborate on interview process to select new interns. Orient eight interns to sites, program policies, procedures, and documentation requirements. Chair weekly staff meeting.

Special projects:
- Planning Committee, Agency Retreat Day.
- Planning Committee, National Catholic Charities Convention.
- Planning Committee, Board and Staff Dinner.
- Co-Leader, Senior Support Group (with gerontology psychotherapy specialist).

*– continued –*

**COORDINATOR, SCHOOL COUNSELING PROGRAM** (approx. 30% of duties)

Coordinate public and private school therapy/counseling services, typically serving three to seven schools at a time. Initiate counseling programs with schools, prepare contracts for principals and boards, coordinate training of site counselors, consult on making counseling services site-managed (i.e., program spin-offs).

Train counselors in assessment and testing (DAP, DAT, DAH, K-F-D), parent interviews, crisis intervention techniques, collaboration with teachers and administrators. Also provide staff/faculty in-service and program orientation.

Special projects:
- Coordinated with Washington, D.C., police and schools in delivery of a drug education program for inner-city schools.
- Panelist, "Depression During the Holidays," Mosaic, Channel 5.
- Organized post-trauma services for victims and witnesses of violence and their families.

**GRIEF COUNSELOR** (approx. 10% of duties)

Provide grief counseling and coordinate grief counseling services.

Special projects:
- Provide grief training twice a year to nonlicensed grief counselors. Member of planning committee for annual retreat for grief caregivers.
- Planning committee and presenter, "Children and Grief" workshop series given to 500+ elementary school teachers.

**SITE COORDINATOR** (approx. 10% of duties)

Ensure proper administrative records and procedures are maintained. Recruit, orient, and coordinate volunteers.

**PRIOR:** Elementary School Teacher, School Principal

**CONTINUING EDUCATION** (representative training only, not an exhaustive listing)

Control-Mastery Theory: Treatment of Incest Survivors, Diane Raisman-Suffridge, Ph.D.

Pharmacology and Mental Health Medications, Terry Wong, Pharm.D.

Object Relations Family Therapy, Jill Savage Scharff, M.D., D.E. Scharff, M.D.

Sexual Abuse Treatment, Lynne Conlin, MSW

Co-Dependency as a Clinical Issue, N. McCollum, MSW

Survivors of Incest, Ellen Bass, M.A.

Countertransference and Relationship in Therapy, J. Goodbread, Ph.D., K. Jove, C.M.A.

Cross-Cultural Issues (Asian, Black, Latino), numerous workshops and classes

Alcohol and Drug Abuse Issues in Psychotherapy, K. Miller, MSW

Post-Traumatic Stress Disorder: Assessment and Treatment, AAMFT Conference

Clinical Issues with Step Families, G. Gregg, MSW

Chemical Dependency, P. Phelps, MSW

Family Violence, J. Hassett, Family Violence Project

Hypnotherapy without Trance, P. Watzlawick, Ph.D.

Myers-Briggs Type Inventory (MBTI) Training, R. Fitzgerald, MSW

# Richard G. Sullivan, M.D.

*Curriculum Vitae*

125 Harbor Complex, C-123
Boston, Massachusetts 02125

dr.sullivan@med.umass.edu
Office: (617) 555-7885
Residence/message/pager: (617) 555-1479

## EXPERTISE

### Medical Research Computing and Medical Administration Computing

State-of-the-art expertise designing medical research and medical administration applications in micro, Internet, main-frame-to-workstation, and LAN/WAN environments. Includes contributions to network utilization design, interactive application design, equipment configuration, operations design/analysis of basic research methodology, data capture, and report/information dissemination planning. Entrepreneurial and forward in approach.

Unusual combination of skills: technical, medical/clinical, communication, financial.

## EDUCATION & TRAINING

**M.D.,** School of Medicine, University of Massachusetts School of Medicine

**B.A.,** Biochemistry, Amherst College

**Fellowship,** Neonatology, Mt. Zion Hospital & Medical Center, Worcester

**Residency,** Porter Memorial Hospital, Denver

**Computer Training:** *extensive* vendor/university training in systems development, project management, applications, programming, operations analysis, and similar. List on request.

## AFFILIATIONS

**Mt. Zion Hospital & Medical Center,** Worcester, 1988–Present

**St. Luke's Hospital,** Boston, 1988–Present

**U.Mass. Med. Ctr. Clinical Faculty,** Boston, 1992–Present

## HIGHLIGHTS

Contracting through **Victoria Medical Group, Inc.:**

**Director, Perinatal Research & Data** (currently, 60%)
**Neonatologist** (currently, 40%)

Medical systems manager. Responsible for computing function, including hardware, software, net-access, LANs, peripherals, and custom-designed data capture devices. Manage research, clinical databasing and recordkeeping, and 25% of applications in administrative computing. Train end-users systemwide. Sample projects:

- Designed the national WWW site for doctor-to-doctor neonatal consultation with U.Mass. Medical Center as host. Won AMA award for "Technology in Service to Medicine," 1996.

- Presented *Use of Computer Database to Predict Outcome of Intensive Care Nursery Graduates,* The Second World Symposium of Computers in the Care of the Mother, Fetus, and Newborn, Kyoto, Japan, 1995.

- Designed and implemented preterm labor monitoring system with on-screen recommendations and information links for Department of Obstetrics. Assisted research director in specifying database function and methodology. Developed data capture system (patient monitor data feed/interpretation program). Programmed screens and links. Administered $15,000 computing budget in compliance with terms of $850,000 umbrella research grant. Computer portion completed on time and under budget.

- Relocated entire billing department and established telecomputing links to maintain real-time billing and ensure hospital cash flow.

- Coordinator for four-hospital study on thyroid releasing hormone. Established central data center; contributed research methodology; designed database and analysis applications. Research will culminate in 1998, and result in 2–4 research papers, e.g., "Prenatal Thyrotropin Releasing Hormone Plus Corticosteroid Decreases Chronic Lung Disease in Very Low Birth Weight Infants," WSPR Meetings, February 1996.

- Research director for March of Dimes project to develop computerized randomly oscillating neonatal water bed device to determine effectiveness of random motion on prevention of neonatal apnea. Built and tested prototypes. Designed and conducted experimentation, data compilation and analysis.

- Created and maintained ICN patient follow-up database, breast-feeding research database, preterm labor research database, alternative birthing center research database, artificial surfactant (EXOSURF) research database, labor and delivery log, and the integrated patient tracking system.

- Programmed and implemented miscellaneous administrative records/database projects, such as billing systems, vacation scheduling, operating theater utilization systems, and similar.

**Clinical Duties:**

- Neonatologist at St. Lukes, Mt. Zion and U.Mass. Medical Center. Responsible for high-risk deliveries and premature infants. Instruct resident physicians and student nurses. Consult to private physicians.

- Specialist on neonatal transport of high-risk newborns. Attending physician for ICN transport of infants from all over New England. Author and instructor on transport technique and theory.

- Coordinator of Teenage Mothers Unit and Well Baby Clinic.

## MILITARY

United States Navy, 1967–1969

- Decorated Vietnam veteran. General Medical Officer, Da Nang Air Base 1st Light Anti-Aircraft Missile Battalion.

- Republic of Vietnam Civilian Award for Medical Civic Action Program. The popular book, *One of Us,* written about work in transferring Vietnamese children to the United States for medical treatment.

## ADDITIONAL

In partnership with another physician and a respiratory therapist, have designed and built prototype clinical equipment that ties together ICN instruments and allows easy entry of data from these instruments into online database. Seventeen prototype systems in beta testing with potential for commercial development.

## BIBLIOGRAPHY

Author or co-author on 18 articles. Cited data analyst and consultant for 49 more. Detailed bibliography available on request.

# GAYLE MERIWETHER

1656 Fisher Road
Roseburg, Oregon 97470

Office direct line: (541) 555-4440
Residence/message: (541) 555-5957

---

## Administration — Managed Care / Marketing & Business Development / Strategic Alliances

---

### SYNOPSIS

- Expertise includes strategic and structural contributions in managed care environments, initiation and control of organizational change, initiation of health care alliances, negotiation of contracts and memorandums of understanding with clinical and business partners, physician-hospital linkage, and antitrust issues impacting the current and upcoming health care environment.
- Extensive new business launch and development background. Accomplished company representative to government, corporate, and community organizations. Effective speaker, lecturer, trainer.
- Fluent in Spanish. Also: cross-cultural business development and promotions experience, especially to Hispanic and Asian communities, both in the United States and abroad.
- Hands-on manager. Full budget and business planning experience. Business writing skills. High energy level and creativity. *Major contributions on behalf of every employer.*

### EDUCATION

**Pepperdine University,** Malibu, California
**M.B.A.,** Executive Program, 1987

**University of Hong Kong,** Hong Kong
**M.A.,** Chinese Porcelain & Household Furniture, 16th–19th Centuries, 1980
(additional emphasis: China-U.S. Trade Relations)

**University of Florence,** Italy
**Graduate Studies,** Art/Furniture Restoration Sciences, 1975–1976

**Royal College of the Arts,** Bloomsbury, W1, London, England
**Diploma,** Art History, 1975

### PROFESSIONAL HISTORY

**UniHealth America / UniMed Division,** Chatsworth, California, 1992–1996
**Regional Director**

In charge of physician advantage opportunities in approximately 30% of a diversified health services corporation with 11 hospitals, two commercial HMO products, two senior HMO products, one PPO product, and several related entities and organizations. Provided strategic direction, recruitment, and marketing support to affiliated physicians, hospitals, IPAs and medical groups within region. Additionally sought health care business alliances within the Hispanic professional health care networks. Delegated to the Coordinator of Practice Enhancement, along with rotating support staffs (depending on project). Analyzed hospital medical staffs, developed medical staff plans, provided advice and support to hospital CEOs. Involved in every aspect of this complex organization. Contributions:

(1) Organized a 110-physician IPA, specifically targeting the Latino population.
(2) Developed a faculty family practice medical group as an off-site hospital feeder, not only increasing bed days and managed care share, but also as a resident retention mechanism.

(3) Developed a joint-venture relationship with a major Latino health services corporation, placing quality primary care clinics in advantageous locations to UniHealth America hospital facilities. Also joint ventured with the health services corporation's "Senior and Activity Center," specifically the primary care geriatric clinic housed within.

(4) Recruited seven new physicians to region in one year, not including the new physicians brought in to affiliate with the new IPA.

**White Memorial Medical Center,** Los Angeles, California, 1988–1992
**Director of Managed Care and External Affairs**

Managed marketing and business development for four business entities: Family Health Center, Family Practice Group, Mental Health Program, and the Chemical Dependency Program. Directed the IPA's growth, and chaired the hospital PPO Association. Contributions:

(1) Conceived, designed, researched locations and launched a "Family Care Specialist" medical group accessing hospital services from three locations. This group generated $1.4 million net increase to the hospital during their second year.

(2) Spearheaded an intensified Hispanic and Asian community relations effort, supporting community associations, hosting several major community health care events, and highlighting the hospital's 10% of budget contracting record with minority businesses.

**Servicios Medicos de la Bahia,** Puerto Vallarta, Jalisco, Mexico, 1984–1988
**Marketing Director/Administrator**

Developed and implemented a high-profile marketing/PR strategy for these medical clinics and mini-hospital, with emphasis on maximum share of wealthy tourist clientele. Acquired in-port medical services contracts with all incoming cruise ship lines, 5-star hotel contracts, and air-evacuation agreements with both the U.S. and Canadian Consuls. Assumed leadership roles in area organizations.

**Baykal & Baykal Wholesale Oriental Antiques,** S.F. & L.A., California, 1979–1984
**Buyer/Marketing and Sales Manager**

Created a West Coast market for antique furniture and porcelains from suppliers in China, Hong Kong, Macao, Burma, and Thailand. Developed a lead list of wholesalers, museums, and serious collectors. Designed a high-end, direct-mail flier that gave credibility to this start-up company overnight (very difficult for this type of trade). Managed two warehouses.

**Save The Children,** Hong Kong, Victoria, 1976–1979
**Supervisor**, Fund-Raising & Development Efforts

Event planning, telemarketing, and public relations.

**Harrod's of London** and **Mitzi Lorenze,** London, England, 1967–1971
**Salon Model**

Modeled to pay educational expenses.

**Macy's Hillsdale**, San Mateo, California, 1965–1967
**Sales**

First California teenager on the now statewide Work Experience Program.

## PERSONAL INTERESTS

Foreign cultures and languages, antiques, opera.

## REFERENCES

References, recommendations, and additional information provided on request. Please keep this information confidential at this time.

# Patricia Vernal Russo

*Curriculum Vitae*

39561 Abercorn Street
Savannah, Georgia 31419

Office: (912) 555-6745
Residence: (912) 555-9933

---

**EXPERTISE**

**Health Care Administration**

*Areas of Expertise:*
- **Surgical Services/Outpatient Services.**
- **Managed Care.**
- **Resource Management.**
- **Utilization Review/Quality Assurance.**

*Strengths:*
- Creative and visionary program development and implementation, including turn-around management when needed.
- Collaborative decision-making and consensus building with internal constituencies.
- Design of programs and policies which serve marketing priorities as well as cost control and quality assurance goals.
- Design of quantitative/qualitative measurement tools to establish statistical control of medical service operations.

**EDUCATION**

UNIVERSITY OF GEORGIA      Athens, Georgia
**Master of Public Administration** (GPA: 3.8)      1988

Thesis: *Time and Cost Study of Maintaining Operating Room Schedule: Timeliness Saves Money and Improves Physician Satisfaction*

ST. MARY'S ON THE HILL      Moraga, Georgia
**Bachelor of Arts, Health Services Administration** (GPA: 3.7)      1978

**EXPERIENCE**

JACKSON & LEE HOSPITAL      Savannah, Georgia
**Director, Perioperative Services**      1993–Present

Hired to modernize, improve, increase efficiency and quality of care in five surgical services departments for 300-bed district hospital:
- **OR**
- **Post-Anesthesia Care**
- **Short Stay Unit**
- **Pre-Operative Testing**
- **Endoscopy**

Develop and manage $10 million annual budget, 55 FTEs, and provide executive direction to all five departments. Report directly to chief of operations.

*Selected contributions:*
- Provided oversight of architects and contractors, including extensive revisions to original plans, for high-tech modernization/reconstruction of OR. Total project: $1.9 million ($1.5 million construction, $382,000 equipment).
- Added endoscopy to perioperative management group.

- Computerized OR, increasing number of automated procedures and departmental efficiency.
- Reduced OR staff approximately 20%.
- Significantly improved employee morale.
- Actively involved with research and implementation of JIT and stockless inventory systems. The OR is responsible for 50% *of the total hospital inventory.*

ST. MARY'S HOSPITAL & MEDICAL CENTER    Savannah, Georgia
**Director, Resource Management** and **Director, Case Management**    1991–1993

Recruited by the hospital CEO to bring a new, institutionwide awareness of resource management to this 550-bed hospital. Served concurrently as department head of two departments, with considerable authority to cross organizational lines and achieve enhancements and improvements to policies and procedures. Reported to the executive director, quality and resource management.

As **Director, Resource Management**, served on hospital committees and conducted special projects to conserve resources, contain costs, and maintain quality. Committees:
- **Resource Management Committee**
- **Risk Contract Management Committee**
- **Medical Quality Committee**
- **Utilization Review Committee**
- **Length of Stay Committee**
- **Managed Care Committee**
- **Financial Committee**
- **Employee Benefits Task Force**
- **Patient Self-Determination Act Task Force**

As **Director, Case Management**, line-managed a department of 12 case managers plus administrative support staff. Planned and administered $750,000 departmental operating budget. Provided executive leadership to utilization review, discharge planning, psycho-social assessment, quality assurance, inservice and educational programs.

*Selected contributions:*
- Brought a fractious group of professionals together into a highly productive department by focusing the efforts of all onto a common goal. (Similar accomplishments across departmental lines.)
- Launched the **Clinical Pathway Program**, including research, design, implementation, and evaluation of clinical pathways. Involved extensive medical staff education to achieve buy-in from clinical, quality, and fiscal perspectives. (Available as a consultant due to the success of this program, see below.)
- Implemented the **Possibly Avoidable Days** program, including design of standardized tools for quantification/qualification, resulting in reduction in length of stay from 7.9 days to 7.1 days.
- Global responsibility for **Medicare Risk Contracts**, ensuring appropriate utilization of resources and quality patient care outcomes.
- Directed the hospitalwide **Managed Care Program**, working with all physicians groups and staff to ensure quality care within fiscal responsible time frames.
- Organized in-service for nurses on contemporary health care issues from a fiscal and managerial perspective.
- Organized educational program for physicians, nurses, and ancillary staff, including a nationally prominent speaker.

PROVIDENCE HOSPITAL    Athens, Georgia
**Director, Surgical Services**    1985–1991

Provided short- and long-range strategic planning and daily operations management for operating rooms, recovery rooms, Ambulatory Treatment Center, G.I. Department, Pre-Admissions, and Perioperative Care Units for this 225-bed hospital. Reported directly to the Administrator of Patient Care Services.

Developed new programs and services, coordinated all issues of staff development, technology, equipment, funding and marketing to bring programs and services on board. Prepared, managed, and analyzed budgets of up to $8 million. Monitored productivity by department and by staff indicators. Designed performance measurement tools. Creatively set staffing plans and scheduled capital purchases to meet conservative capital management goals.

Accountable for developing nursing-based systems to deliver quality patient care in a safe, efficient, and effective manner.

*Selected contributions:*
- Conceived and developed **Center of Excellence for Ophthalmology** at Providence Hospital, including physical plant renovation, operations design, laser equipment, and development of nursing staff. Recruited physicians to participate in the Center, including extensive outreach and education.
- Spearheaded the introduction of laparoscopy to Georgia, establishing a **Center of Excellence for Minimally Invasive Surgery** at Providence. Required extensive relationship-building with area surgeons to promote the technique and our Center. Negotiated agreement to use the Center as a training program. Volume ran to 500+ procedures in the first year alone.
- Launched mobile **Lithotriptor** service through the Department of Urology.
- Expanded and redesigned the **G.I. Department**, resulting in 45% increase in volume (new facilities, equipment, staff development).
- Redesigned admitting practices to achieve 75% reduction in waiting time.
- Reduced sicktime 50% in O.R.
- Orchestrated full computerization of surgical scheduling (staff and facilities).
- Launched cooperative **Perioperative Nursing Education Program** with University of Georgia as an outreach program in support of nurse recruiting.

*Honor:*
- Manager of the Year, 1990. First recipient of this annual award.

DAVIDSON HOSPITAL    Brunswick, Georgia
**Director, Central Processing and Distribution**    1980–1985

Instituted O.R. and C.P.D. systems: trained and oriented professional and semi-professional personnel in its operation. Restored department in chaos to a well functioning service unit. Instilled a sense of purpose and worth to a staff suffering from poor morale. Oversaw the changeover to computerized systems.

Developed a new unit of productivity measurement adopted in this and other hospitals.

*Prior:*

**O.R. Clinical Instructor**
**O.R. Charge Nurse — Orthopedics**
**O.R. Staff Nurse**

| | |
|---|---|
| **CONSULTING** | **Consultant — O.R., C.P.D.** |
| | Consulting engagements with Athens area hospitals in training, operational, and procedural areas of O.R. and C.P.D. Clients: Providence Hospital, Robert E. Lee Salvation Hospital, John Barnett Community Hospital. Available for program review, departmental audits, and general consulting on O.R. and C.P.D. issues. |
| **COMMUNITY SERVICE** | Community outreach, *pro bono*, and volunteer activities, mainly in the areas of health education, development, consortia, and social events for health care professionals—details on request. Memberships and affiliations—list on request. **R.N.**, State of Georgia, current. |
| **REFERENCES** | Extensive personal and professional references available on request. Please keep this information confidential at this time. |

# Theresa J. McNeal

*Curriculum Vitae*

1533 Autumn Drive
Helena, Montana 59601

Office/voice mail: (406) 555-7235, ext. 56
Residence/message: (406) 555-2228

---

**PROFILE**

**Health Care Administration — Finance / Admitting**

*Highlights:*

- Background includes extensive responsibility and success with operations design, staff reorganization, departmental reorganization, and special projects in expense reduction, cost containment, cash flow control.
- Bottom-line contributions on behalf of every employer. Excellent performance reviews. Energetic. Ready for a new challenge.

**EXPERIENCE**

**FOOTHILLS HOSPITAL**     Helena, MT
**Director of Patient Accounting**     1993–Present

Full strategic and operational responsibility for **Patient Accounting**. Supervise staff of 27.5 FTEs, including patient accounting manager, supervisors, billers, collectors, counselors, clerks, and cashier. Ensure close coordination with **Admitting** and **IS** departments at the hospital. Report directly to the CFO. Collaborate on all decisions hospitalwide that impact patient accounting, billing, and collections.

Set policy, establish information flows and reporting formats, develop and document procedures. Interact daily with physicians, patients, third-party payors, and vendors. Forecast, monitor and analyze budgets. Serve on hospital committees, including **Admissions, Utilization Review,** and **Medical Records**.

*Contributions to date:*

- Reorganized Patient Accounting Department, updated and revitalized training programs, provided personal outreach to staff to achieve acceptance of change.
- Reduced staff by 6.5 FTEs with concurrent *increase* in total departmental performance.
- Served on Task Force to establish admission criteria by payor source.
- Implemented Contract Management System (Acculog).
- Automated the Billing Unit. Automated the Collections Unit.
- Reduced patient complaints through more accurate billing.
- Reduced A/R days outstanding from 110 FY90/93 to 60.4 FY94/95.
- Reduced A/R outstanding by $2.5 million and credit balances by $400,000 FY94/95.
- Reduced bad debt by $250,000 FY93/94.
- *Improved cash flow by $1.6 million per month.*

**MONTANA MEDICAL CENTER**     Billings, MT
**Assistant Director of Patient Business Services & Admitting**     1989–1992

Responsible for **Patient Accounting** and **Admitting** functions. Supervised staff of 48 FTEs, delegating through a management team of the manager of admitting, telecommunications supervisor, outpatient registration supervisor, inpatient admitting supervisor, billing supervisor, and collections supervisor.

Monitored and reported on work flow and productivity. Ensured close cooperation with **Utilization Review** and **Medical Records**. Collaborated with director of patient business services on special studies, organizational change, and other strategic considerations. Served on numerous committees.

*Contributions:*

- Implemented defense audits resulting in identification of considerable discrepancies with insurers. Saved the medical center in excess of $200,000 per annum.
- Reorganized the Billing Unit and automated the billing function.
- Standardized an account review process for the Collections Unit.
- Restructured policies and procedures for the Admitting Unit.

**ST. LUKE'S HOSPITAL**   Great Falls, MT
**Manager, NonGovernment Accounting**   1988–1989

Directed the daily activities of the **Billing, Collection,** and **Customer Service** departments. Supervised staff of 14 employees, established policies and procedures, prepared productivity and performance analyses, resolved problem accounting/service issues on behalf of specific patients. Reported to the director, Patient Business Services.

**MOUNT ZION HOSPITAL & MEDICAL CENTER**   Missoula, MT
**Supervisor, Inpatient Accounting** (staff of 20)   1988

**MARSHALL HALE MEMORIAL HOSPITAL**   Billings, MT
**Senior Accounting Representative**   1985–1986
**Patient Accounting Representative**   1980–1985
**Patient Accounting Clerk**   1978–1980

EDUCATION

**Continuing Education in Hospital MIS**

**Computer Studies, Mt. Diablo Adult Education**

**HFMA and HCNC Management Development Courses**

**Studies in Management and Supervision, Diablo Valley College**

**A.A., Diablo Valley College**

PROFESSIONAL
AFFILIATION

**Health Care Financial Management Association (HFMA)**
**American Guild for Patient Accounting Managers (AGPAM)**

REFERENCES

References and performance reviews provided on request, but please keep this information confidential at this time.

# *Legal*

Résumés for lawyers who practice law for law firms have a particular style, as particular as a medical CV, yet this style has no special name. In general, legal résumés do not have a profile, or if they do, it is only a word or two to identify a specialty. They list the number of attorneys at each firm, the type of firm (for example: plaintiff, defense, general practice, PI, insurance defense, and so on), the status of the person the attorney reports to (senior associate, partner, senior partner, managing partner), the type of cases the candidate herself has, and the nature and level of responsibility on those cases. If the cases go to trial, the outcome is usually reported on the résumé for all cases, like a sporting score. If the cases are published, the citations are listed (using the *Uniform System of Citation* {13th ed., 1981}, published by the *Harvard Law Review,* also known as "The Blue Book"). Outcomes of major settled or nonlitigated cases are also stated, good or bad. Education is frequently at the top of the résumé, especially if it is from brand-name schools, and special honors are noted long after the attorney has developed a grey hair or two.

Even the language is peculiar: Use "v." not "vs.," "judgment" not "judgement," "defense" not "defence." "Of counsel," means a senior attorney who is working under contract for another firm. To designate bar memberships, say, "Member, State Bar of California, admitted 1975," never "Member of the Bar, State of California, admitted 1975," as bars are technically extragovernmental. Legal language, Latin and all, is de rigueur.

In addition to minimizing or eliminating profiles, legal résumés generally do not have any bullets or similar accents of any kind. They may feature plenty of white space and can be found with very small type, as small as ten or, god forbid, nine.

Finally, they are understated to the point of being self-effacing. I suppose it's no joke to say that law-firm attorneys ought not brag. (Of course, the examples in this book push the outer limits of this admonition.)

If you want to show promise, mention rainmaking (bringing clients to the firm), successful development of junior associates, major client or symposia presentations, and impressive *pro bono* service, all of which didn't in any way interfere with billing two-thousand hours per year.

Legal résumés must be typographically perfect. The smallest error is grounds for disqualification in most placement situations.

On the other hand, legal administrative résumés are classic, business-oriented, accomplishment-based presentations familiar to you from elsewhere in this book. House counsel and attorneys with extensive administrative, consulting, or business responsibilities will fall somewhere in the middle. There is a complete range of examples following this introduction. Be sure to check the index for résumés in other chapters that may apply to your particular case. (You will find *juris doctor*-degreed careerists in many other sections of the book.)

# Clarence Pittman, Esq.

2130 G Street NW
Washington, D.C. 20037

Telephone / Message:
(202) 555-4366

---

**EMPHASIS**    **Business and Commercial Litigation**

**EXPERIENCE**    **McNAMARA, EVANS, BURMEISTER & STOWE**    Washington, D.C.
**Senior Litigation Associate**    1992–Present

Manage case load of commercial and business litigation for this 150-attorney firm. Case load commonly involves intellectual property, real estate, bankruptcy, employment, disabilities law, director and officer coverage disputes with insurers, and antitrust litigation. Also provide counsel to corporations regarding rights, remedies, liabilities, and exposure. Lead counsel on five to twenty matters at any given time, co-counsel on others.

Contributions: Brought a major client to the firm, a Fortune 500 mortgage company, representing significant, continuing revenues. Co-authored Americans with Disabilities Act compliance manual used nationwide by members of the American Bankers Association. Lectured to business and trade groups on (1) ADA, (2) Protection of Trade Secrets, (3) Creditor Rights and Remedies in Bankruptcy Court. Wrote articles representing the firm for *CFI Compliance News* and *ABA Bank Compliance*. Wrote modules for various seminars offered by banking and trade groups. *Pro bono:* Judge *Pro Tempore*, Washington, D.C. Municipal Courts, Small Claims Division.

Representative cases: Represent lender in bankruptcy court in foreclosure on $14 million acquisition and development loan. Represent buyer of commercial strip center in action for specific performance. Represent former shareholders and officers of circuit board manufacturer in $4 million securities fraud action. Represented DoD-contracted missile parts supplier in $3 million unfair competition and antitrust lawsuit. Represented software distributor in complex breach of contract and securities fraud dispute. Details on additional cases available on request.

**WILSON, GOODRICH, SARONSON & ROSEBERG**    McLean, Virginia
**Associate Attorney**    1988–1991

Managed case load of commercial, business, and malpractice litigation, and provided counsel to corporations, for this 185-attorney firm. Managed one to four major matters at any given time, plus up to 25 smaller actions. Interviewed and hired associates. Brought one major transaction client to the firm, an analytical chemistry corporation.

Representative cases: Obtained summary judgment in $4 million shareholder dispute and wrongful termination of chief executive officer lawsuit. Defended $2 million RICO lawsuit against pension investment manager. Managed $2.3 million malpractice lawsuit against a "Big 6" CPA firm. Managed $350,000 business interruption claim resulting from contractor negligence. Analyzed potential defenses and discovery to negate $181 million breach of contract and fraud lawsuit against a defense subcontractor.

Additional matters included assets foreclosure, breach of commercial aircraft lease dispute, preference avoidance and creditor representation in U.S. Bankruptcy Court, and unfair trade practice litigation.

**BUCHMAN, NEIMEYER, FIELDS & YOUN**    Menlo Park, California
**Associate Attorney**    1987–1988

Represented banks, asset-based lenders and Chapter 7 bankruptcy trustees in U.S. Bankruptcy Court for this 180-attorney firm. Brought and defended proceedings to avoid preferences, disallow claims and administrative expense requests, avoidance of discharge and dischargeability actions. Also represented banks and receivers in Virginia State Courts.

Trial Counsel for *Andrew v. Bell Flavors & Fragrances Inc.*, Adv. No. 3-87-0654 TC(OAK)(Bankr. N.D. Cal.) *aff'd* 107 B.R. 707 (9th Cir. BAP 1989).

**COHEN, ENGLAND & WHITFIELD**    Oxnard, California
**Associate Attorney**    1986–1987

Represented accountants, attorneys, insurance brokers and agents in malpractice litigation in both state and federal courts for this 200-attorney firm. Also represented insurance companies in bad faith and subrogation litigation.

**LEWIS, D'AMATO, BRISBOIS & BISGAARD**    San Francisco, California
**Associate Attorney**    1985–1986

Managed general business and litigation case load for this 15-attorney firm. Emphasis was on business creation, sale and dissolution, and real estate matters (mechanics' liens, construction defect litigation, homeowner association litigation, zoning disputes, water diversion, adverse possession, quiet title and landlord/tenant actions).

**EDUCATION**

**GEORGETOWN UNIVERSITY**
**J.D.**, School of Law    1985
  Law Review, 1984, 1985

**UNIVERSITY OF SAN FRANCISCO**
School of Law    1982–1983
  McAuliffe Honor Society (Top 10%)
  Best Argument, Moot Court Competition
  Moot Court Honors Board

**UNIVERSITY OF CALIFORNIA, DAVIS**
**B.A.**, Economics    1982
  Minor in Philosophy
  Dean's Honors, College of Letters and Science

**ADMISSIONS**

Member, State Bar of California    1985
Member, State Bar of Virginia    1985
Member, District of Columbia Bar    1985
U.S. District Court, Central District    1985
U.S. District Court, Northern District    1986
U.S. District Court, Eastern District    1989

# Morris Granger III

22861 South Highway 38
Knoxville, Tennessee 37920

Home office/voice mail: (423) 555-2248
Private fax: (415) 555-2288
m.granger@mountain.com

## PROFILE

Experience in **financial services management, real estate lending, construction lending,** and all areas of **asset management** and **portfolio management**. Strength: combination of financial and legal expertise. Experience in 47 states. Strong knowledge of regional markets.

Areas of knowledge:

- Origination, underwriting, servicing, and troubleshooting of real estate loans and portfolios, and all related financial analysis (credit, feasibility, pro forma), both as the principal lender and in joint venture arrangements. ADA, FIRREA, FDIC, SEC, and other federal and state requirements (compliance, reporting, due diligence). Commercial, residential, industrial.
- Property management, leasing, rehab, planning and development, records management, investor reporting. REO and asset management, including marketing, packaging, sales of individual and/or portfolios of properties. Legal matters relating to environmental surveys, titles, zoning, entitlement, and condemnation transactions.
- Low-income housing tax credits, Community Reinvestment Act, HUD, FHA, VA, FHLMC, FNMA, securitization, secondary markets.
- Negotiations, work-outs, and settlements involving contract, construction, foreclosure, and bankruptcy law.
- Financial accounting IS, CIMS, Pro-Ject Plus, word processing, and other mainframe and departmental applications. Experience overseeing specification, development, procurement, implementation, staff training, troubleshooting, enhancement.
- Multioffice management, headquarters department management.

## EDUCATION

University of Tennessee School of Law
**Juris Doctor**

University of Tennessee
**Bachelor of Science in Commerce**

Stanford University, American Law Institute, American Bar Association
**Continuing Education in Legal and Real Estate Issues**

Member, State Bar of Tennessee
Member, Urban Land Institute

## EXPERIENCE

Morris Granger Consulting, Knoxville, Tennessee
**Consultant**

1995–Present

Provide financial, legal, and portfolio management consulting to real estate-related companies.

Sample engagements:

- New York-based asset management and real estate company—designed and conducted comprehensive review of a mortgage loan portfolio, graded portfolio quality, advised on disposition proceedings to upgrade and liquidate portfolio.

- Florida-based auction company with offices nationwide—general strategic management consulting related to real estate matters, strategized liquidation of REO, performing and nonperforming mortgage loans, structured procedures, due diligence, and expense controls.
- San Francisco-based real estate developer—designed comprehensive review of leasing strategies, property management practices, and TI operations. Structured a mortgage loan proposal to institutional lender (office/retail property).
- Texas-based asset management company—provided due diligence and valuation analysis (derived investment value) for portfolio.

Tennessee Central Life Insurance Company, Knoxville, Tennessee
**Vice President**

1992–1995

Management diversified portfolio of $350 million in mortgage loans and $120 million in real estate from coast to coast, including but not limited to residential, multifamily, condo, office, mixed-use, retail, warehouse, light industrial, hotel, motel, golf course, restaurant, auto dealership, truck stop, church, school, hospital, and medical clinic properties. Loans ranged from $1 million to $8 million (80% of loans), $8 million to $15 million (15%), and $15 million to $50 million (5%).

Managed staff of 10 in Lexington headquarters, including A.V.P., division manager, financial analysis, loan processors, and accounting clerks. Hired and managed consultants, including legal, engineering, environmental, appraisal, construction and other. Strategized and managed litigation and settlements.

Traveled extensively; interacted with property managers, developers, leasing agents, attorneys, brokers, and lenders. Negotiated and managed property and loan disposition, including restructuring, foreclosure, bankruptcy, and liquidation.

Selected accomplishments:
- Disposed of $100 million in mortgage loans and REOs during a tight market.
- Restructured $135 million in loans on all types of properties.
- Identified $116 million in real estate for immediate disposition.
- Maintained network of relationships with real estate professionals around the country.

1982–1991

Managed staff of 10 servicing and managing real estate and mortgage loan portfolio. Originated selective joint-venture transactions. Portfolio increased from $140 million to $550 million.
- Directed a total of $350 million in construction loans, managed and completed on time and within construction budget costs.
- In a period of financial turmoil, 1980–1981, had only one loan over 30 days past due.

1976–1981

Managed staff of 15. Originated, underwrote, packaged, and presented loans to the Board.
- Increased portfolio to $140 million.

1973–1975

Extensive national travel servicing and closing loans, handling negotiations and settlements, managing sales and dispositions, and working with local counsel.

## ADDITIONAL

**General Practice** of law, with emphasis on real estate transactions, Knoxville, Tennessee.
**U.S. Army, Major** (final rank), honorable discharge.

## REFERENCES

Please keep this information confidential at this time.

# ELIZABETH A. HARPER

*Curriculum Vitae*

East Coast (beginning 8/97):
c/o New York University
240 Mercer Street, Apt. 302
New York, New York 10012

West Coast (until 5/98):
32 Bainbridge Circle
Pleasant Hill, California 94523
(510) 555-1556

## EDUCATION

NEW YORK UNIVERSITY     New York, New York
**LL.M. Candidate (Taxation)**     expected May 1998

Entering class, fall 1997.

UNIVERSITY OF SOUTH CAROLINA     Columbia, South Carolina
**Juris Doctor**     May 1990

GPA — 3.12/4.0; rank — 55/202.
35 units in tax and tax-related courses with GPA — 3.55/4.0.

MICHIGAN STATE UNIVERSITY     East Lansing, Michigan
**Bachelor of Arts in Business Administration**     Dec. 1986

Minor in Pre-Law Study.
Student Advocate, ASMSU Student Legal Services.

## EXPERIENCE

UNITED STATES DEPARTMENT OF JUSTICE
United States Attorney's Office     San Francisco, California
**Assistant U.S. Attorney, Tax Division**     Feb. 1994 to July 1997

Lead attorney in civil and criminal tax cases before U.S. District Court, U.S. Bankruptcy Court, California Superior Court, and the Ninth Circuit Court of Appeals.

*Civil cases:*

District Court — tax refund, wrongful levy, collection (foreclosure, suits to reduce tax assessments to judgment), jeopardy review, injunction, summons enforcement, Freedom of Information Act, writs of entry, Federal Tort Claims Act.

Bankruptcy Court — objection to claims, adversary proceedings, and appeals.

California Superior Court — interpleader, quiet title, partition, eminent domain, and injunction.

Ninth Circuit — Federal Tort Claims Act and bankruptcy appeals.

*Criminal cases:*

Grand jury investigations; prosecution and conviction of Title 26 offenses, including tax evasion, failure to file, and false statements; appeals.

Please see attached summary of decisions.

*– continued –*

INTERNAL REVENUE SERVICE
Office of Chief Counsel    San Francisco, California
**Tax Litigation Attorney, District Counsel**    Nov. 1990 to Feb. 1994

Tax litigation attorney; cross-assigned in general litigation and criminal tax functions. Hired under Chief Counsel Honors Employment Program. Received Chief Counsel Special Achievement Award, 1987, 1988. Pension Plan Litigation Coordinator. Member, National Office Pension Plan Litigation Task Force.

Direct responsibility for approximately 300 docketed cases before U.S. Tax Court.

Please see attached summary of decisions.

RUTH, CLABAUGH & HACK    Hilton Head Island, South Carolina
**Law Clerk**    May 1990 to Nov. 1990

8-attorney firm, general practice specializing in tax matters.

DOWLING, SANDERS, DUKES, NOVIT & SVALINA
**Law Clerk**    Columbia, Beaufort, Hilton Head Island, South Carolina    Summers, 1986, 1987, 1988, 1989

20-attorney firm, general practice.

## ADMISSIONS

Member, State Bar of California

Member, State Bar of South Carolina

Admitted, United States Tax Court

Admitted, United States District Court for the Northern District of California

Admitted, United States Bankruptcy Court for the Northern District of California

Admitted, United States Court of Appeals for the Ninth Circuit

*REFERENCES & WRITING SAMPLES*

*PROVIDED ON REQUEST*

# ELIZABETH A. HARPER

*East Coast (beginning 8/97):*
c/o New York University
240 Mercer Street, Apt. 302
New York, New York 10012

*West Coast (until 5/98):*
32 Bainbridge Circle
Pleasant Hill, California 94523
(510) 555-1556

## SUMMARY OF UNITED STATES TAX COURT DECISIONS

*Estate of Cole v. Commissioner,* T.C. Memo 1994-623; 58 T.C.M. (CCH) 715 (November 20, 1994), *aff'd in part, rev'd in part and remanded,* No. 91-70213, Slip. Op. (9th Cir. 1997) (Consolidated estate tax and related income tax cases involving the estate of Nathaniel "Nat King" Cole and his widow, Maria Cole Devore)

*Estate of Nazarian v. Commissioner,* T.C. Memo 1994-179; 57 T.C.M. (CCH) 188 (April 19, 1994), *appeal docketed* (9th Cir. 1996) (Step transaction and sham arguments asserted in consolidated cases involving sale of convalescent hospital)

*Wehausen v. Commissioner,* T.C. Memo 1993-460; 56 T.C.M. (CCH) 229 (September 22, 1993) (Valuation)

*Rosberg v. Commissioner,* T.C. Memo 1993-267; 55 T.C.M. (CCH) 1114 (June 22, 1993) (I.R.C. Section 6501(e) 25% omission)

*Jackson v. Commissioner,* T.C. Memo 1993-143; 55 T.C.M. (CCH) 537 (April 6, 1993) (Charitable contribution)

*Hirasuna v. Commissioner,* 89 T.C. 1216 (December 28, 1992) (Farm syndicate capitalization rules)

*McMains v. Commissioner,* T.C. Memo 1992-85; 53 T.C.M. (CCH) 118 (February 12, 1992) (Charitable contribution)

*Boswell v. Commissioner,* Memorandum Sur Order (September 8, 1992), *appeal dismissed* (9th Cir. 1992) (Last known address)

*Taylor v. Commissioner,* T.C. Summary Opinion 1992-61 (March 4, 1992) (Innocent spouse)

*Sabin v. Commissioner,* Memorandum Sur Order (October 29, 1991) (I.R.C. Section 6673 damages)

*Ruffner v. Commissioner,* bench decision (July 18, 1991) (Educational travel)

*Mansour v. Commissioner,* bench decision (March 13, 1991) (Foreign income exclusion)

# ELIZABETH A. HARPER

*East Coast (beginning 8/97):*
c/o New York University
240 Mercer Street, Apt. 302
New York, New York 10012

*West Coast (until 5/98):*
32 Bainbridge Circle
Pleasant Hill, California 94523
(510) 555-1556

---

## SUMMARY OF DISTRICT COURT, BANKRUPTCY COURT, AND CALIFORNIA SUPERIOR COURT DECISIONS

*Estate of Hinz v. United States*, 1995 U.S. Dist. Lexis 17967 (N.D. Cal. 1996), *aff'd by unpublished opinion*, 1997 U.S. App. Lexis 13435 (9th Cir. 1997) (Attorney's fees)

*Pangburn v. United States*, C-90-20429-JW, unpublished (N.D. Cal. 1996), *aff'd in part, rev'd in part, and remanded by unpublished opinion*, 1997 U.S. App. Lexis 1575 (9th Cir. 1997), *motion for summary judgment granted*, Slip. Op. (N.D. Cal. 1997) (Quiet title)

*In Re Deer Park*, 136 B.R. 815 (9th Cir. BAP 1997) (Involuntary payment)

*In Re Browning*, A.P. No. 91-4-5338-JP, bench trial, publication pending (B.C.N.D. Cal. 1997) (Schedule C business — profit motive)

*Whitney v. United States*, No. C-83-0584-MHP, publication pending (N.D. Cal. 1997) (Refund deductibility of long-term leasehold expenses)

*In Re O'Neil*, 1997 U.S. Dist. Lexis 7150 (Dist. Ct. N.D. Cal. 1997), *appeal docketed* (9th Cir. 1997) (Bankruptcy appeal — distribution of homestead proceeds)

*United States v. Young*, C-89-2065-MHP, bench trial, publication pending (N.D. Cal. 1997), *appeal docketed* (9th Dir. 1997) (Foreclosure — collection)

*Porter v. United States*, No. 91-10661, unpublished (B.C.N.D. Cal. 1997), *appeal docketed* (Dist. Ct. N.D. Cal. 1997) (Community property)

*C and C Liberty Enterprises v. United States*, No. C-91-6382-EFL, unpublished (N.D. Cal. 1997), *appeal docketed* (9th Cir. 1996) (Summons enforcement)

*United States v. Vroman*, CR-91-0213-EFL, jury trial (N.D. Cal. 1996), *appeal docketed* (9th Cir. 1996) (Tax evasion; failure to file)

*Elliot v. United States*, 91-2 USTC ¶ 50,583 (N.D. Cal. 1996) (Refund — equitable recoupment; mitigation)

*United States v. Contreras*, CR-91-0010-MHP, jury trial (N.D. Cal. 1996) (Assault on federal officers)

*United States v. Waegemann*, No. C-91-7789-SGA, unpublished (N.D. Cal. 1996) (Foreign records consent directive)

*In Re Biggins*, No. 1-86-00591, bench trial, unpublished (B.C.N.D. Cal. 1996) (Bankruptcy application of payment)

*Jacques v. United States*, 1996 U.S. Dist. Lexis 6638 (N.D. Cal. 1996) (Lack of jurisdiction)

*In Re Fondiller*, 125 B.R. 805 (N.D. Cal. 1996) (Bankruptcy appeal — prompt determination discharge)

*Chopp Computer v. United States*, C-91-0226-RHS, unpublished (N.D. Cal. 1996), *appeal docketed* (9th Cir. 1996) (Federal Tort Claims Act)

*Weiss v. United States*, 91-1 USTC ¶ 50,170 (N.D. Cal. 1996) (Interpleader)

*In Re Hardy*, 1-89-01347, unpublished (B.C.N.D. Cal.) (Separate/community property)

*Sheridan v. United States*, 91-1 USTC ¶ 50,130 (N.D. Cal. 1995) (Wrongful levy)

*Kogan v. United States*, 91-1 USTC ¶ 50,126 (N.D. Cal. 1996), *appeal docketed* (9th Cir. 1996) (Refund — statute of limitations)

*Harrell v. United States*, C-90-20510-JW, unpublished (N.D. Cal.) (Tax protester — Rule 11 sanctions)

*In Re Consumers Cooperative of Berkeley*, 4-89-00266-J2, publication pending (B.C.N.D. Cal.) (Section 505 determination — subchapter T cooperative taxation; allocation of patronage-sourced net operating losses and section 1231 gain)

*Sanfellipo v. United States*, 90-2 USTC ¶ 50,567 (N.D. Cal. 1995) (Injunction and refund)

*Eckersley v. United States*, 90-2 USTC ¶ 50,535 (N.D. Cal. 1995), *motion to alter or amend judgment denied*, 1995 U.S. Dist. Lexis 19477 (N.D. Cal. 1995), *aff'd by unpublished opinion*, 1997 U.S. App. Lexis 9534 (9th Cir. 1997) (Refund — validity of 872-A waiver)

*Weiser v. United States*, 746 F. Supp. 958, 90-2 USTC ¶ 50,480 (N.D. Cal. 1995), *aff'd*, 959 F.2d 146 (9th Cir. 1997) (Refund — consolidated cases involving application of tax benefit rule to calculation of alternative minimum tax liability)

*Carter v. United States*, 90-2 USTC ¶ 50,471 (N.D. Cal. 1995), *motion to alter or amend judgment denied*, 91-1 USTC ¶ 50,278 (N.D. Cal. 1995), *appeal docketed* (9th Cir. 1995) (Refund — charitable contribution)

*In Re Saier*, unpublished (N.D. Cal. 1995) (Writ of entry)

*Harrell v. United States*, unpublished (N.D. Cal. 1995) (Injunction - 42 U.S.C. Section 1983)

*Billman v. United States*, 90-2 USTC ¶ 50,428 (N.D. Cal. 1995) (Refund — variance)

*Ortez v. United States*, jury trial (N.D. Cal. 1995) (Refund — 100% penalty)

*Gamma Farms v. United States*, 90-2 USTC ¶ 50,378 (N.D. Cal. 1995), *rev'd by unpublished opinion*, 1995 U.S. App. Lexis 4252 (9th Cir. 1995) (Refund — employment taxes)

*Canyon Bluffs Homes v. Hill*, bench trial, unpublished (Calif. Sup. Ct. 1995) (Quiet title)

*Guy v. United States*, unpublished (N.D. Cal. 1995) (Erroneous refund)

*Bay View Federal v. Amwest Surety Ins. Co.*, unpublished (Calif. Sup. Ct. 1995) (Interpleader)

*Whitson v. Whitson*, unpublished (Calif. Sup. Ct. 1995) (Reformation of Deed)

*Westland Investments v. First Interstate Bank*, bench trial, unpublished (Calif. Sup. Ct. 1994) (Interpleader)

*Whitsitt v. United States*, unpublished (N.D. Cal. 1994), *appeal filed* (9th Cir. 1994) (Injunction — *Bivens*)

*Dynastar Properties v. United States*, unpublished (N.D. Cal. 1994) (Refund — ITC carryback)

*Vosters v. United States*, 89-1 USTC ¶ 9387 (N.D. Cal. 1994) (Refund — 100% penalty)

# LAUREN A. PEABODY

*Curriculum Vitae*

18 Pacific Palisades
San Francisco, California 94131

Offices: (801) 555-8900 or (415) 555-1600
Residence: (415) 555-7366

---

**EDUCATION**

UNIVERSITY OF CALIFORNIA, HASTINGS COLLEGE OF THE LAW:
**J.D., 1981**
**Member,** Hastings Constitutional Law Quarterly, 1980–1981

UNIVERSITY OF ARIZONA:
**Ph.D.,** Government, 1975
Dissertation: *Influence Relationships among State Supreme Courts*

UNIVERSITY OF UTAH:
**M.S.,** Political Science, 1972
**B.S.,** Political Science, 1970

AMERICAN SOCIETY FOR PUBLIC ADMINISTRATION, Washington, D.C.
**Fellowship,** 1976–1977

**TEACHING**

UNIVERSITY OF CALIFORNIA, Berkeley, California
**Lecturer,** (Boalt Hall) School of Law, 1994–Present
"Federal Criminal Law."

GOLDEN GATE UNIVERSITY, San Francisco, California
**Lecturer,** School of Law, 1994
"White Collar Crime."

HASTINGS CENTER FOR TRIAL AND APPELLATE ADVOCACY, San Francisco, California
**Instructor,** 1989–1994
"Trial Practice Workshop."

UNITED STATES DEPARTMENT OF JUSTICE, Washington, D.C.
**Instructor,** Attorney General's Advocacy Institute, 1987–1994
"Trial Practice Workshop."

WESTMINSTER COLLEGE, Salt Lake City, Utah
**Lecturer,** Division of Social Sciences, 1985
"Constitutional Law."

GOLDEN GATE UNIVERSITY, San Francisco, California
**Lecturer,** Graduate School of Public Administration, 1979–1980
"Criminal Justice Information Systems."

WEBER STATE COLLEGE, Ogden, Utah
**Lecturer** (full-time), Department of Political Science, 1975–1976
"American Government" and "Constitutional Law."

UNIVERSITY OF ARIZONA, Tucson, Arizona
**Teaching Assistant,** Department of Government, 1972–1974
"American Government."

**PRACTICE**

UNITED STATES DEPARTMENT OF JUSTICE, San Francisco, California
**Assistant Chief,** Organized Crime Strike Force, 1994–1996
**Attorney,** Organized Crime Strike Force, 1991–1994

Prosecution of organized crime cases, with emphasis on white-collar prosecution of union and corporate officials under RICO and various theft, fraud and internal revenue statutes. Recent reported cases:

*United States v. Tham,* 884 F.2d 1262 (9th Cir. 1994)

*United States v. Holland,* 880 F.2d 1091 (9th Cir. 1994)

(Co-trial counsel)

Special Achievement Award, 1993.

UNITED STATES DEPARTMENT OF JUSTICE, Salt Lake City, Utah
**Assistant U.S. Attorney,** 1985–1991

Criminal and civil litigation including trials of the following cases: bribery of public official, perjury, obstruction of justice, murder, rape, mail and wire fraud, bank robbery, extortion, assault, stolen property, employment discrimination, medical malpractice, national environmental policy act, quiet title, etc.

Special Achievement Award, 1987.

FABIAN & CLENDENIN, Salt Lake City, Utah
**Associate Attorney,** 1981–1985

Civil litigation, with emphasis on trial of commercial cases; some defense of criminal and juvenile justice defendants.

FIRST APPELLATE DISTRICT COURT OF APPEAL, San Francisco, California
**Clerk (Extern),** 1980

OFFICE OF THE DISTRICT ATTORNEY, Alameda County, California
**Summer Legal Assistant,** 1980

**CONSULTING &
POLICY
DEVELOPMENT**

UNITED STATES DEPARTMENT OF JUSTICE, Washington, D.C.
**Consultant,** 1978–1981

In association with U.S. Dept. of Justice and Public Systems, Inc., of Sunnyvale, California, drafted federal privacy regulations related to criminal history information: 28 C.FR §§ 20.1–20.38.

INSTITUTE OF JUDICIAL ADMINISTRATION — AMERICAN BAR ASSOCIATION
JUVENILE JUSTICE STANDARDS PROJECT
**Member,** Drafting Committee on Administration, 1978–1981      Washington, D.C.

Reviewed proposed juvenile justice privacy and management standards. See IJA-ABA, *Standards Relating to: Juvenile Records and Information Systems* (1985); *Planning for Juvenile Justice* (1985); *Monitoring* (1985).

UNITED STATES DEPARTMENT OF JUSTICE, Washington, D.C.
National Advisory Commission on Criminal Justice Standards & Goals
**Deputy Staff Director,** 1976–1978

Directed staff of commission which produced standards for crime reduction and system improvement at state and local levels nationally. Contributed materially to sections on criminal information systems and planning.

Special Achievement Award, 1978.

**SERVICE**

UTAH EQUAL RIGHTS LEGAL DEFENSE FUND, Salt Lake City, Utah
**Member, Board of Directors,** 1983–1987

SECOND DISTRICT JUVENILE COURT, STATE OF UTAH
**Member, Citizens Advisory Committee,** 1983–1985

FIFTH CIRCUIT COURT, SMALL CLAIMS DIVISION, STATE OF UTAH
**Judge Pro Tempore** (pro bono), 1985

AMERICAN CIVIL LIBERTIES UNION, Salt Lake City, Utah
**Member, Legal Panel,** 1983–1985

**PAPERS & PUBLICATIONS**

"Political Scientists as Expert Witnesses," 24 PS: *Political Science & Politics* 521 (September, 1996).

"A Theory of Jury Trial Advocacy," 1989 *Utah L. Rev.* 763.

Note, "Informational Privacy: Constitutional Challenges to the Collection and Dissemination of Personal Information by Government Agencies," 3 *Hastings Const. L. Q.* 229 (1981).

Contributing Editor, National Advisory Commission on Criminal Justice Standards & Goals, *A National Strategy to Reduce Crime & Report on the Criminal Justice System,* U.S. Dept. Just. (1978).

"Crime Specific Goal Setting," paper presented to the National Conference of the American Society for Public Administration (March 21–25, 1977).

**ADMISSIONS**

United States Supreme Court

United States Court of Appeals (Ninth and Tenth Circuits)

United States District Courts (Utah and Northern District of California)

Supreme Court, State of California

Supreme Court, State of Utah

**REFERENCES**

References and additional information provided on request.

# Barbara J. Damlos

1800 Greenwich Street
San Francisco, California 94132

Office: (415) 555-6451
Residence: (415) 555-1636

---

**EXPERIENCE**

**MISCIAGNA & COLOMBATTO,** San Francisco, California, 1990–Present
**Partner**

Insurance defense litigation in the areas of insurance coverage, insurance bad faith, personal injury and products liability. Drafted appellate writs.

Published opinions:
*Bodenhamer v. Superior Ct.* (G.A.B.)(1991)178.Cal.App.3d.180
*Bodenhamer v. Superior Ct.* (St. Paul)(1992)192.Cal.App.3d.1472

Primary responsibility for trial preparation. Assisted lead counsel in four-month trial of insurance bad faith case.

Currently serve as de facto house counsel for firm's largest client, Bodenhamer Industries, a diversified manufacturing and real estate holding company.

**TOLPEGIN, IMAI & TADLOCK,** San Francisco, California, 1989
**Law Clerk**

Directed discovery in toxic tort litigation. Researched and drafted pleadings, motions for summary judgement, and discovery requests.

**BIANCO, BRANDI & JONES,** San Francisco, California, 1988–1989
**Law Clerk**

Researched issues in unfair competition, trade secrets, product liability, and insurance bad faith. Reviewed personal injury and malpractice cases.

**HANCOCK, ROTHERT & BUNSHOFT,** San Francisco, California, Summer 1987
**Law Clerk**

Researched legal issues in bankruptcy proceedings, construction actions, and insurance coverage cases involving asbestos-related claims.

**HANCOCK, ROTHERT & BUNSHOFT,** San Francisco, California, 1985–1986
**Paralegal**

Assisted in preparation of two major construction cases for trial.

**EDUCATION**

**UNIVERSITY OF SAN FRANCISCO SCHOOL OF LAW**
**Juris Doctor,** 1988

Law Review

Semi-Finalist, Advocate of the Year Competition, Moot Court Honors Program First Place Award, Oral Advocacy, Moot Court Competition

**UNIVERSITY OF CALIFORNIA, DAVIS**
**Bachelor of Arts,** Political Science (minor: U.S. History), 1985

Dean's List, Prytanean Honor Society
Intern, State Department of Consumer Affairs, Sacramento
Intern, Public Citizen, Ralph Nader Organization, Washington, D.C.

**PUBLICATION**

"The Duty of Good Faith — More Than Just a Duty to Defend and Settle Claims,"
14 Western State University *L.Rev.*209 (Fall 1986)

**AFFILIATIONS**

Member, State Bar of California
California Trial Lawyers Association
Bar Association of San Francisco

(please keep this application confidential at this time)

# IAN J. FOWLER

*Attorney at Law*

438 Delaware Parkway
Las Vegas, Nevada 89109

Office: (702) 555-2362
Residence: (702) 555-0333
Private e-mail: fowler7@law.unlv.edu

---

**EXPERIENCE**

**D'AMATO, BORCHERT, LONG & SYVERSON**, Las Vegas, Nevada
**Senior Associate Attorney**, 1990–Present

Trial attorney in this civil litigation-defense law firm, a 25-attorney branch office of a Los Angeles-based firm. Handle a broad range of legal disputes: professional malpractice defense of attorneys, architects, insurance agents, real estate agents, and psychologists; personal injury actions, including product liability defense; insurance coverage disputes on professional, trust errors and omissions, commercial, and excess liability policies; eminent domain work (jury trial involving the fair market value of a residence); administrative agency cases (casino employment discrimination complaint before the State Department of Fair Employment and representation of psychologist before State licensing board); construction defect, employment termination, and criminal cases.

Tried two jury trials as lead counsel, prepared for trial in at least 20 other cases, and resolved a large number of other actions through arbitration, summary judgment, or settlement. Examples:

*Churchill v. Partridge Dairy* and *People v. Dan Cook*. Firm originally retained by insurer to defend against wrongful death claim arising out of motorcycle-truck collision. Due to criminal trial experience, was selected by firm to defend truck driver in related vehicular manslaughter case. Police report placed 100% of the blame on the defendant driver, and the Court granted an *in limine* motion excluding intoxication evidence against the motorcyclist. Nevertheless, obtained a not guilty verdict, which assisted in settling the personal injury case as well.

*Camper v. WASCO*. Retained to defend a train brake manufacturer in a wrongful death/personal injury action arising out of an auto-train collision. Discovery established that there was no way the train could stop in time using any conventional braking system. Drafted and obtained a summary judgment based on expert testimony that there was no cause in fact between the design of the braking system and the collision.

*Danzig v. Hinkle*. In legal malpractice case, drafted appellate writ and petition for review to the Nevada Supreme Court, which then ordered the Court of Appeals to reconsider the lower court's denial of motion for summary judgment.

Management responsibilities included supervision and development of junior associates and paralegals, review of billings, personnel evaluations. Also developed clients and brought new business to the firm, both litigation and transaction matters.

**FEENEY, SPARKS & RUDY**, San Francisco
**Senior Associate Attorney**, 1981–1989

Senior associate in this 7-attorney general practice civil litigation law firm. Case load included personal injury, real estate fraud, specific performance, insurance bad faith, liability of corporate directors, employment termination, eminent domain, and probate files.

Conducted numerous depositions and discovery sessions, made law and motion appearances, gained court trial and administrative trial experience, prepared cases for jury trial, arbitrated cases, and negotiated settlements.

Served as legal advisor to a labor union. Advised on apprenticeship program, employee benefits and trust funds, and consent decrees.

OFFICE OF THE DISTRICT ATTORNEY, Alameda County, Oakland
**Deputy District Attorney**, 1976–1980

Prosecuted criminal cases. Gained extensive trial experience, including numerous misdemeanor jury trials, felony preliminary hearings, juvenile court trials, and legal motions.

**COMMUNITY SERVICE**

Member, Board of Directors, Volunteer Auxiliary of Youth Guidance, an organization serving dependent and delinquent children under the jurisdiction of the Juvenile Court.

Trustee, Sandy Foundation, a charitable organization funding programs in education, science, medicine, and community services.

**ACADEMIC**

UNIVERSITY OF THE PACIFIC, McGEORGE SCHOOL OF LAW
**Juris Doctor**, 1975

Ranked top 30% of class.

UNIVERSITY OF CALIFORNIA, Berkeley
**Bachelor of Arts**, History, 1971

UNIVERSITY OF NEVADA-LAS VEGAS, SCHOOL OF LAW
**Guest Lecturer**, 1992–Present (intermittent)

"Contracts: A Real World Perspective."
"Criminal Law: Best Training Ground for Litigation?"

**CREDENTIAL**

Member, State Bar of Nevada, admitted 1989

Member, State Bar of California, admitted 1975

# David Ward Whittier

27768 Fountain Road
Houston, Texas 77074

Office: (713) 555-6773
Residence: (713) 555-5881

*Member, Texas State Bar, admitted 1985*

*Member, Mississippi State Bar, admitted 1975*

*Federal District Court, Ninth Circuit, admitted 1975*

**EMPHASES**

**Civil Litigation**
**Insurance, Construction & Real Estate Matters**
**Criminal Law**

**EDUCATION**

UNIVERSITY OF MISSISSIPPI, University, Mississippi
**J.D.,** School of Law, 1975
**B.A.,** History, minor in Chemistry, 1967

**PRACTICE**

INDUSTRIAL ASSURANCE CORPORATION, Houston, Texas
**Bond Counsel,** 1990–Present

Investigate and defend against contract surety bond and construction defect claims nationwide, individual claims ranging from $500 to $50 million, but mostly in the $5 million to $10 million range. Manage up to 125 matters at one time. Supervise support staff of five.

Handle each claim independently, from initiation through resolution. Evaluate case based on merits; make settle/litigate decision in collaboration with the committee of Bond Legal attorneys. Retain and oversee outside counsel in multiple states.

Inspect job sites, retain expert witnesses (various types of engineer). Negotiate with all parties. Obtain work-out agreements with bond principals to obtain bond salvage. Retain bankruptcy counsel when necessary and pursue matters in bankruptcy courts nationwide. Travel up to 60%.

Part of a team of three attorneys who have collectively brought this department to higher standards. Eliminated claims by roughly one-third, reduced payouts in another third, and one-third are performing at historical norms.

Also plan for and prevent bad faith liability. Supervised successful defense against approximately 45 bad faith claims over a five and one-half year period.

Requires strong administrative management skill, a working knowledge of law in multiple states, and strong negotiating skills.

CHARTER INSURANCE GROUP, Houston, Texas
**Litigation Coverage Evaluator,** 1986–1989

House counsel. Reviewed claims on case-by-case basis, developed strategies, negotiated settlements or managed litigation. Hired and directed outside counsel and/or Cumis attorneys. Motivated insureds to participate materially in claims. Managed cases to conclusion.

Assigned cases with over $1 million potential liability. Legal issues included wrongful termination, product liability, construction defect, and complex litigation.

Contribution: Reduced open cases from over 600 to less than 350. Also revised standards for the department to ensure permanent reduction in backlog.

UNITED INSURANCE, Richardson, Texas
**Litigation Coverage Evaluator,** 1985–1986

> Assigned highly complex and serious personal injury litigation with in excess of $1 million in liability at risk. Similar to above.

LAW OFFICES OF DAVID WHITTIER, Jackson, Mississippi
**Attorney-at-Law,** 1975–1985

> Solo practitioner with a diversified case load of construction litigation, personal injury defense, product liability defense, general litigation. Provided counsel in real estate, employment and labor matters. Also provided criminal defense trial work to sharpen litigation skills. Hired and trained law clerks and secretaries.

> Six civil trials (won four) and twelve felony criminal trials (won eleven).

*Prior:*

CROWLEY MARITIME CORPORATION
**Investigator**

CIGNA CORPORATION
**Assistant Regional Manager**

**SPEAKING**

Over seventy-five public speaking engagements in six years for county bar associations, Texas Trial Lawyers Association Speaker's Bureau, law schools, and others. Sample topic: "Law for the Citizen: What Every American Needs to Know," a three-part program: history of American law, the current legal system, and utilization of small claims court.

# DAVID GREGORY EISENSTAT

Office: (302) 555-1820
2200 Concord Pike, Rear      Residence/message/private fax: (302) 555-8949
Wilmington, Delaware 19803      david.eisen@access.com

---

**EDUCATION**

CORNELL UNIVERSITY, Ithaca, New York
**M.B.A.** emphases: finance, economics      1984
**J.D.** emphases: corporation, partnership, securities, tax      1984

PRINCETON UNIVERSITY, Princeton, New Jersey
**A.B.** major: history      1979

**EXPERIENCE**

MAMA'S INTERNATIONAL, Wilmington, Delaware
**General Counsel**      1993–present

Provide conceptual direction to and daily management of all corporate legal matters for this food products manufacturer with $180 million annual sales, 40% of it export, and owned/leased facilities in New York, Pennsylvania, New Jersey, Texas, Ireland, and Manila.

Provide advice and counsel to senior management. Manage and/or oversee company litigation. Monitor state and federal legislation impacting business lines. Research international law re contractual, financial, regulatory matters. Collaborate with outside counsel. Supervise associate house attorney. Report directly to CEO and collaboratively to president.

Utilize combined MBA/JD skills for M&A, finance, strategic planning, and internal consulting activities. Identify M&A candidates, perform due diligence, negotiate and structure purchase agreements, develop integration and strategic business plans for acquisitions.

*Sample projects:*
- Supervised $15 million shareholder fraud litigation (prevailed).
- Negotiated six multimillion-dollar acquisitions in Asia (five production plants and warehouse site).
- Traveled to Asia with CEO to research business climate (Singapore, Hong Kong, Manila, Bangkok).
- Spent three months in Manila as interim plant manager; selected and oriented new plant manager.
- Acquired $10 million frozen pizza company, Texas.

BIRNBAUM, BROWN & AILSWORTHY, Princeton, New Jersey
**Associate Attorney**      1988–1992

General corporate and securities legal work, acquisitions, private placements of debt and equity, creation and restructuring of partnerships and corporations, negotiation and drafting of contracts, and research of numerous corporate and securities law questions.

U.S. SENATE, Washington, D.C.
Permanent Subcommittee on Investigations
**Staff and Legislative Assistant** to Senator Charles H. Percy      1896–1987

Assisted the Chief Committee Counsel with the Iran-Contra investigation; also wrote speeches, drafted hearing questions, and drafted portions of proposed legislation.

GORSUCH, LTD., Vail, Colorado
**Ski Salesman, Ski Racer**      1979–1980

**PUBLICATIONS**  "Extraordinary Corporate Matters — In General" and "Sale, Lease, Exchange or Other Disposition of Substantially All Corporate Assets" in H. Henn and J. Alexander, *Law of Corporations*, ed. 3 (West 1988).

"Preparing the Proxy Solicitation Campaign — Insurgents' and Management's Pre-Meeting Strategy" in G. Moody and C. Bagley, *Proxy Contests* (Bureau of National Affairs, Corporate Practice Series, Portfolio 20-2) (1988, supp. 1989).

**ACTIVITIES**  LEADERSHIP ADVENTURE PROGRAMS, Paramus, New Jersey
**Member, Board of Directors**    since 1994

Responsible for managing fund-raising programs enabling 600 inner-city, probationary, or disabled youths per year to participate in wilderness leadership education programs.

**ADMISSIONS**  State Bar of New York

State Bar of Delaware

State Bar of New Jersey

# Sidney Stewart Oldham

9 Kenton Drive
Clinton, Connecticut 06413
(860) 555-4551 or (860) 555-1751

---

**EDUCATION**

NEW YORK UNIVERSITY, New York, New York
**Master of Law, Taxation**, 1981

AMERICAN UNIVERSITY, Washington, D.C.
**Juris Doctor**, 1979

LONDON SCHOOL OF ECONOMICS, London, England, U.K.
**Master of Science**, 1976

THE WHARTON SCHOOL OF THE UNIVERSITY OF PENNSYLVANIA, Phil., Penn.
**Bachelor of Science**, *cum laude*, 1974

**EXPERIENCE**

SPENCER, KELSO, SNYDER & STIRLING, Honolulu, Hawaii
**Of Counsel**, 1996–Present

Currently representing General Electric Credit Corporation (GECC) as a plaintiff in Hawaii and federal (San Francisco) bankruptcy court concerning an individual debtor.

WYMAN, BATTLER, CHRISTIAN, KEITEL & SILVAN, Stamford, Connecticut
**Senior Associate Attorney**, 1994–1996

Established the real estate department for the Stamford branch of this 285-attorney New York-based firm. Provided advice, counsel, analysis, due diligence, and transaction services for sales and tax-deferred exchanges of commercial real estate, $1–$180 million, e.g., represented a developer based in Hawaii on purchase of $80 million regional shopping center and residential development located in Minnesota.

Also provided tax litigation services for real estate and financial institutions, drafted new loan documentation for Imperial Bank and E.F. Hutton Credit Corporation, prepared disclosure statements for real estate syndications, and served as a troubleshooter for young associates in all departments.

GENERAL ELECTRIC CREDIT CORPORATION, Stamford, Connecticut
**Regional Counsel**, 1990–1994

Supported 22 business offices located in 18 northeastern states. Drafted and reviewed loan and leasing transactions involving properties, fleets of aircraft, and large industrial equipment, with emphasis on tax consequences of purchase options. Drafted special documentation, including a $20 million revolving credit bail-out for a Ohio manufacturer in Chapter 11, and a $30 million leveraged leasing program for a New Jersey tug and salvage company.

Monitored and interpreted all statutory regulations governing our business in 18 states. Provided senior managers with analysis and counsel. Represented the company in Chapter 11, 13, and 7 bankruptcy proceedings in which the company was a creditor.

Designed seminars, hot lines, and management development program re legal matters (over 200 staff) to identify and avoid legal problems. Saved company over $275,000 in outside legal fees in first year (as verified by management study).

**Associate Counsel**, 1987–1990

Legal advisor to two vice presidents in charge of real estate and large industrial leasing. Drafted real estate financing packages from $10–$85 million, and leveraged leasing packages on fleets of aircraft, oil tankers, and railway equipment from $30–$100 million.

UNITED STATES COMMODITY FUTURES AND TRADING COMMISSION,
**Attorney**, 1981–1986      Washington, D.C.

Conducted complex civil litigation involving fraud, fictitious trading, market manipulation, and technical reporting violations by domestic and international broker-dealers. In charge of reviewing disciplinary procedures taken by self-regulating organizations against their members in order to determine whether federal proceedings were warranted. Served on panel to review new financial products for compliance.

Major cases: the Hunt Brothers' multibillion-dollar manipulation of world silver markets, a coffee price manipulation by the London coffee cartel, a fictitious trading scheme in the NYNEX 400-ounce gold contract with Bear Stearns.

NEW YORK ATTORNEY GENERAL'S OFFICE, New York, New York
**Deputy Assistant Attorney General**, 1979–1980

OPPENHEIMER & STRAIG, New York, New York
**Registered Representative**, 1974–1975

**ADDITIONAL TRAINING**

U.S. Department of Justice — Federal Trial Law Training Program
U.S. Securities and Exchange Commission — Enforcement Training Program

**CREDENTIALS**

State Bar of Connecticut
State Bar of California
State Bar of New York
District of Columbia Bar
Connecticut Real Estate Broker's License
NASD Series 7, 63

# Jean Clauson

3321 North Crawford Avenue
Lincolnwood, Illinois 60645

Residence:
(847) 555-4562

---

## STRENGTHS

Complete administrative and business management. Firm start-up experience, establishing policies, procedures, budgeting, office automation systems. Demonstrated talent for hiring, training, and motivating an intelligent and productive staff. Experienced liaison to vendors, banks, CPAs, consultants. Skilled with client relations.

## EXPERIENCE:

MILTON & WARSAW, Lincolnwood, Illinois, 1995–Present
**Chief Administrative Officer**

Facilitated the amicable dissolution and reorganization of the professional partnership. Planned and managed personnel, financial and accounting, and systems and procedures aspects of the "spin off" of a new firm. Operated double accounting systems during separation of procedures. Was offered permanent positions by both new firms. Oriented and trained new staff at both firms. Designed/installed new systems for billing, call accounting, document flow, and administration. Report to the senior managing partner of the new firm, Graham Milton.

Designed and implemented employee training program, including job design, performance standards, written policy and procedures, employee manuals, and training guide. Orient and develop new attorneys. Train attorneys in supervisory skills. Provide counseling, problem resolution, intervention services.

Negotiated new lease at 47% below market rate by discovery and development of a long-term sub-lease opportunity. Upgraded word processing, including conversion of existing files. Identified operating deficiencies with the proprietary accounting system and worked with programmer to enhance the system.

Currently manage administrative work flow, cash flow, staff. Participate in all management planning. Interact directly with clients, primarily Fortune 500 corporate officers.

HARRIS, BUCHANAN & MILTON, Lincolnwood, Illinois, 1990–1995
**Administrative Manager**

Managed administrative and financial functions for thriving corporate law practice. Reported to five senior partners. Participated directly in strategic planning for the firm. Coordinated legal support staff; scheduled and controlled administrative work flow. Managed all billing and office automation systems. Controlled cash flow, including all statements and projections for review by partners. Interfaced with CPA. Ensured profitability, cost control and operating efficiency at all levels. Hired and supervised a staff of 30 (paralegals, law clerks, legal assistants, secretaries, file clerks, legal word processors, receptionists, librarians, billing coordinators, and bookkeepers).

Accomplishments: Discovered accounting and procedural errors resulting in recovery of $70,000 in monies due the firm. Standardized billing practices reducing total A/R outstanding. Established standard procedures to prioritize and manage computer and word processing functions. Emplaced call accounting system, creating 6% increase in billings. Rewrote job duties, streamlined procedures, reduced administrative operations expense by 14%. Planned and executed successful attorneys' retreat: "Marketing the Law Firm."

*– Continued –*

MANGOLD, JEFFREYS, BUTLER & MARNAK, Highland Park, Illinois, 1986–1989
**Office Manager**

Reported to the Managing Partner. Coordinated with headquarters in Los Angeles. Supervised a staff of 25. Scheduled and controlled administrative work flow. Recruited associates from top universities (Harvard, Princeton, Yale, etc.). Ensured efficiency and profitability of operations.

Selected accomplishments: Achieved estimated $50,000 in annual savings in first year through more effective cost tracking. Facilitated the rapid growth of this firm from a support staff of 4 to a support staff of 25. Instrumental in law office merger. Coordinated three major moves, including facilities, furnishings, space planning. Selected and implemented word processing and call accounting systems.

Greatest accomplishment: Developed a loyal and talented staff, with high regard for the quality of their work. The office had a team atmosphere, high morale, and very low turnover.

THE BUDGET BUSTERS TOUR DEVELOPERS, Chicago, Illinois, 1983–1986
**Administrator**

Managed promotional and administrative aspects of this specialty tour/travel company providing guided shopping tours of Hong Kong, Milan, Paris and other domestic and international destinations.

Planned and coordinated sales/promotional meetings. Gave presentations and signed up travelers. Worked with high-net-worth, leisure, corporate incentive, and other tour populations. Ensured exemplary company reputation.

Also researched destinations and packaged tours. Negotiated for air travel, accommodations, facilities, services. Solved 1001 problems on tour.

SMOKENDERS, INC., Garden City, New Jersey, 1977–1983
**Assistant to the Regional Director**

Planned and facilitated sales and service meetings from Hawaii to Utah. Coordinated up to 150 part-time and full-time employees. Negotiated arrangements for facilities, services, travel, accommodations, etc. Served as a trainer and presenter. Required detailed budget administration and advanced interpersonal skills.

Participated in one-year management and organizational training course with detailed instruction in planning, budgeting, organizational and motivational topics.

## EDUCATION

**B.A., Psychology,** Bryn Mawr College, Bryn Mawr, Pennsylvania

**Certificate**, Financial Management for Managers, Northwestern University, Evanston, Illinois

# Government and Political

Governmental résumés, in particular those for civil-service positions, are frequently long, dry, and way too boring. Nevertheless, there is a rationale for this: These jobs are almost never placed in a hurry. Frequently, a standardized handling and grading system is applied to every résumé, no matter how good or bad. Which means that many of the techniques for good skimming and impressing an intelligent reader become irrelevant.

As a general rule, when writing a résumé for any government job where you think they will use a grading system, which is almost all of them, *leave nothing out; belabor the obvious.* If the grader doesn't read that you managed a budget, even if your title was director of budgeting and finance, she will *not* assume you did. The same rule applies to quantitative figures: List them all, as she will not guess at your accomplishments, and you will get the minimum score if you don't.

Finally, these hiring systems do not allow for error or intentional deviation. If the published deadline is 5:00 P.M. on Friday the 13th, even if you are standing in their office at 5:10, your application will usually not be accepted. If they ask for a salary history and three references, and you write, "References and salary history will be provided upon initial interview," (a perfectly reasonable thing to write in other executive placements) you can just about forget it.

The beauty to this system, however, is that you are entitled to know all about their hiring program. First, you can get an official announcement, which states their hiring criteria, application process, and deadline. By calling them up, you can also usually find out who makes the decision, when, how long they think the process will take, whether there will be a panel interview, when they'll check references, and other such minutiae that no corporation would ever share before admitting an interest in you.

There is one other advantage, and it's no small matter: If you are an older worker, or one who has been displaced for a long time, a government position may make sense for you. Government agencies are frequently bound by their own policies to hire the most qualified candidate! You can kiss good-bye to those young, snot-nosed kids who've been telling you, "Well, Mr. Smith, we'd love to help you out here, but we just don't think you'd be *happy* in this position." Your next job could very well be with a city, county, state, or federal government, or with those ancillary entities which have designed their hiring processes the same way, for example, the United States Postal Service, police agencies, and the like. One minister, after he left the church, looked for a job for over a year before landing a position as a small-business crime prevention educator for a metropolitan police force.

(Note: many governmental agencies have odd ideas of what a résumé should contain. Some require you to state a reason for leaving each position and your beginning and ending salaries. Read all announcements carefully, and do not assume that your existing business résumé fulfills their requirements.)

Political résumés are an altogether different animal. Political résumés are partisan and should contain partisan political activities as well as delineate your regular area of expertise. Do not assume that your contact with the new governor will know you hosted five private fund-raising dinners on her behalf and turned your guest house into a precinct office. Politics is not subtle, and neither should you be. By the way, be careful. Any résumé that the media gets a hold of will be checked right down to the true identity of your father.

Finally, campaign and political consulting résumés are *all* politics, as in the first example following. The other examples depict a range of government and political careerists, including some seeking political appointments (for example, see p. 406 and 416.). Be sure to check the index for résumés in other chapters that may apply to your particular case.

"Fleischman has been organizing campaigns for 14 years … the mastermind of the successful effort to unseat a popular three-term congressional incumbent."
—*The New York Times*, 1996

"Mr. Fleischman … a veteran campaign manager at the age of 27 …"
—*The Wall Street Journal*, 1994

"Fleischman established a reputation as an astute media strategist in congressional campaigns and in county-freeholder races."
—*The Bergen Record*, 1994

"Fleischman has been known to fulfill his predictions.…"
—*The Philadelphia Inquirer*, 1994

"Mahalick's victory was seen as a phenomenal achievement for the Democrats … despite a 96,000 Republican margin in the presidential vote.…Mahalick praised campaign manager Buck Fleischman as having a major impact on the election."
—*The New Jersey Herald News*, 1992

"Buck Fleischman is an extraordinarily bright, indeed brilliant, political strategist and organizer. He is a master of modern campaign techniques, analysis, and tactics."
—Andrew Maguire, former U.S. Congressman

"Buck was our [regional] campaign director and chief political strategist.…Given very limited campaign resources, and in the face of overwhelming 'organization' support for the opposition, Buck was able to put together our best 'grassroots' organization.…I would very readily recommend Buck in any effort at building a political campaign organization in either a 'grassroots' or media effort."
—Paul Gary Bograd, Clinton '92, Ohio & New Jersey Campaign Manager

"I cannot recall the number of requests I satisfied by referring reporters to Buck Fleischman … in short, it was a textbook operation. As Press Secretary, the luxury of having that kind of a 'show and tell' situation was a lifesaver.…To say that he was invaluable is understating it.…Buck is one of the most capable and talented individuals I know.…"
—Emma Byrne, Executive Director, N.J. State Democratic Committee

"Buck is extremely knowledgeable about use of media, polling, targeting, recruiting and motivation of volunteers."
—Matthew Feldman, President Pro Tempore, N.J. Senate

"He is clearly recognized in the county and the state as one of its most able political planners"
—Fredrick Waring, Director of Institutional Research, Ramapo College of New Jersey

"I was in a tough up-hill battle against a popular, better financed incumbent. In the final weeks of the campaign I decided that a hard-hitting campaign piece, dramatizing my opponent's mistakes, should be written and that the person to write it was Buck Fleischman. I won that election.…and was the only Democrat to win in District 38. Buck Fleischman is a thorough professional, and I can recommend his work highly."
—Paul J. Contillo, N.J. Senator

"I had the good fortune of being elected as the lone Democrat and attribute much of that success to his technical knowledge, long hours, hard work.…He has a great understanding of polling data, research analysis, and budgets as well."
—Doris Mahalick, Freeholder, Bergen County

# Buck Fleischman

1715 West Passaic Street
Rochelle Park, New Jersey 07662

24-hour private telephone:
(800) 555-4776

---

## SPECIALTY

Campaign strategic-planning with specific emphasis on image development and communications design. Advanced skills in both free and paid media management. Additional abilities in design and development of successful grassroots organizations. Extensive *successful* experience with lower-budget "underdog" campaigns.

## SKILLS SYNOPSIS

In-depth expertise in *campaign strategic planning* and *competitive analysis*, coupled with demonstrated ability to make adjustments to build market penetration as time and circumstances warrant.

Astute capability to synthesize campaign matrices to optimize concise, persuasive, and targeted *positioning*.

Both design and interpretive skills in *market research*, including questionnaire design, segmentation of target publics, focus group analysis, extrapolation, and demographic research.

Creative vision in production of integrated print, direct mail, newspaper, radio, and television *advertising*: copywriting, thematics, graphic design, color, sound, and photographic imagery.

Familiarity with complexities of cost-efficient *media mix* decision-making and electronic media time-buying.

Extensive tactical experience in development and execution of targeted *direct voter contact programs*: candidate scheduling, get-out-the-vote, phone and foot canvassing, events, recruitment.

Imaginative in integrating *free media* promotion: news media stimulation within context of overall strategic plan and image; use of news releases, special events, conferences, position papers, and debates.

Technical proficiency in *budget design* and *fund-raising* through targeting of individual and PAC contributors at specific dollar ranges as basis for solicitation.

Background in application of *computer technology* to campaign tactical objectives.

## SELECTED ACCOMPLISHMENTS

Career political strategist and campaign specialist with 14 years of successful experience.

Diverse experience augmented by business background in design and placement of financial services, and in academe as college adjunct professor.

Bachelor of Arts Degree, Politics, Princeton University, Princeton, New Jersey.

## SAMPLE POLITICAL POSITIONS

**Caseworker/District Representative**, Representative, U.S. Congress

**Legislative Assistant**, Representative, U.S. Congress

**Assistant to Legislative Counsel**, N.J. Governor's Office

**Executive Assistant**, Representative, U.S. Congress

**Campaign Manager**, county, state, and national elections (won 3 out of 4)

## SELECTED POLITICAL ACCOMPLISHMENTS

As Campaign Manager, won 3 of 4 campaigns, 2 of which were significant upsets. Included full strategic planning, free and paid media management, with focus on print and electronic advertising, fund-raising and budget administration, scheduling, volunteer and voter contact development. Involved as Divisional Project Director or Consultant in over 20 additional primary and general election campaigns.

Designed impactful, last-minute direct mail brochure for State Senate campaign; candidate credited piece for reversing voter trends in *two days* and as key factor in upset win against popular, better-financed incumbent.

As Executive Assistant to first-term U.S. Congressman, directed all aspects of office start-up and staff hiring; designed from scratch and administered complex, multivariable $1.2 million budget; formulated and managed innovative constituency service and communications program.

As Director of Voter Registration for U.S. Congressional campaign, organized a record-breaking door-to-door and central-site voter registration drive that resulted in 11,184 new voters in areas specifically selected to favor our candidate.

As Legislative Assistant to U.S. Congressman, reduced response time to constituent mail from six weeks to one. Overhaul included reordering of computer system, staff reassignment and retraining; consolidation and update of form responses, and improved constituent classification system that increased the direct mail program effectiveness.

## BUSINESS & ACADEMIC EXPERIENCE

**Director of Administration, Director of Marketing**, Investor Surety Division, Integrity Insurance Company, Paramus, New Jersey.

- Recruited by the CEO to assist in development of new division specializing in financial guarantee surety bonds for real estate syndications and similarly structured limited partnership investments.
- Hired staff; created, directed, and made responsible for all operational and documentation systems. Transactions totalled in the aggregate to over one-half billion dollars.
- In association with programming specialists, custom-designed a fully integrated computerized system which streamlined every aspect of business intake, bond production, documentation and marketing. Under constant pressure to perform for clients—system responded *on paper, the same day*.
- After promotion to Director of Marketing, achieved a 198% increase in earned premiums, from $3,452,265 to $6,847,487.
- Personally represented the product to skeptical New York banks, gaining acceptance from Manufacturers Hanover, Chemical Bank, Marine Midland, Mellon and others.
- Received letters of appreciation from clients, highly unusual in the business world, e.g.: "I found Buck's empathy, responsiveness, product knowledge, and attention to detail to be unique amongst company people whom I have encountered throughout my ten year insurance career," David W. Reddington, Account Executive, Marsh & McClennan.

**Adjunct Professor**, Ramapo College of New Jersey, School of American & International Studies.

- Invited by Chair of School of American & International Studies to originate electoral politics curriculum, and teach new course offering: Campaigns & Elections.
- Selected course materials and developed unique hands-on approach in which students formed campaign committee in support of local ballot proposition. Students engaged in actual campaign activities, including polling, fund-raising, advertising design, and publicity. Course generated positive media coverage for college in *New York Times*, *The New Jersey Herald News* (front page), and *The Bergen Record*.
- Chairman's evaluation cited course as "... one of our best political science offerings ... "

## CHRONOLOGY

### Campaign Experience

| | |
|---|---|
| Statewide Campaign Manager, Clinton '96 | 1996 |
| Campaign Manager, Marcia Claimon, Senate Special Election | 1995 |
| Consultant (3 state legislative campaigns, all wins) | 1994 |
| Campaign Manager, Robert Torricelli, U.S. Rep. NJD9 (win against 3-term incumbent) | 1992 |
| Bergen County Campaign Consultant, Clinton '92 | 1992 |
| Campaign Manager, Feldman, Baer, Mazur (one ticket, win) | 1991 |
| Get-Out-The-Vote Director, Degnan for Governor | 1991 |
| Campaign Manager, D. Mehalik, Freeholder (democratic win in republican government election year) | 1990 |
| Pre-Campaign Consultant, Andrew Maguire, U.S. Rep. NJD7 | 1989 |
| Get-Out-The-Vote Director, Andrew Maguire for Congress (win) | 1988 |
| Deputy Campaign Manager, Director of Candidate Activity, Andrew Maguire for Senate | 1988 |
| Bergen County Field Director, Richard Leone for Senate | 1988 |
| Deputy Field Operations Director, Brendan Byrne for Governor (primary only, win) | 1987 |
| Director of Voter Registration, A. Maguire for Congress (win) | 1986 |
| District Campaign Manager, Morris '86 | 1986 |
| Assistant Volunteer Director, A. Maguire for Congress (win) | 1984 |
| Office Assistant/Asst. Volunteer Coordinator, Dem. Hq. | 1983 |
| Student Coordinator, McGowan '82 | 1982 |

### Administrative Experience

| | |
|---|---|
| Executive Assistant, Transition Manager Robert Torricelli, U.S. Congress | 1993 |
| Assistant to Legislative Counsel, NJ Gov. Brendan Byrne | 1988 |
| Legislative Assistant/Advocacy, Andrew Maguire, U.S. Congress | 1987–88 |
| Legislative Assistant/Caseworker, Andrew Maguire, U.S. Congress | 1985–86 |

### Business

| | |
|---|---|
| Director of Marketing | 1994–95 |
| Director of Administration Investor Surety Division, Integrity Insurance Company Paramus, NJ | 1993–94 |

### Education

| | |
|---|---|
| Bachelor of Arts, Politics, Princeton University | 1992 |

# Debbie Fletcher

(800) 555-5333

*West Coast Residence:*
181 Stratton Avenue
Costa Mesa, California 92627

*East Coast Residence:*
46 Sherwood Trail
Saratoga Springs, New York 12866

---

## CAMPAIGN/CANDIDATE INVOLVEMENT

**Coordinator, Orange County, 1988, 1992, 1996 Presidential Campaigns**
Contact: Mr. Benny Taborn (800) 555-7659, Mr. J.T. Karlman (714) 555-3666

- Distributed Republican presidential campaign materials
- Distributed voter's registration forms to convert Democrat voters to the Republican Party
- Provided food and office space to Republican campaign volunteer meetings
- Solicited free services in design and printing of banners, posters and flyers to elect/reelect Bob Dole, George Bush, and Dan Quayle
- Made personal cash campaign contributions and solicited others

**Life Member, Republican Senatorial Inner Circle** (RSIC)
Contact: Ms. Michelle Baker, Life Member Representative (800) 555-6877

- Recruited and solicited prospective candidates to join RSIC
- Converted regular members ($1000 membership fee) to life members ($10,000 membership fee)
- Continue to foster total RSIC commitment to election of republican candidates state/local/national, and to gaining Republican majority in the Senate and Congress!

**Co-National Chairwoman, Republican Women's Senate Victory Committee**
Contact: Senator Nancy Kassenbaum, National Chairwoman (202) 555-4224

- Wrote campaign/fund-raising letters to associates, relatives and political friends across the United States to nominate and elect Republican women candidates
- Stuffed campaign brochures/letters and manned the phone banks

**Associate Member, Republican Committee of Northern California**
Contact: Mr. Bruce Warren (415) 555-7668

- Recruited new members
- Distributed voter's registration forms

**Charter Member, Republican Presidential Task Force**
Telephone: Ms. Sally Marner (800) 555-6772

- Made personal monetary contributions
- Currently campaigning to elect Bob Dole president of the United States and end insanity of Democratic "leadership"!
- Campaigned in two states for George Bush and Dan Quayle

**Chairwoman, Political Action Committee, Mothers for a Future**
Contact: Mrs. Pete Wilson, (800) 555-1762

- Fund-raiser for PAC committed to promoting family values by electing Republican candidates at all state and local levels
- Coordinated campaign meetings under PAC auspices to benefit Republican candidates
- Arranged full-page ad endorsing Republican candidates who exemplify family values
- Door-to-door GOTV to elect Republican candidates

**Member of the Board, Crown Cement**

- Used personal family resources to fund Republican campaign efforts (Crown Cement, largest supplier nationwide of concrete for the road-building industries—started by my grandfather, John Wesley Fletcher—still 100% family controlled)

*Combine* recent political experience with other career history to win a political appointment.

# Melanie Grissé Sabor

19673 Tapo Canyon Road
Malibu, California 93063

Telephone/Message:
(818) 555-9609

---

**NATIONAL ISSUES**

**Communications / Film / Media**

**Children / Education / Schools**

**Realignment of Aerospace Industries to Nondefense Applications**

**Access to Technology for the Disadvantaged**

**Administrative Management & Efficiency in Government Operations**

**RECENT POLITICAL EXPERIENCE**

**Special Assistant to the State Chair, Clinton/Gore '96**
**Los Angeles County Co-Chair, Clinton/Gore '96**
- Generated fund-raising events raising several million dollars (direct and indirect) to reelect Bill Clinton and Al Gore.
- Designed and presided over volunteer organization involving thousands of people and hundreds of the most politically active celebrities in the world.
- Conceived of strategy to export California youth to other, more-contested states to help the campaign.
- Contributed time and funds to make the campaign a success, in Los Angeles County, in California, and across the nation.

**President, SFPDS-PAC** (movie industry Democratic PAC), 1994–95
- Raised over $1,000,000 for Democratic political activities.

**County Coordinator, Defeat 187!**, 1994
**GOTV Chair, Feinstein for Governor**, 1994
**Campaign Co-manager, Ann Klein for City Council**, 1993
**Media Advisor, Don Garvin Campaign for Congress** (Alexandria, Virginia), 1993

Numerous other activities on behalf of Democratic candidates and causes, going back to working a phone bank for Jimmie Carter, 1976

**SKILLS**
- Organizational development / strategic planning
- Media and public relations management
- Staff planning, training, administration
- Budget projections and administration
- Image development, positioning, control
- Volunteer recruitment, organization, motivation
- Fund-raising, corporate and private, cash and in-kind
- Large-scale administrative management

## CREATIVE/MEDIA EXPERIENCE

FULL BORE ENTERTAINMENT, INC., Malibu, California, 1994–Present
**President / Producer**

Develop and produce major film and television projects, orchestrating writers, directors, editors, cinematographers, investors. Permanent staff of only four, project staffs up to many hundred, budgets to tens of millions. Projects are always planned and executed under difficult conditions and the tightest time constraints.

*Sample projects:*
- Developed and produced *The Potato People* about a migrant farm family's attempt to get an education for their brilliant son, released in 1996, nominated for an Academy Award for script, earning $48 million *in its first year* (combined domestic/international) on costs of $25 million.
- Created and co-wrote proposal for television documentary *The Difference of One — The Conservation Movement: WWII to the Present.* Negotiated partnership with Walter Cronkite (Cronkite, Ward, & Co.) to increase project clout for successful sale.
- Currently developing film for television concept, *The Helen Taussig Story.*

HUFFY FILMS, Sherman Oaks, California, 1988–Present
**Vice President, Producer, Associate Producer**

Coordinate development of original screenplays, working with writers, agents, and lawyers to secure rights to projects and move finished scripts to buyers (Touchstone, HBO, USA Cable, Turner Network, Lifetime, Fox, NBC, etc.).

*Sample projects:*
- United States associate producer for two international co-productions: local casting, dialogue coaching, location scouting, catering, media relations, etc.
- *James Bond 007: The Golden Hind.* Associate producer, seven months on location in Rome, 1997 release.
- *The Lunchbox Revolution.* Associate producer, 13 months on location in Paris. Negotiated international distribution rights.

THE UNTOLD STORY, INC., Malibu, California, 1994–Present
**President**

Originate and develop documentary projects on noncommercial subjects (e.g. political and civil rights, hunger, world ecology) for educational distribution.

*Sample projects:*
- Obtained Department of Justice participation in developing case histories and trial information into documentary series.
- Collaborated with Morris Dees of the Southern Poverty Law Center on documentary tracing the links between American and European racist groups.

WORLD WILDLIFE FUND, Washington , D.C., 1991, 1992
**Event Coordinator**

Created first-ever, large-scale fund-raising event for this nonprofit organization. Convinced Los Angeles Zoo to donate facility and docents at no charge for first year, and Los Angeles Museum of Natural History for encore. Recruited celebrity patrons, spokespersons, committee heads. Coordinated press coverage. *Raised over $500,000 for WWF.*

U.S. ENVIRONMENTAL FILM FESTIVAL, Santa Monica, California, 1990–1994
**Judge**

PRIOR:
**Actress** (S.A.G., A.F.T.R.A., EQUITY), New York, Hollywood

## ADDITIONAL EXPERIENCE

LOCKHEED, Burbank, California, 1983–1988
**Project Director**

Started as temporary engineering administrator, earned series of rapid promotions to project director, special projects/public affairs assistant to vice president of engineering.

*Sample projects:*
- Wrote, directed, and produced award-winning industrial films.
- Received *Engineering Product Excellence Award*, the first nonengineer to win.
- Received *Lockheed Management Association Leadership Award*.
- Served as vice president of professional development for Lockheed Management Association, orchestrating management development programs for 6000 professionals.
- Obtained $500,000 corporate funding to launch a pioneering computer training center for Lockheed employees.

NEW YORK HOSPITAL, New York, New York, 1980–1982
**Director, Workers' Comp Unit**

Head of workers' compensation clinic (records, appointments, billing, integration with other departments.) Also administered the department of plastic surgery's resident program.

PRIOR
**Teacher**, 7th through 12th grade, Alexandria, Virginia

## EDUCATION

**M.B.A.**, PEPPERDINE UNIVERSITY, Malibu, California
**M.A.**, **Drama**, CATHOLIC UNIVERSITY, Washington, D.C.
**B.A.**, **English**, LONGWOOD COLLEGE, Farmville, VA

## AFFILIATIONS

World Wildlife Fund, National Council Member
Save the Children, Board Member

*Excellent references and recommendations provided on request.*

# George T. Carrington

c/o U.S. Department of Justice
Office of the U.S. Attorney
1100 Commerce 3rd Floor
Dallas, Texas 75242

Days: (214) 555-7565 or (214) 555-4337
Pager: (214) 555-1788
Eves: (415) 647-4222 or (415) 337-4257
get.tough@usdj.gov

## PROFILE

Senior administrative management skills combined with a lifetime of service in the public sector. Skills in program development and direction, budget development and administration, public/community/media outreach and relations, "sales" and "marketing" of programs and projects, staffing, and daily operations. Excellent trainer, speaker, motivator. Proven team builder and catalyst, capable of starting and sustaining new organizations.

Advanced knowledge of public administration, law, police, and security issues. Sensitive to modern policy issues of concern to women and minorities. Background includes extensive cross-cultural experience; conversationally fluent in Spanish, some basic Japanese.

## EDUCATION

**M.P.A.** (Master of Public Administration), Rice University, Houston

**B.A.** (Police Science / Public Administration), Southwest Texas State University, San Marcos

**F.B.I. Academy** and **Texas Rangers Peace Officers Academy**

## EXPERIENCE VITA

U.S. Department of Justice, Office of the U.S. Attorney, Dallas, Texas, 1992–Present
**Law Enforcement Manager**

Responsible for implementing provisions of the Omnibus Crime Control Act, rev. 1990, 1992, 1994, 1996. Serve as spokesperson for the U.S. Attorney; primary representative to other federal, state, and local law enforcement agencies. Identify and resolve interagency law enforcement problems. Recommend and organize interagency task forces. Identify and develop sources of funding to support all missions. Monitor state and local legislation. Lecture, speak, and testify statewide. Key contributor to all stages of long- and short-term planning.

International Safety Consulting (I.S.C.), Dallas, Texas, 1990–Present
**President** and **C.E.O.**

Founder of this consulting company providing expertise in security and risk management. Clients have included 1996 Olympics in Atlanta, U.S.-based multinational corporations, and significant individuals. In addition to direct services, also broker security contacts and provide referral services to related businesses worldwide.

City of Plattsburg, Plattsburg, Mississippi, 1989–1990
**Director of Public Safety**

Executive leadership of a department encompassing all police, fire, paramedic, and building inspection functions for the City of Plattsburg. Line of command over 2500 total city employees. Managed $100 million budget. Coordinated with seven unions. Initiated a range of projects to increase regional cooperation. Upgraded police computing. Concurrently served as **President, National Association of Town & Borough Chiefs of Police** (NAT&BCP), representing some half-million U.S. peace officers.

City of Denton, Municipal Police Department, Denton, Texas, 1988–1989
**Chief of Police (Interim)**

Responsible for all personnel, budget and operations for city police department with 150 peace officers. Organized task force strategies to meet organized crime and drug threats. Established a variety of aggressive drug demand reduction and community education programs. Included heavy public speaking and media contact. Concurrently served as **Manager, U.S. Attorney's Law Enforcement Coordinating Committee**, for entire State of Texas.

Texas State Police, Austin, Texas, 1987–1988
**Chief of Police**

Responsible for state police force with 500 uniformed officers. Managed $50 million annual operating budget, numerous facilities statewide, plus fleet of vehicles. Directed dignitary protection, disaster planning/response, and crime-fighting efforts. Personally managed some complex and (later) highly publicized investigations of fraud and embezzlement against the State of Texas. Represented the department and the governor in numerous media contacts.

City of Wichita Falls, Wichita Falls, Texas, 1975–1986
**Chief of Police & Fire**

In charge of 100 employees, annual operating budget of $4.5 million. Directed all program development and inter-agency agendas. Wrote the city's master disaster plan. Planned, implemented, and upgraded all computing systems. Authored weekly newspaper column. Concurrently served as **President, North Texas Police Chiefs Association** (NTPCA) and **President, Texas Peace Officers Association** (TPOA).

State of Montana, Office of the Attorney General, Helena, Montana, 1974–1975
**Director, Law Enforcement Services Agency**

Founded State's first Law Enforcement Services Agency. Responsible for strategic planning and daily operation. Included extensive outreach, education, and communication with all existing law enforcement organizations in the state.

Federal Bureau of Investigations (FBI), Washington, D.C., 1966–1971
**Special Agent**

Apprehended more fleeing felons in one year than any other FBI agent in history. Investigated violations of federal law. Trained local police. Managed complex investigations of organized crime under antiracketeering statutes.

United States Marine Corps, Washington, D.C., 1958–1993
**Colonel** (U.S.M.C.R., Ret.)

Decorated in war and in peace-time for activities on behalf of the U.S.M.C. and U.S.M.C.R., including for Valor. One of the most decorated reservists to date.

Last assignment: **Special Staff Officer to Commander in Chief, Pacific Command.**

## REFERENCES

References, list of board memberships, affiliations, certifications, and all additional information provided on request.

# George T. Carrington

c/o U.S. Department of Justice
Office of the U.S. Attorney
1100 Commerce 3rd Floor
Dallas, Texas 75242

Days: (214) 555-7565 or (214) 555-4337
Pager: (214) 555-1788
Eves: (415) 647-4222 or (415) 337-4257
get.tough@usdj.gov

## ADDENDA

### Military Honors

Navy Cross (second highest U.S. military award for heroism in combat)

Bronze Star (2)

Purple Heart (2)

Navy Air Medal

Navy Commendation Medal (2)

Vietnamese Medal of Honor

Vietnamese Cross of Gallantry

Vietnamese Distinguished Service Medal

### Additional Honors

J. Edgar Hoover Gold Medal, Police Officer of the Year (national), 1990

Republic of Korea, Director General's Police Award, 1986

Freedom Foundation, Valley Forge, George Washington Honor Medal, 1985

Republic of China, The Police Medal, 1984

Director General, Japan National Police Medal, 1984

Garda Siochana, Irish National Police Award, 1984

Lifesaving Commendation, Congressman Leo J. Ryan, 1976

### Additional Credentials

Community College Teaching Certificate, State of Texas

*Lifetime Credential for Police Science and Public Services and Administration

Executive Certificate, State of Texas Peace Officers Standards and Training

*Also have attained Management, Advanced, Basic and Technical Certificates

Advanced CPR and First Aid Certificates, American Red Cross

### Additional Affiliations

Society of Former F.B.I. Agents, Texas Chapter

Association of Former Intelligence Officers

American Society for Industrial Security

Insurance Committee for Arson Control

National Arson Task Force

### Publications

List on request.

# Jason Thomas Henry

18175 Southeast Dirt Hill Road
San Bernardino, California 92404

Office/voice mail: (909) 555-8894
Residence: (909) 555-1863
jt.henry@is.fema.com

---

## EDUCATION

**M.P.A.** (Master of Public Administration), California State University at Fullerton
**M.S., Information Systems**, University of California at Irvine
**B.S., Computer Science**, University of San Diego
**Certificate, Telecommunications Management**, University of California at San Diego-Extension

## EXPERIENCE

Federal Emergency Management Administration, Washington, D.C.
Region X, San Bernardino, California
**Division Chief, Program Support Services Division**, 1994–Present

Visionary technical/operations/financial manager with the interpersonal and organizational skills to actualize that vision. Strengths: **Administrative Management** and **Information Services Management** with a purview over **Telecommunications, IS, Personnel, Financial Management, Procurement, Property Management**. Currently in the final stages of a structural reorganization/internal realignment of information, financial, and administrative services for FEMA Region X. This project has been widely acclaimed and is being adopted as a model for other regions and for the national organization itself. Report directly to the Regional Director. Act as Regional Director (SES4) in the line of succession. Last performance rating: "Outstanding."

Saw potential for elimination of organizational redundancies. Presented this information to the Regional Directorate, and in November 1994, was detailed and tasked to develop, organize, and direct a new regional organization, the Program Support Services Division (slated to be renamed the "Operations Support Division," effective November 28, 1996). Was given wide authority to cross organizational lines to create a new, more efficient Region X structure, with emphasis on improved data flow and improved use of financial, material, and human resources.

Developed statistical and narrative data to justify work unit reorganization and position restructuring. Combined the mission and the personnel of the former Regional Administrative Unit (staff of 6) and the Program Support Unit (staff of 6) and elevated the new group to branch status, the Administrative Services Branch. Realigned Information Resources Management (staff of 9) into Information Systems Branch and broadened its purview and mission. These two newly structured branches comprise a new division, total of 21 PFT employees, GS5 to GS14, whose mission is to support the three program divisions: (1) Emergency Management & National Preparedness Programs, (2) Disaster Assistance Programs, and (3) Natural & Technological Hazards. NOTE: Also responsible for additional 75–300 Disaster Assistance Employees, reservists on assignment to disaster response sites.

The critical factors in the success of this endeavor have been: (1) ability to set clear goals and objectives, (2) ability to win employee approval for realignments, or buy-in by the impacted staff, (3) efficient delegation to and communication with line managers, (4) advanced knowledge of FEMA national organization.

In full charge of newly organized **Administrative Services Branch**, responsible for all Personnel, Financial, Contracting, and Administrative Support required by the three Program Divisions and the Office of the Regional Director. Serve as the region's **Senior Financial Officer** (annual administrative budget of $46 million plus annual disaster benefits budget which is theoretically unlimited, aggregate responsibility FY 1993 at $1.3 billion, including multiyear financial planning, annual budget submissions, financial support to the Emergency Response Team, and ongoing justifications for budget allocation). Serve as **Regional Property Officer** tracking fixed assets valued as high as $100 million in FY 1993, including a variety of assets temporarily rented, leased, and otherwise contracted for. Ensure region compliance with all government contracting laws, policies, and regulations. Design and oversee organizational and manpower utilization studies, including analysis of work processes (knowledge, skill, ability, speed, volume, and quality benchmarks) and labor markets (availability, training potential of current forces, potential cost-benefit of job restructuring). Ensure critical readiness, including administrative, financial, and personnel support to deployed units during Presidential Declared Disasters.

In charge of newly organized **Information Systems Branch**, responsible for Telecommunications, ADP, Novell Computer Network, and Audiovisual support required by the three Program Divisions, the Office of the Regional Director, and the Office of the Western District Inspector General. Prepare short- and long-term technology plans. With 24 years of expertise in Information Systems, routinely develop, plan, execute, maintain, and manage complex, state-of-the-art telecommunications, ADP, and media services projects. Proficient in every aspect from specifications development to worldwide vendor evaluation to security issues to training and support for end users. FEMA Region X liaison to Essential Support Functions (Interagency) and National Communications Systems Command (GSA).

In addition to the two branches detailed above, also supervise division-level support staff and divisionwide projects; interpret and ensure appropriate application of FEMA regulations, standards, procedures, and policies; supervise and coordinate the work of subordinates, set goals, time frames and priorities; maintain quality control over all employees and projects under supervision; evaluate employee performance, counsel employees on professional development, manage EEO and grievance procedures, and ensure high morale.

*Sample special projects:*

FEMA response to 1996 Southern California Firestorm: assigned Operations Support Officer and 35 Region X PFTs to set up 8 temporary Disaster Assistance Centers to support FEMA services in the impacted area. Oversaw design and emplacement of remote processing centers (LAN to Pasadena and San Bruno) to support administration and disaster claims services. Established a new computer network using Grid Pad Technology to support expeditious processing of disaster claims, a Beta test on an entirely new technology, including setting up custom LANs. Monitored hiring of 80 temporary employees and assignment of 70 Disaster Assistance Employees to Southern California Operations. Coordinated with Treasury Department to win approval for electronic certification process to expedite checks to victims. Designed emergency Computer Bulletin Board to enhance communication between FEMA workers and victims. Managed $520 million budget request related to this disaster.

Designed tracking and charge-back system to improve FEMA recapture of capital equipment and/or monies in FEMA-executed joint missions involving DoD, GSA, U.S. Army Corps of Engineers, and local government entities. FEMA had failed to install a system to task such organizations under Federal Response Plan guidelines and an internal audit had identified equipment accountability problems. Saved $3,870,000 in the first application of the new system when the U.S. Navy "sold" dump trucks and loaders to FEMA but retained the equipment.

Key point of contact for negotiations between FEMA and the National Park Service for negotiations on a 20-year lease on building in the Presidio of San Francisco. Project involves valuation of FEMA improvements to the buildings as well as federal law against interagency rental (a privilege currently restricted to the GSA). Worked closely with FEMA General Counsel on request to OMB for suspension of regulations to allow lease.

Represented FEMA Region X in two general performance audits in Financial Management for Disaster Operations, which went smoothly.

Appointed to Region X EEO/AA Committee; also instrumental in making changes to Region X policy concerning advancement on merit.

Extensively involved in Agency classified operations. Possess TOP SECRET SECURITY CLEARANCE.

**Chief, Information Systems Branch**, 1994

As Chief, Information Systems Branch, FEMA Region X, had full responsibility over management, operations, and control of **information, telecommunications, audio-visual,** and **security** systems that support all aspects of the Region X mission, including but not limited to permanent and field computer systems

(PCs, LANs, WANs, interagency linkage, standard and special application software packages, security systems, and all peripherals, ranging from computer bulletin boards to color map printers), permanent and field telecommunications (to the switch level, including phone company and longline services, portable phones, field radio communications systems, and other special equipment, and including equipment housed in properties owned by the state or other federal agencies), region audio-visual, videography and film equipment used for public education, outreach, documentary and training purposes.

Supervised staff of seven: Telecommunications Manager, LAN/WAN Manager, Electronics Technicians, Telecommunication Operations Leader, Computer Assistant, Telecommunication Operations Specialist. Supervised the Information Systems Branch through three sections: Operations, Maintenance, Automated Data Processing (ADP). Acted as Regional Director (SES4) in the line of succession.

Directed annual budget submissions for operations and capital projects, submitted recommendations to FEMA HQ regarding information and telecommunications technologies, reviewed agency policy to ensure region compliance. Dealt with worldwide computing technology and telecommunications vendors. Prepared budgets to $4 million.

Brought a structural and proactive vision to a branch that had been primarily reactive in nature. Instituted systematic technology planning, codified procurement processes and cost-benefit analysis used in technology evolution planning, initiated and completed a total upgrade of the region's computer systems, including LAN/WAN upgrades and other measures to ensure capability of meeting expanded requirements of relocation and support of civil service and military personnel during times of natural disaster or war.

Directed region information and telecommunications systems in support of FEMA National Emergency Management System (NEMS), e.g., responsible for the design, periodic testing, and operational readiness of reliable and survivable systems to alert key federal, state, and local officials and warn the civilian population of enemy attack or peacetime disaster, including integration with the National Warning System (NAWAS).

Served as the technical authority over Region X communications and warning systems, FEMA National Radio System (FNARS), FEMA National Automated Message System (FNAMS), FEMA National Voice System (FNVS), FRC Telephonic and Electronic Message Service, and linkage with Defense Switched Network (FSN), Defense Digital Network, National Security Emergency Preparedness, Mobile Emergency Response System (MERS), Decision Information Distribution System, and California FNAVS.

Served as **Regional Physical Security Officer, Regional Information Systems Security Officer**, and **Comsec Officer**. Maintained and enforced information systems policies, procedures and standards related to the safeguarding, access, control, and use of information resources, control and use of sensitive unclassified, classified, and restricted information, including maintenance, security, and utilization of voice encryption systems.

Maintained COMSEC procedures in support of agency classified operations. Possessed TOP SECRET SECURITY CLEARANCE.

(Continue to have line-of-command authority over all these areas in current assignment as Division Chief, Program Support Services Division.)

**Telecommunications Manager**, 1992–1994

Managed the region's communications and warning systems, which are independent, subsidiary functions of the Regional Information Systems Communications Center. Supervised staff of five: Communication Control Technicians and Electronic Mechanics. Prepared communications and warning system budgets, plans, policies, and programs. Dealt with worldwide technology vendors.

Provided expert technical advice and assistance to Branch Chief, Division Chief, and Regional Director. Served as the technical authority over Region X communications and warning systems, FEMA Switch Network (FSN), AT&T System 85 PBX, FEMA National Automated Message System (FNAMS), FEMA National Radio System (FNARS) HF Long Haul System, National Warning System (NAWAS), Federal Telecommunications Service (FTS), Defense Worldwide Voice Network (AUTOVON), Automatic Digital Data Network (AUTODIN).

Provided technical support to Information Systems Manager concerning telecommunications and computing matters. Determined system requirements, coordinated maintenance/repair of information systems, installed software applications, developed training in software and computer operations for region staff.

Collaborated with federal agencies and military units to ensure integration of their emergency plans with FEMA civil defense plans.

Maintained COMSEC procedures in support of agency classified operations. Possessed TOP SECRET/SCI CLEARANCE.

(Continue to have line-of-command authority over all these areas in current assignment as Division Chief, Program Support Services Division.)

**Communications Management Specialist**, 1991–1992

As **Communications Management Specialist**, provided expert technical advice and assistance to Branch Chief, Division Chief, and Regional Director regarding all emergency telecommunications and warning systems. Prepared system budgets, plans, policies, and programs for Emergency Broadcast System (EBS), Electromagnetic Pulse (EMP) Program, Warning and Communications Systems (W&CS), Emergency Operations Center (EOC), FEMA Radio Assistance Civil Emergency Services (RACES) Program. Also managed aspects of routine telecommunications, such as voice mail.

As **Information Systems Coordinator** (ISC), provided technical expertise to Emergency Management Division to ensure forward-looking technology planning, implementation, maintenance, and training for state-of-the-art computer systems and peripherals.

Maintained COMSEC procedures in support of agency classified operations. Possessed TOP SECRET SECURITY CLEARANCE.

(Continue to have line-of-command authority over all these areas in current assignment as Division Chief, Program Support Services Division.)

United States Army
**Telecommunications Chief**, 1989–1991

Coordinated the design, development, and implementation of digital voice/data switch networks supporting major subordinate commands of the U.S. Central Command. Coordinated the design and installation of electronic switching systems, developed and managed the implementation of integrated communications and computer systems. Provided frequency management, satellite access, coordination with civilian agencies, commercial organizations, and foreign governments in support of command missions and exercises.

Provided oversight to J6 staff on balance of Commander-in-Chief, Command and Control Initiative Program, a $20 million annual budget. Managed and operated CCJ6 O&M, R&D budget and provided advice and counsel to the J6 Directorate. Responsible for Travel and Military pay operations during unit deployment.

Assisted staff officers in review of long-range budget requirements; developed operating budget instructions and coordinated financial plan submission from all command directorates.

**NCO, 5th** Signal Command, 1986–1989
**First Sergeant**, Company A 29th Signal Battalion, 1985–1986
**Communications Instructor**, American Embassy (Egypt), 1984–1985
**Senior Enlisted Advisor**, 187th Signal Brigade, New York Army National Guard, 1982–1984
**Communications Chief**, 38th Air Defense Brigade, Republic of South Korea, 1981–1982
**Communication Center Station Chief**, 8th U.S. Army, Republic of South Korea, 1979–1981
**U.S. Army Recruiter**, 1974–1978
**Radio Electronics Instructor**, U.S. Army Signal Center, Fort Gordon, 1972–1974
**Radio Communications Team Leader**, Vietnam and Ft. Benning, 1968–1972

# L. JAMES DUARTÉ

1386 NE Warden Circle
Seattle, Washington 98177

Office/Message: (206) 555-3744
Residence/Message: (206) 555-4268
Holidays/Emergency Message: (206) 555-8329

## AREAS OF EXPERTISE

- **Transportation, Highway Safety**
- **Education, Youth Programs, Drug and Alcohol Awareness**
- **Minority Affairs, Community Relations, Public Relations, Public Speaking**

## EDUCATION

**University of Washington**, Seattle, Washington
**M.A. (Master of Arts), Political Science**, 1971

**Kenyon College**, Gambier, Ohio
**B.A. (Bachelor of Arts), Political Science**, cum laude, 1970
  Honors: Woodrow Wilson Fellow, J. Allen Smith Fellow

## EXPERIENCE

**U.S. Department of Transportation**, NHTSA Region X, Seattle, Washington
**Deputy Regional Administrator**, 1994–Present

Provide daily direction and coordination for the Regional Office staff and programs for AZ, CA, NV, HI, and the territories of American Samoa, Commonwealth of the Northern Mariana Islands, and Guam. Administer regional budget of $27 million. Administer 408, 410, 153 Incentive Grants. Delegate to and supervise a staff of five Regional Program Managers as well as administrative support staff. Fully computerized office (IBM PC, DOS, WordPerfect, Lotus, Harvard Graphics).

Selected accomplishments:
- Coordinate intermodal issues with Federal Highway Administration (FHWA), Federal Transit Administration (FTA), and the Maritime Administration.
- Addressed Police Traffic Services seminar in Monterey, California, representing 80 jurisdictions and the California Office of Traffic Safety.
- Oversaw effort to upgrade California's safety belt law from a secondary to a primary statute (successful).
- Oversaw effort to upgrade Arizona's secondary safety belt law from temporary status to permanent (successful).
- Directed regional participation in National Drunk, Drugged Driving Prevention month, coordinating major media events in San Francisco, San Diego, Sacramento, Los Angeles.
- Selected by the Regional Administrator to produce a single policies and procedures document, codifying policies that had existed prior to this as loose directives.

**Washington Traffic Safety Commission (WTSC)**, Olympia, Washington
**Director**, 1989–1993

Appointed by Governor Booth Gardner. Provided statewide leadership in all traffic safety matters: program management, administration, planning, evaluation and legislative liaison functions. Set and interpreted policy. Developed and managed $7.5 million budget.

Selected accomplishments:
- Represented the governor at National Highway Traffic Safety Administration meetings.
- Developed and published the state's Highway Safety Plan, qualifying for Federal Aid Agreement of $2.1 million.
- Created safety awareness programs resulting in 14% increase in safety belt usage.
- Provided lobbying and public testimony in favor of 1990 motorcycle helmet legislation (successful).
- Successfully lobbied the governor to make Administrative License Revocation (ALR) Governor's Special Request Legislation in 1990–91 session.
- Provided expert testimony on safety issues at legislative hearings.

- Attended Senior Executive Seminar for Leadership and Management of State Highway Safety Programs.
- Certificate of Accomplishment, NAGHSR, Executive Seminar on Program Management.
- Attended Northwestern University Thirteenth Vehicular Homicide DWI Conference.
- Addressed Washington Association of Sheriffs and Police Chiefs.

**National Association of Governors Highway Safety Representatives (NAGHSR),** Wash. D.C.
**Vice-Chair** and **Chair,** 1991–1992

Represented NAGHSR to Congress, U.S. Senate, highway safety advocacy organizations, and federal agencies. Issued news releases and press releases related to NAGHSR business. Appointed committee chairs and vice chairs. Chaired national meetings and executive board meetings. This was an elected position.

Selected accomplishments:
- Addressed national Mothers Against Drunk Driving Leadership Conference.
- Keynote Speaker, MADD, Washington, D.C., 1991.
- Panelist, National Highway Users Federation Conference.
- Addressed FHWA Tri-Regional Conference.
- Addressed National Pupil Transportation Directors Conference.
- Addressed National Lifesavers Conference.
- Addressed high school, middle school, and elementary school groups.
- Provided expert testimony and lobbied key Congressmen and Senators on behalf of highway safety issues, especially during the Surface Transportation Reauthorization process. Lobbying resulted in highest-ever authorization for safety issues and passage of ISTEA (Intermodal Surface Transportation Efficiency Act).
- Maintained expertise in legislation and court cases impacting area of expertise.

**Booth Gardner Committee, Democrat for Governor,** HQ: Seattle, Washington
**Deputy Campaign Manager, Director of Operations,** 1988

Coordinated and managed all functional departments of statewide political campaign: press, advance, field, finance and administration. Planned and managed budget, provided leadership, developed constantly changing strategic and tactical plans.

Selected accomplishments:
- Designed the management matrix used to track all daily campaign activities. Supervised press secretary, field director, chief fund-raiser, advance staff, and principal accountant on all daily activities.
- Facilitated the largest Democratic win in recent statewide electoral history.
- Ended campaign with $300,000 cash reserves.

**Honeywell Marine System Division,** Everett, Washington
**Human Resources Administrator,** 1984–1988

Coordinated training and development programs for 1222 employees, including technical training, management and executive development, supervisory skills development, time management, computer training, and other areas. Coordinator for company participation in university and college extension programs. Collaborated on strategic issues such as management secession and intermediate and long-term planning.

Selected accomplishments:
- Managed implementation of Computer Training & Resource Center.
- Developed the company's Strategic Human Resources Plan.
- Produced all employee relations management communications.
- Provided train-the-trainer for Quality Circle programs, an early version of Total Quality Management using factory-floor feedback and statistical analysis to track and measure performance.

**Honeywell Marine System Division,** Everett, Washington
**Production Program Planner,** 1980–1984

Directed work flow on military and commercial programs. Designed program plans to meet production objectives. Coordinated work order release. Prepared fabrication schedules.

Selected accomplishments:
- Developed budgets from $100,000 to $300,000 as matter of routine.
- Coordinated publication of program summary status reports.

**Seattle Central Community College,** Seattle, Washington
**Instructor, Social Sciences Division,** 1980–1982

Developed and taught curricula for three classes per quarter. Served on academic committees.

Selected accomplishments:
- Selected to coordinate the Action Research Group (ARG), including directing a team of faculty members in the creation of an information guide.
- Created the staff development component for a competency-based education grant.

## ADDITIONAL COMMUNITY SERVICE

Board Member, Interaction/Transition (corrections program)

Advisor, Washington State Governor's Substance Abuse Council

Board Member, Safety Committee Chair, Washington Highway Users Federation

Co-Chair, Seattle Public Schools Full Funding Task Force

Chair, Seattle Desegregation Review Committee
(complete rewrite of the Seattle desegregation plan, 1987)

Co-Chair, Seattle Excellence in Education Committee

Chair, King County Department of Youth Services Advisory Committee (CYAC)

Board Member, Girls Club of Puget Sound

Executive Board Member, Seattle Community College Federation of Teachers (SCCFT)

Founder, Minority Caucus, Seattle Community College Federation of Teachers (SCCFT)

Chair, Central Area School Council, Seattle

President, Beta Theta Pi

## PUBLICATIONS

"Dialectics of School Desegregation: A Western Paradigm," *The Western Journal of Black Studies,* Sept. 1992.

"Desegregation Time Line, Desegregation Overview: History of Desegregation in Seattle, Washington," *Proceedings of the Washington Commission for the Humanities Project,* 1988.

## CONTINUING EDUCATION

Extensive—list on request. Instructor-qualified in supervision and frontline leadership.

## ADDITIONAL POLITICAL SERVICE TO DEMOCRATIC PARTY & CANDIDATES

State Committee, King County, two terms
Precinct Committee Representative, State of Washington
District Chair, Washington State Legislative District, twice
Appointment Candidate, Seattle City Council, Washington State Legislature
Deputy Campaign Director, B. Gardner '88 (largest % win in state history)
Campaign Volunteer every election until Federal Civil Service status (banned by Hatch Act)
State Delegate, State Convention, 1984 and 1988 Presidential Campaigns
Speakers Bureau, Mayor of Seattle
Speakers Bureau, Washington Democrats against Term Limits
Plus approximately 25 other campaigns, with key responsibilities in approximately half of these.

Compare this presentation with the consultants' profiles in chapter 4.

# YOLANDA BILLINGS-LAWTON

1775 Rosebud Hill Circle
Oakland, California 94612
(510) 555-7763 or (510) 555-6658

## PROFILE

**Disaster Planning**

- Program Planning and Development
- Program Administration
- Training

Expertise in Disaster Planning, Evacuation & Emergency Response, for both corporate and civic entities. Emphasis on immediate safety of persons and property, chain of command, and decision-making in emergency situations. Also have ability to integrate disaster preparedness into overall corporate planning, including strategic and long-range master planning and routine operations (such as IS/computing/accounting/records). Ability to work closely with staff to prepare and implement *workable* disaster plans.

Modeling and planning experience with earthquake, fire, emergency evacuations, also: bomb threats, hostage, extortion, terroristic acts. Interested in comprehensive planning, training, trials and testing. Can also prepare feasibility studies, write overviews, and perform other preliminary or follow-up research. Basic knowledge of relevant California laws and regulations.

Strong career skills in project design, project management, administration, and budgeting. Also staff training, development, and supervision. Skilled negotiator, coordinator and motivator. Management experience over research, writing, graphic art, and production staff. Articulate writer and speaker. Outreach and education experience. Sensitive to staff/public/community relations; experience in media relations.

## EDUCATION

MASSACHUSETTS INSTITUTE OF TECHNOLOGY, Cambridge, MA
**Master of City Planning**, 1985

- Thesis: *Types and Effectiveness of Neighborhood Watch Programs*
- Graduate Assistant, Department of Housing & Community Development

UNIVERSITY OF CALIFORNIA, Berkeley, CA
**Bachelor of Arts**, Criminology, 1983

- Congressional Intern, Ronald V. Dellums, Washington, D.C.

## PUBLICATIONS

"Bomb Threat Emergency Response Plan: 450 McAllister," August 1996

"Evacuation Plan: Allen Temple Arms Senior Citizen Home," Nov. 1995

"Evacuation Plan: 450 McAllister," April 1993

"Foreign Trade Zones at Port Authority Airport," July 1991

"Ridesharing Makes Sense," March 1990

## CREDENTIALS

Member, National Black Planners Association

Certified Member, Community Disputes Services Panel, American Arbitration Association, Boston, Massachusetts.

## PROFESSIONAL HISTORY

### PROJECTS:

CITY HALL ANNEX BUILDING, City & County of San Francisco, CA
**Project Coordinator**

Developed a comprehensive disaster/emergency plan for the City Hall Annex Building, a six-story structure. Initiated, designed and managed the entire planning project. Developed questionnaire for the building's tenants, to define their collective evacuation needs and catalog the talents and locations of individuals with special skills who could aid others in an emergency.

Compiled and analyzed the data to produce a computerized listing of all the employees within the building, their routine movements, shift changes, and other predictable behaviors. Developed a model for fire/evacuation officials that would allow them to pinpoint the highest concentration of persons in the building at any one time, with notations for tenants with physical limitations. Also prepared an evacuation plan and produced and distributed a pamphlet explaining it.

ALLEN TEMPLE ARMS SENIOR CITIZEN RESIDENCE HOME, Oakland, CA
**Project Director**

Initiated, designed and executed evacuation planning for this senior home, taking into consideration its many occupants with physical limitations and special needs. Developed the initial proposal for the evacuation plan and presented it to the Development Corporation (the board of directors). Computed the plan's payback rate based on (1) savings available from insurance carrier for implementation of the evacuation plan, and (2) potential savings in actual emergency use. Handled all stages: formulation, dissemination of plan, analysis and integration of feedback, testing under real conditions.

Recruited and coordinated the efforts of professionals and project support staff. Represented the plan and attained its approval before the Fire Marshall of the City of Oakland. Trained the home's administrative and management staff, as well as their designated emergency response team. Presented the plan to residents in easy-to-understand formats, including signing and oral presentations for the sensory-impaired. Held a training drill, complete with medical monitoring of participating residents. Videotaped the drill for training purposes.

### PERMANENT POSITIONS:

CITY & COUNTY OF SAN FRANCISCO, San Francisco, CA, 1990–Present
**City Planner/Transit Planner/Zoning Planner/Neighborhood Planner**

Involved in city's Master Plan process, with special and medium-term assignments into special areas, such as the I-280 transfer program, an $87 million project. Advanced skills in researching and modeling such factors as density and human movement. Includes coordination of other agencies and paid consultants, and research into federal and state regulations. Extensive experience with report writing and presentations before groups.

Presently assigned to Neighborhood Planning, with responsibilities for outreach communication and liaison activities with specific geographical communities. Managing planning and research projects in both Presidio Heights and Hunters Point communities.

PORT AUTHORITY OF NEW YORK & NEW JERSEY, New York, NY, 1988–1989
**Aviation Planner**

Assisted in analyzing the movement of people, goods, aircraft, and associated forms of transport as they involved or affected the airport, for use in long-range development plans. Utilized written and oral communication skills, advanced analytical techniques, and also political and diplomatic skills.

Was placed in full charge of the car pool program. Implemented the program, monitored and evaluated the results. Made a major contribution to the car-pooling concept by integrating human social and motivational factors to increase participation.

Also, on special assignment, developed a white paper exploring the utility of Foreign Trade Zones in cities throughout the United States in order to evaluate their suitability for application at Port Authority Airports.

NATIONAL URBAN LEAGUE INC., New York, NY, 1986–1987
**Project Manager**

Planned, developed, implemented and managed research and technical assistance activities in support of National Urban League projects with criminal justice agencies nationwide. Supervised professional staff of three, as well as support and administrative staff; managed budget of $200,000 per annum.

OFFICE OF THE PRESIDENT, HARVARD UNIVERSITY, Cambridge, MA, 1985–1986
**Project Director**

As Special Assistant to Derek Bok, researched affirmative action policies, procedures and precedents, guided and monitored Harvard's affirmative action program for students and staff. Included extensive research of other institutions and analysis of federal and other government guidelines and regulations.

**REFERENCES**

Professional references and recommendations provided on request. Work samples and portfolio also available for review.

# Nonprofits, Education, and Philanthropy

Nonprofit, arts, and educational administration résumés are classic, business-oriented, accomplishment-based presentations familiar to you from elsewhere in this book.

However, you need to know that academic résumés run a continuum between the general management styles as explicated in chapter 3, the CV styles as seen in the scientific examples in chapter 6, and the examples for primary care providers in chapter 7. If a person's primary duties are teaching or research, they are more likely to use a purely schematic CV style—dates, places, and presentations. You will note that true CVs are practically devoid of accomplishments or any hint of a self-congratulatory tone, and they may include extensive addenda on publications, committees, presentations, and so on, running as many as a dozen pages or more. Traditionally, in academic circles, one never culls early listings from bibliographies; one simply adds to the list, putting new material at the top in reverse chronological order. There are several style guides to bibliographies in the different academic disciplines. Again, ask your reference librarian to help you find the right one.

To complicate matters further, in an academic setting, administrators' résumés are frequently called CVs even though stylistically they are nothing more nor less than business-style résumés. Again, the best guide to which style is just right for you is the style your most successful peers are using.

Résumés for philanthropy are regular business résumés. For benefactors, however, résumés are usually in a CV or vita style, as seen above by Dr. Schaunbaum in chapter 7 (p. 354), and the examples later in this chapter. These latter are properly understated.

Incidentally, I frequently run across the belief among executive job-seekers that they can retreat or hide out in nonprofit endeavors. Promulgated by some of the outplacement firms and an occasional article in a certain otherwise reputable magazine, this idea is absolutely false. There are expected career paths and intense competition in nonprofit administration, just as in any business, and the lower wages can be a shock to those used to corporate pay scales. If you do want to get involved in nonprofit endeavors, come in as a benefactor or volunteer and maneuver yourself to get involved in a paid appointment. It cannot be done in one step, usually. (As an aside, some major corporations have "executive on loan" programs that place executives with nonprofit, educational, and philanthropic organizations. Check into your own company's policies before you take an internal assignment that you simply don't want.)

In the following examples you will find a complete range of styles. Also check the index for résumés from other chapters that may apply to your particular case.

# Tom Landfield

600 Waterford Court
Edina, Minnesota 55424

Residence:
(612) 555-5935

---

## INTERESTS

- Education, Health & Welfare Issues for Children & Youth
- Strategic Planning, Program Development, Financing & Administration
- Policy Development
- Lobbying & Advocacy

## EXPERIENCE

**Edgewood Children's Center**, Flint, Michigan     1982–1996
**Assistant Executive Director** (1991–1996)

Provided strategic planning, new program development, program funding strategies, financial and operations administration, and community, government, and interagency relations for Edgewood's innovative programs for seriously disturbed children: 7-acre main campus, six additional sites, $5 million annual budget, $7 million endowment, 35-member board of directors, 150 staff and 200-member auxiliary.

Strengths encompassed program and budget development, grant-writing, fund-raising, personnel and organizational matters, interagency programs, and public policy development at the statewide and local levels.

Selected recent contributions:

- Key advocate of a broadened mission for the organization, resulting in an increase in the number of children served by a factor of ten (over the last five years).
- Increased agency self-sufficiency (revenues vs. expenses) from 16% to 92%.
- Wrote successful grant proposal generating $850,000 award from state bond funds for expansion of Edgewood facilities.
- Developed program and funding for school-based day treatment demonstration project (Mayor's Award for Innovative Interagency Children's Service).
- Designed and launched Flint's first primary intervention programs for primary grade schoolchildren.
- Directed the development of an affirmative action plan for Edgewood.
- Part of the executive team for a $6 million capitalization program.

Sample program development project:

Guided the development of a legal agreement between the Department of Social Services, Juvenile Court, Unified School District, County Mental Health Services, and Dept. of Probation to create and operate a system of sub-acute residential treatment services for Flint youngsters.

Sample government relations effort:

Appointed to the Mayor's Task Force to design and create a Mayor's Office of Children, Youth and Families. This interagency task force profiled similar local, state, and national programs, analyzed funding strategies and service delivery approaches, and developed a cost-effective plan now in implementation stage.

Sample task force service:

Appointed to the State Interagency Advisory Committee on Systems of Care headed by the State Secretary of Health & Welfare and consisting of Directors and Presidents of statewide educational, health, welfare and other youth services organizations. Assisting in the development of "systems of care" concept to promote integrated services for high-risk children and youth.

Sample additional activities:

- President, Michigan Mental Health Advocates for Children and Youth
- Co-Chair, Council on Children, Flint Department of Public Health
- Co-Founder, Michigan Residential Treatment Agencies Group
- Co-Author, Feasibility Study on Coordinating Children, Youth and Family Services
- Co-Founder, Foster Care Network, Children's Research Institute
- Member, Michigan Health and Welfare Agency Task Force on Out-of-Home Care
- Member, Flint School District Department of Special Education, Alternative Program Planning Committee
- Member, Flint Mayor's Advisory Committee on Robert Wood Johnson's Mental Health Initiative for Children and Youth
- Consultant (statewide, interagency planning and blended funding)

**Executive Assistant to the Director** (1986–1991)

Provided project, operations and financial management functions during a period of growth and dynamic organizational development.

- Participated in the creation, search and placement of three new senior positions: Director, Day Treatment; Director, Residential Treatment; and Medical Director.
- Created the agency's first private school program, serving 70 children and generating $1 million in self-sufficiency funding.
- Part of a team that developed new state public policy mandating mental health services for seriously emotionally disturbed children.

**Program Coordinator, Edgewood Learning Center** (1982–1986)

Provided program development, curriculum development, organizational development, funding and budgeting, staffing, and operational oversight.

- Raised $300,000 in private grants to establish new diagnostic and treatment program for learning disabled children. Also oversaw $200,000 renovation of agency facilities.
- Created the first scholarship program at Edgewood.

Prior:

Fordham Children's Center, Flint, Michigan
**Program Director / Chief Counselor**      1980–1982
**Counselor**      1978–1980

Department of Educational Administration, Michigan State University
**Graduate Assistant**      1975–1977

Devereux Foundation, Santa Barbara, California
**Counselor**      1973–1975

## EDUCATION

**M.A., Educational Administration**      1977
Michigan State University

**B.S., Elementary Education,** with honors      1973
University of Minnesota, Minneapolis

references and additional information provided on request

# C. Gordon Wingate

c/o Faculty Office
Graduate School of Taxation
Seattle State University
Seattle, Washington 98122
Office: (206) 555-7150
Residence: (206) 555-7751

---

## PROFILE

Founder and Dean Emeritus of the Graduate School of Taxation at Seattle State University (now the highest ranked school of taxation on the West Coast), over 20 years professional practice as CPA. Strong contacts in the financial and business community throughout Washington.

## EDUCATION

**M.B.A., Taxation**, Stanford University, 1973

**L.L.B., Law**, University of Colorado, 1960

**B.S., Accounting**, University of Colorado, 1957

## CREDENTIALS

**Certified Public Accountant**, States of Washington, California, Colorado

**Admitted to the Bar**, State Bars of Colorado, Missouri, California

## EXPERIENCE

**Dean Emeritus**, Graduate School of Taxation, Seattle State University, Seattle, Washington, 1992–Present. Represent the School of Taxation to professional groups, government organizations, and the financial/business community nationwide. Maintain relations with the Federal Tax Division of the American Institute of Certified Public Accountants and the Tax Section of the American Bar Association. Also serve on various committees within these two groups. Act as a liaison to various tax groups in Washington, D.C., on behalf of SSU's School of Taxation.

**President**, Wingate Accountancy Corporation, Seattle, Washington, 1969–1992. Started this firm as a sole proprietorship. Built the business into a highly profitable professional corporation with three additional CPAs and two paraprofessional staff. Practice focused on two large family groups, each with assets in the high eight figures. Provided these groups with accounting, tax planning and preparation, financial and investment services. Other business consisted of tax and accounting services for attorneys, physicians, dentists and their professional practices. Sold the practice in 1992 to Laventhol & Horwath.

**Founder & Dean**, Graduate School of Taxation, Seattle State University, Seattle, Washington, 1969–1992. Organized this program as a degree option beginning in 1969 with two classes and 34 students. Within the first ten years the program grew to 150 classes with over 2000 students. We expanded to offerings in six locations, including Idaho and Oregon. This program is still the largest and most comprehensive graduate-level tax program in the United States. The final operating budget under my management was $3.2 million per annum.

## PRIOR EXPERIENCE

**Corporate Officer** and **Tax Advisor**, Stockton Grain Terminal, Puget Sound, Washington

**Accountant** and **Tax Advisor**, Fortney H. "Pete" Stark, San Francisco, California

**Associate Attorney**, Louis Krall, Esq., Seattle, Washington

**Tax Semi-Senior** and **Senior Accountant**, Arthur Andersen & Co., Denver, Colorado

## MILITARY

**U.S. Navy**, 1952–1954

## PROFESSIONAL AFFILIATIONS

Member, American Institute of Certified Public Accountants, Federal Tax Division

Member, American Bar Association, Tax Section

Member, American Accounting Association

Member, Washington State Society of Certified Public Accountants

Member, Seattle Estate Planning Council

Member, Former President, Ex-Officio Member of the Board, Alumni Association of the Graduate Tax Programs, Seattle State University (over 3000 active members)

## SOCIAL/FRATERNAL AFFILIATIONS

Member, Olympic Club, Seattle

Member, World Trade Club, Seattle

## HONORS

Outstanding Graduate, Graduate School of Business, Stanford University, 1990

Outstanding Alumnus, University of Colorado, 1985

## PROFESSIONAL ACTIVITIES

Member of the Board, Pacific Steel & Supply, San Leandro, California, 1972–Present. Corporate Director and Chairman of the Audit Committee.

Founding Member, Tax Transactions Advisory Board, Commerce Clearing House (CCH), Chicago, Illinois, 1983–Present. This Board is presently involved in creating a whole new tax service for CCH.

## REFERENCES

Provided on request.

# MAI LI ZHANG, Ph.D.

*Curriculum Vitae*

*Office:*
The University of Vermont
Department of CSEE
Burlington, Vermont 05405
(802) 555-2656

*Residence:*
4332 Oak Knoll Road
Williston, Vermont 05495
(802) 555-6879
zhang3@uvm.edu

## PROFESSION

Research and Teaching Professor

## EXPERTISE

VLSI, Computer Architecture, Computer Arithmetic

## SYNOPSIS

Graduate and undergraduate professor with eight years experience as faculty member and two years as teaching assistant. Research emphasis currently in areas of VLSI (particularly low-power) design and computer arithmetic, with results of significantly increased processing speed and reduced circuit size. Rare ability to apply theoretical thinking to solve practical application problems. See publications listed below.

## EDUCATION

JOHNS HOPKINS UNIVERSITY
**Ph.D. Electrical Engineering and Computer Science**     1989
**M.S.E. Electrical Engineering and Computer Science**     1986

McGILL UNIVERSITY
**B.Eng. Electrical Engineering** (with distinction)     1983
  Honours Program
  University Scholar

## TEACHING EXPERIENCE

UNIVERSITY OF VERMONT
**Assistant Professor**     1995 to present

DREXEL UNIVERSITY
**Assistant Professor**     1989 to 1995
**Instructor**     1988 to 1989

JOHNS HOPKINS UNIVERSITY
**Research Assistant** to S.R. Kosaraju     1986 to 1988
**Teaching Assistant** to G. Masson, S.R. Kosaraju, V. Sigillito     1983 to 1986

Eight years teaching as faculty member, with two years as teaching assistant.

Instructed at both graduate and undergraduate levels.

*Advanced subjects taught:* digital design, computer architecture, algorithms and theory of computation, mathematics. Also: software, computer languages.

*– continued –*

## RESEARCH ACCOMPLISHMENTS

Created new design procedure for optimum-speed, one-level carry-skip adders, which were originally designed by Charles Babbage and recently found suitable for implementation in VLSI. Greatly improved adder speed by employing gate delays obtained through SPICE simulation. Incorporated gate delays/gate load dependency, contrary to assumption employed by a research team in Grenoble (reference A. Guyot, et. al., "A Way to Build Efficient Carry-Skip Adders," IEEE Transactions on Computers, Oct. 91) which produced adders slower than optimum.

Presented findings (excluding simulation) at the *IEEE International Symposium on Computer Arithmetic*, Grenoble, France, 1995. (Following publication includes discussion of simulation.) M. Zhang, "Designing Optimum One-Level Carry-Skip Adders." Accepted for publication, pub. date pending, *IEEE Transactions on Computers*.

Invented new variant of two-level carry-skip adder: adder sections utilize unimodal rather than bimodal blocks, without increased complexity. M. Zhang, "Accelerated Two-Level Carry-Skip Adders: A Very Fast Type of Adders." Accepted for publication, pub. date pending, *IEEE Transactions on Computers*.

Presented what is presumed to be the first mathematical theory of low-power VLSI design, a rare research paper in this ground-breaking field. Devised first major improvement on D.A. Huffman's classic state assignment procedure for fast, race-free sequential circuits (M.I.T. RLE Tech. Report, 1955), substantially reducing circuit size without sacrificing speed. Result has modern application in low-power VLSI design.

Reference *Proceedings of the 1995 Conference on Information Sciences and Systems.* Experimental evidence and state assignment procedure appears in M. Zhang and A. Andreou, "A State Assignment Approach to Low-Power Synchronous/Asynchronous VLSI Design." Submitted to *IEEE Transactions on Computers*, publication acceptance date pending.

Improved the speed of Lynch and Swartzlander's Redundant Cell Adder, one of the fastest existing adders, the floating-point adder in RISC processor Am29050. Replaced equal-length Manchester carry chains by variable length chains. Currently using SPICE to fine tune the design. M. Zhang, "An Improved Redundant Cell Adder." (in progress)

Invented the first feasible algorithm which calculated whether surface-mount ICs have leads whose lengths are even enough to be mounted onto a circuit board without solder faults. Prior quality control method consisted of manual or part-manual methods. Winner, Drexel University's President's Award, 1994. (With W. Dowling and O. Ekdal.)

Developed robotics algorithms with linear running time rather than quadratic time or greater. (Improvement on algorithms of J. Hopcoft, et. al., "On the Movement of Robot Arms in Two-Dimensional Bounded Regions." *SIAM Journal on Computing*, Vol. 14, No. 2, 1989.) *Journal of Computer and System Science*, 1990, with S.R. Kosaraju, thesis advisor.

Solved an open problem posed in M. Shamos's thesis, "Computational Geometry," which gave name to the field of Computational Geometry. *Information Processing Letters*, Vol. 16, 1987.

## PATENT

U.S. Patent (Pending): "A Fast Method for Coplanarity: Improving the Efficiency of Chip Quality Control." Official filing date: May 3, 1995.

## AWARDS

National Science Foundation, June 1995
    Sponsorship offered for paper presentation in France.
Drexel's President's Award, 1994

## PUBLICATIONS

M. Zhang, "Accelerated Two-Level Carry-Skip Adders: A Type of Very Fast Adders." Accepted for publication, publication date pending, *IEEE Transactions on Computers.*

M. Zhang, "Designing Optimum One-Level Carry-Skip Adders." Accepted for publication, publication date pending, *IEEE Transactions on Computers.*

M. Zhang, "Designing Optimum Carry-Skip Adders." Presented at the *IEEE International Symposium on Computer Arithmetic,* Grenoble, France, 1995.

M. Zhang, "An Improved Redundant-Cell Adder." Submitted to *IEEE Transactions on Computers,* publication accepted, date pending.

M. Zhang and A. Andreou, "A State Assignment Approach to Low-Power Synchronous/Asynchronous VLSI Design." Submitted to *IEEE Transactions on Computers,* publication accepted, date pending.

M. Zhang and A. Andreou, "On a General Design Principle for Low-Power Digital VLSI Circuits." Presented at the *Conference on Information Sciences and Systems,* Baltimore, Maryland, March 1995.

M. Zhang, "Motions of a Short-Linked Robot Arm in a Square." *Discrete and Computational Geometry,* Vol. 7, No. 1, 1996.

M. Zhang and S.R. Kosaraju, "Algorithms for Robot Arm Movements." *Journal of Computer and System Sciences,* Vol. 32, No. 1, February 1990, pp. 136–153.

M. Zhang, "Traveling Salesman Cycles Are Not Always Subgraphs of Voronoi Duals." *Information Processing Letters,* Vol. 16, 1987.

M. Zhang, "A Geometric Proof of Shannon's Result Using Continuous Mathematics." Presented at the *Conference on Information Sciences and Systems,* Baltimore, Maryland, March 1995.

M. Zhang, "Distributed Selection with Limited Memory." Presented at the *Conference on Information Sciences and Systems,* Princeton, New Jersey, March 1990.

M. Zhang and S.R. Kosaraju, "Algorithms for Robot Arm Movements: Improving the Efficiency of Chip Quality Control." Presented at the *Conference on Information Sciences and Systems,* Princeton, New Jersey, March 1988.

M. Zhang, W. Dowling, and O. Ekdal, "A Fast Algorithm for Coplanarity." Winner of Drexel's President's Award, 1994, Drexel Symposium on Scientific Research.

M. Zhang, "Reaching a Point with an Unanchored Robot Arm in a Square." Submitted to journal *Algorithmica.*

M. Zhang, "A Linear-Time, Near-Optimum-Length Triangulation Algorithm for Convex Polygons." Submitted to *Journal of Computer and System Sciences.*

M. Zhang, " A Lower Bound on the Path Length of Binary Trees." *ACM SIGACT News,* Vol. 19, No. 2, Summer 1990.

## ADDITIONAL

Additional details on research gladly provided by mail, fax, or telephone.

Fluent in English, Mandarin, Cantonese, Thai. Conversational proficiency in German.

U.S. citizen.

# MARTA WILLIAMS

7691 Exeter Lane
Sudbury, Massachusetts 01776

Office main line: (617) 555-8800
Office direct line: (617) 555-8779
marta@id.adesign.edu
Residence: (508) 555-7821

## PROFESSION

**Interior Design Education**

**Education Administration**

## HIGHLIGHTS

**Academy of Art & Design**, Boston, Massachusetts, 1987–Present
**Founding Director, Interior Design Department**

Designed, organized, and originated this interior design department as a rigorous four-year program culminating in the bachelor of fine arts degree. Developed the department to 26 instructors and over 300 students in the major. Recruited and retained a faculty of top professionals, all outstanding architects and interior designers currently in practice. Students come from all over the world, 80% from outside Massachusetts. Guide curriculum development, set standards, set departmental policy on an ongoing basis. Plan and administer $500,000 annual budget exclusive of facilities.

Graduates of the program find employment with renowned interior design firms, with architects, in the space planning departments of major corporations, with facilities management corporations, and in the lighting and furniture design industries. The Academy hosts the NCIDQ exam semiannually. Students win IBD- and ASID-sponsored national and regional competitions on a regular basis.

Obtained F.I.D.E.R. provisional accreditation in minimum possible time (six years). Obtained full accreditation in just ten years. F.I.D.E.R. now rates the program one of the top baccalaureate interior design programs in North America.

*Additional Activities*:
- Chairman, IDEC 1995 National Conference
- ASID Teacher of the Year, 1992, California Peninsula Chapter
- Keynote Speaker, 1994 Dallas Winter Home Furnishings Market
- Featured Speaker, 1993 Dallas Winter Home Furnishings Market
- Professional Member, Interior Design Educators Council
- Educational Affiliate Member, American Society of Interior Designers

**Bloomingdale's,** New York, New York, 1973–1983
**Consultant – Designer**

Traveled throughout the country giving interior design presentations in 29 stores. Instructed sales staff in "Decorating Basics and Principles" to improve their ability to market the company's home furnishing products. Planned, organized, and appeared at special events and shows, speaking directly to the consumer.

**Design Trends, Inc.,** Sudbury, Massachusetts, 1973–1987
**President**

Headed an interior design firm which completed 150 major projects ranging from commercial to luxury residential, with a specialty in medical office interiors.

– *continued* –

## EXPERTISE

### Specialist on the use of color

- The Color Connection in Interior Design
- How to Use Color as a Sales Tool
- Psychological Effects of Color in a Medical Environment
- Psychological Effects of Color in Dining Areas
- Color & Fabric
- Color in the Modern Home
  (and similar topics)

Emphasis on environmental effects of color, use of color as a sales tool in selling interior design services and products, and use of color as a rationale for comprehensive, integrated redesign of existing spaces.

Additional expertise in design of medical offices: time-motion analysis, space layout and design, psychological effect of colors, as well as art, fixtures and furnishings. Hospitals, dental offices, clinics, multiuse medical buildings. Also, design of exclusive homes for a discriminating and international clientele.

## TEACHING

### Instructor & Lecturer

- Academy of Art & Design, 1987–Present
- Director, Training Seminars, WESCO Fabrics, 1983–1987
- University of Massachusetts, 1976–1980 (Boston, Amherst)
- Solon Ponds Junior College, 1981
- Tustin School District, Adult Education Program, 1976–1979
- Santa Ana Junior College District, 1970–1972

## EDUCATION

**M.A.** candidate, **Educational Administration**, ongoing
U.S. International University, Boston, Massachusetts

**M.A., Interior Design**
The Pratt Institute, New York

**B.A., Fine Art History**
Indiana University, Bloomington

## REFERENCES

Additional information provided on request. Please keep this information confidential.

# Patricia Gail O'Hara

*Curriculum Vitae*

187 Middleton Lane
Danbury, Connecticut 06512

Direct Line: (203) 555-2766
Message: (203) 555-8476

---

## STRENGTHS

- **Programmatic and Instructional Design & Implementation**
- **Executive Management**
- **Consulting**

Expertise in progressive education, early childhood development, collaborative administration, faculty supervision and development, community involvement. Expertise in inner-city education and minority issues.

## EDUCATION

Xavier University     Cincinnati, Ohio
**M.A., Developmental Psychology**    1977
**M.Ed., Early Childhood Education**    1976
**B.S., Education**    Phi Beta Kappa    1976

Columbia University     New York, New York
Doctoral Candidate in Developmental Psychology ongoing

Dartmouth College     Hanover, New Hampshire
Early Admission Program    1972–1973

## ADMINISTRATIVE & LEADERSHIP EXPERIENCE

St. Agnes School     Hartford, Connecticut
**Principal**    1990–1996

Provided leadership to administration, teaching, curriculum, and budgeting at an inner-city school with a tradition of authoritarian organizational structure and a large percentage of at-risk students. Introduced a collaborative structure involving faculty, parents, and children in virtually every aspect of school life. (K–8, 180 students, 20 teachers, consultants and staff.)

Co-created, along with the faculty, students, and parents, the following programs:

- Family Group Program, a daily meeting of a small group of students representing all grades (the children) headed by a parent (a teacher or administrator). This program was highly successful at creating a feeling of community and belonging within the school, providing a positive venue for conflict resolution, and most importantly, for modeling a functional, supportive family. We also created a support group for the "parents" to deal with their own issues of family which might surface.

- Boyz to Men, a program to bring African-American males into the school to interact with young African-American males, grades 4–8. This group provided positive role models, addressed sensitive topics related to being a successful black male in current times, and looked at the historical context of many of the prevailing attitudes toward African-American males.

- For Ladies Only, a program to provide a forum for girls in grades 6–8, dealing with sexual issues (especially teenage pregnancy and AIDS), respect for women, matriarchal concepts, and challenges to African-American women and families.

- Community Service Program, a program which we developed to introduce concepts of community service, empowerment, and to awaken the idea that we can make a difference in the world. Many of these students had no idea that they had gifts and talents that were needed and valued by others.

- Strong and diversified on-site counseling, psychotherapy, evaluation, and general assistance program, coordinated with four outside agencies.

- Electives: Theatre, Art, Exploring Hartford, Journalism, grades 4–8.

Contributed to and collaborated on creating a new long-term vision for the school. The school created its own supportive atmosphere, earned media acclaim, and continues to provide a viable alternative model for addressing the needs of the urban poor.

Convent of the Sacred Heart  Boston, Massachusetts,  1984–1990
**Co-Head**  1986–1990

Brought a new image and concept to a school with a strong academic program but a reputation for a rather narrow focus. Worked with the faculty and the other administrators to achieve consensus on the goal of educating the whole child (as articulated through the concept of community service through programs which supported the child in making wise moral and ethical decisions) and in designing academic programs to meet students varying needs.

In effect the school became a very child-centered place which addressed and remediated difficult challenges, where curriculum was faculty-generated and collaboratively taught, and textbooks were deemphasized. A large portion of this faculty has since gone on to become instructional leaders and/or to pursue advanced degrees, and those that remain continue to support the program enthusiastically.

Enrollment reached a ten-year high and the accomplishments of the school were recognized in a 96% matriculation rate for students accepted.

**Head of the Middle/Upper Forms (5–8)**  1984–1986

Ensured consensus on and support of philosophical and instructional goals of the division, working closely with administrators, faculty, parents, and students.

Katherine Burge School  Boston, Massachusetts
**Head of Upper School (5–8)**  1983–1984

Provided teacher development, faculty liaison, evaluation and counseling of individual students, and coordination of curriculum and curriculum delivery.

Big City Montessori School  Hartford, Connecticut
**Director**  1980–1983

Designed new school, built enrollment from zero to 105 children (toddler through elementary grades, and including extended care programs). Interpreted and designed curriculum according to Montessori principles. Developed intensive and ongoing staff in-service training. Designed the parent participation component to the school.

## CONSULTING, CURRICULUM & STAFF DEVELOPMENT EXPERIENCE

University of Hartford, Department of Education  Hartford, Connecticut
Teacher Training Program  1986–1988
**Lecturer**

Progressive teaching methods for mathematics, curriculum and child development, environmental design. Intern supervision. Consulting and support to individual students/staff.

American Montessori Society  New York, New York
**Educational Consultant**  1983–1987

Development, evolution and supervision of elementary programs. Acted as a consultant to schools setting up elementary programs.

East River Montessori School     New York, New York
**Program Consultant**     1983–1984

Conducted four independent research studies: Project for the Bureau of Education for Handicapped under grant from H.E.W. Curriculum development project in cognitive areas of mathematics and language for ages 2–5. Designed diagnostic developmental assessment tool. Did preliminary research on implications for alcohol-compromised children in language acquisition.

The Caedmon School     New York, New York
**Coordinator**     1982–1984

Curriculum development and revision for National Association of Independent Schools evaluation.

Beaver College, Graduate School of Education     Philadelphia, Pennsylvania
**Adjunct Professor**     1982–1983

Intensive teacher training program. Taught courses in development of mathematical reasoning and language related to early reading.

Virginia Commonwealth University     Richmond, Virginia
**Seminar Director**     1981

Seminar on designing developmentally appropriate curriculum for the early elementary years, a project under the auspices of the Early Childhood Association.

Xavier University     Cincinnati, Ohio
**Advisory Committee**     1980–1981

Evaluated and advised Department on educational reform.

Cincinnati Public Schools     Cincinnati, Ohio
**Program Development**     1975–1980

Collaborated on the design and implementation of the first public Montessori alternative school in the United States, which won national acclaim and was in part a catalyst to the new educational movement to public school alternative education. This program was designed to create voluntary integration and to abolish need for busing to meet federal mandates. Joint funding provided by the Jergens Foundation, N.A.A.C.P., and federal grants.

## CLASSROOM TEACHING

**Head Teacher**, Big City Montessori School     1980–1981

**Chair, Math, Sciences and Social Studies**, The Caedmon School     1978–1980

**Head Teacher**, The Richmond Montessori School     1977–1978

**Intern**, Xavier University Lab School     1976–1977

## RECENT COMMUNITY INVOLVEMENT

C.H.O.I.C.E. (Consortium of Hope for Outstanding Inner-city Education)
Chairwoman of the Board (support, advice, and funds development)

League of Women Voters
Member of the Board

## BIBLIOGRAPHY

Writings and lectures on education. List on request.

## REFERENCES

References and any additional information required will be provided on request.

# James "Jay" Cleckner

*Curriculum Vitae*

100 Cameron Avenue
Oakland, California 94605

Telephone/Message:
(510) 555-4562

---

## PROFILE

Internationally recognized lecturer and speaker on education and public schools. Topics include year-round schools, troubled schools, multiethnic and urban schools, computer education, learning English by computer, ESL, corporate education, and new roles for business in American education.

## EDUCATION

**University of San Francisco**    San Francisco, California
**M.A., Education**    1983

**Arizona State University**    Tempe, Arizona
**M.A.E., History**    1971

**Arizona State University**    Tempe, Arizona
**B.A., History**    1959

## SPEAKING EXPERIENCE

**I.B.M. — Educational Information Services**    HQ: Atlanta, Georgia
**Speaker** and **Ambassador**    1990–Present

Traveled and lectured on educational topics as part of this I.B.M. public service program with the (very indirect) goal of promoting the use of computers in education. Spoke to teachers' groups, principals, superintendents, school boards, college groups, and print and broadcast media in the United States and abroad, including 32 states, ten nations, and two worldwide satellite broadcasts.

Special strengths: Writing to Read "$W_2R$," Writing Tree, ESL, Bilingual Education by Computer, Year-Round Schools, Educational Trends, Historical Future, Computers in Education, School Management, Parliamentary Procedure. Also worked on numerous other topics.

**U.S. Department of Education**    Washington, D.C.
**Lecturer** and **Advisor**    off and on 1977–1996

Traveled throughout the United States explaining the benefits and logistics of Year-Round Schools. During this period YRE schools increased tenfold. Also traveled to other countries as representative of U.S. Department of Education (Canada, Mexico, Jamaica, Puerto Rico, USVI, Bahamas, and the U.K.), speaking on diverse topics.

**California State Department of Education**    Sacramento, California
**Consultant**    1983–1991

Advisor on Year-Round Education—"YRE is a revenue generating educational concept whose time is overdue"—and numerous other topics.

## SCHOOLS EXPERIENCE

**Oakland Public Schools**    Oakland, California
**Educator** and **Principal**    1977–1997

**Scottsdale Public Schools**    Scottsdale, Arizona
**Educator** and **Administrator**    1964–1975

## COLLEGE TEACHING

**University of California**     Berkeley, California
**Special Adjunct to the Director of Off-Campus Programs**     1981–1985

**Arizona State University**     Tempe, Arizona
**Instructor, Department of History**     1975–1976

## ADDITIONAL EDUCATION

National Year-Round Conference     annually 1987–1996

Postgraduate Studies in Education, University of San Francisco     1984–1989

NEA Verbal Skills Conference in Negotiations     1982

CTA Seminar for Collective Bargaining     1981

NEA Seminar for Contract Negotiations, USC     1979

Summer Program for Doctoral Candidates, King's College, Cambridge University, U.K.     1971 and 1975

Schiffs Executive School (topics: public relations, budgeting, labor negotiations), Mendham, New Jersey     1963

## MILITARY CAREER

**Adjutant** and **Director, U.S. Army Reserve School**     1977–1973

**U.S. Army Intelligence** (Vietnam)     1976–1977

**U.S.A.K.**     1964–1976

**U.S. Army** (Korea)     1959–1964

**Arizona National Guard**     1955–1959

## MILITARY DEGREE

**Command and General Staff College**     Fort Leavenworth, Kansas
**Master in Military Science**     1980

Three Additional Specialty Schools (list on request)

## RECENT ENGAGEMENTS (partial list)

"Writing to Read: The Way to the Future in Education," IBM Computer In-service, Carson City, Nevada, Dec. 4–5, 1996.

"Year-Round Education: The Future for Today's Schools," Northern California Year-Round Conference, Santa Clara, California, Oct. 9–10, 1996.

"Pacifica Health Education in the Public School: Saving the Health of Today's Child," Western States Dental School Program Conference, Sept. 21–22, 1996.

"The Future of Education in America: Failure or Success?" Educator's Conference of the Phoenix Area, Wigwam, Litchfield Park, June 22–25, 1996.

"Report for the Minister of Education on Development of Year-Round and/or Longer School Years," Department of Education in Lisbon, Portugal, Mar. 21–23, 1996.

"Bilingual Education and the Use of Computers to Teach English as a Second Language," University of London, England, Mar. 17–19, 1996.

"English as a Second Language Through Technology," Educational Conference of Japanese Educators, Tokyo, Japan, Nov. 17–19, 1995.

Lecturer and Delegate to the Singapore Educational Innovation and Technology Conference (INNOTECH), Oct. 14–18, 1995.

Guest to the Offices of the French Minister of Education, Paris, France, Sept. 3–5, 1995.

"The Future in Education is the Computer's," (Public School System), IBM Lecture, Seattle, Washington, Nov. 11–12, 1995.

"The Computer is the Greatest Invention in Education since the Lead Pencil," Department of Education, Harvard University, 1995.

"Tomorrow's Leadership in Schools," A Public Schools Conference, Santa Rosa, California, Mar. 24, 1995.

"A Bilingual School in the Year-Round Plan," National Year-Round Conference, San Diego, California, Feb. 13–15, 1995.

Main Speaker and Lecturer at the Southeast Asian Ministers of Education Organization Regional Center, Manila, Philippines, Nov. 12–15, 1994.

Consultant and IBM Representative to the Thailand Government on Computer Education at the Primary Level, Aug. 27–31, 1994.

"Writing to Read Program for Hong Kong School Systems," Guest of the Royal Crown Government and IBM, Aug. 20–27, 1994.

"Educational Changes in Approaches to Basic Teaching Methods," Guest of the Royal Government of Malaysia, Aug. 19, 1994.

"Twenty-First Century Education: An Educational Revolution," Asia/South Pacific Area Education Conference, Singapore, Aug. 14–19, 1994.

"The New Approach to Reading," Educational Conference on Reading, University of Sydney, Australia, Aug. 8–9, 1994.

"Evaluation of the Administrative System," Australian Educational Executive Forum, Gold Coast, Queensland, Aug. 10–12, 1994.

"The Future of Western Education," Australian EXPO, Brisbane, Australia, Aug. 13–14, 1994.

"Development of an Urban/Rural Educational System on Today's India," New Delhi. India, July 27–29, 1994.

"What is New in Today's Urban Schools That Can Be Changed," State and Federal Conference on Education, C.A.L., Mar. 21–24, 1994.

"How to Rebuild a School for Today's Society," National Year-Round Conference, Los Angeles, California, Jan. 31–Feb. 8, 1994.

# KENNETH H. HUFF

*Curriculum Vitae*

315 Oceanside Parkway
Malibu, California 90265

Office: (310) 555-4052
Residence: (310) 555-0351

## SYNOPSIS

Education administrator with extensive training in management, both interpersonal and financial/analytical. Record of accomplishment with responsibility for school and staff administration, curriculum development and direction, community relations, and special programs. Areas of strength include education of minority students, education of language-impacted students, and all issues affecting urban schools.

One of the pioneers of the Year-Round School concept to maximize utilization of facilities and resources. Through education and outreach, was successful in introducing this concept with the support of parents and the community at large.

Strengths: written and oral communications; outreach, liaison, and coordinating functions; program development and implementation; budget development and control; leadership and direction for curriculum.

## EDUCATION

**M.A., Educational Administration**, University of California, Irvine, 1987

**B.A., Political Science-International Relations**, University of Southern California, 1978

## CREDENTIALS

**Administrative Services Credential**, University of California, Irvine, 1987

**Standard Elementary Teaching Credential**, University of Southern California, 1978

## EXPERIENCE

Los Angeles Unified School District, Los Angeles, California, 1979–Present
**Principal**, Garfield Year-Round School, Los Angeles, California, 1993–Present

Guide and direct all aspects of the school's administration and instruction. Delegate through a staff of assistant principal, program facilitators, resource teachers, TSA's, and educational consultants. Also in charge of food service, grounds, maintenance, and security staff. Full budget responsibility, as well as administration of various grants.

Achievements:

- Converted Garfield into a Year-Round School (YRS), including massive public relations effort and resolution of a battery of scheduling and interfacing problems. (See above.) Garfield is now considered a model YRS and is studied by other districts and states considering the YRS concept.
- Gained marked improvements in parental approval as measured by district surveys. Enjoy a high level of participation by parents, with outstanding support from the PTA, volunteers, and advisory councils.
- Presided over largest series of grant awards in school's history: U.S. Title VII, University of California, C-TIIP, AB 803, Sterling Community Service Foundation, Marcus Foster Educational Institute, Project SEED, Centro Juventud, etc. Just selected for Los Angeles County Office of Education Grant to establish a teacher-training computer laboratory.
- Direct a strong bilingual education program, which was honored by a court-ordered auditor as a model for the district. Also selected for a Title VII grant for the education of Southeast Asian students. Total monies for minority education at Garfield exceed $700,000 per fiscal year from both state and federal sources.
- Garfield has become an acknowledged center for Mentor Teachers. Also several Garfield teachers serve as consultants to textbook publishers and otherwise contribute to curriculum and teaching excellence.

**Principal**, Washington Elementary School, Hamstead, California, 1990–1991
Achievements:
- Selected by the community and staff as principal of this 97% minority school. Maintained the full respect, cooperation and support of parents and the community.
- Gained recognition as a model school for maximizing utilization of state and federal programs. Its written instructional plan was used as a model throughout the Los Angeles School District.
- Became a part-time consultant to the State Department of Education due to Washington's stature as flagship school and premier model for the Urban Education Project. Traveled throughout the state explaining the success of the school.
- Maintained strong curriculum and instructional program, winning district contests and placing often in the math olympics, district oratorial competitions, etc.

**Project Director**, State & Federal Programs, LAUSD, Los Angeles, California, 1988–1990
Achievements:
- Supervised and administered funded personnel and projects at different school sites. Monitored activities in detail, and ensured all funds were expended according to rigid guidelines as published by the funding agencies. These funding and administration efforts required advanced *statistical*, *budget*, and *analytical* skills.
- Served as a consultant and expert on proposal and fund writing, assisting many district committees with funding efforts. Included extensive program development concurrent to seeking the funding to implement these efforts. Projects included full range of testing, instructional, materials, environmental, and staffing needs.
- Coordinated successfully with diverse interest groups of parents and school district personnel.

**Teacher**, Los Angeles and Oakland, 1976–1987
Achievements:
- Many, many satisfying accomplishments. Details available on request.

## AFFILIATIONS

Vice President for Programs, Phi Delta Kappa, University of California Chapter

Member, United Administrators of the Los Angeles Schools

Member, Association for Supervision and Curriculum Development

Member, Greenpeace

## REFERENCES

Provided on request.

# KENNETH H. HUFF

315 Oceanside Parkway
Malibu, California 90265

Office: (310) 555-4052
Residence: (310) 555-0351

---

## ADDENDUM

### HONORS:

- Designated "Exemplary Principal" by LAUSD Superintendent. Represented LAUSD at Pacific Telesis Foundation's Managing Excellence in Education Conference, 1996
- Appointed to District Collective Bargaining Team, 1996
- Participant in Pacific Bell's "Influence Management" Management Training Course
- Appointed to Management Council, LAUSD, 1994–1995
- Selected as Recruiter for Teachers, 1994–1995
- Appointed "Peer Principal," Urban Education Project, 1993
- Chair, Urban Education Project, Sub-Committee on State and District Regulations, 1991
- Participant, Urban Education Project (California State Dept. of Ed.), 1990
- Appointed to Writing Sub-Committee, SOAR Program, Malibu Service Foundation Proposal, 1993
- Appointed as "Mentor Principal" in the Mentor/Mentoree Program, LAUSD, 1993
- Appointed to Elementary Schools SB 813 Standards of Achievement Committee for Reading/Language Arts, 1993
- Appointed to the Committee for Organization of Summer Schools, LAUSD, 1993
- Elected to office of Secretary, Principals Advisory Council, 1992
- Elected to the Principals Advisory Council, 1991
- Selected for Board of Education Presentation on the Textbook Needs for Uniform Curriculum Policy, 1990
- Selected to participate in Bank of America's Management Training Program, 1990
- Appointed to represent the LAUSD on Proposal Selection Committee for Bank of America's "Educational Initiatives Program," 1990
- Elected to Board of Directors, OEA, 1989
- Designated "Professionals Plus Teacher," 1987–1988
- Training Teacher, UCLA, 1978, 1984–1986

# LOIS A. KROEMEYER, Ed.D.

*Curriculum Vitae*

4218 South Mountain View Drive
Cascade, Montana 59421

Office/Cascade Consolidated Schools: (406) 555-7700
Residence/private message: (406) 555-7493

---

## EDUCATION

Harvard University, Cambridge, Massachusetts
**Doctor of Education**, 1991

Emphases: Administration, Planning, Social Policy
Urban School Administration

Dissertation: *Gladiators and Heroes: A Comparative Analysis of the Effect of Competitive Athletic and Chess Club Programs on Participant and Schoolwide Attendance and Academic Performance Using New York City Public Schools as a Model.*

Harvard University, Cambridge, Massachusetts
**Master of Arts in Education**, 1989

Emphases: Administration, Planning, Social Policy

University of San Francisco, San Francisco, California
**Master of Arts in Educational Administration**, 1982

Emphases: Leadership and Organization
Multicultural Education

Thesis: *A Survey of Potential Tort Liability Practices of Male Physical Education Teachers in Selected Montana High Schools.*

University of Missouri, Kansas City, Missouri
**Bachelor of Arts in Physical Education**, 1970

Emphases: Social Studies
Physical Education

## EXPERIENCE

CASCADE CONSOLIDATED SCHOOL DISTRICT     Cascade, MT
**Superintendent of Schools**     1992–Present

Provide executive leadership to finance, personnel, curriculum, facilities, and extracurricular programs for a K–12 school district, including responsibility for students, teachers, resource teachers, athletic programs, bus garage and fleet, physical plant, maintenance and support personnel, 1565 students drawn from the county seat, proximate towns, and four rural busing districts (high school only).

*sample contributions:*

Conceived, designed, and promoted a consortium of five area public school districts to share specialty resources, including psychologist, speech-audiologist, learning disabilities diagnostics specialist. First president of this consortium and continuing president for last three years.

Commissioned complete energy use analysis of all facilities. Banned delayed maintenance from district long-range planning. Relandscaped the high school and football field, built bus barn and garage.

Surveyed recent alumni education and career patterns, identifying need for more preparation for local work force. Researched, planned, and ran a successful bond levy generating $1.2 million to expand vocational education in high school and junior high. Also hosted a pilot program to deliver vo-tech classes to 60 rural schools via satellite. Obtained classes in job skills, interviewing, career surveys, etc., which individual schools would not have been able to provide otherwise.

Wrote and won grant from the U.S. Department of Energy to use the school as a test site for wind power generation. Had this written into the curriculum as a didactic tool in all grades' science programs.

Wrote drug prevention and early intervention program sponsored by the federal government, a $36,000, two-year, staff-development exercise located at the University of Montana in Missoula. Guided district policy on drugs during a period of reappraisal away from strictly penal approaches and toward family involvement, early identification, and intervention.

Spent two weeks in China and one week in Russia/Ukraine as part of a delegation of Montana business and civic leaders.

## MOUNTAIN PLAINS EDUCATION AND ECONOMIC DEVELOPMENT PROGRAM   Glasgow, MT
**Program Director (Interim)**   1991–1992

Brought in to fill out the term of Warner Enelow, appointed undersecretary of education. Managed one of the most innovative programs in human services history, recruiting (volunteer) long-term welfare recipient families from five Western states, providing academic and job-skills training in an intensive program setting, with housing and leisure services for the entire family group. Oversaw classroom, drug and alcohol, sports, recreation, and research programs, as well as budget, physical plant, staffing.

San Francisco Unified School District (SFUSD)   San Francisco, CA
**Supervisor of High Schools**   1983–1987

Reported directly to the Assistant Superintendent, indirectly to the Superintendent. Supervised high school principals. Served as the liaison and administrator between high schools and district management. Participated in districtwide special projects. Served as high school office representative to the Division of Integration.

SFUSD had 62,443 students — 19,147 in the High School Division at 18 high schools including 7 alternative schools, 4 continuation schools, the court schools, and the ROP (Regional Occupational Program). High school aggregate budget was approximately $42 million per annum.

*special projects:*

Negotiated staffing allocations with schools, sat in on district budgetary meetings, interfaced with the Department of Business and Fiscal Services. Co-prepared budgets for classified and certificated staffing, and the High School Department's administrative office. Concurrently served as High School Office liaison for the $22 million earthquake rehabilitation project at John O'Connell Technical High School.

Co-Chair, Planning Committee, SFUSD Restructuring Schools Project. Co-authored the three-phase implementation plan. Served as one of the district liaisons for this voluntary transition to site-based management.

Collaborated in the writing of article 21, the shared decision-making component of the SFUSD-UESF contract.

Administrative Representative, SFUSD Restructuring Council. Oversaw the restructuring initiative as it was implemented in the district.

Co-Chair, Safety and Security Advising Committee. Coordinated with Director of Buildings and Grounds and the San Francisco Police Department, and including neighborhood groups and representatives of three unions (teachers/ classified/ administrators). Three recent accomplishments: (1) initiated yearly training program for security aides for all sites, (2) reinforced application of the *Student Behavior Handbook* as a standard, (3) created security aide handbook with "expectations" concerning event and response.

Supervisor, Support Services, J. Eugene McAteer High School. Co-developed a site plan to improve schoolwide academic achievement. Targeted areas: (1) student performance, (2) curriculum, (3) counseling services, (4) parent involvement, (5) staff development, (6) administrative procedures, (7) budget allocations.

Supervisor, Support Services, Woodrow Wilson High School. Co-developed a site plan to improve the performance of "at risk" and underachieving students.

SFUSD Representative, Youth and Education Committee, City & County of San Francisco Human Rights Commission, focusing on education and youth issues.

**Principal,** International Studies Academy      1980–1983

Assigned to take over and turn around the International Studies Academy high school, which had had four principals in one year. Took it from a bottom performer to consistently in top five in the city.

Increased foreign language studies from two to five languages. Linked the school to the San Francisco community through an internship program. Developed ties to the greater international and multiethnic community of the San Francisco Bay Area.

Co-wrote magnet school grant, winning $900,000 federal grant for curriculum development, equipment, materials, and programs. Brought in state-of-the-art computer program. Developed international library and language lab.

**Assistant Principal,** Horace Mann Academic Middle School, 1978–1980

Assistant Principal at one of the first schools to be targeted in court-ordered consent decree desegregation plan. Facilitated smooth implementation with SFUSD Division of Integration, and representatives of the NAACP, SFUSD Office of Student Assignment, parents, teachers, faculty, and the public.

## CLASSROOM EXPERIENCE

**Teacher**      1971–1978

San Francisco Unified School District, San Francisco, California
Horace Mann Middle School
**Teacher,** ESL Bilingual Teacher, Bilingual Counselor, Bilingual Department Chair, Microcomputer Resource Teacher, 1976–1978

San Diego County Department of Education, San Diego, California
Migrant Education Program, Escondido Union and Carlsbad Unified School Districts
**Teacher, Program Coordinator, K–12,** 1975–1976

Peace Corps — Escuela Superior del Profesorado, Tegucigalpa, Honduras
**Teacher,** Phys. Ed., 1974–1975

Escondido Union High School District, Escondido, California
Orange Glen High School, San Marcos High School
**Teacher,** History, Psychology, Phys. Ed., 1971–1974

## CREDENTIALS

Montana Superintendent's Credential, Public School Administration

California Administrative Service Credential

California Life Teaching Credential

Montana Life Teaching Credential

California Bilingual Cross-Cultural Specialist Credential (Spanish)

California Bilingual Teaching Certificate of Competence (Spanish)

Applied Linguistics Certificate, San Diego State University

## SAMPLE PRESENTATIONS

"Montana as Tomorrow's World Leader: What the Information Age Really Means," Montana State Chamber of Commerce annual meeting.

"Leadership, Language, and Communication: Beyond Method," a participatory research and policy colloquium on leadership, socioeconomic change, and gender, Chiang Mai University (Chiang Mai, Thailand).

"Leadership and Inclusion: How Athletic Programs and Affinity Clubs Help Nonmembers," Harvard Department of Education presentation to NACE.

"An Overview of the SFUSD Model for Restructuring Schools," statewide pilot project.

"Creating a Shared Vision of the Future of San Francisco," San Francisco 2000.

"An International High School Model: Promise and Challenge," Bay Area Global Education Project Conference.

"Overview and Utilization of Integrated Software for Administrators," SFUSD.

"Computer Literacy Workshops for Staff Development of Teachers," SFUSD.

"Computer Education for ESL and Bilingual Students," CABE Conference.

"ESL Program Model for Identification, Placement, Monitoring, Exiting," D-Cal Inc.

## REFERENCES

Please see attached.

# Ruby Ausbrooks, Ed.D.

*Curriculum Vitae*

1336 Woodline Place
Bentonville, Arkansas 72712

Office: (501) 555-7703
Residence: (501) 555-0519

**EDUCATION**

**Ed.D.,** Secondary Education, 1994
University of Arkansas, Fayetteville

Dissertation: *Music As a Variable in the Classroom Environment: Effects of Music on Learning and Behavior in Two Classrooms for At-Risk Students*

**M.S.E.,** Secondary Education, 1986
University of Arkansas, Fayetteville

**B.A.,** Geography, 1974
University of Arkansas, Fayetteville

**HONORS**

Certificate in Recognition of Service to At-Risk Students
Arkansas State Board of Vocational Education, Little Rock, Nov. 9, 1989
Top Ranking, Dean's Honor List, Spring 1974
Outstanding Achievement in Geography Award
President, Gamma Theta Upsilon Honorary Geography Fraternity
Graduate Assistantship in Geography

**SUBJECTS**

Certified to teach **Social Studies, General Science, Biology.** Have developed curricula and taught diverse subject matters, including Reading, Writing Skills, Business, Economics, Sociology, Psychology, Career Education, Consumer Mathematics, Basic Mathematics, Art.

**EXPERIENCE**

NORTHWEST ARKANSAS REGIONAL COOPERATIVE, Springdale, Arkansas, February 1995
**Workshop Presenter**

Developed and presented a staff development workshop for principals and teachers on secondary classrooms for at-risk students. The curriculum was adapted in part from the Great Expectations teacher-training program—which has proved particularly successful in Oklahoma elementary schools serving underachieving, inner-city students—developed by Northeastern State University, Tahlequah, Oklahoma.

This workshop was framed to assist those Arkansas school districts complying with the new state mandate to design and open alternative education programs for at-risk students.

UNIVERSITY OF ARKANSAS, Fayetteville, Arkansas, Fall 1994, Spring 1995
**Guest Lecturer**

Presented classroom management and teaching techniques successful with at-risk students to groups of intern teachers.

ROGERS SCHOOL DISTRICT, Rogers, Arkansas, 7/80–Present

Note: In 1990, stepped back from Co-Director role to pursue a program of studies culminating in the doctoral degree and to expand speaking/consulting roles.

**Teacher/Curriculum Coordinator**, 7/91–Present
**Teacher**, 7/90–7/91
Benton County Alternative School, Bentonville, Arkansas

This school provides an innovative dropout prevention program in affiliation with nine area schools in five districts, which includes shared planning and decision-making, a partially integrated curriculum, cooperative learning, peer tutoring, small-group instruction, computer-assisted instruction, and individual tutoring.

Administrative duties include 1) intake, testing, and diagnostics on referred students, 2) supervision of school in absence of the Director, 3) preparation of annual reports to the participating schools and boards of education, and 4) grant writing.

(As Head Teacher, Co-Director, and Curriculum Coordinator, since 1980 I have been a principal writer or co-author for 36 grant proposals, 32 of which have been funded in amounts ranging from $1200 to $35,000.)

*Recent projects include:*

Initiated, structured, and won approval for a cooperative agreement with University of Arkansas, Fayetteville, by which the university provided equipment, staff training, and a graduate assistant to introduce alternative school students to communication and CD-Rom technologies (including Internet and CD-Rom encyclopedia).

In response to increase in Spanish-speaking residents in the area, designed and launched a course in Spanish language and Hispanic culture in which all students and teachers participated. As we had no bilingual teachers on staff, teachers and students learned together using tapes and adapted self-teaching guides.

In collaboration with a retired school superintendent, revised and integrated the Responsible Life Training personal development course throughout the curriculum. Material was adapted with permission from authors of the original course (T-training conducted in business and government organizations for executive-level personnel).

In collaboration with all staff members, reorganized the alternative education program to accommodate team teaching and cooperative learning, as well as small group instruction and individually paced study.

Used a thematic integration to meld language arts into the rest of the curriculum. Developed and/or adapted techniques for teaching language skills which are successful in classrooms with mixed grade levels, mixed learning styles, and various levels of ability.

Co-facilitated highly successful student productions of works by Shakespeare and Mark Twain, open to the general public, raising student esteem and the standing of the school in the community.

**Co-Director**, 7/82–7/90
Benton County Alternative School, Bentonville, Arkansas

Principal on-site administrator for cooperative alternative school with approximately 60 students. Coordinated closely with superintendents from five districts, and principals from nine cooperative schools.

Prepared budgets and grants. Provided program direction. Handled administration. Interviewed teacher applicants; trained and developed staff. Solved daily problems. Taught two classes per day. Represented the program to prospective students, parents and professional and civic organizations.

Worked with new teachers and aides who had no previous experience in classrooms comprised entirely of school-alienated or hostile youth. Organized staff development workshops, implemented daily staff meeting, provided guidance and support to new staff members until they became experts in presenting the school to the community and other educators.

Sample special project:

Co-wrote a grant for a Youth-in-Business Career Education Program which was fully funded as written. Students designed and launched a business enterprise. They made their own decisions, divided profits according to formulae, trained each succeeding class in how to run the business, and paid off their loan on schedule. Spoke by invitation to two community groups and to a state career education convention concerning this program.

**Main accomplishment:**

**During my tenure the average gains in reading and math skills, as shown by pre-enrollment and postseparation standardized tests, were two grade levels per year of enrollment, and one grade level per semester of enrollment.**

**Head Teacher**, Benton County Alternative School, 7/80–7/82

Taught daily classes of 10–20 students in grades 7–12 who were referred to the school as high-risk students. Provided remediation tutoring individually and in small groups. Provided new input to all areas of curriculum; supervision in absence of the director.

Sample accomplishment:

Alternative School science students were invited to participate in the local school's science fair. Our students won first place awards in three categories for the following projects: "How to Make your own Photocopier," "Teenage Suicide," and "Cancer Occurrence in Benton County." Other students won second place awards for "Pinhole Camera Photo Display," and "Model of a Solar Greenhouse." "Cancer Occurrence in Benton County" went on to win first place in the regional science fair.

BENTON COUNTY SUPERVISOR'S OFFICE, Bentonville, Arkansas, 9/78–6/80
**Teacher**
Benton County Alternative School, Siloam Springs

Taught daily classes. Developed and taught summer school program.

Sample accomplishment:

Alternative School science students won first place awards in three categories as the Siloam Springs Science Fair for the following projects: "Making Methane from Garbage," "Pinhole Camera Photography," and "Fossils of Benton County." A second place award was given to a comparative study of natural and artificial light. These award-winning students had been extreme disciplinary problems in their home schools.

ARKANSAS STATE YOUTH SERVICES CENTER, Wrightsville, Arkansas, 9/76–5/78
**Teacher**

This was a residential rehabilitation/education facility for boys under 18 who were tried in juvenile court for felonies. Provided individual remediation tutoring in phonics and small group classes in science. Developed techniques to teach science to nonreading students. Tutored in the only lockup facility in the state for youth accused of violent crimes.

Co-founded the school newspaper. Wrote a proposal for horticulture project to teach horticulture and improve physical environs of the school.

GEOGRAPHY DEPARTMENT, University of Arkansas, Fayetteville, Fall 1973
**Instructor (Graduate Assistant)**

Taught "Introduction to Physical Geography," class of 50, physical science elective. Developed course outline, handouts, and examinations, with guidance from the Department Chairman, Orland Maxfield, Ph.D.

| | |
|---|---|
| **ADDITIONAL** | **COLLEGE OF BUSINESS ADMINISTRATION**, University of Arkansas, Fayetteville<br>**Administrative Aide** |
| | **GEOGRAPHY DEPARTMENT**, University of Central Arkansas, Conway<br>**Administrative Aide** |
| | **ARKANSAS DEMOCRAT**, Little Rock, Arkansas<br>Reporter |
| | **JACKSONVILLE NEWS**, Jacksonville, Arkansas<br>Feature Writer |
| **CREDENTIALS** | Teaching Credential, Secondary, State of Arkansas, current<br>Secondary School Administration Credential, State of Arkansas, ongoing |
| **COMMUNITY SERVICE** | Charter Member and Chairperson (term expired 12/31/89; appointed by the Arkansas State Director of Education)<br>Youth Opportunities Unlimited — Arkansas<br>This is a JTPA-funded statewide program placing at-risk youth on four college campuses for eight-week summer residential program of work, classroom instruction, and enrichment programs. |
| | Member of the Board<br>Office for Human Concern, Benton, Carroll, & Madison Counties<br>This agency oversees senior citizen programs and aid agencies for the poor. |
| | Op-Ed Contributing Writer, *Arkansas Gazette* (on alternative education; also an occasional contributor to local and regional newspapers on educational matters). |
| | Sunday School Coordinator, Member of the Vestry<br>Grace Episcopal Church, Siloam Springs, Arkansas |
| **SAMPLE CONTINUING EDUCATION** | Summer Seminar — Great Expectations Teacher-Training Program<br>Department of Education / Northeastern State University |
| | Seminar on Opening and Managing a Small Business<br>Small Business Administration / University of Arkansas |
| | Marketing Seminar<br>Small Business Administration / University of Arkansas |
| | Teachers' Economic Workshop<br>Bessie Moore Center for Economics / University of Arkansas |
| | Introduction to BASIC Programming<br>Small Business Administration / University of Arkansas |
| | Seminar on Computers in Education<br>Springfield, Missouri |
| | Introduction to Small Computers<br>Small Business Administration / University of Arkansas |
| | Conservation Workshop<br>Forest Industry Association, Monticello |
| | Seminar on Solar Energy<br>Graduate Institute of Technology, Little Rock |

# James Michael Conolly, Ph.D.

115 President Wilson Drive
San Diego, California 92117

(619) 555-6833
(619) 555-7576

| | |
|---|---|
| **EXPERTISE** | **Educational Administration**<br><br>*Synopsis:*<br><br>Lifetime commitment to quality higher education, with emphasis on the integration of intellectual, spiritual, and pragmatic concerns. Over 20 years in highly public positions requiring public relations and fund-raising skills, consistent ability to motivate and direct large staffs of paid professionals and volunteers, and patience. Dynamic communicator, including regular television appearances as host of a religious and educational television show. Over 10 years of full responsibility for budget projection and administration, long-term and short-term development and fund-raising. Experience presiding over comprehensive curriculum reviews. Consistently demonstrated ability to focus the efforts of others onto a common goal. |
| **EDUCATION** | **Ph.D., Holistic Psychology**, 1981<br>University for Humanistic Studies, San Diego, California<br><br>    Dissertation: *Resolving Guilt: A Phenomenological Case Study of U.S. Navy Personnel*<br><br>**M.A., Political Science**, 1967<br>Catholic University of America, Washington, D.C.<br><br>    Thesis: *The Geostrategic Importance of Cyprus*<br><br>**M.A., Sacred Doctrine**, 1961<br>Holy Cross College, Washington, D.C.<br><br>    Thesis: *The English Catholic Reaction to the Seizure of the Papal States, 1870*<br><br>**A.B., Philosophy**, 1960<br>Stonehill College, North Easton, Massachusetts<br><br>**Additional Graduate Studies:**<br>• Educational Leadership Program, 1984–1985<br>  University of South Florida, Tampa, Florida<br>• Family, Child & Marriage Counseling, 1980–1981<br>  University for Humanistic Studies, San Diego, California<br>• Education, 1961–1965, 1970–1972 (part-time)<br>  Fairfield University, Fairfield, Connecticut<br><br>**Languages:**<br>• Proficient reader of French, Italian, Latin. |
| **APPOINTMENTS & AFFILIATIONS** | Board of Directors, King's College, Wilkes-Barre, Pennsylvania<br><br>Board of Trustees, Stonehill College, North Easton, Massachusetts<br><br>Board of Directors, Holy Cross Fathers, Eastern Province<br><br>Governing Board, National Council on Alcoholism, San Diego Chapter<br><br>National Association of Secondary School Principals, National and Connecticut Chapters<br><br>Board of Directors, Family Theatre, Hollywood, California |

**PROFESSIONAL POSITIONS**

**DIOCESE OF BRIDGEPORT, CONNECTICUT**
**High School Principal**

Selected for this position with the mandate to reestablish an emphasis on Christian values and academic achievement. Directed teaching and administration, staff of 40 teachers, budget of $700,000. Coordinated and directed a fund-raising effort for "Educational Stability and Enrichment," leading to $100,000 in new funds. Major accomplishment: Analyzed the needs of the Diocese and engineered the merger of two schools into a single coeducational facility, greatly reducing fixed operating costs. Advanced this concept into the community and got it approved and completed within five months at a time when other dioceses were having major public relations difficulties with consolidations. Continued to maintain close ties with the instructional staff by teaching at least one course each semester. (1990–1995)
• Earned National Catholic Education Association Presidential Citation for Excellence.

**U.S. NAVY**
**Catholic Chaplain**

Direct religious and counseling activities; organize and lead lay ministries and service organizations. In charge of staffs from 4 to 60. Sample accomplishments: (1) Reestablished Parish Council; (2) doubled the number of weekly participants; (3) developed and implemented a bi-weekly T.V. show, "Chaplain's Call," distributed worldwide; (4) implemented and improved drug and alcohol counseling programs at every opportunity. (1976–present, with interruptions)
• Received Navy Achievement Medal for designing and supporting alcohol and drug abuse programs for military personnel.

**Administrative Officer**, Chaplains Religious Education Development Office (CREDO)

Represented CREDO to senior administrative personnel. Effectively doubled funds for programs during a period of major reductions in expenditures. Directed a program of religious retreats for military personnel and dependents. Oversaw a highly successful integrated holistic counseling and treatment program for persons with chemical dependencies. (1978–1981)

**KING'S COLLEGE, WILKES-BARRE**
**Director of Student Activities**
**Assistant Dean of Students**
**Director of Residence Halls**

During the turmoil on college campuses during the 1969–1970 academic year, became the only adult representative to a students' coalition from all four colleges in the immediate area. I feel personally responsible for the fact that there was no violence during that particular year. Also shepherded in a new student government constitution and official guidelines for student operation of dormitories; both of which are still in use today. (1969–1976)

ADDITIONAL INSTRUCTIONAL EXPERIENCE

Sacred Heart University, Bridgeport, Connecticut
**Lecturer**, History Department

King's College, Wilkes-Barre Pennsylvania
**Lecturer**, Political Science Department

St. Peter High School, Gloucester, Massachusetts
**Teacher**

Notre Dame Boys High School, Bridgeport, Connecticut
**Teacher**

**ADDITIONAL INTERESTS**

Have traveled extensively throughout North America, Europe, and the Middle East, as well as some Pacific-Asian countries. Recently published a popular interest book: *199 Ways to Stop Smoking*. This is a humorously presented book with a serious message. Also wrote and produced a 45-minute documentary-instructional for distribution within the Navy rehabilitation system: *Spiritual Aspects of Recovery in A.A.*

Any additional information requested will be forwarded promptly.

**AVAILABILITY**

Spring 1997.

# Matthew Joseph Dolan, Ed.D.

3225 Maylon Road
Toledo, Ohio 43616

Office: (419) 555-0465
Residence: (419) 555-0543

---

**EXPERTISE**

**Educational Administration**

- **Fiscal Management / Fund-Raising & Development**
- **Organizational Development**

**EDUCATION**

UNIVERSITY OF TOLEDO, Toledo, Ohio
**Doctor of Educational Administration**

- Concentration: **Finance**

UNIVERSITY OF TOLEDO, Toledo, Ohio
**Master of Education**

- Emphasis: **Guidance Counseling**

ATHENAEUM OF OHIO, Norwood, Ohio
**Master of Arts, Philosophy**

ATHENAEUM OF OHIO, Norwood, Ohio
**Bachelor of Arts, Secondary Education**

**EXPERIENCE**

DIOCESAN FISCAL MANAGEMENT COALITION, Orent, Ohio
**Executive Director**, 1994–Present

Manage organization of fiscal managers and CFOs of 192 dioceses, with approximately 750 members, throughout the United States and Canada. The DFMC was created to provide innovative technical and administrative assistance to dioceses in the areas of financial management, planning, and development, and assists organizations with annual budgets of up to $100+ million. Represent the DFMC at various national and professional association meetings. Supervise and coordinate annual conferences, and oversee the production of quarterly newsletter.

BISHOP HIGH SCHOOL, Toledo, Ohio
**Principal**, 1991–1994

Recruited to manage school facing severe financial challenges, with main priorities being a balanced budget, retirement of $1.5 million operating debt which had accrued in previous years, and increased enrollment. Instituted aggressive community relations and recruitment plan to spur enrollment. Created and implemented improved financial controls. Supervised 50 employees (teachers, administrators, office workers, athletics directors, custodial workers).

Increased enrollment from 250 to 290 students. Orchestrated diocesan acceptance of plan to eliminate interest charges, reducing monthly liabilities by $7,500. Balanced school budget, and began repayments on operating debt.

THE METANOIA GROUP AT ST. MARY'S COLLEGE, Winona, Minnesota
**Executive Director / Chairperson**, 1987–1991

Instrumental in design and development of creative organizational development and fund-raising consulting service with over 100 educational and NPO clients annually. Emphasis was on effecting organizational changes, improving strategic planning, and implementing more efficient and effective fund-raising programs to increase the long-term health of clients. Provided training and expertise to national client base.

Main accomplishment: Established 3-year master's degree program in philanthropy and development. Program is currently 100% enrolled, 75 students total.

NATIONAL CATHOLIC EDUCATIONAL ASSOCIATION, Washington, D.C.
**Vice President for Development**, 1982–1987

Managed programs providing fund-raising guidance and consulting services for all 7 divisions of nationwide educational organization with 192 dioceses and approximately 15,000 members. Technical assistance included grant writing, planned giving, developing relationships with foundations/trusts, and the institution of various fund-raising programs. Initiated several programs now having an impact on a national level. Served as chairperson, Public Relations Subcommittee; member of the Communications Committee; member of Personnel Relations Review Board; member of Committee to Plan Symposium for the Future.

Sample accomplishments: Project director for study of low-income students financed by the Ford Foundation for almost $1 million. Director of national symposium on development issues. Author and/or publisher for 20 guidebooks for school administrators (fiscal and development issues). Directed national symposium on first amendment issues in private education. Assisted in relocating association headquarters. Liaison to NCEA investment service. Representative, American Association for Corporate Contributions.

**Executive Director, Secondary School Department**, 1980–1982
Designed and conducted administrative, managerial and educational training programs for 1,500 schools.

*prior:*

TIFFIN CALVERT HIGH SCHOOL, Tiffin, Ohio
**Local Superintendent / Principal**

ST. MARY'S CENTRAL CATHOLIC HIGH SCHOOL, Sandusky, Ohio
**Principal**

ST. JOHN HIGH SCHOOL, Delphos, Ohio
**Principal**

CENTRAL CATHOLIC HIGH SCHOOL, Toledo, Ohio
**Instructor**

**ADDITIONAL EXPERIENCE**

ST. MARY'S COLLEGE, Winona, Minnesota
**Adjunct Professor**
Taught courses in the Philanthropy and Development program.

UNIVERSITY OF DAYTON, Dayton, Ohio
**Visiting Lecturer**
Doctoral-level symposium on financial school planning.

SELECTED SPEAKING ENGAGEMENTS

Full list on request, including school graduations and meetings of principals, pastors, parents, students nationwide, such as:

New York Federation of Catholic Parents
Ohio Catholic Educational Association
20th Annual Administrators Conference

**PROFESSIONAL**
**PUBLICATIONS**

BOOKS/GUIDEBOOKS

*Understanding and Implementing Development,* National Catholic Educational Association, Washington, D.C.

*Annual Fund Estate Planning,* National Catholic Educational Association, Washington, D.C.

*Public Relations,* National Catholic Educational Association, Washington, D.C.

*The Case Statement,* National Catholic Educational Association, Washington, D.C.

*Elementary School Finance Manual,* National Catholic Educational Association, Washington, D.C.

*Catholic High Schools: Their Impact on Low-Income Students,* the Ford Foundation

*The Catholic High School: A National Portrait,* the Ford Foundation

*Five Shaping Forces,* National Catholic Educational Association, Washington, D.C.

*Nutrition for Everyone,* National Catholic Educational Association, Washington, D.C.

PERIODICALS

*Pastors Development Newsletter* (5 times per year)

*Private School Law Digest* (quarterly)

DOCTORAL DISSERTATION

*A Replicated Study of Certain Aspects of Business Management in Selected Catholic Secondary Schools in the United States*

UNIVERSITY OF TOLEDO MASTER'S THESES

*Planned Progress Participation: A Public Relations Study*

*The Parochial School: An Entity Before the Law in Ohio*

**REFERENCES**

References, certifications, publications, and additional information gladly furnished upon request.

# Amy K. Divita

32 Woodstock Boulevard SE
Portland, Oregon 97202

Residence/message/fax/pager: (503) 555-9440
amy.divita@aol.com

## PROFILE

Professional volunteer for over 20 years. Experienced motivator, coordinator and catalyst. Can focus the efforts of diverse groups onto common goals. Able to access key decision-makers and benefactors, build effective networks, and create synergistic relationships. Systematic in approach, creating information flows, alliances, and operating procedures that endure to the benefit of the organization. Highly energetic.

## STRENGTHS

### Management, Leadership & Organizational Development

Consistently demonstrated ability to develop and implement detailed strategic plans to meet organizational goals. Greatest strength is team building, bringing together individuals with complementary skills. Invariably able to create a whole that is greater than the parts.

Technical skills include extensive responsibility for design of policies and procedures, organizational development, budget development and administration, and efficient control of resources, human and otherwise. Computer literate.

A major strength is the ability to handle a multitude of simultaneous responsibilities, to delegate effectively, and to meet management objectives without supervision.

### Fund-Raising & Special Events

Ability to plan and direct major special events, especially fund-raising events and live entertainment. Have chaired events for groups up to 2000, coordinated up to 150 volunteer staff, and raised up to $400,000 in a single event.

Personal strength is the development of major donors, both individuals and corporations. Proven ability to initiate contacts, develop relationships, and ensure donor satisfaction with the benefiting organization.

## APPOINTMENTS

HIGHLIGHTS OF SERVICE TO MARY B. EDDY HOSPITAL SYSTEM:

**Mary B. Eddy Corporation**
Trustee, 1988–1990
Executive Committee, 1987–1990
Co-Chairman, Public Affairs Committee, 1990

**Mary B. Eddy-Harmony Community Member**
President, 1993–Present

**Mary B. Eddy Foundation** and **Mary B. Eddy-Harmony Foundation**
Chairman, Board of Trustees, 1987–1991
Vice President, Board of Trustees, 1986
2nd Vice President, 1985
Trustee (former Director), 1983–1994; Consulting Trustee, 1994–Present
Advisory Trustee, 1982–1983
Chairman, Nominating Committee, 1990–Present
Chairman, Friends of Mary B. Eddy, 1982–Present
Capital Campaign Committee, 1986 (part of $3.3 million campaign)
Chairman, High Risk OB Programs, 1982  ($136,688 + matching grant from Kresge Foundation)

**Mary B. Eddy Hospital**
Trustee, 1987–1990
Public Relations Committee, Member, 1983, Chairman, 1984–1992

**Acute Care Affiliates**
Director, 1990–1991

**75th Anniversary Activities**
Chairman, Celebration, 1984
Chairman, Health Festival, 1984
Chairman, 75th Anniversary Task Force (Planning Committee), 1983

**Mary B. Eddy Volunteer Association**
Chairman, Past-Presidents Council, 1980
President, 1979–1980
2nd Vice President, 1977
3rd Vice President, 1976
Member, 1965–Present

**1981 CHA Convention**
Speaker, Long-Range Planning

**1980 Western Hospital Convention**
Speaker, Long-Range Planning

ADDITIONAL ORGANIZATIONS:

**Portland Museum Association Services:**
Women's Board, 1981–Present
Fund-Raising & Development Committee, 1990–1993
Membership Committee, 1982–1983
**White Elephant Sale,** 1981–Present (this event raises up to $400,000, involving a staff up to 150)
　Co-Chairman, entire sale, 1985
　Chairman & Co-Chairman, Women's Wear Division, 1982–Present
　Chairman, Preview Party, 1990 (for 2000 people)
　Director, Promotions & PR, 1983–1984
　Chairman, Personnel, 1982
　Model, Fashion Show, 1982

**American Red Cross, Director,** Portland, 1990, 1992

**YMCA, Portland/Lake Oswego, Director,** 1990, 1992, 1993
Chair, $2 million capital funding campaign, 1996 (in progress)

**Claremont Club,** 1987–Present
Chairman of various Special Events
Singer and Actress in Club Events

**Mt. Diablo Hospital and Providence Hospital,** 1981
Speaker, Hospital Association & Volunteer Organization Management

**Young People's Symphony Association, Vice-Chairman,** Portland, 1971–1972

**Rotary Club,** Portland, 1983–Present

# EDUCATION

**Portland State University**
**B.A.** candidate, expected 1996

Created a special major of **Business Administration / Speech Communication** to capitalize on experience and enhance effectiveness in chosen career.

## ADDENDUM

### GOVERNMENT SERVICE

**Fallen Leaf Community Services District,** El Dorado County, Oregon
**Elected Director,** 1990–Present
**President of the Board,** 1992–Present

### HONORS

Distinguished Service Award, 1991, Mary B. Eddy Corporation Board of Trustees

Outstanding Service Award, 1985, Mary B. Eddy Hospital Board of Trustees

Meritorious Service Award, 1983, Mary B. Eddy Hospital Board of Trustees

Recognition Award, 1980, Mary B. Eddy Hospital Board of Trustees

KABL — Citizen of the Day Award, 1982, 1984

Carnation Award — Volunteer of the Year, 1979
Carnation Corporation Community Service Award /
Multnomah County Volunteer Bureau

Selected Spokesperson and Model for The Diet Center
(*Vogue, People, Redbook, Health, Newsweek,* and other print media)

### HOBBY

Vocalist, The Sound Impressions

Chanteuse, Portland Rotary

Chanteuse, Claremont Club

Vocalist, The Uncalled Four

### REFERENCES

Provided on request.

# ANDRÉ GIBBS

4 Ruby Tower, #1414 • Ruby Tower Square • Chicago • Illinois • 60611 • (312) 555-4648

## PROFILE

### Business Development • Marketing • Sales • Public Relations

Extensive experience representing elite products and services to a discriminating, culturally sophisticated clientele. Proven ability to initiate and extend critical relationships. Personally oriented toward quality, integrity, and long-term view of enlightened mutual benefit.

## EXPERIENCE

**Chicago Ballet,** Chicago, Illinois        1994–Present
**Director, Planning/Development/Marketing**

Plan, organize, and direct operations of the development department, ensuring integration of all activities including fund-raising, marketing, PR, and community programs. Assist in the development of strategic plans to communicate Chicago Ballet mission and programs. Direct fund-raising efforts of the board of directors and assist in identification of major private, corporate, and foundation prospects. Enhance, establish, and maintain relationships with prospective donors. Manage development, production, and distribution of collateral materials to solicit donations and for development activities.

- Created the adult beginning ballet class, a fabulously popular new revenue stream for the troupe.
- Personally developed a $1,000,000+ donor.
- Brought marketing systems up to date, including relationship tracking software.
- Negotiated in-kind legal services, eliminating legal fees to the ballet.

**Tiffany & Co.,** New York, New York        1985 – 1993
**Vice President & Store General Manager**        1990 – 1992

Managed and controlled all aspects of company presence in Manhattan, including public relations, sales, marketing, and customer development. Key player in vastly increased community involvement of the firm and staff, generating much favorable publicity. Consistently exceeded monthly sales goals for the store; personally assisted with key customer relationships. Supervised staff of 50, including sales, operations, and merchandising personnel.

- Increased market share in a very tight market.
- Brought store back to beat Rodeo Drive for first time in five years.
- Recorded annual sales increases ranging from 15% to 32%.
- Controlled expenses to maintain operating profit in excess of targets.

**Operations Manager**        1988 – 1990

Developed and controlled operations budget and accounts. Directed staff of 24, including office management, in stock and inventory control, security, shipping, and maintenance.

- Increased operational efficiency while retaining the cachet of the Tiffany image.
- Orchestrated major store remodel without customer inconvenience.
- Selected for store opening assignment, recruiting, hiring, and training staff.

**Sales Manager**        1984 – 1988

Obtained the highest profit of any branch store within the corporation. Recruited, trained, and supervised staff of up to 15 associates, stressing excellence of customer service. Significant sales contributions resulting in a 34% gross margin.

## EDUCATION

**B.A., Communications,** Rutgers, The State University of New Jersey

*please hold this information in confidence at this time*

# MICHAEL G. ROWLAND

Residence/message: (706) 555-3752
http://hillcor.com/row/

67 Peachtree Riding Path, #22
Athens, Georgia 30605

---

**EXPERTISE**

Health Care

— Organizational Development

— Market Analysis

**EXPERIENCE**

THE HILLCOR CORPORATION / VANGUARD, INC.    Athens, Georgia
**Director of Development (Region 2)**    1990 – Present

Hillcor is the third largest chain of long-term care centers with 450 facilities, 55,000 beds nationwide, $1.2 billion in assets 1996. Overall corporate revenues for this division climbed from $96.6 million to $227.9 million from 1989 to 1995 (last year of full fiscal data). Charged with developing joint ventures with acute care hospitals, acquisitions of existing facilities, and site selection for development of new facilities in the South and Midwest, currently with 90 facilities under management. Report directly to the regional director of operations and indirectly to the full executive committee (quarterly). Supervise five analysts; collaborate with house counsel at national headquarters in Wilmington, Delaware.

Guide the organization's geographic expansion strategy towards expanding market share by surveying consumer buying intentions, analyzing current and projected demographic data, cataloging competitor resources, and developing potential market profiles.

Currently achieving a growth rate in excess of all other regions, with the most profitable sites (new *and* existing) in the entire corporation. Also completely rewrote the strategies for market analysis (adopted nationwide as of this coming quarter).

HILLCOR HAVEN ATLANTA    Atlanta, Georgia
**Area Administrator**    1987 – 1990

Charged with the strategic reorganization of three nursing facilities to become more responsive to changing health care trends and long-term care market demand. Administrator for three facilities including (a) Hillcor Ardmore, a skilled nursing facility with complete rehabilitative services, subacute, skilled, dementia, and intermediate care, (b) Hillcor Pines, specializing in Alzheimer's care, and (c) Hillcor Sugarloaf, offering basic long-term care with a total of 390 beds.

Developed and negotiated contracts with five area HMOs. Significantly changed and enlarged the subacute program, and implemented a major construction project.

HILLCOR WARREN    Warren, Alabama
**Administrator**    1985 – 1987

Led the reorganization of the management staff for this 142-bed skilled nursing facility to turn around a division with poor financial performance.

Turned facility around to a significant financial asset to the corporation from being a major financial loss.

*– continued –*

ST. LOUIS COUNTY HOSPITAL    Clayton, Missouri
**Associate Hospital Administrator**    1982 – 1984

COUNTY REGIONAL HEALTH CENTER    East St. Louis, Missouri
**Administrator**    1980 – 1981

ST. LOUIS CHILDREN'S HOSPITAL    St. Louis, Missouri
**Assistant Director**    1976 – 1980

*prior*

CENTREVILLE TOWNSHIP HOSPITAL    St. Louis, Missouri
**HMO Research Assistant**    1975 – 1976

LITTLE COMPANY OF MARY HOSPITAL    Evergreen Park, Illinois
**Administrative Resident**    1974 – 1975

ST. LOUIS CHILDREN'S HOSPITAL    St. Louis, Missouri
**Assistant Materials Manager**    1972 – 1973

**EDUCATION**    WASHINGTON UNIVERSITY    St. Louis, Missouri
**M.H.A. (Masters in Hospital Administration)**

TULANE UNIVERSITY    New Orleans, Louisiana
**B.A., Psychology**

# Diana J. Holman Wright

2826 Ramona Circle
Santa Maria, Texas 78592

Residence/message: (915) 555-2192
djhw@eng.bartolo.com

---

## EXPERIENCE

**South Coast Big Brothers/Big Sisters, Inc.,** Corpus Christi, Texas          1984–1994
**Executive Director**

Managed development program, greatly increasing revenues for this volunteer organization. Recruited and trained board of directors. Created program strategy, establishing effective marketing and public relations campaigns, cemented relations with area schools, churches, courts, and human services organizations. Repositioned the organization away from a hobby for a few well-meaning individuals and into a committed, thriving, dynamic organization intrinsically linked into the South Texas community.

**Achievements:**
- Gained 1000+ volunteers, 625% funding increase, and quadrupled program service availability.
- Formalized both services *and a volunteer organization* focusing on the Spanish-speaking-only citizens of South Texas.
- Designed and implemented special events, raising $300,000 for mentoring and delinquency prevention programs.

**Tabor Medical Services Company, Inc.,** Corpus Christi, Texas          1990–1991
**Director, Recruitment and Screening — U.S.D.A. Western Human Nutrition Research Center**

Established department to recruit, assess, hire, and supervise volunteers involved in human nutrition research studies. Implemented and executed successful volunteer recruitment efforts including interviewing, assessment, hiring, training, and supervision of a staff of eight.

**Achievements:**
- Directed and controlled budgets of $150,000+ per annum.
- Brought a modern marketing mentality to this volunteer recruiting function.

**Holman & Associates,** Santa Maria, Texas          1989–Present
**Principal**

Consultant to nonprofit and for-profit businesses, providing effectiveness training to boards of directors, establishing or revamping fund-raising and development programs, installing long- and short-term planning functions, and offering other financial, marketing, strategic, and organizational development consulting.

**Achievements:**
- Delivered workshop, "The Care and Feeding of Advisory Boards: The Best Advice You'll Ever Get for Free," at statewide SBA convention, San Antonio.
- Conducted board of directors development training for Big Brothers/Big Sisters of Dallas/Ft. Worth, raising standards to match national requirements.
- Completed long-range strategic plan for Carvel Computing & Business Systems of Houston, an entrepreneurial company with no strategic planning system in place.
- Wrote or edited grants earning $1,865,000 in funding for Texas and Louisiana nonprofits.

**University of Texas,** San Antonio, Texas          1976–1990
**Corpus Christi State University,** Corpus Christi, Texas          1976–1990
**Continuing Education Instructor**

Designed, developed, and conducted educational seminars with diverse topics such as goal planning and stress reduction for professionals, not-for-profit board of directors training retreat, strategic planning for nonprofit boards, motivation in the workplace, and managing change in the independent sector.

**Achievement:**
- Created and implemented the first 30 unit CEU program in Texas for preventive medicine.

**AFFILIATIONS**

> **President, Board of Directors,** Center for Health Advancement
>
> **Member, Board of Directors,** Lexus
>
> **Member, Executive Directors Association,** Big Brothers/Big Sisters of America
>
> **Member, Executive Directors Alumni Association,** Columbia University
>
> **Member, International Service Committee,** Rotary International

**EDUCATION**

> **Ph.D.** (ABD), **Business Administration**
> Purdue University, West Lafayette, Indiana
>
> **Certificate, Nonprofit Management**
> School of Business, Columbia University, New York, New York
>
> **M.A., Health Services Administration**
> Corpus Christi State University, Corpus Christi, Texas
>
> **B.A., Public Service**
> Rice University, Houston, Texas

*References available upon request.*

# ANGELA M. ROSS

19 Beachside Lane, Townhome 15
Panama City, Florida 32401

Office: (904) 555-8760
Residence: (904) 555-4392

---

**PROFESSION**

**Development Officer**

*Strengths:*
- Fund-raising, motivating, networking, organizing, orchestrating.
- Personal strength: major donor identification and development, major gifts (private and corporate), organizational development to maximize benefit of the diverse talents available to the organization.
- Executive experience over database compilation, records and administration, direct mail campaigns, communications development, budgeting, and similar administrative and departmental functions.
- Personal talent for writing development materials (appeals, releases, proposals, etc.) Founding member of several organizations and projects, with start-up and organizational design experience.
- Highly effective liaison and manager, *able to engender enthusiasm and purpose.*

**HIGHLIGHTS**

EDGAR CAGE CHILDREN'S CENTER    Panama City, FL
**Director of Development**    1993–Present

Supervise assistant director of development, development coordinator, and development assistant. Report to the executive director. In full charge of development efforts. Conceptualize, plan, and execute development campaigns. Prepare capital and operating budgets. Write business and marketing plans. Establish policies and procedures. Plan and coordinate special events and meetings. Oversee computer applications (databasing, direct mailing). Produce collateral materials (brochures, solicitations, correspondence). Write grants and proposals. Develop volunteers and support the volunteer organization. Consult with counsel on development and gifting issues. Personally handle relationships with foundation representatives and key donors.

**President, Edgar Cage Auxiliary. Chair, Cage Garden Fair**.

*Contribution:*
- Consistently secure $1.5 million per annum for the center, representing fully 25% of its total annual budget. Also: member of the board during final stages of $6 million capital campaign.

CHRISTMAS YEAR ROUND    Panama Beach, FL
**Board Member**    1991–Present

Established a fund development committee for this new nonprofit service organization providing annual repairs on the homes of the elderly. Created database lists for fund-raising efforts and solicitation of gifts in kind. Identified and developed prospective donors. Served as a liaison to the media and a representative at PR events. Collaborated on volunteer development.

*Contribution:*
- Key member of the founding team. Created the image and reputation necessary to win corporate sponsors. Personally acquired major donations.

*– continued –*

FLORIDA ATLANTIC MEDICAL FOUNDATION      Daytona, FL
**Board Member**      1994–Present

Active member of the development committee. Identify donors, cultivate prospective donors, develop and deliver corporate and foundation presentations, procure or compile donor lists, collaborate with chief development officer.

LIVING/DYING PROJECT OF FLORIDA      Fairfax, FL
**Consultant**      1993

Consulted with the board during a critical reassessment of the makeup of the board. Collaborated with existing board to write a new mission statement. Counseled existing board members. Identified and developed potential board members. Created a new sense of purpose and confidence.

AMERICAN PARALYSIS ASSOCIATION      HQ: Los Angeles, CA
(now the PARALYSIS PROJECT OF AMERICA)
**Executive Board**      1984–1989

Founding member of project that successfully established itself and raised over $600,000 per year in annual campaign.

*also*

GOVERNOR'S HIV TASK FORCE      Miami, FL
**Member**      1994–Present

PANAMA CITY SENIOR TASK FORCE      Panama City, FL
**Member**      1993–Present

NORTH FLORIDA COMMISSION ON AGING      Pensacola, FL
**Commissioner**      1994–Present

FAMILY SURVIVAL PROJECT      Panama City, FL
**Board Member**      1988–1990
Fund Development Committee
Community Relations Committee
Special Events Committee

LITTLE SISTERS OF THE POOR      Panama City, FL
**Executive Board**      1987–1990
**Development Advisory Board**      1990–Present
Fund Development Committee
Special Events Committee

UNITED AIRLINES      Miami, FL
**Special Service Agent**      1970–1977

**EDUCATION**      UNIVERSITY OF NORTH FLORIDA      Jacksonville, FL
**Executive Certificate — Nonprofit Management**

AGNES SCOTT COLLEGE      Decatur, GA
**B.A., Department of Education, Children's Literature**

ST. ROSE ACADEMY      Daytona, FL
**Diploma, College Preparatory**

# Laura Neal Talbott

1937 Blythe Street
Iowa City, Iowa 52240

Telephone:
(319) 555-7620

---

## PROFILE

Effective combination of interpersonal, analytic, and organizational skills. Strengths include (1) program design, development, and direction, (2) management of marketing and promotions, (3) coordination with existing local, area and regional arts and cultural organizations, (4) design of policies and procedures, (5) budget preparation and administration, (6) grant-writing, fund-raising and development, (7) public speaking and community outreach, (8) leadership of volunteer and support organizations.

Experienced motivator, coordinator and catalyst. Can focus the efforts of diverse groups onto common goals. Able to access key decision-makers and benefactors, build effective networks, and create synergistic relationships. Systematic in approach, creating information flows, alliances, and operating procedures that endure. Highly energetic.

## EDUCATION

School of Business Administration, University of Arizona, Tucson, Arizona
**M.S.**, Urban Planning

University of Oregon, Eugene, Oregon
**B.A.**, General Arts & Letters

Renton High School, Renton, Washington
**Diploma**, Valedictorian

## EXPERIENCE

Richard Caplan & Associates, Highland, Iowa, 1994–Present
**Consultant Associate**

*City of Red Bluff, Nebraska*: conducted field research and community analysis for a new 150-room hotel;

*City of Palm Desert, California*: conducted field research and demographic analysis for a feasibility study of a new 18-hole, championship city-owned golf course;

*City of Baton Rouge, Louisiana*: conducted research, interviews, community analysis; contributed to written report and presentation to city council for a feasibility study for a new 2000+ seat performing arts facility.

University of Kansas, School of Fine Arts, Lawrence, Kansas, 1990–1993
**Education/Membership Coordinator**, Office of Concert, Chamber Music, New Directions Series

Developed programs to promote and enhance audience appreciation. Targeted community market segments and developed promotional and educational activities/events to reach them. Initiated and built relationships with area arts organizations. Maximized reach through effective use of resources. Promoted and managed volunteer supporters. Located and developed corporate sponsorship. Promoted and facilitated the Swarthout Society (auxiliary member organization).

Special projects: V.I.P. host to Resident Artists; created the Young People's Performance events; developed the Five-Year Educational Long-Range Plan to expand programs and coordinate with opening of the Lied Center for Performing Arts in 1995; produced annual Swarthout Society Membership Brochures, as well as the regular publication of the Swarthout Society Newsletter.

Concurrent with this full-time position, maintained community service efforts: Chamber of Commerce, Cultural Affairs Committee (Arts Calendar of Events, Business and the Arts Awards); Downtown Lawrence Business Association ("Main Street" Program of Events); and City of Lawrence (Arts in Public Places Program).

Western Wisconsin Regional Arts, La Crosse, Wisconsin, 1983–1990
**Arts Administrator**

Provided leadership, direction, and daily management of a seven-county, tri-state Regional Arts Council. Reported to the board of directors; coordinated all working committees; interpreted and implemented board policies; established daily operating procedures; supervised all staff and volunteers; managed the organization's central facility, a federally designated Historical Landmark building housing arts organization offices, visual and performing arts events, classes and community events. Developed and controlled $100,000 operating budget, including monies from grants, fund-raising activities, corporate donors, and private benefactors.

Initiated and maintained close relationships with member organizations; ensured positive press and public relations within the larger community; served as liaison to City Hall. Executive coordinator of all services to member organizations, schools, and regional communities.

Highlights: Won 17 foundation and government grant awards; founded and served on executive committee for United Fund for the Arts & Humanities; organized the Coordinating Committee of Arts Organizations Representatives; initiated and found funding for a successful building restoration project for organization headquarters, including historic preservation funds; increased visibility for the arts through marketing techniques, frequently using free media exposure and public speaking.

University of Wisconsin, La Crosse, Wisconsin, 1983
**LTE Research Associate**, Center for Regional Studies

Conducted a pilot research project on the impact to and requirements of older adults living in a rural region. Made key contributions to project design. Made contacts, conducted interviews, provided evaluation for potential of P.O.E. (Post Occupancy Evaluation) for a behavior assessment tool. Developed the written summation.

U.S. Department of Housing & Urban Development, Tucson, Arizona, 1981–1982
**HUD Intern**, City Planning Department, City of Tucson

Designed and established a plan monitoring system to give planning staff more precise information and access to resources for use in neighborhood-by-neighborhood planning. Organized the project, conducted original research; wrote, tested and emplaced the system. Wrote guidelines for maintenance and evolution of the system. Also provided related grant research for programs oriented toward families.

Grey Advertising, New York, New York, 1977–1979
**Executive Secretary**

Reported to the Vice President in charge of the Revlon account. Maintained all Revlon account financial spreadsheets, communications and appointments. Supervised office personnel.

## CONSULTANCY

Wyoming Volunteer Assistance Corporation, 1991
Seminar Leader, Time Management/Avoiding Burnout

Lied Center for Performing Arts, Lawrence, Kansas, 1990–1992
Space/Design Consultant

Downtown La Crosse Business Association, 1987–1988
Year 2000 Plan

Eastbank Artists, 1987
Retreat Leader, Organization/Board Development

La Crosse Tribune Readers' Panel, 1986–1987
Panelist and Advisor

Wisconsin Arts Board, 1986–1990
Peer Panelist (also: budget testimony to House/Senate Budget Committee)

General Public Speaking, 1978–Present
Arts Administration, City Planning, Organizational Development (also: media relations and representation/testimony/lobbying to government agencies at city/state/regional levels)

## ADDITIONAL

List of references attached. List of publications on request.

# Laura Neal Talbott

1937 Blythe Street
Iowa City, Iowa 52240

Telephone:
(319) 555-7620

---

## ADDENDA

### Worldview:

Born and raised in Seattle. Have lived in Guatemala City, Guatemala; Eugene, Oregon; Cambridge, Massachusetts; White Plains, New York; Tucson, Arizona; La Crosse, Wisconsin; and Lawrence, Kansas. Extensive world travel. Wide range of knowledge of other cultures, peoples, and their arts.

### Affiliations:

American Planning Association (APA), 1982–Present

Fine Arts Commission, Iowa City, Iowa, 1994–Present

National Society for Fund-Raising Executives (NSFRE), Board Member, 1984–1990

National Assembly of Local Arts Agencies (NALAA), 1983–1990

United Church of Christ (UCC), Wisconsin Conference Board of Directors, 1987–1989

Lawrence Chamber of Commerce, 1990–1993

Area Arts Organizations: La Crosse, WI; Lawrence, KS; and Iowa City, IA.

### Honors:

**Good Citizen Award**
Chamber of Commerce/La Crosse Tribune, 1990

**Outstanding Woman in the Arts**
YWCA, La Crosse, 1987

**Copper Certificate of Appreciation**
Mayor and City Council of Tucson, for development of the city's Neighborhood Plan Monitoring System, 1982

### References:

Ms. Thelma Press
Director, International & Cultural Affairs
The City of San Bernardino
(714) 555-5733

Ms. Jackie Davis
Director, Concert, Chamber Music, New Directions Series
University of Kansas, Lawrence
(913) 555-3869

Mr. Del Brinkman
Vice Chancellor, Academic Affairs
University of Kansas, Lawrence
(913) 555-4655

Mr. Jack Moore
Dayton-Hudson Corporate Headquarters
(First President, United Fund for the Arts, La Crosse)
(612) 555-3874

Mr. Pat Zielke
Mayor, La Crosse, Wisconsin
(608) 555-5785

# Jan Freeman

24 Cardinal Way
Santa Monica, California 90401
24-hour telephone/message/fax/pager: (800) 555-3626
j.freeman@arts.com

---

PERFORMING ARTS PRODUCER • CONSULTANT • DEVELOPMENT

---

## EXPERIENCE

Jan Freeman Associates, Santa Monica, California, 1986–Present
**President**

Produce performing arts programs, cultural events, and media works internationally and in universities and concert venues throughout the United States. Develop specialized programs to promote and enhance audience appreciation. Target community market segments and develop promotional and educational activities/events to reach them. Initiate and maintain relationships with area arts organizations. Maximize reach via effective use of resources. Promote and manage staff, consultants, artists, and collaborating professionals. Locate and develop corporate relationships; perform grant-writing; perform development via estate planning.

Archway Concerts, Berkeley, California, 1982–1986
**Concert Director**

Presented over 800 concerts, events and weekly live radio broadcasts including world-class composers and performers in such specialties as chamber music, jazz, avant-garde, and world music. Full-scale facilities management. Artists included Kronos Quartet, John Adams, and John Handy.

## REPRESENTATIVE PROGRAMS

**Produced** *America on Tap,* a touring production featuring Charles "Honi" Coles as M.C. with legendary tap masters and young stars of the Broadway shows *Black and Blue* and *Jelly's Last Jam.* Sold out performances at University of Minnesota, University of Washington, and Anchorage Concert Association, 1996–1997.

**Producer/Agent** of World Tour for composer Lou Harrison. Performances at the German State Opera, Bonn; Music of the World Festival, Basel, Switzerland; The Holland Festival, Amsterdam; International Mozart Academy, Prague; Pacific Music Festival, Japan, 1996.

**Produced** *In Xanadu,* a critically acclaimed music theater work based on Balinese Shadow Puppet Theater with members of the Tibetan Dance and Opera Company at Theater Artaud, San Francisco, 1996.

**Co-Producer/Consultant for** *The Beat and Beyond,* a poetry reading and fine arts exhibition featuring Lawrence Ferlinghetti, Michael McClure, Joanne Kyger, and Robert Hunter at the Palace of Fine Arts, Los Angeles, 1996.

**Produced** *Sound Design,* the first national conference on the creative use of sound in media at Skywalker Ranch, Nicasio, California. Featured speakers: John Cage and Ben Burtt, 1995.

**Co-Producer and Editor of** *Circles & Cycles, Kathak Dance,* a documentary about classical dance of North India, collection Metropolitan Museum of Art, New York, a PBS broadcast, 1994.

*More . . .*

**Producer/Artistic Director of** *Crossovers,* a performance-interview program featuring traditional master artists from China, Japan, Indonesia, and India along with their American students at The Exploratorium, San Francisco, and University of California, Berkeley, International House, 1990–1994.

**American Producer/Artistic Consultant to the BBC TV production of** *West Coast Story, Frontiers of New Music,* a three-part television series about the history of West Coast composers including more than 20 performances by soloists and ensembles in New York, San Francisco, Los Angeles, and San Diego. Broadcast BBC, Great Britain, 1993.

**Performing Arts Curator/Project Director of** *2000 Years of Indian Music,* a performing arts festival and exhibition with more than 20 events featuring some of the world's finest musicians and dancers of India. International Festival of India, The Exploratorium, San Francisco, 1992.

**International Artist Representative/Producer for Conlon Nancarrow,** Mexico-based composer who received a MacArthur Foundation award. Negotiated all commissions, contracts and produced concert tours through Europe, to Lincoln Center, New York, and Kennedy Center, Washington, D.C., and with the L.A. Philharmonic Orchestra, 1987–1992.

**Producer of music performance tour to the U.S.S.R. and Romania by the Rova Saxophone Quartet.** Negotiated all agreements with the Soviet and Romanian governments, directed fund-raising and produced a three week concert tour to eleven (11) cities in Russia and Romania, 1989.

**Co-Producer of** *Saxophone Diplomacy,* the first nationally broadcast documentary to be made on location in the former Soviet Union. Broadcast PBS and **Producer** of a multimedia work about the tour presented at museums and universities throughout California, 1989–1990.

**Producer of** *The Way Of How,* the first large-scale theater production by George Coates Performance Works.

## GRANTS, AWARDS AND HONORS

**Corporation for Public Broadcasting — Gold,** *Bread & Roses Radio Production,* 1995
**Silver Apple Award, National Educational Film Festival,** *Circles & Cycles, Kathak Dance,* 1994
**San Francisco Critics Award,** *The Way Of How, George Coates Performance Works,* 1987

**California Arts Council**
**Conimcut Foundation**
**Foundation for Contemporary Performance Arts**
**MacArthur Foundation**
**Meet the Composer**
**National Endowment for the Arts**
**Pioneer Fund**
**San Francisco Foundation**
**Thendara Foundation**
**L.J. & Mary C. Skaggs Foundation**
**Zellerbach Family Fund**
**White Light Foundation – Betty Freeman**

*More . . .*

## PUBLIC SPEAKING

**Presenting New Performance,** Conference, California Arts Council, 1988
**Keynote Address, Rural Artists in California,** Conference, Rural Arts Services, 1996

**Moderator/Interviewer:**

**Presenting Ethnic Performing Arts,** Conference, University of San Francisco
**Conlon Nancarrow,** Kennedy Center Stage
**Conlon Nancarrow,** Almeida Theater, London, England
**Conlon Nancarrow,** Center for the Arts, Austria
**Conlon Nancarrow,** Center for Contemporary Art, Santa Fe

**Broadcast:**

**KPIX, PBS, NPR, KKHI, KPFA, KQED, KJAZ**
Radio/television interviews with over fifty (50) artists.

## LANGUAGES

Conversational proficiency in German, Spanish, and French.

## EDUCATION

**Postgraduate Studies:**

**World Music and Dance**
WESLEYAN UNIVERSITY, Middletown, CT, 1987/1990
DUKE UNIVERSITY, Durham, NC, 1984
UNIVERSITY OF WASHINGTON, Seattle, WA, 1979
MILLS COLLEGE, Oakland, CA, 1978

**Undergraduate:**

**World Music and Dance**
UNIVERSITY OF CALIFORNIA, Los Angeles, CA, 1974

**Liberal Arts and Foreign Language**
MERRITT COLLEGE, Oakland, CA, 1972–1974

**Independent Study in Europe, 1975–1978**

# DANIEL R. GUTTIEREZ

114 Jostlery Place NW
Seattle, Washington 98114

Office: (206) 555-0673
Residence: (206) 555-1863

---

## EXPERTISE

### Human Services

Demonstrated ability to create successful service delivery models that promote well-being, facilitate self-sufficiency, and enhance the quality of life for individuals, their families, and their communities.

History of developing productive relationships and partnerships with local citizens, and governmental, nonprofit, and community organizations. Able to focus diverse participants on a common goal.

Committed to providing innovative programs that reflect the values, diversity, aspirations, and priorities of the communities they serve.

*Strengths:*
- Needs/assets assessment based on interaction with those affected
- Grant writing and fund-raising
- Large-scale project development and management
- Team building, training, management, and motivation
- Budget projection and administration

## EXPERIENCE

AMERICAN RED CROSS, SEATTLE AREA COUNCIL, Seattle, Washington, 1987–Present
**Director, Social Services**, 1994–Present

The Red Cross is a $9.5 million-budgeted emergency services organization serving the entire Puget Sound area. As social services director, manage programs and services valued at over $1 million, and the program managers and project coordinators who supervise those services. Currently overseeing seven simultaneous programs, including community-specific services (food, transportation, rental assistance, emergency communications, and international tracing) that are provided to over 5000 households/year.

Develop and maintain relationships with community leaders and service agencies to leverage and increase the delivery of Red Cross services in targeted communities. Provide technical oversight to a county-based services delivery system to ensure the development, implementation, and management of localized social services programs and activities. Identify unmet needs within a community and respond by 1) developing a program within Red Cross; 2) working with other local agencies, neighborhood groups, congregations, or government social services to design an action plan using combined resources; or 3) referring communities to other appropriate agencies.

Personally repositioned the American Red Cross as a leading community service organization within the Seattle-Tacoma-Olympia urban/suburban corridor by expanding scope from emergency response to natural disasters to include response to man-made disasters. Also initiated programs and increased services in extremely low-income, high-risk communities.

*Selected Projects:*
- Pioneered "Homelessness Prevention Program" for at-risk families in Seattle-Tacoma-Olympia. Program has served over 5000 families in its six-year history and has been over 85% successful in keeping families in housing.
- Created "Self-Sufficiency Project" to help families end the cycle of welfare after their rent has been stabilized. Contacted six different social services agencies and orchestrated their participation in programs ranging from male mentoring to foster care. Applied for and received grants, recruited volunteers, hired new staff, and developed and implemented successful model.
- Initiated "Family Support Center Program," which established two sites within the housing authority to serve 1000 additional families annually.
- Created "Low-Income Community Preparedness Project" to train families in low-income neighborhoods on how to prepare for and survive disasters. This ongoing program involved establishing a new partnership with Temple of God First Baptist Church in Seattle and will benefit thousands of households in that area.

*Continued . . .*

**Manager, Social Services, Seattle Chapter**, 1989–1993

Successfully restructured and revitalized Red Cross community services in Seattle proper. Managed an annual budget in excess of $750,000 and a staff of twenty in providing a full range of social and emergency services. Promoted to director of social services.

*Selected Contributions:*

- Pioneered "Homelessness Prevention Program" after sourcing and securing grants and private donations. Within one year, expanded program to include a full-time staff of eight serving over 1000 area families.
- Reorganized and streamlined fragmented "After Hours Services Program" (emergency communications, disaster notification and response). Consolidated staff, saving Red Cross over $15,000/year, while improving quality and efficiency. Established centralized, fully computerized site operating 24 hours/day. Unit covered fifteen counties in Western Washington, and responded to over 3000 emergency requests for assistance each year with zero breakdowns in service. Unit ranked in top five of urban after hours programs nationwide.
- Authored and served as primary consultant for $10 million Red Cross case management program established to respond to scientists' discovery of quake zone off Washington and Oregon. This program is designed to speed services to thousands of victims of any future quake, from homeowners to the homeless.
- Wrote successful grant for funding to establish Red Cross case management services for homeless clients at the new Seattle multiservice centers for the homeless, established in 1990. Became member of the advisory board for shelter operations.
- Wrote a proposal for an additional $275,000 in funds to respond to the ongoing economic disaster of the homeless in downtown Seattle by comparing their conditions to war refugees.

*Award*

**Finalist, Washington Entrepreneur of the Year, Not-for-Profit Category**, 1995

Assessed community need and took initiative to expand Red Cross services to serve people at risk of becoming homeless. Wrote proposals to the Hearst Foundation for $25,000 and to the Department of Social Services for $69,000 which were awarded in full. Raised an additional $32,000 through a special fund-raising event and used monies to establish the "Homelessness Prevention Program."

**Assistant Director, Emergency Services, Seattle Chapter**, 1982–1988

Developed and implemented social service programs and oversaw the use of agency and community resources. Organized and managed a nine-member staff of paid and volunteer caseworkers and an administrative coordinator. Recruited, trained, and evaluated performance of volunteers. Smoothly transitioned services to new chapter. Promoted to manager of social services.

*Selected Programs:*

- Reunification Program: Worked with family members of refugees in camps throughout Thailand, Laos, and Cambodia to prepare proper legal documentation and take all necessary steps to bring their relatives to the United States. Program served over 300 households/year.
- Sports Injury Prevention Program: Wrote grant to secure funding for program focused on local Hispanic soccer teams. Worked directly with Red Cross service center staff and attended advisory meetings to ensure that quality services were maintained in that community.
- Holocaust Tracing Service: Assisted over 200 area residents attempting to discover the status of relatives. Oversaw tracing services in Seattle and coordinated announcement of program in newspapers, directories, and agencies.
- Emergency Assistance to Fire Victims: Provided all essential services necessary to permanently rehouse victims of single-family fires.

*Continued . . .*

*Prior*

AMERICAN RED CROSS, GREATER NEW YORK CHAPTER, New York, New York
**Supervisor, Casework Services**

Oversaw all casework services provided by the Brooklyn service center. Programs included: *Emergency Assistance to Disaster Victims, Assistance to Elderly Victims of Crime, Emergency Communication to Families with Dependents in the Military.*

FEDERATION OF THE HANDICAPPED, New York, New York
**Intake and Assessment Specialist**

Received and assessed all applicants for entry into Nurse's Assistant/Home Health Aide training program. Reviewed fifteen new applicants every two weeks.

ESPADA (Educational Society for Prevention of Adolescent Drug Addiction), New York, New York
**Rehabilitation Counselor**

Performed individual and group counseling for Hispanic and African American teenage substance abusers.

POSTGRADUATE CENTER FOR MENTAL HEALTH, New York, New York
**Rehabilitation Counselor**

Provided individual counseling and daily group counseling for schizophrenic client population.

## EDUCATION

NEW YORK UNIVERSITY, New York, New York
**M.A.**, Counseling

HERBERT LEHMAN COLLEGE, CITY UNIVERSITY OF NEW YORK, Bronx, New York
**B.A.**, History

*Additional*

FORDHAM UNIVERSITY, New York, New York
Postgraduate Studies in **Urban Studies / Urban Education**

## AFFILIATIONS

C.A.R.D. Oversight Team, Co-chair 1994

Seattle Emergency Food and Shelter Board, Board Member, Chair 1991–1993

Seattle Shelter Grievance Advisory Committee, Member

Seattle Homeless Family Service Providers, Member

Seattle Council on Homelessness, Member

Seattle Homelessness Prevention Consortium, Member

*Excellent references and recommendations provided on request.*

Cf. the marketing
and sales résumés
in chapter 5.

# MICHELLE ANN BELL

1022 Avenue of the Americas, #R22
New York, New York 10014

Office: (212) 555-8355
Residence: (212) 555-2164

## PROFILE

Innovative team builder and leader with vision to identify opportunity; strategize, plan, and implement turn-arounds; create self-sufficient, profitable organizations. Skilled financial planner and believer in statistical-based management. Knowledge of commercial real estate.

History of continuing success based on the belief that given the chance, people will outperform all expectations.

## EXPERIENCE

UNITED HANDICAPPED INDUSTRIES OF NEW YORK      1987–Present
**Senior Director of Marketing & Planning**, 1994–Present

Report to the CFO, supervise marketing manager, loss prevention manager, fulfillment manager, and staff. Serve on long-range planning committee and work closely with board of directors to introduce and implement agency improvements. United Handicapped Industries is a nonprofit with donation income of $2+ million (cash and in-kind) and retail revenues in excess of $18+ million per annum. If United Handicapped were a for-profit business, it might very well have the highest gross profit of any major retail business in the New York area.

*Selected Contributions:*

- **Project manager for $11.2 million purchase and renovation of new corporate headquarters, career services training center, and processing plant**. Initiated requests for proposal, selected design team, established budget, assisted in design, and directed engineers, architects, design build contractors, general contractor, and subcontractors.
- Opened agency's first satellite career training center. Targeted under-served areas for service expansion and orchestrated entire project. Located and secured lease for facility, directed renovation, and provided creative and workable solutions to major obstacles.
- Created new marketing department which evolved into new corporate identity program with the goal of establishing a clear public identity for agency. Envisioned, co-created, and led three-phase marketing campaign with $242,000 board-approved budget. Public relations campaign included 2 *Power of Work* videos and an open house awareness event at new headquarters with 2,100 guests in attendance. Planned and coordinated event which resulted in over $500,000 in in-kind donations from community sponsors.
- Formed partnership model with local businesses and other social service agencies to facilitate fulfillment of vision to provide vocational services for 2,000 people/year by the year 2000.
- Instituted safety program which **cut workers' comp rate in half**, a huge savings for the agency. (This loss prevention strategy is now used as a model for nonprofits throughout the United States.)
- Brought sales back on track after 1995 riot in which we lost our largest store, formerly responsible for 40% of total retail revenue.
- **Increased sales** through identifying, leasing, renovating, and opening retail outlets.

**Senior Director of Marketing Operations**, 1987–1994

Reported to the president; supervised a staff of 7, including sales managers, transportation manager, processing manager, loss prevention manager, administrative assistant, and fulfillment manager. Took over administration of transportation department (trucks and donation centers). Renovated entire fleet of 78. Led aggressive vehicle safety campaign resulting in reduced vehicle maintenance, fewer accidents, and lower insurance costs. Improved image of donation centers by increasing site maintenance efforts and focusing on becoming good neighbors to sponsoring businesses.

*– continued –*

Successfully campaigned for creation of long-range business plans and formalized sales goals. Instituted employee-incentive bonus plan based on departmental performance which increased level of cooperation between departments and individual employees. Worked with board of directors and management staff to increase employee salaries, benefits, and wages. Led agencywide safety committee and established safety program involving creation of safety-related reporting systems, goals, policies, and procedures.

*Selected Contributions:*

- **Increased store sales from $2.3 million to $6.25 million** between 1987 and 1992.
- Established material handling system which reduced donor-to-retail turnaround time and decreased operational expenses.
- Located, acquired, and renovated 11 stores.
- Turned around operational profitability. Reached and maintained E/R ratio of 75% or below.
- Partnered with Aluminum Redemption Corp. to establish 6 new sponsored sites, resulting in an additional $1.2 million in annual revenue.
- Directed opening of 10+ new donation centers which assisted in phenomenal sales growth.
- Initiated public awareness campaigns and designed advertisements that resulted in donations and sales and earned agency *Best Donation Advertising Award* for 1992.
- Introduced agencywide monitored security system to protect employees and property.

**Sales / Processing Director**, 1987

Reported to the president; supervised 11 employees, including 5 store managers, 5 workshop managers, and 1 processing manager. Analyzed store functions and provided plans for more efficient processing. Refurbished stores and instructed employees on basic retail, warehousing, and distribution methods to increase profits. Initiated computerized sales-to-shipment report which enabled managers to track product they received and facilitated effective distribution and pricing of goods.

*Selected Contributions:*

- **Immediately increased sales by 23.5%.**
- Located, renovated, and opened profitable store.
- Created capital request lists and pro forma for finance committee.
- Improved morale by listening to staff needs and concerns and implementing policies to give employees a voice in operations. Established regular group meetings and launched incentive programs to encourage healthy sales competition between stores and departments.
- Received promotion based on performance. Assumed responsibility for transportation and entire retail operation.

EASTER SEAL / GOODWILL INDUSTRIES, INC., Great Falls, Montana          1984–1987
**Vice President of Marketing**

Reported directly to the president and oversaw a staff of 5, including store managers, workshop supervisor, contracts supervisor, and retail frame shop manager. Closed unprofitable candleholder manufacturing operation and redoubled efforts in short-term specialty contracts with area businesses. Established marketing plan to increase statewide auditory program services. Obtained workshop contracts through increased personal contact with local business community. Negotiated janitorial/hotel/motel cleaning contracts.

*Accomplishments:*

- Earned *You've Earned Your Spurs* award.
- Charter member of the Montana Manufacturing Association.
- Greatly increased public awareness through media appearances and PSAs.
- **Increased sales and profitability** of retail frame shop by featuring art work by local artists and decreasing service turnaround time.

*– continued –*

BIG SKY AIRLINES, Billings, Montana      1982–1983
**Western Regional Sales Manager**

Hired as station agent, promoted and relocated to H.Q. within first 2 months. Coordinated and directed all sales-related activities in Western United States and Texas. Wrote and edited press releases and travel agency newsletter. Traveled extensively to conduct trade shows at all major regional ticketing centers. Member of speakers bureau. Involved in marketing and public relations programs; appeared in airline television commercial.

*Contributions:*
- **Increased boardings by 12%**.
- Contributed monthly articles to *In-Flight Magazine*.

GOODWILL INDUSTRIES, INLAND EMPIRE, Syracuse, New York      1977–1981
**Marketing Operations Director**

Started as sales manager; promoted twice within first year to become marketing operations director. Reported directly to the president and oversaw a staff of 11, including store managers, transportation manager, workshop leadpeople, processing manager, security manager, and janitorial lead. Streamlined operations resulting in greater efficiency and higher productivity. Established employee purchase policy to encourage solidarity. Installed security systems to protect property and staff. Served as consultant to Easter Seal/Goodwill of New York.

*Selected Contributions:*
- **Increased sales from $1.2 million to $2.3 million**.
- Forerunner of updated retail format.
- Piloted attended donation center system which significantly decreased departmental costs and yielded higher quality of goods.
- Initiated processing plant renovation.
- Guided safety team in institution of program that resulted in **4-year period of zero lost-time accidents**.

ECONO PRINT, Billings, Montana      1969–1976
**Founder / Owner / Manager**

Founded and developed this state-of-the-art "instant" print shop after managing first of its kind in the state. Built business through innovative marketing/public relations/promotional campaigns. Hired, trained, supervised, and motivated staff. Created and implemented safety plan with zero-accident result.

*Accomplishments:*
- Began with 1 employee and first-year sales of $6,000. Developed company into $320,000/year business with staff of 11 full-time press operators, typesetters, clerks, and bookkeeper.
- Sold mature business for substantial profit in 1974. Continued to manage for new owner.

## SELECTED AWARDS AND AFFILIATIONS

*Sales and Marketing Executives International*
 **Regional Vice President**      1992–1994
 **Board of Directors**      1985–1993
 **President, New York Chapter** (first female president in organization's history)      1990–1991
 Received **International Award for Affiliate Membership Growth**      1991

*Unity Christ Church*, **Long-Range Planning Committee**      1994–Present

*New Hunters Point Homeowners Association*, **Board of Directors, Treasurer**      1991–1992

*City of Great Falls, Montana*, **Parking Commissioner** (mayoral appointee)      1983–1985

*Downtown Business Council, Great Falls, Montana*, **Executive Vice President**      1984–1985

Named One of Four **Women Achievers** by *Sales and Marketing Executives of New York*      1991

# Rachel Greene

88 North Park Circle
Highland Park, Illinois 60035

Telephone/Message:
(847) 555-7457

## SUMMARY

Specialist in major gifts. Proven ability to articulate the institutional message with professionalism and sensitivity to diverse constituencies; international, national, regional and local fund-raising and promotions experience.

Program evaluation and management skills, including strategic planning, marketing, operations management, proposal and grant writing, budgeting, team building.

Extensive experience in media relations, public speaking. Former journalist.

## EXPERIENCE

North Shore Jewish Community Federation, 1992–present
**Director of Development**

Leadership and coordination of all operational, budgetary, and staffing functions for fund-raising activities. Direct all aspects of key annual fund-raising campaign. Develop strategies to cultivate prospective and existing donors. Actively develop new constituencies for the organization and perform direct solicitation. Plan public affairs programs for the Jewish legal community. Topics included highly complex, often controversial legal, political, and world issues.

*Highlights:*

Recruited more (and better) fund-raising volunteers than ever before, including one who personally contributed a $100,000 gift. Developed team of over 200 telephone volunteers who generated more than 1500 gifts totalling $721,000 in a single day. Instituted first corporate matching gifts program that raised an *additional* $140,000 its first year in place.

Member of federation task force sent to Israel to research political complexities, economic challenges, social and historical trends. Interviewed top government officials and representatives of various political parties. Conducted on-site visits to health care facilities, emigre resettlement sites, etc.

Significantly increased ratio of actual versus pledged receipts.

American Diabetes Association, 1990–1992
**Director of Development**

Originated and administered major funding programs for Illinois chapter. Prepared reports and policy recommendations and made presentations to the board. Trained and supervised 50-person team comprised of staff, consultants, volunteers. Spearheaded major educational drive for Hispanic and African American outreach programs.

Increased revenues 200% in first six months, and sustained this strong performance throughout the years. Enlisted assistance of celebrity athletes (including Joe Montana) for sports-sponsored fund-raisers. Wrote successful corporate and foundation proposals. Negotiated arrangements for major fund-raising prizes from all major U.S. airlines.

Edited and produced a 36-page quarterly news magazine to educate the public.

New York Marathon, 1987–1990
**Marketing Consultant, Latin America Specialist**

Created and pursued a marketing strategy yielding involvement of business, community, and foreign government and military leaders. Represented organizers in recruiting elite international athletes for participation in the world's largest marathon. Foreign media relations preceding/during event.

*– continued –*

Home Box Office, 1984–1987
**Public Relations Consultant**

Directed national media campaign and promoted company image and name recognition throughout the country.

English Language School, 1970–1976
**Director** (Malaga, Spain)

## EDUCATION

New York University
**Master of Public Policy Analysis,** 1983

Coro Foundation
**Fellowship in Public Affairs,** 1982–1983

Including internships with San Francisco Board of Supervisors (reported to the president), California Roundtable (researched and wrote a 36-page report on high school graduates' preparation for the work place, published by Pacific Bell), Kaiser Aluminum and Chemical Corporation, and North of Market Planning Coalition.

Mills College
**Bachelor of Arts Degree (with honors), Spanish,** 1981

Commencement Speaker, Class of 1981

Phi Beta Kappa

## ADDITIONAL

**Languages:**

Fluent in English and Spanish

**Member:**

First Vice President, Brandeis University Foundation, current
• Recruited Board Members, one of whom founded a $10,000 scholarship.
• Chaired Mission Statement Committee and served as Vice President of Community Development.

Board of Trustees, Mills College, 1986–1989
• Vice President of Educational Life Committee.
• Member on South African Action Committee.

**Journalist/Contributing Writer:**

Contributor, *New York Times* and *Chicago Tribune*

Contributor, *ASU Travel Guide* (a publication for travel industry professionals)

Journalist, *Lookout Magazine* (the English-language magazine of Spain)

Journalist, *Pacific Sun* (a weekly newspaper in Highland Park, Illinois)

# Samuel A. Murray

4100 Third Street
San Francisco, California 94124

14all.all41@com-act.com
Private Line: (415) 555-7521
Private Fax: (415) 555-8837

---

## EXPERTISE

**Program Development & Delivery / Outreach & Advocacy / Management / Supervision**
- Complete needs assessment, program design and development, workshop design, policies/procedures, budgeting, community organizing, staff training, delivery.
- Additional experience in management, supervisory, and public relations roles.
- Personal commitment for delivery of social services to populations at risk.

## EXPERIENCE

**Business Development, Inc. (BDI)**, San Francisco, California        1993–Present
**Project Coordinator**

Business Development, Inc., is a community development agency working on major economic development projects in San Francisco, as examples: Moscone Center, Yerba Buena, San Francisco International Airport Expansion. Provide outreach, liaison, and project implementation. Interface with city agencies: DPW, Architecture Department, Human Rights Commission, and others. Attend and/or organize community meetings. Represent BDI to community groups throughout the Bay Area. Provide minutes, notes, and strategic recommendations to BDI President and CEO.

**Environmental Health Research Consultants**, San Francisco, California        1993–Present
**Founder** and **Principal**

Launched this consulting, lobbying, and advocacy group to address the critical problem of environmental racism. Achieved widespread media coverage of this new issue: documentary, CNN, news stories, KPIX, KRON, ABC, cover story, *San Francisco Weekly*, *San Francisco Bay Guardian*, and many other placements.

Founder, **People's Earth Day Coalition**, the first-ever minority-based Earth Day celebration committee in San Francisco. Co-sponsor of **Earth Day** 1993, with direct linkage to major national and international environmental groups.

Assist in development of **EcoRap**, an independent, community-based organization based in Berkeley with the mission of teaching children about the environment through rap music and the arts.

Lecturer on environmental racism to classes and student groups at U.C. Berkeley, San Francisco State University, Golden Gate University, and others.

Founder, **The Peoples Foundation**, a nonprofit designed to help people of color to understand environmental issues and use political process to improve and protect their communities.

Member, **Environmental Commission** (1993–present) and **Toxic Waste Management Team** (1991–1992), City & County of San Francisco, **Local Assessment Committee** (1993–present) by appointment of the Board of Supervisors.

**Bayview Hunters Point Economical Task Force** (1993–present) created to develop economical strategies for Bayview Hunters Point presented to the Mayor.

Management team member, 3rd Street transportation and economic development study, working with **U.C. Berkeley** and **Urban Habitat**.

Founder, **Toxic Waste Tour** of Bayview Hunters Point, a nationally attended environmental/historical outreach created to educate people about the community.

**Young Community Developers, Inc.**, San Francisco, California        1992–1993
**Executive Director**

Provide policy direction and hands-on leadership to an organization providing job development and school-based career programs for minority communities. Represent the agency to funding sources, Mayor's Office of Economic Development unions, employers, and neighborhood and community organizations throughout the Bay Area. Prepare budgets, write and represent grant proposals, hire and supervise permanent and special project staff.

**Bayview Hunters Point Foundation**, San Francisco, California      1989–1993
**Alcohol & Drug Counselor, Center for Problem Drinkers**

Provide individual counseling and case work, helping clients to solve their personal and interpersonal problems, teaching clients how to help themselves, assisting clients with advocacy and referral. Personally facilitate clients' recovery of sobriety, of loving relationships, and contact with their families. Provide group counseling, creating a group dynamic for growth.

Represent the BVHP Foundation to schools and organizations, providing lectures and outreach about drugs and alcohol, addiction, and recovery.

**New Gethsemane Church of God in Christ**, Richmond, California      1988–1993
**Program Developer**

Created education and outreach program to combat drug and alcohol substance abuse problems utilizing the church as a vehicle for delivery into the community. Organized 50 volunteers to administer and deliver the program. Set policies and operating procedures.

Developed compelling educational presentations on substance abuse, its damage to the individual, the family and to the community. Took production on the road for delivery at churches from Milwaukee, Wisconsin to small towns in Mississippi. Also delivered this and similar presentations before groups of college students up to 200.

Also provided one-on-one counseling, drawing a real-life picture of the choices before the substance abuser.

Developed first-ever AIDS Prevention Program for churches focusing on AIDS's disproportionate impact on minority populations and suggesting appropriate methodologies to reach these populations.

**R.B. Furniture**, South San Francisco, California      1982–1986
**Decorator**

Number one salesperson in Northern California. Developed sales presentations, planned and implemented sales strategies, conducted sales training and motivational seminars for other decorators.

**Greyhound Bus Lines**, Redwood City, California      1978–1981
**Operations Field Manager**

Supervised 300 bus drivers on busy corridor from San Francisco to San Jose. Interviewed, hired, trained and monitored new employees. Handled all discipline and remedial problems. Designed bus routes and schedules; handled other operational duties.

**Jimmy Bee Productions**, Berkeley, California      1975–1977
**Sales & Public Relations Representative**

Utilized every aspect of sales, marketing, promotions and public relations to promote our artists nationwide. Traveled extensively. Promoted with DJs, VJs, and station managers to get TV and radio time for our talent. Devised POP promotions for stores.

## EDUCATION, CREDENTIALS, WORKSHOPS, ETC.

**City & County of San Francisco, Environmental Commission** (1993–present) and **Toxic Waste Management Team** (1991–1992)

**AIDS Prevention Workshop**, Bayview Hunters Point Foundation for Community Improvement

**Relapse Prevention Seminar**, Sunrise House

**Black Family, Community & Crack Cocaine: Prevention, Treatment, Recovery** (national conference)

**HIV Conference** (national conference)

**Economics** and **Liberal Arts** studies, U.C. Berkeley, C.S.U. Hayward, C.C.S.F., and others

**Bayview Hunters Point Homeowners and Residential Community Development Council**, Spokesperson and Chair, **Toxic Waste Committee**, and Chair, **Black Family Day Festival**

**Democratic Club, District 7, Finance Committee**, and Chair, **Toxic Waste Committee**

**N.A.A.C.P., S.F. Chapter**, (former) **Member of the Board**

# Virginia Defoe

2504 South River Road
Richmond, Virginia 23252

Office: (804) 555-3780
Residence: (804) 555-6616

---

## EXPERTISE

**Nonprofit Administration**

—**Program Development**
—**Fund-Raising & Development**
—**Public Relations**

## EXPERIENCE

HEARING DOGS FOR THE DEAF PROGRAM, Richmond SPCA, 1982–Present

**Founding Director** of the Hearing Dogs for the Deaf program, an innovative program to train abandoned dogs as hearing dogs for the deaf. This program is considered a model program throughout the United States.

In full charge of executive direction and daily operations. Supervise administrative staff, training specialists and a communications specialist. Indirectly in charge of 120 paid and volunteer staff of the SPCA. Report to the president of the Richmond SPCA. Member, executive staff and long-range planning committees, Richmond SPCA. Special advisor by invitation of the board, SPCA national organization.

Developed specialized training techniques required for the selection, training, and placement of dogs for the deaf. Developed curriculum for teaching deaf recipients the care and continued training and discipline of their dogs.

Manage all phases of the hearing dog program in Richmond. Establish goals and objectives, plan operations and special projects, direct personnel, represent the program to the public and the press. Administer budget up to $400,000 per year in capital equipment, wages, marketing, P/R, etc. Consult with SPCA branches nationwide on this program.

Personally responsible for a major role in fund-raising activities for the program. Have conducted hundreds of public appearances and demonstrations to groups of all ages.

MANSON DISTRIBUTING COMPANY, Atlanta, Georgia, 1975–1982

**District Sales Manager** for this wholesale carpet distributor. Personally handled key accounts with carpet stores, outlets, interior decorators and designers, and general contractors. With strong organizational skills and consistency of follow-through, was #1 in sales companywide for three straight years. Some accomplishments: Opened new territory from 0 to 130 accounts; generated $350,000 per annum in sales; consistently rated best in the company.

R.T. VAN GARZA TRADING COMPANY, Atlanta, Georgia, 1972–1974

**Sales Manager** of this wholesale carpet brokerage and contracting business. Acted as mill representative to decorators and designers over a three-state area. Wrote specifications and contracts for large-scale installations such as schools and corporate headquarters. Developed company profit planning, implemented annual goals and objectives.

## EDUCATION

Graduate studies in **Marketing**, Georgia State University, Atlanta
**B.B.A.**, **Marketing**, University of Georgia, Athens

# Keith R. "Bobby" Rayburn

120 Madeira Drive NE
Albuquerque, New Mexico 87108

Office: (505) 555-2206
Residence: (505) 555-7644

---

## STRENGTHS

### Housing Development

Knowledgeable in all aspects of administration and financial management related to community-based housing development: public, corporate, private and foundation funding and financing, governmental regulations/requirements, HUD audit requirements, OMB A-133 requirements, social service provision, project assessment and community education. Thorough understanding of real estate finance and acquisition.

Public contact skills, representing community interests to individuals, citizen groups, government bodies, business leaders, media.

Strong administrative record: budget development and administration, reducing/minimizing costs, ensuring legal and regulatory compliance.

## EDUCATION

UNIVERSITY OF NEW MEXICO, Albuquerque, New Mexico
**Master of Public Administration**, *ongoing*

UNIVERSITY OF NEW MEXICO, Albuquerque, New Mexico
**Bachelor of Science, Economics**

## HISTORY

BOSWELL HEIGHTS HOUSING CORPORATION
BOSWELL HEIGHTS NEIGHBORHOOD CENTER, Albuquerque, New Mexico
**Fiscal Manager (CFO)**, 1990–Present

Chief financial officer for nonprofit housing development and social service agency serving low-income clients. Develop and manage combined operating and program budget of $1.2 million, along with current capital budget of $12.4 million. Participate in funding application process, and negotiate all bridge financing. Interact with private lenders and public agencies: Bank of America; Wells Fargo; Low-Income Housing Fund; Mayor's Offices of Housing, Community Development, Criminal Justice, and Children, Youth and Families; New Mexico Commission on Aging; and Albuquerque Redevelopment Agency.

Actively involved with site selection and monitoring, pro forma development and review, bridge financing, all aspects of reporting, consulting with management companies and social service providers. Prepare HUD HOPWA monitoring reports, and CDGB and COA monthly and annual reports.

Focus is on neighborhood housing providing economy of scale, and accessibility to transportation and social services for special-needs populations.

*Key Contributions*:

Member of Board of Directors for New Mexico Reinvestment Committee, monitoring banks' compliance with CRA Act of 1978. Negotiated with team on Bank of America purchase of New Mexico Security Assurance, resulting in Boswell Heights branch being one of only two instances in major corporate merger where bank rescinded plans to close a branch. Negotiating with new owners of First Nationwide, especially on branch issues in low income neighborhoods.

*Continued . . .*

*Sample Projects:*

Secretary of Board of Directors for Boswell Senior Housing Corporation owning 49-unit building for seniors.

Market Heights, a 46-unit affordable tax credit project for working families.

Ten studio units on Woolsey Street purchased with HOME funds and conventional commercial loan from Bank of the West, with bridge financing provided by Low-Income Housing Fund.

119 Holly Park Circle NE and 416 Precita Avenue NE, 4 total units providing 10 beds for persons and families disabled by HIV/AIDS. Bridge financing provided by Corporation for Support of Housing, Low-Income Housing Fund and SFRA, with permanent funding provided by HOPWA.

Moultrie Street, 4-units with 10 beds for persons coming through mental health care system. Bridge financing provided by Bank of New Mexico, with permanent financing from CDBG-Site Acquisition and conventional mortgage from Citibank.

ALAN CLARK, D.D.S., Albuquerque, New Mexico
**Practice Manager**, 1988–1990, 1982–1985

Managed financial and administrative aspects of $50,000/month private dental practice: third party billing and administration, fee collection, cost control, POS marketing. Instrumental in doubling of monthly revenues over 18-month period.

SMILE AMERICA OF NEW MEXICO, Santa Fe, New Mexico
**Office Manager**, 1985–1988

Managed office with 5 dentists, supervising up to 3 support staff. Managed cash flow, financial arrangements, patient and employee scheduling.

## REFERENCES

References, transcripts and additional information gladly furnished upon request.

# Chapter 11

# *Military*

Military résumés for use inside the defense industry, including all defense-related government agencies and defense contractors, are classic, accomplishment-based presentations familiar to you from elsewhere in the book.

These presentations are typically jargon-laden, which is fine as long as any jargon they contain is known to the intended reader. If the jargon is likely not to be familiar to the intended reader, define the acronym or term upon its first use and then use it without explanation for the rest of the document. You can assume that the agency or contractor will know standard military terminology and be familiar with rank, missions, materiel, and facilities for each branch of the service.

If a military officer wants to use a résumé for a position outside the defense community, however, a different approach must be taken. The résumé must be *translated* into standard business English. This is not the same thing as writing a transitional résumé (see p. 33 in chapter 2).

First, remove all reference to armament and materiel, which can make civilians uncomfortable. Instead of talking about guns, tanks, and bombs, talk about equipment, machinery, and supplies.

Then, translate other military terms into business equivalents; for example, change "soldiers" and "sailors" into "employees," change "platoon" to "work team," and so on. Avoid gender references such as "men," even if they were all men. When you have a rank and a functional title, always opt for the functional title: Director, Leadership Development Program. You can also explain rank or title equivalencies in parentheses or in the body of the job description, as in these two examples:

**Sergeant** (equivalent to a first-line supervisor)

---

**Base Commander**

Served in position functionally equivalent to mayor of a small town or president of a large company, staff of 12,800, 3,000-acre facility including all infrastructure, two major transportation fleets, and billions of dollars of capital equipment.

In any military résumé, be careful not to publish classified information. In fact, you can romanticize some older positions by saying little or nothing about them. You know and I know that you drank coffee for a living for two years, but you could say:

**Intelligence Officer**, 1974–1976. Classified assignments.

Finally, in all your assignments try to think like a civilian, and report your accomplishments in reducing overhead, increasing staff productivity, enhancing worker morale, developing subordinate employees, streamlining the budgetary process, and so on. If you can use such nonmilitary words as "marketing" and "profit," you will influence your reader to believe that you have the bottom-line mentality necessary for success in the corporate world.

Be sure to check the index for civilian examples throughout the book with jobs equivalent to your military experience. By borrowing the language you can turn your military experience into a compelling presentation for the private sector.

The examples that follow run the gamut from the ultimate Pentagon insider to an ex-navy man looking for a position designing sexual harassment-prevention programs for corporate America.

# COL. FRANK JAMES R. OLIVET

HQDA ODCSPER
(DAPE-M0)
Room 245BQ2, Pentagon
Washington, D.C. 20310-0300
Office: (703) 555-4642
Fax: (703) 555-3599
Classified fax: (703) 555-4381

Residence:
12 Lockland Avenue
McLean, Virginia 22101
Personal message: (703) 555-9922

## HIGHLIGHTS

- Director of Mobilization for the Office of the Deputy Chief of Staff for Personnel of the U.S. Army. Principal advisor to LTG W. Reno, Deputy Chief of Staff for Personnel. Total of twenty years in mobilization, readiness, strength accounting, and reserve component areas, with emphasis on human resource management, information management, industrial mobilization and crisis management. Focal point on Army Staff for all personnel mobilization matters. Interface with Army Secretariat, OSD, Congress, and MACOMS.

- Directed the call up and stand down of Reserve Components for Panama, Desert Shield, Desert Storm, and Garden Plot (L.A. riots).

- Supervised total revision of Army personnel mobilization policy in light of lessons learned from Desert Shield/Desert Storm, the largest mobilization of reserve forces since WWII.

- Consistently achieve highest ratings in operationally demanding and politically sensitive assignments. (See attached ratings.) Also: related writing and public speaking skills.

## EXPERIENCE

**U.S. ARMY**, 1977–1995
**Director of Mobilization**, HQDA, ODCSPER, Pentagon, 1989 – August 1995

In addition to accomplishments mentioned above:

- Developed mobilization planning within ODCSPER from two-man team to 12-man Mobilization Directorate, now firmly established Armywide as focal point for mobilization policy. Incorporated lessons learned from Desert Shield/Desert Storm in total revision of Army personnel mobilization policy.

- Orchestrated ODCSPER participation in Chief of Staff-directed Integrated Army Mobilization Study (IAMS). Identified $300 million in unfunded requirements for necessary enhancement/improvement of the Army mobilization automation systems and $150 million for clothing and equipment replacement to take Army mobilization into the 21st century.

- Developed Selected Reserve Augmentee (SRA) concept; finalized and implemented CONUS Replacement Center concept; supervised repatriation operations for Army personnel, U.S. citizens, and foreign nationals; presided over rewrite of Emergency Actions Procedures Guide and ODCSPER portion of Army Mobilization and Operations Planning System; designed and coordinated DCSPER conference on Partial Mobilization.

**Assistant Director of Accession Policy**, Office of the Deputy Assistant Secretary of Defense for Reserve Affairs, Pentagon, 1988 – 1989

Represented Deputy Assistant Secretary of Defense for Reserve Affairs in matters related to education policy (including Montgomery GI Bill), National Service Act, Accession Policies, and Army Reserve matters in general. Developed policy and managed programs.

- Guided major programmatic improvements to administration of the Montgomery GI Bill for Reserve Components. Revised DoD guidance of Reserve Incentive Program. Contributed to formative stages of OSD(RA) committee work on National Service Act.

*– continued –*

**Chief, Mobilization Plans Branch**, HQDA, ODCSOPS, Pentagon, 1986 – 1988

Principal staff officer for matters relating to mobilization planning. Responsible for developing and refining the Army Mobilization and Operations Planning System (AMOPS) and the Army portion of the DoD Master Mobilization Plan, including industrial mobilization aspects. ODCSOPS coordinator for the Secretary of the Army Reserve Forces Policy Committee. Army representative on OJCS/OSD-sponsored mobilization exercises.

* Directed civilian contract study on the battlefield of the future and the Army's role in supporting industrial preparedness to meet surge and continuing requirements of that battlefield, for presentation to Vice Chief of Staff of the Army.
* Designed and directed Engineer Study Center analysis of total mobilization requirements for current force.

**Inspector General**, HQ, 7581ST USA Garrison, 1984 – 1985

Confidential representative to the commander, BG F. Santoni, and member of his personal staff, Fort Buchanan, Puerto Rico. Diverse readiness and effectiveness duties on behalf of the General, including the following:

* Established the first full-time, full-service Inspector General office for this command, including designing operating procedures to achieve compliance to strict performance requirements. Developed and initiated three-year rotation of inspections, reinspections, analysis, and assistance programs.

**Chief, Plans and Analysis Branch**, Office of Strength Improvement, HQ, Sixth U.S. Army, ODCSPER, 1981 – 1984

In charge of a range of retention, improvement, and readiness matters, including but not limited to Rapid Deployment Force Units, Sixth U.S. Army Automated Unit Vacancy Program, and seven U.S. Army Reserve Commands.

* Developed and implemented Pre-Initial Active Duty Training Program, reducing basic training failures and saving CONUSA hundreds of thousands of dollars in training funds.
* CONUSA analyst and representative to a major DoD study of retention policies and programs in the USAR.

**Chief, USAR Long Tour Management Branch**, USAR Personnel Center, 1977 – 1980

One of the first officers assigned to the newly created Officer Personnel Management Division at USAR Personnel Center in St. Louis, Missouri. Developed and implemented the administrative machinery required to achieve our mission: proactive career management of all USAR officers serving on special tours of active duty. DoD briefer worldwide.

* Established Long Tour Management Division at the USAR Personnel Center in St. Louis, Missouri, which evolved into the worldwide Active Guard and Reserve (AGR) program. Personally served as career manager to 1500 officers of the Individual Ready Reserve.
* Selected to serve as the original Chief, Officer Distribution Branch, Officer and Enlisted Personnel Management Directorate.

**DEAN WITTER REYNOLDS INC.**, Glendale, California
**Registered Representative**, 1976 – 1977

Financial planning and sales of securities to individual investors.

* Top Quartile Producer.

*– continued –*

## EDUCATION

**U.S. Army War College**, Carlisle, Pennsylvania
**Graduation Diploma, National Security Affairs and Military Strategies**, 1986

**Webster University**, St. Louis, Missouri
**M.S., Business Management** (minor concentration in **Economics**), 1979

**Industrial College of the Armed Forces**, Washington, D.C.
**Graduation Diploma, National Security Affairs**, 1977–1978

**California State University**, Northridge, California
**B.A., Political Science** (minor concentration in **Finance/Economics**), 1975

**New York University of Finance**, San Francisco, California
**Certificate of Completion, Securities, Financial Planning, Brokerage Operations**, 1976

## HONORS, AWARDS, ADDITIONAL CREDENTIALS

Legion of Merit

DoD Meritorious Service Medal

Republic of Vietnam Cross of Gallantry

U.S. Army Latin American Specialist

U.S. Army Special Forces

NASD Licensed Securities Salesman (expired)

Security Clearance: SBI, TS (current)

## REFERENCES

Provided on request.

# WALLACE N. DUCHAMP

2240 Haldane Drive
Petaluma, California 94952

Telephone/Message:
(707) 555-1939

---

## PROFILE

### TRAINING & DEVELOPMENT SPECIALIST

*Strengths:*

**Cultural Diversity • Sexual Harassment • MultiEthnic Workplace • EEO**

**Executive Development • Management Development • Leadership • Supervisory Skills**

**Total Quality Management • Standard Operating Procedures**

Expertise in training and corporate education, needs assessment, design/implementation/evaluation of training programs, train-the-trainer, collateral materials design, documentation, public speaking.

### HUMAN RESOURCES GENERALIST

Experience in most aspects of human resources administration, including employee relations, internal investigations, performance audit, EAP, career counseling, placement, etc.

## EDUCATION

Walden University, Minneapolis, Minnesota
**Ph.D. (ABD),** expected June 1997

Dissertation: *Effective Situational Leadership by Female Leaders in a Male-Dominant System* (in progress)

Naval Postgraduate School, Monterey, California
**M.S.,** Operations Research (Math & Statistics), 1992

Thesis: *A Model That Uses Psychomotor Testing to Predict Naval Aviator Primary Flight Grades*

University of Nebraska, Omaha, Nebraska
**B.G.S.,** Economics, *magna cum laude,* 1984

Narimasu Tokyo American Academy, Tokyo, Japan
**Diploma,** 1972

## PUBLIC & COMMUNITY SERVICE

Bits & Pieces, Oakland, California
**Governing Director**

Member of board of directors for arts administration nonprofit with the mission of identifying and supporting multicultural and disadvantaged peoples' art through individual grants, community events, coordination, outreach, and advocacy.

## EXPERIENCE

**Naval Technical Training Center,** Treasure Island, California, 1993–1997 (separation January 31, 1997)
**Executive Assistant for Total Quality** and
**Director, Leadership & Equal Opportunity Programs**

Serve as total quality "Evangelist" for the Treasure Island Naval Technical Training Center. Design TQM training modules and teach facilitators who in turn are responsible for disseminating the TQM message to over 40,000 management-level employees throughout the northwest region of the United States. Collaborate with line managers to design total quality applications to fit Navy operations. Design and deliver cultural diversity, sexual harassment, and EEO programs. Investigate sexual harassment claims and other grievances. Conduct detailed performance audits.

Oversee staff of 12 full-time facilitators. Plan and manage training materials budget of approximately $25,000. Write and deliver speeches to other regions. Provide specialized training to managers and trainers by invitation nationwide.

*Special Contributions*:

- Wrote a module for the Navywide Leadership Program, an internationally recognized executive-development program. Created the new Communication Model used as theoretical underpinning to leadership training (copyright pending).
- Co-author of regional training response to Tailhook incident. Also invited to co-plan the national response to Tailhook. Rewrote executive training module on "Legitimate Use of Power and Influence." Rewrote ethics and values presentations implemented Navywide.
- Represent employer as keynote speaker to Bay Area business groups, speaking on women in management, statistical tools for total quality, situational leadership, team building, business meeting facilitation skills, and other topics as requested.
- Author of standard for accreditation by Southern Association of Colleges and Schools. Collaborated with CO of training center on first-ever application for accreditation (granted).

**Diego Garcia Naval Base,** British Indian Ocean Territories, 1992–1993
**Operations Officer** and
**Administrative Department Head**

Managed assignment of aircraft and air crews to 14 African, Middle Eastern, Australian, Far Eastern locations. Major project: Handled all logistics for closing a base in Saudi Arabia, including planning relocation and/or decommissioning of physical plant, equipment, supplies, and crews. Critical position, with 24-hour on-call status.

**Naval Air Station,** Brunswick, Maine, 1987–1990
**Instructor/Evaluator, Flight Training** and
**Assistant Department Head, Training Department** and
**Drug & Alcohol Program Advisor**

Wrote ground and flight test components. Conducted training and testing. Supervised up to 40 personnel on a project basis. Managed budgets to $4 million. Provided training, counseling, advice and counsel to managers, career counseling, and drug and alcohol intervention and training.

**U.S. Air Force,** 1972–1983
**Interpreter/Investigator**

Classified assignments utilizing language skills in Vietnamese, Chinese, and German. Could regain conversational fluency in any of these languages if needed.

## AFFILIATIONS

Doctorate Association of New York Educators

Pi Gamma Mu Honor Society in the Social Sciences

Governing Director, Bits & Pieces (detailed above)

# WALLACE N. DUCHAMP

2240 Haldane Drive
Petaluma, California 94952

Telephone/Message:
(707) 555-1939

---

## STRENGTHS

### Total Quality Management

Extensive internal consulting background, including designing and establishing total quality programs and applying total quality concepts to a complex organization with multiple locations and billions of dollars in equipment maintenance/readiness/distribution, logistics, human resources, and training and development aspects. Expertise in statistical analysis, continuous process improvement, statistical process control, logistics, and related information systems. Computer skills: Fortran, APL, Basic, SAS, SPSS, Lotus, dBase, WordPerfect and others. Multilingual.

### Training & Development

Extensive background as teacher, lecturer, and "Evangelist" for TQM, leadership, and other areas. Can design and deliver program modules as needed. Additional HR knowledge in EEOC, diversity training, sexual harassment training, EAP, counseling, and records administration.

## EDUCATION

Walden University, Minneapolis, Minnesota
**Ph.D. (ABD),** expected June 1997

Naval Postgraduate School, Monterey, California
**M.S.,** Operations Research (Math & Statistics), 1992

University of Nebraska, Omaha, Nebraska
**B.G.S.,** Economics, *magna cum laude*, 1984

Narimasu Tokyo American Academy, Tokyo, Japan
**Diploma,** 1972

## EXPERIENCE

U.S. NAVY

Naval Technical Training Center, Treasure Island, California, 1995–1997 (separation January 31, 1997)
**Executive Assistant for Total Quality**

Serve as total quality "Evangelist" for the Treasure Island Naval Technical Training Center. Includes two distinct areas of responsibility: (1) designing total quality applications to fit Navy operations, including complex administrative, logistical, distribution, and human performance objectives; (2) designing TQM training modules and teaching facilitators who in turn are responsible for disseminating the TQM message to over 40,000 management-level employees throughout the northwest region of the United States (Alaska, Hawaii, Northern California, Northern Nevada, Oregon, Washington).

Report to the Commanding Officer of the Naval Technical Training Center. Oversee staff of 12 full-time facilitators. Plan and manage materials budget of approximately $25,000. Write and deliver speeches on TQM to other regions nationwide. Provide specialized training to managers and trainers by invitation nationwide.

Contributions:

- Collaborated with Commanding Officer on mission and vision development to integrate TQM into all elements and departments of the Navy in our region. This effort was recognized as a model by other commands, resulting in requests to assist other regions with TQM mission and vision development.
- Enhanced and strengthened the statistical component of the Navy's TQM training system.

- Taught TQM train-the-trainer at Oakland Naval Hospital by special invitation; continue as regular guest lecturer for professional staff in-service on quality issues.
- Wrote a module for the Navywide Leadership Program, an internationally recognized executive-development program. Created the new Communication Model used as theoretical underpinning to leadership training (copyright pending).
- Received commendations and letters of appreciation from impacted locations.
- Represent employer as keynote speaker to Bay Area business groups, speaking on statistical tools for total quality, situational leadership, team building, business meeting facilitation skills, and other topics as requested.

Naval Technical Training Center, Treasure Island, California, 1993–1996
**Director, Leadership and Equal Opportunity Programs**

Taught two core courses in the executive development program. Selected contributions:
- Completely rewrote communications module, ethics and core values sections of the Leadership course. Also rewrote module on "Legitimate Use of Power and Influence."
- Selected for seven-week national train-the-trainer class on training facilitation. Wrote regional train-the-trainer curriculum.
- Selected for training in performance auditing, a top-to-bottom performance review of commands. Conducted many such audits as special assignments.
- Began integrating TQM procedures into leadership training as part of doctoral studies.
- Taught Equal Opportunity course, including diversity training, cultural differences, minority advancement, and women's issues components.

Diego Garcia, British Indian Ocean Territories, 1992 –1993
**Operations Officer**
**Administrative Department Head**

Managed assignment of aircraft and air crews to 14 African, Middle Eastern, Australian, Far Eastern locations. Major project:
- Handled all logistics for closing a base in Saudi Arabia, including planning relocation and/or decommissioning of physical plant, equipment, supplies, and crews.

Naval Air Station, Brunswick, Maine, 1987–1990
**Instructor/Evaluator, Flight Training**
**Assistant Department Head, Training Department**
**Drug & Alcohol Program Advisor**

Wrote ground and flight test components. Conducted training and testing. Supervised up to 40 personnel on a project basis. Managed budgets to $4 million.

U.S. AIR FORCE, 1972 –1983
**Interpreter/Investigator**

Classified assignments utilizing language skills in Vietnamese, Chinese, and German. Could regain conversational fluency in any of these languages if needed.

## AFFILIATIONS

Doctorate Association of New York Educators

Pi Gamma Mu Honor Society in the Social Sciences

Governing Director, Bits & Pieces (minority arts nonprofit)

# JULIE LYNN HAYDEN

13975 Old Highway
Saint Paul, Minnesota 55111

Telephone/Message:
(612) 555-4898

## STRENGTHS

**Health Care Administration • Human Resources Administration • Administrative Management**

Background of accomplishment in diverse areas of health care administration and personnel/human resources administration. Strengths include organizational development, communications, community and media relations, joint-venture projects, government relations, records administration, IS, long- and short-term strategic planning. Talent for working with diverse staffs (government, military, and civilian; multicultural; international). Management experience in military *and* civilian health care environments.

Human resources background includes job design/redesign, payroll, records, evaluations, staff training and development, program design and administration.

Over 20 years of success with frequent reassignments—flexible, quick to adapt. Seeking a long-term career opportunity with a quality-oriented organization.

## EDUCATION

**M.S., Human Resources Management**, University of Utah

**B.S., Education (Biology/Chemistry)**, Norwich University

Additional 21 hours of graduate studies in **Health Care Administration**

## EXPERIENCE

**U.S. Army Hospital**, Ft. Snelling, Minnesota, 1990–Present
**Adjutant (Personnel and Records Administration, Communications)**

One of the top 20 staff members managing a 1000-bed reserve general hospital, equivalent to civilian **Vice President of Human Resources**. Direct personnel/human resources function for 700 personnel, including records, employee relations, family support program, pay and benefits, job design, staff projections, evaluations, training and development.

Also serve as a communications officer, preparing official responses to congressional inquiries, drafting official correspondence for signature by top administrators, writing/editing/producing the monthly information bulletin, directing the awards program, and responding to outside media contacts.

Part of the team that activated and mobilized 1000 medical and reserve personnel to Ft. Sam Houston in Texas during Operation Desert Storm.

**U.S. Army Reserve Personnel Center**, St. Louis, Missouri, 1988–1990
**Personnel Management Officer (Training and Development, Records Administration)**

In charge of training assignments and records administration for 2000 clinical, technical and health care management personnel. This position is equivalent to civilian **Director of Training and Development**. Required training/development expertise and considerable administrative management ability to identify and coordinate training tours of duty appropriate to develop the skills and abilities of a diverse group of professionals. Also directed complex records administration for reserve officers, all 2000 of which have separate assignment patterns.

*– continued –*

**U.S. Army Hospital**, Providence, Rhode Island, 1985–1988
**Adjutant (Personnel and Records Administration, Communications)**

Position similar to current duties, directing recruitment and retention, HR finance, HR records, employee programs, training and development, and the public relations program for a 1000-bed general hospital.

Part of the team that organized a 1000-bed contingency hospital in Chessington, England, *in less than one month.* This inactive hospital was fully designed including staffing requirements and operating procedures, with pre-packaged and pre-positioned medical equipment and supplies in place.

**Mercy Hospital of Watertown**, Watertown, New York, 1982 –1985
**Assistant Administrator (Marketing, Communications, Special Programs)**

Part of the top management team for a 222-bed acute care regional hospital. Directed public relations, fund-raising and development, volunteer organization, and long- and short-term special programs. Liaison to regional military, law enforcement, and civilian rescue organizations.

Created a marketing function at this hospital, including the hospital's first advertising program, using a health education model. Personally lobbied the military and negotiated long-term joint operating agreements preventing construction of a competing military hospital.

Arranged mobile CAT scan services in joint operating agreement with 3 other hospitals. Upgraded ER services. Organized new outpatient clinics as profit centers and referral sources for acute care system.

Directed development effort targeting corporate and private giving to fund new 6-chair dialysis unit and outpatient cardiac care program.

Chairperson, Education Committee. Chairperson, Disaster Planning Committee. Representative, North Country EMS Council. Contributed to strategic planning.

**Wilcox Hospital Clinic**, Fort Drum, New York, 1981–1982
**Administrator**

Administrator for 25-bed hospital clinic with a permanent staff of 25. Directed administrative functions for inpatient and outpatient services for an extended community of over 60,000 individuals. Coordinated preventive medicine programs, supervised medical supply operation, maintained liaison with civilian health care organizations, represented health services at installation-level meetings. Member, Emergency Action Staff.

**Tri-Medical Information Services (TRIMIS)**, Walter Reed Army Medical Center, Washington, D.C.,
**Patient Administrator**      1979–1981

Primary officer for the Walter Reed Army Medical Center Patient Registration System. Assisted in defining and developing goals and objectives. Planned and implemented an automated patient administration support system developed by TRIMIS. Developed training modules for staff on the new system.

Member of the Army Surgeon General's Staff at the Pentagon implementing policies for military-civilian health care cooperation.

– continued –

**U.S. Army Hospital**, Ft. Polk, Louisiana, 1978–1979
**Assistant Chief, Administration**

Significant responsibility in two areas: (1) Directed the civilian staffing and supervision of the outpatient records section, inpatient records section, hospital admissions / discharge section, CHAMPUS claims processing section. (2) Provided administrative support to several areas of hospital administration, for example, the Emergency Services Department, the Medical Disability Board, and various other committees and boards.

**General Dispensary**, Giessen, West Germany, 1975–1977
**Administrator**

Administrative responsibility for dispensary (outpatient facility) with total staff of 40, providing services to military personnel within 25,000 square mile radius of Giessen, West Germany. Collaborated on design and implementation of mobile health care team to serve isolated NATO bases, requiring close communication / cooperation with German, British, Belgian and Dutch military and civilian organizations. Designed and implemented a civilian employee incentive awards program. Wrote staffing requirements documents resulting in additional staffing.

**Medical Company**, Darmstadt, West Germany, 1973–1975
**Commander**

Responsible for the professional development, training, health, and general welfare of a ground ambulance support organization of 100 employees and 33 ambulances.

**Ireland Army Hospital**, Fort Knox, Kentucky, 1972 –1973
**Medical Company Executive Officer**, promoted from **Administrative Assistant**

Administrative and personnel responsibilities, including dispensing cash payrolls as high as $100,000, extensive training duties, and administrative functions for 200-bed hospital.

## PERSONAL

Energetic and enthusiastic. Seeking a new challenge with opportunity to capitalize on existing expertise and gain knowledge of new areas as well. Consistently proven ability to be effective in positions requiring tact, diplomacy, and collaborative management skills. Availability is negotiable. No restrictions on hours or business travel.

# BURTON ALAN RAMBERT

Residence: (606) 555-9223
5244 Tablerock Lake Road
Lexington, Kentucky 40503

Office: (606) 555-4293
Fax: (606) 555-4293

---

## PROFILE

**Systems Development — Operations Management — Project Management**

Strengths include launching, evolving and managing multifunctional, complex, technical organizations and projects. Effective combination of policy development and direct, hands-on operational responsibility.

Areas of expertise: large and small logistics systems; large and/or highly complex materials control and distribution systems, including maintenance, parts, and distribution aspects; aggressive and proactive technology, information, and automation planning (including directing HW/SW and artificial intelligence/expert systems development for IS, database, logistics, materials control, and distribution applications); maintenance operations, with emphasis on planned maintenance and problem prevention; administrative management; staffing and human resources.

Faculty member for formal and syndicated curriculums in intermediate and advanced training institutions. Advanced skills in communications, technical publishing, decision support and training simulation systems, periodical publishing, and office automation architecture.

## EXPERIENCE

U.S. ARMY

**Director, Materiel Readiness Support Activity**, Materiel Command, 1993 – 1996

Recruited to this worldwide command to write and direct Army policy for acquisition, maintenance, sparing, and readiness sustainment for all Army equipment. In charge of 360 civilian and military employees and a $20.3 million budget. Directed policy, operations, short- and long-range, strategic and tactical planning. Represented agency to industry, Department of Defense (DoD), and Department of the Army. Integrated and coordinated missions across all command lines.

*Highlights:*

- **Acquisition Logistics Division.** Provided systems-based acquisition support for new equipment development and procurement. Developed artificial intelligence/expert systems (AI/ES) software to support Army, Air Force, and Navy program managers and Integrated Logistics Support managers in automating and systematizing the acquisition supportability process. Developed, published, and maintained a series of specifications and standards on supportability engineering and integrated supportability design for new system acquisitions. Certified and validated vendor software to Mil-Spec for internal applications. Designated Executive Agent for the Army's Computer-Aided Logistics Support (CALS), Joint-CALS, Electronic Training Manual, and Interactive Electronic Technical Manual programs.

    - Released versions 2 and 3 of proprietary AI/ES software. Expanded base from 200 Army users to 1000 DoD users. Earned $2.25 million in productivity improvement funding for AI development program.

- **Readiness Sustainment Division.** Designed, implemented, and managed Armywide decision support systems for equipment readiness and maintenance. Managed global Army and DoD aviation- and ground-equipment oil analysis program. Published preventive maintenance magazine, *PS Magazine,* to 200,000 subscribers worldwide. Designed, developed, implemented, tested, and refined unit-level readiness reporting software.

    - Administered $1.8 million contract with outside vendor to enhance systems development for equipment and readiness management applications.
    - Earned $3.2 million in reimbursable funding to design Integrated Weapon Systems Management system.
    - Fielded the only two deployable Army Oil Analysis Laboratories to Desert Shield/Desert Storm theater of operations. Provided critical time-sensitive hardware programming, personnel training, and theater operational technical support to deployed laboratories.

- **Supply Division**. Developed sparing policies, designed sparing models, set pars to spare Army equipment to meet availability objectives. Integrated individual program spare parts practices with the Army Materiel Command's repair and stockage methodology. Developed and published the Army's *Equipment Mandatory Parts List, Combat Prescribed Load Lists,* and *Combat Authorized Stockage Lists.*

- **Management Support Division**. Guided and directed multiplatform MIS (HW/SW procurement/ integration), vendor and in-house systems/applications development and support, and firmware support. Planned and administered annual operating budget, $18 to $24 million. Directed the ongoing training and personnel services for over 300 employees.
  - Specified, procured, and placed into operation state-of-the-art $3.5 million mainframe computer to handle worldwide applications. Integrated system into evolving corporatewide area automation system in minimum time.
  - Converted databases to relational database technology to provide greater flexibility and cost-effectiveness.
  - Modernized office automation and LAN/WAN to provide/support heavily utilized desktop publishing system and integrated information resource management system.
  - Applied innovative reimbursable business program to public sector, allowing reductions in appropriated funding of $1.5 million in 1996 and $2.38 million in 1997 (projected).

- Army Commendation Medal for "Exceptional Support to the Department of the Army."

**Assistant Chief of Staff — Logistics (Corps)**, 1ST United States Army Corps, 1990 – 1993

Directed logistical support, logistical planning, and funding requirements of active and reserve units located in the United States, the Pacific, and Europe, total organization of 85,000 personnel. Introduced automated planning systems for logistics and validated same in three test deployments of over 12,000 exercise participants and 1_ million tons of cargo to the Pacific, $24.7 million operation with well-integrated air, sea, rail, and highway transportation modalities. Developed automated battle simulation logistics support models for staff training. Using computer modeling, produced the first successful execution of a wartime simulated logistics support plan for more than five Army divisions.

- Recognized for this and the preceding assignment with the Army's second highest service award, The Legion of Merit.

**Assistant Chief of Staff — Logistics (Division)**, 9TH Infantry Division, 1988 – 1990

Similar position to above at a lower level, 12,000 personnel, $7 million logistics budget. Provided the logistics integrated design for the Army's Maneuver Control System, the Army's first automated and distributed communications, command, and control system. Fielded modernization equipment to new divisional concept, the Motorized Division.

**Staff Leader (Instructor)**, Command and General Staff College, 1985 – 1988

Wrote and delivered curriculum. Wrote 500-page instructional manual on Logistics and Tactical Sustainment used Armywide. Contributed to other publications.

**Commander, Maintenance Battalion**, 123RD Maintenance Battalion, 1982 – 1984

Commander of organization of 1500 technical personnel deployed over 1100-square-mile area to support 5000 combat systems, annual budget of $6 million. Reduced inventory costs and repair parts stockage by $19 million while maintaining division readiness rate above 94 percent. Earned Meritorious Service Medal and the Army Achievement Medal.

**Commander, Materiel Management Center**, 8TH Infantry Division, 1979 – 1982

Managed six repair parts storage activities with over 18,000 line items of inventory, extended value exceeding $59 million. Fielded and operated modernized automated repair parts management system allowing reduction of stock to less than 8000 line items. Cut inventory cost in *half,* improved equipment operational rate, improved order-ship times. Earned Meritorious Service Medal.

**Commander, Aviation Maintenance**, D Company 8TH Aviation Battalion, 1978 – 1979

Streamlined repair parts activity operations to reduce inventory costs by $4.65 million, while exceeding all Army goals for aircraft mission rates.

*Highlights of prior service:*

**Staff Officer, Installation Aviation Maintenance**

**Commander, Aviation Support Company**

**Maintenance Staff Officer, Director of Industrial Operations**

**Instructor, U.S. Army Transportation School**

**Company Officer** (Combat tour — infantry rifle platoon leader — Vietnam veteran)

## EDUCATION

**M.S.,** University of Southern California, 1976

**B.A.,** Duquesne University, 1965

*Professional Development:*

**Total Quality Management**, California Institute of Technology, 1992

**Artificial Intelligence and Expert Systems Design**, California Institute of Technology, 1991

**Center for Information Research Summer Seminar**, M.I.T., 1991

*Additional Training:*

**Defense Resource Management Course**, Naval Postgraduate School

**Distinguished Graduate**, U.S. Army Fixed Wing Aviator Course

**Honor Graduate**, U.S. Army Rotary Wing Qualification Course

**Honor Graduate**, U.S. Army Aviation Maintenance Officer's Course

**Graduate**, U.S. Army Maintenance Test Pilot's Course

## ADDITIONAL

Affiliation: Society of Logistics Engineers.

Languages: Spanish (fluent), German (conversationally competent).

# ROBERT LEWIS CARMICHAEL

8817 Marlboro Court
Stafford, Virginia 22554

Office: (703) 555-1756
Residence: (703) 555-6720

## PROFILE

### Law Enforcement Management

Twenty-year career in security and systematic police work, including expertise in crime prevention, risk analysis, operational review vis-a-vis loss potential, white collar crime, fraud, contract fraud, criminal investigations, counter-terrorism, executive/VIP security, hostage negotiations, and numerous related areas.

Full charge experience, including staffing, budgeting, computers, policies, procedures, integration with top management priorities. Extensive interstate and international background. Fluent in German.

Strength: Finding structural solutions to structural problems.

*Highlights:*

- Trained and highly experienced in proactive criminal investigations. U.S. Army CID is a fully modern international police organization patterned after the FBI.
- Security Clearance: Top Secret.
- Knowledge of U.S. government contracts. Skilled fraud investigator.
- Comfortable with media, top foreign government officials, and U.S. dignitaries.

## EXPERIENCE

### U.S. ARMY — Criminal Investigation Command (CID)    1974–Present

**Chief, United States Properties**    1994–Present
CID Headquarters, Falls Church, Virginia

Provide oversight, supervision and guidance to a force of 880 Special Agents investigating theft of property, robbery, arson, and terrorism on U.S. Army installations worldwide, and the theft, damage, or destruction of U.S. Government property anywhere worldwide. Further responsible for the conduct of all narcotics interdiction efforts of the U.S. Army, including a large number of overt and covert operations.

Personally maintain liaison with all U.S. and foreign law enforcement agencies involved in the War on Drugs, including planning and oversight of joint operations in the United States and abroad, and resolution of complex interjurisdictional issues. Maintain close liaison with the Department of the Army, Department of Defense, and Department of Justice to conduct successful drug interdiction efforts in compliance with U.S. law and government policy.

- Majority of current projects remain classified.

**Commander — Special Agent in Charge**    1989–1994
San Francisco Field Office

Directed the investigation of crimes of person or property on federal installations and crimes of fraud committed by government contractors in Northern California and the State of Nevada. Supervised staff of 13 investigators, officers, and administrative personnel. Controlled all budgets and administrative aspects, including motor pool; delegated and monitored overt and covert investigations, continued in hands-on role as field investigator and covert operative as needed.

- Directed investigation uncovering $2.5 million in fraud by a U.S. government contractor.
- Awarded Humanitarian Service Medal for actions taken immediately after the 1989 Loma Prieta earthquake.
- Initiated and established systematic training programs, including training staff in computer database applications for investigative operations.
- Designed systems to collect and collate intelligence data, directing the unit database manager to collect, collate, and disseminate information.
- Discovered and prevented a plot for murder of U.S. officer in Saudi Arabia using the above analytical systems.

### Field Investigations Coordinator / Drug and Black-Marketing Coordinator   1987–1989
7th Region, Seoul, Korea

- Identified systematic black-marketing of customs-free and stolen goods in Korea, Japan, and the Philippine Islands.
- Uncovered $50 million in drugs and drug monies in a single operation.
- Designed Lotus 1-2-3 application to control departmental planning, operational data, and budgeting. Indirectly supervised approximately 150 criminal investigators.
- Earned Army Meritorious Service Medal for keeping critical investigations on track during period of excessive personnel turnover and transition.

### Special Agent in Charge   1985–1987
San Francisco Field Office

- Identified and restructured organizational weaknesses resulting in estimated annual savings of $200 million. Supervised 13 personnel — 4 administrative and 9 investigators.
- Investigated four homicide cases with 100% solve rate.
- Earned Army Meritorious Service Medal for Level II covert drug operation resulting in apprehension of GS-15 Dept. of Defense employee for drug trafficking, and seizure of $350,000 in cocaine.

### Special Agent in Charge   1982 –1985
Resident Agency, Mannheim, West Germany

- Supervised 18 investigators, interpreters, and administrative personnel.
- Earned Army Achievement Medal for investigation of helicopter crash with 47 fatalities, involving coordination with several foreign national governments.
- Earned Meritorious Service Medal for professionalism in office and for exceeding target ratios for solved crimes.

### Team Chief / Operations Officer   1979–1981
Fort Benning District, Columbus, Georgia

- Identified, investigated, arrested, and subsequently convicted the ".22 calibre killer" who killed and wounded several African Americans in New York City and Buffalo, New York.
- Earned Army Meritorious Service Medal for professionalism in office and for exceeding target ratios for solved crimes.

### Drug Suppression Team Chief   1976–1979
Resident Agency, Bamberg, West Germany

- Earned Army Commendation Medal for uncovering and building a case against a large-scale international cocaine operation based in Florida, and for apprehension of three German national terrorists supplying LSD in quantity to U.S. personnel.

### Special Agent   1974–1976
Ft. Hood, Killeen, Texas

## EDUCATION

**FBI Academy,** Hostage Negotiations Training (*numerous* other courses on-site)
**U.S. DEA,** Drug Law Enforcement Training
**U.S. Army Military Police Schools** (investigations, forensic science, management, logistics)
**Secret Service/U.S. Army,** Personal Security Training
**Bethel College,** History
**Western Michigan University,** History
**Troy State University,** Criminal Justice

## REFERENCES

Supporting information of any kind presented upon request.

# Lance T. Rosenberg

ltr33@hr.bus.ggu.edu
77 Buffalo Avenue
Medford, New York 11763

c/o Rosenberg

Message number: (516) 555-1640
Until June 10, 1997: (415) 555-0170

## PROFILE

**Corporate Human Resources / Personnel**

Human resources generalist with knowledge of recruiting/retention, management theory and practice, modern employee motivation and incentive programs (including pay-for-performance), EAP, benefits and compensation, staff forecasting, downsizing strategies, IS for HR, and general financial/statistical analysis.

Possess effective combination of interpersonal and analytical skills. Qualified for both analyst/specialist positions and generalist/company representative positions. Seeking long-term career opportunity.

## EDUCATION

Golden Gate University, San Francisco, California
**M.B.A., Human Resource Management,** May 1996

Coursework / Areas of Special Interest:

- Topics in HR Management
- Management Theory
- Employment Law
- Benefits Analysis
- Compensation Theory & Practice
- Issues in Outplacement & Downsizing

- Training Science
- HR Information Systems
- EAP
- Labor Negotiations

University of Tampa, Tampa, Florida
**B.A., History,** 1980

## EXPERIENCE

UNITED STATES ARMY

**Chief of Staff, Recruiting Region**
Fort Baker, California, 1992 –1994

Provided planning, implementation, and organizational development related to recruiting efforts in 10 Western States and U.S. bases on the Pacific Rim (including Alaska, Hawaii, Japan, Guam, the Philippines). Delegated through senior staff of 8 with following functional titles: Advertising/Sales Promotions Manager, Marketing Manager, Personnel Administrator, Training Officer, Comptroller, Information Systems Specialist, Legal Counselor. Planned and analyzed multimillion-dollar budget.

- Created the regional response to 10% budget reduction order. Achieved a 99.7% budget performance for the fiscal year, coming in below the lowered budget targets.

**Commander, Recruiting District**
San Francisco, California, 1990–1992

Selected to serve as line manager over recruiting activities in the Greater Bay Area. Planned recruiting events, interpreted strategies set by regional management. Planned million-dollar budget for advertising/promotions, travel, training, and administrative support. Analyzed cost-benefit and efficacy of various recruiting programs on an ongoing basis.

- Through increased motivation of sales force and better application of monies, raised district from bottom 10% to top 10% in just one year.

**Operations Officer, Recruiting Region**
Fort Sam Houston, Texas, 1988–1990

Supported recruiting efforts in eight southwestern states, including Special Programs campaigns for officers and nurses. Oversaw market analysis. Developed specific programs and strategies to counter negative trends and capitalize on positive trends defined in market research. Directed the training program for recruiters, including sophisticated sales and motivation training.

• Co-author of the "How To" manual (how to manage a recruiting district) for new and prospective District Commanders.

**Executive Officer, Recruiting District**
Jackson, Mississippi, 1985–1987

Support position to C.O.O. on district level.

**Personnel Director / Adjutant**
Fort Campbell, Kentucky, 1983–1985

Processed assignments/reassignments and all related personnel actions.

## ADDITIONAL

Helicopter pilot. Amateur sailing (cruising and racing). Racquetball.

## AWARDS

Legion of Merit for Outstanding Service

Meritorious Service Award for Outstanding Service (four)

# Special Cases, Unusual and Nontraditional Career Paths

There are résumés for odd people and there are odd résumés. Everyone in the employment placement industry has a personal collection of weird résumés. I once received a résumé that folds out like a menu and has a caricature of the candidate in a little diner apron, holding a large tray over her head. The copy goes on to explain how she can balance a multitude of simultaneous responsibilities. I have another résumé that features a pie chart showing the relative weight of various character traits possessed by the candidate and a separate pull-tab table showing how each character trait is of benefit in solving a standard set of business problems. Another involves an animated CD-Rom showing the candidate flying through the air, presumably coming to my rescue. Yet another was printed on a very large plaster foot. My favorite of all time, however, was crudely handwritten on a yellow legal pad. It contained this amazing qualification: "I can be a bitch when I don't get my way."

I don't recommend weird résumés. There are résumé traditions in certain industries. To ignore these traditions is to appear as an outsider, which is hardly the best way to win a job offer. Standard business, medical, legal, academic, and technical styles were described in prior chapters. This chapter contains a grab bag of other styles, including advertising, film, television, and theater. By the way, acting résumés are typically printed on 8 x 10-inch paper, and glued, printed directly, or clipped onto the back of an 8 x 10-inch headshot.

The odd thing about successful résumés for unusual people is that they tend to look just like successful résumés for regular people. The exorcist's résumé that follows could just as easily be for a retail store manager, at least stylistically. If you are faced with writing a résumé for an unusual person, it is best to present the unusual material in some standard format. I've written résumés for strippers and professional skateboarders, but these résumés were not odd in appearance.

No guide could be exhaustive, but we have tried. Whether you are an undercover agent or a certified public accountant, be sure to check the index for examples throughout the book that may apply to your particular case.

# DARWIN ENOLVA II

1922 Prather Street, Suite 600
San Francisco, California 94109
Telephone/Message: (415) 555-6931

## QUALIFICATIONS SUMMARY

- **Supernatural Consultant** — over 17 years of successful experience.
- Recognized internationally for command of theoretical, practical, and artistic issues related to supernatural phenomena, including generation of original research, models, and presentations.
- Highly knowledgeable in related scientific fields.
- Advanced interpersonal skills. Commanding presence—able to interact well with and influence key decision makers, business people, community groups.

## PROFESSIONAL HISTORY

### MACROCOSMOLOGIST      1985–Present

Developed comprehensive, illustrated theoretical model of the supernatural, including perception and actuality throughout history. This exhaustive research project covers the spheres of biological evolution, human physiology and reproduction, the psychic body, supernatural art history, a history of the supernatural in film, and development of a highly specialized technical lexicon.

- Created/developed extensive supernatural video library.

### PSYCHIC COUNSELOR      1977–Present

Provided both generalized and issue-specific consultations in highly successful private practice:

- Psychic Consultation
- Past Life Consultation
- Channeled Consultation
- Bio-Energetic Consultation
- The Alexander Process©

### PSYCHIC BUSINESS CONSULTANT      1982–Present

Performed analytical and consultative services for wide range of business clients:

- Stock Market Analysis
- Geological Surveying
- Business Consulting
- Company Connection©
- Key Decision-Making

### PSYCHIC HOMICIDE DETECTIVE      1977–Present

Assisted police departments in California, New York, and Hawaii with numerous aspects of homicide investigations. Developed exceptional reputation for ability to find vital physical evidence and provide valuable information on seemingly intractable cases.

### PSYCHIC CRIMINOLOGIST      1977–Present

Provided investigative assistance and personal analysis to lawyers and police investigations:

- Homicide
- Missing Persons
- Theft
- Fraud
- Embezzlement
- Sexual Harassment
- Divorce

### PRESIDENT/DIRECTOR OF RESEARCH AND EDUCATION      1983–1985

International Psychic Investigations (IPI)

Conceived original vision for, founded, and managed all phases of successful nonprofit education and research organization. Planned and oversaw acquisition and implementation of 501(c)(3) nonprofit tax status. Administered all development efforts. Supervised all public relations and community outreach efforts. Conducted Board of Directors' meetings and ensured compliance with requisite NPO laws and regulations. Spun the organization off in 1985.

As **Director of Research and Education**, developed psychic studies curriculum. Created consciousness studies library. Compiled list and information on domestic and international psychic institutes. Established methodologies and proposals for psychic research experiments. Evaluated psychophysical laboratory equipment for applications.

**PSYCHIC EDUCATION INSTRUCTOR**     1983–Present

Beginning with IPI and continuing in a variety environments and formats, developed curriculum and taught classes. Sample topics:

- Tarot
- Mediumship
- Telepathy
- Clairvoyance
- The Laying of Hands
- Ritual Magic
- Astral Projection

**PARAPSYCHOLOGICAL RESEARCH PARTICIPANT**     1980–1985

Participated in parapsychological experiments with **Psychophysical Research Laboratories** (Princeton, New Jersey), **Mobius** (Los Angeles, California) and **International Psychic Investigations** (Palm Springs, California).

- Tested extremely well in all settings, ranking in top 1% for all phenomena.

**POLTERGEIST AND HAUNTING INVESTIGATOR**     1981–Present

Spearheaded field investigations, spirit contact and removal, and cleansing of the surrounding environment on cases generated by referrals from police departments and personal referrals in California, New York, and Hawaii.

**EXORCIST**     1983, 1987, 1992

Conducted comprehensive exorcism, witnessing classic supernatural phenomena with highly successful results.

**GEOMANTRIC CONSULTANT**     1977–Present

Utilized a variety of techniques including psychocartographical evaluation surrounding a given environmental issue.

- Natural Resources
- Location of Lost Objects
- Geomantric Centers
- Energy Fields

**PSYCHIC HEALER**     1977–Present

Generated healings via bio-energetic manipulation:

- The Laying of Hands
- Reading Auras and Chakras
- Bio-Energetic Balancing
- Crystal Healing

**PSYCHIC EVENT FACILITATOR**     1979–1985

Facilitated and coordinated psychic events:

- Group Channeling
- Psychic Parties
- Séances
- Full Moon Celebrations
- Spirit Guide Introductions

**PSYCHIC VOLUNTEER**     1983–1985

- Lectured to police departments, community centers, schools.
- Provided community demonstrations.
- Worked with comatose patients in hospital settings.
- Presented supernatural fairy tales to preschoolers.

**ADDITIONAL**

- Frequently requested radio talk-show guest, public speaker, public demonstrator.

- **Additional information and references furnished upon request, but client confidentiality prevents description of many activities and engagements.**

# DIANE KETCHIE

## SOPRANO

### REVIEWS

From the première of the opera *Orpheus in Love*:

Diane Ketchie, in a stunning display of multimedia virtuosity, whizzes through difficult piano music, sings lustily, and employs deftly funny body English all at the same time. If Mr. Lucas and Mr. Busby want to keep ORPHEUS IN LOVE in circulation, I suggest that they sign Ms. Ketchie to a lifetime contract. I can think of no one in the popular, Broadway, or classical world who could do all the things she does and do them simultaneously and so well.

— Bernard Holland, *New York Times*

Diane Ketchie is the opera's greatest treasure.

— *New Jersey Star Ledger*

Diane Ketchie is a triple threat, combining her skills as an actress, pianist, and soprano.

— *Back Stage*

... a bitter combination of stern taskmaster and lascivious seductress, equal parts sadism and loneliness, Diane Ketchie gets the mix just right.

— *Variety*

From *Phantom of the Opera*:

Most of the secondary roles are beautifully performed with particularly nice work by Diane Ketchie as the resident diva.

— Robert Hurwitt, *San Francisco Examiner*

Diane Ketchie's Carlotta is a skillful parody of a coloratura diva.

— Steven Winn, *San Francisco Chronicle*

Diane Ketchie is a superb singer.

— Jeff Kaliss, *Marin Independent Journal*

Ketchie sings well and has fun with the role without overdoing the prima donna bit.

— Judy Richter, *San Mateo Times*

From *Christopher Columbus*:

Professional, big-voiced soprano Diane Ketchie is his lovely latest fiancée. Looking and sounding like a young Beverly Sills, she adds a major touch of class to the production.

— *Stockton Record*

New York import Diane Ketchie plays Columbus' fiancée, dispatching the operetta's showiest arias with polish and expressiveness.

— *Modesto Bee*

From Mozart's *La Finta Giardiniera:*

> Diane Ketchie has a flair for recitative, and she handled her big second act scene with aplomb.
>
> — Wilma Salisbury, *Cleveland Plain Dealer*

From *Pirates of Penzance:*

> The show has some fine singing. Diane Ketchie's voice was the biggest pleasure.
>
> — *Milwaukee Journal*

> The singing actors served both directors well. Diane Ketchie and Nicholas Saverine are superbly matched as Mabel and Frederick. Ketchie uses her brilliant coloratura as a weapon to cow her competing sisters.
>
> — *Milwaukee Sentinel*

In New York recital debut:

> Diane Ketchie is a soprano whose interest, understanding, and appetite for the art-song literature, on the evidence of her performance last Sunday afternoon at Weill Recital Hall, have blossomed. . . To a long program of Purcell, Schubert, Strauss, Ravel, Obradors, and Lee Hoiby, she brought enthusiastic projection and no small measure of specific comprehension of the songs and poems.
>
> — Will Crutchfield, *New York Times*

In solo recital in Milwaukee:

> Keep an eye and ear on soprano Diane Ketchie. She put her compelling instrument on display Sunday at the War Memorial Center. But the recital, sponsored by the Civic Music Association, was more than a vocal display. It was an afternoon of song.... Ketchie's voice compels the audience to sit up and listen because it is so powerful. Yet it is flexible, too.
>
> — Roxanne Orgill, *Milwaukee Journal*

In concert with the Rankweil Chamber Orchestra of Austria:

> Diane Ketchie enchanted the audience with her mature interpretation of Mozart's "Exsultate, Jubilate." She possesses a luminous, very cultivated soprano voice—her coloratura was virtually captivating through its immaculate precision. . . . Diane Ketchie emerged victorious as the radiant favorite of the public in this concert series.
>
> — Dr. Edgar Von Schmidt, *Vorarlberger Nachrichten*

In concert with the Milwaukee Symphony:

> Diane Ketchie was in splendid voice, filling the auditorium with a sound of unpretentious clarity, superbly supported throughout the dynamic range.
>
> — Jay Joslyn, *Milwaukee Sentinel*

In concert with the Allentown Symphony:

> "Glitter and be Gay" was brilliantly funny. In this parody of divadom, Ketchie strung melismas like diamond necklaces and struck white-noise notes with crystalline authority.
>
> — Geoff Gehman, *Allentown Morning Call*

# Joseph Phillippe

ART DIRECTION • 283 Martini Drive, Bergen Village, NJ 07662, 201-555-2454

## PROFILE

Increased billings from $8 million to $40 million before buyout by DDB Needham. Increased retail catalog business for another agency from $15 million to $24 million in just 3 years. On account team with first agency ever hired by Microsoft Corporation. On account with first agency ever hired by Voice mail. AWARDS: 1 Clio nomination, 4 Addys (1990 Gold in Print, 1990 Best of Division in Print, 1984 in Broadcast, 1984 in Print), 2 Readership Awards.

## EXPERIENCE

**Joseph Phillippe**, Bergen Village, NJ          1992–Present
**Art Director, Creative Director**

Handle print and television campaigns, catalog design/production, collaterals, signage, outdoor, logo and image development, packaging. Collaborate with writers and hire/supervise artists, photographers, and film crews as needed.

Agencies:

- Saachi & Saachi
- DDB Needham
- Aschor & Associates
- Hal Riney

- BBD&O
- Chiat Mojo
- J. Walter Thomson

- Foote Cone
- Grey Advertising
- Fischer & Associates

Accounts:

- Levi's 501 Jeans
- Mizuno Sports
- U.S. Sprint
- Rainier Ale

- Sterling Motorcar
- Dole
- Clorox
- Chevron

- Emil Villa's Restaurants
- Lonestar Beer
- Anheiser Busch
- KWAM Radio

**Fischer & Associates**, San Francisco, CA          1990–1992
**Associate Creative Director**

- California Table Grapes
- *San Francisco Examiner*

- KSFO Radio
- Canterbury of New Zealand

- Emil Villa's Restaurants

**Doyle Dane Bernbach (DDB Needham)**, San Francisco, CA / New York, NY          1984–1990
**Senior Art Director**

Tripled revenues with zero increase in staff. Assigned to New York office and exclusive responsibility for Atari/Warner Communications for 2 full years. Part of highly successful start-up agency bought by DDB Needham.

- Atari/Warner Comm.
- Volkswagen Dealers Assn.
- Microsoft

- CGM/Incotrans
- Golden Gate Ferry System

- Morrow Designs
- GTE Microcircuits

Academy of Art College
Instructor

Walger's Advertising
Art Director

Furniture Marketing Concepts
Graphic Designer (freelance)

2001 Productions
Assistant Art Director

## EDUCATION

Art Center College of Design

San Jose State University

Annapolis Naval Academy (merit scholarship)

Santa Clara University (merit scholarship)

San Francisco Academy of Art (merit scholarship)

*Portfolio on request.*

# Mary McHale

615 Marina Way                                    Office: (415) 555-2000
Sausalito, California 94965                     Residence: (415) 555-7166

---

## EXPERIENCE

FOOTE CONE AND BELDING, San Francisco, California, 1975–Present
**Senior Broadcast Buyer / Spot Account Manager**

*Place over $15 million per year in broadcast time for such clients as*:

- Mastercard
- Levi Strauss
- Pacific Bell/Pacific Telesis
- Mattel
- Alaska Tourism
- C&H Sugar
- Adolph Coors
- Citicorp
- ARCO
- Long John Silver's
- California Milk Advisory Board
- Orion Pictures
- Farmers Insurance
- California Raisins
- Mazda
- Supercuts
- Ashton-Tate
- Albertson's
- Colgate-Palmolive
- Universal Studios
- Clorox
- Eddie Bauer
- Dreyer's Ice Cream
- Hughes Airwest
- Payless Shoe Source
- First Interstate

*Buy for up to 47 markets simultaneously. Have bought over 200 rated markets in the United States and Canada, with emphasis on*:

- San Francisco
- New York
- Cincinnati
- Dallas
- Philadelphia
- Sacramento
- Tampa
- Atlanta
- Cleveland
- Seattle
- Phoenix
- Honolulu
- Kansas City
- Reno

*Skills include*:

- Analyzing, negotiating, purchasing, maintaining, and monitoring radio and TV buys. Additional skills include post analysis, client contact, and training of assistant buyers.
- Negotiating radio and TV sports sponsorship packages for clients, including TV and radio schedules, promotions, and merchandising programs.
- Serving as liaison with buyers, planners, account management and clients, including contact with FCB regional offices.

*Prior experience provides well-rounded background*:

- Assistant Media Buyer (one year), Commercial Production Account Coordinator (two years), Print Production Coordinator (two years).

## EDUCATION

**Holy Names College**, Oakland, California

# ANDREA TIPTON

(SAG, AFTRA)
Frederick & Templeton Agency, Inc.
6608 Hollywood Boulevard, Hollywood, CA 90028
(213) 555-8506 {in New York, call (212) 555-6100}

---

## DATA

| | | | | | |
|---|---|---|---|---|---|
| Height: | 5'7" | Hair: | Blond | Ages: | 23–35 |
| Weight: | 115 | Eyes: | Blue | Lang: | Italian, Polish, Greek |

## FILM

| | | |
|---|---|---|
| *When Harry Met Sally* | Waitress | Rob Reiner, Dir./Castle Rock |
| *Zelda* | Zelda | Paul Scott Reuter, Dir./NYU Student Film |
| *Bye Bye Budapest* | Mrs. Borbas | Margeaux Wasommer, Dir./WSU Student Film |

## THEATRE

| | | |
|---|---|---|
| *The Snow Queen* | Snow Queen | Long Beach Players/Long Beach, CA<br>Deborah La Vine, Dir.<br>"A visual delight — a female Mr. Spock," Heffley, L.A. Times<br>"A beautiful, regal Snow Queen," Warfield, Drama-Logue |
| *The Woolgatherer* | Rose | New Studio Theatre/Detroit, MI |
| *A Midsummer Night's Dream* | Titania | Mullady Theatre/Chicago, IL |
| *Uncommon Women* | Rita | Mullady Theatre/Chicago, IL |
| *Lysistrata* | Corinthian | Mullady Theatre/Chicago, IL |
| *Rattlesnake in a Cooler* | Ellen | Detroit Repertory/Detroit, MI |
| *Who Killed Richard Cory* | Mistress | Fourth St. Playhouse/Royal Oak, MI |
| *Quail Southwest* | Kerra | Fourth St. Playhouse/Royal Oak, MI |
| *The Late George Apley* | Lydia | Henry Ford Theatre/Dearborn, MI |

## COMMERCIALS

List upon request.

## STAND-UP COMEDY

| | | |
|---|---|---|
| At My Place | 1990 | Santa Monica, CA |
| Igby's Comedy Cabaret | 1990 | Los Angeles, CA |

## TRAINING

| | | |
|---|---|---|
| The Groundlings | Improv | Los Angeles, CA |
| Judy Carter | Stand Up Comedy | Los Angeles, CA |
| Greg Dean | Stand Up Comedy | Los Angeles, CA |
| Lawrence Parke | Scene Study | Los Angeles, CA |
| Loyola University | B.A., Drama, 1986 | Chicago, IL, and Rome, Italy |
| Lodz Film School | Acting | Lodz, Poland |
| Kosciusko Foundation | Acting | Warsaw, Krakow, Wroclaw, Poland |

Producers and directors, etc., also just list credits. Cf. next example.

# Bruce Golin

4366 Monroe Avenue, #107
Studio City, California 91604

Telephone:
(818) 555-0575

---

## PRODUCER / CO - PRODUCER

### STRENGTHS

- Twelve years in television — great record for on-time and on-budget.
- Good communicator with writers, talent, crew, production and post-production techs.
- Strong on directing/shooting inserts and 2nd Unit filming.

### SAMPLE CREDITS

*Adam-12/Dragnet* (New Syndicated Series), The Arthur Company, 1996–Present
Position: Producer
Executive Producer: Burton Armus

*The Smothers Brothers Comedy Hour — 200 Year Reunion* (CBS), Comedic Productions, 1994
Position: Associate Producer
Executive Producers: Tom and Dick Smothers — Producer: Ken Kragen

*Pee Wee's Playhouse: Banned for Life* (MTV), BRB Productions/Pee Wee Pictures, 1993
Position: Production Manager
Executive Producer: Steve Binder — Production Executive: Howard Malley

*We Are The World* (USA for Africa), Golin-Malley Productions, 1992
Position: Stage Manager
Exec. Producers: Ken Kragen, Ken Yates — Producers: Craig Golin, Howard Malley

*Knight Rider* (NBC Series), Universal Television, 1984–1990
Position: Associate Producer
Supervising Producers: Burton Armus, Bruce Landsbury

*Simon & Simon* (CBS Series), Universal Television, 1982–1984
Position: Assistant Associate Producer
Executive Producer: Phil DeGuere — Producer: Richard Chapman

*Legends of the West* (ABC Special), Marble Arch Productions, 1981
Position: Production Coordinator
Producer: Eric Lieber

*The Gambler* (CBS Movie of the Week), Kenny Rogers Productions, 1979
Position: Production Coordinator
Producer: Ken Kragen

*The Lily Tomlin Show* (NBC Special), Tomlin Productions, 1979

Position: Production Coordinator

Producer: Rocco Urbisci

### EDUCATION

**Pre-Med**, University of California, Los Angeles

# Ron Dollar

1800 North Genesee
West Hollywood, California 90046

Telephone:
(213) 555-7670

## ANIMATOR

**STRENGTHS**

**Clay — Cel Animation — Stop-Motion**

**CREDITS**

**Michael Jackson "Moonwalker"** (Music Video), Hollywood Tokyo Film Group, 1988
Director: John Sheele

Project: storyboards; design/animation of female robot figure; clay sculpture and animation of "A B C" segment; stop-motion wings on television spaceship for "When I Come of Age" segment.

***Pee Wee's Playhouse: The Original*** (CBS Series), BRB Productions, 1987
Director: Kevin Dole

Project: storyboards for Penny, refrigerator, dinosaurs and strata-cut segments; stop-motion animation for dinosaur family segments.

***Ruthless People*** (Feature), Touchstone Pictures, 1986
Chief Animator: Sally Cruickshank

Project: animation in the opening titles.

***Robocop*** (Feature), Chiodo Brothers, 1986
Director: Steve Chiodo

Project: dinosaur animation sequence.

***Jane Fonda's Complete Workout*** (Video), BRB Productions, 1988
Directors: Steve Binder, Kevin Dole

Project: concept, storyboards, sculpture and animation of Jane Fonda puppet.

***Mannequin*** (Feature), Playhouse Pictures, 1987
Chief Animator: Sally Cruickshank

Project: animation in opening titles.

**Playboy Channel** (Inserts), Playhouse Pictures, 1987
Animation Director: Gerry Woolery

Project: cel and clay animation for various Playboy Channel segments, including Gahan Wilson cartoon characters.

***How We Feel About Taste*** (Educational Short), Playhouse Pictures, 1987–1988
Animation Director: Ade Woolery

Project: cel animation of children.

**Burt Ward's "Early Bird Theatre"** (MultiMedia), Playhouse Pictures, 1987
Animation Director: Gerry Woolery

Project: cel animation of Early Bird character.

***Runaway Ralph*** (ABC Children's Special), ABC/Churchill Films, 1987
Director: John Matthews

Project: art direction, concept development, design/animation of TV cartoon; also provided voice for the cartoon cat.

***Frog and Toad Together*** (Film Short), Churchill Films, 1986
Director: John Matthews
Project: set construction and animation of frog character in garden scene.

***You Know I Love You*** (Music Video), Howard Jones, The Company, 1986
President: Curt Marvis
Project: director of animation in six segments of the video.

***The Aphid*** (Cartoon), Don Waller Productions, 1983
Project: writer and animator.

## COMMERCIALS

**"Kool Aid"** (2 releases), Limelight Productions, 1987
Project: art direction, character design, animation of sea creature segments, radio.

**"California Cooler,"** Limelight Productions, 1988
Project: character design and animation of "fruit man."

**"Six Flags,"** Kevin Dole Productions/Six Flags Productions, 1988
Project: concept sketches; design/animation of couch potato characters.

## ADDITIONAL

Storyboards on music videos for Boogie Boys, Ozzy Ozbourne, Cutting Crew, Hank Williams Jr., Mason Rufner.

## PUBLICITY

"Clay Figures Animate Pee-wee's Playhouse," by Charles Solomon, in the *Los Angeles Times*, Part IV, Page 10, June 29, 1988.

"Pee Wee Herman: The Pee Wee Principle," by N. Kourtney Kaye and Marcia Urbin, in *Animation Magazine*, Vol. 1, Issues 2/3, December 1987.

"Shooting Robocop," by Paul M. Sammon, in *Cinefex Magazine*, No. 32, November 1987.

"Singing Image," by Jay Blotcher, in *How: Ideas & Technique in Graphic Design*, Vol. II, No. 5, July/August 1987.

## BIOGRAPHY

14 years in animation. Attended the Art Institute of Pittsburgh for two years after high school. Spent four years with The Animators studio in Pittsburgh, primarily working on commercials. Spent five years with Hellman Animates, a division of Hellman Associates, working primarily on commercials. Moved to Los Angeles and pursued the credits listed above. Avocation: semi-professional musician. Hobbies: rock climbing, volleyball, travel. Available for travel and relocation as needed.

## REFERENCES

References on request. Reel on request.

# JOHN BART APPLEBY

*Curriculum Vitae*

17 - 12th Avenue
San Francisco, California 94110

Telephone/Message:
(415) 555-3285

---

## PROFILE

**Theatre Instructor, Director** and **Acting Coach** with unusual combination of psychology/ psychotherapy background with extensive training and experience in the theatre.

Over 20 years teaching, directing, producing: New York University, Boston University, Skidmore College, State Theater School of Denmark, State Theater School of Sweden, Ringling Bros. Barnum & Bailey Clown College, Commedia dell'arte and acting, and private studios.

## EDUCATION & TRAINING

Research Society for Process-Oriented Psychology        Zürich, Switzerland
**Seminar in Process Work** (with Arnie Mindel)        1987

California Institute of Transpersonal Psychology (ITP)        Menlo Park, CA
**Master of Arts, Psychology**        1986
Teaching Assistant, "Personality Theory" (graduate course)

Carnegie Institute of Technology, School of Fine Arts        Pittsburgh, PA
(now: Carnegie-Mellon University)
**Bachelor of Fine Arts, Directing**        1966

## LICENSURE & AFFILIATIONS

Licensed M.F.C.C. (Marriage, Family, Child Counselor), State of California, # 29845

Member, California Association of Marriage and Family Therapists (CAMFT)

Member, Theater Bay Area (TBA)

## THEATRE TEACHING

San Francisco Actors Studio/City Actors Workshop        San Francisco, CA
**Acting Teacher**        1994–1995

Teach acting technique, scene study, character analysis, stage presence, stage space, monologues and audition pieces, sense memory, emotional memory, relaxation, improvisation (as a didactic tool), actor-actor interplay, and working with directors.

Use psychotherapy background to provide character insight and to enrich presentation of major acting theories (Grotowski, Stanislavsky, Meisner, et al.).

Theatre Therapists        San Francisco, CA
**Chief Instructor / Founder / General Manager**        1993–Present

Provide theatre training to psychologists, psychotherapists, and other mental health care professionals from throughout California. Develop and deliver curriculum on acting, improvisation, play writing, scene writing, and related arts.

Provide professional development with particular emphasis on incorporating acting, role-playing, and scene studies *into the therapeutic process.* These classes provide professionals with new therapeutic tools, access to their own creativity, and empowerment.

## ALSO

### Producer

*Starting Here, Starting Now,* lyrics and direction by Richard Maltby Jr.; music by David Shire; with co-producers Mary Jo Slater, Scott Mansfield (original cast album—RCA Records & Tapes)

### Broadway Investments

*Veronica's Room,* by Ira Levin; Ellis Rabb, director, Morton Gottlieb, producer; starring Eileen Heckart and Arthur Kennedy

*A Little Night Music,* by Hugh Wheeler; music and lyrics by Stephen Sondheim; Hal Prince, director/producer; starring Glynis Johns, Hermione Gingold, Len Cariou

*Chicago,* by Fred Ebb and Bob Fosse; music by John Kander, lyrics by Fred Ebb; Bob Fosse, director/choreographer; Robert Fryer and James Cresson, producers; starring Gwen Verdon, Chita Rivera, Jerry Orbach

### Administration

Morton Gottlieb, producer: *Same Time Next Year,* Gene Saks, director; starring Charles Grodin, Ellen Burstyn.

New York's City Center: 55TH Street Dance Theater Foundation, theatre development.

### Director

*Hot'l Baltimore,* Staircase Community Theatre, Soquel, California

*Peter and the Wolf,* adapted by Steve Abrams, Staircase Theater

*La Celestina or The Spanish Bawd,* La Mama Theater, Off B'way, New York

*Improvisations on a Theme,* Taped in West Germany for La Mama Theater

*Lost and Found,* adapted from a Pirandello short story by Steve Abrams & John Ford Noonan, Jr., Carnegie Institute of Technology, School of Fine Arts

*Till Eulenspiegel's Merry Pranks: A Mime Play,* by Steve Abrams, based on the music of Richard Strauss, Carnegie Institute of Technology, School of Fine Arts

*Three Penny Opera,* by Bertold Brecht, Pittsburgh YM-YWCA

*Macbeth* (assistant directed), by William Shakespeare, Boston University

*The Three Sisters,* by Anton Chekhov, Boston University

*The Emperor's New Clothes,* by Charlotte Chorpenning, adapted by Steve Abrams, Gateway Playhouse, Long Island, New York

*Tom Sawyer,* by Paul Kester, Gateway Playhouse

### Stage Management

*Antigone,* by Jean Anouilh, Actors Conservatory Theater, Bill Ball, director

*Arms and the Man,* by George Bernard Shaw, Cincinnati Playhouse, Donald Moffat, director

*Don Perlimplin,* by Frederico Garcia Lorca, Cincinnati Playhouse, Brooks Jones, director

*The Burnt Flower Bed,* by Ugo Betti, Cincinnati Playhouse, Stephen Porter, director

*The Bacchae,* by Euripides, Carnegie Institute of Technology, School of Fine Arts, translation and direction by Minos Volonakis

*Mother Courage,* by Bertold Brecht, Caravan Theater, Boston

*Once Upon a Mattress,* by J. Thompson, Dean Fuller, and Marshal Barer, Millbrook Playhouse, Millbrook, Pennsylvania

### Technical

WQED TV, Pittsburgh, Floor Manager

New York Shakespeare Festival, with Joe Papp: *A Winter's Tale, Antony and Cleopatra, As You Like It, King Lear, The Merchant of Venice, The Tempest*

### Additional Teaching

New York University, Director for Student Acting Finals

Boston University, Graduate Teaching Fellow, Acting

Skidmore College, Summer Program for Youths, Acting

Ringling Brothers, Barnum & Bailey Clown College, Mime

Williamstown Theater, Apprentice Program, Movement

State Theater School, Copenhagen, Denmark, Acting

State Theater School, Malmø, Sweden, Acting

Private Studios, U.S. and Europe, Acting

## CLINICAL EXPERIENCE

Private Practice      San Francisco, CA
**M.F.C.C.** (individuals, couples, families and groups)      1991–Present

Family Service Mid-Peninsula      Palo Alto, CA
**M.F.C.C. Staff Clinician** (couples, families and individuals      1992–1993

Live Oak Counseling Center      San Francisco, CA
**M.F.C.C. Intern** (couples and individuals)      1988–1991

Therapy Group for Men      Palo Alto, CA
**Guest Facilitator**      1989

Catholic Charities      San Francisco, CA
**M.F.C.C. Intern** (adolescents and families)      1989

KARA      Palo Alto, CA
**Peer Counselor** (terminal illness support services)      1989

Haight-Ashbury Psychological Services      San Francisco, CA
**M.F.C.C. Intern**      1987–1988

Gestalt Therapy Group      Menlo Park, CA
**Assistant Group Leader**      1986

ITP — Grof Breath Workshop      Menlo Park, CA
**Assistant Workshop Leader**      1986

ITP — Personal Growth and Relationships      Menlo Park, CA
**Assistant Workshop Leader**      1985

Esalen — Marathon Weekend Therapy Group for Men and Women      Big Sur, CA
**Assistant Group Leader**      1985

Skidmore College — U.S. Gov. Title VI Program      Saratoga Springs, NY
**Group Leader** (urban kids program)      1969

New York City Dept. of Welfare — Emergency Division      New York, NY
**Case Worker** (family services)      1966–1967

## PERSONAL THERAPY

Over 500 hours, including two years with Laura Perls.

## REFERENCES

All additional information provided on request.

# *Cover Letters*

Most cover letters consist of self-centered blather followed by a diffident request that the reader call if interested. How could they be interested in something like that?

First, when writing an *unsolicited* letter, it is a good idea to have a strong opening that grabs the reader's attention. Here are two openings that hook the reader in to read further:

> "Are you tired of excuses?"

> "Everyone knows that the credit card market is a mature market, with all the players chasing the same creditworthy 13 million households."

Other ways to keep your letter from being tossed include mentioning in the first paragraph that they requested your résumé or dropping the name of a mutual acquaintance. If the letter is sure to be read, then a bold opening is not so essential.

To keep the targeted executive's secretary from automatically screening out your letter, try appealing directly to her business sense, as in the first sample letter following.

If you are writing to a headhunter, *always* include some version of the following statement: "Of course it is understood that you would not forward my résumé to any employer without discussing the specific opportunity with me first."

In all your letters, end with a **call to action**; that is, specify exactly what you want to happen next. The best call to action is to specify that you will call them on a certain day at a certain time, as in: "I will call you on Thursday at ten o'clock. You can count on me to be prompt, so please advise your secretary to expect my call." If that is too precise, say you'll call on Thursday before noon.

Cover letters at the executive level are routinely one to two pages long, and occasionally can be much longer, as in the example beginning on p. 527.

Unfortunately, cover letters are complex documents, easily as complex as résumés, and cannot be but briefly explicated in a chapter like this. For a large assortment of cover letters, including broadcast letters, query letters, response letters, and headhunter letters, see my *Overnight Job Change Letter,* full of executive-level examples.

Robert G. Donner
334A Echo Park Avenue
Los Angeles, California 90036
(213) 555-2834 or (213) 555-9103


24 April 1997


Ms. Rita Cole
Executive Assistant to the President
Pony Express & Company
120 Montgomery Street
San Francisco, California 94103

Dear Ms. Cole:

The enclosed is a letter of inquiry concerning purchasing operations at Pony Express in light of the merger with Calhoun & McCoy. It also includes a résumé of my career.

I realize that your normal procedure is probably to insulate Mr. Hazen from employment applications and to forward the enclosed directly to personnel.

Please consider that in this case he may wish to review my letter himself, as the rationale I am presenting is politically sensitive and is one that only he could implement.

My experience as Vice President & Head of Purchasing at Chemical Bank should be of direct interest to him.

Finally, the material is brief and to the point. He will know almost immediately whether he is interested in further contact with me.

I thank you for your consideration in these matters, and I hope you will present the enclosed to Mr. Hazen for his review.

Sincerely yours,

*Robert G. Donner*

Robert G. Donner

# J ROBERT BLOOM

25 Divisadero Place
San Francisco, California 94115

Office direct line: (415) 555-6200
Residence: (415) 555-5200
Fax: (415) 555-7200

---

September 1, 1996

Attn: Andrea Miskow, Division President
Ardmore Housewares Corp.
2219 China Basin, Bldg. H-218
San Francisco, California 94112

Dear Ms. Miskow:

Are you tired of excuses? Do your top managers blame foreign competition, lazy workers, Bill Clinton, and a punitive tax structure for a lack of profits? You don't have to listen to this kind of negativity.

In my last operating position, I created a 15% increase in gross revenues in an industry that was experiencing a 30% decline. The company had a mature product line, encroaching foreign competition, a  management team in disarray and still we resolved these problems to add 15% to gross and 5.3% to margins.

In my current position, I have set up national account relationships between major companies that had not previously been business partners, generating millions of dollars in new business. In short, I can approach your business problems from both sides, i.e., creating greater profits through attention to both revenues and cost containment.

If you'd rather hear positive ideas than excuses, then let's have a "get acquainted" discussion. It won't cost you anything, and it could lead to the type of management you really want.

I'll call your office within 24 hours of your receipt of this letter. Please advise your secretary to expect my call. Thank you for your consideration, and I certainly look forward to our conversation.

Sincerely,

J Robert Bloom

Enclosure
JRB/da

**Carmen Solano**

30 East Superior Street, #2
Chicago, Illinois 60611
Office: (312) 555-7969
Residence: (312) 555-3782

August 16, 1997

William L. Breidelman
CEO
Americom Tech

Dear Chairman Breidelman:

Everyone knows that the credit card market is a mature market, with all the players chasing the same credit-worthy 13 million households. There are some keys to success, however, and when I heard about your company's planned calling card/consumer credit card venture, my first thought was "What a great opportunity!" I'll tell you why in just a moment.

As the engineer of several highly successful product enhancements and marketing strategies on behalf of Citibank Visa/MasterCard, I believe I have a unique perspective on the market you are targeting and both a qualitative and statistical understanding of your consumers. Your card has the potential to serve your strategic objectives on several levels.

First and foremost, a successful card could be a very sweet contributor to both revenues and profits. A rapid and decisive launch would be key to achieving this goal, however. I believe I can facilitate such a goal, balancing the twin objectives of successful marketing and sound organizational development. I am proud of my track record of success on similar projects, and you will note that my experience has primarily been in large, sophisticated organizations, where major contributions are usually a combination of well-balanced technical, business, and interpersonal skills.

Also, the card would allow you to cement your relationship to your consumers, allow you to build a sophisticated database on those consumers, and provide a platform from which to launch continued financial products and information services.

With the benefit of millions of dollars of directly related research, and the experience of designing and launching successful projects almost exactly like the one your company has proposed, I believe I have something to contribute. If you have a moment to discuss this, I'd like to see if we have a mutual interest.

Would you be available to speak by phone on Wednesday, August 21, at 10:30 a.m.? Please advise your executive assistant to expect my call.

I thank you for your attention.

Sincerely,

Carmen Solano
CS/da

# WILSON PARSONS

1 Parsons Lane
Golden, Colorado 80401

Office: (303) 555-7445
Residence: (303) 555-7822

January 31, 1997

**Attn: John M. Shallott, President**
**Re: Mountain Municipal Insurance Fund**

Shallott Associates
1601 Target Road, Suite 390
Sacramento, California 95815

Dear Mr. Shallott:

Thank you for your letter of January 19, 1997. Your query has fallen upon an interested party. After significant success where I am now, Executive Director of two public entity self-insurance groups, I have begun to realize that I've done about all I can here. Perhaps you—and your client—will be interested in the accomplishments outlined in the enclosed c.v.

My contributions have been primarily in the following areas: (1) improved financial performance, in particular, a careful alignment of the competing priorities of plans, rating, and reserves, (2) improved administrative function, allowing increased services with zero increase in staffing and expense budgets, (3) improved communication with Boards and constituencies, of both a "hard" nature (financial data/ strategic planning) and a "soft" nature (access, accountability and public relations). Finally, I use my law and mediation background on a daily basis, to solve the competing demands that are inherent in this field. I think one of my talents is simply the ability to be effective without burning any bridges.

Although I am in no hurry to change positions, I certainly want to explore this opportunity. If you think we may have a basis for mutual interest, please let us continue this dialogue. I will contact you within a week to see what your thoughts are on the matter, and to see where we go from here.

Thank you for your consideration. Meanwhile, I look forward to speaking with you soon.

Sincerely,

Wilson Parsons
enclosure

## NORA L. BERTSCHI COOK

700 South Church Street
Lexington, Massachusetts 02173

Office/voice mail: (617) 555-6545
Residence/message: (617) 555-7921

October 22, 1996

Attn: William Chip
Eli, Chip, Chris & Albrain
200 Nassau Street, Suite 2010
New York, New York 10012

Dear Mr. Chip:

After considerable success with DEC, I find myself without an interesting challenge on the horizon.
Do you have a client who may be interested in my services? I am seeking a consulting position, a
turnaround assignment, or a position as permanent or interim operating officer for a company with
$20 million to $100 million in annual sales.

As you can see from the enclosed, I have a background of full P&L responsibility for a business unit
generating $450 million in annual revenues, with a total staff of 650. My most recent accomplish-
ments are:

- Designed the paradigm shift now underway at DEC — away from selling boxes and toward
  selling solutions and availability guarantees.

- Developed market management and segmentation studies for 24 different markets (brand, industry,
  service), with business and financial plan for each market.

- Increased market share in mature product lines, doubled revenue in service business, reversed
  negative revenue trends.

My success to date is strictly based on my ability to adapt to changing business conditions—and
persuade others to adapt and change as well. Even a large and cumbersome organization can be
transformed if the changes are correctly sold to employees. My background includes assignment after
assignment that was in one way or another an experiment. So far, all those experiments worked.

If you know anyone who is seeking a market-driven operating executive with a proven track record,
who can make an immediate *and* an enduring contribution, then your timely introduction could be
beneficial to all concerned. DEC is very happy with me, so I need your utmost discretion at this time
and, of course, please do not forward my materials to any employer without discussing the particular
opportunity with me first.

I will call you within 48 hours of your receipt of this mailing to answer any preliminary questions
you may have about me and to hear what ideas, leads, or referrals you may have.

Thank you for your consideration. I look forward to our conversation.

Sincerely,

Nora L. Bertschi Cook

encl.
NLBC/da

# MARTIN MOREHOUSE

11305 Long Branch Road
Bath, New York 14810

Office (discreet): (607) 555-6438
Residence (message): (607) 555-2441

May 9, 1997

Yankee Marine
AD# GT760SJ
500 Dock Side Drive, Bldg. 17
Providence, Rhode Island 02904
fax: 401-555-2728

Dear Yankee Marine Executive Team:

I was interested to notice your advertisement for a **Distribution Center Operations Manager**. Using the same skills that would make me a success on your team, I've been a key contributor at each of my last three companies, taking them to *record profits* without reinventing the wheel. My contributions are outlined on the enclosed résumé.

My method was to review every aspect of operations. I came up with internal processes design to improve efficiency in some big ways and 1000 little ways. Then I took the design changes to the rest of the executive team, adding their suggestions and gaining their commitment to the improvements.

Then I *personally* sold the new policies and practices to impacted staff. I currently ship UPS, common carrier, and air freight, and have found significant reductions through (a) aggressive negotiation of rates and (b) more creative use of various modes of transportation (e.g. 2nd day air service to New York/Chicago/Dallas cheaper than UPS ground rates). We ship 10,000 products to 7000 customers worldwide, with a daily shipping schedule.

Take a look at my track record. Are you poised for growth or increased profitability? If so, I could provide you with the distribution management you need now, *and throughout the coming period of success and growth*. I'd like to discuss your plans and my background to see if we can develop a mutual interest. I'd appreciate a call at your convenience.

Thank you for your consideration. I look forward to speaking with you.

Respectfully,

*Martin Morehouse*

Martin Morehouse

enc: résumé
*via fax, hard copy to follow by mail*

**JOHN M. FLOSS, JR.**
186 Craton Lane
Hacienda Heights, California 91745
Home: (818) 555-5477
Office: (818) 555-0965
Fax: (818) 555-0547

October 12, 1996

Dr. Beth Solis
Solis Executive Search and Selection
2764 Diamond Street
New Brunswick, New Jersey 08543

Dear Dr. Ross:

I am writing you to provide information regarding my qualifications for a senior marketing position.

| | |
|---|---|
| Objective: | Director or Vice President of Marketing |
| Present Position: | Group Marketing Manager |
| Compensation: | Presently $176,000 |
| Geography: | Open |
| Industries: | Experience with customer products and packaged goods including: beverage, healthcare, drug, flavors/ingredients. Additional interest in healthcare/hospitals, forest products, furniture, and hardware. |
| Experience: | Experience with the full range of marketing responsibilities: direct, broker, and distributor sales networks; domestic and international markets; licensing and royalties. |
| Knowledge: | Project management, strategy, planning/analysis, budget control, product development and expansion work, advertising and promotion programs, marketing mix and product positioning decisions, sales and merchandising programs. |
| Style: | Committed to developing clear objectives and getting results. Responsive to high standards. Believe in building a shared sense of purpose. |

My resume is attached for your review and consideration. Of course it is understood that you will not forward my materials to any employer without discussing the specific opportunity with me first. I look forward to talking with you.

Sincerely,

*John M. Floss, Jr.*

John M. Floss, Jr.
JMF/rf
Enclosure

# Dawn G. Danning

61 Pond Drive
Palisades Park, New Jersey 07650

Telephone:
(201) 555-9440

February 10, 1997

Paul Faber, Chairman, and Members of the Search Committee
Pershing Hospital Foundation
3001 Colby Street
Palisades Park, New Jersey 07650

Dear Members of the Search Committee:

Please accept this letter and the enclosed resume in application for the position of C.E.O. of the Pershing Hospital Foundation.

As most of you know, I have been actively involved with Pershing since before the inception of the Foundation. In the last 30 years, with assignments encompassing practically every committee and function available, I have worked many productive hours on behalf of both Pershing Hospital/Pershing Hospital Foundation, and now after the merger, Pershing-St. Mary's Foundation.

I believe that most members of the search committee are aware of my strengths: fundraising, motivating, networking, organizing, orchestrating. Since 83.1% of all charitable giving is direct from individuals, these are especially critical traits. This letter is intended to address some of the other screening criteria you may use in evaluating candidates: administrative skill, technical understanding of legal and tax matters, education and cumulative knowledge, and ability to engineer a smooth transition.

Administrative experience is a basic requirement and is evidenced in my own extensive background of setting up offices and initiating and managing fund-raising projects. This has often entailed creating administrative systems, forms design, work flow planning, training of administrative and volunteer staff, setting up networks and sharing data with others. Records control and database compilation and maintenance also have been part of my experience. I am able to write specifications and work with computer specialists to achieve necessary results.

Planning, coordinating, and managing such projects to completion are some tasks our next C.E.O. must be able to do well.

With regard to tax and legal aspects of nonprofit foundation work, I have been studying and reviewing state and federal charitable tax requirements with my accountant. This preparation, coupled with my experience relative to my own family foundation and finances is a strong step toward gaining the level of expertise required for this position. Recently I have spent some highly instructive time discussing all aspects of planned giving opportunities with David Hanaman and Jeffrey Close at Desert Hospital Foundation in Palm Springs, California. Mr. Hanaman, well known to many of you, is a lecturer on planned giving and one of the foremost leaders in NAHD. (Desert Hospital Foundation generates approximately $4.5 million in giving on a yearly basis.)

An important aspect of my candidacy is that I know my limitations and do not expect to be an expert in every area. I will always be willing to utilize the services of specialists when appropriate, with a clear mission to have the services of these professionals donated to the foundation. With my proven ability to enlist others to participate in projects, I expect that my knowledge of tax and legal matters will be sufficient to excel in this position.

As to the matter of my educational status, I am a mature student with fully grown children. A requirement of a college degree is always meant to be a test of knowledge and maturity. My levels of energy and commitment to every enterprise have always been 100%. I will excel in my efforts on behalf of the foundation while completing my degree studies on a part-time basis. I would ask that the search committee consider my contributions to the foundation and other area organizations as more than sufficient evidence of my ability to perform as a seasoned, dedicated professional.

Concerning the transition from peer to employee, the committee is aware that any person coming to this position will have to make transitions. I understand and expect the changing relationships that would be appropriate with this new status and should I be selected for the position, I will facilitate those transitions. Ours is a unique community, with greatly varied interests and donor groups. I submit to you that because I know so well the community and many individual donors, I am a strong candidate. Significantly, donors will not have to experience a transition to an unknown manager. They will already know their new foundation C.E.O. (I introduced Feinbaum, Watters, and Raymer to the foundation, our top three donors and close personal friends of mine). We can all move quickly and smoothly past this small change to the more pressing business of raising money and future development of a strong foundation, in image and in fact.

Finally, I would like to say that I am at the point in my life where I desire more challenge and a more formal role in an organization. I will be seeking a position such as this with some organization. My greatest desire is to continue to contribute to the success of Pershing Hospital Foundation and our community.

My interest in the future of the foundation includes an eagerness to participate in the assessment process, and to let that process guide the direction of the organization. I believe the foundation needs a leader, not just an administrator—a motivator more than anything else—to create and implement a plan for the future. To increase giving efforts which reflect the regional nature of the patient populations for the hospitals, and to integrate a recognition of the greater financial and social strength of the new and proud cities surrounding the hospitals, are exciting prospects for me. I am willing, also, to help guide the foundation through the assessment and planning process on an 18-month assignment, and then reassess my position at that time with the board. My ultimate goal is, of course, the benefit of the foundation and the institutions that it serves.

I am hopeful that you will support my candidacy. My goal is to welcome all members of the greater community of Pershing-St. Mary's Hospitals to contribute to the development of a comprehensive new vision for our foundation.

Thank you for your consideration, and I look forward to working with you in a new, mutually rewarding relationship.

Yours sincerely,

*Dawn G. Danning*

Dawn G. Danning

Enclosures.

**C. Roger Snowden**
106 West 45 Street
New York, New York 10013
(212) 555-6471

---

May 5, 1997

Sir David Chorley
Chorley Associates
Hanover House, 73-74 High Holborn
London WC1V6LS

Dear Sir Chorley:

I was very interested to read your advertisement in the *Financial Times* of April 19, 1997. I would like to explore employment opportunities with your group, and I think my background may be of interest to you.

My outlook has always been very international. Even though my first employer was a small firm, I was the main catalyst for going international with offices in Australia, Europe, and Hong Kong. Also, I have traveled extensively throughout Europe, Africa, and the Far East. Finally, my wife is German, and I have family in Europe. It has long been my desire to continue my career in Europe, especially the U.K., so I am very intrigued by the opportunity available with your company.

My resume details my career growth. With my first employer I earned rapid promotions from financial operations to responsibility for strategic concerns. Even though I was employed by the same company for six years, I participated in a challenging series of business evolutions involving new product launches, several M&As (including two LBOs), several capitalizations, a complete reorganization, and a turnaround. To put it simply, I was retained and promoted by every change of management.

I enjoyed corporate finance, strategic planning, and merger and acquisition activities so much that I decided to pursue a career in financial and management consulting where I could focus entirely on these activities.

For my current employer, Venture Associates, Inc., of Los Angeles, I am a senior associate with responsibility for planning and executing complex consulting engagements. Although not a V.C. firm, we are associated with several venture capital sources. Working with start-up companies and organizations in transition has been the most satisfying work that I have done to date. I also enjoy the related activities of identifying, analyzing, structuring, and negotiating mergers and acquisitions.

I attribute my success to date to several key factors: (1) a capacity for continued personal and professional growth, (2) advanced financial and analytical skills, (3) ability to find structural solutions to business problems, and (4) command of presentation and negotiation skills at multiple levels. I would be very interested in an opportunity that would provide consistent challenge for my combination of financial, marketing and management strengths. It is my belief that working for a V.C. group will provide such challenge.

With my background I find it easy to access and communicate with client managers and staff at all levels. Combined with my advanced financial and analytical skills, this ability to access a client company at multiple levels has allowed me to be a particularly versatile and effective consultant.

Here are some details of the four major engagements I've managed over the last year:

- On behalf of a high technology start-up, assisted in defining market niche, developed start up business plan, supported implementation of marketing and operational strategies, and obtained a $1 million venture capital infusion to bridge the company between R&D stage and revenue-producing stage.

- Developed an acquisition strategy to facilitate continued growth for a diversified multibillion-dollar corporation. This included developing criteria and methodologies by which to identify and evaluate acquisition candidates. Evaluated six companies and successfully completed one purchase, a $50 million transaction.

- Decentralized a government organization creating 26 distinct business units out of one $250 million department. Included comprehensive project planning and management (business plans, operational restructuring, financial restructuring, market and competitive analyses, assessment of management and staffing strengths, logistics, etc.).

- On behalf of a state government, developed a cash management strategy that created a one-time credit of $50 million through better utilization of existing assets.

There is much more that I could say concerning accomplishments, philosophy, and skills, but I am most interested in learning more about your needs. Hopefully, these points will support my candidacy for a position. I would like to meet with you to discuss your business, and my skills, in greater detail. I'll be calling you soon, or you may contact me. As you can imagine, I need your complete confidentiality.

I look forward to our conversation.

Respectfully yours,

*C. Roger Snowden*

C. Roger Snowden

CS/yw

## Nancie O'Connell

1370 North Filon Street, #1
Princeton, New Jersey 08540

Telephone:
(609) 555-4474

---

October 7, 1996

### Confidential Communication

Attn: Charline Brown
Recruitment Coordinator
Crosby, Heafey, Roach and May
1999 South Harrison Street, 22nd Floor
Princeton, New Jersey 08540

Dear Ms. Brown:

I have been recommended to you by Michael Brown. He suggested that I forward the enclosed resume to you immediately.

As you can see, I am a competent litigator with expertise in wrongful termination and employment discrimination law. In addition to this specialty, I have a range of experience in insurance defense. My performance to date has included significant accomplishments on behalf of clients assigned to me. I presently handle 6 to 15 matters at any one time, and I have had no trouble meeting my objective of 2000 hours per year.

Crosby, Heafey, Roach, and May is well known for the quality of its litigators. An important criterion in considering another position is the quality of the other attorneys, and Crosby would be an ideal environment for me. I am also aware of the congenial nature of the office, and would consider it a privilege to be a part of the Crosby team.

I would like to discuss my past performance and successes in some greater detail. May I call you to arrange an interview?

Sincerely,

*Nancie O'Connell*

Nancie O'Connell

PS: When the time comes I am positive that my present employer will give me an outstanding recommendation, but please keep this application confidential at this time. Harbeck et al are quite happy with me, and I would not like to compromise my position here without a firm offer.

# Salary Histories and Reference Sheets

Employers want references who are loquacious and easy to contact. Do not list a reference without getting approval from the person listed as a reference. In general, employers need a name, business title, business address, and business telephone number. Providing home phone numbers, when approved to do so, can be of benefit to both the reference and the potential employer. Be careful of distributing the address and phone number of any references who may be famous or place a high value on their privacy. This has been a faux pas committed by more than one ambitious careerist, and the error is not usually forgiven.

References can be incorporated into the résumé, as in the example on p. 468, or separated as an addendum or stand-alone communiqué, as in the examples following.

At the middle-management level, salary histories focus on guaranteed cash compensation, plus any likely bonus. At the executive level, however, salary histories can become complex documents involving stock options, perks, and a range of contingencies. For more on this, see Jack Chapman's *How to Make a Thousand Dollars a Minute: Negotiating Salaries & Raises*. The following salary history example is typical, providing a base for the salary-negotiation stage.

Even if this material is requested, it is perfectly acceptable to withhold references and salary data from preliminary communications. Simply notate your cover letter or résumé, "Salary information and references will be provided upon interview." Providing the data before you have established mutual interest can only count against you. This is treated in greater detail in my *Overnight Job Change Strategy*.

Since a great deal of time can pass in an executive placement, try to notify your references if you find out they are about to be contacted concerning you.

# Henry James Hudson, Jr.

1258 St. Charles Avenue
New Orleans, Louisiana 70112

Telephone/message: (504) 555-5387
hank.hudson@mailhost.bus.tulane.edu

## Compensation Sheet

Former:     $78,800 base
  15,760    incentive on base (20%, routine for grade)
  39,650    1994 restricted shares (650 @ $61)

**$134,210**


At beginning of leave, had promotion in hand:

  $85,222    3% base increase time-in-service plus additional 5% for increase grade level (grade 15 exec class)
  21,305    incentive on base (25%, routine for grade)
  44,530    estimated 1995 restricted share award (730 @ $61)

**$151,057**


Plus generous package of benefits. Objective: $160k to $200k+ reflecting immediate potential upon returning to Kraft.


Will need minimum signing bonus of $20,000 to reimburse education agreement with current employer.

# Henry James Hudson, Jr.

1258 St. Charles Avenue
New Orleans, Louisiana 70112

Telephone/message: (504) 555-5387
hank.hudson@mailhost.bus.tulane.edu

### References

Jason Hardaway
Operations Business Leader
Pillsbury Company-MS 3200W5
200 South 86th Street
Minneapolis, Minnesota 55402
H: 612-555-4523
W: 612-555-4330
jhardaway@pillsbury.com

Rich Slaughter
Plant Manager, Champaign
Kraft Foods
14600 West Bradley
Champaign, Illinois 61821
H: 217-555-2352
W: 217-555-19378, ext. 68
rich33@kraftfoods.com

Georgette Tobiasson
President
Tobi Productions
183 Harbor Terrace
Columbia, Maryland 21046
W: 301-555-5596
georgette@2b.com

# MICHAEL HOLMES

168 Monte Cristo
Chicago, Illinois 60611
Office: (312) 555-4398 / Residence: (312) 555-9259

## REFERENCES

John Quirt
Senior Vice President
Park Place Hotels International
(312) 555-4491

David Khapchick
Chief Financial Officer
C&L Financial / Fu Investment
(312) 555-1989

Carole Cooper
Director of Human Resources
Park Place Hotels International
(312) 555-4000

Richard Frankl
Senior Vice President
Innco Hospitality, Inc.
(913) 555-1300

# Personal and Work History Forms

# Personal History Worksheet

Name: _____

Address: _____

City/State/Zip: _____

Home Phone: _____

Office Phone (if any): _____

Car Phone (if any): _____

Fax No. (if any): _____

Message No. (if any): _____

Internet Address (if any): _____

High School: _____  City/State: _____

Graduate? _____  Year: _____

Honors, Activities: _____

_____

_____

College/University: _____  City/State: _____

Major: _____  Minor: _____

Graduate? _____ Degree: _____  Year: _____ GPA: _____

Honors and Awards: _____

_____

_____

_____

_____

Activities: _____

_____

_____

_____

# Personal History Worksheet

Additional College/University: _____ City/State: _____

Major: _____ Minor: _____

Graduate ? _____ Degree: _____ Year: _____ GPA: _____

Honors and Awards: _____

_____

_____

Activities: _____

_____

_____

Additional College/University: _____ City/State: _____

Major: _____ Minor: _____

Graduate ? _____ Degree: _____ Year: _____ GPA: _____

Honors and Awards: _____

_____

_____

Activities: _____

_____

_____

Other Education/Continuing Education/Training/Seminars: _____

_____

_____

_____

_____

_____

_____

_____

# Personal History Worksheet

Available for Travel (give %): _____

Professional Licenses: _____

_____

_____

_____

Computer Skills: _____

_____

_____

_____

_____

_____

_____

_____

_____

_____

_____

Other Machinery and/or Equipment I Can Operate: _____

_____

_____

_____

_____

_____

_____

_____

_____

# Personal History Worksheet

Professional Organizations and Affiliations: _____

_____

_____

_____

_____

_____

Charitable, Religious, Educational, and Other Organizations: _____

_____

_____

_____

_____

_____

_____

_____

_____

_____

Hobbies: _____

_____

_____

_____

_____

_____

_____

_____

_____

# Work Experience Worksheet

Company Name: _____

City/State: _____

My Title: _____

Dates I Held This Title: _____

My Supervisor's Title: _____

Number of People I Supervised: _____

Their Titles and/or Functions: _____

_____

_____

Key Business Relationships (suppliers/vendors/customers/consultants/venture partners): _____

_____

_____

_____

_____

_____

Special Training/Continuing Education: _____

_____

_____

_____

_____

Honors, Awards, Commendations: _____

_____

_____

_____

_____

_____

# Work Experience Worksheet

**What I did** — Include daily and seasonal routine duties. Be brief and to the point. Use numbers and percentages. Quantify budgets. Describe team and independent responsibilities:

_____

_____

_____

_____

_____

_____

_____

_____

_____

**What I accomplished** — Include all accomplishments and contributions above and beyond the basic job description: problems you solved, special projects you handled, trips you may have taken, etc. Quantify your impact on the company's bottom line whenever possible. _Be specific_, and feel free to turn this page and write more:

_____

_____

_____

_____

_____

_____

_____

_____

_____

_____

_____

# Bibliography

### Résumés

*The Overnight Résumé*. Donald Asher. Berkeley, CA: Ten Speed Press, 1991.

### Cover Letters

*The Overnight Job Change Letter*. Donald Asher. Berkeley, CA: Ten Speed Press, 1994.

*200 Letters for Job-Hunters: Every Possible Way to Get Job Offers*. Wm. Frank. Berkeley, CA: Ten Speed Press, 1990.

### Strategy

*High Impact Telephone Networking for Job Hunters*. Howard Armstrong. Holbrook, MA: Bob Adams, Inc., 1992.

*The Overnight Job Change Strategy*. Donald Asher. Berkeley, CA: Ten Speed Press, 1993.

*New Rules of the Job Search Game: Why Today's Managers Hire...And Why They Don't*. Jackie Larson & Cheri Comstock. Holbrook, MA: Bob Adams, Inc., 1994.

### Interviewing

*Sweaty Palms: The Neglected Art of Being Interviewed*. Rev. ed. H. A. Medley. Berkeley, CA: Ten Speed Press, 1992.

*Knock 'em Dead: With Great Answers to Tough Interview Questions*. Martin John Yate. Holbrook, MA: Bob Adams, Inc., 1996.

### Salary

*How to Make a Thousand Dollars a Minute: Negotiating Salaries & Raises*. Jack Chapman. Berkeley, CA: Ten Speed Press, 1987.

### Headhunters

*The Recruiting & Search Report* (a constantly updated database). Panama City Beach, FL: Ken Cole and Company, (904) 235-3733 or (800) 634-4548.

*Executive Search Research Directory*. 5th rev. ed. Kenneth J. Cole and Joan S. Cole. Panama City Beach, FL: Recruiting & Search Publishers, 1994.

*The Headhunter Strategy: How to Make It Work for You*. Ken Cole. New York: John Wiley & Sons, 1985.

*The Directory of Executive Recruiters* (aka *The Red Book*). Fitzwilliam, NH: Kennedy Publications, annual, (603) 585-2200 or (603) 585-6544.

*Rites of Passage at $100,000+: The Insider's Lifetime Guide to Executive Job-Changing and Faster Career Progress*. Rev. John Lucht. New York: The Viceroy Press, 1995.

### Launching Your Own Consulting Practice

*No B.S. Sales Success: The Ultimate No Holds Barred, Kick Butt, Take No Prisoners, & Make Tons of Money Book*. Dan Kennedy. Bellingham, WA: Self Counsel Press, 1994.

*Getting Sales: A Getting-into-Business Guide*. Dan Kennedy. Bellingham, WA: Self Counsel Press, 1991.

*Guerilla Marketing On-Line: The Entrepreneur's Guide to Earning Profits on the Internet.* Jay C. Levinson and Chalres Rubin. New York: Houghton Mifflin Co., 1995.

*Guerilla Marketing for the Nineties: The Newest Secrets for Making Big Profits from Your Small Business.* Jay C. Levinson. New York: Houghton Mifflin Co., 1993.

*Five Hundred Fifty-Five Ways to Earn Extra Money.* Rev. ed. Jay C. Levinson. New York: Henry Holt & Co., 1992.

*Earning Money Without a Job.* Rev. ed. Jay C. Levinson. New York: Henry Holt & Co., 1991.

*Guerilla Marketing Attack: New Strategies, Tactics & Weapons for Winning Big Profits.* Jay C. Levinson. New York: Houghton Mifflin Co., 1989.

*Guerilla Marketing.* Jay C. Levinson. New York: Houghton Mifflin Co., 1985.

*National Business Employment Weekly Guide to Self Employment: A Round-up of Career Alternatives Ranging from Consulting & Professional Temping to Starting or Buying a Business.* David Lord. New York: John Wiley & Sons, 1996.

*Running a One-Person Business.* Claude Whitmyer and Salli Rasberry. Berkeley, CA: Ten Speed Press, 1994.

## Self-Assessment & Self-Directed Career Planning

*What Color Is Your Parachute?* Richard Bolles. Berkeley, CA: Ten Speed Press, annual. (This is the best-selling career book in history. You *must* read it at least once during any major job search.)

## Older Candidates

*The Forty-Plus Job Hunting Guide: Official Handbook of the Forty-Plus Club.* Rev. ed. P. Birsner. New York: Facts on File Publications, 1990. (Warning: Do not follow the résumé advice in this otherwise excellent book.)

*Finding a Job After 50.* Terry Harty and Karen Kerkstra Harty. Hawthorne, NJ: Career Press, 1994.

*Getting a Job after 50.* J. S. Morgan. Blue Ridge Summit, PA: Tab Books, Inc., 1990.

*Job Hunting After 50: Strategies for Success.* S. N. Ray. New York: John Wiley & Sons, 1991.

## Burnout

*Unnecessary Choices: The Hidden Life of the Executive Woman.* E. Gilson with S. Kane. New York: Paragon House, 1989.

*Career Burnout: Causes & Cures.* A. Pines and E. Aronson. New York: Free Press (Macmillan), 1988.

## Other Resources

*JobShift: How to Prosper in a Workplace Without Jobs.* William Bridges. Reading, MA: Addison-Wesley, 1994.

*Seven Habits of Highly Effective People.* Stephen R. Covey. New York: Simon & Schuster, 1989.

*Working for America: Employment Opportunities in Federal Civil Service.* James C. Gonyea. Hauppauge, NY: Barron's Educational Series, Inc., 1992.

*Government Job Finder.* 2nd ed. Daniel Lauber. New York: Planning Communications, 1994.

*Designing and Managing Your Career.* Harry Levinson, ed. Boston: Harvard Business School Press, 1989.

*Outplace Yourself: Secrets of an Executive Outplacement Counselor.* Charles H. Logue, Ph.D. Holbrook, MA: Bob Adams, Inc., 1993.

*End of Work: The Decline of the Global Labor Force & the Dawn of the Post-Market Era.* Jeremy Rifkin. New York: Putnam Publishing Group, 1994.

## Reference

*America's Corporate Families & International Affiliates* (formerly *Billion Dollar Directory*). Mountain Lakes, NJ: Dun & Bradstreet.

*Business Periodicals Index.* Bronx, NY: Wilson Publishing.

*Business Rankings Annual.* Detroit: Gale Research, Inc.

*The Career Guide: Dun's Employment Opportunities Directory.* Parsippany, NJ: Dun's Marketing Services.

*Commerce Register* (geographical guides to manufacturers). Midland Park, NJ: Commerce Register Co.

*Corporate 1000 and International Corporate 1000.* Washington, D.C.: Monitor Publishing.

*Corporate Yellow Book: Who's Who at the Leading U.S. Companies.* New York: Monitor Publishing Co.

*Directories in Print.* Detroit: Gale Research, Inc.

*Directory of Corporate Affiliations.* 2 vols. Wilmette, IL: National Register Publishing Company.

*Directory of Human Resources Executives.* Cos Cob, CT: Hunt-Scanlon Publishing Co., Inc.

*Encyclopedia of Associations.* Detroit: Gale Research, Inc.

*Encyclopedia of Business Information Sources.* Detroit: Gale Research, Inc.

*Guide to American Directories.* West Nyack, NY: Todd Publications.

*Hoover's Handbook of American Business.* Austin, TX: The Reference Press, Inc.

*How to Get a Job in _____.* Chicago: Surrey Books.

| | |
|---|---|
| Atlanta | New York Metropolitan Area |
| Greater Boston | Pacific Rim |
| Chicago | San Francisco Bay Area |
| Dallas/Fort Worth | Seattle/Portland |
| Europe | Southern California |
| Houston | Washington, D.C. |

*The _____ JobBank.* Holbrook, MA: Bob Adams, Inc.

| | |
|---|---|
| Atlanta | New York |
| Boston | Ohio |
| Carolina | Philadelphia |
| Chicago | Phoenix |
| Dallas-Ft. Worth | San Francisco Bay Area |
| Denver | Seattle |
| Detroit | St. Louis |
| Florida | Tennessee |
| Houston | Washington DC |
| Los Angeles | National |
| Minneapolis-St. Paul | |

*Job Hunter's Sourcebook: Where to Find Employment Leads and Other Job Search Resources.* Detroit: Gale Research Inc.

*Million Dollar Directory* series. Parsippany, NJ: Dun & Bradstreet.

*Moody's Industrial Manual and News Reports.* New York: Moody's Investors Service.

*NASDAQ Yellow Book: Who's Who at the Leading Younger Growth Companies in the U.S.* New York: Monitor Publishing Co.

*National Directory of Addresses and Telephone Numbers.* Kirkland, WA: General Information.

*The National Jobline Directory: Over 2000 Companies, Government Agencies, and Other Organizations that Post Job Openings by Phone.* Holbrook, MA: Bob Adams, Inc.

*Reference Book of Corporate Managements: America's Corporate Leaders.* 4 vols. Parsippany, NJ: Dun & Bradstreet.

*Standard & Poor's Register of Corporations, Directors, & Executives.* New York: Standard & Poor.

*Standard Directory of Advertisers: Geographical Edition.* Wilmette, IL: National Register Publishing Company.

*Thomas' Register of American Manufacturers.* New York: Thomas Publishing Co.

*Ward's Business Directory of U.S. Private and Public Companies.* Belmont, CA: Information Access.

*Where the Jobs Are: A Comprehensive Directory of 1200 Journals Listing Career Opportunities.* Garrett Park, MD: Garrett Park Press.

*Who's Who in America.* Wilmette, IL: Marquis.

*Who's Who in American Women.* New Providence, NJ: Marquis.

*Who's Who in Finance & Industry.* Wilmette, IL: Marquis.

*Who's Who in Science and Engineering.* New Providence, NJ: Marquis.

*Who's Who in Venture Capital.* New York: John Wiley & Sons.

Yellow pages directory published for your community.

# Index

# Also by Don Asher . . .

### The Overnight Résumé

When you absolutely, positively *must* have the perfect resume overnight, this book tells you how. Supported with ace job-hunting advice, and dozens of sample resumes for inspiration. The ultimate starter kit for everyone from entry-level to the executive suite.

8½ x 11 inches, 136 pages

### The Overnight Job-Change Letter

A collection of proven, effective cover letters that will get the job-hunter through a wide range of situations, from getting the proverbial foot in the door to crafting the perfect thank-you.

8½ x 11 inches, 128 pages

### The Overnight Job-Change Strategy

Most job-hunters waste the first few weeks of a job hunt following false leads, using ineffective strategies, and otherwise losing out to the better-prepared competition. This book cuts to the chase, highlighting only the hottest, most effective, most sophisticated strategies for the dedicated, aggressive go-getter. And, if you're not that go-getter, it shows you how to become one.

7¼ x 9 inches, 136 pages

### The Foolproof Job-Search Workbook

Just open this book up, follow the instructions, and you *will* get job offers . . . **guaranteed.** The systematic, proven methodology in this book will enable you to build an effective job-hunting network, get the offers you want, and the salary you deserve. If not, you can just return the filled-in workbook to the publisher and receive a full refund. No one has had to take us up on it yet!

8½ x 11 inches, 272 pages

### Graduate Admissions Essays—What Works, What Doesn't, and Why

The definitive book on writing a unique, innovative essay that will get any student noticed by even the most exacting admissions committees.

8½ x 11 inches, 128 pages

### From College to Career

A collection of entry-level resumes and savvy job-hunting hints for students making the jump to their first "real world" jobs.

8½ x 11 inches, 96 pages

For more information, or to order, call the publisher at the number below. We accept VISA, Mastercard, and American Express. You may also wish to write for our free catalog of over 500 books, posters, and audiotapes.

Ten Speed Press
P.O. Box 7123
Berkeley, CA 94707

800-841-BOOK